PSYCHOLOGY
BRIEF EDITION

ROBERT E. SILVERMAN   *New York University*

PSYCHOLOGY

BRIEF EDITION

2nd edition

Prentice-Hall, Inc., Englewood Cliffs, New Jersey

CHAPTER-OPENING ILLUSTRATIONS

Chapter 1 Early anatomists dissected the brain seeking clues about its function. Woodcut by Andreas Vesalius, 1514-1564, from *De humani corporis fabrica.* (Library, New York Academy of Medicine)
Chapter 2 Twinning: identical twins (top); fraternal twins (bottom). From *Birth atlas,* published by Maternity Center Association, New York City; reproduced with permission.
Chapter 3 Anatomical drawing of human musculature by Andreas Vesalius, from *De humani corporis fabrica.* (Library, New York Academy of Medicine)
Chapter 4 Lunar gravity training at Wright Patterson Air Force Base, Dayton, Ohio. Astronaut John Young is not at zero gravity, but at one-sixth that of the earth. (NASA)
Chapter 5 Devils or angels? (M.C. Escher—Haags Gemuntemuseum, the Hague)
Chapter 6 Starling at feeding machine. (Courtesy of the American Museum of Natural History)
Chapter 7 Computer-assisted instruction. (IBM)
Chapter 8 Monkeys learning tasks and satisfying their curiosity drive. (Harry F. Harlow, University of Wisconsin Primate Laboratory)
Chapter 9 Loneliness. (NCA photo)
Chapter 10 Washoe uses signs to name objects. (Beatrice T. Gardner and R. Allen Gardner)
Chapter 11 Test materials for the Stanford-Binet test. (Courtesy of Houghton Mifflin Company)
Chapter 12 Sex-typing: girls imitate their mothers. (Jan Lukas—Rapho Guillumette)
Chapter 13 Fit of demoniac fury. From Abraham Palings, *'t Afgerukt Mom-Aansight der Tooverye.* (Huntington Library, San Marino, California)
Chapter 14 Projective drawing: manic clown.
Chapter 15 Men's lib: Texas Bell System's first male operators. (A.T.&T. Co.)

Library of Congress Cataloging in Publication Data

Silverman, Robert E
   Psychology.

   Bibliography: p. 442-450
   Includes indexes.
   1. Psychology. I. Title.
BF121.S52 1975   150   74-19430
ISBN 0-13-734004-4

This book has been composed in linotype Electra, with headings and research abstracts in Helvetica. Production by Bert N. Zelman and Helen Maertens. Typographical design by Rita Ginsburg.

10 9 8 7 6 5 4 3 2 1

Prentice-Hall International, Inc., London
Prentice-Hall of Australia, Pty. Ltd., Sydney
Prentice-Hall of Canada, Ltd., Toronto
Prentice-Hall of India Private Ltd., New Delhi
Prentice-Hall of Japan, Inc., Tokyo

Preface

This revised Brief Edition, like its predecessor, aims at broad systematic coverage of basic psychological concepts and principles—an aim that has been approved by users of the first edition in over 300 colleges. Important trends in psychological research are reviewed, with emphasis on practical applications. Psychology's many branches are surveyed so that students who later wish to take advanced courses will be familiar with the major fields of specialization.

Psychology is continually growing, changing, and moving in different directions. To keep pace with these changes, a textbook must also alter its coverage, tightening up material in some areas while expanding in others. A number of improvements have been made here without adding to the book's length. A chapter is now added on intelligence and ability testing (Chapter 11). There is new material on cognitive psychology, altered states of consciousness, and drugs and their effects. More is presented on social and personality development, on language development (especially grammar), and on signal detection theory. Helpful comparisons of behavioral, cognitive, and psychoanalytic approaches to therapy are included. The discussions of physiological psychology (Chapter 3) and sensation (Chapter 4) are now improved and tightened up. And the final chapter (15) has been expanded to include consideration of the developing fields of community psychology, human relations training, crime prevention, and environmental psychology.

There is, of course, no one right way to teach a course. The book is ordered in a way appealing to this author, but each teacher may adapt the material to suit his own special abilities and his students' needs. The use of this text can be flexible. Chapters are sufficiently independent so that they may be rearranged.

v

A course with emphasis on science		A basic course using supplementary materials	
Chapter 1	Psychology: its approaches, methods, and origins	Chapter 1	Psychology: its approaches, methods, and origins
Chapter 2	Heredity and development	Chapter 2	Heredity and development
Chapter 3	Physiology of response	Chapter 5	Perception
Chapter 4	Sensation	Chapter 6	Learning processes
Chapter 5	Perception	Chapter 7	Complex learning and retention
Chapter 6	Learning processes	Chapter 8	Motivation
Chapter 7	Complex learning and retention	Chapter 10	Language, thinking, problem-solving, and creativity
Chapter 8	Motivation	Chapter 12	Personality
Chapter 10	Language, thinking, problem-solving, and creativity	Chapter 13	Behavior pathology
Chapter 11	Testing intelligence and ability	Chapter 14	Therapy
Chapter 13	Behavior pathology	Chapter 15	Psychology and society
Chapter 14	Therapy		

Two alternative sequences are listed here, and others are feasible, depending on the instructor's orientation and objectives. All are geared to a course lasting one semester or one quarter.

This book is designed, together with its accompanying *Study Guide and Workbook* and *Test Item File*, for courses utilizing personalized self-instruction (the Keller Plan). While these supplementary aids lend themselves well for use in P.S.I/Keller Plan courses, they are also valuable in more traditionally organized courses.

A number of other aids have been included to assist the student in his work: Suggested Readings after each chapter and the Bibliography at the back of the text will assist those who wish to delve deeper into relevant books and journal articles in preparation for class discussion. A listing of Research Abstracts (encapsulated descriptions of major studies and current experimentation, printed in color in the text) follows the Contents. When new terms are introduced, they are italicized and clearly defined. An expanded Glossary at the back of the text serves as a convenient reference and study aid. For any terms not found in the Glossary, the reader should consult the comprehensive Subject Index.

Every effort has been made in this revision to maintain the level of *clarity* and *readability* that I am happy to note was much praised by users of the first edition.

R.E.S.

Contents

RESEARCH ABSTRACTS

1

Psychology: its approaches, methods, and origins

Psychology is the science that seeks to describe and explain and, on occasion, to change the behavior of man and other animals. Compared to such older sciences as mathematics, physics, biology, and chemistry, psychology is a rather young science, a surprising fact, considering man's age-old curiosity about himself. There is evidence that from the beginning of recorded history man has wondered about the things that have affected his behavior. In the more recent past, for hundreds of years, he has searched for understanding of something he called mind—looking for answers sometimes in magic, often in philosophy and religion. Yet, not until recently did he develop a science of psychology to answer his questions about why he behaves as he does. Before this could happen, man had to go through a revolution in his attitudes.

Earlier generations saw the mind of man in relation to God, to the state, to art and reason, to accident and disease—but never as a subject for scientific study. Medicine studied the flow of blood through the body and philosophy systematized thought—but there was no scientific discipline to study the interrelationship of the physical and mental processes to show that they often acted together in highly predictable ways. In short, man studied himself in bits and pieces. He believed that man in his totality was too complex for the understanding of mere mortals.

Today, of course, we are no longer deterred by this view. To be sure, behavior is very complex, but so is the universe, which has long been subject to scientific interpretation. Now, we have every reason to believe that the science of psychology will enable us to measure and explain behavior—and to modify it in ways that will affect us significantly, individually and as a society.

Most psychologists do not limit their study of behavior to that which is directly and immediately observable. For contemporary psychology, the concept of behavior is broad, and it includes levels of behavior that are not immediately apparent. In addition to observable or *overt* behavior, there are *covert* and *unconscious* levels of

1

behavior. Psychologists today realize that while they are observing one form of behavior, other forms may be occurring simultaneously in the same individual. For example, although the individual is smiling on an overt level, he might at the same time have the covert thought that his companion is acting like a fool. On an unconscious level, he might be deeply jealous of the other person. The smile is obvious, but only the individual himself is aware of his internal thoughts, and perhaps even he does not realize that his jealousy exists.

THE LANGUAGE OF PSYCHOLOGY

Each discipline tends to develop its own special language in order to provide accurate and rapid means of communication. When one physician tells another about the "ventricular fibrillation as seen on lead 3 of an EKG," he is quickly understood. Similarly, when an experimental psychologist says that "an operant is being emitted at a high rate, because it has been maintained on a variable-ratio schedule," he is readily understood by other psychologists.

The language of psychology is made up of many languages. It consists in part of our everyday language, for psychologists also use such familiar words as motivation, emotion, intelligence, and ability. From time to time, however, these words are given special technical meaning, as when the word "anxiety" is reserved for the condition produced when one fears his own basic instincts (Freud, 1926).

Psychologists freely use technical terms from other branches of science, particularly mathematics. We speak of means, medians, and correlation coefficients when we use statistics. We refer to functional relationships between variables. We describe our graphs in terms of the slope of the curve and sometimes use elaborate mathematical language to describe curves in terms of equations.

The language used by psychologists also identifies the specific problems they choose to study. Some psychologists talk about *reinforcers that maintain responses*, and their research is directed toward the study of reinforcers (see Chapter 6). Other psychologists are interested in the *structure of knowledge*, and they turn their attention to untangling the processes that may underlie the development of knowledge. A psychoanalyst (who adheres to Freudian theory of personality) looks for unconscious conflicts, while a behaviorist (who advocates the study of overt behavior) looks for the discriminative stimuli (cues) that may trigger particular patterns of behavior.

The language of psychology will become increasingly familiar to you as you study the subject areas of interest to psychologists and learn how they proceed with their investigations.

PROBLEM-FINDING IN PSYCHOLOGY

Psychology, like any other science, must begin every inquiry by clarifying and sharpening the questions to which it seeks answers. We cannot answer the most complex questions first; we must begin with relatively simple questions and gradually work our way to more complex ones. Neither can we jump from question to conclusion. The scientist must always follow specified procedures. He chooses a problem, selects the questions to be answered, and makes a series of systematic observations to gather the facts needed to answer the questions; finally, he organizes and interprets the facts. In so doing, he may answer the questions or he may raise new questions.

Questions psychologists ask

Psychologists study behavior by asking questions that each of us may have asked at one time, such as the following:

To what extent is the way we think and act predetermined by our heredity?

What makes a baby learn? What creates a talent or genius in the adult? What are the problems of old age?

What determines our awareness of our world? Are some people more aware than others? What accounts for the differences in the ways we perceive?

What motivates behavior? Are we aware of our own drives?

How do we think? What is the role of language in thought?

What accounts for personality differences among people?

What makes a person lose control? Why does one person develop an anxiety neurosis, and another a hysterical disorder?

How can the therapist modify or change maladjustive behaviors?

It should be noted that none of the above questions asks such things as: Why did John shoot his commanding officer in the back? What prompted the senator not to seek a sure-fire second term? Why did Rosemary decide to marry an old friend instead of a current lover? Such questions are too complex; they involve too many variables and are not precise enough to enable the psychologist to seek an answer. But if the psychologist is able to find answers to our sample questions, and if he is able to study the particular individual in relation to the broader questions and their answers, perhaps he can then say what caused John to shoot his officer and, more important, what might be done to prevent other young men from doing the same thing.

The search for answers: selecting problems

Sometimes we choose a problem; sometimes a problem chooses us. Most often our own observations raise questions; we find further questions to ask; and, in this way, we define a problem. The scientific search for knowledge often begins naturally.

Let us illustrate this process. A psychologist in a high school observes that one group of students has a record of delinquent behavior, a series of unhappy encounters with police and local citizens, and that another group does not have such a record. Having made this simple observation, the psychologist becomes concerned over the troubles of the first group. He has identified a problem that he must study and solve. The psychologist makes further observations. He finds that many of the troubled youngsters have been ignored or rejected at home—or have been abandoned altogether by one or both parents. On the basis of this observation, the psychologist chooses to consider the following question: Is rejection by parents a key factor in the development of delinquency in the students in his school? He cannot be satisfied with generalizations or guesses. He must seek specific ways to arrive at an answer. Let us assume, in this case, that the psychologist decides to design a test to discover if a large number of the troublesome students feel rejected by their parents. He develops the test, administers it, and learns that rejection *is* a key factor. Most of the delinquent students do feel that they have been rejected by their parents, whereas very few nondelinquents express this feeling so strongly.

This observation leads to a further question: What accounts for the relationship between rejection and delinquency? He develops a test that asks: Do the rejected students tend to turn toward their friends for approval and satisfaction? Do they then turn away from their parents and authority figures in general? Questions like these lead him to develop an additional test in which he seeks new answers.

We can see in this brief, simple example how the psychologist's initial observations led him to the problem. The problem in turn gave rise to specific questions, and the questions produced a system or a method of systematic observation. In this case, the observation required the use of a specially designed test. The first set of systematic observations (the test) led to some answers, and these answers gave rise to an additional question. On the basis of the additional question, the psychologist proceeded to develop a new test.

In our example, the choice of problem was governed by the psychologist's immediate situation—his professional involvement in the school. A number of psychologists argue that the choice of problems and questions should be determined by a *theory* (Hull, 1943); that is, these scientists insist that the most useful questions are based on some organized set of guesses as to what the answer may be. They gather facts in order to support or refute a theory. If the facts do not support the theory, they revise or reject it. One can say that the theorist has a kind of map or guideline that he follows in choosing the questions he seeks to answer.

Some psychologists, however, argue that theory-building is premature. They say that we do not have enough facts to develop sound theories, and that if we create theories too quickly, we will have faulty maps that will lead us astray. One such psychologist, B. F. Skinner, has argued that curiosity rather than theory should be our guide—that we should search out answers to any questions that interest us. Skinner has stated, "When you run into something interesting, drop everything else and study it." He has argued that curiosity about nature is the best motive for scientific research.

Whether we feel drawn to theorists, such as Hull, or to nontheorists, such as Skinner, the fact remains that scientific activity begins with questioning. The next step is systematic observation, and we shall see that both curiosity and theory contribute to the observation and interpretation of facts.

Role of theory

We have seen that a theory can direct the psychologist in his choice of questions. So too can a theory serve as a way of organizing observations into a set of summary principles predicting relationships we have not yet observed. Theories are neither true nor false; they are either useful or not useful. A useful theory is one that helps us understand what we have observed and points to new questions and possibilities. To illustrate the role of theory, we shall consider a simple theoretical formulation that begins with straightforward observations and ends in a theoretical statement.

Let us place a laboratory rat in a simple maze shaped in the form of the letter *T* (see Chapter 6). One arm of the maze contains food, the other does not. We observe that the rat goes increasingly to the arm that contains the food. Let us assume that, in a different situation, we notice that a dog will push open a door in his cage if, by pushing it open, he gains acces to drinking water. These observations interest us, so we make some additional observations: We find that the rat learns to go to the arm of the maze containing food if—and only if—he has been deprived of food earlier, and the dog learns to push open a door for water if—and only if—he has been deprived of water. We may represent these two observations as facts; and, if we were to seek additional information, we would find that most rats and most dogs perform as described.

Because the food and the water seem to play important roles in learning, our observations suggest a general underlying principle. We are led to consider the possibility that learning depends on the presentation of needed *stimuli*; perhaps the *reduction of a need* plays an important role in the behavior we call *learning*. For example, the dog needed water and he learned to push open the door to get it; the rat needed food and he learned to go to the arm of the maze that contained food. Therefore, we may now propose a theoretical statement: Some forms of learning depend on need reduction. We might wish to make this statement in a stronger form and say: All forms of learning depend on need reduction. However, if we were to make such a strong statement, we would be going well beyond the bounds of our initial observations. Either statement, the strong one or the more cautious one, qualifies as a theoretical statement. Both go beyond facts to suggest a summary principle.

We have made our observations and translated them into a theoretical statement. Now that we have done this, we need to see whether or not this statement will apply to other observations. For example, if we identify approval as a strong need in children, our theoretical statement leads us to predict that children who have been deprived of approval will learn better than nondeprived children when the rewards for learning are in the form of approval. If we now perform an experiment to test this prediction and find that our prediction is correct, we have additional support for our theoretical statement about need reduction and learning. Furthermore, we have added an important new bit of knowledge; we have observed that children deprived of approval will learn to make responses in order to obtain approval. We now know that a social reward such as approval functions in much the same way as do the more basic rewards of food and water. The theory (theoretical statement) has not only summarized our former observations, but it has also led us to make new observations.

THE SCIENTIFIC METHOD

In his search for answers, the psychologist follows a definite sequence of steps. This sequence is known as the *scientific method* because it is characteristic of virtually every scientific endeavor. The scientific method involves two steps: *systematic observation* of important factors or *variables*, and *organization and interpretation* of emerging facts.

Systematic observation

The procedures of systematic observation are intended to eliminate the subjective influence of bias and prejudgment and to insure that the observing process will be repeatable. Systematic observation is carefully planned and described, so that other investigators can follow the same procedures to check the observer's conclusions.

Two techniques of systematic observation are basic to psychology. The first is the *experimental method*, in which we manipulate events in order to observe what will happen; the second is the *correlational method*, in which we observe naturally occurring events. The sample study of high school delinquency illustrates the correlational method. The psychologist does not create delinquent behavior in one group and not in another; the problem already exists. His first step, therefore, is to discover a means to determine the factors causing delinquency, to *hypothesize* (or forecast) certain relationships, and to test for their existence.

In the experimental method, however, the observer *manipulates* a set of conditions (or variables) in order to determine if those conditions have some effect on a particular form of behavior (another set of variables.) If an experimentalist-observer has questions about the effects of hunger on learning, he might arrange conditions so that the *experimental subjects* (rats) are made hungry, while another group of subjects, the *control subjects*, are put on a normal diet. Each group is given a learning task to perform, and the experimenter then compares the performances of the two groups. On the basis of this comparison, he should be able to make some statements about the effects of laboratory-induced hunger on learning.

Lab findings versus survey findings Psychologists recognize the many advantages of laboratory experimentation, but they are cautious about applying results to life experiences because conditions in the outside world often produce somewhat different results. Hovland (1959) has pointed out, for example, that the findings of laboratory experiments on attitude change differ from those of surveys conducted outside the laboratory. Changes in attitudes occur more clearly in research conducted in a laboratory than in survey research performed in real-life situations. Hovland suggested that findings from the two kinds of research should be integrated and that each has its advantages. The carefully controlled conditions of experimental research in a laboratory help to identify basic principles, and the less-controlled survey setting serves as a testing and proving ground for such principles.

The experimental method

When a scientist wishes to study the direct relationship between variables, when he wants his observations to be precise, he prefers to use the experimental method. For example, if an observer wants to answer questions about the effects of fatigue on problem-solving ability, he needs, first, to devise ways to increase and decrease fatigue, and, second, to devise a means of measuring problem-solving ability. It is not enough for him simply to observe that people who report being fatigued do not solve problems well, for those people might be unable to solve problems for reasons other than fatigue. To obtain direct information, it is necessary for the observer to control the events that he studies and to minimize extraneous and interfering factors.

Although the experimental method is found largely in laboratory settings, it is frequently applied to problems outside the laboratory. The basic feature of the experimental method is the *control of relevant variables*; that is, the control of all factors that affect the experiment. The experimentalist identifies the variables that are of interest to him. He then seeks the means by which he can manipulate these variables and,

at the same time, controls other factors that may interfere.

It is helpful to classify the variables involved in experimental observation as either independent or dependent. The *independent variables* are the variables that we manipulate, and the *dependent variables* are the variables in which we expect to see the results of our manipulations. In an experiment designed to study the effects of fatigue on problem-solving, fatigue is the independent variable and the measure of problem-solving is the dependent variable, because we expect that it is in some way affected by fatigue. Thus, the experimenter expects the dependent variable to change as a result of his manipulation of the independent variable. (Of course, the experiment may prove him wrong.)

If the experimenter is a theorist, he will make a prediction; that is, he will formally indicate the changes he expects in the dependent variable as a result of certain manipulations of the independent variable. If the experimenter is not theoretically inclined, he may simply have some general idea that there is a relationship between the variables, and so he designs an experiment to determine the nature of that relationship.

Whether or not the psychologist has set down a prediction, he must record in detail a description of the conditions under which he carried out his experiment. If he does not, no one will be able to repeat his experiment or relate his results meaningfully to other work in the

Figure 1.1 *Experimental psychologists spend many research hours in the laboratory where the experimental situation and subjects are controlled. Here Professor Neal E. Miller and his associate Dr. Leo V. DiCara prepare a rat for training in the operant conditioning of changes in heart rate.* (Dr. Neal E. Miller)

6

Table 1.1   Experimental designs for the investigation of anxiety and learning

A	Experimental group		Control group
Independent variable	Shock threat		—
Dependent variable (average number of errors)	(38.85)		(43.77)

B	Experimental group		Control group
	Avoidance	*Nonavoidance*	
Independent variable	"May" be shocked	"Will" be shocked	—
Dependent variable (average number of errors)	(35.85)	(47.80)	(43.77)

field. *Repeatability* is a basic condition of any science and of every experimental method. Only by repeating the conditions of experiments performed by someone else can we determine whether or not our observations and conclusions agree with his.

If, for example, a psychologist wished to determine the relationship between learning and anxiety, he might set up the following experiment, using variables that can be repeated in any laboratory. The learning task consists of a list of eight nonsense syllables—letter combinations with no meaning whatsoever. The syllables are presented on a device called a *memory drum*. The drum rotates every two seconds, and on every rotation a nonsense syllable appears. The subjects (college students in this case) are expected to memorize the nonsense syllables.

Each subject is interviewed individually and is then assigned to either the experimental group or the control group. Anxiety is created in the experimental subjects only: the experimenter attaches electrodes to their ankles and tells them that during the experiment they may receive a painful electric shock for each wrong answer. The control subjects are neither strapped with the electrodes nor threatened with shock, but in all other respects they are treated exactly like the experimental group. Although no shock

is delivered to either group during the course of the experiment, it is assumed that the electrodes and threat produce a condition of anxiety in the experimental group—an anxiety not felt by the control subjects (Figure 1.1).

The experimental design almost always involves the two groups mentioned here: The experimental group is subjected to the independent variable, anxiety, in the form of shock threat. This is the independent variable, because it is the one thing we have manipulated in setting up the experiment. We have defined the dependent variable as the factor that we expect will be affected by the independent variable. In this case, the dependent variable involves the subjects' ability to memorize nonsense syllables. We measure this ability by counting the errors made by each subject on the first ten trials. The number of errors, then, is what we have to observe—it is the dependent variable.

The design for this experiment is depicted in Table 1.1A. The numbers in parentheses show the average number of errors made by each group. These averages indicate that the experimental group made fewer errors than the control group; threat of shock evidently motivated the subjects in the experimental group to pay careful attention and to learn well. We will be discussing the motivating effects of anxiety in

Chapter 8, but it is worth noting here that this particular experiment showed that one type of shock threat may have a positive effect on simple memory learning.

It is possible to have more than one independent variable and more than one dependent variable in an experiment. Again testing for the relationship between learning and anxiety, we shall now consider two independent variables, rather than one. With the addition of another independent variable, we must use three groups: the control group described above; a group threatened by shock, called the avoidance shock group; and another group threatened by shock, called the nonavoidance shock group. The subjects in the nonavoidance group have electrodes attached to their ankles, and each subject is told

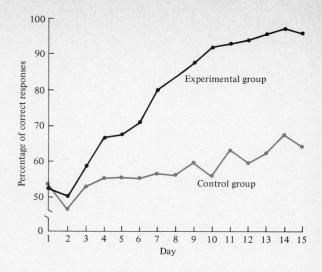

Figure 1.2   *The experimental group received prolonged exposure to circles and triangles (on the walls of their cages). The control group had no such exposure. All animals were then taught to discriminate between circles and triangles by receiving a reward each time they pushed open a small door identified by the correct stimulus. (Gibson and Walk, 1956)*

The overeager experimental subject   In psychological research, the experimenter assumes that subjects' responses will depend on the manipulation of predetermined experimental variables. Orne (1962) however, suggests that there are other very powerful forces at work—appearing when compliant subjects actively attempt to respond according to their own interpretations of the experiment's purpose.

Orne asserts that this phenomenon is partially a result of well-defined role expectations shared by subjects and experimenter. For example, subjects will agree to endure even considerable amounts of discomfort, boredom, or actual pain because of their generally high regard for scientific experimentation. (Orne reports that he failed in his attempts to devise a task so boring or so meaningless that subjects would be discouraged enough to discontinue their efforts. Instead, they invariably attributed some scientific purpose to the experimenter's demands.)

As a consequence, subjects must be considered very active factors in the outcome of an experiment. Because they usually feel they have a vested interest in the project's success, they are motivated to be "good" subjects. Almost invariably, subjects will respond—both consciously and unconsciously—in a way that will tend to validate the experimental hypothesis *as they perceive it*. Cues that offer hints for an experimental hypothesis are labeled *demand characteristics* by Orne. He warns psychologists that they must account for the powerful effects of demand characteristics, and even learn to manipulate them as another kind of experimental variable. To disregard his warning is to risk producing false results

that during the course of the experiment he *will* receive a shock. The emphasis on "will" is designed to indicate to the subject that the shock is unavoidable, that he will get a shock no matter what he does in the course of the experiment. The intent is to create a high degree of anxiety in which the subject has no control over the shock. In the avoidance group, you will remember that the subjects are told that they *may* receive a shock. For these subjects, the implication is that if they perform well, they can avoid the shock. Thus, the two independent variables are avoidance of shock and nonavoidance of shock. Table 1.1B shows the design and results of this larger experiment. These results are more interesting than those of the experiment in which only one independent variable was used. It shows that the threat of shock may have very different effects, depending on how it is administered. The subjects in the avoidance group made fewer errors than the control group, but the subjects in the nonavoidance group made more errors than the avoidance group. This experiment offers a new conclusion: learning is hindered by anxiety, if the threat that causes anxiety is not controllable by the subject.

Very often the results of experiments such as these are represented graphically, particularly when the experimenter wishes to show the effects in terms of time, number of trials, or some other changing conditions. In such research it is sometimes useful to compare the increase in learning in one or more experimental groups, or to compare the experimental groups with control groups. Figure 1.2 shows the different patterns of learning in an experimental and a control group of laboratory rats. The graph clearly shows that the experimental group learned more quickly and to a higher degree than the control group. By the fourth day of training, about 67 percent of the experimental group's responses were correct; by the fourteenth day they were close to 98 percent correct. The control animals did not get to 67 percent until the fourteenth day.

Statistics In reporting their research results, psychologists often use *descriptive statistics* as a convenient and efficient way to summarize data and compare one set of measurements with another. It is certainly easier and more convenient to show, as in Table 1.1, that the average scores of the experimental groups are 35.85 and 47.80 than it is to present all the scores of both groups and require the reader to summarize the data for himself.

To find the average scores and thus to describe the *central tendency* of a group of scores, psychologists frequently use the arithmetic mean or median. The *mean* is the average of a set of scores, computed by adding all the scores and dividing by the total number of scores. The *median* is the score that is midway between the highest and lowest scores. It is found by listing the scores from highest to lowest, counting them, and, if there is an odd number of scores, finding the middle score. When there is an even number of scores, the median is an average of the two middle scores. See Figure 1.3 for sample computations of mean and median.

Measures of central tendency such as the mean and median are often used to enable psychologists to organize and reduce their data to manageable size. If, for example, we studied problem-solving ability in two groups of 50 students, we would find it difficult to analyze and report our findings if we had to describe the performance of each subject. A measure of the central tendency for each group allows us to view an overall picture of our findings. We can see whether, on the average, one group does better than another group, and then we can proceed to concern ourselves with the meaning of group differences if they do occur.

The first and most important meaning to be attributed to a difference between central tendencies is the probability (p) that it did not occur by chance. The difference is significant only if the probability of chance is less than .05 $(p < .05)$. An insignificant differences $(p > .05)$ usually indicates that the experimental manipulation had no real effect.

Correlational methods

While the experimental method permits the manipulation of independent variables, correlational methods are used to investigate events that cannot be manipulated effectively. It has been said that nature has always been experi-

Figure 1.3   Computing the mean and median.

Mean	Median
3	3
5	5
7	7
9	9 = median
11	11
13	13
15	15
63	

9 = mean

7 ⟌ 63

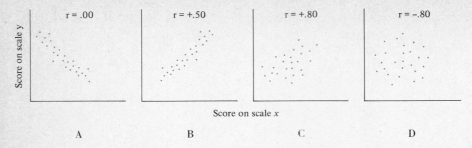

Figure 1.4 Four scatter diagrams, formed by placing a dot for each individual at the point of his x score and his y score.

menting with a courage and complexity that goes beyond science. The correlational methods enable us to study the results of nature's experimentation. For example, we use correlation to compare the IQ scores of identical twins.

The measurement of the mutual relationship between two variables is their correlation. We may say, for example, that the IQ scores of identical twins raised in the same home are highly correlated (see Chapter 11). If one of the pair has a high score, the other typically has a high score; if one has a low score, the other also has a low score.

One method of determining whether or not some degree of correlation exists is to plot a *scatter diagram* as in Figure 1.4. One set of scores is plotted along the x (horizontal) axis; the other scores are plotted along the y (vertical) axis. Each point represents an individual with an x and a y score. Figure 1.4 shows four scatter diagrams. In diagram A the dots are scattered at random and the correlation is zero. There is no relation between the two sets of scores. In diagram B there is some degree of relationship between the sets of scores, and in diagram C the relationship is very close—a high score for x corresponds with a high score for y. Diagram D also shows a close relationship between the two sets of scores, but the relationship is a negative one. In D low scores for x correspond with high scores for y. Thus, we see that correlations may be positive or negative. Where high scores in one variable correspond with high scores in another variable, the correlation is positive. For example, the size of one's vocabulary and the ability to express one's thoughts in writing are positively correlated. Where low scores correspond with high scores, the correlation is negative. For example, body weight and the ability to run fast are negatively correlated. Neither correlation is perfect, but both signify a high degree of relationship.

The relationship between the x and y scales (representing two sets of characteristics) is expressed as a decimal number called the *correlation coefficient*, usually signified by the letter r. A correlation coefficient can range from ±1.00 to .00. An r of +1.00 indicates a perfect positive correlation, and an r of −1.00 indicates a perfect negative correlation. An r of .00 indicates that there is no relationship between the two sets of scores. (Note that these decimal numbers are not percentages; they do not indicate specific multiples of the characteristics under study. For example, .60 does not imply twice as much as .30.)

All correlations found in psychological research fall between ±1.00 and .00, but there are very few, if any, perfect correlations. Correlation coefficients in the vicinity of ±.80 are very high and generally indicate a high degree of relationship, especially if such coefficients are obtained from a sample of 30 or more individuals. If the IQ score for a sample of 30 pairs of identical twins correlates +.80, we can fairly accurately predict one twin's score when we know the other twin's score. Our predictions will not be perfect, but they will be much better than chance.

While highly correlated variables allow us to predict from one to the other, they do not permit us to conclude that one causes the other. Correlations say nothing about causation. A high correlation between the number of flying insects observed and the thickness of a lawn does not mean that the insects caused the lawn to thicken or that the thick lawn attracted the insects. In point of fact, insects begin to appear as the weather warms, and lawns are stimulated to grow in warm weather.

There are instances, however, when correlations do indicate a causal relationship. In such cases, proof requires additional evidence—usually, but not always, of an experimental nature. An obvious example is the correlation between the number of hours of food deprivation and the amount of food consumed after deprivation; the longer the period between feedings, the more food will be consumed at each meal.

Three correlational methods are of interest in current psychological research: psychometric techniques, naturalistic observations, and clinical methods of observation. *Psychometric techniques* are simply tests. Psychological testing occupies the attention of psychologists in a wide variety of settings; in fact, probably no other application of psychology is so widely known to the general public, particularly to students in high schools and colleges. *Naturalistic observation* is the study of behavior in real-life settings. This method has recently become increasingly interesting to those involved in psychological research. The *clinical methods of observation*, as the phrase implies, may be set in a hospital, medical office, or similar treatment center. Such methods have long been popular and controversial, for they provide interesting information in situations that are difficult to control. Each correlational method has a special use in psychology.

Psychometric techniques Essentially, psychological tests are samples of behavior. These samples are obtained in special ways in order to predict behavior and to measure changes in behavior. Tests may be used to distinguish among the characteristics of several individuals or to distinguish changes within one individual. In practical situations, tests are used to provide decision-making information. For example, a reading test may be used to decide which child should be given remedial help in reading; a mechanical aptitude test may be used to place students in a technical course; a personality test may help to select candidates for a difficult and demanding job; and so forth. Tests are used in correlational research to identify particular independent variables. For instance, if we wished to select emotionally stable students for a learning experiment, we might rely on a test that has been known to separate the anxious person from the calm one.

If a test is to be useful, it must be standardized; that is, the test designer must somehow make certain that the test is always given in the same way and that every score can be compared fairly with every other score.

Psychometric tests are found in a variety of formats. Some tests—like the familiar intelligence, aptitude, and personality tests—are designed for the individual. Others are administered to groups whose members must then interact to complete the test. Tests may require paper and pencil, or they may involve elaborate equipment and complex performances from subjects.

The questionnaire is another type of psychometric technique that is useful in large-scale research. Carefully designed questionnaires are often used in social psychology, when attitudes and attitude change are studied by what is called the survey method. Public-opinion surveys play an important role in predicting voting behavior, and survey research is commonly used in analyzing the behavior of the buying public.

Naturalistic observations Some psychologists argue that conventional experimental methods and correlational methods that rely primarily on psychometric techniques are too limited. These scientists feel that naturalistic observations have much more to offer. Specifically, naturalistic research—the observation of behavior in real-life settings—offers three advantages:

1 It does not require the cooperation of the subject.
2 It usually does not let the subject know he is being studied in any special way.
3 It therefore does not change the behavior being measured.

In naturalistic observation, we might observe a child or a group of children playing in the street, the nest-building of birds, or the social behavior of gorillas in their natural habitat. The study of large-scale social phenomena, such as the behavior of crowds, also requires naturalistic observation. The Swiss psychologist Jean Piaget made extensive use of naturalistic observation in formulating his theory on the development of thinking in children. Piaget, in fact, studied his own children in his own home as intensely as he studied other children in their natural surroundings. (See, for example, Piaget, 1969.)

Piaget and other well-known psychologists have achieved far-reaching and important results from naturalistic observation; however, if not carefully conducted, naturalistic observation can produce misleading or inaccurate conclusions. Like the clinical method, it is most easily subject to individual bias or interpretation.

Clinical methods of observation The clinical method, especially the use of the case history, has played an important role in the development of psychology. The *case history* technique involves the gathering of information about the significant events in the life history of a person or persons. This information is sometimes very sketchy, and the investigator is required to piece together bits and pieces to create a meaningful biography of his subject or patient. Some investigators do a considerable amount of interpreting of their observations.

Perhaps the most famous case histories are to be found in the writings of Sigmund Freud, who based most of his theory of personality on observations and interpretations made in the clinical setting. Freud did not perform experiments. He systematically observed his patients and tried to identify conditions that seemed to influence their behavior. Freud wanted to get as much information as he could without interfering with what he was observing. He was flexible, adapting the techniques as the situation demanded. The following quotation from one of Freud's case histories provides some insight into his procedure and interpretation of observations.

But I have examples at my disposal which seem to prove the genesis of hysterical symptoms through symbolization alone. The following is one of the best and relates once more to Frau Cacilie M. When a girl of fifteen, she was lying in bed, under the watchful eye of her strict grandmother. The girl suddenly gave a cry; she had felt a penetrating pain in her forehead between her eyes, which lasted for weeks. During the analysis of this pain, which was reproduced after nearly thirty years, she told me that her grandmother had given her a look so "piercing" that it had gone right into her brain. (She had been afraid that the old woman was viewing her with suspicion.) As she told me this thought she broke into a loud laugh, and the pain once more disappeared. In this instance I can detect nothing other than the mechanism of symbolization, which has its place, in some sense midway between autosuggestion and conversion.

My observation of Frau Cacilie M. gave me an opportunity of making a regular collection of symbolizations of this kind. A whole set of physical sensations which would ordinarily be regarded as organically determined were in her case of psychical origin or at least possessed a psychical meaning. A particular series of experiences of hers were accompanied by a stabbing sensation in the region of the heart (meaning "it stabbed me to the heart"). The pain that occurs in hysteria of nails being driven into the head was without any doubt to be explained in her case as a pain related to thinking. ("Something's come into my head.") Pains of this kind were always cleared up as soon as the problems involved were cleared up. Running parallel to the sensation of the hysterical "aura" in the throat, when that feeling appeared after an insult, was the thought "I shall have to swallow this." She had a whole quantity of sensations and ideas running parallel with each other. Sometimes the sensation would call up the idea to explain it, sometimes the idea would create the sensation by means of symbolization, and not infrequently it has to be left an open question which of the two elements had been the primary one.

It is probably true that most clinically based statements about human behavior cannot be so general as statements made on the basis of extensive psychological testing or controlled and repeated experimentation. However, there are instances when the statements from the clinic and the laboratory are similar or even identical. It is such points of agreement that will ultimately enable us to develop a comprehensive understanding of behavior.

Both experimental and correlational methods can sometimes be used to investigate the same problem. For example, to study the effects of anxiety on learning, we could select, test, and compare a group of students who are anxious with a group of relatively nonanxious students. Or, in the laboratory, we could use electric shocks or other threats to create an anxious group, whose performance might then be compared with that of a control group. The first approach utilizes the correlational method; the second, the experimental method. Both are scientific, and either might be used.

Sometimes, however, the nature of a given problem may limit the scientist in his choice of method. We cannot truly observe the parent-child relationship in the laboratory, because it operates only in a natural setting. Nor would we be justified in taking an identical twin from his family simply to study a heredity-environment question. In each case the psychologist has alternatives. The parent-child relationship can be observed in the home or in the clinic. The scientist interested in heredity will need to locate twin pairs whom life has already separated, through adoption or through accident. In such cases, a correlational approach is used, because the conditions to be studied cannot be created experimentally. In other cases, where it is not feasible to use human beings, scientists use animals. To study the effects of brain surgery on behavior, for example, we might retain the experimental method and settle for animal subjects rather than human subjects.

DIMENSIONS OF PSYCHOLOGY

Figure 1.5 depicts the structure of psychology in three ways: (1) the kinds of subject matter studied; (2) the aims and methods of psychologists; and (3) the settings in which they work.

Subject matter

In discussing the subject matter of psychology, we shall identify 12 general areas. (You will note that for the sake of brevity some of these areas are combined in Figure 1.5. For example, the area of physiological processes includes the sense organs and the nervous and muscle systems.) Each of these areas is discussed in detail in the chapters that follow. Here we shall briefly identify each area:

1 The development of the individual organism, including heredity and maturation;
2 The role of the sense organs, including vision, hearing, smell, taste, touch, pain, and temperature, as well as the senses that detect bodily movement and balance;
3 The nervous system, including the central and the peripheral nervous systems and the muscles and glands that cooperate with the nervous system;
4 Perception, the process by which we come to understand the world in which we live;
5 The processes of learning and memory that enable us to adapt and cope with our environment;

Figure 1.5   This matrix is arranged to indicate the variety of combinations that make up the structure of psychology. One hundred and fifty combinations are shown here. However, because we have combined some of the subject matters, this is probably a conservative estimate. For example, physiological processes include the sense organs and the nervous and muscle systems. In addition, learning and memory, motivation and emotion, and language, thinking, and problem-solving are each combined under one heading; and a wide variety of topics may be lumped together under social behavior.

    Each block in the matrix represents a subject matter, an aim, and a setting in which psychologists work. For example, the block identified as number 1 indicates that the development of the individual is the subject matter, basic research is the aim, and the setting is the laboratory; block number 7 indicates that the subject matter is development, the aim is applied research, and the setting is the clinic; block 15 indicates that the subject matter is development, the aim is practical application, and the setting is the community.

6 Motivation, the unlearned and learned drives that impel action or inaction;
7 Emotion, the bodily conditions that we identify with feeling and that affect everything we do;
8 The higher processes of language, thinking, and problem-solving;
9 The observable and unobservable behavior that we call intelligence and its testing;
10 The specific characteristics of the individual that we refer to as personality;
11 The many varieties of behavior pathology (disturbance);
12 Social behavior, the interaction of people in groups.

Aims and methods

Three different aims absorb the psychologist. One is *pure research*, another is *applied research*, and the third is *practical application*.

Pure research   Pure, or basic, research is research pursued for the sheer love of discovery; it is the foundation of any science. Psychological

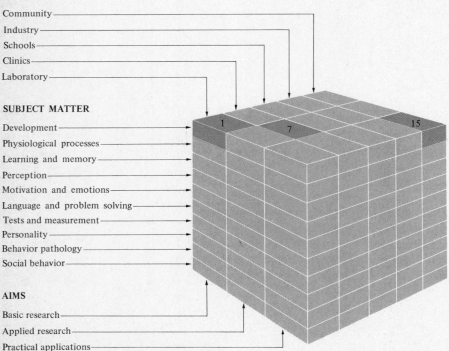

SETTINGS

Community
Industry
Schools
Clinics
Laboratory

SUBJECT MATTER

Development
Physiological processes
Learning and memory
Perception
Motivation and emotions
Language and problem solving
Tests and measurement
Personality
Behavior pathology
Social behavior

AIMS

Basic research
Applied research
Practical applications

researchers seek to discover the fundamental laws of behavior—both human and animal behavior. The pure researcher considers himself to be politically, ethically, morally, and socially neutral. This does not mean that persons doing pure research are unaware of social issues and social needs. However, their research interests focus on specific problems that may or may not have an immediate applicational value to society. They do not deliberately avoid application, but they seek to discover knowledge without allowing personal prejudices or the prejudices of others to interfere with their inquiry.

Basic research is conducted in virtually all areas of psychological inquiry including such areas as learning, perception, the study of intelligence, developmental psychology, personality, behavior pathology, physiological psychology, social psychology, and psychological measurement.

Applied research Psychologists involved in applied research are usually interested in solving practical problems to serve an immediate purpose. A typical applied research problem might be: What effect does prolonged weightlessness (as might be experienced by an astronaut) have on an individual's ability to solve problems and to use good judgment in decision-making? This is obviously an important practical problem, for it has implications for our space program as well as for the individual astronauts who participate.

Such a problem is approached in a systematic, well-controlled way, for applied research requires as careful a use of the scientific method as does basic research. The two forms of research are in fact closely related. They differ only in that one seeks immediate answers to practical problems, while the other has a longer-range view. The history of science tells us that the understanding of basic processes usually leads to significant practical applications. In other words, pure research typically generates applied research.

Applied research is found in educational psychology, clinical settings, industry, group and community relations, and in many other areas where practical answers to psychological questions are sought.

Practical applications Although *applied research* and *practical applications* are practiced in many of the same settings (in the clinic, school, industry, and community agency), these areas involve two different groups of psychologists. One group seeks answers to practical problems, and the second group applies these answers to uncontrolled, "real-world" situations. The most highly populated practical group is in the area of clinical psychology, in which the psychologist diagnoses and treats patients who display breakdowns in behavior. In Chapters 11, 13, and 14 we shall discuss some of the ways in which clinical psychologists apply the researchers' theories.

Because many psychologists are interested in the problems of education, they apply their knowledge and skills to the educational setting. Some of these *educational psychologists* deal with learning problems, some specifically with reading problems, some with the problems of adjustment found in young children. Many use the methods and techniques of psychological testing. *Industrial psychologists* apply their knowledge to personnel selection, vocational guidance, the training of workers, the maintenance of job satisfaction and morale, and to problems having to do with relationships between men and machines.

An increasing number of psychologists and *psychiatric social workers* are applying their skills to problems in community mental health, community change, intergroup relations, social action within the community, the problems of the aged, and relationships between law-enforcement agencies and the citizen.

The settings

Psychologists work in a number of different settings. Many do research and teach in universities and colleges. Close to 50 percent of all psychologists have some professional affiliation with a college or university. Another large group of psychologists is found in clinical settings. Some of these are in hospitals or in child-guidance clinics; some are in schools, where they work with disturbed children, diagnose learning problems, and are concerned with methods of testing in general; and a substantial number have private practices, maintaining their own offices and seeing patients on a fee basis. More and more psychologists are moving into industry, where they may be involved in personnel selection and placement, industrial training, and the design of equipment—the area often referred to as *human engineering*. Many psychologists in industry are involved in market research to determine the effectiveness of advertising or the desirability of certain products. Community psychology is also a fast-developing area. Many psychologists are now working in community mental health centers, suicide-prevention centers, drug-addiction treatment centers, or rehabilitation centers for patients discharged from mental hospitals.

RELATION OF PSYCHOLOGY TO OTHER SCIENCES

No science stands apart from other sciences. There always is overlap, both in content and in method. Psychology has always had a close relationship with the biological sciences, and today there is an increasingly strong link between psychology, anthropology, and sociology.

Physiological psychology is closely associated with the biological sciences—particularly physiology, neurology, and biochemistry. In order to understand the behavior of an organism, we must know something about the behaving organism's anatomy and physiology. We cannot talk about behavior as if it takes place in a vacuum, for behavior is often related to the individual's biological makeup, his hereditary predispositions, his maturational level, and his bodily conditions at the moment that he is behaving. No serious student of human or animal behavior can afford to ignore the biology of the organism.

Nor can we ignore the meaning of the social environment. Psychologists who are primarily interested in human behavior have become increasingly interested in cultural and social variables. *Anthropology* is the science that emphasizes the study of the origins of man and the manner in which he has developed culturally. The naturalistic observations of anthropologists contribute much to the understanding of individual behavior, for cultural variables play important roles in every facet of human behavior.

Sociology studies people in groups; the group rather than the individual is the unit of study. *Social psychologists* study the individual's participation in the group and the group's influence on the individual. Social groups, business groups, political groups, and religious groups attract the interest of the sociologist. While the data of sociology are concerned principally with groups as such, it is often difficult to separate social psychology from sociology, and very often no distinction need be made. Many sociologists are well trained in social psychology, and many social psychologists have extensive training in sociology. It is likely that in the near future we will see an increasing tendency to merge these two disciplines.

HISTORICAL ORIGINS OF PSYCHOLOGY

Psychology is a modern science, but its origins are found in the earliest days of written history. Man has probably always speculated and wondered about himself and his kind, and some of these speculations have been systematic and informative.

In tracing the history of psychology, we shall emphasize the individuals who have played an important role in the development of psychology. We have chosen this approach as a means of identifying significant developments in psychology. Like any other science, however, psychology has moved forward because of changes in society and through the accumulation of knowledge. Great ideas are not recognized if society is not ready for them. And the great ideas of individuals often arise out of earlier ideas. The physicist Isaac Newton once said, "If I have seen a little farther than others, it is because I have stood on the shoulders of giants." Great as Newton's contribution was, it represented the culmination of the work of many others.

Early philosophical influences

Although psychology did not exist as a formal and separate discipline until the last half of the nineteenth century, its roots were established many centuries ago in writings of the Greek philosophers, particularly *Plato* and *Aristotle*. The early philosophers were largely antiscientific and, with the possible exception of Aristotle, they tended to discourage man from seeking objective answers about himself. Plato specifically denied the value of experimentation. He felt that whatever knowledge man was to have about himself already resided within him, and that by thinking and reasoning alone man would come to understand what he was capable of understanding. Aristotle, in contrast to Plato, was an observer. He was among the first to state explicitly that the understanding of natural phenomena, including man, must begin with systematic, objective observations. It is easy to see why some psychologists refer to Aristotle as "the first psychologist."

When the Greek culture disintegrated and the writings of the Greek intellectuals were temporarily forgotten, religious teachings began to dominate man's intellectual activities. Philosophy and religion were for many centuries one and the same. Perhaps the most influential thinker in the tradition of religion and philosophy was *St. Thomas Aquinas*. Aquinas took it

Aristotle Aristotle believed that research begins with careful observation; he felt that one should study anatomical structures in order to understand their behavioral functions.

We must therefore not recoil with childish aversion from the examination of the humbler animals. . . . If any person thinks the examination of the rest of the animal kingdom an unworthy task, he must hold in like disesteem the study of man. For no one can look at the primordia of the human frame—blood, flesh, bones, vessels, and the like—without much repugnance. Moreover, when any one of the parts or structures, be it what it may, is under discussion, it must not be supposed that it is its material composition to which attention is being directed or which is the object of the discussion, but the relation of such part to the total form.

Figure 1.6   Aristotle. (The Bettmann Archive)

Figure 1.7   St. Thomas Aquinas. (The Granger Collection)

upon himself to interpret the work of Aristotle and, in so doing, he attempted to reconcile Aristotle's objectivity with the intellectual dogma of the church in the thirteenth century. Whereas Aristotle made no distinction between man and the lower animals, Aquinas emphasized such a distinction; whereas Aristotle discussed mind in terms of behavior, Aquinas considered mind as an entity separate from the body. This view of man is called *dualism*. Aquinas's belief in the separation of mind and body was to challenge psychology for many centuries to come.

Figure 1.8   James Mill. (The Granger Collection)

Revival of scientific inquiry

In the fifteenth century man's style of inquiry began to change. During this period, known as the Renaissance, man began to cast aside some of his old beliefs. He actively sought new knowledge. Literature was reborn, as were political philosophy and other forms of philosophy. The Renaissance provided a new spirit for scientific inquiry, and although no new significant events in science occurred at this time, the stage was set for development in the years to follow. Early in the seventeenth century, *Francis Bacon*, truly a product of the Renaissance, argued persuasively on behalf of the importance of objective observation. Bacon identified the important connection between theory and research. Theory, he said, provides the guidelines, but research provides the answers.

For three centuries after Bacon, many philosophers were preoccupied with questions about the nature of the mind. These questions emerged largely from the work of *René Descartes*, who carried forward the ideas of Plato and the dualism of Aquinas. For Descartes, ideas were innate; they were placed in the mind by God. He held to a rationalistic view of knowledge; and, as opposed to Bacon, he felt that we could discover the truth by reason alone. He was a dualist; he believed that the mind and body are separate. The mind is the "thinking matter," a nonphysical substance, and the body, the physical machine, does the work of the mind. It was clear that psychology would have to answer to these views if it were to emerge as a science.

During the philosophical period of the middle seventeenth century to the middle nineteenth century, two streams of influence played prominent roles in shaping psychology. One influence was a movement often referred to as *British empiricism*. British empiricism, exemplified in the writings of *Thomas Hobbes, John Locke, David Hartley, James Mill,* and James's son *John Stuart Mill*, argued against Descartes's view of innate ideas. For the empiricist, knowledge comes through the medium of the senses. The "mind," according to Locke, is a *tabula rasa*, a blank slate on which experience writes. We know only what we have experienced or what man generally is able to experience.

The British empiricists wanted to know how ideas occur, how they influence each other, and what prompts one idea to combine with another idea. Locke felt that the "mind" consists of combinations of ideas. Simple ideas are acquired passively, but the mind combines these ideas to produce complex ones. This view was extended by James Mill, who argued that the association of ideas is the basic principle by which we can come to understand how man learns and how he thinks. The speculations of the British empiricists played a significant role in the later development of *associationistic psychology*.

The biological influences on psychology were represented by the movement called *materialism*. This movement is seen in the research of *Charles Bell* and *François Magendie*, who identified the difference between sensory and motor nerves; *Pierre Flourens*, who used surgical techniques in which he removed brain tissue to localize certain brain functions; *Johannes Mueller*, who formulated the doctrine of the specific energies of nerves (specific senses are mediated by particular sensory nerves); and *Marshall Hall*, who identified the anatomical properties of the reflex.

Perhaps the most significant contributions were made by *Hermann von Helmholtz*, who was a physicist, mathematician, philosopher, physiologist, and a forerunner of experimental psychology. Helmholtz insisted that human activity could be explained solely in terms of physical principles. He was a scientific giant who studied an amazing variety of phenomena, ranging from the speed of the nerve impulse to visual and auditory processes and perception.

Helmholtz was opposed by a philosopher-physicist, *Gustav Fechner*, an *antimaterialist* who developed a method that was later to become a part of experimental psychology. Fechner sought to prove that the nonphysical mind could be studied, and his search led him to create the methods of *psychophysics*. These methods are used to measure relationships between the physical characteristics of stimuli and the sensory experiences reported by subjects.

Hermann von Helmholtz Helmholtz felt that perception develops as a result of experience:

My conclusion is, that nothing in our sense-perceptions can be recognized as sensation which can be overcome in the perceptual image and converted into its opposite by factors that are demonstrably due to experience.

Whatever, therefore, can be overcome by factors of experience, we must consider as being itself the product of experience and training.

Figure 1.9   Hermann von Helmholtz. (The Granger Collection)

Psychology emerges

The first psychological laboratory was established by *Wilhelm Wundt* in 1879 in Leipzig. Wundt, who had been trained by Helmholtz, was influenced by the British associationists, and his psychology was based on their views of the associations of ideas. Wundt established a school of psychology (that is, a systematic point of view) known as *structuralism*. The structuralism of Wundt was based on the argument that psychology should begin its study of the mind in terms of the elements comprised in it, the fundamental building blocks of which ideas and other mental events are composed. Wundt's point of

E. B. Titchener Titchener's reliance on introspection stemmed from his view that it was simply a more difficult—but not less accurate—method of observation:

In principle, then, introspection is very like inspection. The objects of observation are different; they are objects of dependent, not of independent experience; they are likely to be transient, elusive, slippery. Sometimes they refuse to be observed while they are in passage; they must be preserved in memory, as a delicate tissue is preserved in hardening fluid, before they can be examined. And the standpoint of the observer is different; it is the standpoint of human life and of human interest, not of detachment and aloofness. But, in general, the method of psychology is much the same as the method of physics.

Figure 1.10 E. B. Titchener. *(The Granger Collection)*

view was brought to the United States by *E. B. Titchener*, the foremost spokesman for the structuralist point of view. Titchener argued, as did Wundt, that the basic method of psychology is self-observation. It differs from the observation of physical science in that it involves looking within oneself, a method that is called *introspection*. Titchener felt that this could be done objectively and scientifically.

The introspective method became the cornerstone of structural psychology; and structuralism became vulnerable to criticism from those who argued that introspection is too subjective to be reliable. In spite of Titchener's best efforts to demonstrate the objectivity of introspection, little objective verification could be found, and because science depends on verifiability, most psychologists ultimately chose to seek more objective methods.

The publication in 1890 of *Principles of Psychology* by *William James* signaled the beginning of another significant movement in psychology, a movement often referred to as *functionalism*. The functionalists did not agree with the ideas of structuralism. They felt that psychology should be the study of man's methods of adapting to his environment, the ways in which

he satisfies his needs and increases his abilities. James was particularly interested in consciousness, which he saw as a tool that enables the individual to select his courses of action. The more intelligent the organism, the greater is his consciousness; the less intelligent, the less is his consciousness. James felt that consciousness is an ongoing process that cannot be analyzed into elemental units. He and other functionalists were not interested primarily in overt behavior. They studied behavior, but they were more interested in speculating about its causes.

The period of structuralism and functionalism also marked the appearance of *Sigmund Freud*, an Austrian psychiatrist who proposed a powerful and complex theory of personality. Freud's psychoanalytic theory did not develop from philosophy, as did the other schools of psychology we have encountered; rather, it drew from medical and psychiatric practice. For example, Freud's early thought was influenced by medical experiments with hypnosis, and by the work of *Jean Martin Charcot*, a Parisian neurologist who believed that all nervous disorders could be traced to sexual problems. In addition, Freud drew from the writings of Johann Friedrich Herbart and Gustav Fechner, both of whom had speculated about the role of unconscious ideas in human behavior.

which involved some form of pleasurable physical stimulation and were thus "sexual" in nature. Specifically, he believed that many disturbances arose from the frustration of the sexual needs in early childhood. Convinced of the importance of childhood experiences, Freud postulated a series of sexual stages through which the child passes. He found that if the child did not progress properly through these stages, he would experience behavior disorders in adult life. (The so-called Oedipus complex and related hypotheses were part of Freud's attempt to define the drama of infant sexuality in terms of its effect on adult behavior.)

Though professionally involved with emo-

William James James's discussion of habit is a classic in psychology:

Habit is thus the enormous fly-wheel of society, its most precious conservative agent. It alone is what keeps us all within the bounds of ordinance, and save the children of fortune from the envious uprisings of the poor. It alone prevents the hardest and most repulsive walks of life from being deserted by those brought up to tread therein. It keeps the fisherman and the deck-hand at sea through the winter; it holds the miner in his darkness, and nails the countryman to his log cabin and his lonely farm through all the months of snow; it protects us from invasion by the natives of the desert and the frozen zone. It dooms us all to fight out the battle of life upon the lines of our nurture or our early choice, and to make the best of a pursuit that disagrees, because there is no other for which we are fitted and it is too late to begin again.

Sigmund Freud Freud developed ways and means to probe beneath the surface of consciousness:

When I set myself the task of bringing to light what human beings keep hidden within them, not by the compelling power of hypnosis, but by observing what they say and what they show, I thought the task was a harder one than it really is. He that has eyes to see and ears to hear may convince himself that no mortal can keep a secret. If the lips are silent, he chatters with his finger tips; betrayal oozes out of him at every pore. And thus the task of making conscious the most hidden recesses of the mind is on which it is quite possible to accomplish.

Figure 1.12 Drawing of Freud by Schmutzer, 1926. (© Presse und Informationsamt der Bundesregierung, Bonn)

Freud proposed that the unconscious actively influenced behavior to an extent that earlier thinkers had never conceived. He found evidence of this in his observations of hysterical patients—patients in whom an unconscious problem seems to manifest itself as a physical disorder. In treating these patients, Freud thought that most of their unconscious problems were due to the frustration of basic universal needs, all of

tionally disturbed patients, Freud was also concerned with the psychology of average people and everyday happenings. He felt that even the lives of the well adjusted are filled with "accidents" caused by unconscious wishes and with dreams rich in suppressed thoughts and symbols. Freud worked his colorful observations into a comprehensive theory that attempted no less than a total explanation of the behavior of man.

Freud's role in the history of psychology is controversial. For some he looms as the most important figure of modern times; others regard his contributions as largely negative and would deny him a place in the scheme of scientific psychology. Many of Freud's critics—including some of his disciples—regret his emphasis on early childhood and declare that he underestimated the ability of the adult personality to be changed. Others object to Freud's belief in basic universal drives, maintaining that culture and society are the major influences on behavior. Some critics feel that Freud's theory is useful in dealing with certain types of disturbed personalities, but not with ordinary personality development.

The usefulness of Freud's observations is judged differently by psychologists with different objectives. A clinical psychologist faced with a suicidal patient is likely to be more interested in Freud than is an experimental psychologist with a laboratory full of rats.

While psychoanalytic theory has dominated behavior pathology, experimental psychology has dealt with sensation and the sensory processes. At the beginning of the twentieth century, the work of the experimentalists virtually exploded into the significant areas of learning, memory, and perception. The research breakthrough was most strongly influenced by *Ivan Pavlov* in Russia and *E. L. Thorndike* in the United States. These two men, proceeding in very different ways and with different interests, set the stage for the development of behaviorism and for the experimental psychology of learning. The study of learning came to dominate much of American psychology during the 1930s and 1940s, and Pavlovian conditioning still dominates psychology in the Soviet Union.

As a result of the work of Pavlov and Thorndike, and in reaction to Freudian and structuralist psychology, respectively, behaviorism and Gestalt psychology developed. Both groups moved away from clinical observation to endorse the principles of *empirical* science. The emperical scientist bases his conclusions on planned observation. In psychology, the empiricist is often, but not always, an experimentalist, because the experimental method is the most refined method for making objective, careful observations. Where he cannot experiment, he tries to systematize his observational techniques,

Figure 1.13   E. L. Thorndike. (Mrs. E. L. Thorndike)

E. L. Thorndike Thorndike was not a behaviorist, but his studies of learning were among the examples of the behavioral method:

Human learning consists of changes in the nature and behavior of human beings. Changes in nature are known to us only by changes in behavior. The word behavior as used here and later means anything which the human animal does. It includes thoughts and feelings as truly as movements, and makes no assumptions concerning the deeper nature of any of these. It takes them as they are found.

for if others are to check his observations, they must be able to repeat them in the same way that he carried them out.

We shall consider the contributions of behaviorism and Gestalt psychology separately; they have different origins and very different implications.

No movement or development in psychology has been more vigorous or more influential than *behaviorism*. In the early twentieth century, *John B. Watson*, an American psychologist and founder of behaviorism, urged that psychology break with the past. He was a forthright, aggressive, and enthusiastic spokesman who argued that psychology had been looking at the wrong problems in the wrong ways. Watson concluded that the study of consciousness or conscious experience was severely limited, for it relied almost exclusively on the technique of introspection, and he insisted that introspection was not an adequate tool. It made a pretense of careful observation, and was futile and hopeless from the start; observers who studied only themselves could not produce reliable data for comparison. Watson felt that psychology should turn its attention away from consciousness and toward the goal of predicting and controlling behavior. He reasoned that psychology had many objective methods available, perhaps the most important of which was the methodology developed by Pavlov in Russia. Watson, Pavlov, and other forerunners of behaviorism thought that psychology should be concerned exclusively with overt behavior—and not with unobservable

thought processes or unconscious wishes. Watson studied the ways organisms responded to stimuli in the environment. His observations led him to believe that by controlling the environment he could control behavior. Watson held that all forms of human and other animal behavior ultimately could be accounted for by environmental conditioning.

Watson did not accept the classical distinction between mind and body, nor did he accept the idea that man was qualitatively different from lower animals. He turned to Darwin's view of the continuity of species and rejected the views of Plato, Aquinas, and Descartes. So, too, did he challenge the popular theory that emotional patterns are instinctive; he stated that only fear, rage, and love exist prior to learning.

Watson was an extreme environmentalist, virtually rejecting the idea that hereditary factors play a significant role in human behavior. He is widely remembered for the following statement about environment:

Give me a dozen healthy infants, well formed, and my own specified world to bring them up in and I'll guarantee to take any one of them at random and train him to become any type of specialist I might select—a doctor, lawyer, artist, merchant, chief, and yes, even into a beggarman and thief regardless of his talents, penchants, tendencies, abilities, vocations and race of his ancestors.

This quotation is more of a challenge than a statement of scientific principle, but Watson was an attractive, flamboyant personality who enjoyed teasing his critics and detractors.

Watson was not only the founder of behaviorism but also the man who influenced the full-scale development of applied psychology. Furthermore, he paved the way for much of the research now being performed, particularly in the psychology of learning. In insisting that psychology be applied and useful, Watson directly opposed many of the classical psychologists who preceded him.

Approximately the same time that behav-

Figure 1.14   John B. Watson. (Historical Pictures Service, Chicago)

John B. Watson   Watson wrote vigorously and persuasively. He had this to say about meaning:

From the behaviorist's point of view the problem of "meaning" is a pure abstraction. It never arises in the scientific observation of behavior. We watch what the animal or human being is doing. He "means" what he does. It serves no scientific or practical purpose to interrupt and ask him while he is in action what he is meaning. His action shows his meaning. Hence, exhaust the conception of action—i.e., experimentally determine all of the organized responses a given object can call forth in a given individual, and you have exhausted all possible "meaning" of that object for that individual. To answer what the church means to men it is necessary to look upon the church as a stimulus and to find out what reactions are called out by this stimulus in a given race, in a given group or in any given individual.

iorism was beginning in the United States, *Gestalt psychology* was developing in Germany. Gestalt psychology, like behaviorism, arose as a protest movement. The Gestalt psychologists—*Max Wertheimer, Wolfgang Köhler,* and *Kurt Koffka*—opposed the structuralists and favored James's belief that the workings of the mind of component elements. When we analyze, says could not be understood through the analysis the Gestaltist, we artificially break things down into elements. Gestaltists insist that such analysis is incorrect, because "the whole is more than the sum of its parts." They say that the *whole* (*Gestalt*) is the basic unit, and that perception is the basic tool by which it is studied. The way to understand an individual is to understand how he perceives. The interests of Gestalt psychologists are thus directed to the principles of perceptual organization.

Wolfgang Köhler   Like most Gestalt psychologists, Köhler rejected the importance of past experience in perception:

It would be extremely unfortunate if the problem were thrust aside at this point as being after all only another case of the influence of past experience. No one doubts that past experience is an important factor in *some* cases, but the attempt to explain all perception in such terms is absolutely sure to fail, for it is easy to demonstrate instances where perception is not at all influenced by past experience.

Gestalt psychology originated in Germany, where Wertheimer, Köhler, and Koffka studied and taught. This movement was not favorably received, nor was it influential in the United States until American psychologists began to turn some of their attention to problems of perception and to the fields of problem-solving and

Figure 1.15   Wolfgang Köhler. (Swarthmore College)

personality. By emphasizing the complexity and the importance of perception, Gestalt psychology played a prominent role in the development of *cognitive psychology*. It gave to this new approach the ideas that cognition begins with sensory input (stimuli) and that to understand perception, the psychologist must account for the organization, transformation, storage, and use of the sensory input. The study of cognition concerns itself with the internal mechanisms, such as sensation, perception, and imagery, that may account for overt behavior.

Psychology asserts itself

In the early 1930s, psychologists began to concentrate on theory and research that was specifically and uniquely psychological. By this time, most universities had established departments of psychology that were no longer affiliated with philosophy or biology. Textbooks in psychology were written, and university students took increasing interest in the new discipline. During the 1930s and 1940s, psychological research flourished, and psychological theories, particularly in learning, were developed.

Many of the learning theories were directly influenced by Watson, Thorndike, and Pavlov. These theories are usually referred to as *stimulus-response (S-R) theories*, because they ana-

lyze behavior in terms of the responses of which behavior consists and the stimuli that evoke or set the occasion for these responses. For a number of years S-R psychology was equated with "rat psychology," because so much of the research performed by S-R psychologists entailed the use of rats as laboratory animals.

The major contributors to S-R psychology during this period were *C. L. Hull, E. R. Guthrie,* and *B. F. Skinner.* Hull proposed a formal theory of learning that served to stimulate considerable research as well as considerable debate. Many of Hull's students are active today, having developed modifications or offshoots of the original Hullian theory, published in 1943. Guthrie is referred to as a theorist, although he never presented a formal, organized theory. His writings are often anecdotal, but always perceptive and provocative. Skinner refuses to be designated as a theorist, for he emphasizes the empirical approach, arguing that the gathering of factual information must of necessity precede theorizing. Whether or not we call Skinner a theorist, he has developed a highly organized system of analyzing and controlling behavior, and he is among the most influential contemporary psychologists.

B. F. Skinner Skinnerian descriptive behaviorism avoids the use of theory. Skinner insists that we should seek to explain behavior by studying behavior and not by inventing unseen processes:

I never faced a Problem which was more than the eternal problem of finding order. I never attacked a problem by constructing a Hypothesis. I never deduced Theorems or submitted them to Experimental Check. So far as I can see, I had no preconceived Model of behavior— certainly not a physiological or mentalistic one and, I believe, not a conceptual one.

Another influential psychologist of the late 1920s and the 1930s was *E. C. Tolman,* who combined behaviorism with some of the concepts of Gestalt psychology and helped to pave the way for cognitive psychology. While the

Figure 1.16   B. F. Skinner.
(© Karsh, Ottawa)

behaviorists rejected purpose as an explanatory device, Tolman felt that stimulus-response analysis was not adequate to explain complex human phenomena and that the concept of *purpose* was necessary for analyzing behavior. Tolman's point of view served to stimulate interest in the psychology of thinking; his critical comments caused both S-R and Gestalt psychologists to take to their laboratories to prove or disprove his arguments. It is not clear how well the research that resulted served to unify psychological thinking. Psychology is certainly not unified today, but there is more and more evidence of a movement toward integrating ideas from S-R psychology with those of cognitive psychology. What is emerging is still not clear, but many of the old doctrinaire arguments between the militant S-R and Gestalt psychologists have faded. Behaviorists and cognitive psychologists alike are interested in thinking, language, problem-solving, perception, and learning.

From the early 1930s until recently scientific psychology was dominated by the behaviorist model, or *paradigm*. Within this paradigm, emphasis is almost exclusively on external situations, overt behavior, and the environmental events that govern this behavior. But there are signs that the behaviorist model is beginning to share center stage with the paradigm of cognitive psychology. Some writers (Neisser, 1972; Segal and Lachman, 1972) even suggest that there is a paradigm shift, in which the behaviorists' concentration on external observation and rejection of mental processes is giving way to interest in such higher mental processes as ideas, imagery, and cognition.

The distinction between the behaviorist model and the cognitive model is best described in terms of their different emphases. The behaviorists take the position that man's behavior, however complex, can be reduced to the principles of learning. The associations of stimulus and response is a fundamental concept, and the study of learning is basic. Behavior is explained in terms of the environmental events that shape responses. The scientific observer studies what the learner does and the observable variables that influence his actions.

Cognitive psychology is concerned with covert, or concealed or disguised, responses. Covert behavior is dealt with in terms of the cognitive processes that determine the behavior. Cognition as described by Neisser (1967) "refers to all the processes by which the sensory input is transformed, reduced, elaborated, stored, recovered, and used. . . . Such terms as sensation, perception, imagery, retention, recall, problem-solving, and thinking, among many others, refer to the hypothetical stages or aspects of cognition." The cognitive psychologist interests him-

Figure 1.17   E. C. Tolman. (Mrs. T. J. Kent)

E. C. Tolman Tolman's modified behaviorism rejected a mechanistic view of learning. He felt that too much emphasis was placed on the passive aspects of learning and not enough emphasis was given to goals and purposes.

My objection to Thorndike's Law of Effect was not to the importance of motivation as a factor in learning, but rather to his wholly mechanical notion as to its operation by way of effect. According to Thorndike, an animal learned, not because it achieved a wanted goal by a certain series of responses, but merely because a quite irrelevant "pleasantness" or "unpleasantness" was, so to speak, shot at it, from a squirt gun, after it had reached the given goal-box or gone into the given cul de sac.

Figure 1.18   Erik Erikson. (Olive R. Pierce)

self in hypothetical mechanisms. He seeks to identify the variables that affect these mechanisms and the ways these mechanisms affect behavior.

The behaviorist paradigm emphasizes the history of the individual—how past events influence present behavior. Cognitive psychology looks at how the present environment is interpreted (transformed, reduced, elaborated, and so forth) by the individual. Within the cognitive paradigm the emphasis is on the present.

The two paradigms are not necessarily competitive. They focus on somewhat different problems, but they also overlap. Both behaviorists and cognitive psychologists study retention, problem-solving, and thinking, and both recognize the necessity for scientific objectivity. The repeatability of observation holds for the two approaches, and both seek to discover the variables affecting behavior.

In personality theory, the Freudian influence is still major. Some of Freud's disciples—notably *Alfred Adler* and *Carl Jung*—left the Freudian school to pursue original theories. Adler explained the personality in terms of the individual's constant attempt to overcome inferiorities. Jung postulated, among other things, that the individual has a collective unconscious from which he draws memories held in common by humanity in general.

More recently, post-Freudians have adapted psychoanalytic theory to the needs of modern therapy. Usually this has meant replacing Freud's emphasis on sexuality with a new emphasis on the frustrations imposed by the social structure. Thus, *Karen Horney* felt the need to describe the neurotic personality of our time in her study of the same name (1937); *Erich Fromm* investigated the personality types that tend to be created by different societies; and *Harry Stack Sullivan* described the ways in which the self is defined through interpersonal relationships. Especially current is the work of *Erik Erikson*, the personality theorist who first made us aware of the "identity crisis." Erikson describes development in terms of social stages, each of which is characterized by a different personality crisis.

In recent years two new approaches have interested some psychologists. One is the *existential viewpoint*, advocated by *Rollo May*, which centers on the way man deals with the reality of his own existence in the face of anxiety and death; another is the *self-actualizing view of Carl Rogers*, which aims at individual growth and fulfillment (self-actualization).

SUMMARY

The student of psychology will acquire a vocabulary of terms that holds a special meaning in this discipline. They have been devised for quick and accurate communication.

The psychologist selects a problem for study, formulates sharp, clear questions, and makes systematic observations.

Some psychologists argue that the choice of problems and questions should be based on an organized theory. B. F. Skinner, a nontheorist, has argued that curiosity should be the psychologist's guide. However, both curiosity and theory have a place in psychological investigation.

A theory can serve as a way to summarize what we have observed and to predict as yet undiscovered relationships.

The scientific method involves systematic observation of important factors, or variables, and organization and interpretation of emerging facts.

In the experimental method, the observer manipulates variables to determine how such conditions affect behavior. He uses independent variables, those he can manipulate, and dependent variables, those he expects to be affected by his manipulations.

Experiments usually involve an experimental group (a group to which some special treatment is applied) and a control group (a similar group exposed to the same experimental environment but not given the special treatment).

Psychologists often use descriptive statistics to summarize research data and to compare one set of measurements with another. To find the central tendency in scores, psychologists may use either the mean or the median.

Correlational methods are used to investigate events that cannot be manipulated effectively. A correlation measures mutual relationship. It may be positive or negative. The relationship between two sets of scores is the correlation coefficient r, ranging from ± 1.00 to .00.

Three important correlational methods are psychometric techniques, naturalistic observation, and clinical methods.

Those who work in the field of psychology may be engaged in pure research, applied research, or practical application.

Psychology is closely related to other scientific disciplines: biology, sociology, and anthropology, for example.

Early philosophical influences are found in the writings of the Greek philosophers Plato and Aristotle, and later in the teachings of St. Thomas Aquinas.

Psychology began to take shape following the Renaissance. Bacon saw the connection between theory and research. Descartes, a dualist in the tradition of Plato, argued that ideas were innate. The British empiricists Hobbes, Locke, Hartley, James Mill, and John Stuart Mill denied Descartes's view of innate ideas; they asserted that ideas (knowledge) came from experience. The materialists, among them Helmholtz, studied the biological variables affecting man. Fechner performed experiments to measure sensation.

Psychology emerged as a full science when Wundt established the first laboratory in 1879 and the school of thought known as structuralism, which was brought to the United States by Titchener. Other systems of psychology also flourished: the functionalism of William James; Freud's psychoanalysis; the behaviorism of John B. Watson; and the Gestalt school led by Wertheimer, Köhler, and Koffka.

During the 1930s and 1940s, Hull, Guthrie, and Skinner contributed to the development of stimulus-response (S-R) theories. Tolman combined behaviorism with Gestalt psychology to pave the way for cognitive psychology.

The behaviorist paradigm, or model, emphasizes overt responses and the influence of past events on individual behavior; the cognitive paradigm emphasizes covert responses and the interpretation of the present environment by the individual.

Adler explained personality in terms of the inferiority complex. Jung postulated the collective unconscious. Other leading post-Freudians are Horney, Fromm, Sullivan, and Erikson. The existential view of May and the self-actualizing school of Rogers are also influential.

SUGGESTED READINGS

Texts

Boring, E. G. *A history of experimental psychology* (2nd ed.). New York: Appleton-Century-Crofts, 1950. Survey of historical movements in a modern context.

Ellenberger, H. F. *The discovery of the unconscious.* New York: Basic Books, 1971. Traces the chain of development of psychiatric systems from exorcists, magnetists, and hypnotists to the evolution of Janet, Freud, Adler, and Jung.

Guilford, J. P. (Ed.) *Fields of psychology.* Princeton, N.J.: Van Nostrand, 1966. Profiles of various areas in psychology.

Hernstein, R. J., & Boring, E. G. *A source book in the history of psychology.* Cambridge, Mass.: Harvard University Press, 1965. Collection of 116 excerpts from the writings of philosophers and psychologists living between 300 B.C. and A.D. 1900.

Hutt, S. J., & Hutt, C. *Direct observation and measurement of behavior.* Springfield, Ill.: Charles C Thomas, 1970. Description of the use of naturalistic observation to study the behavior of children.

James, W. *Psychology* (Gordon Allport, Ed.). New York: Harper & Row, 1961. This revision of William James's original (1890) work is "must" reading for its insight and scientific verve.

Kaufman, H. *Introduction to the study of human behavior.* Philadelphia: Saunders, 1968. Excellent discussion of the concepts and logic of psychological research.

Marks, R. W. (Ed.) *Great ideas in psychology.* Collection of articles by Freud, Lewin, James, and other leading psychologists.

Scott, W. A., & Wertheimer, M. *Introduction to psychological research.* New York: Wiley, 1962. Handbook dealing with the practical uses of psychological research.

Sidman, M. *Tactics of scientific research.* New York: Basic Books, 1960. Practical account of the approach to research based on the experimental analysis of behavior.

Wertheimer, M. *A brief history of psychology.* New York: Holt, Rinehart and Winston, 1970. A comprehensive but condensed survey that provides a good overview of the history of psychology.

Popular books

Edinger, E. F. *Ego and archetype.* A provocative book, offering a lucid survey of Jung's psychological concepts.

Fincher, C. *Preface to psychology.* The scientific method as it appears in experimental and clinical techniques.

Joncich, G. *The sane positivist: A biography of Edward L. Thorndike.* A biography of an olympian figure in the history of psychology.

Klein, D. B. *A history of scientific psychology.* An account of the efforts of psychology to achieve scientific status. Excellent research tools for beginners, because it includes replicas of useful historical materials.

Murchison, C. *History of psychology in autobiography.* Autobiographical accounts by several famous psychologists.

Spector, J. J. *The aesthetics of Freud.* A study of psychoanalysis and art, and a fresh look at the impact of Freud on our times.

Watson, J. D. *The double helix.* A frank and refreshing account of how scientists work.

Watson, R. I. *The great psychologists: Aristotle to Freud.* A readable account of the backgrounds and ideas of psychology's most important historical figures.

2

Heredity and development

At one time people were quick to say that we are what our heredity causes us to be. The pendulum of opinion then swung away from heredity toward environment, and we were said to be more a product of our environment than our heredity. Neither the heredity nor the environment position, however, has come out on top. The issue of heredity versus environment has been replaced by the question of how heredity and environment interact to contribute to individual differences.

HEREDITY AND BEHAVIOR

How does heredity influence our behavior? The term "heredity" is used to describe the biological transmission of characteristics or patterns from parents to child. For example, a child inherits the potential for either blue or brown eyes, and for straight or curly hair. We say "potential" because the individual inherits the patterns for a given characteristic rather than the characteristic itself.

Heredity involves the transmission not only of complex potentials but also of growth patterns that will cause the potential characteristics to appear. Transmission of hereditary material occurs at *conception*, the moment at which the female's *egg cell* (*ovum*) is fertilized by the male's *sperm cell*. The union of the egg and the sperm within the mother's body results in a new fertilized cell, called the *zygote*. In the nucleus of the zygote, the hereditary material of mother and father is combined, and within 24 hours of conception, this hereditary material begins to direct the development of a new individual. The zygote divides as the mechanisms of heredity activate a series of cell divisions that transform the single cell into a human infant, born about 9 months later. During the prenatal period, when the fetus is in the mother's womb, the systems and structures it will need to function as a separate being are developing.

Hereditary material is transmitted through submicroscopic units called *genes*. The gene is the basic unit of heredity. Each gene controls the development of a specific characteristic in the new individual; in concert, the genes determine the nature and growth of virtually every bodily structure. Singly or in groups, genes determine thousands of subtle, almost imperceptible characteristics—the shape of an earlobe, the curve of an eyebrow, the distance between knuckle and fingernail—as well as many characteristics that are not visible. At least 46,000 genes contribute to the making of an individual, and no two individuals receive the same selection of genes (except for identical twins).

Since identical twins are the only individuals who inherit exactly the same genetic makeup, they are frequently used as subjects for genetic studies. Observed differences between identical twins cannot be due to heredity, since both individuals have inherited exactly the same characteristics; therefore, the environment must be held accountable for any differences in growth and development. To determine the influence of environment, scientists have studied the development of identical twins reared together and contrasted those findings with information about identical twins reared apart.

As another aspect of environment-heredity research, scientists also study *fraternal twins* (individuals born of two different zygotes, each separately fertilized at conception). Since in fraternal multiple births each zygote is fertilized by a different sperm, the sex of each fraternal twin is determined independently. Thus, fraternal twins may be of different sexes, whereas identical twins, fertilized by the same sperm, must necessarily be of the same sex. Fraternal twins, indeed, have a genetic composition no more alike than that of ordinary siblings. But because they have a similar environment, coupled with unlike genetic material, they provide a good source of data for comparison with studies of identical twins, who share the same environment as well as the same genes.

Nature versus nurture

Heredity-environment studies investigate questions of enduring interest. When we see an overweight child, for example, we are quick to wonder which is responsible—his mother's genes or his mother's cooking (usually, it is a little of both). This is the kind of question involved in what has come to be known as the *nature versus nurture controversy*. Participants in the controversy have attempted to find out whether nature (heredity, as determined by the genes) or nurture (environment) plays the major role in human behavior. It should not surprise us to learn that neither force has been identified as the dominant influence.

In the past, psychologists, biologists, and philosophers often chose to adopt extreme positions. By setting out to prove that environment (nurture) is the determinant of the individual's ultimate behavior—his personality, intelligence, aptitudes, and so on—adherents to the nurture theory discounted the role of inherited characteristics. They argued that in some subtle, natural process of heredity, inherited characteristics balanced each other in the statistical sense, so that every individual was the same at birth. Adherents of the nature theory argued the opposite: that an individual is what heredity makes him, and that the environment plays an insignificant role in shaping behavior.

There is no longer scientific justification for maintaining either of these extreme views: it is increasingly clear that the individual is a product of the interaction of his environment and his heredity. Both factors operate in ways that researchers cannot always identify; there are causal relationships, interrelationships, and perhaps even isolated influences stemming from nature to nurture. The connections are subtle indeed. A child may inherit the sensory organs that enable him to make precise discriminations between tones of a different pitch—and this sensitivity may predispose him to demonstrate the behavior we call musical talent. Such talent, however, involves more than the inherited sensory capacity; it requires such appropriate environmental conditions as opportunities to listen to music and the encouragement of parents.

An unbiased investigation into the nature-nurture issue begins with objective observation.

Influence of heredity

The influence of heredity upon behavior cannot be directly observed, but we assume that the genetic code controls the various maturational processes and that these processes have an observable effect on behavior. Let us consider, for example, the behavior we call walking. The development of the the legs to support the body and of the upper body to balance on the legs; these abilities are triggered by the genetic potential within the individual's cells. At the time that the infant is maturationally ready to walk, the genetic codes have prepared the bodily structures to accommodate his first uncertain steps.

Since function depends on structure, function, as well as structure, is influenced by heredity. The behavior of a seemingly clumsy person may be attributed to the simple fact that he is nearsighted and does not realize that he needs corrective lenses. In another person clumsy behavior may be due to underdeveloped motor coordination. In both cases, certain structures malfunction because of inherited characteristics. The eyes of the first person and the nerves and muscles of the second developed according to the message from the appropriate genes—thus setting the stage for nearsightedness or "clumsiness" in whatever form it is expressed.

The genes transmit or fail to transmit certain chemical substances ("messages") to the proper bodily structures or systems. The absence of such substances or their unbalanced presence often produces a physical characteristic that affects behavior.

Behavioral characteristics almost always result from multiple-gene determination. The ability to remember, for instance, is governed by many genetic factors, including the ability to perceive what is to be remembered, the efficiency of the nerves in relaying the information to the brain, the storage capacity of the brain, and so forth. In this instance, no direct linkage has been made between specific genes and behavior. At best, researchers can hope to trace inherited characteristics by observing various psychological processes and taking into account the physiology of the individual involved.

The role of instinct

Thus far we have discussed inherited characteristics; now we will focus on inherited behavior. The term *instinct* is commonly used to describe behavior that appears to be inherited genetically in every individual of a given species. Baby chicks, for example, peck at seeds without having learned to do so (Figure 2.1). A mother sparrow builds a nest, lays eggs, secures food, and returns to the nest to feed her young. Salmon migrate thousands of miles through ocean waters to spawn in the rivers in which they were born. The nectar-bearing honeybee,

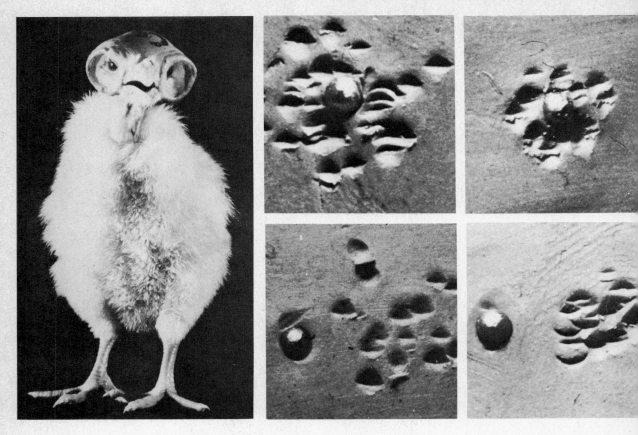

Figure 2.1 *Studies performed with chicks wearing goggles show that the*
ability of chicks to localize objects is innate. Prisms in the goggles
deflect the chick's vision to the right and, unlike a human being whose
spatial localization is largely learned, the chick does not learn to
adjust for this deflection; he continues to miss the seed after 3 days
of attempting to peck it. Peck marks aimed at a seed prove the point.
The two top patterns were made 3 days apart by a normal chick,
the bottom two by a chick wearing the prisms. In each case, aim
improved with maturity, but after 3 days the chick wearing the prisms
still pecked to the right of the seed. (Chick: Wallace Kirkland,
Time-LIFE Picture Agency; Peck marks: Eckhardt H. Hess)

upon returning to the hive, indicates the route
to the source of nectar by engaging in a complex
dance that lasts for 30 seconds or longer. A cat,
upon bearing her first litter, eats the placenta
(the "afterbirth" membrane) to remove it from
the newborn, kills kittens that have been born

deformed, then nurses the healthy young. All
these behavior patterns are referred to as instinctive because they have three features in common:

1 All members of a given species exhibit the behavior (or, in cases where the instinctive behav-

ior is sexual in nature, all members of the same sex in a given species exhibit the behavior).

2 The behavior is not learned; if the organism has reached the appropriate level of maturation, it will exhibit the behavior the first time conditions require it.

3 The behavior is complex and conforms to a fixed pattern.

Exactly what instinct is, no one can say for sure —but many can argue. After the height of the controversy over instinct in the 1930s, a group of European *ethologists* (scientists who study animal behavior within the natural setting, or habitat) sought to avoid further controversy by avoiding the controversial term; some, like N. Tinbergen, have called all undeniably instinctive behavior *species-specific*. Although scientists disagree on what constitutes an instinct, they can now identify and discuss specific behavior patterns that appear in a given species.

By classifying a particular type of behavior as instinctive (or species-specific) we have sim-

ply given it a label; we have not explained it. The word "instinct" is a descriptive term rather than an explanatory one. Having described a behavior as instinctive, we are still left with the problem of identifying the conditions that produce the behavior and of determining whether the behavior pattern is rigidly fixed or can be changed. Consider the example of the honeybee. Bees raised in a cellar where light is supplied by a stationary lamp are unable, when moved outdoors, to orient their dance to the sun as do bees raised under natural conditions. However, after 5 days of outdoor living, they dance in the usual beelike fashion. It appears, therefore, that the so-called instinctive dance depends in part on previous experience with the movement of the sun's light (Van der Kloot, 1968).

Environmental factors evidently play a role in instinctive behavior. The extent of this role depends on the particular pattern of behavior and on the organism involved (Figure 2.2).

The instinct concept plays little part in the analysis of human behavior. Human beings do have reflexes (simple, unlearned responses to immediate stimulation, such as drawing away from a painful stimulus and blinking in response to a loud noise), but these are not the complex

Figure 2.2 *Members of different species in the same environment. In domesticated animals such as the dog and cat pictured here, the curiosity drive is often strong enough to overcome the animals' mutual fear. (Stanley Rotman)*

patterns of behavior that qualify as instincts. Nor can we consider as instinctive human maternal behavior or fighting for self-preservation, for many types of behavior and "misbehavior" are used to express motherhood and self-preservation. We need only refer to the many different ways in which women throughout the world care for their newborn babies for an example of maternal inconsistency. Some women breast-feed, some bottle-feed, some depend on others to feed their babies, and some even abandon their babies. Differences may be due to cultural or emotional factors. In any case, the existence of such differences casts doubt upon the usefulness of the concept of a human maternal instinct.

Maternal behavior in the rat Rosenblatt (1967) has made a noteworthy contribution to the continuing controversy about instinct. Maternal behavior in the rat, as measured by retrieving, crouching over pups, licking, and nest building can be elicited in castrated male rats (hormone lacking), in females who were never pregnant (lacking experience with pups), in females who had either their ovaries or pituitary gland removed (hormone lacking), as well as in normal rats, by repeatedly exposing them to rat pups over a 15-day period. Rosenblatt interprets his results to indicate that maternal responsivity is not dependent upon hormones for its arousal.

Similarly, many examples contradict the idea that self-preservation is instinctive in human beings. Too many martyrs throughout history have traded this option for an ideal. The Japanese idealize honor and pride. If a Japanese person "loses face" (is dishonored), tradition dictates that he commit *hara-kiri*, suicide; and so he sacrifices his own self-preservation for his ideal. Japanese kamikaze pilots (who dived with their planes into enemy targets) also challenged the theory of a supreme self-preservation instinct.

Personality theorists have continually tried to find what they call the "primary instinct" in man. However, with each supposed discovery, someone was always able to point to a class of human acts that contradicted the so-called instinct. Thus, the search for a primary instinct seems to be a fruitless endeavor.

It is probably more accurate and useful to emphasize the modifiability and adaptability of human behavior than to speak of its instinctive features. If there are instinctive patterns in human behavior, they are quickly and effectively overshadowed by learning.

PRENATAL DEVELOPMENT

The newborn infant has many well-developed systems that function immediately—upon his first breath of air. Other systems, evident at birth, will develop later as he grows into adulthood. Growth—whether of a single organ or of the entire organism—is determined genetically by the controlling process of *maturation*. Maturation is an unfolding or "acting out" of the various systems of the body, each at its own proper time. That time may be during infancy, childhood, adolescence, or adult life; there is no one point when we may say that maturation is absolutely complete.

Generally, development is described by its various stages or periods. Psychologists identify each stage of maturation by changes manifest in certain body systems or structures. Some of the stages in development will be explained in the sections that follow.

The first stages of human development are *prenatal*; that is, they occur before birth. The major developmental stages of the unborn child are as follows:

1 *Ovum* The individual is first a fertilized ovum, or *zygote*. During the first 2 weeks of life, early stages of cell division transform the single cell into a cluster of cells called the *gastrula*, which then becomes a hollow sphere or *blastula*. By this time, the cell colony has traveled from the mother's Fallopian tubes to the uterus (womb), where it becomes secured to the uterine wall.
2 *Embryo* From about the third to the ninth

week, the organism is called an *embryo*. During this period the blastula forms into three cell layers:

(a) *ectoderm* (outer layer), which forms the sense organs, skin, and nervous system;

(b) *mesoderm* (middle layer), which forms the bone, and muscle;

(c) *endoderm* (inner layer), which forms the digestive system.

These layers continue differentiating until the embryo takes on roughly the form of a human being.

3 *Fetus* From the time that the human form becomes recognizable (about 9 weeks after conception) until its birth as an infant, it is known as a *fetus*. During the fetal period, the primitive structures become more refined, and such definite behaviors as kicking and sucking are evident.

The prenatal development of any system is important, especially within the context of overall fetal growth, for a number of reasons. Because the timing of development differs for each system, the many human parts connect or grow together according to a wonderfully complex "master plan" or timetable. The nervous system, for example, develops from unattached sections of the ectoderm and mesoderm. Muscles, nerve structures, sense organs—all the parts that will cause the fetus to act like a human being—develop independently, on separate schedules. Slowly the parts interconnect, with the sense organs at last locking into the system. By the seventh month, the fetus is equipped to carry out an extensive repertoire of responses. Table 2.1 shows the timing of the development of reflex activity in the human fetus.

Never too early to learn Evidence of learning before birth in a species of duck (*Anas platyrhynchos*) has been reported by Gottlieb (1971). He found that while these ducks are still embryos, they learn to recognize and respond to the mother's assembly call. Consequently, when they are hatched the ducklings can already discriminate their mother's call from similar calls of other species.

By wiring an embryo for laboratory monitoring, Gottlieb found that as early as 5 days before hatching, the unborn duckling will make physical responses to the low-frequency tones in the mother's call. Once the embryo has begun respiration and can vocalize, its responses broaden to include the high-frequency component of the maternal call. In addition, the learning process relies in part on the ability of the newly hatched duckling to hear its own responses (as well as those of its siblings): deprivation of normal exposure to self- or sibling-vocalization results in faulty discrimination in subsequent responses to the vital assembly call.

In studying the systems developed in the fetus, our interest in their influence on behavior makes us focus on the nervous system. We shall consider the complex operations of the nervous system in Chapter 3; here, we shall simply observe how the developing nervous system directs the earliest behavior of the newborn child.

The nervous system consists of the brain, the spinal cord, and the network of nerve cells (*neurons*) that transmit impulses from a stimulated area of the body to the brain and back again. Thus, by means of the nervous system, the individual can both perceive and respond to stimuli. We have observed that the baby is incapable of accurate discrimination; this is because the nervous system develops more slowly than other parts of the body. The brain area known as the *cerebral cortex* (commonly called the *gray matter*) is the slowest to mature. The cerebral cortex controls motor and sensory responses (body movements, speech, body senses, vision, and hearing). Proper maturation of the cortex is essential for an infant to learn to turn over, sit up, crawl, and walk. Experiments have shown that at birth the cortex is far from ready to direct such coordination. Although most cortical maturation is complete by the age of two, some maturation continues until the middle teens.

Similarly, the other bodily systems develop in ways that permit the introduction of new behavior patterns throughout childhood and the young adult years. The system of endocrine glands (which secrete hormones) is responsible for sexual changes during adolescence. Malfunction of these glands can cause severe personality disturbances.

Table 2.1   The development of reflex activity in the human fetus

Week	Activity
0	Conception
1–8	Embryonic stage (nervous system begins to develop)
9	Beginning of fetal stage (trunk bending, sensitivity in mouth region)
10	Grasp reflex, head turning
14	All reflexes found in newborn infants are present except breathing and vocalization
16	Prerespiratory movements
18	Hand closure and grip, leg movements ("fetal kick"), respiratory movements can be evoked
20	Tonic-neck reflex (when head is moved, limbs change their position)
24	Sucking reflex

Maturation of swimming ability   Infant rats are born quite helpless; many of their reflexes and physiological mechanisms develop after birth. Swimming, for example, involves complex coordination, and the process involved does not mature until the fifth day. In order to swim, the infant rat must learn to hold its nose above water and to extend and flex its front legs. Schapiro, Salas, and Vukovich (1970) have shown that injections of the hormone thyroxine advance the maturation of the swimming process, while another substance, cortisol, delays it. Electrical activity of the brain's cortex also showed acceleration or retardation as a result of the injected hormones. The experimenters also concluded that the hormones act over a long period of time. The rat normally begins swimming without moving its legs at the age of 16 to 22 days, after which swimming is performed with the legs extended. The hormones influenced the maturation of this second stage, as they did the first, although the injection had not been repeated.

MATURATION AND BEHAVIOR

The relationship between maturation and behavior is easy to observe in the human infant. With charts and baby books, a parent can anticipate when the baby will lift his head, sit, crawl, and so forth.

Infant behavior is so predictable partly because much of it depends solely on maturation determined by the genes. Such behavior is called *unlearned* because it does not depend on training or practice but is rather an innate characteristic of organisms that mature to the infant stage. Patterns of reflex behavior present in the newborn are considered unlearned. For instance, the infant does not have to be taught how to cry or swallow.

Maturation as a behavior factor in salamanders   The importance of maturation in the development of some basic behavior patterns was demonstrated by Carmichael (1927) in his study of two groups of salamanders placed in separate tanks. One group was placed in an untreated water tank, and the other group, in a tank that had an anesthetic added to its water. (Feeding was available by way of the yolk sac with which they had been born.) After the salamanders in the untreated tank had exhibited swimming behavior for 5 days, Carmichael shifted his anesthetized animals to plain water. Within 30 minutes, the "frozen" salamanders were swimming as actively as the normal ones. Carmichael found that it also took his normal group 30 minutes to recover from anesthesia and begin swimming. He was therefore able to conclude that maturation, rather than learning, makes this basic behavior possible.

Certain other behaviors are absent at birth, but they develop as soon as the individual matures to a state of *readiness*—the ideal time for learning the behavior. Such behavior patterns are *learned* in that they require a certain amount of experience and preliminary practice. But when the child is ready to learn a certain type of behavior, he will usually do so with incredibly little practice, although the initial efforts may present difficulties, as we see in a toddler on his feet for the first time. Walking, running, and jumping are kinds of behavior prompted by maturation but requiring practice.

Fear and playfulness: learned or innate?   Some kinds of behavior, such as the use of language, are learned. Other behaviors, such as the digestive processes, are *innate* (inborn). Between these extremes is a large group that cannot be so easily classified. Experi-

Heredity and development   **38**

menting with monkeys, Sackett (1966) attempted to determine the source of two puzzling types of behavior—fear and playfulness. Infant monkeys were raised in isolation, never seeing or coming in contact with human beings or other monkeys; for several periods each day, they were shown colored picture slides of other monkeys in situations depicting either play, threat, exploration, fear, sexual activity, mother and infant interaction, or infant isolation. Between the ages of 2½ and 4 months, the infants became disturbed at the sight of the threat pictures—withdrawing, rocking, or hiding whenever these pictures were shown. The subjects had been taught to press a lever to turn pictures on. Although they pressed at other times, they ceased pressing the lever whenever threat pictures were shown. When pictures of infants were shown, the monkeys became very playful—climbing, exploring, and chattering more than they did at the sight of other pictures.

These results suggest that specific visual stimuli may act as releasing mechanisms for certain responses that are apparently inborn (fear and playfulness). The study also showed that such releasing mechanisms are most effective for monkeys at a specific age (2½-4 months).

Readiness to learn

We have seen that various forms of learned behavior depend on the maturational timetable. Observation tells us that a newborn infant cannot sit up, although we know that he possesses a skeletal and a muscular system; his systems are not yet strong enough or sufficiently developed. It usually takes about 8 or 9 months of development before the infant can sit alone. This is the *range of readiness* for this behavior.

The concept of readiness is important in the analysis of behavior because it makes us aware that certain skills may be difficult or impossible to learn before a given age. A parent who tries to rush the training of his child—because he wants the child to get ahead of his playmates, or because he wants to "show off" the child's prowess—may be wasting his time and needlessly frustrating the child. A child is not able to learn a task before certain structures or systems are sufficiently mature for the learning to take place. For example, an infant usually cannot walk at 6 months of age, no matter how much training is forced upon him; most infants begin to walk between the ages of 11 and 14 months—the usual age range of readiness.

Ideally, each child should be allowed to learn at his own pace, but this is not always possible. Instead, educational, social, and legal institutions generally insist that individuals follow a social timetable, one that benefits society in general—and not necessarily the individual. A child is required to enter public school at age 6, whether or not he is ready to deal with first-grade concepts. Some youngsters are, in fact, ready for school at 4; others are not ready until age 8. This forced readiness has created many problems for educators. Every classroom usually contains students who are ready to learn, those who are not ready to learn and who will consequently be frustrated, and those who are "over-ready" and who will learn, but not so well as they might have earlier. Much research has been conducted to find effective ways of dealing with individual differences in the classroom.

Readiness Darnell and Bourne (1970) conducted a study to determine whether or not the training of children in one task would transfer to improve the children's performance on a similar task. Two groups of children, aged 6 and 8, were taught to classify cards by the color and size of figures drawn on the cards. Immediately thereafter, the children were given jars of different colors and sizes and asked to arrange them in an orderly way. It was clearly evident that the training had been of greater benefit to the older children.

Most psychologists would say that the younger children did not learn so well because they had not matured and were not ready to learn. Similar studies have shown that with simplified and extended training, the younger children might also have done as well at learning the task. Thus, if a child starts school at 5, he may benefit from the training, but only if his teacher reaches him at his level, not if she teaches him as she would a 6-year-old.

Mastering a task

It is rare for two children of the same chronological age to be ready to learn a specific skill at exactly the same time (except identical twins, who have the same maturational timetable). But psychologists are able to specify the average age of readiness for the learning of various tasks. For example, reading readiness usually occurs at the age of 6. Some 3-year-olds, however, have been taught to read by means of a special device called a "talking typewriter" (Moore, 1962). Averages are useful to the parent and the professional child observer, but of even greater value is the ability to recognize readiness in the individual child. Too often, learning is withheld from the precocious child simply because the books say he is too young to learn. Learning is often presented too early to the "late bloomer," frustrating him with tasks that are still beyond his capabilities.

Unless parents, teachers, and psychologists are sensitive to the period of readiness, they may miss the optimum, or most favorable, age at which to introduce new learning. If the *optimal period* is missed, learning may be impaired or may never occur. There is much speculation as to why learning of specific tasks—by man and other animals—must occur at an optimal age. Speculation focuses on the following possibilities: (1) if the bodily systems do not perform the operations appropriate to their level of maturity, they may become stunted and prevented from ever performing correctly; or (2) if the individual waits too long to learn, responses may develop in the meantime that interfere with his learning (for instance, the older child may develop a fear of learning or lack of interest).

Passing the optimal period to learn One extreme example of the effect of delayed learning was shown in Singh and Zingg's (1942) account of two children found living in a den of wolves in India. The older girl, Kamala, was estimated to be 8 years old. The younger child (1½ years old) exhibited behavior very much like that of the older girl, but showed a greater readiness to adjust to her new environment in an orphanage. However, study of her adaptability was cut short by her death 10 months after her transfer to the orphanage.

Kamala's behavior, however, remained wolflike for a long time; she moved around on all fours, and, when approached, would make faces and show her teeth. Her knee and hip joints had lost their flexibility, and she could not stand upright. It took her 15 months to stand on her knees without support, and it was 44 months before she could stand on her feet. She could not learn to run in an upright position, however. It was 33 months before she stopped sleeping with her legs drawn up to her body. She hated baths, and it was 5 years before toilet training became effective. Her early vocalizations were merely growl-like sounds and howls. In 4 years, she acquired a vocabulary of only a few partial words. In 5 years, she spoke 30 words. In 6 years, she seemed to understand most of what was said to her, and shortly after, she formed her first sentence: "Momma come." Her eighth year at the orphanage was marked by accelerated learning and a flowering of her human personality. Kamala was said to have become a new person (shortly before her death, at approximately 16), manifesting the maturity of a 3- or 4-year-old child.

Development of responses during an optimal period also occurs in other animals, as Konrad Lorenz has reported. In experiments with goslings and chicks, Lorenz found that early in the maturation schedule, baby geese followed their mother. But even if the mother is not present, the goslings, in a state of readiness for this behavior, will nevertheless follow any moving object that is presented to them. Lorenz found that when he appeared among the goslings during this critical period, in the mother's absence, they followed behind him wherever he went (Figure 2.3).

To describe the follow response, Lorenz coined the word *imprinting*. Further experimentation showed him that imprinting had its strongest impact a few hours after birth. If the moving object was first presented before or after the critical period, the goslings followed their substitute mother far less often.

Imprinting seems to resemble a learned response in that it requires environmental stimuli (in this case, the moving object). But it depends far more on the presentation of the stimulus during the *critical period of development*.

Research in imprinting has focused on the follow response in various species, but other imprinted behaviors have also been observed.

There is no evidence that human beings are subject to the follow response. Yet in human beings—as in geese—if learning does not occur at an optimal period, a lifelong maladaptation may result that interferes with the mastery of a particular task or creates an emotional obstacle to learning. For example, most children can easily be taught to swim; their bodies are ready to learn, and their attitudes are enthusiastic and fearless. Thus, in children, a little practice or training will usually produce an active swimmer. But those who attempt to teach adults to swim find that they are not as limber and flexible as children, and that frequently they have developed interfering responses, such as a fear of water. Because psychological factors affect the learning of new skills, adults may even have difficulty beginning the study of music, art, a foreign language, and so on. Adults who have not developed interfering responses, however, may be well suited to begin new pursuits, whatever their age may be.

SENSORY DEVELOPMENT

Sensory development is perhaps more closely related than any other maturational process to readiness behavior. For it is the individual's senses that pick up the external cues that implement readiness. It is believed that behavior patterns cannot be developed normally if the individual is deprived of the stimuli that feed him awareness of the world.

Clearly, many forms of behavior depend on the individual's development of perception and the ability to organize sense impressions (as in

Figure 2.3   Konrad Lorenz takes a swim accompanied by his brood of goslings, who from infancy have learned to follow him as their mother. (Nina Leen, Time-LIFE Picture Agency)

reading). Where stimulation is limited or absent, perceptual development may be impaired. Laboratory chimpanzees reared in total darkness make a reflex response when exposed to light, but they cannot react to complex visual patterns (Riesen, 1950, 1961). Similarly, blind people who are surgically given a first look at the world are able to see but must then learn how to use and interpret what they see (Von Senden, 1960).

At birth, the infant experiences a new world of sensory awareness: he must cope with noise, light and dark, and heat and cold; he begins to nourish his body with food and to excrete wastes. If the infant is to become increasingly able to deal with his environment, he must also learn to perceive stimuli, and the sharpening of his perceptual abilities depends on maturation and learning. An infant who has been much stimulated shows earlier sensory development than one who has lacked the stimulation of brightly colored toys, fondling, and voices. In the following sections we shall discuss the usual development of sensory abilities in *neonates* (infants less than 2 weeks old) as well as older infants.

Taste and smell

It is difficult to draw conclusions about the neonate's ability to *taste* and *smell*, for physical responses related to these senses cannot be accurately measured. We can make certain assumptions, however. If we assume that sucking indicates pleasure, the neonate is pleased by salty or sweet taste sensations; and if disturbed behavior indicates displeasure, the neonate dislikes bitter and sour sensations. We use the word "sensation" rather than "taste" because evidently something other than taste is involved. The *taste buds* (the taste receptors that appear as crevices on the tongue surface) have not yet begun to mature in the neonate. Similarly, although the sense organs responsible for the sense of smell are not mature in the infant, some experiments with infants have elicited definite responses to

specific odors—of ammonia and acetic acid, for example. At first it was thought that the infant could smell these substances. However, it is now believed that the infant reacts to their irritating quality without perceiving them as distinct odors.

Touch and skin sensations

Four skin sensations—each activated by different receptors—have been found in human beings. They inform us of *touch*, *warmth*, *cold*, and *pain*. The neonate seems fairly sensitive to touch and temperature. He reacts to fondling; he rejects milk that is too hot; and he is generally aware of temperature changes in the environment. But immediately after birth, the neonate seems blissfully free of pain; he does not respond when the doctor pricks him for his first blood test. Soon afterward, the same stimulus will produce a loud wail. It is probable that the intricate nerve networks are not fully matured at birth but function fully a few weeks later.

Kinesthesis

The kinesthetic sense tells the individual where his body is and where and how it moves. It informs him of the relative position of his bodily parts—for instance, that he has moved his leg or tensed a muscle in his right arm. Without a kinesthetic sense, we would have great difficulty in maintaining posture, reaching for an object, walking, and so on.

The kinesthetic sense seems to be absent in the neonate. He cannot locate his toes or direct his arm movements. Experiments have not been devised to test the response mechanism for kinesthesis.

Audition (hearing)

Hearing varies greatly from infant to infant. Many neonates are unable to hear for the first several days because their ears are filled with fluid collected during birth. Most of those who can hear will respond only to loud, startling noises; conversation, music, or baby-crying in the nursery go unperceived. By the end of the first week, however, most infants can hear a wide range of tones and some ordinary rattling sounds. About one month later, the infant's auditory sense has developed to the point where he can hear almost everything—particularly human voices.

Vision

Vision is by no means acute at birth, requiring from 6 to 7 years to mature fully. It is extremely difficult to trace the development of this sense, for responses to subtle visual stimuli are difficult for a child to convey before he is able to speak. Nevertheless, experimenters have had some success in testing vision in the neonate. They have learned that neonates cannot see precise shapes and colors but that they can detect brightness and can follow the path of a bright light with their eyes. Perceptions of pattern, shape, and possibly even color are thought to be present just a few days after birth.

The infant cannot see objects clearly at close range, however. He sees them only as blurred images. This inability to focus on close objects and to perceive things clearly in general is due to the lack of a developed *retina* (the part of the eye whose elements are sensitive to light).

Vision in infants First with infant chimpanzees, later with human infants, Fantz (1961) recorded the amount of attention each subject gave to particular sets of stimulus patterns. Fantz used four pairs of patterns in decreasing order of complexity, testing infants weekly, from their first week of life. He found that the amounts of time spent looking at the various pairs differed sharply. The more complex the stimulus pair, the more attention the infant paid to it. He also found that the relative attractiveness of each member in a pair depended on pattern design. For example, all ages showed a preference for stripes, a bull's-eye, and a checkerboard square. From this we may infer that a normal one-week-old infant is able to differentiate forms.

MOTOR DEVELOPMENT

A second area of infant development is the coordination of *motor responses*—movements of any part of the external body structure. Moving a joint of the finger is motor behavior, as is moving the entire finger, the hand, or the arm.

The infant's motor skills are more easily observed than any other bodily development. It is evident that the movement exhibited by the neonate is not really coordinated motor behavior. His early responses are relatively uncontrolled reflexes—kicking, flailing the arms, grasping aimlessly.

Coordination develops in a nearly identical sequence for all infants, although the age at which different infants acquire each skill will vary. Figure 2.4 shows the average times of maturation of the motor responses. These averages are presented in age ranges or time spans because of the tremendous variation in individual mastery.

In connection with averages, let us examine the useful concept of norm. In psychology, *norm* refers to average or standard performance under specified conditions—for example, the usual age at which the child first grasps an object. Generally, the norm, or average, is established for purposes of comparison; identification of an average enables the psychologist to compare human behavior, in quantifiable terms. Norms should be used with caution, however, since they do not describe every individual. Obviously, many individuals perform above the norm and many below it. Moreover, norm statistics from one study cannot necessarily be applied to another area. Nor should they be.

The study of motor development is significant (Figure 2.5), not so much for determining the age at which different infants learn certain skills, but rather to show the sequence in which these skills are universally acquired. Each learned skill is built upon a preceding one—until, after years of maturation, learning, and practice, the young child masters the skills required for the playground, the bicycle, the swimming pool.

Prehensile motor development

The infantile form of motor coordination known as *prehension* can be observed in the grabbing and grasping movements characteristic of babies.

Figure 2.4   *At each stage of motor development, the infant becomes better able to manipulate and coordinate his complex systems. All infants follow the same sequence—from simple reflexes to standing, walking, and so on: (A) 1 month; (B) 4–6 months; (C) 8–10 months; (D) 10–12 months (Vivienne— dpi)*

A   B

C   D

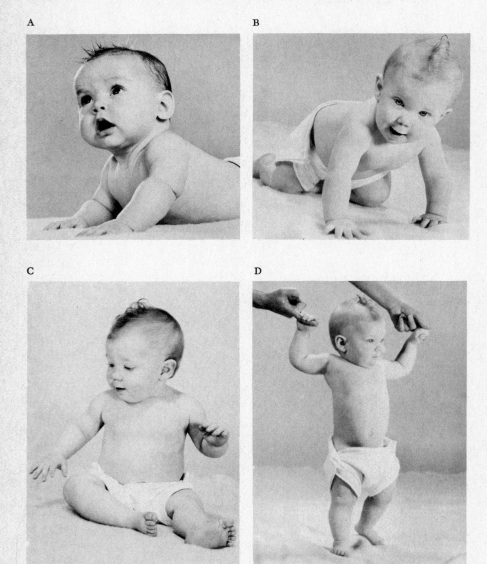

Figure 2.5　Children improve their motor
coordination as their muscles mature
and develop. This development proceeds
from the relatively simple task of holding
onto and moving with an object
to more complex tasks. (Vivienne—dpi)

However random such movements may appear,
they are part of the initial stage in the sequence
of prehensile development and thus function
significantly in the overall process of motor development. In adults, prehensile skills appear in
refined movements, such as picking up a needle
or managing a knife and fork. Only the primates
—monkeys, apes, and human beings—are able
to oppose the thumb (move it in the opposite
direction to the other fingers). This flexibility
makes fine prehension possible.

　　Psychologists believe that the more accurate the early learning and mastery, the better
the later skill. It appears that the child learns
best when he has reached prehensile maturity
at approximately 12 months of age; the environment is less threatening and the infant is then
less afraid of experimenting with the new behavior. He is likely to reach for nearly anything
bright and interesting.

　　Prehensile movements begin with random,
circular reaching movements of the entire arm.
Although the infant reaches for an object, at
first he is unable to grasp it; if he does touch
the object, he will probably succeed only in
knocking it down. Soon after, the infant can use
his entire arm to surround the object and pull
it toward him. In such attempts the arm still
functions as one unit, and the infant is not able
to direct the parts of it separately. When the
muscles in the arm develop and the infant learns
that he can control them, he is able to manipulate the parts of his arm separately, using the
wrist to pull objects toward him. The loose,
random movements are replaced by more direct
or organized movements. Figure 2.6 illustrates
the sequence of prehensile development.

　　At the same time that the infant develops
wrist coordination, he begins to learn the more
complex tasks of finger manipulation. The fin-

Heredity and development　　**45**

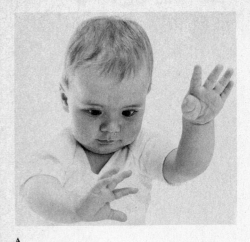

A

B

C

D

Figure 2.6   Several stages of prehensile development:
(A) Random reaching (Tana Hoban—dpi)
(B) Straight-line wrist coordination (Ralph Breswitz—dpi)
(C) Finger-thumb grasping (Vivienne—dpi)
(D) Finger clutching (Vivienne—dpi)

gers are at first used without the thumb to encircle an object. As the infant becomes more certain of his abilities, he closes his fingers tighter about objects he wishes to grasp. Next, he begins to wrap his thumb around the opposite side of the object, so that it meets his fingers and clutches the object. Last, the fingertips become highly manipulative, grasping tightly and, with the aid of the thumb, holding objects securely.

Reaching behavior in early infancy When a new baby reaches toward an object he sees, is he doing so deliberately, or is the movement simply accidental and caused by excitement? Bower, Broughton, and Moore (1970) demonstrated that the behavior of babies, even before they are one month old, does indeed indicate that they intentionally reach out to touch particular objects in their line of vision.

After observing that babies only 1 or 2 weeks old can consistently direct their reach to less than an inch from a nearby orange sphere presented in various positions, the investigators used lifelike images produced by specially filtered light to test for intentional behavior. They reasoned that if babies deliberately reached to touch an interesting object but found no object to be grasped, they would respond with apparent signs of distress.

As predicted, when the lifelike images were projected so that they seemed to be within touching distance, each experimental baby reached out—and, when unsuccessful in touching the apparent object, expressed frustration by crying within 15 to 75 seconds of the first reach. Control babies, on the other hand, did not cry when presented with real objects for longer lengths of time, nor did the babies in the experimental group cry during their posttesting session. It seems reasonable to conclude that the observed behavior was caused by frustration of the babies' intentions.

SPEECH DEVELOPMENT

Speech is a special, systematic behavior that develops only with proper learning and maturation. By *speech* we mean here the approach to vocal expression with specific intent to convey meaning.

At a very early age, an infant makes spontaneous babbling noises. An infant placed in isolation, however, where no sounds could penetrate his auditory organs, would not be able to talk or babble in a normal way. In fact, speech development can be permanently retarded by a lack of hearing experiences and opportunities to imitate. Later, speech is learned through the assimilation of systematic language patterns. A child does not speak, however, until his organs of speech have matured so as to permit verbalization.

Early development

Nearly every infant begins to babble at approximately 3 months of age. Babbling is regarded as the first stage of speech development. Although many parents see the crying and grunting of their 1-month-old infant as efforts to say something to them, early noises are more likely to be the infant's way of relieving his discomfort or voicing contentment.

Babbling differs from earlier noises in that it is characterized by repetitive sounds of an immense variety. Infants babble all the sounds in the world's many languages. American infants may babble sounds like German vowels, French nasals, or singsong Chinese. Later they will stop using such sounds, because they are not heard in the American home. Clearly, the sounds of voices delight the infant and make him continue his babbling. The deaf infant does not babble in the same way normal infants do; he makes altogether different sounds.

During the babbling stage, the infant learns that certain sounds mean certain objects. Most often the first recognizable sound— "ma-ma" or "da-da"—is an imitative response to the parent's utterance of the same word. Eventually, the infant comes to associate the sound with the adult who always seems to get excited when he says it. Parents normally encourage first words by pointing to, or offering to the infant, the thing or person he appears to have named. From such practice sessions with his parents, the infant begins to comprehend speech. Table 2.2 describes the early pattern of speech development.

Table 2.2	Development of speech in infants[a]
Age	Vocabulary
8 months	No words—babbling reinforced by parents
10 months	First word
12 months	3 words
18 months	22 words
24 months	272 words

[a]Based on Terwilliger (1967).

Level of early understanding

Simple tests with infants show that they make definite responses to various kinds of sounds. At about the time that babbling begins, the infant learns to turn or raise his head toward a sound. Soon after, he learns to distinguish various tones of voice—soft, scolding, happy, and so on—and can react appropriately to the signals his ears receive. At this age (about 10 months), the baby may be taught to obey simple commands, such as "stop" or "no," especially if they are strengthened with gestures. The infant quickly learns to understand gestures paired with commands of a more complicated nature. He may obey "Bring me the ball," for example, if the parent points to the ball.

In all instances, the infant's comprehension is increased when signals and sounds are associated with the words the parent wishes to teach. People who work closely with children teach with gestures and facial expressions as well as with words, and come to recognize unspoken as well as spoken signs of understanding.

Word development

When the baby first speaks a word without prompting, we may truly say that he has formed his *first word*. The first word is typically one syllable, and is meant to communicate a request for some person or plaything. Once the first word is spoken, others follow quickly. As each new word brings a new toy or companion to the baby's side, his vocabulary widens.

The infant normally picks up nouns first and uses them as substitutes for whole sentences. A simple word like "dog" may convey the complex idea "I want you to bring me the stuffed dog." Verbs generally appear next, and the random use of other parts of speech follows. Pronouns are usually most difficult to learn, and often are not mastered for several years.

According to the norm, the first word is spoken at between 10 and 13 months. However, some infants utter their first words earlier, and others do not communicate until 18 months or later. Although late speech development often worries parents unnecessarily, speech problems may serve to alert parents to developmental malfunctioning.

Other influences on speech

Along with maturation and learning, many other factors influence speech development in the growing child. The major ones are the following.

Sex For reasons not completely understood, girls develop speech patterns earlier than boys, and until about 4 years of age or older, seem more adept at vocalization and word usage.

Intelligence Intelligence tests given to very young children indicate that children with high scores show early speech development. This is not surprising, since such tests are often heavily weighted with verbal material. Nevertheless, it is known that early speech development depends only partially on intelligence, for other factors also affect the forming of the first word. Only when an infant speaks unusually early or late, or not at all, are we likely to find that some exceptional intelligence factor is at work—be it genius or retardation.

Environment Interactions with people and the environment, in general, speed the development of the infant's comprehension and use of words. The child exposed to various environments and the company of adults willing to spend time talking to him is likely to attain a wide range of language skills. Exposure to the world outside the playpen and to persons other than the parents increases the infant's sensory experiences and spurs him to new language learning. Adult conversations with the child somehow have an influence, as do the parents' activities, friends, travels, and artistic and cultural pursuits. Generally speaking, the more experiences the better. (There are, however, experiences that may retard or block speech; such instances of behavior pathology are considered in Chapter 13.)

Unfortunately, not all homes can provide an environment that stimulates verbal development. In poor families—where travel and cultural luxuries are scarce—the infant's speech development may be limited, particularly in vocabulary (McCarthy, 1954). In addition, parents at the poverty level are sometimes uneducated or unsympathetic, and do not encourage conversation in their children; they are often saddled by long working hours from one or two jobs and so rarely have the time or energy to cope with all their children's questions and problems. Similarly, some well-to-do and educated parents lack time or interest to encourage childhood speech. Thus children deprived of environmental stimulation may grow up with only limited verbal skills, despite high intelligence.

The more fortunate children are those whose infancy is spent with attentive adults who encourage them to imitate by patiently rehearsing words. The speech development of such children is usually accelerated. Of course, an infant who is usually disregarded overhears words spoken by his parents and others; but he is not directly involved, and his word development therefore tends to be slow. Attentive parents thus serve as the primary environmental force for language learning—both in practicing with the child and in encouraging him to abandon baby talk in favor of fully pronounced words.

As might be expected, infants who remain mostly in the company of other infants do not develop verbal skills so early as those usually in adult company. Indeed, research has shown that speech is delayed in twin babies who spend more time alone together than with the attending adult (Day, 1932). Twins take mutual pleasure in babbling to each other; single children have no particular encouragement to babble and are motivated instead to talk in adult language. Moreover, twins tend to be left without adult supervision more frequently than single infants, and this, of course, decreases the twins' opportunities for imitative speech practice. The fact that speech development is delayed in twins does not affect the quality of speech once the phenomenon has begun; twins may start late, but they quickly catch up.

Baby talk Schwartz, Rosenberg, and Brackbill (1970) recently experimented with auditory, visual, and tactile stimulation to see how everyday social reinforcements affect the rate of vocalization in infants of from 2 to 4 months.

The investigators first established a baseline rate of vocalization by having an adult with an expressionless face lean over the crib while two judges scored the baby's vocal response. Subsequently, during conditioning sessions, the vocalizations of each baby were rewarded with one or more of three kinds of social reinforcement: a tape-recorded female voice that said "Nice baby" (auditory); a smile and nod of the head from the adult leaning over the crib (visual); and patting of the baby's abdomen (tactile). (When nonvisual stimuli were applied, the experimenter's face remained expressionless in the baby's visual field.) The "score" was the number of conditioning minutes required before each infant's vocalization rate reached 2.5 times the baseline rate. When this rate was reached, two extinction sessions followed during which the experimenter simply leaned over the crib without expression, as in the baseline periods.

It was found that the three social reinforcers—singly or in any combination—were equally effective in increasing babies' vocalization rates. Similarly, no one reinforcement condition proved most resistant to extinction. Apparently, then, babies are equally receptive to any sort of social reinforcement for vocalization, an important aspect of their early behavioral repertoire.

Another environmental factor that affects speech development is *bilingualism* (the use of two languages) in the home. Bilingual families are common in cities where large immigrant populations have settled. Immigrants tend to speak their native tongue in the home, but adopt the new language to deal with the new outside environment. If both languages are spoken in the home, the infant may confuse them and be delayed in developing good linguistic skills in either. He may be overwhelmed by the confusing similarities and inconsistencies of what appears to be a single language. For the child to develop speech skills, one language should be taught first; once it is learned, the child will be better able to master the second.

THEORIES OF DEVELOPMENT

The study of human growth has been marked by a continuing interest in the concept of *stages of development*. Man shows a high degree of regularity in the sequence and timing of his ability to carry on specific types of activity, as indicated by studies of the development of motor activity in infants. These studies suggest that behavior develops in a series of identifiable and biologically determined steps or stages.

The concept of stages of development is not limited to simple motor activity such as the stages ranging from creeping to crawling, to standing, and to walking, but may be applied to all human activities, including those pertaining to emotional, cognitive, personality, and social development.

Freud's theory of personal development

One of the best-known theories is Sigmund Freud's classification of *psychosexual development*. The term "psychosexual" comes from Freud's view that instincts play a key role in human development and that the sexual instincts are dominant. Freud gave a very broad meaning to sexual activity, however. He believed that sensual gratification is derived from the pleasures obtained in satisfying such basic survival needs as eating and defecating, as well as from acts that are obviously sexual in nature.

Freud saw development as progression in the satisfaction of basic needs. He defined the first stage as the *oral* stage, in which the form of satisfaction involves the mouth. During his first year of life, the infant is satisfied by such oral activities as sucking and, later, biting and chewing, and he is motivated to find objects to suck to satisfy his oral need. Next comes the anal stage. From approximately 1 to 3 years of age, the child derives satisfaction from the act of expelling or withholding his feces. The third stage, the *phallic* (or *Oedipal*) stage, lasts from about 3 to 5 years of age. During the phallic stage, the child finds satisfaction in exploring his genital organs. In the fourth stage, the *latency period*, from about 5 years to the beginning of adolescence, the child is dominated by his social and intellectual development, and his attention is drawn to the world around him. The fifth stage occurs at puberty. This is the *genital* stage, and it marks the onset of adult sexual desires and behavior, dominated by emotional patterns formed in infancy and childhood. (Freud's psychosexual stages will be discussed in greater detail in Chapter 12.)

Piaget's theory of cognitive development

In the stages outlined by Freud, motivational and emotional features of behavior are emphasized. Jean Piaget, the eminent Swiss psychologist, has focused his attention, instead, on the development of cognitive activity—the use of language and thinking. Piaget worked with children of all ages, creating experiments to observe and measure the child's awareness of the natural world about him. From these he concluded that cognitive development is best described by its stages, rather than as a continuous, unbroken progression. Piaget theorized that cognition develops as the individual masters certain *mental operations* characteristic of each stage—operations that are nonverbal, unlearned, and universal. The following summarizes the stages of cognitive development, as seen by Piaget.

Sensorimotor operations (*birth to age 2 years*) From birth to 18 months, the infant functions almost exclusively by means of reflexive responses; few of the behavior patterns that exist at birth are cognitive in nature. For example, a baby can neither perceive objects as different from himself, nor himself as different from an object.

When he sees his arm bobbing about the crib, he cannot differentiate between his arm and a toy, because he does not have in his repertoire the concept of self that allows him to make the differentiation.

Because movement is almost all the infant is capable of doing at this age, the first cognitive stage is called *sensorimotor operations* (the exercise of sensory and motor awareness).

At approximately 18 months, the infant demonstrates some ability to solve problems. He can figure out how to get at a distant toy or how to pull a covering off his face. The infant is aware of objects and can consistently identify some of them. He can use the same solution for different situations, or adapt a learned solution to a new problem.

Preconceptual thought (age 2 to 4 years) As we have seen, speech is developed through the association of word and object. At the stage of *preconceptual thought,* the power of association is further developed by the use of "mental" representations. Thus, something a child sees can

be imagined as something else. A doll becomes a real child, a fence post is a person, a tree is a large animal. The child's imagination creates a world of objects for his own mental exercise. But the child does not yet think in terms of concepts or generalities.

When a cat is not a cat One of the most imaginative studies of the Piaget variety was carried out by DeVries (1967). Children from 3 to 6 years old were shown a live and "very tolerant" cat. The cat was fitted with extremely realistic masks, one of a rabbit and one of a ferocious-looking dog. Measurement of both verbal and nonverbal fear responses showed that to the younger children the cat became a rabbit or a dog, but to older children, although they were at the preconceptual stage, the animal was still a cat.

Intuitive thought (ages 4 to 7 years) The child develops keen perceptual sensitivity. Especially, he gains the ability to see several objects as a group characterized by some obvious similarity. At this stage, given a box of pegs he might perceive round pegs as one group and square pegs as another. The child may know nothing about circles or squares but acts on intuition.

One concept generally tested at the intuitive stage is known as *conservation* (or what Piaget calls the *principle of invariance*). In essence, according to the conservation concept, we perceive that the same amount, mass, weight, or volume is being conserved even when it is placed in a different position, poured into a different-sized container, or molded into a different shape. The conservation concept does not seem to operate in children at the intuitive stage. If the child is given two identical balls of clay and asked to roll one into a sausage, he will say that the sausage contains more clay than the ball simply because the sausage is longer. Figure 2.7 shows a typical conservation test.

If the child observes gradual alterations in the shape of a mass, he is likely to think he has seen more than one object. He cannot see the moon as an object that changes from a whole circle to a sliver of a circle and back again; he sees the moon in its stages as three different ob-

Figure 2.7 The middle jar contains more candy than the identical jar on the left. The taller, narrower jar on the right contains the same amount of candy as the standard jar on the left (from "A Study of Development of Conservation by a Nonverbal Method," by Irwin Silverman and Dale Schnieder. The Journal of Genetic Psychology, 1968, 112, 287–291. Reprinted by permission of the author and The Journal of Genetic Psychology)

jects. The child in the intuitive stage is, in addition, unable to understand cognitive processes as they exist in others. For example, we might ask him what his mother would think if he were to cry, but he simply is not mature enough to imagine the thoughts of another person.

Concrete operations (age 7 to 11 years) During the stage of *concrete operations*, the child acquires many concepts that escaped him at earlier stages. He can now comprehend the concept of conservation and can even work conservation experiments in reverse order (Figure 2.8). For example, given a ball of clay and instructed to roll it into a long sausage, he is able to reason that the quantity of clay has remained unchanged.

At this stage, learned behavior responses are part of the child's repertoire. As long as a problem is concrete and involves physical objects or processes, the child is able to apply previous learning to its solution. He is able to think through transformation problems—that is, problems that involve sequential developments, such as successive increases in size. And he can perceive points of view different from his own.

Despite these developments, the child is still unable to deal effectively with abstract problems. Although he may see and understand elements of an abstract problem, and can even relate it to someone else, he is unable to formulate a solution.

Formal operations (age 11 to 15 years) The peak of cognitive development is approached during the stage of *formal operations*—the stage at which the child begins to think abstractly. In older children, the early sign of formal operations is the ability to think scientifically, to approach a problem with several solutions and weigh them by reasoning, discussion, or putting them to practical tests—until the correct solution is found.

Once logical thought begins, a great deal of subsequent learning is needed for the young adult to attain the cognitive maturity required

Figure 2.8 A Piagetian test to determine cognitive development during the concrete operations stage. The boy demonstrates his ability to determine whether two objects are the same size and weight. (The New York Times)

for complex intellectual tasks. Not all individuals make the effort to develop the faculty of dealing with formal operations. Ideally, cognitive development continues until late in life. There are no limits to the creative use of the cognitive function in man.

A challenge to Piaget's theory Kingsley and Hall (1967) have questioned Piaget's theory that mental development occurs naturally and in a predetermined sequence in all children. As an alternative interpretation of Piaget's findings, they suggest that learning takes place *through experience*. They contend that only because children must learn simple concepts before they can learn complex ones has the order appeared to be predetermined; and because the acquisition of concepts takes time, one may have the incorrect impression that each learning stage unfolds at a particular age.

To support their formulation against Piaget's theory, they

1 taught children to understand the conservation concept, thus contradicting the hypothesis that the

concept cannot be taught at all but matures naturally;

2 taught children to understand conservation quite rapidly, contradicting the hypothesis that the concept matures slowly;

3 taught conservation to children aged 5 and 6, considerably younger than the 7-to-11 stage designated by Piaget;

4 taught conservation concepts out of Piaget's natural order.

Although the work of Kingsley and Hall has attracted attention, Piaget's theory has been verified by a large body of data and has proved very useful to educators. More conclusive evidence would be required to modify or nullify his theory.

Erikson's psychosocial stages of development

Erik Erikson, unlike Freud or Piaget, emphasizes the social development of the individual. Erikson's *psychosocial stages* of development are eight areas of crisis in the course of individual development:

1 Trust versus mistrust During his first year of life the infant depends on others for care. His mother feeds him, carries him about, dresses him, and constantly exposes him to new stimuli. His mother and father both cuddle him, talk to him, and play with him. These social interactions determine his later attitudes. If the infant is cared for affectionately, and if his physical needs are adequately met, he learns to trust his environment. If he is not cared for properly, or if his parents are inconsistent in their treatment of him, he will become fearful and will mistrust himself as well as others.

2 Autonomy versus doubt During the child's second and third years, he learns to walk, talk, and act independently; he is capable of learning at his own rate of speed and exploring the world on his own. If the child's parents are inconsistent in their disciplinary techniques, tend to be overprotective, or show disapproval when the child acts on his own initiative, he will become uncertain and ashamed of himself and his behavior. If, on the other hand, parents encourage initiative, act consistently, and allow the child a certain amount of independence, he will be better able to deal with later situations requiring choice, control, and autonomy.

3 Initiative versus guilt Between the ages of 4 and 5, the child's motor skills begin to develop, and he is thrown into a growing number of experiences, including relationships with school friends, neighbors, and relatives. If activities, questions, and general creative play are encouraged by parents, he will find it easier to go out on his own. The more experiences he is allowed to have, the more he will try to have on his own. If the child's activity and inquisitiveness are restricted by his parents, he will develop feelings of guilt whenever he tries to move out on his own.

4 Industry versus inferiority From 6 to 11 years, the child becomes fairly competent at manipulating objects and creating his own activities. Boys, as a rule, are taught to use this new-found ability to make or build things, and girls to cook or sew; the sexes are equally free to study, read, and learn about anything that interests them. If encouraged by parents and teachers, the child will develop a sense of industry and curiosity and will seek intellectual stimulation. If the parents or teachers become annoyed with the child's first fumbling attempts at industriousness, the child will develop a sense of inferiority and possibly a disinclination to complete future tasks.

5 Identity versus role confusion Adolescence, between the ages of 12 and 18, has traditionally been identified as a time of emerging sexuality and related crises. Erikson, however, is less concerned with this aspect than with the adolescent's crisis in finding his place in society. The adolescent must integrate all he has previously experienced in order to develop a sense of ego identity—determining what he wants out of life, what he believes in, and who he is. If he cannot integrate these earlier experiences, he cannot gain a sense of his own identity and becomes confused over what his role should be. Erikson believes that this is the single most significant conflict that the individual must face.

6 *Intimacy versus isolation* Dating, marriage, and early family development are all part of young adulthood. If the individual has achieved a sense of identity, he is able to form close relationships; he is able to share himself as well as his possessions with others. If the individual is unable to relate intimately to others, or if he has never achieved a full sense of identity, he may develop a sense of isolation and feel that he has no one but himself in the world.

7 *Generativity versus self-absorption* Middle age is the time when the individual must resolve his conflict with the external world, the future, and his willingness to contribute to its betterment. By *generativity* Erikson means the individual's ability to look outside himself and to be concerned for others. If the individual cannot do this, perhaps because he was unable to resolve earlier conflicts, he tends to be self-centered, rather than productive and happy.

8 *Integrity versus despair* The older person enters a period of reflection; he realizes that most of his life's work is complete and that he must bring his active pursuits to a close. If the individual remembers his life with pleasure, he establishes a sense of unity in himself and with others. If an individual feels that his life was a series of disappointments and failures, realizing that he cannot relive a new life at this age, he develops a sense of despair.

Comparison of the three theories

While all three major theorists assume that there are specific stages of development, each deals with a somewhat different area of behavior. Freud was concerned with emotion, Piaget with cognition, and Erikson with the individual in his environment. Erikson's position further differs from Piaget's and Freud's in that he does not see the stages he outlines as biologically determined but as determined by the individual's interaction with others. While Freud leans heavily on instinct doctrine, and Piaget on the concept of a gradual unfolding of biologically determined

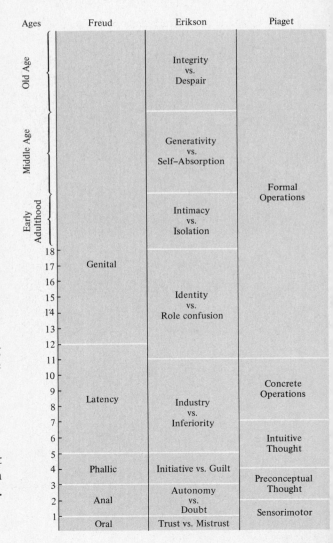

Figure 2.9   A comparison of the stage theories of Freud, Erikson, and Piaget.

capacities, Erikson gives as much weight to the environment as to factors within the individual. A comparison of the three stage theories is given in Figure 2.9.

DEVELOPMENT OF SOCIAL BEHAVIOR

Man is a social animal. He depends totally on other people during infancy and most of childhood, and during almost all of his life he continually interacts with others. The development of social behavior prepares him to live among his fellow individuals.

Social behavior does not develop passively; its development depends on the child's interaction with his social environment. A child affects and is affected by others, in a *dynamic interaction* that begins early in life. It probably starts the moment the newborn infant moves and someone responds to his actions. When the infant cries and his mother reacts to comfort him, mother and child are modifying each other's behavior. The way the mother initially reacts depends on the infant's bodily characteristics. The reactions elicited by a vigorous, overactive infant will usually be different from those elicited by a quiet, passive child.

Parental behavior

Characteristics of parents play an important role in the socialization of children. Parents set examples for their children, although not always intentionally. For instance, most parents do not want their children to display aggression; yet a parent will punish a child by spanking, thereby unwittingly encouraging the child to make use of aggression. Sears (1951) has shown that children who are frequently punished by parents show a great deal of disguised aggression. In another study, Sears, Maccoby, and Levin (1957) showed that very aggressive children come from

homes in which (a) there was much physical punishment; (b) parents condoned overt aggression; (c) parents disagreed frequently; and (d) the mother was not satisfied with her role in life and held a low opinion of her husband.

Parental characteristics influence the social development of children in subtle ways. Imitation plays a role, but the influence may be more complex. An aggressive father is sometimes imitated by his son; but if the father is very aggressive and dominates his son, the son may develop timid patterns of social behavior. The son may assume the role of a dominated individual and carry that passive role through life. A mother who takes pride in her own beauty may be imitated by her daughter; but if the mother is more vain than maternal, her daughter may see herself as inferior to her mother and take little pride in her own appearance.

Feeding and toilet training As we know, infants are totally dependent upon their parents for feeding, clothing, cleaning, and the satisfaction of all other basic needs. Thus, parental response to these needs strongly influences the infant's social development. The feeding situation represents the first crucial test of the parent-child interaction. If the child's experiences are gratifying and relatively free from discomfort, they become a source of contentment and satisfaction. These feelings of contentment generalize (spread) from the parents to other adults. If the feeding situations are unpleasant, as might happen if the mother is rough with the child and typically hurries with the feeding, then the feeding situation and the mother come to arouse feelings of discomfort and tension. These negative feelings may generalize to other adults.

Toilet training, which generally begins when a child is 18 months old (when he is physiologically mature enough to control the appropriate muscles), often represents the child's first contact with punishment. It is difficult to toilet train a child, because the child is required to restrain a natural urge, expressing it only in socially approved ways. Many parents think it necessary to use some form of discipline in the training, rewarding the child when he successfully controls his urge to urinate or to move his bowels and/or punishing him when he fails to do so. Few parents are able to tolerate for long a child's inability to control his need to eliminate.

If toilet training is accompanied by frequent punishment, a child may come to fear the situation and become confused about what he should and should not do. His biology is in conflict with his immediate society. Fears relating to toilet training can generalize to the point where the child feels insecure about everything he does. His feelings of insecurity will depend on how much emphasis his parents place on the training and how they react to him in other situations. It is not likely that childhood insecurity will arise solely from toilet training. Parents who are severe and harsh in toilet training are likely to be severe and harsh in other situations as well.

Affectionate behavior and attachment

There is little question that the development of affection is related to the interaction of parent and child, but this relationship is difficult to study in human beings. Animal research has been very useful in suggesting the effects of the presence or absence of a mother during early infancy. It has indicated that infants have a basic need for attachment to a mother that does not seem to depend on such variables as hunger and fear.

Harlow's experiments with young monkeys have been influential in developing the concept of attachment of affection (Harlow, 1958, 1970; Harlow, Harlow, and Suomi, 1971). Harlow set out to determine whether or not there is a drive for affection or attachment that is independent of hunger and other drives. He observed the reaction of baby monkeys with surrogate (substitute) mothers. One surrogate mother was made of wire mesh with a wooden block at the head posi-

tion. The other surrogate mother was of the same size and shape, but its wire body was covered with soft terry cloth backed by sponge rubber and its wooden head was painted and glued with false features. Both mothers were heated by electric bulbs of equal warmth. Both contained a hole through which the nipple of a nursing bottle could be protruded to provide nourishment at feeding time. The baby monkeys had no experience with their real mothers, with other monkeys, or with human beings. They were individually placed in a cage containing two artificial mothers.

One group of monkeys was fed by the cloth mother; another was fed by the wire mother. Harlow reasoned that if affection in monkeys was caused by the satisfaction of a basic drive, such as hunger, each group would show affection for the mother that fed it; each group of monkeys would stay with its surrogate mother. This did not happen, however. Regardless of previous feeding experience, all monkeys preferred to cuddle up to the cloth mother. The monkeys fed by the wire mother would go to her for feeding but they soon returned to the cloth mother, even though it did not provide them with food. The monkeys fed by the cloth mother hardly ever approached the nonfeeding wire mother. Both groups clung to the terry cloth mother with all the outward signs of affection. Figure 2.10 shows one of these monkeys. Harlow also found that any fear stimuli caused the infant monkeys to reach out and cling to the cloth mother.

In a follow-up study of the monkeys, Harlow made an important discovery: when the monkeys used in the experiment reached adulthood, they failed to show any interest in normal sexual behavior. The males showed no interest in copulation; females did not voluntarily mate. When the females did become mothers, they showed no maternal behavior. They ignored or mistreated their own babies. Evidently, the contact comfort that they received in infancy was not enough for them to become normally functioning adults. They were incapable of transfer-

Figure 2.10 *The monkey clings to the cloth surrogate mother while feeding from the wire mother. Clearly, the warmth and comfort of the terry cloth is more important than the source of food. (Harry F. Harlow, University of Wisconsin Primate Laboratory)*

ring the affection they felt for their cloth mother to the opposite sex or to their own children. While these studies demonstrated that the development of affection involves more than comfort, the more complex variables in affection are yet to be identified.

Charm of the unnatural mother In recent experiments with monkeys and surrogate mothers, Harlow and Suomi (1970) demonstrated several new aspects of the affectional drive. Given their choice of mother, the monkeys indicated the following preferences:

1 A cloth mother is prefered not only to a wire mother but also to a vinyl or rough sandpaper mother.
2 A mother with breasts and lactate (milk) is preferred to one without either.
3 A rocking mother is preferred to a stable, stationary mother.
4 A warm mother is always preferred to a cold mother. In fact, monkeys raised by a cold mother develop a coldness for mothers in general.
5 A mother with no face is preferred to a mother who at first has no face and then is given a face. One monkey, who had been raised by a mother with a blank face, started screaming when his mother was given a face. However, he found that

he could turn the face around and get his "no-face" mother back. When the experimenters persisted in turning the face around each time he turned it away, the monkey finally ripped the whole head off and threw it into a corner.

Sex roles

Sex roles, which play a major part in social behavior, are established very early in life. Unfortunately, the treatment of boys and girls is often based on stereotypes: boys are expected to be aggressive and active, and girls submissive and passive; boys are expected to be good with tools, but girls are not. The fact is that the expectations of parents and society play a significant part in determining the extent to which a child adopts a particular sex role. Basing their battle against sex discrimination on this fact, those in the women's liberation movement know they can succeed only if society modifies the sex roles imposed on youngsters at a very early age.

Women's lib among the fish The wrasse, a small fish in the coastal waters of Australia, lives in small families consisting of two to five females and one dominant male. The females arrange themselves in order of dominance behind the male. When the male dies, the leading female literally becomes a male. Within a few days, female sex tissue changes to male tissue, and the new male is able to fertilize the eggs of the females in his family. Evidently, the male tendencies are always present in the female, coming to the surface when no male is present to serve the needed male functions.

There are, however, important basic physiological differences between males and females that cannot be ignored. Recent research suggests that hormones secreted into the bloodstream by the sex glands during the fetal stage of development help to determine later tendencies toward masculine or feminine behavior.

In laboratory experiments, female rhesus monkeys born to mothers who were given male sex hormones during their pregnancy behaved more like males. These masculinized female monkeys had external male sex organs and engaged in the rough and tumble play typical of males (Goy, 1970).

Similar findings have been reported for human beings. Of ten young girls whose mothers were accidentally exposed to a masculinizing hormone (progestin) during pregnancy, nine were born with male-like sex organs that were modified surgically during infancy. And as they grew, the girls tended to exhibit typically male behavior, sharing more interest in active sports than in playing with dolls (Ehrhardt and Money, 1967).

Social deprivation

In the developing child, the absence of normal social contacts often has a dramatic effect on later social behavior. The effects of such deprivation have been observed in laboratory monkeys reared apart from other monkeys. These isolated monkeys show extremely deviant behavior and become very aggressive adults. In cases involving long periods of isolation in infancy, the adult monkeys exhibit fear of any form of social contact and, in fact, appear incapable of performing any social function. Female monkeys raised in social isolation fail to demonstrate normal maternal activity, usually behaving indifferently or cruelly to their offspring (Harlow, Harlow, and Suomi, 1971).

There is little formal research on the social isolation of humans since such cases are not common, and ethical considerations make unlikely their creation in the laboratory for long-term study. There have been reports about children raised in relative isolation from other children, but these reports are generally sketchy and inconclusive. We must therefore rely on the monkey studies for clues to the effects of long-term human social isolation.

SUMMARY

Heredity involves the transmission through genes of the potential characteristics of the individual.

A major technique used in studying the influence of heredity and environment in human behavior involves the comparison of identical twins reared together with identical twins reared apart.

Neither heredity nor environment alone determines the characteristics of the individual. The individual's behavior is a product of the interaction of his heredity and his environment.

Instinct or species-specific behavior is behavior that appears to be inherited in every individual in a given species. The instinct concept, however, is not very useful in the analysis of human behavior.

Maturation is the genetically determined process that controls the growth of the organism as a whole and the various systems of which it is composed.

Prenatal development occurs from fertilization of the ovum to birth. It includes the ovum stage; the embryonic stage, during which the ectoderm, mesoderm, and endoderm develop; and the fetal stage.

The infant stage begins at birth, and during the 2 years of infancy the nervous system continues to develop. The endocrine system is also incomplete at birth.

After birth, development takes three forms: reflexive behavior; a pattern built in by genetic potential; and the combined effect of maturation and learning.

Maturation determines an individual's readiness to engage in a particular activity or learn a particular task.

Studies of imprinting have led to the idea of an optimal period for the learning of particular responses.

At 7 months the fetus possesses such prenatal sensory responses as kicking, flexing, and turning.

Taste and smell are underdeveloped at birth. The skin sensations of touch, warmth, cold, and pain are stronger in the newborn (neonate) than taste or smell. Very little experimentation has been done on the neonate to test for kinesthesis, the sensory feedback from muscles, joints, and tendons. By the age of 1 month, a strong auditory sense develops. The neonate cannot see precise shapes and colors. However, he can follow a path of light with his eyes. Complete vision requires 6 or 7 years to mature.

Prehension is the ability to grasp, hold, and manipulate objects manually. Prehensile motor development follows a sequence from random general arm and hand movements toward an object to gradual refinement of the use of the fingers, thumb, and fingertips.

Speech development depends on maturation of the organs of speech and exposure to sounds that the infant can imitate. The initial stage begins at about 3 months and is marked by babbling of a large variety of repetitive sounds.

Various theories of human development are based on the concept of stages of development. Sigmund Freud's theory of psychosexual development focuses on emotion and motivation. Freud viewed growth in terms of stages directly related to sexual needs, which he said dominate all behavior.

Jean Piaget's theory of cognitive development holds that the use of language and thinking grows as the child masters certain mental operations step by step, rather than in a continuous progression. His theory includes the following stages: sensorimotor (from birth to age 2); preconceptual thought (age 2 to 4); intuitive thought (age 4 to 7); concrete operations (age 7 to 11); and formal operations (age 11 to 15).

Erik Erikson has altered and broadened Freud's psychosexual theory of development to include conflicts related to social adjustment. He defines eight psychosocial stages in the life of the individual in our society: trust versus mistrust; autonomy versus doubt; initiative versus guilt; industry versus inferiority; identity versus role confusion; intimacy versus isolation; generativity versus self-absorption; and integrity versus despair.

Social development depends on a dynamic interaction of the child with his social environment, particularly his parents.

Parental affection appears to be an important factor in shaping future attitudes, as indicated by Harry Harlow's experiments with monkeys.

Sex roles are set forth by parents and society, but basic studies indicate that physiological differences between males and females also influence the display of sexually differentiated behavior.

The effects of deprivation of social contacts in infancy and early childhood are suggested by experiments with isolated young monkeys who were found to be socially dysfunctional.

SUGGESTED READINGS

Texts

Baldwin, A. L. *Theories of child development.* New York: Wiley, 1966. A comprehensive exploration of contemporary prominent theories of human development.

Bijou, S. W., & Baer, D. M. (Eds.) *Child development: readings in experimental analysis.* New York: Appleton-Century-Crofts, 1967. Child development studies with an orientation toward a Skinnerian point of view.

Cratty, B. J. *Perceptual and motor development in infants and children.* New York: Macmillan, 1970. An interesting and well-illustrated account of development, particularly noted for its description of motor development.

Ginsberg, H., & Opper, S. *Piaget's theory of intellectual development.* Englewood Cliffs, N.J.: Prentice-Hall, 1969. An excellent and readable introduction to the comprehensive development theory of Jean Piaget.

Kagan, J. *Change and continuity in infancy.* New York: Wiley, 1971. This report of a large-scale longitudinal study provides not only data on infancy but a rich description of the methodology of infant study.

Langer, J. *Theories of development.* New York: Holt, Rinehart & Winston, 1969. A lively comparison of psychoanalytic, learning, and cognitive-developmental approaches to human development.

Money, J., & Ehrhadt, A. *A man and woman, boy and girl.* Baltimore: Johns Hopkins University Press, 1972. A thorough exploration of the processes of sexual differentiation from conception to maturity.

Schaffer, H. R. *The growth of sociability.* Baltimore: Penguin, 1971. A comprehensive introduction to the critical importance of early social behavior in later social and cognitive development.

Werner, H. *Comparative psychology of mental development.* New York: International Universities Press, 1948. A classic and readable account of comparative structural principles of mental organization.

Popular books

Fraiberg, S. H. *The magic years.* A delightful overview of the changes and problems of the early childhood years.

Golding, W. *Lord of the flies.* Allegorical novel about the shedding of cultural characteristics by boys stranded in a primitive environment.

Goodall, J. *In the shadow of man.* An anthropologist's report on her field studies of chimps, their development and social behavior.

Lewis, O. *The children of Sanchez.* The autobiography of a Mexican family, told in stories taken down by tape recorder over a period of years.

3
Physiology of response

To understand man, we need to know him as a biological organism, for all human behavior is influenced by biological variables. It is possible to study behavior without knowing much about the sense organs, the muscles, or the nervous system, but this is like learning to operate a car while remaining ignorant of what happens under the hood. In either case, one does not know how to forestall problems or what to do about them when they occur.

In this chapter we shall deal with aspects of *physiological psychology*, sometimes called psychobiology, which is emerging as an exciting and separate discipline concerned with the biological bases of behavior. Here we shall examine the body's response systems and how they translate stimulation into action. With this information as a basis, you may want to learn more about the intricate means used by the body to protect itself and respond to the environment. For this purpose, several excellent books are listed at the end of this chapter.

RESPONSE SYSTEMS

Although most of us know something about how our bodies function, we rarely appreciate the complexity of the organization and interrelation of systems within the body. We tend to take the efficiency of our bodies for granted. Study of the response systems makes us aware of how finely tuned the body is. When an organism is called upon to perform an emergency function, it must signal and coordinate many different organs and systems to generate the necessary response, one that involves the whole body. Psychologists who have analyzed complex behavior have found that the human being responds and adjusts to the demands of his environment. The environmental demands are *stimulus events*, which may or may not call for immediate response. It is reasonable to assume that, since stimuli are received by many sensory organs and each sensory organ reacts independently to stimuli, an individual can receive many stimuli at once. For example, we taste and smell simultaneously. It is also true that we may hear, see, sense cold or warmth, and feel our heart beat and our back muscles ache at the same time that we taste and smell.

Although the sensory organs are affected by many different stimulus events at once, the body can respond to only one set of stimuli at a time. The bodily systems organize and coordinate various incoming stimuli through a process called *integration*. This coordination is accomplished by an elaborate balance of systems within the body and, for the most part, by integrated patterns of activity in the brain.

Once the brain interprets a stimulus event, it relays a message through the nervous system to the muscles and the glands; this message dictates to the body how to respond to the stimulus. The nerve impulse thus describes a complete circuit—from the point of stimulus origin to the brain and to the reacting parts of the organism. Before we can understand the nervous system, we need to understand how the muscles and glands work in response to stimuli.

Tuning in and tuning out The ability to tune into one of many conversations in a room while ignoring the others is familiar to all of us. You cannot, however, tune into more than one conversation at a time without its all becoming a senseless din. Yet, most people are able to read a book while listening to the radio. In this situation, your system integrates the different stimuli.

Poulton (1956) designed an experiment to explore the integrating mechanisms of the human system by asking his subjects to listen to two messages at the same time. The subject was to write down all the messages he heard. There were two conditions: (1) one message was very simple and often repeated while the other was difficult; (2) both were difficult.

The results showed that, because of the increased difficulty of the two messages, the subjects made more mistakes in condition 2. Thus, although we can often integrate two or three different speech channels and respond to all of them, we can only do so if the messages are not too complex (that is, do not contain too much information).

The muscles, together with the skeleton, are chiefly responsible for body movement. Normally, muscle cells remain in a semiactive (partially contracted) state. In response to direct stimulation or to motor nerve impulses from the brain, the muscles contract, causing movement of the limb or organ of which they are a part. An active (or fully contracted) muscle is therefore shorter than a muscle at rest. After responding to stimuli, muscles return to their partially contracted state in order to maintain the most efficient condition of their cells. This condition, known as *muscle tone*, varies in each individual according to the elastic strength and vigor of his muscle cells. Muscle tone usually is maintained automatically by reflexive movements within the body and, additionally, by exercise.

Those of us who spend a great deal of time exercising and lead active lives have high muscle tone, which is excellent for health and well-being. However, a person may have muscle tone that is too high, and this will endanger a portion of his bodily functioning by hindering and/or destroying the smooth, effortless actions made by muscles with a lower tone. Psychologists frequently encounter otherwise well-functioning individuals whose muscles are tense, and who are unable to relax. Such tension may be identified as an involuntary tightening and may indicate that the individual is troubled or disturbed.

There are three kinds of muscles: (1) *striated muscles*, which control the posture and movement of the skeleton and movements of the tongue and eyes; (2) *smooth muscles*, which control the internal organs, including blood vessels; and (3) *cardiac muscles*, which control heart action (Figure 3.1).

1 *Striated muscles* (so called because they appear striped under the microscope) are often referred to as skeletal muscles because they usually connect to the body skeleton. For the most part,

skeletal muscles function in pairs, one muscle contracting while the other relaxes. These muscle pairs, known as *antagonistic muscles*, are used for movement of the joints in walking, dancing, or any "free-flowing" movement. The principle behind the function of antagonistic muscles is known as *reciprocal innervation*, a balance of impulses that leads one of a pair of antagonistic muscles to relax as the other muscle contracts.

2 *Smooth muscles* control internal bodily organs. They derive their name from the fact that, unlike the striated muscles, they have a relatively smooth surface. Smooth muscles contract more slowly than the striated muscles, but their response lasts comparatively longer. You are no doubt familiar with the responses produced by both types of muscles. Suppose you have to brake your car quickly to avoid a crash. You rapidly forget the feel of the striated muscles you used in shifting your foot to the brake, but the perspiration and queasy feeling caused by the response of the smooth muscles does not stop until some time after the danger is past.

3 *Cardiac muscles* are located exclusively in and around the heart. They resemble skeletal muscles in that both are striated. They contract more slowly than do striated muscles and, like the smooth muscles, their response lasts relatively longer.

Although the striated muscles have been called the *voluntary* muscles, and the smooth and cardiac, the *involuntary*, these labels are misleading. Few people can hold back all signs of a smile when something amuses them or can refrain from blinking when hands are clapped in front of their eyes. These are striated-muscle responses, but they are not always under voluntary control. On the other hand, some people can control the so-called involuntary muscles of their circulatory or digestive systems. Cases are on record of people who could lower or raise their heartbeat or blood pressure at will.

Controlling the "involuntary" muscles Most of us think that because our autonomic functions are "involuntary," they are completely beyond our control. Yet some of those who practice yoga (a system of meditation and exercises based on Eastern philosophy) claim that they can control such autonomic functions as the heartbeat. Similar claims have been made for fire walking and needle penetration without bleeding.

Wenger and Bagchi (1961) traveled to India, home of the yogi, to take physiological measurements to test such claims. They found no fire walkers or heart stoppers, but they did find a man who possessed voluntary control of an autonomic function.

Figure 3.1 *Muscle cells as seen under a microscope: left, striated muscle, such as in the arm; center, smooth muscle, such as in the stomach; and right, cardiac muscle. (Turtox General Biological)*

This yogi could, without physical exertion, cause sweat to break out on his forehead. The subject explained how he learned to do this.

One winter, he lived in Himalayan caves. When the cold distracted him from his meditations, his teacher advised him to visualize himself in extremely high-temperature situations to make himself feel warm. After about 6 months of practice, he gradually succeeded in obtaining this feeling of warmth. Later he found that in a moderate climate, the same kind of effort produced not only feelings of great warmth, but also perspiration.

The authors explained this as a conditioned response pattern to visual imagery. They concluded that, generally, where direct voluntary control of autonomic functions is claimed, intervening mechanisms usually are employed.

The endocrine system

The endocrine glands, like the muscles and the nervous system, play a major role in maintaining bodily well-being. In conjunction with the area of the brain called the *hypothalamus* (to be discussed later; see Figure 3.8), endocrine glands participate in most aspects of human behavior and development by activating internal organs to respond appropriately.

The endocrine glands are ductless; this means that they lack structured passageways to the organs they serve. The glands discharge their

Figure 3.2 *Diagram illustrating the endocrine glands, the hormones they secrete, and the function of each. (Drawing "Natural History," by Ralph Kellmer, May 7, 1972. Copyright © 1972 by The New York Times Company. Reprinted by permission.)*

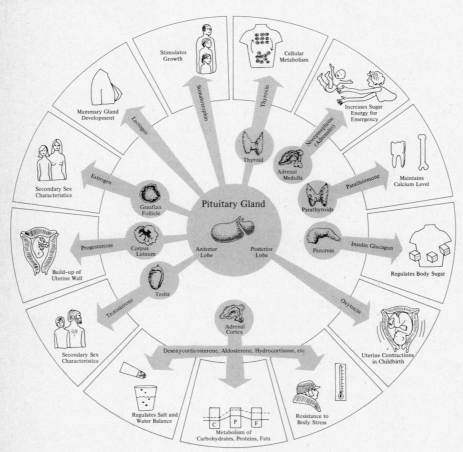

secretions, called *hormones*, directly into the bloodstream. The circulatory system, therefore, is the passageway that carries hormones from the endocrine glands to the various body organs and parts that need them.

Specifically, the endocrine glands and the hypothalamus contribute to *homeostasis*—the proper balance and rate of internal activities. Although the endocrine glands do not, by design, function simultaneously, they do function relatedly. Chemical messages pass among them. Should one gland need to be adjusted, the others regulate its functioning by hormone secretion. The endocrine glands are so closely interrelated that injury to or removal of one gland may cause the entire system to malfunction. The endocrine system operates in conjunction with the nervous system: endocrine glands are stimulated by nerve impulses.

The perfectly functioning body is like a well-kept neighborhood: when the streets get dirty, they are cleaned; when the fire hydrant leaks, it is fixed; the lawns are fertilized, trimmed, or watered when they need it. The body also patrols itself in that it is able to recognize its malfunctions and deficiencies, especially as they may relate to the normal metabolic level of everyday functioning. When, for example, there is too little salt in the bloodstream, the altered chemical composition of the blood stimulates certain fibers, a message is relayed, and the adrenal cortex acts to stimulate the release of salt deposits stored in "tissue pockets" in the body. Surgical removal or damage to the adrenal cortex disrupts this balancing action, and the organism must consume large amounts of salt to maintain the proper balance of salt in its bloodstream.

Figure 3.2 shows the functions of the principal endocrine glands. Although much is known about the endocrine system, many questions remain about the role of hormones in determining behavior. The study of *endocrinology* is important both for this reason and because the malfunctioning of endocrine glands often carries serious physiological and psychological consequences.

STRUCTURE AND FUNCTIONS OF THE NERVOUS SYSTEM

The nervous system plays an essential role in the individual's response to his environment. Hence, we shall devote the rest of this chapter to its structure and functions. We shall examine the movement of a nerve impulse as it travels through the nervous system to the brain in order to activate a response mechanism.

Neurons

Impulses are conducted by specialized cells called *neurons*. Other cell types also exist in the nervous system, but they appear to function only to assist the neurons—for example, *glial cells*, which nourish and support neurons. (However, recent evidence indicates that the glial cells also may function independently in the metabolic process.) Although neurons may take many shapes, every neuron functions in essentially the same way. Differences in shape apparently depend on location; the neuron has to fit. Figure 3.3 shows a typical neuron.

The neuron is composed of a *cell body*, which contains the *nucleus* of the cell, and two types of fibers that branch off from the cell body. The branching fibers are called *dendrites* and *axons*. Dendrites receive nerve impulses from adjacent neurons or directly from some physical source and conduct them to the cell body. After nerve impulses are received from the sensory organs, the dendrites start these impulses on their way to the brain. *Axons* relay or send impulses from the cell body to the other neurons or to muscle tissue.

Dendrites and axons may be arranged in a variety of ways depending on the special requirements of the body area they service. Dendrites are usually short, but axons can be quite long, depending on the connecting cells in the

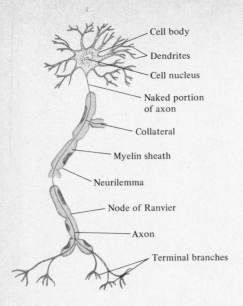

Cell body

Dendrites

Cell nucleus

Naked portion
of axon

Collateral

Myelin sheath

Neurilemma

Node of Ranvier

Axon

Terminal branches

Figure 3.3   Diagram of a typical motor neuron
located in the spinal cord. The dendrites, which
carry impulses into the cell, are the short fibers
around the cell body. The axon is the long fiber,
which carries impulses away from the cell to the
dendrites of another neuron.

area. In areas of great density of neurons—gen-erally in the brain or in places of complex con-nections—both fibers are relatively short and bushy. In outer areas of the body, neurons tend to be elongated; an axon running from the cortex to the base of the spinal cord may be as long as 3 feet.

Axons in the brain and spinal cord are often covered by a white, fatty layer of cells, the *myelin sheath*. Nerve fibers outside the brain and spinal cord may be covered by an additional thin layer of cells called the *neurilemma*. Figure 3.3 shows the myelin sheath and the neurilemma. The myelin sheath acts as an insulator and facili-tates the conduction of impulses through the axon portion of the neuron; for this reason, the myelin sheath is essential for the timing and pat-terning of nerve impulses. Myelin develops slowly on the human neuron and in some cells may not be well formed until the individual is approx-

imately 7 to 10 years old. This late development bears a direct relationship to the fact that certain motor skills and sensory processes do not mature until middle childhood. Perhaps the maturation of these systems depends on full development of myelin.

The myelin sheath does not cover the axons of all neurons and there are interruptions in the myelin surface at regular intervals along the course of every nerve fiber. Little has been learned so far about the function of these inter-ruptions in the sheath, which are known as the *nodes of Ranvier*.

Some neuron cell bodies are gathered in large clusters throughout the nervous system; these clusters are called *nuclei* and generally ap-pear grayish in color because of the presence of many dark nuclei in the cell bodies. Other gath-erings of smaller numbers of cell bodies are called *ganglia*. Many axons from neurons in the same location of the body tend to travel together as *nerve fibers* to form *tracts* (*nerve pathways*). Such tracts always appear as bundles of axons within the brain and the spinal cord. Similar bundles of axons called *nerve trunks* connect neurons running from within the brain and spinal cord to the outer body areas.

Types of neurons   The neuron depicted in Fig-ure 3.3 is a *motor* or *efferent* (outgoing) *neuron*. It is directly responsible for each movement, each response we make, by relaying messages from the brain to the muscles or glands. In efferent neurons, the cell body is located in the spinal cord and the axon is long enough to reach a neighboring neuron or even as far as the muscle or gland to which it relays impulses. Ef-ferent neurons are *long-conducting* neurons.

Another type of long-conducting neuron is the *sensory* or *afferent* (incoming) *neuron*, which receives the stimuli and carries impulses to the brain for interpretation (or sensing). The cell body of the afferent neuron is located on the *nerve root*, which is outside the spinal cord. It receives external stimuli through its dendrite fibers and then, through a dendrite approximately equal in length to the motor neuron's axon, relays the impulses through the cell body into the spinal cord. Once within the spinal cord, impulses either travel to the brain or pass to the efferent neurons that return them directly to the muscles and glands.

Another type of neuron, the *interneuron* or *association neuron*, is located in the brain and the spinal cord. Interneurons often connect the impulse from the axon fibers of the afferent neuron to the dendrite fibers of the efferent neuron. It has been shown that the interneurons also form alternate circuits, or pathways, for impulses to take. If one circuit is busy or damaged, another path is thus made available. The interneurons, which are short and stubby at both ends, are merely connectors, neither accepting sensory stimuli as the afferent neurons do, nor stimulating muscle cells as efferent neurons do.

Afferent neurons, efferent neurons, and interneurons may possess axon fibers that branch off from the main stem to make connections with other types of nerve cells. Since the axon transmits the nerve impulse, these branches, or *collaterals* as they are called, are also able to transmit the nerve impulse. Because of the collaterals, axon fibers of one neuron are able to connect with dendrite fibers of more than one neuron. Similarly, the dendrite fibers of one neuron may well be receiving impulses from many other neurons.

The nerve impulse

The nerve impulse results from changes in the thin membrane that covers the nerve cell. In its usual state, this membrane is electrically *polarized*; that is, there are positively charged ions on the outside and negatively charged ions inside. This polarization occurs because the membrane is semipermeable (able to be penetrated only by certain smaller substances: it does not let the positive and negative ions through).

The nerve impulse is set in motion when a stimulus causes the membrane at a given point to become permeable. When that happens, the

ions pass through the permeable gap and neutralize each other; the result is a loss of polarization of the adjacent membrane. The loss of polarization causes the membrane at that next point to become permeable and the whole process repeats itself, with the nerve impulse seeming to roll along the surface of the nerve fiber. Figure 3.4 represents the sequence of events that take place in the transmission of the nerve impulse.

Figure 3.4   Transmission of an impulse along a nerve fiber.

+ + + + + + + + + + + + + + + +
— — — — — — — — — — — — — — — —

(A) *Resting:* The nerve fiber is electrically polarized (the positively charged ions on the outside balance the negatively charged ions on the inside), because the membrane is semipermeable and does not let positive ions through.

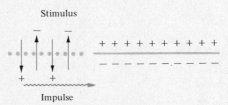

(B) *Activated:* A stimulus causes the membrane to become permeable. The impulse is set in motion as the positive ions flow rapidly through the membrane into the cell and a smaller number of negative ions flow out.

(C) *Recovery:* The membrane is polarized; semipermeability is restored after the impulse passes.

The following further explains the nerve impulse and how it operates:

1 The strength of the nerve impulse does not depend on the strength of the stimulus that started the impulse. This fact is the *all-or-none law*; it states that nerve fibers respond completely or not at all. The stimulus must be above a certain minimum strength, referred to as the *threshold*, if the nerve is to react. If the nerve fiber reacts at all, it reacts fully, just as a firecracker fuse burns in a certain way whether it was lit by a blowtorch or a match. The strength of the nerve impulse is maintained throughout its journey along the nerve fiber.

2 There is a limit to the number of times a nerve fiber can respond each second. Immediately after a nerve fiber responds to stimulation, there is a period of time during which the membrane remains permeable and unpolarized, hence completely unresponsive to new stimulation. This period of time, called the *absolute refractory period*, lasts from 0.001 to 0.01 seconds, depending on the nerve fiber. This is followed by a *relative refractory period* that lasts two to three times as long as the absolute refractory period. During this time, only very strong stimuli, well above the threshold, will excite the nerve fiber. Because complete repolarization of the membrane has not yet occurred, these refractory periods limit the rate at which a nerve fiber can respond. The most rapidly recovering fibers cannot be stimulated more often than 1,000 times per second.

3 Nerve impulses travel relatively slowly. The fastest impulses in large-diameter myelin-covered fibers travel about 130 yards per second, and in small-diameter unmyelinated fibers, the impulses may be as slow as 2 yards per second.

Let us return for a moment to the first point, the all-or-none law. We know that individual neurons cannot respond to nerve impulses in degrees: nerve cells must be either all on or all off. How, then, does the nervous system enable us to experience various intensities of sensory stimulation? Physiologists have determined that some nerve fibers have lower thresholds than others. A stronger stimulus will break through the stimulation threshold of larger numbers of nerve fibers, causing them to respond. A weak stimulus will excite few nerve fibers, and hence may not excite at all. During the relative refractory period, only very strong stimuli are passed along by the nerve fibers.

The synapse

We have not yet explained how electrochemical nerve impulses pass along from the axon of one neuron to the dendrite of another. The passage occurs without the nerve endings actually touching; instead, nerve impulses are transmitted chemically across gaps to be received by the next neuron in the chain. These gaps, called *synapses*, are usually found between the axon tip of one neuron and the dendrite or the cell body of another neuron. Two characteristics of synapses have an important bearing on the functioning of the nervous system: (1) *one-way conduction*, whereby impulses pass from axon to dendrite or cell body, but never in the opposite direction; and (2) *delay of transmission*, whereby slightly more time is required for an impulse to cross a synapse than to pass along a nerve fiber. Evidently, a buildup of chemical and electrical excitation must occur at the synapse before transmission takes place. Often this buildup requires that impulses from more than one fiber converge on a synapse.

The transmission of impulses across synapses does in fact involve electrical and chemical reactions in the synaptic region. When an im-

Figure 3.5 The impulse is transmitted across the synapse from axon to dendrite by a transmitter substance secreted by the synaptic vesicles.

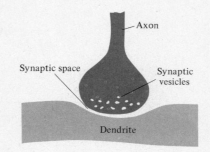

Axon

Synaptic space

Synaptic vesicles

Dendrite

pulse arrives at the end of an axon, tiny sacs called *synaptic vesicles* release a transmitting substance that crosses the synaptic space (Figure 3.5) and causes the membrane of the receptor dendrite to react and produce an impulse in the dendritic fiber. One of the transmitting substances identified in synaptic activity is *acetylcholine*, a chemical found in much of the nerve tissue of the body.

Synaptic activity does not always encourage the transmission of nerve impulses; it may also involve blocking or inhibition of the impulses. Some synaptic vesicles release a substance that makes impulse transmission more difficult; only the stronger impulses get through. The fact that blockage may occur at synapses is further indication of the complex organizing and integrating function of the nervous system.

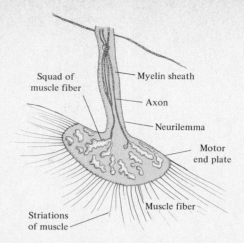

Figure 3.6 *At the motor end plate, the axon branches and spreads into squads of muscle fibers.*

Motor connections

The axon branches extensively as it approaches a muscle; and when it enters the muscle, it branches even more. Each axon branch ends at a muscle fiber. Thus, each motor neuron controls a squad of muscle fibers (Figure 3.6). These squads vary in size from a few muscle cells in small muscles, such as those of the eyes or the fingers, to as many as 200 in large muscles, such as those of the arms and legs. The axon branches contact the muscle cells at the *motor end plate*. It is interesting to note that curare, the drug that South American Indians put on arrowheads to paralyze and kill animals or enemies, blocks transmission of impulses at the motor end plate. Curare has been used in controlled dosages in the laboratory to study the effects of temporary muscular paralysis on conditioning.

A temporary paralyzing agent *Curare* has been useful in psychology laboratories for many years for its action as a neuromuscular blocking agent. Normally it is used for very localized effects: it can temporarily inhibit the passage of impulses from nerve to connecting muscle—without interrupting either the nerve's normal conduction of impulses or the muscle's ability to respond to direct (artificial) electrical stimulation. For experimental purposes, the local administration of curare is normally as effective as cutting the nerve in the area to be studied; and, since curare is only a temporary paralyzing agent, it has the added advantage of permitting study of the same animal under normal conditions. For example, Girden and Culler (1937) were able to condition dogs to make two different responses to the same stimulus—one under normal functioning and one under curarization.

Intravenous curare injections were at one time used to treat tetanus, spastic paralysis, and the convulsions suffered by psychotics undergoing electric shock treatment. The drug's unreliability in such situations, however, prompted the use of alternative treatments, and curare is now best known for its usefulness in the experimental animal laboratory.

THE CENTRAL NERVOUS SYSTEM

The neurons we have discussed are a part of the nervous system. We generally classify the nervous system into two divisions, the *central nervous system*, composed of the brain and spinal cord, and the *peripheral nervous system*, which consists of those nerve fibers, or bundles of axons, found outside the brain and spinal cord. The peripheral nervous system connects the central nervous system to the rest of the body. First we shall discuss the central nervous system and the ways that the spinal cord and brain function as part of the body's response mechanism.

The spinal cord

The central nervous system is primarily a place of impulse transference. Across the spinal cord and upward to the brain, bundles of nerve fibers (tracts) and bundles of cell bodies (nuclei) populate the central nervous system. The spinal cord has two major functions. Its first function is to serve as a pathway through which nerve impulses from sensory organs (affectors) pass to the brain and impulses from the brain return to the muscles and glands (effectors). Figure 3.7 shows a simplified cross section of the spinal cord. The outer area of the cord appears white, because white is the color of the fatty myelin sheath that encases the nerve fibers that run along the spinal cord. Sensory impulses are conducted upward to the brain through tracts located in these outer regions of the cord. Motor impulses travel down from the brain through the tracts located along the cord's cleft and on the side. The central H-shaped area of the spinal cord is of a grayish color because it is composed of clusters of nuclei, or cell bodies.

The second function of the spinal cord is to govern certain types of reflexive movements by processing sensory impulses to the effectors without the assistance of the brain. Principally, it is the instantaneous reflexes—such as withdrawing the hand from a pinprick, blinking the eyes, or extending the muscles of the trunk to support the body's weight when standing up—that are controlled by the spinal cord.

Scientists have learned much about the role of the spinal cord in reflex activities through experiments with animals. By severing connections between the spinal cord and the brain and observing subsequent behavior patterns in the

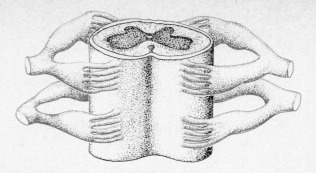

Figure 3.7   *Cross section of the spinal cord. The cleft is the part of the column facing the front of the body. The gray matter shows the location of cell bodies that control certain reflex actions (the nuclei give the gray coloring).*

subject, it has been possible to determine which reflex activities are governed by the brain and which by the spinal cord. When a response is controlled by the spinal cord, the subject is able to react to stimuli, even if connections between the spinal cord and brain have been severed; if the response is controlled by the brain, the subject is unable to react. A standard experiment in high school biology courses involves severing a frog's legs and lower portion of the spinal cord from the rest of the body; the student notes that when the leg muscles are stimulated, they continue to flex without the aid of the brain.

Spinal-cord-controlled activities   The earliest and clearest analyses of the "spinal animal" (one whose brain has been severed from its spinal cord) were given to us by James (1890), the American philosopher-psychologist, and Sherrington (1906, 1947), who has been called the "father of modern neurophysiology." Sherrington found that by applying a weak electric current ("electric flea") to a "spinal dog's" shoulder, he could get the dog to scratch the irritated spot with his paw. If he then irritated a different spot, the animal would move its paw to that spot. From this he concluded that, since it is obvious that the animal applies some "will" in directing its own movement, spinal-cord-controlled movement is not entirely without purpose.

James, in observing a "spinal frog," noted that

although the spinal cord could produce many different movements when stimulated, it still did not initiate any action on its own; there were no spontaneous movements.

The line between spinal-cord-controlled and brain-controlled movements is not firmly drawn. It seems safe to say that the differences between them are only in degree of complexity. Thus, it would be wrong to say that the spinal cord cannot accomplish some of the functions of the brain proper.

The brain

An analogy is often drawn between the brain and a computer, but such a comparison is misleading. For the brain is far more complex than any computer developed to date; if a machine could be developed to perform the work of the brain, it would probably be larger than the Empire State Building—and even then would be less efficient than the human brain. Hundreds of pages would be required to explain all the functions of the brain and the theories and facts about how it works. For our purposes, it is enough to understand the function of the brain, which is to identify, code, interpret, store, and respond to the experience of sensory stimulation.

Much of what we know about the brain has come from careful studies of the brains of human beings and animals. Medical researchers have performed numerous experiments with animal subjects and have examined brains donated by human subjects for scientific investigation. (Albert Einstein, the great physicist, left his brain to research.) Researchers have developed surgical procedures to map out areas of the brain and determine which parts of the body they control. These studies of brain tissue offer the psychologist wide opportunities to investigate the neural base of human behavior.

Three divisions of the brain

The brain consists of three cavities, or cores: the *hindbrain*, the *midbrain*, and the *forebrain* (Figure 3.8). In many respects, the development of the brain in an individual human fetus parallels the evolutionary development of the brain in man; studies of fetal brain development and comparison of the structures and functions of the brain common to man and other species have helped researchers gain an understanding of how the human brain evolved.

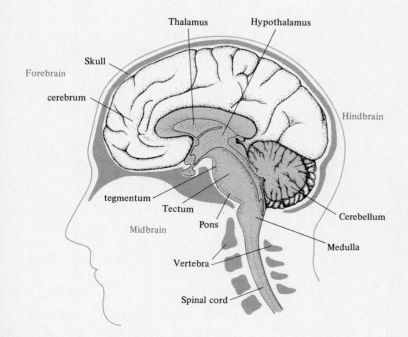

Figure 3.8 The three divisions of the brain and their structures. The reticular activating system, which is a system of neurons running through the hindbrain, the midbrain, and up into the forebrain, and the limbic system, which is a large system of nerve cells encompassing the hypothalamus, are too diffuse to be labeled clearly.

71

Hindbrain The hindbrain appears to have been the first, or most primitive, brain to evolve. It is present in the simplest vertebrates. It contains structures essential for the organism's survival. Structures of the hindbrain are the *medulla*, which controls respiration, digestion, and circulation; the *cerebellum*, which governs balance, posture, and muscular coordination; and the *pons*, which appears to contain nerve fibers from both sides of the cerebellum as well as the tracts of sensory and motor nerve fibers that connect the upper brain to the spinal cord.

Midbrain The midbrain is relatively small in human beings and in most other species. In primitive animals the midbrain is of great importance because it controls simple motor responses by regulating certain motor neurons. In man, however, the midbrain is comparatively less important, for the more complex patterns of his behavior are controlled by the forebrain. Like the hindbrain, the midbrain maintains tracts between the cerebrum and the spinal cord and functions as part of the overall impulse-conduction system. In addition, the midbrain controls some auditory and visual responses (for example, it regulates the size of the pupil of the eye). Two structures of the midbrain, the *tegmentum* and the *tectum*, have been identified, but except for their general location, little is known about them.

Forebrain The forebrain, largest of the three divisions of the brain, occupies the entire upper portion of the skull. It is composed of the most complex structures in the brain. These structures control complicated patterns of behavior and are the source of those higher-level activities that differentiate man from other animals. Three major structures constitute the forebrain: the *thalamus*, the *hypothalamus*, and the *cerebrum*.

The *thalamus* interprets and sorts afferent and efferent impulses traveling to and from the cerebrum. Scientists believe that it relays sensory impulses to specific areas in the cerebral cortex. Recent research has disclosed that although certain thalamic cell bodies emit impulses, they do not appear to be able to receive sensory stimulation. The precise nature of thalamic activity has yet to be determined, however.

The area known as the *hypothalamus* is a collection of nerve cells that controls such processes as body temperature, metabolism, hunger, and thirst. The hypothalamus also plays a key role in emotional behavior, for stimulation of the hypothalamus can produce highly organized emotional behavior patterns. For example, studies have shown that stimulation of the appropriate hypothalamic area in a cat will enrage the animal. In other experiments, removal of the hypothalamus has caused animals to eat voraciously, gorging themselves until they were barely able to move.

The hypothalamus is part of a large, diffuse system of nerve cells called the *limbic system*. Because the limbic system is more primitive than the cortex from the standpoint of evolutionary development, is it often referred to as the "old cortex." The limbic system appears to be involved in emotional behavior because it participates in the actions of the autonomic nervous system, a system intimately associated with emotional activity (see Chapter 9).

The *reticular activating system* is a diffuse group of neurons that occupies a portion of the hindbrain and midbrain and also extends into a lower part of the thalamus in the forebrain. The system, a netlike bundle of collateral nerve fibers, acts as a relay station, delivering impulses to large areas of the cortex. It serves as an activating or arousal system, constantly alerting the cortex to data from the sensory organs. The reticular activating system operates even when the individual is asleep or very inactive. When this area of the brain is destroyed accidentally or surgically, the individual falls into a coma.

The *cerebrum* is the main area of the forebrain; it is responsible for emotion, learning, thinking, remembering, and sense perception. The *cerebral cortex* (which we mentioned in terms of sensory behavior in Chapter 2) forms the outer layer of the cerebrum. The cortex is the section of the cerebrum that directs the activities of the central nervous system. We shall describe the cerebrum and its cortex in greater detail.

The cerebrum

The cerebrum consists of two halves, or hemispheres, that are mirror images of each other. The *right hemisphere* is separated from the *left hemisphere* by a straight groove that cuts from front to back along the outer layer of the brain (Figure 3.9). The right hemisphere of the cerebrum controls the sensory and motor activity in the left side of the body, and vice versa.

Connecting the hemispheres of the cerebrum and lying inside the cerebral cortex is a large whitish area known as the *corpus callosum*. As its white color indicates, it is composed of myelin-sheathed axons that converge in this area from several parts of the body. Among the nerve fibers that populate the corpus callosum are some of the afferent and efferent tracts that transverse the spinal cord longitudinally. Sensory impulses move along these tracts through the central nervous system to the corpus callosum, then to the cortex, where they are translated into motor impulses. Conversely, motor impulses begin at the cortex and pass through the corpus callosum on their way to the muscles. The corpus callosum also contains nerve fibers that conduct impulses from the cerebrum to other parts of the brain and link parts of the cortex to other areas within the cerebrum. Thus, the corpus callosum coordinates the activities of the two hemispheres; surgical cutting of the corpus callosum can split the brain so that activity in one half does not affect that in the other half (see Chapter 7, Figure 7.16).

The cerebral cortex The outer surface of the cerebrum is the cerebral cortex (the "rind" of the brain). The cerebral cortex is gray, like the center of the spinal cord, and for the same reason: it is also composed of nerve cells and small blood vessels.

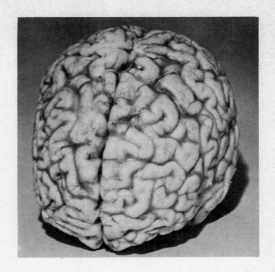

Figure 3.9   *This view of the cerebral cortex clearly demonstrates its sharp division into two hemispheres. (Tringali—dpi)*

The surface of the cerebral cortex is deeply grooved, folded, and flapped over and into itself. Perhaps the fold-over growth (convolution) occurred because of the limited space left in the skull; the cortex is the last evolutionary addition to the brain and may have grown in this way because the skull could not expand to encase it.

Because of its grooved and convoluted surface, the human cortex is larger than its appearance might indicate. Through comparative studies with lower species, neurophysiologists have determined that the higher the level of functioning of the species, the greater the amount and depth of the cortical grooves. Human beings have deeper and more numerous convolutions than lower animals and undoubtedly exhibit the most advanced development of cerebral cortex of any species. However, the cerebral cortex is not the single source of man's intelligent behavior, as is commonly believed. The cortex could not function without subcortical structures for support, conduction, and interaction.

Scientists use the deepest, most pronounced fissures in each hemisphere to delineate the major regions of the cortex. The *fissure of*

Rolando, or *central fissure,* runs from left to right across the brain beginning at the top of the cerebrum in each hemisphere and running downward and slightly forward. The *fissure of Sylvius,* or *lateral fissure,* begins at the base of each hemisphere about halfway between the front and center side of the cerebrum and angles back and slightly upward toward the rear; it terminates about midway between the center side and the back of the cerebrum.

Figure 3.10 shows the four major anatomical areas of the cortex as defined by the fissure of Rolando and the fissure of Sylvius:

1 the *frontal lobe,* located forward of the fissure of Rolando across the front of the brain;
2 the *temporal lobe,* lying along the lower sides of the cerebrum behind and below the fissue of Rolando and just inside the portion of the forehead called the temple;
3 the *occipital lobe,* situated at the lower back of the cerebrum behind the point where the fissure of Sylvius ends;
4 the *parietal lobe,* located in the upper rear of the cerebrum, behind the fissure of Rolando.

Cortical function Psychologists and neurologists have developed a fairly accurate picture of cortical function. We will discuss some of the main aspects of it here. Different surface areas of the cortex are responsible for specific experiences or sensations: before the individual can "feel" a stimulus of pain to the left knee, nerve impulses must reach the one area of the cortex that influences the mechanism to interpret this experience. Thus, we say that functions are *localized* in the cortex.

Through research, the concept of *localized functions* has been tested and corroborated consistently. The most common experimental procedure is to stimulate various portions of the brain electronically, observe the resulting responses, and map out the area of the brain that affects different behaviors. Some of these "mapping" experiments have been conducted with human beings in the course of brain surgery. In such studies the subject is usually placed under

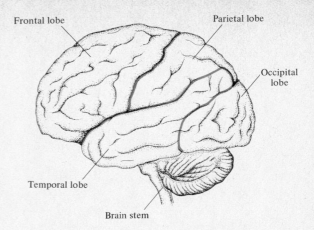

Figure 3.10   *Lateral view of the four lobes of the cerebrum of the human brain.*

a local anesthetic so that he is conscious and can report his "feelings" as his brain is stimulated at the various points. For example, if the taste area for sweets can be properly stimulated, a subject will report that he "thinks" he tastes something sweet, when, in fact, he has nothing in his mouth. Motor responses as well as sensory experiences can be created without actual external stimuli. However, only a limited variety of responses or sensations can be aroused by brain stimulation, for the cortex alone does not control all bodily functions.

Localized functions   Penfield and Roberts (1959) experimented on the localization of speech functions. Each subject was asked to count or name a series of objects while the experimenters electrically stimulated his cortex. Depending on the part of the cortex stimulated, Penfield and Roberts obtained two types of results:

1 Stimulation caused an otherwise quiet subject to make a sound, such as a groan or a longer vowel cry. No full words were ever elicited.
2 Stimulation prevented a subject from vocalizing or using words.

Thus, the subject's involuntary response was uncharacteristic of his usual behavior; he either said nothing at all or something other than what he wanted to say.

Projection areas of the cortex

Psychologists have used the results of electrical stimulation to produce a map of the cortical area identifying locales for almost all human sensory and motor experiences. (Some experiences, as we shall see, continue to defy specific localization.) This type of map shows *projection areas* of the cortex, which are specialized areas for sensory and motor functions (Figure 3.11).

Since each hemisphere of the brain is a mirror image of the other, we need only locate the functional centers of influence of one hemisphere; those of the other hemisphere can be assumed to be identical.

Motor area   The area of the cortex responsible for *primary motor functions* is located in the frontal lobe, just in front of the fissure of Rolando. The specific motor functions appear in an order upside down to that in which their corresponding body parts appear; that is, the cortical centers for the feet are localized at the top of the fissure of Rolando, whereas the cortical

Figure 3.11   Diagram of the primary projection areas of the cortex and their functions. (From The Cerebral Cortex of Man by Penfield and Rasmussen, The Macmillan Company, Inc. 1952)

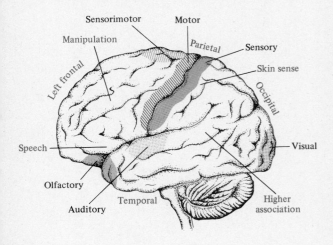

centers for the face are localized at the lower sides. Every feature of the body, including each finger and toe, has a corresponding cortical center of influence.

Sensory impulses are translated into motor impulses at the cortical center and by means of dendrite stimulation travel through the motor neurons to become retranslated into bodily movements at the appropriate muscles. As already stated, motor neurons appear as tracts through the spinal cord, with exit points to various muscles. Axons of neurons traveling to the regions of the body below the spinal cord, such as the legs and feet, exit the spinal cord at the base and travel in nerve fibers to the outer areas. Along this route, the impulse travels from the cortex to the site of primary motor activity.

In addition to the area of primary motor functions, two other cortical areas influence motor activity. Although very little is known about these two areas, we do know that one is located on the temporal side of the longitudinal fissure (fissure of Sylvius), and the other appears a short distance in front of the primary area along the top of the central fissure. These are the so-called *secondary motor areas*. In contrast to the arrangement of the primary area, body regions controlled by the secondary areas are represented rightside up and on the same side of the body. Neither of the two secondary motor areas directly connects to the axons that run all the way through the spinal cord; instead, they are composed of neurons with short axons that connect to other neurons located at the inner portions of the cerebrum. These cerebral neurons link up to others in the brain stem, and then they, in turn, maintain a connection of short-axoned neurons down through the spinal cord. This system of short neurons is the first such tract found in the nervous system, and currently is subject to considerable experimentation.

Body sensory area   Often called the *somatosensory area*, the cortical centers for body senses are located from the top to the sides of the parietal lobe along the central fissure. These sensory centers duplicate almost exactly the localization of the motor areas along the cortex, with slight adjustments for those features constructed to accommodate body sensation, such as the gums, the throat, and the teeth. The cortical representation is primarily a map of the sensory receptors, and secondarily a map duplicating the motor functions. It is more than coincidence, however, that the motor and body sensory areas face each other along the central fissure.

A doctrine concerning sensory function was developed about a century ago by Johannes Müller, a German physiologist. Müller proposed that a sense organ could only respond to stimuli in a particular way. For example, pressure on the eyelid will result in the "seeing" sensation (usually colors); a slice of apple pie on the arm will feel cold or sticky, but of course the arm will not be able to respond to the taste of the apple pie. Müller's proposal is known as the doctrine of the *specific energy of nerves*, and it simply means that the sensation originating in each individual sense organ will always be peculiar to that sense and hence characteristic of it. The cerebral cortex plays a crucial role in the specific energy of nerves because the characteristic interpretation of sensory stimuli depends on the part of the cortex that received the sensory impulse.

Specific energy of nerves Close one eye and gently press the eyelid on the spot nearest your nose ridge. Most people see either a colored arc or a circle in the eye opposite to the area on which pressure is applied. These colored figures are called *phosphenes*. They are of special interest to psychologists, who wonder how we can "see" anything when our eyes are closed and there is no visual input.

Oster (1970) reports different ways of producing phosphenes. One is electrical stimulation of various areas on the surface of the brain. Stimulating the visual cortex at the extreme rear of the brain causes the subject to see specks of light. As the stimulation is moved forward in the brain, the subject sees progressively more vivid and clearly shaped phosphenes. At the most forward point stimulated, one subject actually saw a scene from his recent experience.

Research of this nature is being advanced today in the hope that by electrical stimulation of the visual nerves we may someday be able to help those blinded by injury to the eye or optic tract to see. (People born blind do not see phosphenes.) This might be achieved by the development of a code whereby each visual stimulus will electrically stimulate the optic tract in its own way, aiding the blind to see various visual stimuli.

Visual area The important centers of vision are located in the occipital lobe. Some visual controls are also found along the central fissure in the parietal lobe. Although specific mappings of visual areas have not yet been possible, it has been determined that the visual sensation is regulated by the response of neural receptors to variations in light.

Auditory area The principal area for translating auditory stimulation lies along the upper portion of the temporal lobe. The auditory cortex is arranged so that higher-frequency tones stimulate neurons deeper in the cortical surface, whereas low-frequency tones stimulate neurons on the surface of the auditory cortex. Note also that both ears are linked to the auditory cortex in each hemisphere, so that deafness will not occur if the cortex of one cerebral hemisphere is destroyed.

Physiological psychologists and neurologists have been able to locate the cortical areas responsible for activities much more specific than the general areas shown in Figure 3.11. Figure 3.12 shows the more detailed localization of motor functions.

As Figure 3.12 shows, the size of cortical area responsible for a given region of the body is directly related to the use and sensitivity of that region. The area for lips, jaw, and tongue is far greater than that for the rest of the face. The area for the hand is much larger than that for the trunk of the body.

Association areas of the cortex

More than three-fourths of the cerebral cortex is occupied by areas that are neither so well mapped nor so well understood as the projection

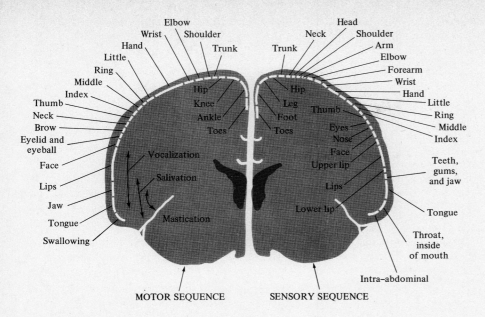

Elbow
Wrist — Shoulder
Hand — Trunk
Little
Ring
Middle
Index
Thumb
Neck
Brow
Eyelid and
eyeball
Face
Lips
Jaw
Tongue
Swallowing

Head
Neck — Shoulder
Arm
Elbow
Forearm
Wrist
Hand
Little
Ring
Middle
Index

Hip
Knee
Ankle
Toes

Vocalization
Salivation
Mastication

MOTOR SEQUENCE

Trunk

Hip
Leg
Foot
Toes

Eyes
Nose
Face
Upper lip

Lips

Lower lip

Teeth,
gums,
and jaw

Tongue

Throat,
inside
of mouth

Intra–abdominal

SENSORY SEQUENCE

Figure 3.12   A projection map of the cortex. Note that the area at the top controls the lower extremities, the toes, ankles, and legs; the area at the bottom controls the facial muscles, including the mouth and lips. (This diagram does not show the actual depth of the areas; it only points out their location as viewed in a cross section of the cerebral cortex.)

areas. These large areas, known as the *association areas*, are evidently responsible for the organizing, processing, and storing of information entering and leaving the brain. Association areas produce much of the behavior we call language, speech, learning, remembering, and thinking. In man these areas are highly developed, but they are less well developed as we descend the evolutionary scale. Except for isolated findings in experimental situations, very little of a specific nature is presently known about the association areas in man.

One of the findings about the association areas (also called the *association cortex*) that is extremely interesting to psychologists is that the area is highly integrated and that damage to one specific portion does not necessarily cause a total

sensory or motor deficiency. Malfunction depends more on the extent of damage to the association cortex than on the specific place of damage. Through observation of brain-damaged individuals and through the technique of mapping, physiological psychologists have determined that when injury does occur there, it may produce language, perceptual, or motor impairment or some combination of these. The language functions controlled by the association areas include the ability to formulate meaningful words or word combinations and use them appropriately, the ability to hear words and understand them, and the ability to recognize and identify the meaning of printed words. The association cortex also enables the organism to recognize objects and associate them with their use. Certain motor functions, such as performing purposeful movements and using the jaw and tongue in speech, are also known to be controlled by these areas.

Surgical lesion of the brain Clinical patients occasionally furnish a great deal of information about brain function. This has been true of patients who have undergone surgical separation of the two brain hemispheres to prevent severe epileptic seizures. After the brain has been split in this fashion, the patient's general behavior appears to be much the same as it was before surgery. Using very refined techniques, Gazzaniga and Sperry (1967) discovered clear and important differences in the functions of each of the hemispheres.

The experimenters verified that the ability for speech is located in the dominant hemisphere, which, for most people, is the left hemisphere. The subjects performed all their usual verbal tasks through the left hemisphere. They could describe a picture transmitted to the left hemisphere or name an object placed in the right hand. The other half of the brain, the right half, had no effect on speech. The subjects were totally unable to name pictures transmitted to the right hemisphere or objects placed in the left hand. However, the right hemisphere was capable of affecting a form of understanding. For example, when a picture of a nude female was transmitted to his right hemisphere, one patient smiled appreciatively although he could not say what it was.

The authors concluded that the major speech functions are confined to the left or dominant hemisphere. The right hemisphere displays the ability to influence speech comprehension and a rudimentary ability to handle language. In response to material sent to the minor half of the brain, subjects expressed themselves entirely nonverbally, through pointing or retrieving. Material sent to the left half of the brain showed that the organization of speech was unimpaired by the split-brain surgery. It is therefore clear that language normally is processed in the left, or dominant, hemisphere.

Speech has been localized in one region of the association cortex by Pierre Broca, a neurologist. He examined a patient who was unable to use language (a disorder called *aphasia*) and found that a portion of his left frontal lobe, now known as *Broca's area*, had been damaged. For some time after Broca's discovery, scientists believed that language functions invariably occurred in this area. However, it was eventually found that some individuals unable to use language properly or at all had instead suffered damage to the right frontal lobe, the hemisphere opposite Broca's area. Further research disclosed that most aphasic persons who are right-handed show damage to the left hemisphere, whereas most who are left-handed show damage to the right

hemisphere. As we learned in our discussion of projection areas of the cortex, the right hemisphere controls the responses of the left side of the body and vice versa; thus, neurophysiologists have concluded that the specialized neural center for speech behavior is located in the hemisphere that controls that side of the body to which there is a motor inclination. In other words, the left association cortex of right-handed persons contains the center for speech behavior, and vice versa. Because most individuals are right-handed, the majority of speech impairments are traced to damage in the left hemisphere.

An injury to the association area of the cortex can result in any one or a combination of several types of disorders. We have already noted aphasia, a disturbance characterized by language impairment that results from either sensory or motor inabilities. Aphasic disturbances often follow a brain hemorrhage or other injury to the speech association areas of the cortex. In sensory aphasia, or *alexia*, the individual may be unable to recognize printed words; he can see and trace words but cannot identify their meaning. Sensory aphasic disturbances can afflict a person in different degrees: sometimes a person can read or understand one word but not a group of words; sometimes he can only understand when he sees and hears the word. The inability to use spoken language is known as *motor aphasia*: the person can make speech sounds, but cannot formulate meaningful words or word combinations. He may say one or two words such as "yes" or "no," but he cannot use them appropriately. Individuals suffering from *auditory aphasia* (*word deafness*) hear but do not understand words.

A language problem The brain, if functioning properly, tells us what sounds we are making and how we are forming them. Luria (1970) found that damage to the central region of the left hemisphere disturbs the ability to speak. People with lesions in this area cannot distinguish between *d*, *n*, and *l*, since these letters are all made with similar tongue and lip movements. Children with lesions, accustomed to pronouncing words a certain way, reveal their difficulty when writing. They may write "*d*ollipop" instead of "*l*ollipop," because they are unable to distinguish one pronunciation from the other.

It would seem, therefore, that the admonition, "Be sure brain is engaged before putting mouth into gear," can be taken quite literally.

Apraxia is another disorder that affects motor abilities. Persons suffering from apraxia cannot perform purposeful movements. Their motor pathways are not damaged, but they cannot make the responses they desire. For example, a person's finger and hand coordination may be unimpaired, yet he cannot tie his shoelaces; he may be able to hold a pen but not be able to write with it.

Injury to the association areas of the cortex may also cause perceptual disorders in which the person cannot recognize common objects. In some cases, recognition occurs when the person is provided with hints. For example, when shown a set of keys, the perceptually damaged person may not recognize them, but if one key is placed in a lock, he is able to say "key." Or, when shown a pen, he cannot identify it, but when he sees someone writing with it, he calls it a pen.

The largest section of the association areas is found in the frontal lobes of the cerebral cortex. These are the areas that lie directly under the forehead. The frontal lobe area is often referred to as the "silent area," because damage here does not produce any sensory or motor loss. Experiments within recent years suggest that these areas of the frontal lobes may be concerned with abstract reasoning and problem-solving, the so-called higher intellectual processes. The association areas of the frontal lobes have excited the interest of man for centuries because of their anatomical prominence and because so little is known about them. We often tend to speculate on the significance of a high forehead.

Creativity lost In about 1848, a Vermont quarryman, Phineas Gage, suffered a wound in both frontal lobes when the gunpowder with which he had been working exploded, sending a crowbar through his cheek up to both frontal lobes. After a few months, the wound healed and the man returned to work. He did not show any loss of memory or skill.

This case is reported by Gray (1948) in his discussion of the function of the frontal lobes. He contrasted it with the case of an eloquent clergyman who was known for the penetrating thought he showed in his sermons. After injury to his frontal lobes, the clergyman could not go back to his parish. When invited to deliver a sermon, he could not write a new one, but had to piece together one of his old sermons.

These two cases led Gray to conclude that an individual with damage to his frontal lobes could continue to function using old acquired skills. He could not, however, be creative or improvise, particularly in the use of language.

THE PERIPHERAL NERVOUS SYSTEM

The second division of the nervous system, the *peripheral nervous system*, is comprised of those nerve fibers or bundles of axons that lie outside the central nervous system. The peripheral nervous system includes the *somatic nervous system* and the *autonomic nervous system*. The somatic system is composed of the motor-nerve fibers connecting the spinal cord to striated muscles and sensory-nerve fibers. The autonomic nervous system (ANS) is primarily a motor system serving the smooth muscles. The autonomic nervous system will be given special attention here because of its importance in the regulation of the internal bodily organs.

Autonomic nervous system

Although we classify the autonomic nervous system as a peripheral system, most of the controlling characteristics are found in the brain, particularly the hindbrain and the hypothalamus of the forebrain. For purposes of clarification, it is necessary to divide the autonomic system into a *sympathetic division* and a *parasympathetic division*. Although both divisions conduct impulses to the same viscera and glands, they function reciprocally; for example, when the sympathetic system overreacts, the parasympathetic comes into play and slows down the sympathetic's activity. Figure 3.13 shows a simplified version of the two divisions of the autonomic nervous system.

Autonomic balance The relationship between an individual's sympathetic and parasympathetic nervous activity is called his *autonomic balance*. Individual differences in autonomic balance are of interest to research because of their implications for personality and behavior pathology.

There are two ways to measure individual differences in autonomic balance: (1) relative balance under nonstressful conditions of rest; and (2) patterns of autonomic reactivity to strong stimulation. It seems reasonable to assume that these measures might be quite different, indicating much about a person's style of coping—both physiologically and psychologically—with everyday events.

Wenger, Jones, and Jones (1956) report, for example, that studies of autonomic balance have demonstrated that there is a tendency for persons showing sympathetic dominance to be easily excited to emotional behavior. Interesting implications appear when one matches these findings with data which indicate that many patients with anxiety neuroses or various other forms of psychological distress are often found to have sympathetic nervous system dominance. It is not yet known whether this autonomic imbalance causes the disorder or whether the disorder causes the relative imbalance.

Sympathetic division of the autonomic nervous system The sympathetic division, sometimes called the *thoracico-lumbar system*, runs longitudinally along both sides of the spinal cord and adjacent to the thorax and lumbar regions. Each side of the sympathetic division services its corresponding side of the body. It was first thought that, because the structure of the sympathetic system appeared to be a whole, chainlike "other cord," the autonomic nervous system served as an aid to impulse conduction to the central body region. Scientists thought that it caused internal organs to function in "sympathy" with the central nervous system. Instead, however, research has shown that the sympathetic division is a neural system that is active in situations of fear, emotion, violence, and extreme cold. It is a highly integrated system functioning as a unit.

The sympathetic system responds to bodily emergencies by preparing the body for energetic action, a reaction that has been called the "fight or flight reaction." When an emergency situation occurs, this integrated neural function calls up the body's stored energy reserves in the following order:

1 Blood is transferred from internal organs to external muscles.
2 Sugar is released by the liver to feed the active muscles.
3 Tiny structures within the lungs expand to take in more air.
4 The heart beats faster to add more blood to the system.
5 The blood added is richer in oxygen because of the increased intake by the lungs.
6 Digestion and intestinal contractions cease in order to protect these functions and their operating organs from danger, and to divert blood that might otherwise be needed for more vital functions.
7 The adrenal glands are stimulated to produce adrenalin and other hormones.

The sympathetic division performs many other activities in addition to those listed; essentially, all its functions involve diverting the normal body processes quickly and efficiently, by action of a unified system of neural connections. Although we do not know exactly what part of the brain originates the stimuli that heighten emotions, it is known that much of the autonomic nervous system, including the sympathetic system, is controlled by nerve cells in the hypothalamus and brain stem.

Parasympathetic division of the autonomic nervous system The *parasympathetic division* assumes the day-to-day task of maintaining the individual functions of body organs; it does not integrate the activities of the organs and glands. After an emergency has passed, it is the function

Figure 3.13 A simplified schematic of the two divisions of the autonomic nervous system: the sympathetic division and the parasympathetic division. This same network of fibers is repeated on the other side of the spinal cord. Note that because the parasympathetic division is concerned with the daily functioning of individual organs, its ganglia (not fully shown) are closer to the organs it services. The sympathetic division, on the other hand, serves an integrating function, and its ganglia are further from the organs.

of the parasympathetic division to return the body to its normal functioning.

The parasympathetic division is composed of nerves situated in two places: *cranial nerves* in the brain stem, and *sacral nerves* below the lower back (thus its identification as the *craniosacral system*). The sacral and cranial nerves conduct impulses to the viscera and are similar in structure to nerves that conduct impulses to the skeletal muscles. Organs influenced by the

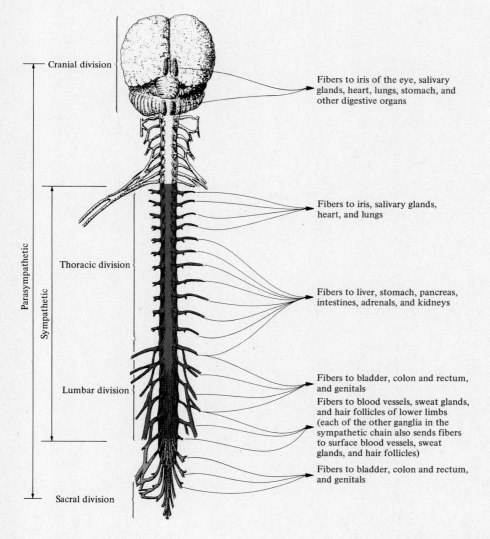

Cranial division

Fibers to iris of the eye, salivary glands, heart, lungs, stomach, and other digestive organs

Fibers to iris, salivary glands, heart, and lungs

Thoracic division

Parasympathetic

Sympathetic

Fibers to liver, stomach, pancreas, intestines, adrenals, and kidneys

Lumbar division

Fibers to bladder, colon and rectum, and genitals

Fibers to blood vessels, sweat glands, and hair follicles of lower limbs (each of the other ganglia in the sympathetic chain also sends fibers to surface blood vessels, sweat glands, and hair follicles)

Fibers to bladder, colon and rectum, and genitals

Sacral division

parasympathetic division include the heart, tear glands, salivary glands, stomach, pupil of the eye, rectum, bladder, and male genitalia.

Although no structural relationship exists between the sympathetic division and the parasympathetic division, both serve the same smooth muscles and glands of the body organs. The two divisions often create opposite signals. The sympathetic increases heart rate, the parasympathetic decreases it; the sympathetic inhibits digestion, the parasympathetic facilitates it; the sympathetic dilates the pupil of the eye, the parasympathetic constricts it. Of the two systems, the parasympathetic is more responsible for the idea that the autonomic nervous system operates in an "automatic" way, since the usual functioning of our internal organs does not involve our control or awareness.

Table 3.1 summarizes the functional characteristics of the central and peripheral nervous systems. It may be said that each system is in the service of the other system. Neither has any function without the other. Thus, in psychology, when we discuss behavior we do not limit ourselves to the activity of the brain or the spinal cord or the sense organs or the muscles and glands; we regard behavior as a function of the whole organism.

THE REFLEX

One of the simplest forms of behavior involving sensory input, connecting links, and motor output is the *reflex*, which is a fixed response to a particular stimulus that occurs regularly. A reflex act is involuntary and generally occurs very quickly after stimulation. Reflex responses are produced automatically by the body, and they serve to protect the organism and preserve its life.

Many familiar responses are classified as reflexive. Some reflex actions common to human beings are the knee jerk, pupil constriction, pulling away from a very hot or cold object, and yawning. All reflex behavior involves a similar chain of events; a stimulus activates a receptor cell; the receptor cell sends a nerve impulse through an afferent neuron to a place of control; an efferent neuron receives a response impulse from the place of control and carries it to an effector (the muscle or gland that responds to the stimuli). In this respect, reflex behavior is not unlike more complex behavior patterns.

Table 3.1   Functions of the major divisions of the nervous system

System	Function
Central nervous system (brain and spinal cord)	Receives impulses from the sensory nerves, provides interneuron connections, transmits impulses to motor nerves
Peripheral nervous system Somatic (sensorimotor nerves)	Transmits impulses from receptors to brain and spinal cord, transmits impulses to striated muscles from brain and spinal cord
Autonomic (sympathetic and parasympathetic divisions)	Transmits impulses from brain to smooth muscles

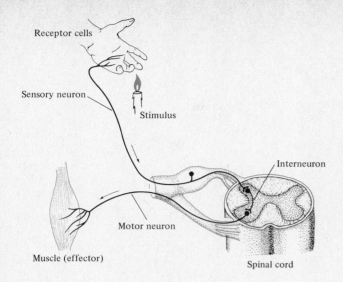

Receptor cells

Sensory neuron

Stimulus

Interneuron

Motor neuron

Muscle (effector)

Spinal cord

Figure 3.14   Schematic of the sensorimotor arc.
If the stimulus is strong enough, it causes the
receptors to react. The nerve impulse created in
the receptors travels the afferent neuron to the
spinal cord, where it passes to an interneuron
and then to the efferent neuron. From the
efferent neuron, the impulse travels to the
effector muscle where the response is made. Note
that this arc is not usually one long smooth
passage; the impulse must cross many synapses to
reach its destination.

However, the reflex differs in two ways: (1) the reflex circuit operates fairly automatically; and (2) in most cases the center for processing the impulses of reflex stimulation is in the spinal cord, not the brain. The reflex circuit transmits impulses up and down the spinal cord and may involve the interconnections of collaterals and interneurons. The circuit through which the nerve impulses travel is called the *reflex arc*. When the brain does not participate in a reflex response, the process is descriptively known as a *spinal reflex* and the circuit is the *sensorimotor arc* (Figure 3.14). Brain-controlled reflex arcs provide for more intricate and variable combinations of responses than those controlled by the spinal cord.

In the *sensorimotor arc*, receptor cells may be located either in sense organs, where they are in contact with external stimuli, or in internal organs or joints, where they receive stimuli from the body. Thus, stimulation for simple reflex activity can be either external or internal. In some reflex arcs, the impulse passes directly from the afferent to the efferent neuron through a synapse; in others, it passes through many interneurons and synaptic transfers. Reflex arcs are formed throughout the nervous system, and

some of these interconnect to form alternate pathways for impulses. The more interneurons and synapses there are, the slower the traveling time of the impulse; this difference in impulse speed, however, is imperceptible to the individual.

In *spinal reflex activity* (Figure 3.15), there are many ways in which nerve impulses might travel. Because of the numerous synaptic possibilities within the spinal cord, many muscles may be activated by the stimulation of only one afferent neuron. Other neurons, connecting with this afferent neuron, may become transmitters of the original impulse and ultimately activate many efferent neurons (*divergence*). Conversely, the spinal cord might distribute many incoming impulses to a single efferent neuron, causing one muscle to respond to many stimuli (*convergence*). However, perhaps the most interesting aspect of impulse activity in the spinal cord involves closed loops of neurons that create independent, self-exciting circuits.

Connecting neurons and collaterals may become arranged in such a way as to reconnect within the same circuit and recirculate an impulse again and again. The neurons create an "arc" or "arcs" within the spinal cord. In this type of circuit, known as a *reverberating circuit*

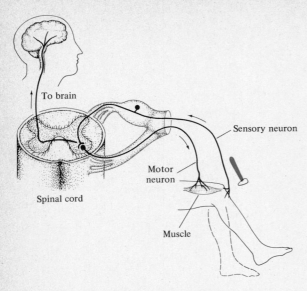

Figure 3.15   A schematic of the spinal reflex arc. When your knee is tapped, the message follows this route.

(Figure 3.16), the recirculated impulse continually stimulates the efferent neurons; the result is a continuous surge of muscle excitation. The length of time that the self-exciting circuit is active appears to vary from impulse to impulse and from circuit to circuit; there has been con-

Figure 3.16   A reverbrating circuit in the spinal cord. The impulse travels around the circuit several times, each time stimulating the effector muscle. The result is a continuous stream of muscle excitation.

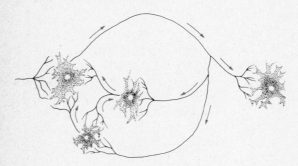

siderable speculation as to what controls its duration. Reverberating circuits also occur in the brain, where they are believed to play a part in more complex processes, such as short-term memory.

Ideas may reverberate   Hebb (1972) uses the concept of reverberating circuits in proposing his theory of the cell assembly. According to Hebb, a cell assembly may be thought of as a number of reverberating circuits that have become connected with each other as a result of the association of stimuli. An assembly is organized initially by a particular stimulus or a group of stimuli. For example, the image of a tree organizes a particular cell assembly.

A given cell assembly, once aroused, is capable of maintaining its activity (the reverberating circuit) for a period of time in the absence of the stimulus. A cell assembly may also be excited into action by other cell assemblies, even when the original initiating stimulus is not present. The tree cell assembly may be excited into action by the sound of rustling branches or by the sight of an acorn.

Hebb suggests that the cell assembly can be conceived as the basis or locus of ideas. An idea, after all, can occur in the absence of the stimuli originally responsible for it.

Reflexes involving regions of the nervous system above the spinal cord are called *higher-level reflexes* and their circuits are called *cranial sensorimotor arcs*. Breathing is a higher-level reflex, for although it is a response that can be controlled by higher brain centers, it cannot be completely inhibited by these centers. A person can hold his breath voluntarily, seemingly overcoming the reflex control of breathing, but once the carbon dioxide level of the blood becomes too high, the medulla reacts reflexively and breathing resumes. A person cannot commit suicide by voluntarily holding his breath. The reflex is too powerful.

Function of reflexes

Reflex actions serve the organism by providing adaptive mechanisms that maintain body efficiency. The common reflexes noted earlier are responses that protect the individual from injury or increase his bodily comfort. Actually, almost all reflex action is adaptive in this way. Internally stimulated muscles and glands are least noticed because their responses are more subtle.

Reflex actions are also adaptive in that they correspond in location and intensity to the particular stimulus being presented. The more widespread or intense the stimulation, the greater the response. Also, reflexive behavior always produces a reaction in exactly the same location that received the stimulus. This localization is especially necessary for self-protection as it enables the organism to react quickly to protect any vulnerable limb or organ.

Many other unusual adaptive characteristics of reflexes contribute to the normal functioning of the body. For example, if a stimulus is too weak to cause an impulse to cross a synapse, the impulse will generally be confined in the neuron in which it was last conveyed. However, repeatedly weak stimulations tend to build up to an intensity capable of causing an impulse to cross a synapse, and these remain strong as they pass through the nervous system. The accumulation of weak impulses is known as *summation*, since, in effect, it is a "summing up."

Summation is a complicated process, and involves more than weak impulses. It can also be involved in multiple related stimulations, especially to the skin. For example, two or three quick stimulations, such as pinpricks, to the same general area of skin tend to arouse different afferent neurons, but the interneurons interpret these as one impulse; ultimately, only one efferent neuron responds. We see, then, that the interneurons collect and sort impulses and are capable of grouping related spatial stimulations.

It is convenient to discuss reflexes as if they occur in pure form; in fact, however, the pure reflex is only found in the laboratory where the scientist surgically isolates the reflex arc he is interested in studying. In the intact animal or person, reflexes do not occur independently of other events taking place within the organism. For example, if the left knee of a person is tapped at the same time his right leg is pinched, a more pronounced knee jerk results. It is also true that reflexes can be influenced by events in the environment, as we will see in our discussion of *conditioned reflexes* in Chapter 6.

METHODS OF STUDYING THE BRAIN AND NERVOUS SYSTEM

Many areas of the brain and nervous system are yet to be explored. Scientists are currently devoting considerable time to experiments and research aimed at increasing man's understanding of the neural bases of behavior. In these studies, the use of precise scientific techniques is essential. In the following section, we discuss several experimental methods used by researchers to uncover facts about the brain and the nervous system.

Electrical stimulation

The technique of electrical stimulation of the brain, as we have seen, has enabled researchers to identify and map the various functional areas of the brain and, in human research, is usually administered during surgery. Because the patient is conscious and able to report his "experiences," he can describe simple sensations of sight and sound as well as complex memories. Experiments with memory are particularly interesting, for individuals undergoing stimulation can recall stories or events that they never realized they remembered.

In human beings and animals, stimulation to the motor cortex excites muscles to respond. Since these responses are easily observed, this technique has yielded useful information. Animals can be observed in experiments in which electrodes are implanted in the brain and a particular motor function is observed over a continuous period of time. Some implantation surgeries have been performed on human beings, not for specific scientific observation of behavior, but for experimental treatment of various disturbances.

Ablation

The method of surgically removing a portion of an organ or a system of organs is known as *ablation*. In animal research, the animals may be trained to make particular responses; the ablation is then performed, and the animals are studied to determine how much of the training is lost as a result of the ablation. Another procedure is to perform the prescribed ablation and then see how much the ablation affects the acquisition of new responses.

Ablation studies have been carried out in the course of treating patients undergoing brain surgery for illness, injury, or tumors. Human studies are often much less precise than animal studies, because the amount and type of brain tissue removed is governed by the patient's disorder and not by any scientific hypothesis. However, the findings from human studies, when checked in the animal laboratory, do provide useful information about the various functions of the nervous system.

Anatomical methods

Observation of the structural appearance of various parts of the nervous system (the *anatomy* of the system) is a useful method of research. Of course, the anatomy must be exposed to view before it can be observed. Although we can recognize the white myelin sheaths covering the axon fibers and the gray nuclei of the cell bodies without the mechanical help of microscopes, we cannot see a single neuron with the naked eye. Thus, we rely on microscopic techniques to view these cells; for this purpose the cells must be removed from the organism but kept alive in a chemical solution.

Many different cells have been observed under a microscope by means of standard staining techniques (a stain is a special purpose dye that is made to be absorbed by certain types of cell structures and not by others). If an individual neuron is stained, the path of its impulses can be traced by following the spread of that stain through the group of neurons. Another type of stain may be absorbed by cell bodies to distinguish the structure of the nuclei. When a portion of a fiber is severed, we can watch the course of its degeneration. By observing the degeneration occurring in a single cut fiber, we may ultimately identify the center of control and the routes of the pathways leading to it.

Electrical recording

Some well-developed techniques exist for detecting and recording the electrical activity of the nervous system. One of the most commonly used types of recording is the *electroencephalogram* (EEG), an electrical record of the brain. EEG recordings are made by means of electrodes attached to the scalp. The electrodes detect changes in the electrical activity of the cortex, and these changes are recorded graphically as so-called brain waves.

Different types of brain-wave patterns appear, depending on whether the person is awake or asleep, active or passive, calm or disturbed. Among the wave patterns most frequently studied are the *alpha waves*. These waves have a frequency of about 10 hertzes and characteristically occur when the person is awake and relatively relaxed. The alpha rhythm becomes "blocked" (drops out) when the person is stimulated by a sound, a light, or any other effective stimulus. Figure 3.17 shows an alpha pattern and the blocking phenomenon.

The EEG is routinely used in neurological examinations because it can assist in locating tumors or gross neural damage. As a research tool, the EEG has excited much interest, particularly with respect to possible relationships between EEG patterns and intelligence or personality. The findings in these areas of interest

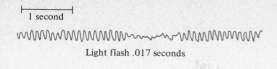

Light flash .017 seconds

Light flash .760 seconds

Figure 3.17   Blocking of the alpha rhythm by a light flashed for varying periods of time.

are only suggestive at best. There is no real correlation between EEG patterns and intelligence in normal children, but some evidence suggests that EEG patterns may be related to intelligence in adults (Mundy-Castle, 1958). There is also some evidence that EEG patterns may be related to personality characteristics, but here again the facts are not clear and further research is needed.

Use of the MEG   Cohen (1972) describes the use of the magnetoencephalogram (MEG) for detection of the brain's activity. Instead of measuring the electrical activity of the brain, as the EEG does, this technique measures the magnetic field produced by the electrical activity of the brain. Cohen finds that recordings of the magnetic field can yield information in a number of ways not available to the EEG. First, the direct current generated in the brain can be measured. (When the EEG is used, the electrodes on the scalp interfere with measurements.) Second, during some events there is no current flowing within the head although some current appears on the scalp, and the only way to deal with this problem at present is through measurement of the magnetic field. Third, the MEG can pick up currents to which the magnetic field is sensitive but which cannot be detected by the EEG.

Also of great importance in neurophysiology is the highly refined technique of surgically implanting tiny electrodes (*microelectrodes*) in the brain at points that give off impulses that can be recorded by sensitive machinery. In this procedure, the subject is more or less free to function normally; he is not confined to one spot as he is during EEG recordings. Recordings are given off constantly—not just at a specified time during or after stimulation. Hence, microelectrodes are more precise in recording nerve impulses and in comparing impulses of different neurons. This method has been used in the study of sensory and motor impulses, and it promises to be even more informative than the EEG technique.

Microelectrode readings   Every time we see an object in our visual field, the cortical cell activated by this particular stimulus fires. Depending on the strength of the activation, the cell will fire with a greater or smaller frequency of firing.

Hubel and Wiesel (1962) used microelectrode recordings to provide us with information about the organization of information at the cellular level. To study the effect of the visual stimulus orientation on vision, Hubel and Wiesel placed a rod in front of a cat's eye. They then systematically changed the orientation of the rod (for example, from horizontal to vertical) and took readings of the frequency of firing of cortical cells that had microelectrodes stuck into them. Their readings showed that a cell that would fire at high frequency when stimulated by a vertically oriented rod would fire progressively less and less as the rod was being displaced toward a horizontal position, with a complete halt in firing at that point.

Microelectrode readings of this sort are a great help in visual research. By this technique we can study the functions of different points in the visual system and see how they integrate and act as a whole.

Chemical methods

Direct injection of certain chemicals into the brain is another method used in studying the activity of the nervous system. The chemical method is frequently used to study synaptic transmission. For example, the theory that a substance such as acetylcholine is involved in synaptic transmission can be checked by injecting an amount of acetylcholine into a region of the nervous system and observing whether or not there is an increase in neural activity at the place of injection.

The technique of chemical injection is constantly being perfected. At present the technique has been developed to the point where tiny amounts of a chemical can be injected microscopically into a single nerve cell. This very precise method is likely to provide important information about the functioning of individual nerves and of the nervous system as a whole.

SUMMARY

The types of muscles are striated, smooth, and cardiac.

Skeletal muscles that control the movement of limbs by reciprocal innervation are called antagonistic muscles.

The endocrine glands, which are regulated in the hypothalamus, secrete hormones to regulate and balance the internal activities of the body (homeostasis).

Neurons (composed of cell bodies, dendrites, and axons) conduct impulses through the nervous system.

Nuclei are large clusters of neuron cell bodies, whereas ganglia are smaller clusters. Axons from neurons in the same location of the body travel together as nerve fibers, forming tracts in the brain and spinal cord. Nerve trunks connect neurons from the brain and spinal cord to outer body areas.

Neurons are either efferent (motor), afferent (sensory), or interneurons (association neurons). Collaterals branch off from these neurons.

The membrane covering nerve fiber cells is electrically polarized. An energy charge moves through successive nerve fibers and carries an impulse along. The all-or-none law states that only stimuli above the absolute threshold will enable a nerve to react.

Nerve impulses pass from one neuron to another through the synapse.

The central nervous system is composed of the brain and the spinal cord.

There are three sections in the brain: the hindbrain, which includes the medulla, cerebellum, and pons; the midbrain, which contains the tegmentum and tectum; and the forebrain, which consists of the cerebrum, the thalamus, and the hypothalamus.

The cerebrum is divided into right and left cerebral hemispheres, which are connected by the corpus callosum. The cerebral cortex is the outer surface of the cerebrum.

There are four lobes in each hemisphere of the cortex: occipital, temporal, parietal, and frontal. Three of the lobes are separated by the fissure of Rolando (central fissure) and the fissure of Sylvius (lateral fissure).

There are localized functions in the cortex. The specialized projection areas are the motor, somatosensory, visual, and auditory areas.

Müller's doctrine of specific energy of nerves states that the sensory event created by each sense organ will always be characteristic of that sense organ.

The association areas (also called association cortex) appear to be responsible for organizing, processing, and storing information that enters and leaves the brain.

Broca's area is just left of the frontal lobe. In left-handed individuals, the speech area is usually just to the right of the frontal lobe.

The frontal association area appears to be involved in higher intellectual processes.

The peripheral nervous system consists of the somatic nervous system and the autonomic nervous system (which includes the sympathetic and parasympathetic divisions).

In a spinal reflex, impulses do not go to the brain; the circuit is a sensorimotor arc. In cranial sensorimotor arcs, impulses travel to the cerebrum and then connect with muscles.

Divergence is the distribution of a single impulse to many neurons, while convergence involves the transmission of many incoming impulses into a single efferent neuron.

Self-exciting pathways joining neurons and collaterals in the spinal cord are called reverberating circuits.

Summation is a process by which a weak impulse builds in intensity until it is able to cross a synapse.

Some of the methods for studying the brain and nervous system are electrical stimulation of the exposed cerebral cortex, anatomical analysis, the electroencephalogram (EEG), surgical implantation of microelectrodes in the brain, and injection of chemicals into the brain.

SUGGESTED READINGS

Texts

Gardner, E. Fundamentals of neurology (5th ed.). Philadelphia: Saunders, 1968. Well-illustrated book on the structure and function of the nervous system.

McGaugh, J. L., Weinberger, N. W., & Whalen, R. E. (Eds.) Psychobiology: the biological basis of behavior. San Francisco: Freeman, 1969. Discussion of behavior from a physiological point of view.

Sechenov, I. M. Reflexes of the brain. Cambridge, Mass.: MIT Press, 1965. Discussion of the basic brain functions.

Teitelbaum, P. Physiological psychology. Englewood Cliffs, N.J.: Prentice-Hall, 1968. Introduction to the biological basis of behavior.

Popular books

Ausubel, D. P. Drug addiction. Discussion of the effect of various drugs on the response mechanisms as well as the senses themselves.

Burroughs, W. Naked lunch. Novel concerning macabre modifications of the response mechanisms and their effects on a society.

Maurer, D. W., & Vogel, V. H. Narcotics addiction. Popular description of the effects of drugs on the nervous system and response mechanisms.

4

Sensation

The sensory processes enable us to make contact with the world in response to stimuli. Now that we have discussed the mechanisms of human response, we can proceed to an understanding of how our sense organs—eyes, ears, nose, skin, and taste buds—through the excitation and co-operation of the nervous system, make us aware of a face, a melody, a fragrance, a caress.

There is more to the sensory system, however, than the five senses. Contrary to common belief, there are at least ten senses: *vision, hearing, smell, taste, touch, pain, cold, warmth, kinesthesis, and the vestibular sense* (balance).

Another common misconception is that our sense organs are responsible for the whole task of perception—that we "see" with our eyes, "hear" with our ears, "feel" a hot stove with our fingers. Actually, our sense organs perform only part of the task of perception. Each is a highly specialized organ whose sole function is to receive and transmit a particular kind of stimulus. After the stimulus is received in the sense organ, it must be transmitted through the nervous system to the brain, where it is coded and categorized. It is the brain's task to identify the stimulus and to produce the appropriate sensation. And it is the nerve patterns in the brain that enable us to perceive, for example, that a stimulus of a certain weight, color, shape, and size is a collection of information and is, in fact, this textbook. The sense organs are simply the advance scouts in the sensory processes. The nervous system provides the pathways and message runners; the brain is the headquarters and decision-maker, telling us whether what we smell is bacon frying or rubber burning, or whether a traffic light is red, yellow, or green.

The accomplishments of the sense organs should not be underrated, however. Try to imagine what the world might be like for a man without sense organs. He would have no knowledge of light, time, sound, joy, sorrow, pleasure, or pain. Nothing we value would have meaning to him. He could not learn as we do. He could not even forget as we do, for what are the things we forget but lost sensory impressions?

Those of us with sensory processes that function normally partake of a world of unending wonders. In an imperceptible fraction of a second, a stimulus registers on a sense organ and impulses flash through the nervous system to the brain for evaluation. In scarcely the time it takes to hear a bar of music, we distinguish between Bach and Beethoven, Mick Jagger and Glenn Campbell. A mere silhouette against a sunset can tell us whether a bird drifting through the sky is a hawk or a gull.

His curiosity whetted by his senses, man has sought to identify stimuli beyond the reach of his sense organs. With the help of special instruments (sonar, radar, telescopes, microscopes, and so forth), scientists have detected sounds that cannot be heard by the human ear and things that cannot be seen by the human eye.

THE CHARACTERISTICS OF SENSATION

Before examining the sensory systems separately, let us discuss the general characteristics of sensory behavior. First, each sensory organ is stimulated by a specific form of external or internal energy—vision is stimulated by electromagnetic energy, i.e., light; hearing by sound waves; the skin senses of warmth and cold by thermal energy; and the skin senses of touch and pain by pressure. There are two other characteristics common to all sensory systems: (1) the process by which information is transmitted to the brain; and (2) the method of locating the point at which a stimulus is perceived and of measuring its intensity.

Transduction and the sensory pathways

Energy, whatever its form, must be converted by the sense organs into data that the nervous system can transmit to the brain. This converting process is called *transduction*. It takes place at *receptor cells*, which receive the physical energy produced by the stimuli and convert it into electrical energy; the electrical energy then activates the nerve endings connected to the receptor cells. (The nerve endings generally wrap together, attaching the organ to the central nervous system.) The electrical energy becomes nerve impulses that journey along *sensory pathways* in the nervous system, en route to the brain. In the brain, impulses are sorted (in ways that are not yet clear) and routed to the appropriate sensory areas.

Measuring sensation

Sensory psychologists have found that many human subjects cannot give accurate, scientifically measurable accounts of their sensations. The science of *psychophysics* was developed to deal with this measurement problem. In psychophysics, changes in the physical stimuli that act on an individual are measured against changes in the sensations experienced by the individual. Interesting discrepancies observed under varying laboratory conditions have spurred new research in the areas of sensation and psychophysics.

Threshold

Threshold is the approximate point at which a stimulus is strong enough to produce a response in an individual. An important psychological measurement, threshold generally refers to the level or intensity of physical energy that activates the sensory organs. Each sense has a different threshold, and the thresholds differ from situation to situation.

The *absolute threshold* is the least amount of stimulus necessary to produce a response in a given individual. An absolute threshold is the stimulus intensity that is reported by the subject 50 percent of the time. To determine this, he is exposed to varying intensities and asked each time to say whether or not he detects the stimulus. His responses are recorded, and a graph can be plotted to show the intensities he reports and those he does not (Figure 4.1).

When a subject's absolute threshold is reached and measured, the experimental psychologist can measure the *difference threshold* —the smallest detectable change in stimulus intensity the subject is capable of perceiving. The difference threshold is often called the j.n.d., or *just noticeable difference*. Difference thresholds vary from situation to situation because no two situations involve the same intensity of stimulation. We can detect certain changes in the sound level in a relatively quiet room; the same sound changes are not detectable in a noisy room. Thus the difference threshold depends on the magnitude or intensity of the stimulus as well as the size of the stimulus change.

The relationship between stimulus intensity and difference threshold is referred to as *Weber's law*. In 1934, E. H. Weber discovered that in comparing stimuli of different intensities, the important difference is not arithmetical but proportionate. Weber stated that the difference threshold depends on the ratio of change in a stimulus over the initial stimulus intensity and that the ratio needed to effect a difference is constant for all intensities of the same type of stimulus. Later research showed that Weber's law is true only for the middle range of stimulus intensities.

To illustrate Weber's law, let us consider difference thresholds for loudness. If a subject is presented with a tone of 50 decibels, he will recognize a tone of 55 or more decibels as louder but will not recognize a tone of 54 decibels as louder. If presented with a tone of 70 decibels, a 7-decibel difference is needed for a second tone to be recognized as louder; and for a 30-decibel tone, only a 3-decibel difference is needed for a second tone to be recognized as louder. In these cases, the constant ratio for the difference threshold is 1:10 (5:50, 7:70, 3:30). In other words, for loudness changes to be recognized, the intensity of change (in the middle range of loudness) has to be at least 10 percent.

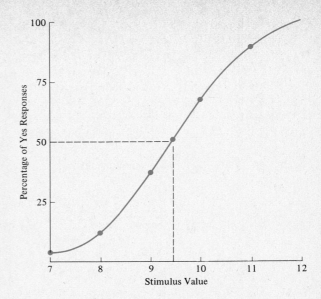

Figure 4.1 *Graphical determination of an absolute threshold. The threshold is approximately 9.4, the point where the signal is perceived 50 percent of the time. In this example, a signal of 9 units was perceived about 35 percent of the time and one of 10 units about 68 percent of the time. (After Underwood, 1949)*

Weber's law Examples of Weber's law were identified by Boring, Langfield, and Weld (1948). They found that the minimum percentage of change necessary for detecting differences in brightness was 1.2 percent; for lifted weights (1 or 2 pounds), 2 percent; for smell (rubber), 10 percent; and for taste (salt), 20 percent.

Many measurement samples are required to estimate individual thresholds of a sensation because an organism's responses will vary from moment to moment. The classic psychological methods of threshold measurement are referred to as the *psychophysical* methods because their inventor, Gustav Fechner (1860), saw them as possible ways of measuring the relationship between psychological events and physical events. These methods are the following:

1 *Method of average error (or adjustments)* The subject adjusts the stimulus until he thinks that

it bears some stated relationship to a standard. (For example, he might be asked to adjust the stimulus until it is equal to a previously administered stimulus.)

2 *Method of limits* To determine the difference threshold, the experimenter controls the stimulus and varies the amount of change above or below the intensity of the original stimulus. The subject must report whether the stimulus he perceives is equal to, greater than, or less than the original stimulus.

3 *Method of constant stimuli* The stimulus is presented to the subject, and he must report whether it is present or absent. In a series of trials, various intensities are used.

Signal detection theory

Psychophysical methods are useful, but they are not entirely satisfactory because many factors may influence a subject's report of a stimulus. Because of this dissatisfaction, the *signal detection* approach to the study of threshold was developed (Green and Swets, 1966). Signal detection theory regards threshold identification by a subject as a form of decision-making. The subject must decide whether or not he detects the stimulus, and his decisions depend on (1) his sense organs, (2) his expectations about the stimulus, (3) the nature of the stimulus, and (4) his motivation to be accurate in his decisions. The decision concerning the presence or absence of a stimulus is most difficult to make when the stimulus is very weak and subjects are uncertain.

Because a subject's decisions depend on a number of variables—some of them related to the subject's self-confidence, expectations, and motivation—it is helpful in establishing thresholds to use a system that includes *signal trials* and *catch trials*. A *signal trial* is one in which a signal (a stimulus) is presented; a *catch trial* is one in which no signal occurs. When a subject answers yes on a signal trial, it is a *hit*; when he answers yes on a catch trial, it is a *false alarm*.

According to signal detection theory, a false alarm is a stimulus created by some form of sensory activity, perhaps spontaneous neural activity, often referred to as *noise* to distinguish it from the signal. It is assumed that a continuum of sensations results from either noise alone or signal plus noise. When the signal is very weak, it is easy for the observer to mistake noise for the actual signal. Because the subject has continuously variable sensations ranging from the lowest produced by the noise to the highest produced by the signal, he must set some criterion level of sensation that will enable him to identify sensations above this level as signals, and sensations below it as noise. That is to say, the criterion he sets for himself tends to determine the point at which he agrees that he detects a signal. The subject is aware of the varying magnitudes of sensations he classifies as noise, but because they fall below his criterion, he identifies them all as noise, replying that he did not detect the signal.

Because a subject wants to maximize his hits, he will set a relatively low criterion if the signal is presented on a large proportion of trials and a high criterion when the signal trials are infrequent. However, the variation in the percentage of signal presentations does not automatically produce corresponding changes in the ratio of hits to false alarms. Signal detection theory assumes that the subject changes his criterion in one direction or another when presentation probabilities are manipulated.

Hits and false alarms To determine a subject's threshold for the detection of a weak auditory signal, Galanter (1962) administered a series of trials that included both signal and catch trials. The subject was asked on each trial whether or not he heard a signal.

The results of this series of trials were plotted in a matrix like the one in Figure 4.2A. Each entry in this figure represents the proportion of times the subject answered yes or no when asked whether or not the signal occurred. The signal was actually presented on 90 percent of the trials, and the subject answered yes in 97 percent of these signal trials. When no signal was presented—in the catch trials—the subject also answered yes in 62 percent of the trials. Instead of hits, he registered false alarms.

When the proportion of signal trials to catch

trials was varied, the number of hits and false alarms both changed, depending on the change in proportion. As shown in Figure 4.2B, the situation was changed so that the signal was presented in only 10 percent of the trials. In this case, the subject registered hits on 28 percent of the signal trials and false alarms on 4 percent of the catch trials. The experimenter concluded that, because the subject wants to maximize his hits, he will vary his yes responses in proportion to the percentage of signals he believes are being presented. Motivation and expectation, then, play an important role in signal detection.

We can plot a graph for the hit and false alarm probabilities of a subject. Figure 4.3 is an example of such a graph. In it, the probability of hits and false alarms is presented for four different percentages of signal trials: 10, 30, 60, and 90 percent. The figure shows that the rate of hits increases as the percentage of signal trials increases. The rate of false alarms also increases as the percentage of signal trials increases, but the probability of hits increases at a greater rate.

The diagonal line in Figure 4.3 represents a signal of zero intensity, or no signal at all; the plotted curve represents, for a particular subject, the *receiver operating characteristic* (ROC) curve using a signal well above zero. Strong signals depart from the diagonal. A subject's sensitivity to a particular signal is determined by calculating the extent to which the ROC curve differs from the diagonal.

Sensory adaptation

A variety of external conditions can change us so that a stimulus that once excited our sense(s) is no longer detected by us. This *adaptation* of the sensory organs is a common occurrence. It contributes greatly to an organism's survival. A construction worker operating a pile driver day in and day out grows accustomed to the noise. A man working underground in almost total darkness becomes accustomed to the lack of light and learns to function very well. People can adapt to many situations—even to severe pain, as in the case of the athlete who plays in spite of an injury.

	(A) Responses		(B) Responses	
	Yes	No	Yes	No
Signal trials	.97	.03	.28	.72
Catch trials	.62	.38	.04	.96

Figure 4.2   The results of two signal detection procedures showing the proportion of yes and no responses when the signal is presented (A) on 90 percent of the trials and (B) on 10 percent of the trials. (From "Contemporary psychophysics" by Eugene Galanter, in New Directions in Psychology by Roger Brown, Eugene Galanter, Eckhard H. Hess, and George Mandler. Copyright © 1952 by Holt, Rinehart and Winston, Inc. Adapted and reprinted by permission of Holt, Rinehart and Winston, Inc.)

Many examples of human sensory adaptability can be found in more usual situations. Young people have adapted to hard rock music that cannot be endured by adults (who may have grown up in an era of melodic dance music). Psychedelic poster art and light shows have been criticized as overly stimulating visual

Figure 4.3   A receiver operating characteristic (ROC) curve for four different percentages of signal trials.

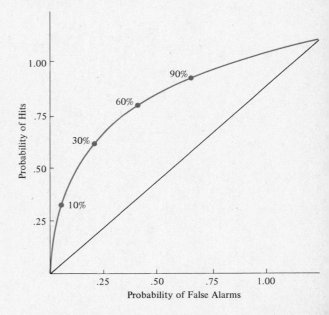

exercises. Yet, as people grow accustomed to them, they begin to enjoy the experience. Our vision gradually adapts to such experiences. The boundaries of human sensation are being challenged in this age, and the challenge is being met by sensory adaptation.

LIGHT SENSATION: VISION

The human visual system is the product of a lengthy evolution. Through our eyes we sense the *visible spectrum*—light waves that carry to us the many colors in our environment.

Structure of the eye

The eye is a sphere-shaped structure composed of the visible outer portions and an inner chamber in which the earlier-mentioned transduction process occurs. Figure 4.4 shows a three-dimensional view of the eye. The outermost cover is called the *sclera*, or "white" of the eye. Its relative hardness enables it to maintain the shape of the eye. The middle layer, the *choroid*, protects the inner chamber of the eye from outside, interfering light, much as the body of a camera protects the film from light.

The quantity of light that enters the eye is regulated by the size of a center opening, the *pupil*. The size of the pupil in turn is controlled by the muscles that pad the inner circular boundary of the *iris*, the colored portion of the eye. In bright light, the pupil contracts, decreasing the amount of light entering the eye. In dim light, the pupil widens, increasing the amount of light entering.

The iris area is protected by a chamber of clear, fluidlike chemicals. The outer coating of this protective layer is the *cornea*. The cornea is transparent; light passes through it and then through the pupil toward the *lens*—a transparent focusing mechanism. After passing through the lens, light rays penetrate the inner chamber to the *retina*, the area of the eye that receives the light stimulus and transforms it into electrical impulses, then into nerve impulses. The retina contains the receptor cells and nerve endings required for transduction.

On the retinal surface is the *fovea*, a recessed area positioned almost exactly behind the lens. Because of its many neural endings, the fovea is the most visually sensitive area of the eye. The *cone* cells—the receptor cells that are activated under high illumination—are more numerous in the fovea than anywhere else in the retina. Distributed throughout the retina, except in the fovea, are the *rod* cells; these are used primarily under low illumination. Both rods and cones are essential to vision as we know it.

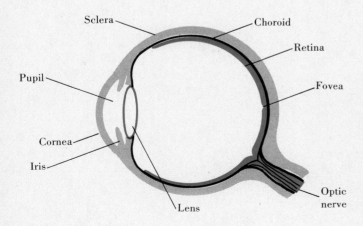

Figure 4.4   The structure of the human eye. Light rays pass through the cornea and are focused by the lens. The light rays then pass through the inner chamber of the eye to the retina, which is composed of rods and cones that transform the light rays into electrical, then nerve, impulses. These nerve impulses are then transduced by the optic nerve to the brain for interpretation.

Rods and cones Cone cells, when stimulated, mediate color. They are responsible for keenness of vision (*visual acuity*) in daylight. Cones do not function well at night, for their chemical makeup is not aroused in dim light. Rods, on the other hand, translate light energy only into white, black, and gray; they provide night vision but do not enable an individual to distinguish colors in the dark. In moving from a dark environment to a light one, the cones take about one minute to become adapted and function efficiently. In moving from light to dark, adaptation by rods takes much longer—usually 30 to 40 minutes. We are aware of this switchover when we turn off the light before going to bed; at first, we cannot see objects in the room and feel that we are in total darkness. But after our eyes become *dark adapted*, we can see and maneuver fairly well, regardless of the dark. It has been reported that eyes adapted to the dark over a long period of time can detect the illumination of match flames 3 miles away (Cohen, 1969b). Figure 4.5 shows the typical development of dark adaptation. The curve indicates that the break in threshold is caused by decreased activity of the cones and increased rod activity.

Figure 4.5 indicates that the dark-adaptation process primarily involves the rods. The process depends on *rhodopsin*, a chemical pigment found in the rods. Light causes rhodopsin to break down into two substances, *retinene* and *opsin*; and this reaction sets off the nerve impulse. Retinene and opsin spontaneously change back to rhodopsin, readying the rods to respond again to light. Their visual cycle is faster under low illumination than under high illumination, because rhodopsin builds up more rapidly in darkness or dim light than in bright light.

Intense illumination converts retinene into vitamin A, which during dark adaptation reverts back to retinene, which, in turn, recombines to form rhodopsin. A deficiency of vitamin A retards dark adaptation because retinene is slow to reconstitute without a sufficient reserve of vitamin A. A severe, long-term deficiency may result in *night blindness*, a defect of vision

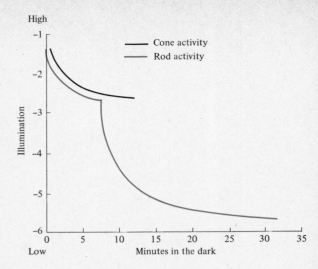

Figure 4.5   *The development of dark adaptation. Under high illumination the cones are activated. Under low illumination the rods predominate. As shown here, when going from high to low illumination, it takes at least 30 minutes for the rods to become adapted and to function at an appropriate level. (Based on Hecht, 1934)*

marked by very poor visual sensitivity under low illumination.

A deficiency which occurs in all human beings is a lack of vision in an area known as the *blind spot*, where no rods or cones are present (Figure 4.6). When light waves are projected to the blind spot, nothing is seen. The blind spot is actually a break in the retinal lining where the nerve endings meet and tie together into the *optic nerve*. The optic nerve joins the eye to the central nervous system.

Nerves and the brain connection In the visual sensory process, nerve cells attached to the rods and cones receive the nerve impulses into which light waves have now been converted. The nerve cells vary in number and position. In the fovea every cone cell is connected to a matching nerve cell. Outside the fovea, however, nerve cells interconnect any number of rods and cones. The entire system is intertwined to organize the impulses that represent a single visual experience.

Figure 4.6 *Find your blind spot. Cover your left eye and look intently at the dollar sign with your right eye. Slowly move the book toward or away from you until the coin disappears. The coin disappears when it falls on the blind spot of your right eye. Reverse the procedure to find the blind spot of your left eye.*

Figure 4.7 *Schematic of how vision occurs. Half of each visual field is received by the opposite half of each eye. The left visual field is projected onto the right side of the retina of both the right and left eyes. The two halves combine at the optic nerve and are carried by the optic tract to the opposite side of the brain— the left field to the right side, and the right field to the left side.*

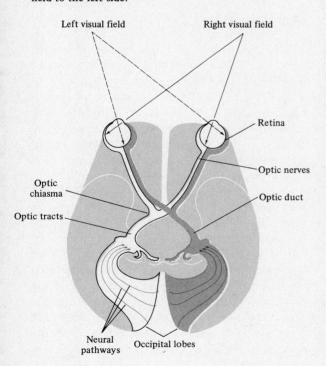

Left visual field

Right visual field

Retina

Optic nerves

Optic chiasma

Optic duct

Optic tracts

Neural pathways

Occipital lobes

Psychologists believe that research on the nerve cell interconnections will lead to increased understanding of more complex visual sensations.

From each eye, the impulses travel along two different nerve tracts to the brain. Each tract transmits only half of the light pattern received by its eye. This is why we speak of an eye's *left field of vision* and *right field of vision*: the nerve tracts are split so that impulses from the left and the right fields of vision of each eye travel in separate messages to the visual area of the brain, there to be encoded. The visual field for the right area of external sight is carried to the left lobe of the brain, and the visual field for the left area of external sight is carried to the right lobe of the brain. As we saw throughout the study of human response mechanisms, the area of the brain that records nerve impulses is usually opposite the side of the body that receives the stimulus.

The sight impulses go to the *occipital lobes* of the brain, located in the cortex (see Chapter 3, Figure 3.10). Figure 4.7 shows how this process takes place. Note that one-half of each tract crosses over to its mate's side, after passing the junction known as the *optic chiasma* at the base of the brain.

Damage to the optic nerve or to the brain has been carefully studied in cases in which such damage occurred both before and after the crossing-over. Cuts or damage to parts of the optic nerve before the cross cause complete blindness in the corresponding eye; severance of the left optic nerve means loss of vision in the left eye. But any destruction of an area of the occipital cortex, *after* the crossing-over of the nerve, will cause loss of vision in the opposite field of both eyes. In other words, damage to the right side of the occipital cortex will cause loss of vision in the left visual field of each eye.

Cutting the optic chiasma When Myers (1955) destroyed the optic fiber crossing in a cat by cutting the optic chiasma, he found that the two eyes functioned separately in the opposite halves of the brain. He trained cats to discriminate between patterns with one eye. When that eye was covered and the other eye tested, the cats were able to make the same pattern discrimination. Thus, he concluded that the cat's ability to discriminate was transferred from one eye to the other by means of a pathway other than the optic chiasma.

In 1956, he severed the corpus callosum (the bundle of nerves connecting the two hemispheres of the cerebrum) of cats and tested the cats using other discrimination problems. He found that with the corpus callosum and the optic chiasma severed, there was no transfer from one eye to the other. When the eye patch was shifted after the discrimination was well learned, there was an abrupt drop in performance as compared to the same condition with the corpus callosum intact. These experiments showed that the two hemispheres function independently—at least for visual learning and retention.

Although damage to the brain may cause blindness, the prebrain processes of transduction and nerve transmission continue to occur. It is also interesting to note that while complete destruction of the occipital cortex means blindness in humans, this is not true of apes. Apes with complete visual cortical damage continue to maintain some degree of dark-light vision, although they cannot differentiate between patterns or colors.

Visual acuity

Visual acuity is the ability to discriminate details and fine differences in the field of vision. This ability can be measured in a variety of ways; one way is through the familiar eye chart. Before discussing the techniques of measurement, let us explore the biological basis of visual acuity.

The rod and cone receptor cells, as already noted, are found in varying densities throughout the retina of the eye. An individual's vision may range from poor or unfocused to perfect, depending on the density of the cones in the area of the retina that is stimulated. If the fovea is stimulated, vision is sharp, since in the fovea the cones are thinner and more densely packed. When the stimulus appears in bright daylight or well-lit artificial light, acuity is usually excellent too. From a biological standpoint, the better the lighting, the more cone cells are activated. When both conditions occur together—good light and good foveal reception—there is maximum sharpness of vision.

Immediately adjacent to the fovea, where cones dominate, is an area dominated by rods. In the rest of the retina, the *periphery*, there are fewer rods and cones, and these are interconnected by multipurpose nerve cells. Since there are fewer receptors and fewer nerve cells, it is obvious that visual acuity decreases when light stimuli strike the periphery.

We see best by focusing the fovea on external stimuli; to see something clearly we turn our head to it, so that the light penetrates the center of the lens and hits the fovea directly. The peripheral areas of the retina receive those stimuli which are not observed directly through the center of the lens. Seeing "out of the corner of the eye" is thus called *peripheral vision*. Figure 4.8 presents a simple visual experiment that demonstrates peripheral vision. (At night, or in dim light, visual acuity is best when the object is viewed slightly off center, where the rods are most numerous on the retina.)

Movements of the eye are generally important in directing the fovea toward light. Observe the movement of the eye as it scans an object. These small movements, or oscillations, occur very rapidly. We are not usually aware of them. They stimulate many receptor cells in the retina, improving visual acuity, especially when tiny objects are being viewed.

Figure 4.8   An experiment demonstrating peripheral vision. Stare at the X for a while. The two lines that you see out of the corner of your eye seem to blend into one line. Peripheral vision results from activity of the rods and, especially under low illumination, is much less sharp than central vision.

When overall visual acuity is strong, we may conclude that the image of what we see has somehow been reproduced by the receptor cells. To understand how this happens, take a closer look at a television picture; just as the black and white or colored dots define a picture, so do the stimulated and unstimulated receptors produce a retinal image. The size and shape of an external stimulus is recorded by stimulated *receptor cell units*—a unit being a group of rods and cones connected to one nerve cell. The retinal image of a pattern (or of objects and spaces between them) consists of a combination of stimulated and unstimulated receptor units in a pattern that approximates the external stimulus. If, for instance, the external stimulus is a checkerboard, the retinal receptor units also pattern themselves in checkerboard fashion. (Were all the adjacent retinal units to react, then the pattern might be seen as a solid block, not a checkerboard, and we would say that the acuity was poor.)

Peripheral vision   Mackworth (1965) presented three alphabetical letters to his subjects. One letter was presented centrally so that its image would fall directly on the fovea. The other two letters were presented peripherally. The subject's task was to determine if the letters presented peripherally were the same as those presented centrally. The task was found rather easy. When Mackworth added more letters, however, not only was the accuracy in peripheral vision greatly impaired, but the foveal presentations also suffered somewhat. When only three letters were presented in the visual field, there were no errors (at any width); when more letters were added, the subjects were correct only 10 percent of the time.

Measuring visual acuity   Measuring devices have been developed to examine and identify visual problems or defects in human beings. The most familiar is the standard acuity measurement. This is often called the "20/20" test. In it, the individual stands 20 feet from a standard *Snellen eye chart.* If his eyesight is normal, he sees the material on the eye chart clearly. If he does not see normally, some or all of the material may be blurred. He may see objects 20 feet away only as clearly as a person with normal vision sees objects 60 feet away; in this case, he is said to have 20/60 vision. A person with 20/10 vision, on the other hand, sees things 20 feet away as sharply as the person with normal vision sees objects 10 feet away. The man with 20/10 vision may also need corrective lenses. His eyesight is *too* acute and may cause him difficulties in body coordination and balance.

The *Ortho-Rater test* measures visual acuity by means of a chart that depicts patterns of decreasing size. In this test, a small checkerboard appears randomly in a square of a large checkerboard. As the checkerboard patterns decrease in size, it becomes more and more difficult to locate the small checkerboard. When two locations are missed in succession, the test is over, and a visual acuity score is assigned.

Another testing device, the *Sight Screener,* tests eye muscle coordination, depth perception, and the coordination of left-right, or binocular, vision.

Defects in visual acuity   There are many types of visual disorders. Some, such as *nearsighted-*

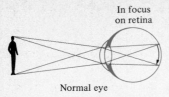

In focus
on retina

Normal eye

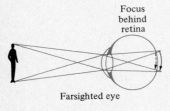

Focus
behind
retina

Farsighted eye

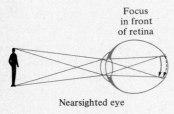

Focus
in front
of retina

Nearsighted eye

Figure 4.9   In normal vision, light rays are focused right on the retina. In farsightedness light rays are focused behind the retina—the eyeball is shorter than normal. In nearsightedness, light rays are focused in front of the retina—the eyeball is longer than normal.

ness and *farsightedness*, are very common. These disorders are due to abnormalities in the shape of either the eyeballs or the corneas. Figure 4.9 depicts the structure of normal, nearsighted, and farsighted eyes. All these disorders can be measured by the standard test for visual acuity.

In nearsightedness (*myopia*), the abnormally long eyeball causes light rays to be deflected to a point somewhere just short of the retinal surface, so that the rods and cones are not sufficiently stimulated. The nearsighted person usually has little trouble in seeing close objects clearly, since the light rays are focused at an angle that allows them to penetrate the lens sufficiently to focus on the retinal surface.

The reverse is true for farsighted persons. In this condition (*hyperopia*) the eyeball is shorter than normal, so that the deflected light rays fall somewhere beyond the retinal surface. The angle of reflection is better for objects far away, and the retinal surface is properly stimulated by reflections from such objects.

Middle age often brings on increasing farsightedness, caused by hardening of the lens. As the lens loses elasticity, the individual finds it more difficult to focus clearly, because the lens cannot contract to allow objects to come into proper focus. This condition is known as oldsightedness, or *presbyopia*. Generally, old-sighted persons experience deterioration of vision in the years following age 40. At around age 60, the "blur point" for the old-sighted person is about 39 inches from his eyes. Without the aid of eyeglasses, the individual must hold objects 39 or more inches away to see them clearly.

The defect known as *astigmatism* is also fairly common. Astigmatism is an inherited characteristic that affects the curvature of the cornea. For normal vision, the cornea and lens must be exactly circular in shape so that reflection of light rays comes into sharp focus through the center of the lens. In astigmatic individuals, either the vertical or horizontal degree of cornea curvature is inconsistent with the lens curvature. Astigmatic eyes distort the light rays either vertically or horizontally.

Diplopia (double vision) occurs because of unequal action by the muscles of the eyes. Consequently, an incoming light stimulus produces two retinal images and the brain receives two different nerve impulses—one from each eye —therefore producing two unmatched sensory experiences. In normal vision, of course, the experiences are matched. The weak eye muscles that cause diplopia can be inherited, caused by disease, or temporarily brought on by injury, alcohol, or drugs. Sometimes, for reasons we do not yet understand, one of the two diplopic images disappears and the diplopic individual experiences normal vision. But when this takes place, the machinery can become permanently damaged; prolonged disappearance of the diplopic image will cause permanent blindness in the eye that is not transmitting its image.

Still another common visual defect is *scotoma*, a recurring blind spot in one's field of vision. Scotoma may be brought on by damage to the retina or to the optic nerve.

Color vision

The human being can see only a small number of all electromagnetic waves. For instance, he cannot see ultraviolet rays, X rays, radio and television waves, or radar. He is limited to the *visible spectrum* of color, which can be shown by passing sunlight through a prism. This procedure converts the beam into bands of light, with four bands preeminent: red, yellow, green, and blue (see Plate 1). This beautiful color experience is a measurable scientific phenomenon —a matter of wavelengths and absorption intensities. It is probably the most studied of all physical phenomena. In approaching color from the psychological point of view, we require some background information from the artist and the physicist.

Color mixing   Colors are described in terms of *hue, saturation,* and *brightness. Hue* refers to the wavelength of a color. It is usually the basic name given to a color—green is a hue, for example. *Saturation* is the degree of pure color, the amount of hue in a particular color. Pink is less saturated than red. *Brightness* refers to how dark or light a color is; apple green is much lighter than forest green. The three terms are often represented as a "color solid," as shown in Plates 5 and 6. All combinations of hue, saturation, and brightness are shown on the color solid. A very bright color is likely to be of medium saturation. White and black are colorless; they have no hue.

The psychologist deals with color in somewhat the same way that the physicist does. He is concerned with color in terms of light waves, rather than pigment intensities. In *wavelength mixing* (the mixing of different-colored lights),

the complementary colors and elementary (primary) colors are not the same as those used in pigment mixing. The pigment artist uses red, yellow, and blue, but the lightwave artist uses red, green, and blue—three wavelengths that he can combine to create a virtual rainbow of colors. Plate 2 shows that a wavelength mixture of red and green produces yellow; a red and blue mixture, purple; and blue mixed with green, blue green.

Some of these mixtures are surprising to people who have mixed paint pigments and seen different results. They may have mixed red and green paint and produced gray. But when beams of red light and green light are projected together onto a plain white surface, the resulting hue is yellow, as Plate 2 shows. Mixing wavelengths is an *additive process,* for the eye receives both wavelengths. Mixing pigments, however, is a *subtractive process,* because one pigment absorbs the wavelengths of the other. The red pigment absorbs the wavelengths of the green, and the green absorbs the wavelengths of the red. The two absorptions leave only a gray hue.

Color naming   The qualities of colors depend on the length and intensity of the light waves that produce them. Under identical conditions, persons with normal vision will all perceive the same hue, saturation, and brightness of a color. Names for colors are artificially imposed, of course, and quite undependable as evidence for an experience with a physical light wave. The same color may be called "egg-shell," "off-white," "champagne," "natural," "buff," and so on. Each year the cosmetic industry alone creates an entirely new color vocabulary.

Cultural influences on color naming We usually identify the purest (most saturated) hues by the names red, yellow, green, and blue. We often use name combinations or other names for the less pure colors. We refer to yellow green, red orange, blue violet, and so on. Names such as these reflect our cultural influences, but they are too few to reflect our highly refined abilty to discriminate colors. It has been estimated that the human being is able to discriminate more than 7 million colors (Triandis, 1964). No culture has names for more than a relatively few colors, however, and their names are a product of the culture.

Ray (1953) studied the basic color names used in ten different North American cultures and found differences in the names used and in the parts of the color spectrum emphasized by the names.

Afterimages If you look steadily at a red disc and then shift your gaze to a plain gray rectangular surface, you will see a green circle superimposed on the gray surface. This phenomenon is known as *negative afterimage*—so termed, because green is the complement of red. Negative afterimage can last as long as 30 seconds. Not all afterimages are negative. You can also see a *positive afterimage*—an image that is the same color as the original stimulus. Positive afterimages occur when the stimulus appears for just a brief time and is very intense. Plate 4 demonstrates the afterimage effect.

Negative afterimages affect other color sensations and therefore account for the phenomenon of *successive contrast*. If we are in a room that is reflecting red light and then enter a room that is illuminated by ordinary white light, the second room will appear greenish. This differs from *simultaneous contrast*, in which simultaneously presented complementary colors affect each other. For example, blue on a yellow background will appear more bluish than blue on a gray background. Simultaneous contrast accounts for the fact that the Christmas colors of red and green appear so vivid when seen together.

Inhibitory processes

As color sensations influence each other, so do different brightness sensations. Experiments performed on the eye of the horseshoe crab have shown that if a single light receptor is stimulated, followed by stimulation of an adjacent receptor, the first receptor will be inhibited and will respond more slowly than if stimulated alone (Ratliff, 1965). The brightnesses of two adjacent visual sensations simultaneously modify each other. Each is inhibited and, in turn, inhibits the other. This process, called *recurrent* or *lateral inhibition*, is thought to account for the fact that the border between a half-light, half-dark visual stimulus will be seen as highly emphasized. On the dark side of the border, a dark band appears; on the light side, a light band appears. These bands at the inside border are called *Mach bands* after the physicist Ernst Mach (1839–1916), who first called attention to them. Figure 4.10 presents an example of the Mach-band phenomenon.

Theories of color vision

We know that the cone receptor cells in the retina are used in perceiving color. Several theories have been developed to explain how cone cells enable us to see color. One popular theory was developed by Thomas Young and later adapted by Hermann von Helmholtz. The Young-Helmholtz theory states that the three psychological primary colors—red, green, and blue—are the basis for three corresponding types of absorption in the cones. In other words, there are three types of cone cells, and they display three distinct types of sensitivity; one for red, another for green, and a third for blue. Sensitivity to all other colors is caused by varying combinations and proportions of these three

Figure 4.10 Mach bands are apparent streaks between adjacent areas of different brightness. These bands occur as a result of recurrent or lateral inhibition between adjacent receptors. (The bands are slightly exaggerated here for effect.)

types of cones. Equal activity in all three cones is believed to produce the color sensation of white. The Young-Helmholtz theory of color vision (which is remarkable in that it was developed early in the nineteenth century before specialized testing instruments were developed) is supported by the fact that any hue found in the spectrum can be produced by mixing these colors. The theory is weak, however, in that it fails to explain such visual phenomena as red-green color blindness. The presence of red and green cones is necessary to explain the detection of yellow, yet a red-green color-blind individual can see yellow.

Another theory of color vision, developed in the early twentieth century, is the *opponent-process theory* of Ewald Hering. It is so named because it deals with three sets of receptors in which one member of a set opposes or cancels the other. The members of each pair are complementary: blue-yellow, green-red, and black-white. The pair can respond to only one of its colors at a time. When the green-red receptors are stimulated, they can only react to provide a green sensation or a red sensation, not both.

In the opponent-process theory, each set of cones is thought to be one of the three pairs. Any members of a pair can interact with any member of another pair, thus producing such variations as yellow green or blue green. The black-white pair provides the contrasting effects. This pairing also explains the visual phenomenon of negative afterimage. If, for example, the appearance of green signified the inhibition of the other member, then the cessation of the visual stimulation that produced green would tend to result in a strong reappearance of the inhibited member, red. The opponent-process theory seems to explain color blindness somewhat better than the Young-Helmholtz theory, since red-green color blindness does not prevent either color from combining with a third.

Recent research in which cones are examined by means of a *microspectrophotometer* has clearly shown that three color receptors do exist in the cones (MacNichol, 1964). Using the microspectrophotometer to direct different wavelengths of light through individual cones, MacNichol and his associates were able to identify three light-sensitive substances: one sensitive to blues, one to greens, and one to yellows. The yellow-sensitive substance is sensitive as well to the red end of the spectrum.

The work of MacNichol and others lends strong support to the Young-Helmholtz theory. Their view of three color receptors appears to be essentially correct. But how the color code is interpreted in the central nervous system is still not well understood. Studies of the visual nervous system have shown that an opponent process of some type may be operating. DeValois and Jacobs (1968) found that some nerve cells in the *lateral geniculate nucleus* (a portion of the thalamus involved in vision) respond antagonistically to blue and yellow light: one type is inhibited by blue and stimulated by yellow, and another is inhibited by yellow and stimulated by blue. And in the same way, some nerve cells respond antagonistically to red and green light.

This suggests that color vision occurs in two stages. Stage 1 entails differential responses in the retina. Stage 2 entails differential responses in higher receptor cells that process the opponent colors of the blue and yellow, and red and green.

Color blindness   One person in 25 is color-blind. He is unable to see some or all of the colors. Color blindness is a sex-linked characteristic, appearing more often in men than in women. In the most common type of color blindness the person's color vision is normal in respect to only two of the three primary colors. The most common deficiency is related to the red-green complementary pair. Such persons typically will confuse purples, blue greens, reds, and yellow greens —the various shades of the red-green area of the visible spectrum. Occasionally they can distinguish between highly saturated reds and greens, but they have considerable difficulty with the grayer mixtures. People who are mildly color-blind are said to be *color-weak*.

Individuals who do not have cone cells in their retinas are completely color-blind, a rare affliction known as *achromatism*. Achromats see only black, white, and shades of gray. They also have severe visual problems resulting from the absence of cones, which normally populate the fovea. In viewing objects, they may have to keep the object image away from the fovea, where it would normally be focused, in order to see at all.

Many people are not aware that they are color-blind, having no accurate color perceptions to match against their inaccurate perceptions. Several tests for color blindness exist, but there is disagreement over their usefulness and efficiency. Most tests involve the subtle use of complementary colors. Plate 3 shows stimuli typically used in tests for color blindness.

SOUND SENSATION: HEARING

In the auditory (hearing) system, the external stimulus is the *sound wave*, manifesting itself as a pressure change that emanates in all directions from a vibrating object. Sound waves

Figure 4.11   Typical sound levels. (From Man's Control of the Environment. Washington, D.C.: Congressional Quarterly, Inc., August 1970, p. 56, © 1970 by The Congressional Quarterly, Inc.)

travel much like the ripples produced by a pebble thrown into a pond. Objects that vibrate set off sound waves of varying frequency and intensity. We measure the sensations produced by these waves in terms of pitch, loudness, and timbre.

The characteristics of sound

Pitch is the "high" or "low" quality of a sound. It is determined by the frequency of wave vibrations per second, or *hertzes*; the more hertzes, the higher the pitch. Human hearing ranges from a low of about 20 hertzes to a high of 20,000 hertzes. As in sight, there are limitations on perception in hearing; some sounds are above or below the sounds our ears can detect. A tone is made up of regular wave vibrations. A *pure tone* consists of a single frequency, but most of the tones we hear consist of a fundamental frequency and multiples of that frequency called *harmonics*. *Noise*, in contrast to a tone, is the auditory effect of many frequencies that are not in harmony with each other. The wave vibrations are irregular and the sound is unpleasant. A "white" noise is the hissing sound one hears when all the wave vibrations occur at once. It is comparable to white light, which consists of all the wavelengths of light.

Loudness is the amplitude of the sound wave—the amount of expansion and contraction

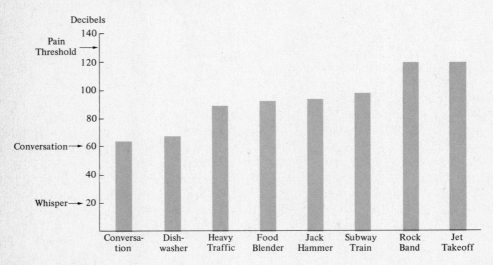

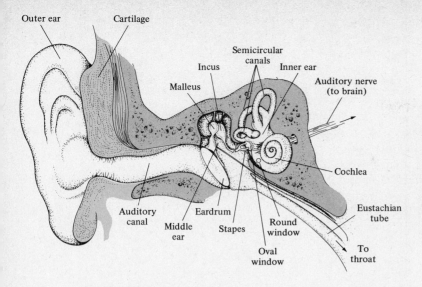

Outer ear Cartilage

Semicircular
canals

Incus Inner ear

Malleus

Auditory nerve
(to brain)

Cochlea

Eustachian
tube

Auditory
canal Eardrum

Middle Stapes Round
ear window

Oval To
window throat

Figure 4.12 *Diagram of the structure
of the ear. The ear is divided into
three major sections: the outer ear,
which is the external covering and the
canal into the ear's mechanism; the
middle ear, including the eardrum, the
hammer, the anvil, and the stirrup;
the inner ear, which is separated from
the middle ear by the oval window, and
which contains the cochlea, the round
window, and the vestibular organ.*

of the pressure changes that form a sound wave. When we turn up the volume of a radio, we increase the amplitude of the vibrations from the speaker, and louder sounds result. Loudness is derived not only from amplitude; it also depends on pitch. A higher and lower tone will not be heard as equally loud if they have the same degree of amplitude. The lower tone will require greater amplitude to sound as loud as the higher.

For lack of a more precise term, we call the distinctive quality of a sound *timbre*. Tones are usually complex; they are composed of combinations of pitches and as a result have widely varying qualities. As a matter of fact, two musical instruments that produce the same fundamental tone will produce sounds of different quality: an A played on a violin will not sound the same as an A played on a flute, though both are 440 hertzes.

Human beings have the ability to hear a vast number of different kinds of sound. In the study of human hearing, it has become customary to describe sound intensity in terms of a scale that has no absolute zero point. Zero is arbitrarily defined as the intensity at which a tone of 1,000 hertzes is not strong enough to be heard. The scale progresses upward, measured

in units of intensity called *decibels*. Sounds above the *threshold of pain* produce discomfort (Figure 4.11). The decible is a somewhat awkward measurement constructed on the basis of the relationship between two aspects of sound waves—amplitude and frequency.

The structure of the ear

Figure 4.12 illustrates the structure of the ear. Sound waves entering the ear exert pressure against the *eardrum*, the thin, stretchable, vibrating membrane that separates the outer ear from the middle ear. The eardrum must be properly pressurized both externally and internally or it will burst. The pressure is maintained by means of the *Eustachian tubes*, which open into the middle ear from the inside back of the mouth, allowing air to press on the inside of the eardrum. Since this balanced pressure is essential for normal hearing, any damage to the eardrum results in a hearing impairment. Generally, we can equalize pressure by swallowing or yawning when rapidly changing external pressure affects us.

In the middle ear are three hinged, bony structures—the *malleus*, the *incus*, and the *stapes*

—that receive pressure impulses from the eardrum; these structures are commonly called the hammer, the anvil, and the stirrup, respectively, because of their shapes. The hammer is attached directly to the eardrum; the anvil is attached to the hammer at one end and to the stirrup at the other; the stirrup is loosely connected to the *oval window*, the membrane to the inner ear.

The oval window lines the surface of the *cochlea*, the inner-ear mechanism that further transmits sound waves to the auditory receptors. The cochlea (so called because of its snail-shell shape) is about the size of a pea. The stirrup's position against the oval window builds up pressure in the fluid inside the cochlea, causing vibrations to be pulsed through the fluid. To prevent pressure from bursting the cochlea, a small *round window* opening just below the oval window equalizes pressures. The auditory receptors in the cochlea are activated by displacement of the *basilar membrane*, a thin tissue that is set vibrating by the pulsing cochlear fluid. The basilar membrane transmits the varying frequencies of sound to the actual receptors—hair cells located on the *organ of Corti*, a structure that is attached to the basilar membrane. The hair cells move with the vibrations and stimulate the nerve cells to which they are linked. These nerve cells are the beginning of the auditory nerve.

The complex structure of the inner ear includes the *vestibular organ*—an organ which is not used in hearing but is essential to the vestibular (balance) sense, which we will discuss later in this chapter. Here we are concerned primarily with the auditory channels in the inner ear. Figure 4.13 shows the cochlea as it would appear if unwound.

Transduction and transmission of impulses to the brain

The organ of Corti, shown in Figure 4.13, is shaped so that the hair cells are stimulated by the energy of the fluid inside the cochlea; consequently, they transmit the energy as a nerve

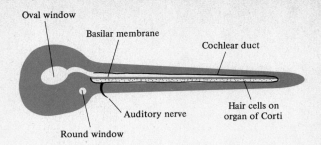

Figure 4.13 *Schematic of the cochlea, the pea-sized, snail-shaped organ in the inner ear, as it would appear if uncoiled. Pressure from the stirrup's position on the oval window builds up in the fluid inside the cochlea. This built-up pressure causes vibrations to be pulsed through the fluid. The basilar membrane reacts to these vibrations and stimulates the receptors hair cells on the organ of Corti. These hair cells in turn stimulate the nerve cells to which they are attached and thus transfer the sound waves into nerve impulses that travel through the auditory nerve to the brain.*

impulse to the nerve cells of the auditory nerve. There are millions of these receptor cells in each ear. They accommodate nearly infinite variations of pitch, loudness, and timbre within the range of human hearing. Differences in pitch produce different patterns in the receptor cells. It is believed that discrimination of the intensity of the stimulus is based on the number of nerve cells activated and the timing of the impulse sending, or "firing," along the auditory nerve. This factor is important. It holds true as a principle for all the sensory processes: *To discriminate the increased intensity of a stimulus, the number of nerve impulses transmitted to the brain must be increased or the pattern must be changed.* Thus, the less intense the stimulus, the fewer will be the nerve impulses transmitted to the brain—fewer both in number of cells activated and in the firing frequency of each nerve cell.

It has been speculated that the impulse patterns for different intensities of sound stimuli not only are unlike but also maintain separate projections on the brain's cortex. It is also believed that the cortex is more deeply penetrated by the auditory stimulation of high-frequency sounds. This reception pattern is believed to be similar to that of the cochlea. The auditory portion of the brain, in other words, can be said to resemble a map of cochlear sensitivity.

Before the auditory impulses reach the temporal lobes of the cerebral cortex, there is considerable, but not complete, crossing-over of sides; that is, the left side of the brain receives almost all the impulses from the right ear and vice versa. The remaining impulses are routed to the side of the brain that corresponds to the location of the ear that hears the sound. We know this happens because severing one tract of nerves will not cause total deafness in the opposite ear.

Theories of hearing

Several theories of hearing account for some aspects of the hearing process, such as transduction, the maintenance of differences in stimulus intensities, and the operation of receptor cells. So far, no one theory has successfully accounted for every aspect of hearing.

Place and traveling-wave theories An early theory of hearing was developed by Helmholtz, the physiologist who helped to develop the color-vision theory discussed in the preceding section. Helmholtz suggested that the basilar membrane resonates and produces vibrations—high tones at the smaller, narrower end and low tones at the wider end—like the strings of a piano or a harp. Nerve fibers attached along this membrane correspond to the resonance emanating from their respective membrane cells. According to this theory, the nerve fibers transmit an exact duplication of the sound to the brain because they are positioned at the point of corresponding resonance. Helmholtz's theory has come to be known as a *place theory*, because it suggests that pitch is determined by the place stimulated on the basilar membrane.

Helmholtz's concept of place was retained in a newer theory, developed by Von Békésy (1957). According to his *traveling-wave theory*, as the sound wave travels through the cochlear fluid, it is responsible for displacing, or moving, the basilar membrane at a place corresponding to the frequency of the sound wave.

The frequency and volley theories Another theory of hearing, known as the *frequency theory*, holds that the basilar membrane, as a vibrating unit, corresponds in number of vibrations per second to the original frequency of the sound wave stimulus. Stimulation of the nerve fibers exactly reproduces the frequency of the sound. However, there cannot be a one-to-one correspondence in this relationship, because the nerve fibers simply are not able to fire as frequently as the fastest sound waves vibrate. To account for this, the *volley theory* states that the nerve fiber discharge is a combined operation. Groups of nerve cells fire impulses into the auditory nerve in a direct relationship to the frequency of the stimulus sound wave by alternating with one another to carry the total surge of the impulse. In this way, no one group is overworked. The process resembles a variety of minor explosions. Put more simply, it is a matter of sharing among several groups the task of impulse transmission normally carried by one group. Firepower is merely increased.

A joint theory of hearing will probably be adopted someday that will combine elements of the volley and place principles. It has been discovered that the volley theory is valid for frequencies below a certain number of hertzes (5,000); above that number, the nerve fibers are unable to group together fast enough to muster a properly coordinated fire pattern. Thus, at higher frequencies the place principle better explains man's auditory capabilities.

Auditory defects

Conduction deafness results from an injury or defect in the sound-conducting mechanism of the middle or outer ear. Some individuals who suffer from conduction deafness cannot hear above a murmur. Some are unable to distinguish between similar words. In such cases, any one of the delicate parts of the conduction mechanism may be damaged; for example, the eardrum may be ruptured by poking an object too deeply into the ear. Temporary hearing deficiencies may be brought about by wax deposits in the ear, or by a severe cold or other illness that has affected the auditory channels. Sounds of every frequency are affected. Most individuals with conduction deafness can be helped, because the damage is not in the inner ear. Hearing aids help to reconduct sounds through the middle ear. *Nerve deafness* is caused by malfunction of the inner ear, often because of damage to it or to the auditory nerve. Individuals affected by nerve deafness suffer from greater hearing loss of high-frequency sounds than of low-frequency sounds. If there is complete destruction of either the cochlea or the auditory nerve, the individual will be deaf forever in the ear in which the destruction occurs.

CHEMICAL SENSATION: SMELL AND TASTE

Stimulation to smell and taste is provided by chemical substances. As in both vision and audition, once the stimulus penetrates the sense organ, the receptor cells carry out the transduction process to alter the stimulus to a form that can be transmitted to the brain. We know far less about smell and taste than about sight and hearing, but we do know that the transduction process is also at work in these sensory processes.

Smell

Little is known about smell. We cannot even determine which types of odors man is able to distinguish. Some theories say that there are four basic odors: acidic, fragrant, burnt, and caprylic (like limburger cheese); others say that there are six: fruity, flowery, burnt, spicy, resinous, and putrid. We usually end up describing odors by comparing them to some particularly aromatic stimulus. We may say something smells like a rose or like a dead fish.

Fair or foul Cultural preferences and variations exist for the stimuli of smell, just as they do for food. W. J. Junker mentions this in his *Travels in Africa.* When Junker ate some Edam cheese in the presence of one particular tribe, the reaction was lively. The tribesmen were repelled by the odor of the food and were astonished that anyone would eat such a thing. Some Americans might agree with the natives on that count, but few would also be repelled by the scent of eau de cologne or perfumed soap, as were these natives.

Different societies have favored or disliked particular scents. Our society appears obsessed

Figure 4.14   Results of a study in which experimental subjects were visually deprived for a period of 7 days, while control subjects were allowed normal stimulation. Note the gradual decline of olfactory sensitivity of the experimentals, their marked increase in sensitivity after the 7 days, and the renewed decline on "post day 2." (From Schutte, W. and Zubeck, J. P. Change in olfactory and gustatory sensitivity after prolonged visual deprivation. Canadian Journal of Psychology, 1967, 21, 337–345. Reprinted by permission of the publisher and authors.)

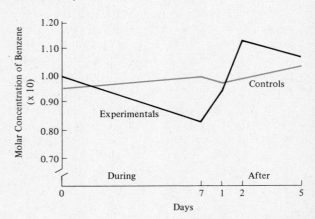

with the elimination of certain body odors—witness the superabundance of mouthwashes and deodorants in our stores. Most other societies do not share this obsession. Some cultures regard the odor of garlic as especially savory; in others, a whiff of curry arouses appetites. Obviously, olfactory (smell) preferences are not permanent, and humans adapt to odors, learning to tolerate those they found unpleasant at first.

More than any other sensory system, the olfactory system is capable of adaptation. New stimuli presented to the system increase the system's sensitivity to its environment. Under continuous stimulation, however, olfactory acuity is reduced. It has also been shown that the sensitivity of the olfactory system may be equally affected by visual stimulation. For example, subjects deprived of visual stimulation for 7 days showed a gradual decrease in olfactory sensitivity during the experiment and a marked increase at its conclusion (see Figure 4.14).

Structure of the olfactory system   The structure and function of the olfactory sensory channels are not well defined. Very little is known about the processing, or transduction, of chemical stimuli, though much is speculated. Figure 4.15 shows the structure of the olfactory system. The *nostrils* are passageways through which the chemical stimuli must pass. The hairs in the nose have nothing to do with the sensation; they serve as filters. The *olfactory sense organ* is recessed high up on the walls of each side of the nasal cavity. It is the sense organ closest to the brain.

Often a stimulus must be sniffed rather vigorously to draw it up the length of the nasal passageway because, as Figure 4.15 shows, the main flow of air goes from the nose to the throat rather than to the olfactory receptors. The upper part of each nasal cavity contains a membrane to which are attached *ciliated* (hairy) *receptor cells.* To receive the chemical stimuli from the nasal passage, the receptors penetrate the fluid, or *mucus,* that covers the membrane; long and

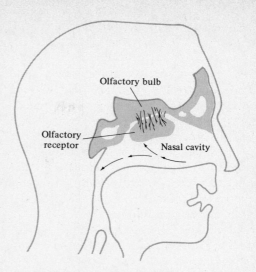

Figure 4.15   Diagram of the olfactory sense organ. Note how far the olfactory bulb is from the nostrils. Because of this distance, strong sniffs are necessary for sensation of stimuli.

spindly, these cells serve as their own conductors of impulses to the olfactory nerve. They admit chemical stimuli at one end and transfer them to nerve impulses at the other.

Olfactory nerve impulses travel a short path to the brain and are received into the *rhinencephalon,* located in the frontal lobe of the cerebral cortex. Olfactory impulses are believed to penetrate the front portion of the rhinencephalon. Attempts to map the olfactory impulses have failed thus far, however.

Measuring a smell   Because fibers from the olfactory structures are inaccessible, no one has succeeded in directly measuring the electrical activity within them. Adrian (1951), however, inserted wire electrodes into the olfactory bulb of animals and recorded the activity that resulted from the presentation of odoriferous stimuli. When he presented odorless stimuli, such as carbon monoxide or carbon dioxide, activity (electrical potential) did not result. Adrian also noted interesting differences among animal species. Fruity smells caused the greatest amount of activity in rabbits' olfactory bulbs, while decaying animal matter was most effective in activating the olfactory bulbs of cats.

Taste

To a great extent, taste depends on smell. Most of us know that when suffering from a head cold, we sometimes cannot tell what we are eating because we cannot smell the food. With our nostrils closed, we usually cannot tell the difference between ice cream and pudding. Try it. By itself, the tongue is really sensitive to only four broad tastes: sweet, bitter, salty, and sour. We may say that olfactory senses provide the details for the eating experience.

Taste, like smell, is quite adaptable. After the first bite of food or sip of a drink, we no longer perceive the strength of its flavor. When someone says that the taste of a particular food lingers in his mouth, he is, in fact, only continuing to smell the food.

Research has shown that the sharpness of the *gustatory* (taste) *sense* declines with age. Children and young adults are at the peak of gustatory activity, while middle-aged and older people become progressively less aware of taste sensations. Incidentally, taste sensitivity is decreased markedly by smoking.

Structure of the taste buds The chemical stimuli for taste sensations are received by the *taste buds* of the tongue. The buds are complex structures, found only on certain areas of the tongue. It is believed that the taste buds deteriorate and regenerate frequently. (The deterioration is probably due to the chemical action of saliva.) Taste bud cells do not necessarily regenerate in the place at which the earlier cells were destroyed. The surface of the tongue changes, but very minutely.

Clusters of taste buds form bumps on the tongue called *papillae*. Each rounded taste bud is composed of many elongated *taste cells* that form an opening at the top of the bud known as the *taste pore*. Through the taste pores the chemical stimuli penetrate the gustatory sense organ.

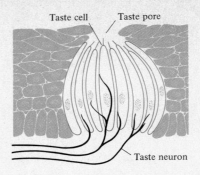

Figure 4.16 *Diagram showing the structure of a single taste bud. The stimuli (hamburger, pizza, or such) enter through the taste pore. Changed to nerve impulses, they pass through the taste cell to the taste neuron. The nerve impulse carries the taste message to the brain.*

Figure 4.16 shows a taste bud lying within the surface cells of the tongue. The effect of chemical stimuli upon nerve impulses is carried through the taste cells into the *taste neurons*. In turn, the taste neurons relay the impulses through the sensory nerve fibers to the brain. The taste neurons group together in several small tracts, depending on the location of the neurons in the tongue. It has been found that the tracts travel to the brain together with other nerve fibers from the skin and facial region, but that upon arriving at the gustatory area of the cerebral cortex, previously separated taste impulses are all received in the same general area.

Measurement of taste Techniques to measure taste have been more successful than those devised to measure smell. Experiments that identified the four basic taste sensations also provided a basis for mapping the areas of the tongue for each type of sensitivity. Sweetness is detected best by the tip of the tongue; bitterness, at its base; saltiness, by the tip and sides; and sourness, along its sides.

If a stimulus is dropped on a surface area of the tongue other than the one best able to receive it, the stimulus does not taste the way it usually does. Almost any sweet stimulus tastes bitter, for instance, if dropped on the taste buds at the base of the tongue.

SKIN AND BODY SENSATIONS

Our final classification of human sensation is a broad one. The skin senses of touch, pain, cold, and warmth are grouped together with kinesthesis and the vestibular sense because each involves stimulation to the skin or body by pressure, pain, or temperature.

The four skin senses

Once it was believed that the skin was sensitive only to touch (or pressure); now it is understood that the skin is actually receptive to four different stimuli: touch, pain, cold, and warmth.

In developing a theory of how the four skin senses function, it has been necessary for psychologists to take into account the fact that 90

Figure 4.17   A simplified cross section of skin showing free nerve endings, basket nerve endings, and Meissner's corpuscles. Free nerve endings are sensitive to pain, warmth, and cold; basket nerve endings are sensitive to touch; and Meissner's corpuscles are sensitive to pressure.

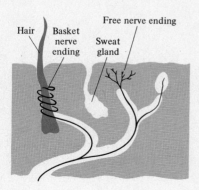

Hair   Basket nerve ending   Free nerve ending   Sweat gland

percent of the human body is covered with hair. The skin in the hairy regions contains two types of nerve endings: a *free nerve ending* and a *basket nerve ending.*

The free nerve endings are loose, unsystematized structures below the surface of the skin. They branch and tangle to cover the undersurface area. Any area of skin may be shown to possess the free nerve endings of a host of separate fibers. The basket nerve endings, on the other hand, are enmeshed in the base of each hair. Figure 4.17 presents a cross section of hairy skin showing both types of nerve ending.

The free and basket nerve endings assume different roles in the sensory processes of the skin. Basket nerve endings are receptors for touch; movement of the hair stimulates these nerves, causing a skin sensation capable of detecting the location, intensity, and direction of the stimulus. The free nerve endings are assumed to be responsible for detection of pain, warmth, and cold, plus touch to a lesser degree. Although the exact method by which the free nerve endings are stimulated is not known, some scientists believe that each stimulus forms a different pattern of impulses in the receptors and that these patterns are subsequently interpreted by the brain. This theory is similar to those that purport to explain other sensory processes, especially taste.

The nonhairy parts of the body, for example, the palms of the hands and the soles of the feet, contain free nerve endings, responsive to touch. The hairless regions also contain *Meissner's corpuscles,* pressure-sensitive receptors also found on the lips, eyelids, and tip of the tongue.

Skin sensations are transmitted to the brain through the spinal cord. Nerve tracts cross over at several junctions but are not entirely opposite their areas of stimulation until they leave the spinal cord and begin their journey through the areas of the brain. Once received by the cerebral cortex, sensory impulses for the right side of the body are processed in the left lobe, and vice versa. Severance of the *cutaneous neurons* (skin neurons) is a form of surgical therapy used as a last resort to relieve extreme pain in cancer victims and persons suffering from deep skin burns. Removal of the cutaneous cortex cancels the effect of all four skin sensations for any area of the skin.

Touch Touch sensitivity is a reaction to pressure exerted on the skin. In human beings, only a mild touch stimulus is necessary to produce a sense of pressure. Some areas are more sensitive than others: the lips, the fingertips, the tip of the tongue, and the face respond to the lightest touch. The upper arms, the calves, and the back require a greater intensity of pressure to create the sensation of touch. As with the other senses, the sense of touch is adaptable to our life-style. Certainly, clothes exert pressure on almost every part of the body, but we seldom notice this pressure because it is constant.

The sense of touch seems to be more intense in some individuals than in others. Craftsmen, such as jewelers, stone cutters, engravers, and glass makers, require an exquisite sense of touch. Blind readers, too, must sensitize their fingertips to the small raised dots of Braille printing.

Pain The sense of pain is often coupled with other senses; pressure can bring pain, and so can intense heat or cold. When the free nerve endings are stimulated by pain, the body is aware of an injury or illness affecting a particular area. Certain areas of the skin are more sensitive to pain than others. The same stimulus that evokes pain when applied to the lips or the tip of the nose may not be as painful when applied to the shoulders or forearms.

Interesting psychological studies have been made to determine the degree of stimulus required to cause pain. Warm water is not painful, but when water reaches a certain degree of heat, it can cause great pain. The explanation is that, at a certain temperature, water destroys skin tissue. The most consistent cause of pain is the destruction of body tissue—when water scalds and burns the skin, when the needle penetrates, and so on.

Pain warns us of tissue destruction. Many pain receptors lie near the skin surface, and this strategic position allows them to act as a warning system for those internal organs of the body that do not experience pain as a sign of trouble and are therefore unable to signal us when they need help.

The word "pain" evokes a stronger reaction in some individuals than in others. Some individuals are oversensitive to painful reactions—reporting more pain than they are actually experiencing and feeling pain before it actually occurs. Conversely, mountain climbers, boxers, automobile racers, football players, and others engaged in strenuous physical activity tend to ignore pain. Football players often injure muscles, joints, or tendons and remain on the field. They frequently undergo corrective surgery for serious injuries and are back on the football field in a week or two.

Temperature senses: cold and warmth We feel a cold or warm stimulus if its temperature differs from normal skin temperature by at least 2° or 3°F. Warm and cold stimuli apparently do not depend for their effect on the activation of separate cold and warm receptors. The different sensations may be due to the pattern of impulses transmitted to the cortex by the nerve fibers after they have received the stimulus sensations. We know that a functional difference occurs because we can distinguish between cold and warmth. Therefore we infer either that there are differences in the techniques of transduction of impulses or that the pattern of nerve stimulation encodes the stimulus sensation for the brain.

A test with three basins The thermal senses are divided into cold and warmth receptors. The experience of either warmth or cold depends on the temperature existing in the skin at the point of examination. This temperature is arbitrarily taken to be a zero point around which perceptible differences may be noted. Thus, if the skin temperature is 33°C, a warmer stimulus (34 or 35°C) is felt as warm, and a cooler stimulus (31 or 32°C) is felt as cool or cold. The classic example demonstrating the adaptive process through temperature change is the following: If one hand has been in cold water, and the other hand in hot water, when they are simultaneously placed in water at room temperature the water feels cool to the hand previously immersed in hot water and warm to the hand previously immersed in cold water. Try it.

The cold and warmth receptors in the skin adapt readily to different base temperatures. If, in an experiment, you place one hand in cold or warm water, the sensation of cold or warmth gradually disappears as you accommodate to the water. The receptors no longer receive stimuli and transmit information about them. Technically, the normal temperature of the skin is called the *indifference point* or the *physiological zero point*. During a simple experiment such as the one just described, the individual is said to

reach a new indifference point—that of the water temperature.

We have discovered through experiments that the cold and warmth receptor cells react very differently to stimuli. A cold receptor cell may react to a warm stimulus as if the stimulus were cold—not just cool, but utterly cold. Receptor cells for warmth react similarly when stimulated by a cold object that is below the indifference point; they produce the sensation of intense heat. These phenomena are known as *paradoxical cold* and *paradoxical warmth*, respectively.

Kinesthesis

Kinesthesis denotes consciousness of our own body movement and position. We know we are walking, sitting, or lying down because of feedback from kinesthesis. This vital sensory capacity is located in cells in the muscles, joints, and tendons throughout the body; there is no one specific organ of kinesthesis.

Kinesthesis informs us that we are in upturned or unbalanced position. It tells us when our muscles are straining, our arms are out of control, and our torso is unbalanced. If any change occurs in the direction taken by a limb or its rate of movement, it will be sensed by the kinesthetic receptors.

Generally, the receptor cells are simple neurons that branch off from the central nervous system and lead into muscles, tendons, and joint linings. Kinesthetic receptors join with nerve fibers from the organs of the skin and go through the spinal cord to the brain, much as with the skin receptors.

The vestibular sense

Another sense—one that is also primarily sensitive to pressure changes—is the *vestibular sense*. Its organs are located in the vestibular area of the inner ear. The vestibular sense is related to body balance and position. It is also called the *equilibratory sense* or the *labyrinthine sense* (the inner ear is also called the *labryinth*). The best example of vestibular sensitivity is the individual's perception of his position with respect to gravity and space. The position of the head is of utmost importance. If you stand with your eyes closed, you tend to lose this vestibular awareness.

Figure 4.18 is a diagram of the structure of the vestibular organs. The *semicircular canals* are not used in hearing but are necessary for vestibular balance. There are three canals, all responsible for informing the body of its motion in space. The base of each canal contains a bulging structure called the *ampulla*. The ampulla houses a gelatinous, bud-shaped mass called a *crista*, in which hair cells are embedded. The hair cells of the crista are similar in structure to the hair cells on the organ of Corti, discussed in the section on hearing. However, the ampulla is stimulated by the pressure from the fluid in the semicircular canals. Since the semicircular canals are located at right angles to each other—in three planes, or dimensions—they can react when the body is rotated. The canal fluid, called *endolymph*, becomes displaced by bodily rotation and its movement affects the hair cells in the crista. The hair cells react by bending or otherwise moving, and thus stimulate the nerve fibers at the base of the ampulla. Figure 4.18 also shows a cross section of an ampulla, the structure where transduction of stimuli to nerve impulses begins.

A second structure is a double sac that appears below the ampulla between the base of the semicircular canals and the beginning of the cochlea. These two sacs are called the *utricle* and the *saccule*; the former is closer to the ampulla and the latter is closer to the cochlea. The bodies of the utricle and saccule contain stonelike structures, known as *otoliths*, which balance in the fluid to signal the position of the body in space. The otoliths do not exert pressure on the hair cells unless the body or head is tilted. Thus, through the hair cells in the sacs, we receive stimuli that help us maintain the upright position.

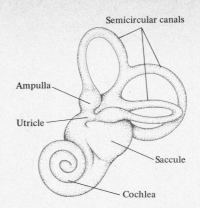

Figure 4.18   The structure of the vestibular organ.

The nerve fibers from both the ampulla and the vestibular sacs travel toward the brain with the auditory nerve. Although it is not known exactly how impulses reach the cerebral cortex, it is significant to note that the vestibular nerves end at the base of the brain in structures called *vestibular nuclei*, which are gray masses of matter. At this point the impulses break up; some are relayed to the eye (for righting the balance and position of the body), others to the internal organs, and still others to the brain.

The vestibular organs are most sensitive to rotation of the head; thus, any movement that causes the head to swerve around can bring on an unpleasant sensation. The most common results of an upset in vestibular sensitivity are seasickness, motion sickness, and dizziness. In a situation that causes dizziness, such as rapid rotation of the body, the unpleasant feeling can be controlled by preventing the head from whirling or spinning. This is done by fixing the eyes on a particular object once in every turn—once every 360 degrees. The eyes are fixed and then the torso is turned so that it is in line with the gaze. If the balance of the head and eyes is maintained, then the labyrinthine organs will not be unbalanced. The ballerina's ability to whirl around for several minutes at a time without becoming dizzy is due to her mastery of this technique.

SUMMARY

Transduction, the process whereby particular forms of energy are converted for transmission to the brain, takes places in the receptors.

Psychophysical methods were developed by Fechner to measure the relationship between physical stimuli and the sensations they produce.

Threshold is measured by the method of average error, the method of limits, and the method of constant stimuli.

Signal detection theory looks upon the identification of thresholds as a form of decision-making because a variety of factors influence a subject's report of a stimulus.

Sensory adaptation refers to decreased sensitivity to a particular stimulus through continued exposure to it.

The parts of the eye include the sclera, choroid, pupil, iris, cornea, lens, and retina (containing the fovea). Receptor cells are rods and cones.

Nerve impulses travel over the optic nerve to the occipital lobe of the cerebral cortex. Greatest visual acuity occurs when the light rays fall on the cones in the fovea. In the area outside the fovea, peripheral vision occurs. The blind spot is the point at which the optic nerve leaves the retina.

Cone cells mediate color vision and do not function well in dim light. Rods translate light energy into white, black, and grays; they function in dim as well as bright light. Adaptation to darkness primarily involves the rods.

Visual impulses go to the occipital cortex after passing the optic chiasma. The visual field for the right-hand area of sight goes to the left lobe of the brain, and the visual field for the left-hand area goes to the right lobe.

Visual defectiveness may take the form of nearsightedness, farsightedness, presbyopia, astigmatism, diplopia, or scotoma.

Colors are described in terms of hue, saturation, and brightness. The human eye can detect only a small range of light waves.

Staring at a color for a long time may produce a negative or a positive afterimage on a gray or white square, viewed immediately afterward.

Recurrent or lateral inhibition causes two adjacent visual sensations to simultaneously modify each other. The border between a light and dark area is called a Mach band.

There are two basic theories of color vision—the Young-Helmholtz theory and Hering's opponent-process theory. MacNichols has used a microspectro-photometer to provide evidence for the Young-Helmholtz theory.

The characteristics of sound are pitch, loudness, and timbre.

The parts of the ear are the eardrum, Eustachian tubes, oval window, round window, cochlea, hammer, anvil, and stirrup, organ of Corti, and basilar membrane. Impulses travel over the auditory nerve to the brain.

Conduction deafness results from defects in the outer or middle ear. Nerve deafness usually involves defects in the inner ear.

The four theories of hearing are Helmholtz's place theory, Von Békésy's traveling-wave theory, the frequency theory, and the volley theory.

It is believed that olfactory impulses activate the receptors in the front portion of the rhinencephalon.

The gustatory sense (taste) largely depends on the sense of smell. The taste receptors are small taste buds grouped together to form the papillae (bumps) on the tongue.

The skin is sensitive to pressure, pain, cold, and warmth. Sensitivity is mediated by the basket nerve endings, free nerve endings, and Meissner's corpuscles.

Kinesthesis is activation of the receptors in the muscles, tendons, and joints to provide information about position and movement.

The vestibular sense (also equilibratory or labyrinthine sense) depends on activities of the semicircular canals in the inner ears.

SUGGESTED READINGS

Texts

Cain, W. S., & Marks, L. E. (Eds.) *Stimulus and sensation: readings in sensory psychology.* Boston: Little, Brown, 1971. An overview of historical and current sensation problems. Many of the articles are classics.

Gregory, R. L. *Eye and brain: the psychology of seeing.* New York: McGraw-Hill, 1966. Finest book on visual perception to appear in a very long time. It is visually pleasing and well written by a known authority in the field.

Kling, J. W., & Riggs, L. A. (Eds.) *Woodworth and Schlosberg's experimental psychology* (3rd ed.). New York: Holt, Rinehart & Winston, 1971. Chapters 5 through 11 provide a brief but thorough introduction to methods, trends, and issues in current sensory research. Individual chapters on aspects of taste, smell, audition, and vision.

Morgan, C. T. *Physiological psychology* (3rd ed.). New York: McGraw-Hill, 1965. Contains good coverage of the physiology of the sense organs.

Stevens, S. S., & Davis, H. *Hearing.* New York: Wiley, 1938. Classic work on the sense of hearing.

Underwood, B. J. *Experimental psychology.* New York: Appleton-Century-Crofts, 1966. Includes a comprehensive, well-organized, and interesting discussion of the problems of psychophysics.

Popular books

Hall, E. T. *The hidden dimension.* Account of perceptual peculiarities of different societies and cultures around the world.

Keller, H. *My story.* Autobiography of a woman blind, deaf, and dumb from infancy.

Montague, A. *Touching.* A comprehensive discussion of the significance of skin to human beings.

Trevor-Roper, P. *The world through blunted sight.* The author playfully advances the hypothesis that blunted vision (particularly nearsightedness) is responsible for many of the world's great works of art.

5
Perception

Our environment is made up of stimuli that are constant and insistent. Stimuli seldom reach our sense organs singly; most compete with other stimuli for our attention, or they are linked so that we perceive them in patterns. Rain, for example, is a stimulus that occurs as part of a pattern of stimuli that includes dark clouds, a pattern perceived as a whole.

Perception is an individual's awareness of and reaction to stimuli. Perception is a highly individual aspect of behavior, for it is the way each person processes the raw data he receives into meaningful *patterns*. Individual perceptions of the same event may vary. For example, a man waiting for a bus and a farmer standing at a window are likely to perceive rain in quite different ways. An individual can also have different perceptions of the same stimulus pattern on different occasions. Rain may evoke sadness, or joy, or go unnoticed. Slight variations in the pattern —such as an increase in wind velocity during a storm—can also cause the pattern to be perceived differently.

It is easy to provide examples of perception. But it is very difficult—and very essential— to isolate and define the principal factors in perception. Perception depends on the nature of the stimuli, the individual's sense organs, his attention, the organization of the stimuli, the context in which the stimuli occur, his past experiences with the stimuli, and his bodily conditions at the moment. This chapter will show how complex activities inside and outside each individual act and interact to produce perception.

ATTENTION

No one could possibly react to all the stimuli simultaneously occurring around him. Perception therefore requires *selectivity*, the act of paying attention to one stimulus or pattern of stimuli while ignoring others. Attention is a complex act that involves the central nervous system, motivation, the individual's set (his expectation that he will perceive a stimulus of a certain type), various external factors, and the absence of distractions.

Effect of noise on attention Given a choice, most people would prefer to study in a quiet room rather than among three younger brothers, a television, and a barking dog. But noise is not always a hindrance to study, as Mech (1953) discovered when he set out to determine the effect of noise (the sound of a phonograph record) on students' performance in solving mathematics problems. Students studied under a quiet condition and under a noisy condition. Two groups were used: one group was told that they were expected to do better either in the quiet or in the noisy situation; the other group received no such instructions.

Subjects tended to perform according to the instructions. The group that had been given no instructions showed no difference in performance under noisy and quiet conditions. Mech concluded that: (1) subjects will respond to instructions and tune out or not tune out the noise, depending on the instructions; and (2) when no instructions are given, performance is the same in noisy as well as quiet situations. These conclusions, however, cannot be generalized. They will vary, depending on the motivation to perform the task and the interest held by distractions. Thus, for most people, reading in a noisy home is probably much harder at the beginning of a semester than on the day before the finals.

Sensory gating

A process in the central nervous system known as *sensory gating* is thought to be responsible for the selective reception of stimuli. Still not fully understood, sensory gating appears to occur when strong input in one sensory channel interferes with input from another sensory channel. It is as if a gate were opening and closing to permit entry of only one set of sensory impulses at a time. For example, if you were standing on a beach watching the sun set over the ocean, you might not hear the water, feel the spray of the waves, or notice the increasing cold of night until you lost interest in the sunset or until the sun went down.

Motivation

Motivation is an important factor in the selection of stimuli. Let us see how it works. If, for example, a student has just failed a test, he may focus his attention on the instructor's lectures after the test, since the lectures will provide the information to satisfy his current need to improve his grade. Another student who failed the test may avoid the lectures for several days to escape the stimuli that remind him of the failed test. Motivation, then, is as subjective as the overall act of perception.

There are basic motives, however, that most people share in varying degrees (the desire to feel well, to be popular, to look good, and so on). When stimulus patterns are related to these motives, most individuals are likely to be attentive. This, of course, is why advertisers aim to arouse the basic human desires; they get more attention than if they describe only the utilitarian use of their products.

Bodily orientation and set

Ivan Pavlov, the eminent Russian neurophysiologist, noted that during the conditioning of animals, the conditioned stimulus produced changes in the animals' bodily orientations. Responding to one stimulus caused animals to ready their sensory receptors for the reception of other stimuli. These changes represent an *orienting reflex* that enables an animal to be more attentive to new stimuli. A man in a concert hall, eyes closed, body turned, ear cocked, provides a human example of this orienting reflex, or *set*: he is set for the auditory stimulation of the music.

It is often difficult to separate set from motive. But experiments indicate that the set condition—sensory channels open and ready to respond—may occur whether or not a motive exists. For example, a subject in an experiment is set to respond; he may not know what he is to respond to, but he is attentive anyway. We often refer to set as an *expectancy*.

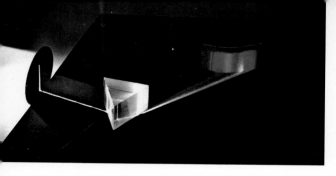

Plate 1 *When sunlight is passed through a prism, a spectrum results. Sunlight contains all wavelengths, which are separated into individual wavelengths by the prism's angle of deflection. Each wavelength, from the shortest (violet) to the longest (red), has its own hue. (Fritz Goro, LIFE Magazine © Time Inc.)*

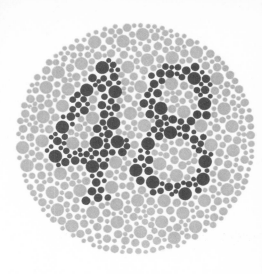

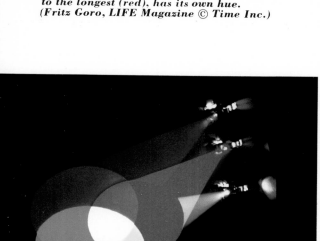

Plate 2 *Color mixing is shown by the effects of combining beams of light from three projectors. Mixing wavelengths is an additive process; the eye receives both wavelengths. For example, when red and green are mixed, yellow results. White results from the mixing of all the wavelengths. (Fritz Goro, LIFE Magazine © Time Inc.)*

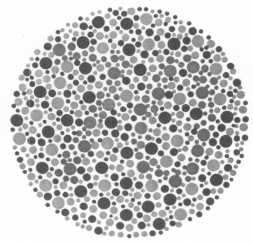

Plate 3 *The Dvorine Pseudo-Isochromatic Plates are used to detect color blindness. Because color-blind individuals differentiate colors by degrees of brightness, certain plates include colors of equal brightness. The person with normal vision can read the number or see the pattern, but the color-blind person cannot. (Stoelting)*

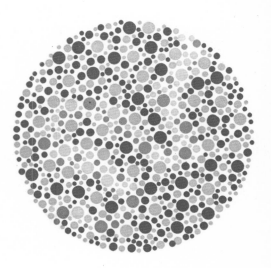

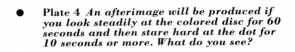

Plate 4 *An afterimage will be produced if you look steadily at the colored disc for 60 seconds and then stare hard at the dot for 10 seconds or more. What do you see?*

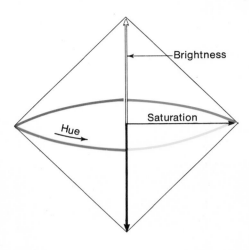

Plate 6 *The color solid. The dimension of hue is represented by the circumference, saturation by the radius, and brightness by the vertical pole.*

Plate 5

Plate 7

Individuals possess sets toward some stimuli and not toward others; a mother is set to respond to the sounds her child makes, but probably not to a ringing doorbell. It is possible to evoke a particular response by establishing a consistent set. Read these words aloud: *MacDuff, MacPherson, MacDonald, MacMahon, MacHines.* How might you pronounce the last word if you saw it standing alone, without the others? (Incidentally, the expectation of being tricked is also a set.)

Stimulus factors and attention

Several external factors contribute to what you may perceive at any given moment. They are, briefly:

1 *Intensity*—the degree or strength of the stimulus. A loud sound calls attention to itself; a soft sound often passes unnoticed.
2 *Size*—the physical dimensions of the stimulus. Depending on the context, either a large or a small stimulus can call attention to itself.
3 *Movement*—a moving object usually compels attention. It is noticed much sooner than a stationary object.
4 *Contrast*—that which is different from its surroundings attracts attention.
5 *Repetition*—continued presentation of the stimulus captures attention but can have a dulling effect if carried on too long.

Distraction of attention

Distractions are urgent stimuli that the individual cannot disregard. They occur because the attention span is limited, and many stimuli compete for our attention. Distractions are an acute problem where employees are expected to produce maximum output with a minimum waste of time and energy. Many studies have been conducted in the effort to establish working conditions that promote efficiency. It has generally been observed that distractions interfere with efficiency both during and after their presentation to the worker. But after prolonged exposure to distracting stimuli, individuals tend to become accustomed to them.

A distracted cat Attention controls perception in very powerful ways. An event that commands our attention can sometimes shut out all other events. To show this, Hernández-Peón, Scherer, and Touret (1956) implanted electrodes in the auditory nerve of a cat and recorded the electrical activity of the nerve. At regular intervals, a noise was sounded and the electrical activity in the cat's auditory nerve increased. However, when mice were placed in front of the cat to attract its attention, the noise no longer had any effect on the electrical activity in the auditory nerve. Once the cat's attention had been attracted by something else, it did not hear the noise.

PERCEPTUAL ORGANIZATION

In processing sensory data, we all find it necessary to organize a multitude of environmental stimuli into meaningful structures and forms. Unless our world consists of familiar shapes, it is unpredictable, and we are rarely comfortable in unpredictable situations. Therefore we see patterns of stimuli, as noted earlier, rather than random collections. When we look at a chair, we are responding to the various patterns we perceive, such as shape, texture, and design. We feel confident in describing the chair as having sides, a front, and a back, even though we cannot see all these parts at the same time. Learning is important in the organization of perceptions—quite as important as the functions of the sense organs and nervous system (Figure 5.1).

The founders of Gestalt psychology—M. Wertheimer, W. Köhler, and K. Koffka—devised principles to explain the organization of perceptions. *Gestalt* means "whole" or "configuration," and the Gestalt psychologists study perception in terms of wholes. To them, the whole is more than the sum of its parts. They find that the individual organizes stimuli into objects according to certain principles, and that these principles—

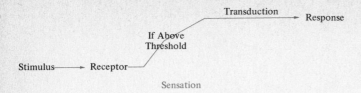

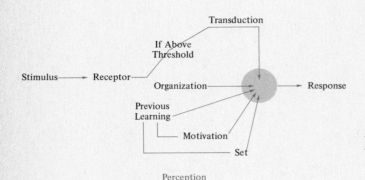

Figure 5.1 *Comparison of sensation and perception.*

figure and ground perception, contour, grouping, camouflage, and figural aftereffects—largely account for how we perceive.

Figure and ground

The *figure-ground* relationship, which is illustrated in Figure 5.2, is basic to all forms of perception. A tree is a figure that appears against a ground of sky or forest. The figure stands out because it has a defined shape, whereas the ground does not. Because the figure stands out, it appears to be at the front of our field of vision, while the ground appears more distant. Many factors contribute to figure and ground perceptions: among them are color, size, shape, and intensity.

Frequently, figure and ground are so shaped that either can be seen as the object. When there is no contrast between the figure and the ground, the relationship is said to be *reversible*. Figure 5.3 shows a reversible figure and ground; although it does not matter which object is perceived first, the object that the individual is set to perceive will probably be perceived first. It is not possible to perceive both figure and ground simultaneously. If figure and ground are reversible, it would seem that perception depends as much on the characteristics of the perceiver as on the characteristics of the stimuli.

Other sensory experiences may be perceived as figure and ground. A person who is eating a meal that tastes too salty will perceive salt as a figure on a ground of meat and potatoes. We listen to what the person sitting next to us at a party is saying (figure) and at the same time are aware of conversations going on throughout the room (ground).

Contour

The *contours* that separate figure from ground also enable the individual to organize stimuli into patterns. A contour is the boundary between a figure and its ground. To a blind person, the boundary may be tactile; a sighted person perceives contour as a visual sensation.

We often have great difficulty perceiving

Figure 5.2   An example of a figure-ground relationship.

Figure 5.3   Reversible figure and ground perception. You can perceive devils or angels, but you cannot perceive both at the same time. Nor can you truly identify which is the figure and which is the ground. (Escher Foundation— Haags Gemeentemuseum, The Hague)

contours. Too much light or too little light can easily affect the ability to distinguish between a figure and its ground. It is important to remember that contour provides a boundary to a shape but is not itself a shape.

Grouping

The term *grouping* applies to the tendency to perceive stimuli in meaningful patterns. Figure 5.4 shows various examples of grouping. (Note that you see an organized pattern in each part of the figure—not clusters of isolated stimuli.) The following types of pattern are illustrated:

1 *Likeness or similarity* (item A)—Objects of like appearance will be grouped as a unit. Objects of

Figure 5.4   Five examples of how stimulus patterns become organized. Each of these clusters of stimuli will appear as a pattern of stimuli. The patterns shown are (A) likeness, (B) nearness, (C) symmetry, (D) continuation, and (E) closure.

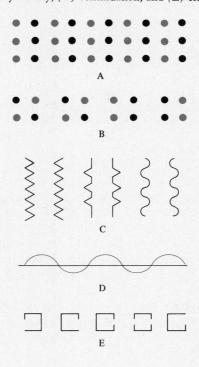

dissimilar appearance will not be grouped. Notice that the black dots group into columns and the colored dots into other columns.

2 *Nearness* or *proximity* (item B)—The objects closest to each other appear as a group. Notice that the dots appear as four groups of square patterns. Although each pattern consists of different color arrangements, the proximity of the dots forces us to perceive four patterns rather than a random collection of black and colored dots.

3 *Symmetry* (item C)—The more symmetrical the set of contours, the more likely it is that the region bounded by these contours will be perceived as a figure. In item C, do you see six vertical crooked lines or do you see three figures? Most people see three figures.

4 *Continuation* (item D)—We tend to group the stimuli that have the fewest interruptions in contour. The pattern in item D is usually perceived as a smoothly curved line crossing a straight line because the curved line and the straight line are both continuous.

5 *Closure* (item E)—The ability to perceive a whole object when the object itself is not whole is *closure*—because of the characteristic "closing" of incomplete lines. Although closure is primarily based on the individual's past experience, it may be caused in part by an effort to see a symmetrically whole object (called a "good" figure). A person's age plays a major part in his ability to close perceptions. Young children and adolescents will close a figure fairly quickly and accurately, while adults (especially those over 40) are less likely to perceive a closed figure.

Camouflage

The principles of grouping also apply to the camouflaging of objects. Figure 5.5 provides examples of concealment based on the principle of good continuation. Camouflage is important to many animals whose coloration blends in with their accustomed background to hide them from predators. Figure 5.6 shows an example of natural camouflage. Note that it is difficult to perceive camouflaged objects—until they are pointed out. This suggests that camouflage tricks can be played with many organizational factors.

A   B   C

Figure 5.5 Examples of camouflage. The principle of continuation is operating to conceal three different numbers in (A), (B), and (C). What are they?

(A) 4 (B) 5 (C) 8

Figural aftereffects

If a specific sensory region, such as a part of the retina, is stimulated for a long period of time, a distortion in perceptual organization can occur, and the individual's response—either to the original stimulus or to a subsequent stimulus—may become distorted. We can only speculate as to whether this distortion is caused by tiring sensory receptors, boredom, or some process of satiation in the central nervous system. The distorted perceptions are called *figural aftereffects*. Figure 5.7 provides an example.

CONTEXT

Context is the setting in which the stimuli appear (Figure 5.8). The perception of a stimulus may change substantially when its context changes. A word or phrase, for instance, can mean different things in different contexts. Consider these examples: The joke was very *funny*. He had a *funny* look on his face. He felt *funny* when he saw the headless chicken. (When people complain of being quoted out of context, it is often with good reason.)

Figure 5.6   Natural camouflage. It is
advantageous for the frog not to be perceived.
In this way, it is hidden from its natural enemies.
(Leonard Lee Rue III—Monkmeyer)

Figure 5.8   Context determines our perception.

Figure 5.7   Follow the steps as labeled and a
figural aftereffect can be perceived: Stare at
the X in A for approximately 60 seconds; then
quickly shift to the X in B. Note that the
circles surrounding the X in B appear to be
spaced unevenly; the right-hand circles seem to
be closer together than the left-hand circles.
As you can see from C, the large amount of space
between the right-hand circles in A causes the
right-hand circles in B to appear closer together
—the outside circles push the inside circles
toward the center.

"Maybe it would look bigger if we used a smaller boy."

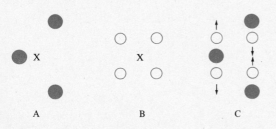

A   B   C

Context effects

Read this line: **A B C D**

Now read this line: **I2 I3 I4**

If what you read was a group of letters followed by a group of numbers, look closely at the "letter" B and the number 13: they are identical. Yet because of their context, you saw one as a letter and one as a number. Does this tendency to judge stimuli according to their context also apply to the judgment of people? It would seem so.

Maslow and Mintz (1956) had subjects inspect pictures of people's faces to judge whether the people were energetic or fatigued, displeased or in a state of well-being, and so on. The subjects performed this experiment either in a room that resembled a maintenance man's untidy closet or in an attractive, comfortable study.

Significantly more faces were rated as showing energy and well-being when the subjects were in the beautiful room than when they judged the photos in the ugly room. In this experiment, context certainly made a great difference.

Aesthetic judgments are affected by context, as museum directors know when they display important works of art in the most appropriate surroundings. Moreover, people place a greater value on things that someone else (in this case, an art expert) obviously values highly.

Contrast

Attention is often drawn to stimuli that are in sharp contrast to nearby stimuli. *Contrast effects* depend entirely on the contexts in which stimuli occur. A large object stands out in the context of smaller objects (Figure 5.9); a small object may attract attention in the context of larger objects. Contrast effects can occur for all the senses.

Context particularly affects perception of color; how a color is perceived usually depends on other colors near it. Our perceptions of color change: a gray patch on white paper appears much darker than the same gray patch on black paper; red appears vivid in contrast to its complementary color, green; blue is vivid in contrast to yellow.

Adaptation level

One psychologist, H. Helson (1964), maintains that we tend to develop an *adaptation level* that acts as a standard against which we judge stimuli, that is, we measure stimuli against an adaptation to similar stimuli. To the person who has grown accustomed to lifting heavy weights, a medium-weight object will be perceived as relatively light.

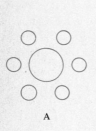

A

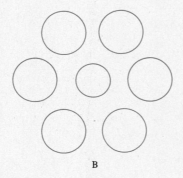

B

Figure 5.9   An illusion based on contrast effects. The surrounding circles in B make the central circle appear smaller than the central circle in A, even though the two are the same size. (After Lindgren and Byrne, 1961)

Figure 5.10A   These representations of objects create a retinal image. However, no meaning is given to each object by the retina. In order for the individual to recognize the object, the other part of the constancy relationship must be perceived. (Turn the page to discover what these objects are.) (Beckwith Studios)

PERCEPTUAL CONSTANCY

To cope successfully with our environment, we must see certain aspects of the environment as stable and unchanging. These are *perceptual constancies.* For example, if a man stands 40 feet from you, he forms an image on your retina that is exactly half the size of a retinal image of him when he is 20 feet away. But you perceive him to be a certain size whether he is 20 or 40 feet away. This is the *size-constancy* phenomenon. Like the other forms of perceptual constancy discussed in this section, it helps us maintain stable sensory images.

As we have seen, our perceptions of an object are not simple reflections of the retinal image of the object. You may perceive a tabletop as rectangular even though the angle of your vision may make it fall on the retina as a diamond shape. Look at the retinal images in Figure 5.10A. You will need more data if these stimuli are to be meaningful. Turn the page and look at Figure 5.10B. Now you can easily recognize what the objects in Figure 5.10A are.

Perception of an object is what we actually see combined with what we already know about the object. When we see a shape of a certain size or color, we perceive it in its true and constant appearance regardless of how an angle of vision distorts this true appearance. To sum up, perceptual constancy, insofar as it pertains to vision, is the phenomenon that characterizes the way we perceive an object as opposed to the object's retinal image. Perceptual constancy applies to our other sense organs as well.

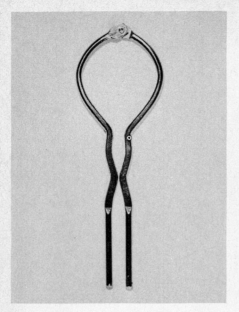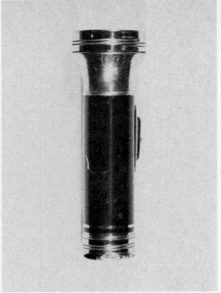

Figure 5.10B   The object on the right is a
flashlight; that on the left, a pair of pliers.
(Beckwith Studios)

Size constancy

We have said that known objects tend to be perceived at a constant size, no matter how far or
near. What occurs in the visual process to permit this perceptual adaptability? We know that
the retinal image alone gives no clue as to size
constancy, since the image size varies according
to the distance.

The pygmy who learned to see   Turnbull (1961) relates an interesting experience he had with a Bambuti pygmy in the Congo. The Bambuti rarely leave
their forest homes and so do not know of the existence of mountains. Turnbull, who had a pygmy guide
with him on a trip, took the guide up a mountain to
show him what it was like. The pygmy looked down,
saw a herd of buffalo, and asked what type of insect
they were! When Turnbull explained that they were
buffalo, the pygmy refused to believe him. As they
drove down the mountain, the pygmy watched in dis-

belief as the buffalo grew larger, claiming that this
was witchcraft. Gradually Turnbull was able to convince him of what was happening, and slowly
throughout the trip the pygmy learned to take distance, as well as retinal image, into account.
    Turnbull explains that because the pygmy had
lived in forests and had rarely looked over distances
greater than a few yards away, he was ignorant of
effects of distance on perception. Like us, he learned
to compensate for retinal image by taking distance
into account, something we have learned to do
through practice.

We rely, first of all, on our own experience
to perceive the true size of an object. When
we cannot estimate an object's distance from
other cues, our knowledge of its actual size helps
us gauge its distance. The perceiver must actually operate in two types of distance: *apparent*
distance and *real* distance. In determining the
size of an object, the individual considers its apparent distance.

Marital distance   "A woman is not easily fooled
about her husband." This rather tired maxim has
only recently been shown to be scientifically correct.

Figure 5.11A *The Ames Room. From left to right, we appear to be moving from a short man to a tall man. This illusion is created by the distortion of context (see Figure 5.11B). (William Vandivert)*

Figure 5.11B *This diagram illustrates how the room shown in Figure 5.11A, which looked like a square room, is actually constructed, and how the observer can be tricked. Note that the observer is required to peep at the entire scene with one eye; monocular vision further impairs distance and depth cues.*

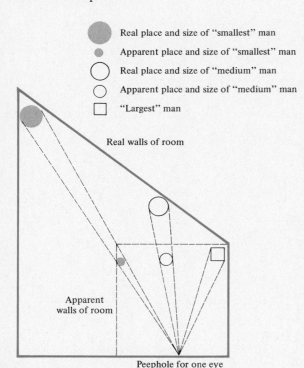

⬤ Real place and size of "smallest" man

• Apparent place and size of "smallest" man

◯ Real place and size of "medium" man

○ Apparent place and size of "medium" man

▢ "Largest" man

Real walls of room

Apparent walls of room

Peephole for one eye

In 1952, Wittreich had a woman look at her husband in the tilted room shown in Figure 5.11. She exclaimed, "Honey, that's a very funny room you are in. It's crooked." Thus, instead of receiving a distorted view of the person in the room, as is usually the case, this wife refused to distort her husband; rather, she saw a distorted room. This experiment was later tried with many other couples. It was found that couples will sooner distort the room than each other. This came to be called the *Honi phenomenon.*

This effect is usually explained as follows: we are accustomed to seeing people of different sizes, but are not accustomed to seeing rooms with crooked floors, walls, and ceilings. We will, therefore, tend to distort the person's size rather than the room's size. If, however, we know the person very well, we are less likely to distort his size. Thus, familiarity breeds . . . perceptual stability.

As seen in Figure 5.11A, size constancy may be distorted by context. An object that appears close to the perceiver (but is not) is perceived to be smaller in size than it actually is. In the context of the room, the apparent distance of each occupant from the perceiver is the same. The *real* distance, however, is *not* the same, because the far wall is angled in such a way that the small man is standing against a far corner, many feet away from the tall man in the near corner. Figure 5.11B provides an explanation of this perceptual illusion.

Shape constancy

Perceptual cues help maintain *shape constancy* in much the same way as size constancy. The actual shape projected onto the retina is the stimulus. To recognize the object, we must estimate the apparent tilt of the object and combine this estimation with what we see. Usually it is relatively easy to judge apparent tilt. The judgment depends largely on *texture, coloration,* and *density*. For example, the plate diagrammed in Figure 5.12 can easily be recognized and its shape constancy easily maintained. Misleading cues for apparent tilt may, however, produce an illusion.

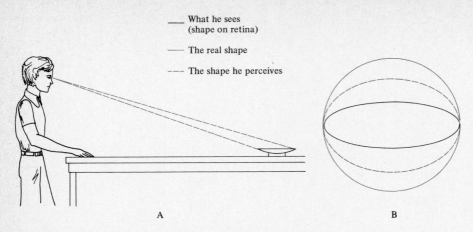

_____ What he sees
(shape on retina)

—— The real shape

- - - The shape he perceives

A

B

*Figure 5.12   When a subject observes a circular plate as in A, he perceives
a shape more like the real circle than like the ellipse that actually falls
on his retina. See B. His perception is determined by asking him to "draw
what he sees." (After Thouless, 1931)*

Brightness and color consistancy

Changes in illumination have relatively little
effect on our perceptions of the actual lightness
and darkness of objects. This phenomenon is
due to *brightness constancy*. A white shirt is
perceived to be the same shade of white in
bright sunlight as in the pale light of evening;
a lump of coal appears as black in daylight as in
the dim recesses of a coal cellar. Nonetheless,
the context in which objects are seen does contribute to constancy. If we look at the white
shirt or the lump of coal through a *reduction
screen*, a simple device made by punching a
quarter-inch hole in a piece of paper, we see that
the shirt is darker in the evening than by day,
and the coal looks blacker in the cellar than outdoors.

We stated in Chapter 4 that color is determined by the wavelength of light and that an
object is a certain color because it absorbs certain
light waves and reflects others. A camera reflects
color in an absolute way, as contrasted with how
we ourselves perceive colors. Photographed outdoors, a scarlet object will not appear to be the
same color as it is in a photograph taken indoors.

But when we look at an object, we perceive it
as the same color indoors or outdoors, because
we are familiar with it and compensate for the
varying intensities of light reflected from it at
different times in different places.

Effect of surroundings on color   Here is an experiment that you can do on your own.

First, obtain from any art supply shop (or perhaps from one of the school's art instructors) papers
of graded shades of gray. Then cut out squares of
each of the grays and smaller squares of a medium
gray. Place one medium-gray square in the middle
of each of the other squares. Show the squares to
your subjects and ask them to judge the shade of
the smaller squares. Depending on the shade of the
background gray, the smaller gray square will look
either darker or lighter to your subjects. Since the
smaller square is always a medium gray, what explains the difference?

To demonstrate the principle underlying this
phenomenon, carry your experiment a step further.
Place a small square of the lightest gray on a larger
square of the medium gray. Also, take a small square
of the medium gray and place that on a larger
square of darkest gray. Tack these to the wall or
place them on a table and ask subjects to judge
which small gray square is darker or lighter. Although the grays in this case are indeed different,
your subjects will think that they are the same.

Hans Wallach (1963) based his "ratio" theory of brightness constancy on these experiments. The actual lightness or darkness of an object, Wallach explains, is a property of the light reflected by the surface of that object. The perceived lightness and darkness of an object depends on the amount of light it, as well as its surroundings, reflect. Thus, a patch of gray on a dark background will look light because its background gives off little light. On a light background, that same patch will look dark because its background gives off more light. Therefore, the perceived brightness of a surface depends on the brightness ratio of the object to its background.

Thus, if two different surfaces are in the same ratio to their surroundings, they should appear to be of the same brightness. This, in fact, is what happened in the second part of your experiment. The two small patches are not the same, but since both surroundings are about twice as dark as the patches, the patches appear the same.

Thus, while a piece of paper is still white inside a coal mine, and a piece of coal is still black in the sunlight, the absolute brightness of both changes when the brightness of the surroundings changes. Also, even though the paper gives off less light in the cave, its surroundings give off still less.

ILLUSIONS

The term *illusion* derives from a Latin word that means "to mock" or "to make fun of." Incorrect perceptions that we call illusions are everyday occurrences. Each time we attend the movies, we seem to see three-dimensional scenes with people, animals, and objects in motion; what we are really seeing—what is being projected on our retinas—is actually a series of two-dimensional still pictures in rapid sequence.

The moon illusion Have you ever looked up at the moon when it is straight above you in the middle of the sky? How does it compare in size to the way it looks when it is ahead of you on the horizon? To most people, the moon appears much larger at the horizon than at the zenith, even though the moon always subtends the same visual angle (retinal image) to the eye. Psychologists call this the *moon illusion.*

Many theories have been offered to explain this illusion. The latest was offered by Restle (1970). Restle holds that we should consider the sky as the background against which we judge the size of the moon. Since at the horizon the sky is bounded by the earth, there is less sky at that point. Therefore, the background is smaller than when the moon is in the middle of the sky, which is a great expanse. We know that a circle drawn on an index card, which will look larger than the same circle drawn on a large poster, and that a football in your little brother's hands looks larger than one in a professional football player's hands. In both cases, a larger background makes the object look smaller. Thus, says Restle, the larger background at the zenith will in the same way make the moon seem smaller.

Figure 5.13 shows three well-known illusions. Item A is the Müller-Lyer illusion in which the line segments appear to be of different lengths but are actually the same length. Item B is the illusion of Ponzo. This is a very compelling illusion, for even after we are told

Figure 5.13   The three well-known illusions described in the text.

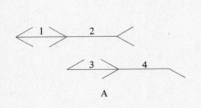
A

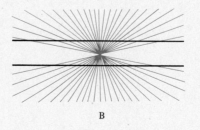
B

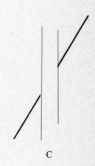
C

that the two horizontal lines are parallel, it is impossible to perceive them as parallel. This illusion is based on the principle of linear perspective described in the next section. Item C is the Poggendorff figure. The illusion is that the diagonal lines will not meet if extended through the two parallel vertical lines.

VISUAL PERCEPTION OF DEPTH

We perceive objects in the third dimension—depth—by means of fairly simple cues, for example, clarity and shading. Man has been investigating these cues for a long time. The prehistoric cave paintings in the Lascaux region of France are mute witnesses to human curiosity about depth perception. But not until this millennium did painters begin to display an accurate understanding of depth cues. Let us explore some ideas about depth perception.

Monocular depth cues are stimuli that operate independently on each eye. The simplest monocular cues arise directly from the stimulus patterns. Therefore, let us first consider the properties of the visual field as they contribute to depth perception. (Figure 5.14 diagrams the different monocular depth cues.)

1 Clearness—A clearly seen object appears closer and an unclear object further away. If you have looked across a dry desert at mountains, or looked at the bottom of that rarity, a clear pool of fresh water, you know how clarity affects distance.
2 Linear perspective—The further away two objects are in the visual field, the closer they will appear to be to each other. The converse is also true. Parallel lines, such as railroad tracks, provide a classic example; the lines appear to converge in the distance.
3 Interposition—An object partially blocked by another object seems further away than the obstructing object.

Figure 5.14   Examples of monocular depth cues: (A) clearness; (B) linear perspective; (C) interposition; (D) texture-density gradient.

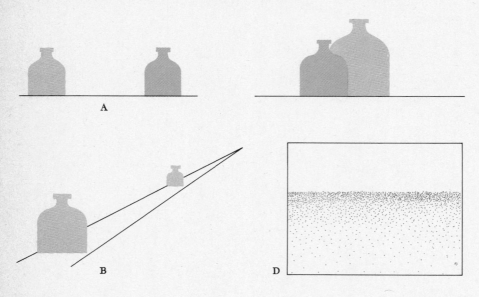

4 *Shading and shadows*—When a pattern of light creates shadows on objects, it generally makes further objects darker and nearer objects brighter.

5 *Texture-density gradients*—the more detailed and rougher textures give the impression of nearness, and finer textures, the impression of distance. The change in texture may be continuous and the changes in its gradations barely visible, but the overall impression of depth will be quite strong.

Monocular depth cues: accommodation

Accommodation is the role played by the muscles in and around the eye lens in monocular focusing. These muscles are responsible for the curvature of the lens. To enable the lens to focus on nearby objects, they make it rounder; to make it focus on objects further away, they flatten it. Since the lens muscles move in accordance with the distance of the objects in the field of vision, the kinesthetic sensations provide the individual with further monocular depth cues. We feel muscle strain in focusing on an object close by; we feel little muscle strain when we focus on faraway objects.

Binocular depth cues: retinal disparity

Binocular vision is far more important than monocular vision in depth perception. There are two major reasons: the first is *retinal disparity*. Retinal disparity means that the right and left eye each receive a different, or disparate, image. You can test this by looking at an object close to you. First cover the right eye, then the left. The position of the eyes will cause you to see one image slightly to the left and the other slightly to the right. The joining of the two geometrically inexact images produces true depth perception—even in the absence of *any* other monocular or binocular depth cue.

The distance between the object and the eye is a factor in retinal disparity. The closer the object, the more unlike the images. A faraway object will produce only slight retinal dis-

parity, since both eyes focus almost identically on distant objects.

Binocular depth cues: convergence

Convergence is the joining of the different images produced by retinal disparity so that a single image is seen. Here the binocular cue is a kinesthetic sensation similar to accommodation in monocular vision. The eye muscles involved in convergence turn the eyes to focus together on close objects. But if the object is too close, the two images remain separate, because the eyes cannot converge. This results in the familiar "cross-eyed" sensation.

The stereoscope A *stereoscope* is a device through which two separate one-dimensional objects, each projected on a different eye, seem to be coming from one three-dimensional image upon which the eyes are converged. This is accomplished by distorting the rays coming to the two eyes from the two different objects so that they seem to come from only one object.

The rays can be distorted by placing prisms in front of the two eyes. These prisms will bend all light rays coming to the eyes, so that two different one-dimensional objects will look as if they are coming from one three-dimensional object.

There is an interesting demonstration of stereoscopic vision that you can easily do by yourself. Take a piece of exposed film or colored glass and place it over one eye while someone swings a pendulum in front of you, back and forth on a frontal plane only. As you look at it, the pendulum will appear to be moving in an ellipse! This is known as the *Pulfrich phenomenon.*

We usually explain this phenomenon by noting that the two eyes seem to be stimulated at different times by the pendulum; this is due to the filter over one eye. Thus, it is as if two different objects are stimulating each eye. The eyes, however, resolve the different rays as coming in from the same point in space, causing apparent motion through an ellipse.

Conflicting depth cues

Monocular and binocular depth cues usually operate simultaneously and harmoniously. Various combinations of cues provide us with an ongoing series of depth and spatial perceptions. However, experiments have shown that sometimes the depth cues conflict (Figure 5.15). This occurs when conditions of perception are unfavorable, as when light stimulation is inadequate or unusual; in spatial situations where completely unfamiliar relationships are created; and under conditions of weightlessness, as experienced by astronauts in space. Here men learning to function in a new spatial atmosphere must develop new sets of estimations for position, distance, and luminescence. As we will see later, man is extremely quick to learn and adjust to new sensory orientations.

Figure 5.15 *Conflicting depth cues can result in distortion of perception. The straw appears to hit the water, disappear, and reappear along a different diagonal. The top half of the straw appears to be farther away from us than the bottom half.* (Beckwith Studios)

AUDITORY PERCEPTION OF DISTANCE AND DIRECTION

To a great extent, depth perception is also a function of the auditory sense. Both distance and direction can be accurately perceived by the sense of hearing alone. There is evidence, in fact, that hearing without vision is more acute than it is with vision. Each of our senses probably becomes keener when it cannot depend on the help of other senses. The blind man usually has an extremely keen sense of hearing (he can hear the slight movements of a person nearby), while the deaf man develops an acute sense of vision (he reads lips and sees slight, soundless movements). In the absence of visual cues, your perception of sound becomes much fuller, music seems to be more powerful, and human voices reveal more tonal quality.

There are two significant differences in the use of auditory and visual cues to perceive distance or direction. In the perception of distance, vision usually requires *binocular* cues for true distance perception, while audition requires *monaural* cues. When perceiving direction, the situation is somewhat reversed: *binaural* cues are necessary for audition, and *monocular* cues

for vision. In other words, two eyes and one ear are needed to perceive distance, but one eye and two ears are needed to perceive direction.

Perception of distance

We estimate the distance of a sound primarily by its loudness and to some extent by its clarity. Loud, clear sounds are perceived to be nearby, and weak or indistinct sounds are usually heard as being far away. This does not always produce an accurate gauge of distance. If an object—such as a wall—intervenes between the source of the sound and the receiver, the sound source will obviously appear to be further away than if there were no obstruction.

Perception of direction

As already pointed out, both ears are needed to perceive the direction of a sound. This is a fairly complex process, usually involving at least three types of cues to produce accurate perception. In each case, the cues will not work if the sound is directly above, behind, or in front of the listener; the listener is always making adaptive movements of head and body to be in the position most receptive to sound direction. Let us examine these cues.

Time differential   Because the ears are on opposite sides of the head, a sound wave (traveling at 1,100 feet per second) coming from either side will reach one ear before it reaches the other (Figure 5.16). Although only a split second is involved, this *time differential* permits the hearer to gauge the directions of the sound source.

Intensity differential   When a sound originates on one side of the head, the full strength of the sound wave penetrates the ear on that side. The *intensity* diminishes by the time the sound is heard by the other ear. Much of the sound wave is detoured by the head itself, which acts as a

sound shadow, absorbing some of the sound's intensity. Because of this reduction in intensity, the individual can generally locate sound direction within an angle of 20°.

Ripple   The wave character of sound, including its familiar ripple (phase differences), was described in Chapter 4. The ear on the same side as the sound source usually picks up one part of the ripple, and the ear on the other side picks up a different part. This gives the listener still another means of identifying the direction of the sound.

THE PERCEPTION OF MOTION

In physics, "motion" generally refers to the change of an object's position in space. In psychology, the word "motion" is used to refer to the successive stimulation of different areas of the retina. But the perception of motion is not always caused by changes in the location of retinal excitation; some motion perception comes from the rapid presentation of fixed stimuli (for example, movies). This *apparent motion* has occasioned great interest in psychologists who study the perception of motion.

Figure 5.16   Sound waves that reach a perceiver from one side (rather than from front or rear) are perceived first at the closest ear, then travel around the head to the farthest ear. In the path around the head, part of the sound is absorbed by the shadow and a lower intensity of sound is perceived by this shadowed ear.

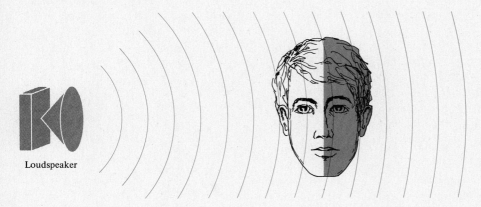

Loudspeaker

Apparent motion

Apparent motion is the perception of motion when the stimuli involved are not actually moving. It is a common experience, one that shows that what we perceive does not simply mirror whatever reaches our sense organs. For example, if we are sitting in a train and the train on nearby tracks is moving, it sometimes seems as though we are moving.

Phi phenomenon If you arrange two spots of light in a totally darkened room and then illuminate them alternately, you can create what appears to be a single light moving from one position to another. This effect is known as the *phi phenomenon*. It is the kind of motion we perceive in neon-light signs having arrows that appear to move. For motion to be perceived under such circumstances, the illumination must be of a certain *intensity*; the lights must be a certain *distance* apart; and the *time interval* must be correct.

Stroboscopic motion The movement we perceive in motion pictures and television is the result of the presentation of separate visual stimuli, each slightly different, in rapid succession. The perception of motion in such cases depends on *visual persistence*, brief afterimages that remain when the stimulus is removed. Rapid presentation permits the successive individual stimuli to be organized into a perception of smooth motion.

Induced motion Watch the sun "pass behind" a cloud. The sun appears to be in motion, although in fact it is the clouds that are moving. In the framework of the sky, we perceive the clouds as the ground and the sun as the figure. Our vision erroneously tells us that the figure is moving through the ground.

Direction of induced motion Wallach (1959), a psychologist of the Gestalt tradition, demonstrated that induced motion was a product of the relationship of a figure to its surroundings, or a *figure-ground relationship*.

Wallach illustrated his point by placing a dot inside a rectangle. When the rectangle was moved to one side, the subjects "saw" the dot move in the opposite direction, while the rectangle appeared to remain motionless. When a circle was placed around the rectangle, the subjects thought they saw both the rectangle and the dot move, for the rectangle was then surrounded by the circle.

To demonstrate that induced motion occurs also in directions other than those opposite to the actual movement of the surroundings, Wallach moved the circle downward and the rectangle to the right. The subjects "saw" the rectangle move diagonally up to the right and the dot diagonally up to the left.

Autokinetic motion A fourth type of perceived motion occurs when we have too few cues and these cues conflict. Known as *autokinetic motion*, this perception involves only one stimulus. If you sit in a darkened room and stare at one continuously shining spot of light, you will soon see it move in different directions, at different speeds. No matter what you *know* about the light source, you will continue to see it as being in motion. Asked to point to the light source, you will probably discover, once the room has been brightened, that you were wrong.

Having too few visual cues, you lost your frame of reference for perceiving the light because there were virtually no boundaries to support the image. If one or more additional spots were presented with the original spot of light, the spots would remain stationary—because the introduction of the other spots would provide the boundaries needed to keep the image stable.

Night pilots without cues Because a pilot flying at night has few visual cues in the sky ahead, the danger of his having an accident is far greater than during the day. Suppose, for example, that his only cue in the dark sky is one star directly in front of him. After a while, because of the autokinetic effect, the star will appear to move. The pilot may decide that this means one of two things: (1) his plane is moving without his control; or (2) there is another plane out there. In either case, he may make corrections to put himself back on the straight course that he actually never left. These corrections are potentially dangerous, for they may cause the pilot to make the wrong move at the wrong time.

EFFECTS OF LEARNING
AND DEVELOPMENT ON PERCEPTION

Perception plays an important role in behavior and, like the other behaviors we have discussed, is determined by an individual's biological makeup and experiences. Let us consider the effects of learning, innate factors, and maturation on perception—remembering that they are by no means easy to separate.

Scientists still disagree about which is more important in perception, innate factors or learning. Gestalt psychologists emphasize a *nativist* position, arguing that we are born with certain fundamental perceptual abilities. The *empiricist* position favored by others (Brunswick, 1956; Ittelson and Kilpatrick, 1952) emphasizes the influence of previous experience. However, less and less attention is being given to the nativism versus empiricism issue. There is more interest today in studying the variables that affect the development of perception.

The constancies

Studies indicate that 8-year-old children do not show the same degree of size constancy as do adults (Zeigler and Liebowitz, 1957). Adults tend to perceive objects at their real size as far as 100 feet away, but 8-year-old youngsters perceive the same objects as smaller than life-size at this distance. This suggests that size constancy develops through learning. Shape constancy and brightness constancy effects are slower to occur in children than size constancy effects. Children tend to use the most obvious cues available and may ignore context or other stimuli that influence the perception of constancy. Their perceptions depend more on the stimulus itself. A trap-ezoidal shape is perceived as trapezoidal, not rectangular. A white shirt in dim light is perceived as less white than one in bright light.

Pattern and depth perception

Maturation (particularly of the sense organs) and heredity also play a part in perception. Whether or not some perceptions are hereditary (innate) is less clear, and the answers have been sought through systematic experimentation. There is evidence that infants perceive patterns as early as 5 days after birth and show preferences for patterns that resemble the human face.

Children respond to the most distinctive stimuli in a pattern of stimuli. Given a complex pattern, they perceive its simple features. Wohlwill (1960) points out that whenever a stimulus pattern can be perceived in different ways—as, for example, in an ambiguous drawing —the young child will see the easiest percept. For instance, a 4-year-old child will have great difficulty in finding a figure that is embedded in another figure (see Figure 5.5). His eyes are held by the continuous lines and he does not perceive the less organized parts.

Experiments with infants who are between 6 and 14 months old offer evidence for very early depth perception, however. A typical testing device is the *visual cliff*, which presents an illusion of depth (Figure 5.17). The device is a raised platform, half patterned surface, and half glass. Under the glass half, a sharp drop in the patterned surface produces the perception of a cliff. The infant placed on the shallow patterned side is called to the deep side but will not cross, even when he feels the solid glass beneath him. Clearly, he perceives depth.

Deprivation of stimuli

To distinguish between learned and innate perceptions, psychologists have isolated newborn infants from certain stimuli and have then tested for their immediate perception of these stimuli. These experiments have produced some evi-

Figure 5.17 The visual cliff, a device that tests depth perception in infants and animals. For an explanation, see the text. (William Vandivert)

dence that perception depends in part on inherited perceptual abilities.

Rats totally deprived of light were found, when light was provided, to be capable of leaping a specific distance through space from one raised platform to another to obtain food. This indicated that the rats could use light to define space regardless of their lack of previous experience with this stimulus. Cats deprived of light, however, do not respond immediately to visual cues when light is introduced; they require a period of learning.

When chimpanzees are deprived of sensory experience, they do not develop certain perceptual abilities. For example, chimpanzees raised with restraints on their hands and feet are unable to learn simple sensations of touch when freed. After release from their bonds, they are unable to discriminate among tactile stimuli administered to their freed arms and legs. These findings remind us of the critical period concept (see Chapter 2).

Several interesting but inconclusive studies have been made of human beings born blind who received normal vision through surgery later in life. After spending years in a sightless world, the newly sighted could not make sense of the visual environment. They could not discriminate among patterns and shapes, or perceive depth and form. They had to relearn all their auditory and tactile associations to accommodate their new visual frame of reference.

Sensory distortion

Experiments with special goggles that invert and reverse the visual image show that we adapt to such dramatic visual distortion and can very quickly begin to respond appropriately. Snyder and Pronko (1952) repeated an experiment done in 1897 by Stratton. They had a subject wear a set of *anamorphic* lenses (lenses that invert and reverse the retinal image), and they observed his behavior and received descriptions of how he reacted. They found that there is an initial period of confusion during which the subject reaches to his left for an object on his right and reaches upward for an object at his feet. But this kind of confusion gives way to a series of adjustments leading to very accurate visual and motor coordination.

Seeing is believing This old maxim is supported by current research in the area of perception.

Rock (1966) has described an interesting experiment conducted in his laboratory. A subject wore a pair of glasses whose prisms distorted vision so that straight lines appeared to be curved. The subject was then shown a straight wooden board and told to run his hands back and forth over it. Only after a while could he say whether the board was straight or curved. Although the subject was running his hands over a straight board, he said that he felt a curved board and that the board must, therefore, be curved.

It seems that, even when all other evidence is to the contrary, we believe what our sight tells us. Sight can affect the discoveries of our other senses.

Some investigators interpret such findings as indicating that a change in visual perception can occur. According to Ivo Kohler (1964), the subject's visual perception adapts; his vision, and thus his behavior, are reoriented. He comes to see the reversed, upside down world as "normal," "natural," and "familiar." Other investigators take a different view of this form of visual distortion. Harris (1965), for example, holds that when vision and position provide contradictory information, it is the position sense that changes. The subject still sees the world as upside down and reversed, but he comes to make postural adjustments to compensate for these reversals. He moves his hand when he reaches for an object by responding to the feedback provided by his *proprioceptive sense* (response of internal stimuli); the sense organs thus pick up muscle movements. According to Harris, the adaptation occurs because position perception is flexible; it responds to environmental demands, more so than does visual perception.

Auditory cues, too, can be reversed. This can be demonstrated in an experiment using an instrument called a *pseudophone*. The pseudophone covers each of the subject's ears with a tube that opens at the opposite ear. A sound cue from the left side of the head reaches the right ear, and vice versa. The individual must learn to look to the left when he hears a sound from the right. Within a few days, he makes this adjustment.

EFFECTS OF MOTIVATION ON PERCEPTION

"You see only what you want to see" has often been said as a reproach. The fact is that an individual's perceptions may indeed be colored by his motivations. Stimuli are perceived in terms of our drives, interests, and values. Our dog is the best-looking canine in the dog show, win or lose. A woman sees only her child's beauty, only her father's wit. A sailor is much more receptive to slight changes in weather than is a landlubber.

An examination of the effect of various values on perception provides clues to the relation between motivation and perception. Money, for instance, is a highly valued stimulus, consistently coming out ahead among objects that elicit attention and cooperation (as might be expected). Experiments with money show that individuals often perceive a high-value object as larger than it actually is. Children have demonstrated this. When asked to match a spot of light to the size of a certain coin, poor children tended to match the coin with a light spot much larger than the coin. Rich children, who need money less, identified a light spot that was closer to the actual size of the coin.

Perception and social pressure Social pressure, in large enough doses, can make most people change their opinions on an issue. Asch (1955) showed that our perceptions as well can be molded by society.

A group of subjects sitting around a table were presented with two cards; one had three lines drawn on it, and the other, one line. Subjects were to pick out the one line of the three that was equal in length to the line on the other card. One of the subjects seated at the table did not know that the other "subjects" were actually accomplices of the experimenter. These subjects would consistently and unanimously give the wrong answer to each comparison of lines. Asch was trying to determine whether the subject, in order to be agreeable to the others, would yield to group pressure and pick the wrong line. Or would he remain independent and pick the line that he himself believed equal to the single line on the other card?

In a situation of this sort, subjects are expected to make errors in judgment less than 1 percent of the time, but in this case wrong judgments that conformed to group pressure were given 36 percent of the time. Thus, social pressure clearly was shown to influence perception, as reported by the subjects.

Other sources of motivation have been studied, and the findings support the general view that motivation affects perception. Hungry people perceive food-related stimuli readily; thirsty people keenly perceive water.

Other motivations besides value affect perception. Man's need to reduce the ambiguity in his perception of the world around him is a strong motivator. He prefers structured to unstructured situations. This intolerance of ambiguity seems to be related to anxiety, for it has been found that anxious subjects are more likely to perceive closure in ill-defined objects than are nonanxious subjects. The anxious are more prone to fill in the gaps in incomplete pictures.

The intolerance of ambiguity Frenkel-Brunswick (1949) showed subjects a series of pictures that gradually changed from one clear percept to another, for example, from a dog to a cat. Midway through the series, the pictures were very ambiguous, and some subjects were quite willing to make such statements as "It might be a dog or a cat, but I am not sure what it is." However, other subjects who were evidently unable to tolerate ambiguity tended to cling to one percept until the other percept became very clear, and at that point they would switch to the new percept. These subjects preferred to be wrong part of the time rather than to accept an ambiguous percept as simply ambiguous.

Since most of us wish to behave in socially acceptable ways, we frequently perceive situations in the way that we imagine someone expects us to. This is very apparent in experimental situations in which human subjects act in a manner that they think will be acceptable to the experimenter.

Studies of the perception of socially unacceptable words reveal our motivation to behave acceptably. In one experiment, obscenities and neutral words were recited in the same series; tests showed that the subjects recognized and remembered fewer obscenities. The subjects also tended to be uneasy when the obscenities were recited. (This uneasiness was measured by the *galvanic skin reflex*, a measure of the sweat gland activity in the palms.)

CONSCIOUSNESS

Scientific psychology began with the study of sensation and perception in an attempt to analyze consciousness. With the advent of behaviorism, the problem of consciousness was temporarily put aside. Behaviorists preferred to deal directly with objective behavior and to leave the issue of consciousness to philosophers. Recent developments in psychology, however, have led to a renewal of interest in consciousness and its various states.

Consciousness may be thought of in terms of the awareness of one's own internal processes. We are conscious when we can perceive our own thoughts and feelings and can report, at least to ourselves, what our internal stimuli mean. Consciousness is a continuum, for there are degrees of consciousness. We can be highly conscious, less conscious, minimally conscious, or unconscious. There are also probably degrees of unconsciousness; and some theorists, such as Freud (see Chapter 12), have attributed considerable importance to the role of unconscious activity.

The states or degrees of consciousness undergo changes in the normal course of a day. There may be times during the day when a person is sharply aware of his inner processes, and other times when he is less aware. Upon awakening from a night's sleep, we are still partially drowsy and are less aware of our thoughts and feelings than after we have had our breakfast coffee. As the day wears on, we may experience periods of drowsiness or boredom and are again less aware than when we are wide awake. And then as we approach sleep once again, our awareness diminishes. Most of us tend to maintain such regular patterns of sleep and wakefulness.

Biological clocks Sleep-waking cycles are relatively constant; we sleep for approximately the same periods of time in each 24-hour cycle, and we are awake for approximately the same period from cycle to cycle. While the cycles persist in most situations, they may be modified somewhat if the individual's environment is changed drastically—for example, if he moves to the Arctic, where darkness prevails for 20 hours of a winter's day and daylight remains for 20 hours of a summer's day.

The sleep-waking rhythms of man and lower animals depend in part on internal events, often referred to as the *biological clock*. Aschoff (1965) reports that human beings who are deprived of time cues because of isolation from the outside world continue to show regular sleep-waking cycles. The isolated subject initially retains the cycle he had when he lived normally in the outside world. After a period of adjustment, the subject's cycle of sleep and waking and other biological rhythms, such as urine excretion and body temperatures, become remarkedly regular.

Sleep

One end of the continuum of consciousness is occupied by the state we know as sleep. Sleep has been analyzed into four stages, with dreams occurring during stage 1. Figure 5.18 shows the distinctive electrical patterns recorded by the electroencephalograph (EEG) as characteristic

Figure 5.18   EEG characteristics during the four stages of sleep. (W. Dement and N. Kleitman, Cyclic variations in EEG during sleep and their relation to eye movements, body motility, and dreaming. Electroencephalography and Clinical Neurophysiology, 1957, 9, 373–390, Figure 2)

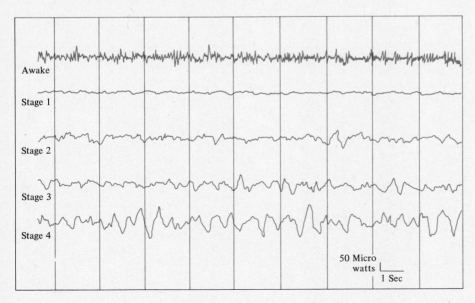

of each sleep stage. During stages 1 and 2, the sleeper is more responsive to external stimuli than during stages 3 and 4. As sleep becomes deeper, the sleeping person is relatively unresponsive to external events. During stage 1, visual dreaming may take place; when this happens, the stage 1 period is marked by the presence of *rapid eye movements* (REMs).

Figure 5.19 shows the stages of sleep during a 7-hour sleep period. This figure indicates that the sleeper frequently goes from one stage to another. Stage 2 is most prevalent and stage 1—REM sleep (dreaming)—occurs most often in the last half of the sleep period.

According to the EEG pattern, stage 1 is a period of relatively light sleep; but when REMs occur, it is difficut to awaken the sleeper. REM sleep is sometimes called *paradoxical sleep* because the EEG indicates that there is cortical activity and yet the sleeper does not easily awaken. Roffwarg, Muzio, and Dement (1966) suggest that the REM sleep serves as a source of internally developed stimulation. According to their hypothesis, dreaming may be some form of internal perception.

Active sleep Most of us think that deep sleep is a completely restful state. Several experiments have made psychologists doubt this very much. In these experiments, EEG recordings were obtained from subjects in different stages of activity and sleep. When the subjects were in a transitional state between wide awake and asleep, the EEG changes indicated a variation from much activity in the brain to little activity. As the subject slipped into a deep sleep (so defined by difficulty in waking the subjects), the EEG recordings indicated the same sizable amount of activity as in the waking state.

Dement and Kleitman (1957) found that when sleep is characterized by "active-type" EEG recordings, there are also rapid eye movements. Subjects reported dreaming more often and could remember dreams much better when awakened in the rapid-eye-movement stage than in the no-eye-movement stage. Analyzing the dream content, Dement and Kleitman also found that eye movement is related to dream activity. Thus, a subject who reported dreaming that he was climbing a ladder and looking up and down also showed vertical (up-down) eye movements during sleep.

REMs and dreaming

Most dreams are primarily visual, and the presence of REMs suggests that there may be a direct relationship between the eye movements and the recalled dream. Recorded eye movements of sleeping subjects have been found to correspond to their reported dreams (Roffwarg, Dement, Muzio, and Fuher, 1962). For example, one subject reported dreaming of walking up steps, and the eye movements recorded just before he was awakened showed clear up-

Figure 5.19 Stages of sleep across a night. Dotted lines show periods of Stage 1—REM. (From W. B. Webb, Sleep: an experimental approach. Reprinted with permission of Macmillan Publishing Co., Copyright © 1968 by Wilse B. Webb)

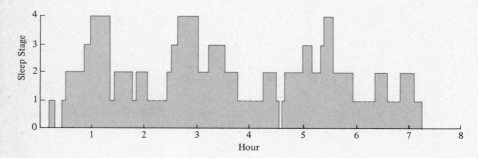

ward motions of the eyes. All REMs do not indicate visual dreaming, however. Cats whose visual cortices have been removed and newborn infants (who cannot yet see clearly) show REM sleep.

Sleep and memory Many psychologists have long suspected a relationship between sleep and memory, although the evidence has been somewhat contradictory. A recent experiment by Fowler, Sullivan, and Ekstrand (1973) attempts to clarify some earlier sources of confusion. Their findings indicate that deep stage-4 sleep, which occurs largely in the first half of each night, substantially facilitates the consolidation of memory, whereas dream-filled REM sleep, which occurs largely in the second half of each night, is far less effective in this respect.

Their experimental subjects were awakened either as they began to fall asleep or after they had slept soundly for 4 hours. On awakening, some subjects were required to learn paired-associate words and paired visual forms, while others were asked to learn lists of high-imagery or low-imagery words. Subjects were then allowed to go back to bed for 3½ hours, at which time they were again awakened for recall sessions. Control subjects in all conditions learned similar material with no prior sleep and a 3½-hour normally active interval between learning and recall.

Those who were awakened early and whose 3½-hour interval was filled with a large proportion of stage-4 sleep (as measured by monitoring devices) forgot far less of their material than either of the other groups. Those who were awakened later, and whose 3½ hour sleep included a large proportion of REM sleep, remembered their material somewhat better than the fully awake controls, although the differences were not nearly so conclusive as for the "early risers."

One possible explanation is that sleep of any sort prohibits other stimuli from impinging upon subjects so that there is less interference in the memory process. Even more speculative is the possibility that the stimulation and activity experienced during REM sleep itself serves as interference for the memory process.

The available evidence indicates that the dreaming person moves his eyes around imagined visual stimuli. His dream perceptions are apparently based on symbolic images rather than objectively identifiable stimuli, while the dream itself may incorporate some identifiable stimulus. For example, the sound of a siren may lead a sleeping person to dream that he is on a fire engine rushing to a fire. His dream perception is similar to other forms of perception in that it organizes stimulus input into something more than a collection of stimuli. The input becomes meaningful in some fashion.

Dreamlike sequences What is the nature of the dreamlike sequences people often experience as they are falling asleep or sleeping lightly? Are they sufficiently similar to the traditional (REM-period) dreams that they should be considered real dreams? Or are they qualitatively different and therefore on a lower level than REM dreams? Foulkes and Vogel (1965) recently reported that the two are more similar than previously believed.

In their experiment, subjects came to the laboratory at their normal bedtime, dressed for bed, were equipped with facial and scalp electrodes, and went to sleep in a darkened room for several hours. Each time the experimenters' monitoring equipment revealed one of the initial phases of sleep, however, the subject was awakened and asked to describe whatever he had been experiencing (if anything) just before being aroused. After inquiry, the subject was permitted to go back to sleep, only to be reawakened during subsequent drowsiness or falling off to sleep. Each subject participated in four experimental sessions, totaling about 25 observations per subject.

Foulkes and Vogel report that 95 percent of all observations contained reports of some experience of imagery—mostly visual, mostly without any strong accompanying emotional feeling, often absorbing enough to engender a sense of action "really" happening, and mostly including the hallucination of the subject's own active participation. In addition, the experimenters found these light-sleep (hypnagogic) dreams to be very similar to REM dreams.

Who dreams?

Webb (1968) reports that everyone dreams. His laboratory observations indicate that dreams occur on the average of from one to six times per night for a total duration of about 1½ hours. He found that every subject showed some evidence of dreaming, but that the rate of forgetting was very fast. About 80 to 90 percent of the subjects reported dreams if they were awakened while they showed signs of dreaming. Only

10 percent of subjects who were awakened 5 minutes after showing the signs of dreaming recalled their dreams, and their recall was usually fragmentary.

Recall 10 minutes after a REM period is very rare. If you remember a dream when you awaken in the morning, it is probably because you awoke during or just after the dream.

ALTERED STATES OF CONSCIOUSNESS

The renewal of interest in the study of consciousness comes, in part, from curiosity about altered states of consciousness. Much attention is being given today to the techniques of drug-induced changes of awareness, the methods of meditation, and the age-old problem of hypnosis and its effects.

Drugs

Man has used drugs medicinally since the beginning of recorded history. He has also experimented with drugs to find ways to change his relationship to his environment or, as he often puts it, "to expand his mind." These subjective experiments always have in common the search for something—for some ecstasy of experience, some new dimension. This search reflects a desire on the part of some to increase perception or perceive more vividly, perhaps to be more creative or to gain understanding. For others, drugs have been used to cloud or reduce perception, perhaps to blot out reality or escape from disturbing stimulation. In each case, the individual seeks to alter his consciousness through the use of drugs.

The hallucinogens Drugs such as LSD (lysergic acid diethylamide) and mescaline have been found to produce strange and unreal perceptions similar to *hallucinations*. The distorted or exaggerated perception induced by these drugs is not, however, a typical hallucination. Hallucinations are imaginary perceptions that are regarded by the subject as real. (He sees a wolf although there is no wolf there.) The drug-induced images, on the other hand, are usually recognized as unreal by the subject. The typical perceptual phenomena include strange changes in the size and shape of objects, very vivid color experiences, and often dancing or undulating patterns of lights or dots. Many people feel "a new awareness of the physical beauty of the world" (Barron, Jarvik, and Bunnell, 1964).

The imagery that takes place is not confined to changes in visual perception. Auditory effects occur, and there are often dramatic changes in the perception of time. The drug-influenced subject sometimes experiences a feeling of separation from time; time does not change for him.

Barron and his colleagues also reported that drug-induced perceptions are not always pleasant. Disturbing or depressing sensations of gloom and "emptiness" may occur. Bad reactions ("bad trips") are more frequent than was first realized, and it is now clear that unsupervised experimentation with the hallucinogens is dangerous. Some individuals experience reactions to LSD or mescaline that are so overwhelming as to require intensive professional treatment.

Marijuana The drugs derived from the hemp plant—marijuana and its stronger form, hashish—are well known for their consciousness-altering properties. The effects of these drugs are less dramatic than those of LSD or mescaline, but they do produce changes in perception and perceptual sensitivity. Colors appear brighter and more vivid; sounds seem fuller; and time sometimes appears to stand still. The subject often feels relaxed and may experience a drifting or floating feeling.

There is considerable public controversy over the use of marijuana. It has been argued that the drug may be addictive; that it leads its users to hard drugs such as heroin; that it incites people to violence; and that it causes behavior pathology. None of these allegations has been supported by evidence (Grinspoon, 1969). It is clear, however, that marijuana, like alcohol, is often used regularly by people who are seeking to escape from personal frustration or from feelings of inadequacy. They use the drug to ease their frustrations and blot out their feelings of discomfort. Use of the drug is less of a social problem than are the stresses that have widened its popularity.

Methaqualone In the early 1970s, drug manufacturers began to market methaqualone, a sedative hypnotic (sleep inducer), as a prescription drug for insomnia. Methaqualone pills were widely picked up by the youth culture as a means of reducing anxiety and producing pleasurable calm. Interest was further boosted by the misguided belief that the pills were aphrodisiac. Commonly called "sopors," they were at first less expensive than other drugs and easily available at the local pharmacy. Many users who began with 1 or 2 pills a day worked up to 15 and 20 as they developed a tolerance for the drug, which led to hospitalization in numerous cases and sometimes death, especially when the pills were taken with alcohol. As a result, druggists restricted the sale of methaqualone severely, and scores of users turned to black market distributors.

While methaqualone was originally reported to be nonaddictive, its full effect on the human body is now controversial. Recent findings indicate that methaqualone may be addictive; that it affects the central nervous system, causing a slowdown of the response mechanisms and respiration; and that it may build up in the nervous system with damaging results. Unlike heroin, methaqualone, taken in overdose, may send the individual into convulsions; like heroin, abuse of this drug produces destructive consequences that may eventually lead to death.

Meditation

It has been shown that altered states of consciousness can be produced through meditation. Practitioners of Zen Buddhism are known to develop states of meditation in which their EEGs indicate thorough relaxation (Wallace and Benson, 1972). Other investigators have found that yogis are able to induce in themselves states in which they are minimally responsive to stimuli. These special states of consciousness are usually produced by means of exercises involving relaxation and concentration. In the technique known as *transcendental meditation* (Mahesh Yogi, 1969), the subject sits crosslegged and proceeds to attend to a selected stimulus, a sound or a thought. As he does this, he is to allow his mind to be "free." This is not so easy to accomplish as it may seem. But those who have mastered the technique report that they experience a highly pleasurable state in which they rise to a "finer and more creative level" of thinking and perceiving.

Wallace and Benson point out that subjects in a transcendental meditation state do not appear to be physiologically similar to persons who are asleep or under hypnosis. The physiological activity represents a state of quiescence in which the subject is awake, thoroughly relaxed, yet responsive to his inner stimuli. It is a kind of heightened consciousness in the absence of tension. Recently, transcendental meditation has been put to use in treating drug addicts and other disorders based on psychological disturbances.

Hypnosis

Hypnosis involves the use of verbal suggestion to produce a trance or dreamlike state. There are a variety of techniques used by hypnotists to induce (bring on) the hypnotic state. Most induction procedures generally include the following three features:

1 a preliminary orientation designed to put the subject at ease and to remove any fears that he may have about the procedure;
2 use of some stimulus, an object or a sound, on which the subject can focus his attention;
3 repeated suggestion to the subject that he feels comfortable and relaxed and that he is to think of nothing but what the hypnotist is saying.

As the induction proceeds, the hypnotist usually tests the subject to determine whether relaxation is occurring. For example, he may lift the subject's arm and then let go—if the subject is relaxed, the arm will fall limply.

The hypnotized subject does not go to sleep. The subject may become drowsy and may even doze for a moment or so, but he is not sleeping when the hypnotic induction is successfully completed.

The scientific study of hypnosis has had to contend with an aura of magic and mystery that has long enveloped this phenomenon. The notion of trances and trancelike states has suggested to some that the hypnotized subject is in some separate mental world. It has also been believed that under hypnosis subjects somehow develop superhuman powers and that their ability to remember long-forgotten events and to ignore pain is well beyond normal human capacity. Recent research (Orne, 1959; O'Connell, Shor, and Orne, 1968) has shown that these beliefs about hypnosis are incorrect. The actions of hypnotized subjects were compared to those of subjects who were simply told to act as if they were hypnotized, and it was found that there was nothing that the hypnotized subjects could do that those who were not hypnotized could not also do. The acting subject withstood pain, behaved as if he were a dog, a child, or a monkey, and did as well as the hypnotized subject on any other assigned task.

Hypnosis and relief of pain The potential pain-relieving benefits of hypnotic suggestion have long intrigued medical science. To what extent, if any, hypnotic suggestion can act as a better pain killer than other means of psychological persuasion has been seriously debated for much of the last century. McGlashan, Evans, and Orne (1969), however, argue that there are two components to pain-reducing hypnotic suggestion: one which affects subjects in a very general way, somehow reducing tension or "convincing" them that their pain is lessened—much like the experience of reduced pain in subjects who believe that a fake drug (a *placebo*) administered to them is a strong pain reliever; and another, induced during deep hypnosis, which actually distorts some people's perceptions of pain.

To test their hypothesis, these investigators selected subjects who were either highly susceptible or unsusceptible to hypnosis. Each subject was asked to perform a painful task three times—once with no "pain reliever," once under hypnotic suggestion that they would feel no pain, and once after being given a fake "pain-relieving drug." The results indicated that the unsusceptible subjects under placebo and hypnotic suggestion and the susceptible subjects under the placebo condition experienced a slight degree of pain reduction. Half of the highly susceptible participants, however, succumbed to deep hypnosis and were able to perform the task with much less pain than was experienced by the nonhypnotized subjects.

Although the reasons why only half of the highly susceptible subjects became deeply hypnotized could not be determined, the investigators argue that the experience of pain reduction in those subjects who did go into deep hypnosis holds important implications for medical treatment.

Barber (1969) asserts that hypnosis does not produce a special state of awareness. He and his co-workers have shown that highly motivating instructions can be as effective as the traditional methods of hypnotic induction.

However persuasive Barber's position, he has not explained why hypnosis works as it does. Undeniably, hypnosis has an effect. For the hypnotized subject, reality is what has been suggested to him (Orne, Sheehan, and Evans, 1968). His reactions are different because his perceptions have been altered. Under hypnosis, he does not feel the pain, while the subject who is merely acting feels it and controls his reaction. Like a dreamer, the hypnotized subject seems to accept the odd and unusual. He can believe he is 3 years old again and having a party, or that he is standing nude on top of a floating iceberg.

His attention is fixed on what he is told to do, and he perceives in terms of this narrowing of attention. He sees what he has been asked to see and hears what he has been asked to hear. These are phenomena that deserve considerable further research.

Increasing memory through hypnosis There have been many reports of the clinical use of hypnotic suggestion to facilitate the recall of significant childhood events. One might ask, then, if hypnotic suggestion can also induce increased memory (hypermnesia) for other kinds of material. Actually, the findings suggest that, in most cases, the effect of hypnosis on memory is not nearly so dramatic as in certain cases reported by clinicians that have dealt with highly emotional material.

Learning that is both nonmeaningful and non-emotional (like learning nonsense syllables, for instance), seems to enjoy no hypermnesic advantages from hypnotic suggestion. However, there are cases that have demonstrated hypermnesia through hypnosis. For example, Marcuse (1959) reports the case of a dancer who forgot the movements to an important dance she had performed a year earlier. Under hypnosis, both the dance concert and her performance were vividly suggested. She was told that she would recall everything she had done when she awoke. The suggestions proved effective, and the dancer resumed her career.

Just how hypermnesia operates remains a mystery. It has been suggested that the extraordinary relaxation attained under hypnosis may make possible a lowered chemical or electrical resistance between the brain's nerve junctures, somehow giving remote memories better access. This, however, is merely speculation.

EXTRASENSORY PERCEPTION

Most psychologists regard the concepts of extrasensory perception (ESP) with suspicion at best and as hokum at worst. But ESP continues to attract attention, and such aspects as *telepathy* (thought transference between two people), *clairvoyance* (detecting objects or events without the use of the usual senses), and *telekinesis* (apparent control of objects without touching them) continue to be investigated. This research raises some interesting questions and answers none.

Extrasensory perception in identical twins Duane and Behrendt (1965) elicited similar changes in electroencephalograph (EEG) recordings in a pair of identical twins. The EEG changes were induced by having the twin close his eyes when he was signaled to do so. The other member of the twin pair sat in a lighted room some distance away, and his EEG changes were recorded as his twin was being stimulated. In 2 out of 15 pairs of identical twins, the nonstimulated twin showed EEG changes similar to those induced in the stimulated twin. No similar extrasensory influences were seen in any of the unrelated subjects who were tested. These findings are only suggestive, and the authors of the study carefully refrained from drawing any general conclusions.

The evidence produced by such research is slight and tenuous, and elaborate statistical manipulations are often required simply to deny that whatever was reported was not due solely to chance. In a typical ESP study, a subject is asked to determine, by ESP, the symbols on cards hidden from him. Packs of 25 cards containing 5 different symbols are usually used. Five correct guesses would occur according to the laws of chance. If you guessed the same symbol for all 25 cards, you would be correct 5 times. But few subjects for whom ESP is claimed do better than 6 correct guesses per pack. A study of one subject over a series of 2,600 trials showed he was correct, on the average, 6.8 times per trial. His accuracy was sometimes as low as 4 per 25 guesses, sometimes as high as 8 per 25. New ways of testing ESP are perhaps needed.

SUMMARY

Attention is the focusing of the sensory organs to select a particular stimulus or pattern of stimuli. It is selective, and at an internal level may be due to the neural process called sensory gating.

The orienting reflex is the postural adjustments that we make in order to help us perceive stimuli with greater ease and clarity. At the same time, an individual is ready, or set, to respond to a stimulus in some way.

Attention is influenced by such external factors as the intensity, size, or movement of a stimulus; the amount of contrast between a stimulus and its surroundings; and the repetition of a stimulus. Stimulus repetition may at first capture attention, but after prolonged repetition, an individual adapts, or habituates, to the stimulus. At other times, a distraction may occur.

Gestalt psychologists have discovered that perception is organized according to figure-ground relationships, contour, grouping, closure, and figural aftereffects.

Context is the frame of reference or background against which a specific perception occurs. A stimulus may be perceived differently because of contrast or adaptation level.

Because of perceptual constancy, we tend to perceive given objects as always the same size, shape, and color even though they stimulate our sense receptors in a variety of ways.

A reduction screen eliminates context cues. The object is then perceived in accordance with the size, shape, or color appearing on the retina.

Perceptual illusions are inaccurate perceptions that do not correspond with objective measurement of the perceived situation.

Depth perception consists of seeing objects in three dimensions and at a distance.

Monocular depth cues occur in the form of linear perspective, interposition, and differences in shading and texture gradients, or may be a result of accommodation.

Binocular depth cues involves the convergence of the different images produced by retinal disparity.

Conflicting depth cues contradict each other and alter or weaken depth perception.

In auditory depth perception, monaural or one-ear depth cues aid perception of distance, while binaural or two-ear depth cues aid direction perception. Distance can be determined by the relative loudness or softness of the sound. Direction is perceived when the sound source is at a different distance from each ear; that is, the time differential between the moment the sound reaches the first ear and the moment it reaches the second ear gives a direction cue. Other direction cues are provided by an intensity differential between the sound wave's ripple picked up by each ear. A sound source equidistant from both ears will give no auditory cue to its location.

The four types of apparent motion include the phi phenomenon, stroboscopic motion, induced motion, and autokinetic motion.

Gestalt psychologists argue that we are born with innate perceptual abilities (nativism); empiricists hold that perception comes from experience. Interest has shifted from this debate to the variables in the development of perception.

Learning appears to play a crucial role in many of our perceptions. Maturation and heredity each play a part in perception, but how much is not known.

Man can perceptually adapt to unique environments. This has been demonstrated by the use of sensory equipment such as anamorphic or "reverse-world" goggles, or a pseudophone that reverses auditory cues.

Motivational studies indicate that highly valued or much-needed stimulus objects will appear larger to the perceiver than they actually are.

Intolerance of ambiguity appears to be related to anxiety.

Under normal circumstances, an individual's consciousness, his perception of his own thoughts and feelings, operates on a continuum, with sleep at one extreme and alert wakefulness at the other.

There are four degrees of sleep in which the sleeper becomes progressively less responsive to external stimuli. Rapid eye movements (REMs), noted in stage 1, appear to be related to dreaming.

Drugs, such as LSD, mescaline, methaqualone, and marijuana, tend either to distort perception or to reduce perception and blot out reality.

Transcendental meditation produces a relaxed state in which consciousness is altered. Hypnosis alters the subject's reality but cannot empower him to carry out extraordinary tasks.

Extrasensory perception (ESP) refers to methods of perceiving that do not depend on the usual sense organs.

SUGGESTED READINGS

Texts

Barber, T. X. *Hypnosis: a scientific approach.* Princeton, N.J.: Van Nostrand, 1969. A scientific effort to operationalize and explain the phenomena historically associated with "hypnotism."

Boring, E. G. *Sensation and perception in the history of experimental psychology.* New York: Appleton-Century-Crofts, 1942. Authoritative history of concepts, problems, and experiments in the field of perception.

D'Amato, M. R. *Experimental psychology: methodology, psychophysics, and learning.* New York: McGraw-Hill, 1970. Good treatment of perception and related topics.

Gibson, E. J. *Principles of perceptual learning and development.* New York: Appleton-Century-Crofts, 1969. A comprehensive overview of perception theory and research from a developmental point of view.

Gibson, J. J. *The sense considered as perceptual systems.* Boston: Houghton Mifflin, 1966. An expert in the field explains how we perceive.

Hartmann, E. (Ed.) *Sleep and dreaming.* Boston: Little, Brown, 1970. A far-ranging survey of the exciting issues raised in the last 15 years of research.

Hochberg, J. Perception. In J. W. King and L. A. Riggs (Eds.), *Woodworth and Schlosberg's experimental psychology* (3rd ed.). New York: Holt, Rinehart & Winston, 1971. Chapters 12 and 13 of this basic manual provide a brief but thorough introduction to current methods, trends, and issues in perception research.

Hochberg, J. E. *Perception*. Englewood Cliffs, N.J.: Prentice-Hall, 1964. A brief but fairly detailed discussion, excellently illustrated.

Klein, G. S. *Perceptions, motives, and personality*. New York: Knopf, 1970. Classical and current studies on the theory of consciousness.

Köhler, W. *Gesalt psychology* (rev. ed.). New York: Mentor, 1947. Perception and other phenomena from the Gestalt standpoint. A classic.

Leibowitz, H. W. *Visual perception*. New York: Macmillan, 1965. Eight topics dealing with perception, each group of readings is preceded by an introduction explaining their background.

Neisser, U. *Cognitive psychology*. New York: Appleton-Century-Crofts, 1967. A detailed discussion of the cognitive, information-processing aspects of man in his interaction with his environment.

Schmeidler, G. R. (Ed.) *Extrasensory perception*. New York: Atherton, 1969. A balanced reference work on parapsychology.

Zubek, J. P. (Ed.) *Sensory deprivation*. New York: Appleton-Century-Crofts, 1969. A collection of papers covering the range of research in this fascinating area of psychology.

Popular books

Bester, A. *The demolished man*. Science fiction novel about people who can perceive thoughts.

Gombrich, E. H. *Art and illusion*. Treatment of the use of illusions to create art.

Gunter, B. *Sense relaxation*. A discussion of new levels of awareness through new modes of sensation.

Joyce, J. *Ulysses*. Remarkable novel using "stream-of-consciousness" technique, of interest here because when he wrote it, Joyce was nearly blind, and so for most of his perceptions and descriptions he depended on his other senses and on his phenomenal memory.

Knight, A. *The liveliest art: a panoramic history of the movies*. Includes the technical prehistory of movies, from optical toys to projected images.

Otto, H. A., and Mann, J. (Eds.) *Ways of growth*. A selection of readings including several approaches to heightened perception and expanded awareness.

Still, H. *Of times, tides, and inner clocks*. An exploration of the ways in which inner "biological clocks" may dictate many of the physiological and psychological rhythms of human life.

Vernon, M. D. *The psychology of perception*. A popular introduction to the subject.

Wohlberg, L. R. *Hypnosis*. An authoritative account of hypnosis from its beginnings to its present uses in medicine and psychotherapy.

6

Learning processes

Learning is a critical process in human development. Understanding this process is an important key to understanding human behavior. Like all other animals whose behavior is not entirely instinctive, man survives through learning. Most of what he does or refrains from doing is influenced by learning.

Let us begin with a broad definition: *Learning is a process in which past experience or practice results in relatively permanent changes in an individual's repertory of responses.*

"Change," by this definition, may be either desirable or undesirable. You change by learning to hang up your clothes—or, by learning to throw them on the floor. "Experience" or "practice" indicates that the change in responses is not attributable to maturation, illness, injury, or bodily growth. By limiting the definition to those changes that are "relatively permanent," we exclude tentative behavior changes, such as those caused by fatigue, drugs, or alcohol, which are not classed as learning.

There are many ways to learn. From situation to situation, and from individual to individual, the combination, sequence, and presence or absence of these ways varies, but the ways themselves are clear. During many years of experimentation and study, psychologists have isolated some of the basic principles of learning—and caught glimpses of the essential order that underlies the learning process.

A number of studies of the learning process have dealt with animals. In the search for effective controls over laboratory learning situations, psychologists have used animal subjects extensively because learning is often easier to control in animals than in humans. Many of the principles of learning advanced by scientists have, in fact, been based on experimentation with animals.

In this chapter, we shall discuss the *associationistic* approach to the study of learning, including *classical* and *operant* conditioning, the *cognitive* approach to learning, and the major learning theories.

ASSOCIATION

The earliest learning process to be identified was *association*. When an event or an object is observed to occur at the same time, in the same place, or under the same circumstances as another event or object, the two tend to become associated. Thus "night" and "day," "man" and "woman," "thunder" and "lightning" are all associated. The appearance of the dentist and the patient's anticipation of pain are associated, as are the sight of a good steak and the response of salivating. There are two major types of associative learning: *sensory association* and *stimulus-response association*.

Sensory association

The earliest theory of association was developed by philosophers who stated that stimuli are stored in the brain as paired sensations. Each of the two events was thought to produce a separate sensation in the brain. The sensation of one event might be recalled simply by the recurrence of the other. In other words, there was a direct connection between the different brain sensations caused by two events, and the repetition of only one of the events could evoke brain sensations related to the other; a person could thus experience the sensations of the second event even when it did not actually take place. The product of this process, the sensation of the second event, was technically called an *idea*. The key concept in sensory association is that a connection made in the brain brings about ideas associated with other ideas.

Association of ideas   James Mill (1829) regarded the association of ideas as a means of combining and binding together experience. Mind, said Mill, is composed of combinations of ideas and sensations. A complex idea is merely the sum of simple ideas. For example, the idea of a wall is complex; it is made up of the idea of bricks and mortar, and it includes the idea of quantity.

Mill felt that some ideas are so closely associated that they cannot be separated. He stated:

If one exists the other exists along with it, in spite of whatever effort we make to disjoin them. For example; it is not in our power to think of colour, without thinking of extension; or of solidity, without figure.

As scientific method was used more frequently in psychology, it became obvious that no experiment could be devised to measure or define ideas, and the concept of the association of ideas gave way to other theories founded on experimental approaches. Nonetheless, the basic concept of sensory association remains; there is evidence that stimulus-stimulus associations, as sensory associations are termed, play an important role in learning. As often happens, as experimental work grows more sophisticated, an earlier intuitive or philosophical approach to psychology is found to have some correct insights.

Stimulus-response association

The pairing of stimulus and response is a form of association that is commonly discussed and studied today. According to the concept of stimulus-response association, learning is not simply a matter of responding; for learning to occur, the correct response must come at the correct time, and the individual learns by associating responses with stimuli. By means of such associations, for example, a child learns to label the objects in his environment—the appearance of a dog is associated with the word "dog," and so on. Psychologists refer to these learning situations as stimulus-response, or S-R, associations.

Often there is a chain of stimulus-response associations. In such cases, a response produces a second stimulus; that stimulus, a new response; and so on, in serial fashion. The series may continue indefinitely. For example, repeating the alphabet involves a chain of associations. Saying A becomes a stimulus for the response of saying B, B for C, and so on.

CLASSICAL CONDITIONING

In *classical conditioning*, a neutral stimulus, such as the sound of a buzzer, is systematically paired with another stimulus, such as an electric shock, that regularly produces a strong, uncontrolled response in the subject. The pairing of the stimuli is repeated, with the result that the mild buzzer comes to elicit the same response as the violent shock. The subject's response might take the form of increased heart rate, higher blood pressure, and so on.

Classical conditioning is also referred to as *Pavlovian* conditioning, after Ivan Pavlov (1849–1936), the Russian neurophysiologist who developed the method. Still another term for this form of conditioning is *respondent conditioning*, because of its emphasis on the properties of reflex (respondent) activities (Skinner, 1938).

The conditioned response was discovered partly by accident. Pavlov was experimenting with dogs to learn more about their digestive and salivary functions, particularly to determine the connection between the presence of food in a dog's mouth and the dog's salivary flow. Pavlov isolated the salivary glands, connected tubes directly to them, and created measuring devices to record the salivary flow. He then noticed that the dogs salivated not only at the sight of the food, but even when they heard or saw the experimenter who had been feeding them. These observations caused Pavlov to introduce new stimuli—such as the musical tone of a tuning fork—before the dogs were fed. Eventually, the sound of the tuning fork alone elicited the salivating response. Pavlov's work was the beginning of highly significant research in psychology.

In the Pavlovian conditioning experiment, there are four clearly identifiable variables. The first is the *conditioned stimulus* (CS). This is a neutral stimulus that, after repeated use, or conditioning, evokes a response in the subject. In Pavlov's experiment, the CS was the tone produced by a tuning fork. Initially, the dog did nothing but perk up his ears when he heard it; after several soundings of the tone, the dog habituated (became accustomed to the situation) and his responses to the bell became less noticeable.

The second variable is the *unconditioned stimulus* (US). When this stimulus is presented to the subject, it causes a reflexive *unconditioned response* (UR). In Pavlov's experiment, the US was food powder placed in the dog's mouth, and the UR was the dog's salivation.

The CS (tone) is presented in association with the US (food powder), which naturally causes the UR (salivation) to occur. Note that the CS is always presented first. After repeated trials, the US (food powder) is not presented and the CS (tone) is presented alone. Salivation similar to that evoked by the US occurs; but it is now called the *conditioned response* (CR), the fourth variable. We refer to the response of salivating to the tone as a conditioned response because it has been conditioned to a stimulus (the CS) that did not originally elicit it. Figure 6.1 diagrams the events of the classical conditioning situation. Figure 6.2 shows a simplified version of the experimental apparatus that was devised by Pavlov.

CS-US pairing Pavlov noted that the connection between the conditioned stimulus and the conditioned response was strengthened by repeated pairings of the US and the CS; he referred to this process as *reinforcement*. The more CS-US pairings, the better the conditioning. Although most learning psychologists now reserve the term "reinforcement" for operant

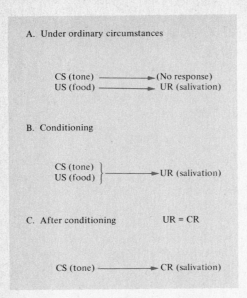

A. Under ordinary circumstances

CS (tone) ——————→ (No response)
US (food) ——————→ UR (salivation)

B. Conditioning

CS (tone) ⎫
US (food) ⎬ ——————→ UR (salivation)

C. After conditioning   UR = CR

CS (tone) ——————→ CR (salivation)

Figure 6.1   Diagram of Pavlov's classical conditioning sequence of learning.

conditioning, we may sometimes see it used in discussions of classical conditioning.

Time relationships   The time relationships between the CS and the US are important, because experiments have shown that if the US is presented either too soon or too long after the CS, learning efficiency decreases. The most successful *interstimulus interval* (time lag between

onset of the CS and onset of the US) is approximately half a second for human beings. This is the standard time relationship for *trace conditioning*, in which the CS precedes the US. For other types of conditioning experiments, depending on the objectives of the study and the type of UR to be elicited, there are other time relationships: *simultaneous*, in which both CS and US are given together; *delayed*, in which the US is given while the CS is still being presented; and *backward*, in which the US is presented first, ceases, and then the CS is presented. Backward conditioning has been shown to be ineffective in learning. Figure 6.3 shows these time relationships.

The interstimulus interval   Pavlov (1927) found that animals could often "inhibit" the onset of the conditioned response for many minutes. If, for example, a CS were presented in a trace conditioning procedure 5 minutes before the US, the animal would gradually condition in such a way that the CR would not occur until 5 minutes after the CS. It appeared that the CR was a response made in anticipation of the US, for the CR appeared at or just prior to the time the US was presented.

Strength of the variables   Whatever time sequence is used, the critical factors remain the US and the CS. If the conditioning is to be effective, the US must be strong enough to evoke a UR; otherwise, conditioning simply will

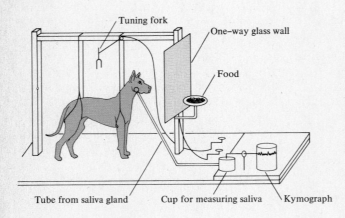

Figure 6.2   The typical harnessing apparatus used in Pavlov's classical conditioning experiments. A tube attached to the salivary glands was used to drain the saliva into a cup. The liquid in the cup could be measured by reading the record made on a moving drum (kymograph). The experimenter could remotely control the appearance of food and the sounding of the tone. The dog and the apparatus were in a soundproof room, and the experimenter was located on the other side of a one-way viewing glass.

not occur. In addition, the CS must be strong enough to be sensed by the subject. An inaudible bell or a light too weak to be visible can hardly be an effective conditioned stimulus.

Measuring the effects of classical conditioning

There are four measures of the effectiveness of classical conditioning. *Magnitude* is a measure of the amount, force, or size of the CR. It is used when we want to know if the CR is grow-

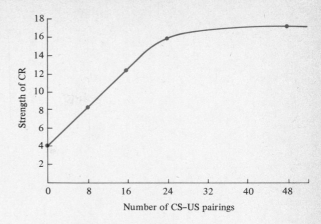

Figure 6.4   Graph of a classical conditioning experiment. The strength of the CR increases rapidly at first. With succeeding CS-US pairings, the increase lessens. From 0 to 24 pairings there is a steep increase; from 24 to 48 pairings there is a negligible increase. (Based on Hovland, 1937)

Figure 6.3   The four time relationships between the CS and US in classical conditioning, as depicted on a time continuum. The plateaus depict the duration of each stimulus. Interstimulus intervals are indicated by the arrows.

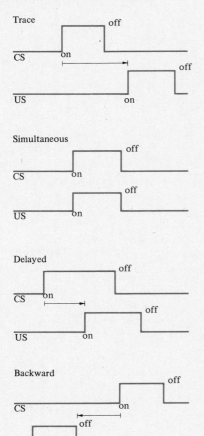

ing stronger as conditioning continues. *Probability* is a measure of the likelihood that a CR will occur when the CS is presented. *Latency* is the elapsed time between the presentation of the CS and the appearance of the CR. The shorter the time between the CS and the CR, the stronger the CR. The fourth measure, *resistance to extinction*, will be covered in the next section.

Figure 6.4 is a graph illustrating a typical classical conditioning experiment. Note that conditioning is rapid at first, but gradually slows down.

Extinction

The process by which an established conditioned response is weakened or eliminated is called *extinction*. Extinction results when the CS is presented frequently without being paired with the US. When this happens, the CS becomes increasingly unable to elicit the CR; the subject appears to have returned to his original preconditioned state. Experimenters use extinction pro-

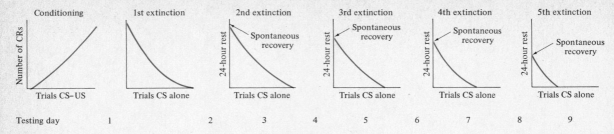

Figure 6.5 Schematic of the conditioning, extinction, and spontaneous recovery of a conditioned response. After rest, the CR recurs, but with each day of presenting the CS alone, the CR is maintained for a shorter and shorter period of time. (Adapted from Mednick, 1964)

cedures to test the strength of conditioning, since the more effective the conditioning has been, the more difficult it is to extinguish. Extinction procedures, then, also measure resistance to extinction.

Spontaneous recovery

A conditioned response that has been extinguished can reappear without additional conditioning. This phenomenon is known as *spontaneous recovery*. In laboratory testing, a rest interval is allowed to follow the extinction of a CR. Then, the CR typically reappears in somewhat weaker form. Figure 6.5 shows the process of conditioning, extinction, spontaneous recovery, additional extinction, recovery, and so on.

It has been found that renewed conditioning through the original CS-US association will quickly strengthen the original response. As a matter of fact, it appears that continued conditioning at this time may produce an even stronger CR than before. Reconditioning is known to be a faster learning process than original conditioning. Thus, reconditioning is quite desirable in some situations—both to intensify the response pattern and to insure more lasting behavior.

From his observations of spontaneous recovery, Pavlov argued that the CR is never completely extinguished—that it is only blocked from being actively produced. This blocking process is known as *inhibition*. Experiments that test the spontaneous recovery phenomenon provide a basis for the theory of inhibition; they suggest that an inhibiting state develops during extinction, and that this state disappears with rest. Successive trials of spontaneous recovery in which the CR is not reconditioned show a lower level of recovery at each trial. After many trials, without reconditioning, spontaneous recovery becomes insignificant. The more often the CR is extinguished, the more difficult reconditioning will be—until finally the learning rate for the CR is just as slow as it was during the original CS-US trials.

It should be noted that there is no direct evidence for the inhibition process; discussions of such a process are entirely speculative.

Stimulus generalization

Once the CR is learned, a CS that is similar to the original CS will also elicit the CR. This process is known as *stimulus generalization*. Pavlov's experiments with stimulus generalization showed that a dog who was conditioned to respond to the tone of a tuning fork would also respond to the ringing of a bell and other sounds similar to the original tone. Many experiments related to stimulus generalization have been conducted since Pavlov's.

Although generalization sometimes occurs between stimuli that are not particularly similar (for instance, an auditory and a visual stimulus), the more similar the stimuli are, the more frequently the process occurs. Figure 6.6 shows a stimulus-generalization curve.

We find that stimulus generalization decreases somewhat as our perceptual abilities mature and become better trained. It is more common for a young child than for an older child to confuse similar stimuli. A 4-year-old may refer to all four-legged animals as dogs. An older child has learned to make sharper distinctions.

A furry generalization Watson and Rayner (1920) conducted a now-famous experiment in stimulus generalization. Albert, an infant, was allowed to play with a white rat. He showed no signs of fear of the rat. While he was playing with it, a loud noise was suddenly sounded, and Albert was frightened. The noise was paired with the rat several times. Thereafter, Albert showed signs of being afraid of the rat and all similar objects, including his mother's white fur neckpiece. His fear had generalized. (In Chapter 9, we further discuss the fact that the emotion of fear can easily generalize to similar objects.)

Stimulus generalization is at work in all of us, however, and it may account for a variety of puzzling human responses. Generalization is operating when a child reacts to his school-teacher as though she were his mother; or when an employee hates his boss because he reminds him of his old army sergeant.

Response generalization

Responses can also be generalized. If a stimulus demands a response from a subject and he is unable to make that particular response, he will very likely make a substitute response. For example, a dog may learn a CR involving his left front paw, but if that paw for some reason cannot be used, he will probably generalize his response to the CS by making the CR with his right front paw. Conditioning does not deteriorate because a response mechanism no longer functions. The ability to generalize a response makes it possible for learning to become highly adaptive; and this is especially important in human learning.

Discrimination

A subject can be selectively conditioned to respond to one very specific stimulus. Such training is called *discrimination*. To achieve discrimination, a number of stimuli are presented to the subject. Only the stimulus chosen to be the CS is systematically followed by the US. Animal subjects can learn to discriminate between tones

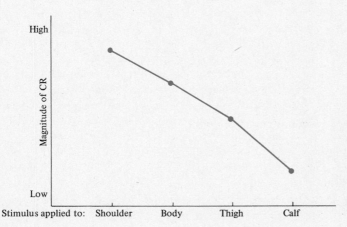

Figure 6.6   Generalization of a CR. The CS was a tactile (touch) stimulus to the shoulder, the US an electric shock, and the UR and CR palm sweating, an emotional response. Note that the farther the test stimulus is from the original CS, the weaker the CR. (Based on Bass and Hull, 1934)

of bells, light intensities, object positions, and so forth.

In human training, much adaptive behavior is learned through discrimination—for example, a person insures his own safety by learning to discriminate between vitamin pills and sleeping tablets, or between liquid cough medicine bottles and bottles of cleaning fluid. However, stimuli that are very similar to the CS usually continue to evoke some response by the learner —how much depends on the conditions of training.

Discriminating between stimuli Fuhrer and Baer (1965) used two clearly different stimuli: one, a tone of 700 cps (cycles per second); the other, a tone of 3,500 cps. The CR was the galvanic skin response (GSR—changes in electrical conductivity of the sweat glands of the palm). Initially the GSR was the same regardless of which stimulus was presented. The US was an electric shock applied to the left forefinger after the presentation of just one of the stimuli. After several trials, large increases in the GSR for that CS were noted, whereas the GSR for the never-shocked stimulus decreased. This study demonstrates how, through training, the capacity to elicit a conditioned response may become specifically restricted to a stimulus that has been systematically paired with an unconditioned stimulus.

Higher-order conditioning

It is possible to use a conditioned stimulus as an unconditioned stimulus in establishing a conditioned response to a third stimulus. This process is known as *higher-order conditioning*, because the new CS is one step removed from the original US. For example, a bell may be the CS, food the US, and salivation the UR. Once the bell regularly elicits salivation, it can be used as the US—and a light can be established as a new CS. When the light is paired with the bell often enough, it, too, will evoke salivation.

But the salivation evoked by the light will be comparatively weak and hard to achieve. The conditioning sequence in higher-order conditioning is difficult, because it is competing with the extinction process we mentioned earlier. For

higher-order conditioning to be successful, the original CS-US pairing should be reintroduced at intervals to maintain the strength of the CR.

Images as conditioned stimuli Many words create images for us. Staats (1968) has analyzed the process in terms of classical conditioning, using the following example. An individual who hears the word "blue" imagines a color. If at the same moment he were given a shock, his heartbeat would accelerate. His image of the color (CS) would have preceded the shock (US) and the heart rate response (UR), but if this pairing of stimuli should happen one or more times, he becomes conditioned so that the word "blue" elicits the heart rate response. When a blue light is paired with the word "blue" during conditioning, the light will also arouse the heart rate response. Thus, seeing a blue light, the subject will feel the sensations that were related to the shock and that were first conditioned to the word.

Can you substitute frightening words from your own experience for those in Staats' example and trace the history of your own reaction? Recall the original fright-producing stimulus (US) and the first and subsequent (if any) CSs that were paired with it. If you have succeeded this far, separate the fright response from the image that accompanies it.

OPERANT CONDITIONING

Operant conditioning involves responses controlled by the individual. In classical conditioning, the subject may be passive; the stimulus acts upon the subject to elicit a response and the subject responds automatically. But in *operant*, or *instrumental*, *conditioning*, the subject is active; the individual affects the stimulus, which in turn affects his response. The original activity in operant conditioning need not be elicited by any observed stimulus; it is emitted by the subject.

In classical conditioning, the aim is to use an unconditioned stimulus to elicit from the subject a response that will be associated with a conditioned stimulus—a stimulus that would not naturally elicit such a response from him. In operant conditioning, there is no unconditioned stimulus that from the beginning forces the subject to make the response sought by the experimenter. Instead, the learner's original activity produces an environmental effect that results in a repetition of the activity (the response). Continued repetition of the response brings about a repetition of the environmental effect, reinforcing the learner's tendency to make the response. For example, if a hungry animal pushes open a door and finds food, the probability of his pushing the door open again will increase. If a child solves a problem correctly and is praised by her teacher immediately, the responses that led to the solution of the problem will more likely recur when she encounters a similar problem in the future. If, in other words, her response produces reinforcement (praise), the response will become stronger. And the more frequently the response is reinforced, the more it will be emitted.

Operant conditioning is based on the *law of effect* propounded by Edward L. Thorndike (1911). The law states that *responses may be altered by their effects on the environment.* Responses that lead to satisfying effects are strengthened; responses leading to annoying effects are weakened. Operant conditioning is very much a part of our daily lives, as can be seen from the following examples of common behaviors and their reinforcing effects (alternatively the same activities might have annoying effects that could weaken each response): a dog begging (reinforcer, food); a child going willingly to bed (reinforcer, mother's praise); a girl dyeing her hair (reinforcer, attention); a person answering a ringing doorbell (reinforcer, someone at the door); a panhandler seeking a handout (reinforcer, money, food, clothing, whiskey).

Any event that strengthens a response is called a *positive reinforcer.* Reinforcement may also be effected by *negative reinforcers.* These cause the subject to respond so as to avoid or terminate a stimulus. For example, when a bell is sounded, a shock is applied to a dog's leg. The dog can terminate the shock by lifting his leg.

Figure 6.7   *The experimental chamber is used for operant conditioning of rats. In the background can be seen the complex equipment used to record the animal's behavior. The recording of its responses is transferred to and depicted on the cumulative recorder also attached to the experimental chamber. (Eliot Elisofon,Time-LIFE Picture Agency)*

Consequently, he learns very quickly to lift his leg whenever the bell sounds. Here the termination of the shock provides a negative reinforcement that strengthens the leg-lifting response.

Reinforcement in operant conditioning

Reinforcement is the pivotal concept in operant conditioning. The subject learns the correct response because his response is reinforced. Whether or not he would learn in the absence of reinforcement is still open to question. Some psychologists believe that all learning requires reinforcement. Others, such as Guthrie, have argued that reinforcement is not required—subjects learn by responding to stimuli; they learn by doing, whether or not what they do is reinforced.

The experimental chamber

A piece of laboratory apparatus called an *experimental chamber* is the setting for experiments in operant conditioning with rats and pigeons, the most frequent subjects of this type of research (Figure 6.7). The chamber is often called

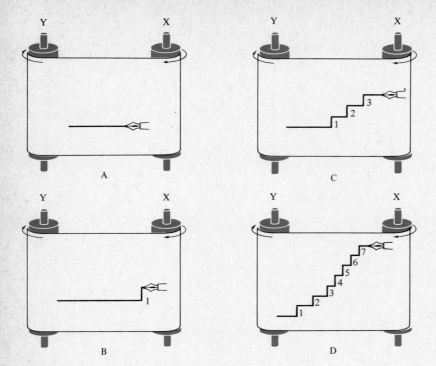

Figure 6.8   The construction of a cumulative record: (A) shows the paper moving from right to left, from the roll at X to the takeup roll at Y As the paper moves, the response pen inks a continuous line. (B) shows that each time a response is made, the pen deflects upward. (C) shows three successive responses. (D) shows seven responses; the first three are slower than the last four—that is, more time elapsed between responses 1, 2, and 3 than between 4, 5, 6, and 7. The faster the rate of responding, the steeper is the record.

a *Skinner* box, after B. F. Skinner, the psychologist who invented it and developed most of the techniques of operant conditioning.

The basic structure and function of the experimental chamber is standard, although slight variations allow for differences in the animal species being conditioned and in the responses being learned. On the chamber's inside wall is a device the subject can operate—a lever for rats or a pecking key for pigeons. Below the device is either a tray or an opening. Here the reinforcer appears. The typical rat chamber has either a tray on which small pellets of food can be delivered or an opening permitting the animal access to a water dipper. The pigeon chamber is usually provided with an opening below which a tray of grain is placed. The floor of the chamber may be covered with metal rods through which electric shocks can be administered for escape or avoidance conditioning (discussed in the next section).

Outside the chamber is a measuring device that records the number of responses (presses of the lever or pecks on the key); this device is a *cumulative recorder*. The cumulative recorder enables the experimenter to obtain a graphic record of the rate of response that occurs during learning. The cumulative record is different from any of the curves we have shown thus far. It appears as a straight line which is deflected upward each time a response is made (Figure 6.8).

The experimental chamber In Skinner's original conditioning experiment (1932), bar-pressing was the response to be reinforced. First, Skinner allowed his animal to adapt to the experimental chamber by feeding him there frequently. Then he began to train the animal to press a bar. Finally, he put the animal, which had been deprived of food for 24 hours, into the box. The animal engaged in exploratory behavior and finally pressed the bar, causing a food pellet to be dropped into the feeder tray. The response was recorded on the cumulative recorder outside the box. A second bar-pressing response followed, and soon the animal was bar-pressing and eating food pellets at an optimal level.

Once rats learn to press the bar, the response rate becomes steady. When the animal is deprived of food for 24 hours and is then placed in the experimental chamber, he begins responding at a relatively high rate. As his hunger is satisfied, he gradually slows down. If the animal were permitted to live in the Skinner box and eat on an unrestricted schedule, a cumulative recording of his eating responses would probably be on a straight line, since he would eat more slowly and at regular intervals.

In each new operant situation, a period is allowed for the animal subject to be freely active —to respond to and randomly explore his environment. When an animal is first placed in the chamber, it is likely to be afraid; this fear may at first cause inactivity, defecation, and other signs of alarm. After becoming habituated (accustomed) to the box, the animal begins to explore, sniffing or pecking randomly. It will soon find the key or lever, since there is little else in the box, but may hesitate for a time before pressing it. When it does, the food appears. Initially, the animal will not associate pulling the lever or depressing the key with the appearance of the food. But usually by the second trial, and invariably by the third, the association is made. The animal presses the lever, eats the pellet, presses the lever, eats the next pellet, and so on. Since the food is a positive reinforcer, it strengthens the lever-pressing response. The rat in Figure 6.9 presses a lever twice his weight to obtain his food reward.

Can "laziness" be learned? Some recent work with pigeons indicates that, under certain conditions, both "laziness" and "industriousness" may be products of operant conditioning.

Engsberg, Hansen, Welker, and Thomas (1972) used three groups of pigeons: one group was trained originally to open a food hopper by pressing a treadle (the treadle group); one group was given periodic access to the food hopper irrespective of any particular behavior (the hopper group); and a control group was handled daily and fed normally throughout the others' training period. After initial training, all subjects were tested in a situation in which the food hopper was periodically opened without the subjects' having to make any particular response (noncontingent reinforcement)—but a luminescent response key lit up several seconds before each hopper opening. Normally such a procedure encourages pigeons to make pecking responses (to the lit key) *as if* the food reward depended on those responses.

In this case, the controls reacted as expected, acquiring the key-pecking response in less than 80 trials. The hopper group—initially trained in a situation where their own behavior had no effect on access to the food hopper—took more than 120 trials to acquire the pecking response. These pigeons had learned to be "lazy." The treadle group, however—

Figure 6.9 A rat presses a lever twice his weight in return for reinforcement—food. (Allen Stubbs)

initially trained to work for reinforcement—took just 60 trials to show the same level of response. These pigeons had learned to be "industrious."

Beyond the laboratory, operant conditioning techniques that include positive reinforcement are particularly useful in the treatment of disturbed behavior, especially in children. Providing the child with social reinforcement—such as approval or attention—strengthens socially acceptable responses. We shall discuss these procedures more fully in Chapter 14.

Escape and avoidance conditioning

In some forms of operant conditioning, a shock from the floor grid of the experimental chamber may serve as the stimulus for which the animal learns an *escape response*. When the shock is administered, the animal may respond in various ways: it may squeal, run, jump, or crouch. The shock is continued until the animal presses the lever on the chamber wall; when it does so, the shock stops. In this situation, the negative reinforcement is the termination of the shock.

In another type of operant conditioning, the subject learns an *avoidance response*. This experiment typically includes a warning stimulus, such as a light or a buzzer, that is activated by the experimenter before the shock is turned on. After the first trial or two, the subject learns to respond by pressing the lever when the *warning* stimulus occurs, in this way avoiding the shock altogether.

Rats learn to avoid shock Miller (1948) placed rats in an apparatus with two compartments, one black and one white (see Figure 8.10 in Chapter 8). When the rats placed in the white compartment were shocked, they immediately fled to the black compartment. After several trials, the rats automatically ran to the black compartment, as soon as they were placed in the white compartment, even before shock was administered.

For the next series of trials, Miller placed the rats in the same white compartment; this time, how-

ever, the door between compartments was closed. A wheel was added to the white compartment, which, if rotated, would open the door. The rats eventually learned to rotate the wheel and to escape from the white compartment, although they no longer received the aversive shock while in the white compartment. Then Miller made this escape response dependent upon a second new activity—bar-pressing. The rats learned to press the bar that opened the door between compartments. These animals were responding to an aversive stimulus that was no longer present. Even after shock was removed from the situation, the animals sought the reinforcing effects of escape from the white compartment itself, which had acquired aversive properties.

Escape and avoidance learning are closely related. A subject undergoing operant conditioning must learn the escape technique before it can learn the avoidance response. Some psychologists identify two sequential steps in avoidance learning. The first is a classical conditioning situation in which the warning signal becomes a conditioned stimulus. As the CS, it is associated by the subject with the shock or pain of an oncoming stimulus, which the animal fears and tries to escape from. Subsequently, when the warning signal is presented, the subject displays the same fearful behavior that it displays when actually being shocked. In the second step, the animal makes the escape response (hitting the key) on presentation of the warning signal, thereby reducing his fear and avoiding the shock.

Escape and avoidance learning are not uncommon in the daily lives of people. A bully frequently hits a smaller classmate. The smaller boy comes to expect to be hit by the bully. The bully's punch is the painful stimulus; the sight of the bully is the warning signal; and the smaller boy learns to avoid a blow by running away from the bully (the painful stimulus) whenever he sees him.

Learned helplessness Seligman and Maier (1967) have demonstrated *learned helplessness* in an experiment with two groups of dogs. The first group was placed in a situation in which they could not escape from the shocks administered by the experimenters.

Thus, they did not learn either to avoid or to escape shock. The second group was placed in a situation in which they could escape the shocks; that is, they could terminate the shocks by movements of their heads. When they were subsequently placed in the shock compartment, they quickly learned to jump out to avoid the shock.

Apparently, avoidance training teaches more than the specific response; it enables the animal to learn a generalized response—to *do something* to avoid or escape shock. By the same token, animals who are initially given inescapable shock learn to be generally helpless. This seems to occur when unavoidable punishment occurs early in the animal's experience.

Seligman and Maier point out that the reaction of the helpless dogs is not unlike the behavior of people who cannot seem to help themselves—chronically unemployed persons in society and depressed patients in mental hospitals, for example.

Figure 6.10   Pigeons are conditioned to discriminate between lights of two different colors, usually red and green. If the pigeon responds correctly, it is allowed to feed from the small opening in the wall of its chamber. (H. S. Terrace)

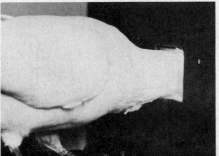

Successive approximations

Successive approximations, or *shaping,* is the term for a process in which the experimenter develops a series of responses that lead to a final, desired response by the subject. A rat placed in an experimental chamber does not rush to the lever and press it. The experimenter *shapes* the lever-pressing response. He gives the rat a food pellet initially for coming *near* the lever; next for *touching* the lever; and finally, for *pressing* the lever. The desired final response—in this case, pressing the lever—has been achieved by a series of *successive approximations,* in which only the responses that approximate the desired response are reinforced.

These shaping techniques are especially helpful in educating children. Appropriate attitudes and responses in learning situations are rewarded to shape the child's progress toward a certain, often very long-range, goal—for example, praising a third-grader's scholastic efforts might very well be part of a parental program of encouraging the child to go to college later on.

Shaping power Professor X had a habit of pacing about the room while lecturing to his graduate class in learning psychology. Without his knowledge, his students agreed to look interested and wide awake only when he was in a particular corner of the classroom. As soon as he ventured away from that spot, the students yawned, doodled, stared out the window, and generally looked bored. As soon as he moved toward the corner, they seemed to become more interested and alert; they were most attentive when he was actually in the corner. By the end of the lecture, Professor X spoke only from that particular corner.

Discrimination

If operant conditioning is to be successful, the correct responses must be emitted in the presence of *particular stimuli.* For example, the pigeon must peck the key when the light is green, but not when it is red (Figure 6.10).

Consequently, it is important to teach discrimination among stimuli.

In *discrimination-learning* situations, the subject is taught to distinguish between two or more stimuli, or to distinguish between the presence and absence of a stimulus. This is achieved by reinforcing only the responses that are made in the presence of the correct stimulus—and by *not* reinforcing any responses made in the presence of other stimuli. The correct stimulus is frequently referred to as the *discriminative stimulus*, or S^D ("ess dee"), and the incorrect stimulus as S^Δ ("ess delta"). Figure 6.11 shows a discrimination-learning situation.

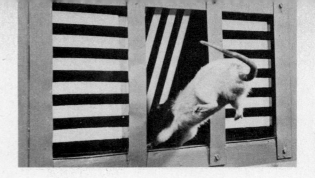

Figure 6.11   Rats learn to discriminate among three doors. They select the door that differs from the other two. (Frank Lotz Miller—Black Star)

Stimulus generalization

Stimulus generalization occurs in operant conditioning as well as in classical conditioning. Stimuli similar or identical to the original discriminative stimulus serve as cues for the responses made in the presence of that first stimulus. If a child opens a cookie jar and finds a cookie, he is quite likely to open other containers (cans, jars, boxes) that might look to him like cookie jars.

Extinction

In operant conditioning, a response is extinguished by withholding the reinforcer. As this withholding is repeated, the subject responds with decreasing frequency, until he ceases to respond altogether. In the experimental chamber, the lever-pressing activity will ultimately be extinguished if the reinforcing food pellets cease to be delivered. The time required for extinction of a response pattern varies according to the frequency and pattern of reinforcement. The stronger the conditioning, the more difficult it is to extinguish. Complete extinction, as in classical conditioning, is said to occur when the subject's response pattern reverts to its original, preconditioning level. Figure 6.12 shows a cumulative record of conditioning followed by extinction.

It is more difficult to extinguish behavior learned under negative reinforcement. Obviously a shocking, painful, or otherwise unpleasant stimulus does not "wear off" so easily—and neither does the response to it. The subject's fear of an unpleasant experience makes avoidance learning especially difficult to extinguish; although the subject does not experience the original, painful stimulus, he has learned to fear the stimulus and to avoid it anyway. The warn-

Figure 6.12   A cumulative record of conditioning and extinction. Note that for a short time after extinction begins (at A), the rate of responding continues to be high, but then it diminishes until it approaches zero. Between B and C, no responses are made.

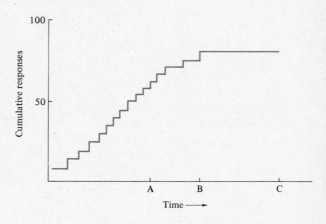

ing stimulus continues to be effective because the subject responds before he finds out if the shock will occur.

Counterconditioning Lutenberg, Rawson, and Bath (1970) have raised some questions about the fate of responses suppressed by counterconditioning, that is, by a reward for competing responses. In their experiment, they withdrew reinforcement after a response was established. During extinction, an experimental group was rewarded for making a competing response, while a control group was conventionally extinguished. The experimental group made fewer of the responses that were being extinguished. In the next phase of the study, reinforcement for the competing response was withdrawn from the experimental group. The experimental subjects resumed making the original response, even though it was not being reinforced. It appears that the response was not really extinguished during counterconditioning; the competing response had merely been substituted for it. The experimental animals still needed to learn *not* to make the response.

Measuring the effects of operant conditioning

Operant conditioning situations usually involve *free responding*. The experimental chamber in which a rat presses a lever or a pigeon pecks at a key allows the subject to respond or not to respond, and to respond frequently or infrequently. After the subject makes the appropriate response, it is free to make the same response again, to rest, or to make some other response. In the free-responding situation, the effects of conditioning are measured in terms of the correct response. The more correct responses the subject makes in a given period of time, the faster is his rate of responding. Rate of responding can be read from a cumulative record.

In some types of operant conditioning research, resistance to extinction is used as a measure of the conditioning effects. When the experimenter is especially interested in the persistence of a conditioned response, he will probably count the number of responses a subject emits after extinction is begun. The more responses

Figure 6.13   Rats will wander the alleys of a maze to find food at the end—for the previous response of running the maze correctly has been reinforced with food. (Allen Stubbs)

there are, the more effective has been the conditioning.

Some operant conditioning is performed in *discrete trials*. The discrete trial method is seen in experiments in which a rat is placed in a T maze and trained to find his way into one particular arm of the maze. At the end of the correct arm there is a goal box containing a positive reinforcer, such as food or water. The effects of conditioning are measured by determining the number of trials it takes the rat to learn to get to the food. In more complicated mazes where there are many incorrect alleys, either the number of trials to learn or the number of errors made during the learning may be used as measures (Figure 6.13).

Unconditioned and conditioned reinforcement

We distinguish between *unconditioned reinforcers* (those which are effective without benefit of previous association with other reinforcers) and *conditioned reinforcers* (those which become reinforcers only after the subject associates them with previous reinforcers). Food, water, and the termination of pain are some unconditioned reinforcers; the sound of a buzzer that has been paired with food is a conditioned reinforcer. Such stimuli as money, good grades, and spoken praise are examples of human conditioned reinforcers. Although the differences between unconditioned and conditioned reinforcers are often subtle, they are real, and it is possible to distinguish between the two types. For example, praise seems to be rewarding by itself, but if we trace back, we are likely to find that praise became a reinforcer because it was frequently associated with such unconditioned reinforcers as food and the reduction of discomfort. A mother often says such things as "good boy" or "nice girl" as she feeds and cares for her child. And in this way, words of praise are conditioned to become reinforcing.

Conditioned reinforcement of a chimpanzee In working with a chimpanzee, Wolfe (1936) used a poker chip as a reinforcer, which, when inserted into a vending machine, released a grape to the animal. After using this method successfully to teach the chimpanzee to associate the poker chip with grapes, Wolfe initiated the training of simple operant responses, such as lifting a lever or pulling a small tray by a cord. The chimpanzee continued to make these operant responses for the chips, despite the fact that they could not be exchanged for grapes until later.

Cowles (1937) found that chimpanzees worked as hard for conditioned reinforcement (poker chips) as they did for food. When Cowles attempted to teach a chimpanzee a position habit (always choosing the stimulus in the same place despite the fact that several different stimuli were used), as many as 20 trials were sometimes needed. However, he found that poker chips alone were enough to sustain the chimpanzee's behavior through the 20 trials.

Partial reinforcement

The reinforcements we have discussed were continuous because in every case a correct response was reinforced. Although continuous reinforcement is often attainable in experimental situations, real-life learning situations seldom provide continuous reinforcement. Reinforcement simply does not occur every time an animal or a human being makes a particular response to a given stimulus.

Psychologists, therefore, rely on studies of *schedules of reinforcement* that are closer to real-life learning situations. These schedules are based on the concept of *partial reinforcement*, or reinforcement that occurs intermittently. Experiments have indicated that responses learned under a partial reinforcement schedule take longer to be extinguished than do responses learned with continuous reinforcement. For example, in a typical experiment the rats in one group are reinforced each time they press a lever (100 percent reinforcement), while another group is reinforced 50 percent of the time on a random basis. During extinction the 50 percent group will make more lever-pressing responses than the 100 percent group. The 50 percent group will show greater resistance to extinction even though they received one-half as many reinforcements as the 100 percent group.

The fact that partial reinforcement increases resistance to extinction has significant implications for human behavior. A child who is reinforced for every correct response is more likely to show quick extinction of these responses than a child who is on a partial reinforcement schedule. The child on the 100 percent–reinforcement schedule does not have an opportunity to learn to persist in the face of some nonreinforcement. He may experience frustration when he is not reinforced and give up because of that feeling of frustration. The child on a partial reinforcement schedule learns that a nonreinforcement does not necessarily signal the end to reinforcement altogether. Occasional nonreinforcement does not frustrate him. However, it is important to recognize that efficient learning usually begins with a 100 percent–reinforcement schedule, which then, as the learning becomes strong, is gradually switched to a partial reinforcement schedule.

The effects of partial reinforcement on extinction may be attributed to the way the individual learns to respond. He learns that every correct response is not reinforced. He learns to respond in the presence of stimuli that are associated with nonreinforcement, and thus the extinction situation is not very different from the learning situation.

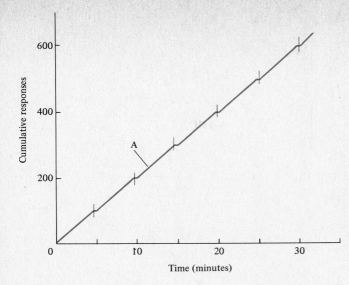

Figure 6.14   Graph of a fixed-ratio (fr) schedule. One hundred responses are required for each reinforcement (fr 100). The vertical marks indicate points at which reinforcement is given. The pauses, the flat part of the record (see A), indicate a slowing of response rate. These pauses are typical of fixed-ratio schedules. In this record, 600 responses were made in a 30-minute period.

Another view of reinforcement Premack (1959, 1965) has suggested that almost any activity can serve as a reinforcer; it simply must be preferred more than the activity that it is reinforcing. He discovered that 6- and 7-year-old children would sometimes prefer to play with a pinball machine rather than with a candy dispenser and sometimes would prefer the dispenser to the pinball machine. Whichever device was preferred at a given moment could be used to reinforce responses to the nonpreferred device.

Homme (1966) and Homme, De Baca, Devine, Steinhorst, and Rickert (1963) extended the "Premack principle" to the teaching of young children in the classroom. They arranged situations in which the students agreed to perform some low-probability (nonpreferred) behavior in order to perform a high-probability (preferred) behavior. If, for example, the probability of playing with clay or finger paints were higher than the probability of writing out a list of spelling words, the conditions were arranged so that the student had to write the spelling words before he could play with the clay or the paints.

Partial reinforcement schedules can be established on the basis of time, number, rate of response between reinforcements, or combinations of these factors. The four most common methods are the following:

1 *Fixed-ratio schedule*—Reinforcement is administered after a fixed number of correct responses.

The ratio is the number of nonreinforced trials to reinforced responses. If every twelfth correct response were reinforced, the fixed-ratio schedule would be 12:1. The response rate under this schedule is high because it is to the subject's advantage to make many responses. It is like being paid on a piecework basis: the more you produce, the more you are paid. Figure 6.14 shows the response rate under fixed-ratio reinforcement.

2 *Fixed-interval schedule*—Reinforcement is administered for the first correct response after a fixed time has elapsed. The subject learns to respond when a specific time has passed, anticipating the occurrence of reinforcement. The subject can be trained to a time schedule, so that his rate of response begins to increase as the time for reinforcement approaches. Often students behave in this way: their studying decreases immediately after an exam; as the time for the next exam approaches their studying increases (Figure 6.15).

3 *Variable-ratio schedule*—Reinforcement is administered after a varying number of nonreinforced correct responses. The ratio schedule is an average based on the overall length of performance under the schedule. For example, the variable ratio may be 12:1; this means that over the entire range of performances, there is an average of 12 correct responses for 1 reinforcement. Varying from trial to trial, however, are reinforcements scheduled at anywhere from 1 to 24 responses—forming a built-in averaging system.

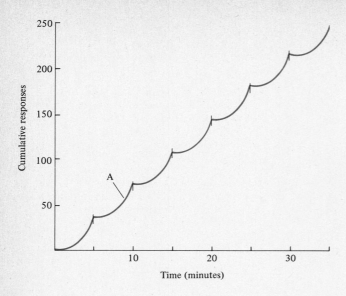

Figure 6.15   Graph of a fixed-interval (fi) schedule. Five minutes must elapse between reinforcements. The postreinforcement pauses are obvious. Also note that the rate of responding tends to increase toward the end of each interval, just before a reinforcement is due (see A).

Sometimes a reinforcement is given after 1 correct response, sometimes after 4 or 5, or after as many as 20. Variable-ratio schedules maintain high rates of response for long periods; because the subject never knows when reinforcement may come, he "keeps trying." Slot machines provide excellent, if costly, examples of variable-ratio schedules of reinforcement. Because the gambler is sure the machine will eventually pay off, he hates to leave it (Figure 6.16).

4 *Variable-interval schedule*—Reinforcement is administered after varying time periods of nonreinforced correct responses, based on an average time period between reinforcements during the entire schedule. Intervals above and below the average are created to maintain the average. In this schedule, the subject works at a relatively high and constant rate in order to be responding correctly when a reinforcement is due. Figure 6.17 shows the response rate of the variable-interval schedule.

The techniques of partial reinforcement are extremely effective in maintaining behavior for long periods of time. The subject learning under a partial reinforcement schedule does not simply learn what he must do to receive reinforcement; he learns when and how frequently he must re-

spond to get the most reinforcements. Of the four schedules, the variable-ratio is the most effective, because it produces the highest response rate. Since the subject under variable-ratio reinforcement never knows exactly when reinforcement is coming, and since the reinforcement depends on the number of correct responses he makes, he often performs at an almost frantic level.

Punishment

We know that the consequences of a response usually affect the response. Responses leading to reinforcement are strengthened. Responses leading to punishment—to painful or unpleasant stimuli—are less likely to appear again. Punishment, therefore, is used to suppress particular responses. If, when a child reaches into the cookie jar, his mother slaps his hand, he will discontinue the reaching response while his mother is present. The slap has changed the child's behavior—it has caused him to replace the response of reaching into the cookie jar with another response, that of not reaching into the cookie jar.

Although negative reinforcement and pun-

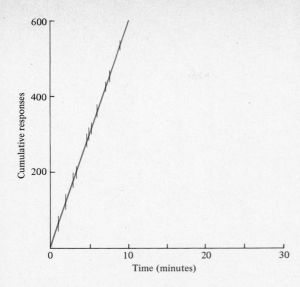

Figure 6.16   Graph of a variable-ratio (vr) schedule. Reinforcement is given intermittently, but on the average of every 60 responses. The rate of responding is very high; in a 10-minute period, 600 responses are made. Notice that there are no postreinforcement pauses here. Since the subject never knows when to expect reinforcement, this schedule is the most effective in maintaining strong and constant responses.

Figure 6.17   Graph of a variable-interval (vi) schedule. Reinforcement is given at intermittent intervals on an average of one reinforcement every 5 minutes. There are no postreinforcement pauses.

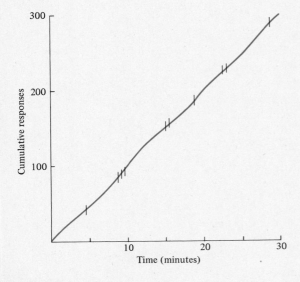

ishment both involve the use of aversive (painful or unpleasant) stimuli, there are important differences between the two techniques. In negative reinforcement, the termination of the aversive stimuli. Negative reinforcement strengthens a response; punishment weakens or suppresses it (Table 6.1).

Punishment, which is undeniably effective in controlling behavior, does have two disadvantages. First, unless the punishment is very severe, its effects may be only temporary. Experiments have shown that the punished response will ultimately return at full strength. Second, punishment introduces into a learning situation stimuli that are capable of disrupting the learning process. A child is being taught to read and his teacher scolds him severely every time he mispronounces a word. The scolding is meant to stop him from mispronouncing words, but its primary effect is to frighten him. He becomes frightened and confused. He mispronounces more words, receives more scolding. At length, he grows so frightened that he is no longer able or willing to read aloud—and very likely forgets all that he has already learned about reading.

How strong is punishment? Skinner (1938) conditioned two groups of animals for 3 days. Extinction was then carried out in two periods of 2 hours each. The lever-press responses made by Group I in the first 10 minutes of the first period of extinction were punished. Whenever an animal pressed the lever during this period, a sharp return kick of the bar slapped against the animal's forepaws. The responses of this group were not reinforced during the rest of the extinction period. Group II's responses were merely not reinforced during each of the extinction periods. Group I's punishment only served to suppress the behavior temporarily, for the bar-press behavior returned, and at full strength. The total number of responses emitted before extinction occurred was the same for both groups, however, thus indicating that punishment does not subtract from the overall strength of response in extinction.

It is obvious that punishment, if it is used at all, must be used carefully. One way is to provide a possible alternative response to the re-

Table 6.1   Relationship between positive and negative reinforcement and punishment[a]

Reinforcer	Presentation	Withdrawal
Positive	Positive reinforcement	Punishment
Negative	Punishment	Negative reinforcement
An example:		
Praise	Positive reinforcement	Punishment
Scolding	Punishment	Negative reinforcement

[a]Adapted from Holland and Skinner (1961).

sponse that is being suppressed. The alternative response, if made, should be answered with positive reinforcement. In experimental situations, the subject can be given an alternative: it can be trained to consider a light of one color as a stimulus to which it should respond. Another example of alternative responding is the often used T maze. The subject is required to find its way to one or the other arm of the maze. In one arm of the maze it will find a punishment, in the other a reward. The subject learns to go to the reward.

In human situations, punishment seldom needs to be harsh to teach avoidance of one response in favor of another. Many people respond very swiftly to certain types of mild punishment, which they interpret as signals to begin new response patterns. Such mild punishments as verbal criticism, frowning, shaking one's head, or clearing one's throat may signal undesirable behavior very clearly. As long as alternative correct behaviors exist, mild punishments have a reasonable chance to be effective.

Operant conditioning of involuntary responses

Would it be possible by operant conditioning to change the rate at which the heart beats or the intestine contracts? The question is related to a very basic theoretical problem: is there a difference between classical and operant conditioning, or are they simply two aspects of the same process? In practical terms, the question relates to the study of psychosomatic illnesses, such as stomach ulcers or certain forms of high blood pressure. If the subject could be "taught" to produce a lower blood pressure in response to the presentation of a stimulus—what a boon to medicine that might be!

What is involved is finding a way to reinforce an involuntary response (such as the normal heartbeat) without presenting stimuli that in themselves influence the response. An interesting example, far reaching in its possible consequences, is at hand. Neal Miller and his associates have solved the problem experimentally by using a form of electrical brain stimulation as a positive reinforcer (Figure 6.18). Miller has been able to condition heart rate, stomach contractions, and blood flow within the body. His research shows that involuntary responses can be conditioned by means of a positive-reinforcement procedure.

The theoretical question can now be partially answered, too. It seems clear that operant conditioning can affect responses previously thought to be the exclusive province of classical conditioning.

Control of blood pressure and heart rate Schwartz (1972) applied operant conditioning to autonomic responses in humans. He conditioned two closely related autonomic responses—blood pressure and heart rate—to vary independently or at the same time. Some subjects were reinforced when both responses increased, whereas others were reinforced when both decreased. Two other groups were reinforced when one response decreased while the other increased. The subjects were told only that the purpose of the experiment was to determine whether or not they could control certain physiological responses. The specific response was not mentioned.

The subjects in the experiment learned in one session to control their blood pressure and heart rate. A major practical difficulty is that the natural pattern of responses makes some combinations more difficult to condition than others. However, these findings suggest that some day people who suffer from heart irregularities and high blood pressure may be conditioned back to health.

Overview of operant conditioning

Many psychologists believe that operant conditioning is the basic means by which new responses are formed. A vast number of experiments, covering a wide variety of complex behaviors, have corroborated this opinion. Social responses, personal goals, cultural beliefs, to name but a few types of complex behavior, are seen as examples of operant conditioning. Common to all these forms of behavior is the fact that reinforcement—positive or negative—has been a necessary part of the learning process. Levels and kinds of reinforcement have varied, but the behavior has been learned because of the pending reinforcement. Consider the following illustrations:

Social activities—A man holds a door open for a woman because he has learned that it is the "gentlemanly" thing to do. This behavior is reinforced by social approval. To cite another example, a child learns the mechanics of language, grammar, composition, and so forth, because they enable him to communicate and also because society provides recognition and approval if he completes these tasks satisfactorily.

Personal goals—A tall girl may want to become a ballet dancer to prove that she is as agile and graceful as shorter girls; her accept-

Figure 6.18 Animal behavior can be controlled by electrical stimulation. At the same time that the cat is experiencing the stimulation, its brain waves are being monitored. (Tringali/Palmeri—dpi)

ance by the ballet troupe and by the public is her reinforcement, for she has proven to her own satisfaction that she is the equal of girls of medium height, the more usual height for ballet dancers.

Cultural beliefs—The American child is generally respectful of and passive toward his parents because he is reinforced for good behavior—a concept he shares with most other American children. The Yanomamö child of Brazil is encouraged to be aggressive, even to hit his parents if he wishes, because his culture is geared toward warfare and this reinforces the child's concept of manliness.

Since reinforcement can occur in so many different ways at so many different levels, it is easy to see why operant conditioning is effective. For instance, if a teacher discovers the appropriate positive reinforcer for a student in a given learning situation, and if he uses that reinforcer correctly, he can achieve startling results—even when the student seems not to be a promising one.

Effects of operant conditioning on brain chemistry
The influence of brain chemistry on behavior has been well established. Lewy and Seiden (1972) found that the reverse is also true: behavior influences brain chemistry. Water-deprived rats were trained to press a lever to get water, while identical control rats were either water deprived without lever-press training or had free access to water and were untrained. After training patterns were well established, all rats were injected with specially treated doses of norepinephrine, a chemical naturally present in rats' brains. Two hours later, all the rats were destroyed and examined. The investigators found that the group of trained rats had metabolized substantially more of the injected chemical than either of the two control groups. Since water deprivation was a control condition, it was concluded that only the behavioral difference—i.e., the operant lever-press training—could be held accountable for the change in metabolism.
Previous experiments had established that aversive stimulation affected norepinephrine metabolism, but this study was the first to show that operant conditioning also had this effect.

THE COGNITIVE APPROACH TO LEARNING

Behavioral psychologists view learning primarily as the association of stimuli to responses. They emphasize the observable environment and observable responses. While they do not ignore the possible events that may link stimulus and response, they are primarily interested in the external variables. *Cognitive* psychologists, on the other hand, emphasize what is or may be going on perceptually. They concern themselves with the processes that intervene between the stimulus and the response. The learner is not merely a receiver of stimuli and a maker of responses. He processes what he receives and his responses are determined by the processing. This processing involves the organization of information into meaningful or understandable wholes. Thus, cognitive psychologists conclude that learning involves changes in the processing—or, more specifically, in the perceiving.

Latent learning

E. C. Tolman was among the earliest investigators to reject the position that learning consists of a chain of stimuli and responses. He felt that learning consists of finding out what stimuli are associated with what other stimuli. He formulated the concept of *cognitive maps*, relationships among stimuli, and stated that rats as well as men learn through such relationships (Tolman, 1948). To support his contentions about cognitive learning, Tolman developed the idea of *latent learning*. Latent learning is operant learning that apparently takes place without the usual sequence of response leading to reinforcement. Tolman's position led him to suggest the kind of learning that occurs when the learner is able to see relationships among stimuli; he need not make the specific responses and does not require reinforcement.

The classic latent learning experiment was reported in 1930 by Tolman and Honzik. An experimental group of rats explored a complex maze on 10 successive days without any reinforcement for their responses. There was no apparent way for them to learn what constituted a correct route, for there was no goal box as such. A control group of rats also went through the maze on 10 successive days, but they were reinforced for each correct response. On the eleventh day, the experimental animals were reinforced for correct responses. The experiment showed that (1) the animals whose responses were reinforced (control group) performed better during the first 10 days than did the non-reinforced animals (experimental group); and (2) the introduction of reinforcement led to an immediate improvement in the performance of the experimental animals. Immediately after the experimental rats began to be reinforced, they performed as well as had the control animals, who had been receiving reinforcement all along. Thus, it was indicated that the rats in the experimental group learned the maze in the absence of reinforcement. Tolman believed that the experimental animals, on the basis of their experience in the maze, had learned which routes were the blind alleys. They had a cognitive map of the maze.

Insightful learning

An individual may be confronted with a problem that appears to be insoluble, and he may make no progress toward a solution until, suddenly, the solution comes to him. This common experience of sudden awareness is known as *insight*. Many psychologists believe that during the period of "no progress," when the problem seems insoluble, the individual reshuffles his past experiences and learning from similar problems in searching for a solution to the current one.

The moment of awareness comes when the past learning is recalled and applied effectively to the new situation.

Numerous experiments describing insightful behavior have been conducted with animal subjects, particularly chimpanzees. In one of Köhler's classic experiments (1925) a chimp in a cage is shown food, located beyond arm's reach. Sticks are placed in or near the cage, and the chimp soon examines and manipulates them. As soon as the food is presented, the chimp tries to reach it; when he cannot, he exhibits signs of frustration, anger, and perhaps even resignation. The insight experience occurs the moment the chimp reorganizes his perceptual field, so that he realizes how to reach the food: he can use a stick to push the food within arm's reach, and then he can grasp it successfully. Figure 6.19 illustrates insightful behavior in a similar situation.

Köhler also experimented with chickens, which are far less intelligent than chimpanzees. He trained chickens to find food on the darker of two paper squares placed side by side. Once the chickens learned to "expect" food on the darker square, he substituted for the originally lighter square one that was even darker than the original dark one. On 70 percent of the test trials, the chickens showed a preference for the new darker square. They switched their preference from the originally rewarding square to one that was darker. This suggested to Köhler that the chickens had perceived the relationship of the different degrees of darkness. They had an insight that the darker of two squares is the one with food.

Insight in human learning often involves the organizing or fitting together of information in a way that is meaningful to the learner. A child may learn the multiplication tables by memorizing them and only later recognize that multiplication is essentially addition. This recognition is a form of insight in which the child suddenly perceives that multiplication fits together with other things that he knows. Or a

Figure 6.19   Photographs of an ape's sudden insight that the food that was out of arm's reach can be obtained by stacking the boxes in his cage, one on top of the other. (Three Lions)

child may memorize the multiplication tables and later perceive some pattern to them. For example, he may suddenly see that in the 9s table, the sum of the digits in the answers is always 9: $9 \times 4 = 36 \ldots 3 + 6 = 9; 9 \times 8 = 72 \ldots 7 + 2 = 9$, etc. (Bigge, 1964). This is the type of insight in which a new meaningful relationship emerges.

Figure 6.20   See the text.

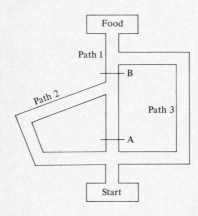

The long road home Tolman and Honzik (1930) studied a form of insightful learning in rats. Using an elevated maze like the one diagrammed here (Figure 6.20), they trained rats to take path 1, the shortest path to the food box. When the rats were trained, path 1 was blocked at point A. The rats proceeded to the block, then turned back and took path 2. The question was: What would happen if the block were placed on path 1 at point B and the rats started from the beginning again? Would they take path 2 again? What occurred was that 14 out of 15 rats "insightfully" chose path 3, the longest path but the only route open to the food box.

Constructing a coatrack Is insight related to other behavior or cognitive functions? Burke and Maier (1965) indicate that, if such a relationship exists, it is more complex than any psychologists have yet discovered.

In the Burke and Maier study, college men were asked to construct a coatrack in the middle of an empty room, using only two long sticks and one C clamp large enough to join the two boards. The only useful solution required the insight to clamp the sticks together so that they could be wedged between floor and ceiling, allowing the clamp handle to serve as the coat hook. Of the 18 psychological

Learning processes   **172**

measures available on many of the subjects (including SAT scores, measures of creativity and intellectual flexibility, and several opinion, attitude, and interest measures), none proved systematically correlated to successful completion of the coatrack insight problem. Insight seems to be a special psychological phenomenon that is not predicted by any of the usual intellectual or personality measures.

THEORIES OF LEARNING

All learning theories are systematic sets of guesses, by fallible men, about the nature of learning—how it occurs, when it occurs, and what factors cause it to occur. These theories, like all others in science, are based on observation and tested by observation. If a learning theory is useful, it increases understanding; if accurate predictions of experimental results can be based upon it, we value it. If it is not useful, if it does not clarify, if it does not help us to make accurate predictions, we discard it.

Note that there is no one learning theory. This chapter on learning is not a closed chapter, for we certainly have not discovered all there is to know about learning. Nonetheless, we know quite a lot about learning theories. We can class them, for example, into two groups: the stimulus-response or associationist theories, and the cognitive theories. There are points of agreement between the two groups, but it is generally easy to see the differences between them; they emphasize different features of learning.

Associationist theories

The associationist theories have their basis in the work of Pavlov and Thorndike. They are often referred to as S-R theories because they typically present learning in terms of changes in the association between stimuli and responses.

Guthrie's contiguity theory The simplest (in appearance) of the association theories is that of E. R. Guthrie. Guthrie's contiguity theory (1935) is based on the principle that a combination of stimuli that has accompanied a movement will, when it occurs a second time, tend to be followed by the same movement. According to Guthrie, once a stimulus has been associated by the learner with a response, the stimulus will thereafter elicit that response. This theory holds that efficient teaching can occur when the proper stimulus can be associated with the proper response without any interference from competing responses. (For a discussion of interference, see Chapter 7.)

Guthrie paid little attention to the problem of reinforcement. He held that we learn because we make responses in the presence of stimuli. We learn what we do, and we learn by doing. If you wish to know what a person is learning, look at what he is doing.

Hull's theory The most elaborately developed associationist theory is that of Clark L. Hull (1943). This theory makes use both of Pavlov's conditioning and of Thorndike's "trial-and-error" learning. Two of the key concepts in Hull's theory are "habit strength" and drive. A habit is a permanent connection that develops between a stimulus and a response. It grows stronger each time a stimulus and response are associated and the association is accompanied by the reduction of a particular drive. For example, a child learns to find candy in a round box because the stimulus (the round box) is associated with the response (lifting the top of the box), and the association is accompanied by a reduction of the hunger drive when the candy is eaten.

This theory stems in part from Thorndike's *law of effect.* The law of effect states that a modifiable connection between a stimulus and a response is strengthened when the association between them satisfies the organism. Hull does not speak of satisfaction. He speaks about the reduction of bodily needs and the consequent reduction in drives. For Hull, learning depends on association and drive reduction; drive reduction is the basis of the reinforcement.

Skinner's system   B. F. Skinner is the originator of a major school of thought in psychology. Skinner (1938) really founded a system rather than a theory. His system relies on *descriptive behaviorism* and the concepts of stimulus, response, and reinforcement. His reinforcement concept is defined in nontheoretical language: a positive reinforcer is any stimulus that strengthens responses that lead to the stimulus. Anything that increases the likelihood that the desired response will occur is regarded as a positive reinforcer. Food, praise, money, a nod of the head, and a smile are all examples of positive reinforcers.

Skinner distinguishes between two types of learning—respondent and operant. The respondent type is classical Pavlovian conditioning, as we noted earlier. For Skinner, the operant type of learning (operant conditioning) is more important since it involves more complex forms of learning. In operant learning, situations must be arranged so that the desired response is properly related to the reinforcement. This is a basic feature of the system of programmed instruction developed by Skinner.

Skinner's system lends itself well to application—not surprisingly, for it has been developed with an eye to application. Operant conditioning is a kind of behavioral engineering that constantly offers new ways to modify and control behavior. Because it is application oriented, the system has attracted the interest of many teachers. The applications of this system (with respect to programmed instruction and teaching machines) will be discussed in Chapter 7.

Pigeon inspector   Thomas Verhave used operant conditioning to teach pigeons to perform a complicated industrial task—to point out dented and defective gelatin capsules (*skags*) from a daily line of almost 30 million such capsules. He constructed a moving belt, on which the capsules came into the bird's view behind two keys. In discrimination training, the pigeon was given a food reward for pecking the key that indicated the appearance of a skag. If the capsule was acceptable, the pigeon pecked the other key, moving the belt but producing no food. Reinforcement in the form of food was given only after the correct identification of a skag. Incorrect judgments were not rewarded; instead, each one resulted in a 30-second blackout (the belt carrying the capsules was hidden from the pigeon's view for 30 seconds). In one week, the birds learned to inspect with 99 percent accuracy. The drug industry, however, objected to the employment of pigeons and did not hire them.

Cognitive theories

The cognitive theories are derived in part from Gestalt psychology. The theories in this group are closely related. Each emphasizes perception and perceptual processes. The cognitive theorists take the position that learning is a change in perception, a change in the way that an individual views a given situation. Their basic question is usually, "How has the learner's perception of a situation changed?" Whereas the S-R theorists emphasize the individual's association of stimulus and response, cognitive theorists emphasize the processes whereby the stimuli are perceived to be different from one another.

Lewin's theory   The best-known Gestalt psychologists, Wertheimer, Köhler, and Koffka, were more interested in perception than in learning; however, they exerted strong influence on Kurt Lewin and E. C. Tolman, both of whom developed theories of learning. Lewin's theory (1942) makes use of the Gestalt concept of *field*. The field is likened to a magnetic field whose key property is that every part of it depends on every other part. As learning occurs, the field changes and the learner behaves differently because he now perceives the stimulus situation in a different way. This change in the field comes about very swiftly, and when it does, the new behavior emerges quickly in an "insightful" manner.

A favorite field-theory example is found in motor skill learning. An action cannot be performed properly until a learner gets the hang of it, that is, until he perceives what it is that he must do. A person may work at learning to swing a golf club for a long time, apparently making no progress, until suddenly he finds (perceives) the correct muscular relationships in the swing and does it correctly.

Tolman's theory The cognitive theorist E. C. Tolman attempted to combine parts of cognitive theory with aspects of associationist theory (1932). Tolman's theory is often referred to as *purposive behaviorism* because of his emphasis on goal-directed behavior and his attention to the details of stimulus and response. According to Tolman, the learner's activity is always directed toward a goal. When he learns, he does so by finding out what leads to what. He develops a cognitive map of his environment. When a response is followed by a reward reinforcement, a cognition is produced—in other words, the learner perceives that making the response will lead to reward. We know that we will be rewarded with food if we go to the refrigerator. If we are hungry, we develop a picture (cognitive map) of the path to the refrigerator, the way to open the door, and the contents that await us.

Tolman's theory is a compromise between the two approaches. Moreover, it makes use of language and ideas that are reasonably familiar to the layman. But, although it is interesting to researchers in cognitive learning, it is not well supported by research.

The role of perception in learning will be discussed further in Chapter 10, where we examine problem-solving.

You discovered earlier in this chapter that psychologists disagree about learning. These disagreements are particularly troublesome to people who are primarily concerned with the practical problems of teaching. Many teachers would prefer to say, "So-and-so is correct," or "Thus-and-such learning theory is the way it really is." This is rarely possible. But we must bear in mind that the basic disagreements of psychologists are not necessarily related to the everyday problems of learning and teaching. Most of them are not; among the ones that are, the disagreements tend to be over what should be emphasized rather than over what actually happens during learning. For example, Guthrie emphasized the stimuli that evoke responses at one end, and Skinner emphasizes the reinforcers that strengthen responses at the other. Hull was primarily concerned with how reinforcers do their job. Lewin's emphasis was on the relationships between stimuli. Both Lewin and Tolman wanted to know what the learner perceives and what he does as a result of that perception.

Thus, we may feel assured that, although these differences in emphasis lead to different methods in the experimental study of learning, they need not, and generally do not, lead to different methods of teaching. There are principles on which the theorists agree, and these provide useful guidelines for both student and teacher.

SUMMARY

Learning is a process that brings about a relatively permanent change in an individual's repertory of responses as a result of experience or practice.

According to the principle of association, when two events or objects occur together in time or space, they tend to become associated. There are sensory associations and stimulus-response associations.

Classical conditioning (also known as Pavlovian or respondent conditioning) occurs when a neutral stimulus is systematically paired with another stimulus that produces a strong, uncontrolled response, resulting in a similar response to both stimuli. It involves four variables: (a) the conditioned stimulus (CS); (b) the unconditioned stimulus (US); (c) the reflexive unconditioned response (UR); and (d) the conditioned response (CR).

Pavlov used the term "reinforcement" to describe the process of strengthening the relationship between the CS and the CR by repeated pairings of the US and CS.

The ideal interstimulus interval is half a second, which is standard for trace conditioning. Other time relationships are simultaneous, delayed, and backward conditioning.

The measures of classical conditioning are magnitude, probability, latency, and resistance to extinction.

The weakening of an established conditioned response is called extinction.

When a conditioned response that has been extinguished reappears after rest without additional conditioning, it is a spontaneous recovery.

Stimulus generalization occurs when stimuli similar to the original conditioned stimulus evoke the conditioned response. When a subject cannot meet the particular demands of a stimulus, he is likely to make a substitute response, or a generalized response.

Discrimination is the process whereby the individual learns to respond to one and only one stimulus, even though similar stimuli may be present.

Higher-order conditioning takes place when a conditioned stimulus is used as an unconditioned stimulus.

In operant (or instrumental) conditioning, the consequences of a response to a stimulus determine whether the response will persist.

A positive reinforcer is an event that strengthens a response. A negative reinforcer causes a subject to respond so as to avoid or terminate an unpleasant stimulus.

Operant conditioning, based on Thorndike's law of effect, relies on the concept of reinforcement—the subject learns because his response is reinforced.

A basic tool of operant conditioning is the experimental chamber, or Skinner box. Responses of an animal pressing a lever or pecking a key in the box are measured by a cumulative recorder.

In escape and avoidance conditioning, reinforcement is termination or avoidance of a painful or unpleasant stimulus.

Successive approximations, or shaping, is the development of a series of responses in the direction of a desired final response.

Discrimination learning in operant conditioning involves responding only to particular stimuli. The correct stimulus is designated S^D; the incorrect stimulus, S^Δ.

Stimulus generalization in operant conditioning involves responding to stimuli similar to the conditioned stimulus, as well as to the original stimulus.

In operant conditioning, extinction is achieved by withholding reinforcement.

The effects of operant conditioning are measured by the rate of correct responses in the free responding situation. Some researchers use resistance to extinction to measure conditioning. In discrete trials, the effects of conditioning are measured by the number of trials required by the animal to make the correct response.

An unconditioned reinforcer is a reinforcer that is effective without its having been associated with other reinforcers. A conditioned reinforcer becomes effective only after it has been associated with other reinforcers.

Schedules of reinforcement are either continuous or partial. Partial reinforcement schedules may be fixed ratio, fixed interval, variable ratio, or variable interval.

Negative reinforcement strengthens the response that terminates the negative stimulus. In punishment, a response is suppressed by the presentation of an aversive stimulus.

Cognitive psychology views learning as a change in perception. It involves the organization of information into meaningful wholes.

Tolman developed the principle of latent learning, which maintains that learning occurs when the learner sees relationships among stimuli, without the need for specific response and reinforcement. The learner develops a cognitive map.

Insight in an individual is the sudden emergence of a solution to a problem after he has given much thought to it without making any apparent progress.

Learning theories may be classified as either stimulus-response (S-R) or cognitive theories. They differ in their views of what should be emphasized rather than over what actually happens during learning.

Associationist theories, based on the work of Pavlov and Thorndike, are S-R theories. The simplest associationist theory is Guthrie's contiguity theory. The most elaborate is Hull's, whose key concepts are habit strength and drive.

Skinner founded a system based on descriptive behaviorism; he considers a positive reinforcer to be anything that increases the likelihood of the desired response.

Cognitive theories of learning are based on principles of Gestalt psychology and take the position that learning is a change in perception. They emphasize the process whereby changes occur in the perception of stimuli. Lewin's field theory and Tolman's purposive behaviorism come under this category.

SUGGESTED READINGS

Texts

Estes, W. K., Koch, S., MacCorquodale, K., Meehl, P. E., Mueller, C. G., Jr., Schoenfeld, W. N., & Verplanck, W. S. *Modern learning theory.* New York: Appleton-Century-Crofts, 1954. Clear and readable discussion of the theoretical systems of Hull, Tolman, Skinner, Lewin, and Guthrie.

Gagné, R. M. *The conditions of learning.* New York: Holt, Rinehart & Winston, 1965. Excellent text on how the psychology of learning can be used in improving education.

Hilgard E. R., & Bower, G. H. *Theories of learning* (3rd. ed.). New York: Appleton-Century-Crofts, 1966. Best text available on the theories of learning.

Hill, W. F. *Learning* (2nd ed.). San Francisco: Chandler, 1972. A short, readable survey of psychological interpretations of the learning process from behaviorism to cybernetics.

Keller, F. S. *Learning: reinforcement theory* (2nd ed.). New York: Random House, 1969. A thorough introductory discussion of reinforcement theory.

Mowrer, O. H. *Learning theory and behavior.* New York: Wiley, 1960. Discusses conditioning with applications to various aspects of human behavior.

Munn, N. L. *The evolution and growth of human behavior* (2nd ed.). Boston:

Houghton Mifflin, 1965. Chapters 4 and 7, on learning in animals and children, are especially recommended.

Pavlov, I. P. *Conditioned reflexes.* New York: Macmillan, 1972. Classic statement (in English) of the Pavlovian position.

Skinner, B. F. *Cumulative record* (3rd ed.). New York. Appleton-Century-Crofts, 1972. Contains reprints of many of Skinner's most significant studies.

Popular books

Beltz, S. E. *A new learning environment: a case for learning.* An operant-conditioning reward system produced substantially accelerated academic growth among incarcerated juvenile delinquents.

Borger, R., & Seaborne, A. E. M. *The psychology of learning.* Nontechnical introduction for the general reader.

Cohen, H. L., & Filipczak, J. *How to make Johnny want to obey.* Application of basic learning principles to contemporary child-rearing practices.

Hill, W. F. *Learning through discussion.* Description of the process of learning in a group discussion situation.

7

Complex learning and retention

In the last chapter we began to study the principles of learning by looking at the fundamental processes. Much of what we know about learning has come from the evaluation of animal learning experiments under controlled conditions; and many of our examples were necessarily drawn from these experiments.

Perhaps it is difficult for you to associate the factors discussed in the previous chapter with the realities of learning as you have experienced them. The controlled world of the laboratory animal may seem remote from the real world, and the process of learning in our own lives may appear to bear little resemblance to classical and operant conditioning situations in the experimental laboratory.

But as we extend our examination to learning outside the laboratory, you will see the relevance of the principles we have discussed to the human learning process and grasp their relationship to such things as learning efficiency and retention.

LEARNING OF SKILLS

As in Chapter 6, we begin with the *response*—the overt behavior that is elicited by or associated with stimuli. All responses, if they are more complex than the simplest reflex or instinct, must be learned. Hence, the study of responses provides us with information about how skills are learned.

Motor skills

A *motor skill* is defined as the ability to coordinate a series of muscular movements. Motor skills involve a relationship between muscular movements and sensory input. We should also remember that perceptual variables affect motor skills and that, in some cases, motor skills are also affected by verbal behavior and cognitive factors.

Experiments that measure motor skill learning usually involve an unfamiliar situation. In a mirror-drawing experiment, for example, the subject is asked to trace a design without looking directly at it; he sees the design as it is reflected in a mirror. Because mirrors reverse the objects they reflect, the subject must learn to reverse his eye-hand coordination (Figure 7.1); lines that appear to be on the right are actually on the left and so on. Usually, the subject fumbles about for a while, but eventually he learns the task.

The subject's motor skill learning, in this and other experiments, is measured in terms of his correct responses and/or errors. The method of measuring may vary, depending on how the experimenter wants to chart the learning situation. He may record the number of errors and correct responses on a trial-by-trial basis. He may record the number of correct responses in each trial and relate them to the total number of responses; or he may record the number of errors in each trial and note the decrease as learning progresses. Whichever method he uses, the experimenter ultimately organizes his data graphically on a *learning curve*.

In the example of the mirror-drawing experiment, the psychologist records the number of correct responses and/or errors per trial and plots a learning curve. Figure 7.2 is a learning curve of a subject's progress in a series of mirror-drawing trials.

Motor skill learning begins in infancy—witness the child who randomly reaches, then grabs, and finally manipulates objects in his environment. It is most evident in the learning of active sports. For example, the bowler trying to make a strike learns a little more on each throw (trial)—how to stand, how to direct the ball, and so on.

The learning of any motor skill—mirror drawing, bowling, baseball, knitting, and so on —requires *feedback* from the sense organs. Feedback helps us coordinate our muscular movements. Visual feedback, for example, tells the mirror-drawing subject that he has crossed a line; it tells the bowler that he must stand at a certain position in the alley and at a certain distance from the tenpin.

Figure 7.1   Subjects are tested on motor skills in unfamiliar situations. The subject here must reproduce the design by looking at its reflection in the mirror. (Van Bucher, courtesy University of Florida Clinical Psychology)

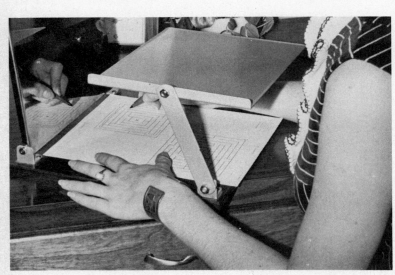

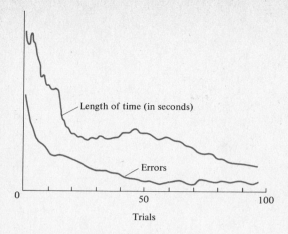

Figure 7.2 A learning curve to show the individual's record of progress in learning to draw the mirrored design in Figure 7.1. The scores are determined by the length of time each tracing takes and the number of errors made on each tracing. As an individual improves, his score decreases. (After Starch, 1910)

A person can improve his performance of a motor skill by *conceptualizing* the task before he performs it, that is, by first picturing what has to be done and how to control his motor responses. Just as we practice a speech in front of a mirror, so we can practice a motor task in our minds and see ways to improve our performance.

Conceptualization in tennis We may imagine that Billie Jean King, awaiting the first service of a tennis match, has already programmed herself by reviewing in her mind all she knows of her opponent and noting the court conditions. When the court is wet, the balls are heavier and have less bounce. If the server is left-handed, she will hit the ball to Billie Jean's backhand. The normal overspin on the service will be accentuated by the ball's heaviness. Billie Jean, awaiting service, will conceptualize the action of the ball.

Verbal skills

Verbal learning typifies much of our learning. Its study is especially important since the tech-

niques by which we acquire words, associate meanings, transfer learning from one experience to another, and maintain (or remember) learning are common to many other learning situations. Studies of verbal learning thus provide information about a wide variety of human learning situations.

Rote memorization In an important study of word learning, the German psychologist Hermann Ebbinghaus (1885) deliberately used repetitive verbal learning, *rote memorization*, as a model for all learning. Ebbinghaus devised *nonsense syllables*—letter combinations that have no meanings. With these made-up "words," he could eliminate certain uncontrollable and interfering factors, such as meanings, associations to other words, and other similar distractions.

Ebbinghaus created his nonsense syllables by selecting three-letter words of a consonant-vowel-consonant form: *YIP, GUP, XEX,* and so on. But these almost-words were not entirely free from connotations (*XEX* might connote "sex"). Later psychologists created triple-consonant nonsense syllables: *XVB, KGC, PBJ,* and so on. The use of triple-consonant syllables—or of number combinations—freed the nonsense material from most meaningful interpretations.

In memory experiments, nonsense syllables are presented on a slowly moving *memory drum,* which reveals one word or one word pair at a time (Figure 7.3). The subject is given a limited length of time to look at the word before the drum rotates to the next word. When nonsense syllables are to be memorized in a given order or series, we say that the task involves *serial memorization* or *serial anticipation* (Figure 7.4). When syllables are to be learned by *paired-associate learning,* they are shown in pairs (Figure 7.5) and the subject learns a single pair at a time.

Serial memorization In serial memorization experiments, the first trial is usually run with a standard interval of about 2 seconds between syllables. Since the subject has never before seen

Figure 7.3   The memory drum, a device used in serial memorization and paired-associate learning tasks. The drum rotates slowly and shows either a sequence of single nonsense syllables (as in Fig. 7.4) or a sequence of single nonsense syllables followed by a pair of nonsense syllables (as in Fig. 7.5). (Photo by Van Bucher, courtesy Wagner College Department of Psychology)

the list of syllables, he will obviously be unable to provide the proper response for any of the stimuli. Nevertheless, it is on the first trial that the subject begins to learn. The first nonsense word becomes a stimulus for the second, and the second word is both a response to the preceding stimulus and a stimulus for the third word. By means of the stimulus-response chain, the subject learns the cues for anticipating the complete list of words in their correct order.

It is often useful to memorize serially. You may recall that you learned the multiplication tables by serial memorization. Each number became a cue for the next as you ran through the products of 8 × 1, 8 × 2, and so on.

Paired-associate learning   In paired-associate learning, the syllables are learned in isolated pairs; there need not be any stimulus-response relationship between one pair and the next. The first member of each pair appears on the memory drum as the stimulus. The complete pair—the

Figure 7.4 (Left)   A typical list of nonsense syllables for serial memorization.

Figure 7.5 (Right)   A typical list of nonsense syllables for paired-associate learning.

BOQ
VUX
SEM
GAZ
XUJ
LUP
NEF

GEZ
GEZ–BUH
WAL
WAL–ROV
PIF
PIF–LER
XUT
XUT–QAC

stimulus and the response—is shown next. Consequently, the subject sees immediately whether or not his response was correct.

Paired-associate learning may be used effectively in many disciplines. It is, for example, the principle behind all "matching question" tests. The technique is particularly helpful in foreign language vocabulary learning. The stimulus word is the foreign term, and the response word is the equivalent word in the learner's native language (or vice versa).

Paired-associate learning is similar to classical conditioning methods. Indeed, it is safe to say that *any* method of learning that involves the association of a stimulus and a response is similar to classical conditioning.

Foreign language potential Governmental and educational institutions on the lookout for people with foreign language skills need a quick and accurate method to test for potential ability. In response to this need, Cooper (1964) designed a study to determine whether the results of a paired-associate task could be used to predict success in learning a foreign language. He administered paired-associate tests to a group of college students who had completed one semester of a foreign language. When he compared his results with the scores obtained from the college entrance exam, an English grammar test, and the final language grade for each subject, he found that the scores obtained for paired-associate learning correlated highest with grades received in the foreign language course. Also, the scores for the most difficult paired-associate items, in terms of meaningfulness and similarity, correlated even higher with grade scores in language courses. Thus, the data suggest that success on the paired-associate task indicates an individual's potential for learning a foreign language.

Imagery and verbal learning

The serial and paired-associate methods are most useful to associationist psychologists because of their emphasis on the connections between stimuli and responses as the basis of all learning. Cognitive psychology, however, emphasizes other processes in verbal learning. One such process is imagery. *Images* are internal sensory representations of objects in the absence of those objects; they may represent objects previously perceived, or they may be symbolic creations of new objects. Images do not reflect the present experience; rather, they only make us feel as if we are having an experience.

Imagery may take many forms, depending on the sensory mode the individual associates with the image. An image may be visual, auditory, or perhaps olfactory.

The clearest type of imagery is known as *eidetic imagery*, or *photographic memory*, whereby individuals are somehow able to re-create entire visual experiences. Although much more common in children, eidetic imagery does appear in some adults. People who have this ability may remember the most minute detail of a scene, or entire pages of a book.

Images can bring to mind words, and words have the property of arousing images, some more easily than others. Concrete words, such as "pig," "bicycle," and "pencil," are good image-arousers, but words like "liberty," "happiness," and "honesty" do not easily arouse images. A list of image-arousing words is usually learned more quickly and retained better than a list of words that do not easily arouse images.

The formation of images appears to help in learning and retaining what has been learned. According to Paivio (1971), imagery provides an additional source of association. The learner has access to associations between words, between images, and between words and images. If an individual learns to associate two words, such as "boy" and "fence," and each word arouses an image, then the number of available associations is greatly increased.

Afterimages seen by children To obtain more reliable information on the frequency of eidetic imagery, Haber and Haber (1964) tested three-fifths of the students in a Connecticut elementary school. Each child was shown four solid-colored squares and four pictures against a neutral gray easel. The investigators elicited from each a detailed report of what, if anything, he saw in that spot after the stimulus was removed, and evaluated the quality of each subject's afterimagery. Subjects were questioned about color, movement, clarity, duration, and detail of their afterimages. A measure of memory for each stimulus was obtained by asking for another detailed description of the stimulus after the subject reported complete fading of his image.

Only 8 percent of the total sample were found to have the capacity for eidetic imagery, although more than half of all subjects reported some type of afterimage. The ability of the children with eidetic imagery to report the detail and vividness of the experimental stimuli was so complete that the investigators judged their capacities to be qualitatively different from normal afterimage phenomena. Interestingly, no great difference was found in memory for stimulus detail after the fading of the reported image among the various groups of children—the exceptional eidetic-imagers, those who had normal afterimagery, and those who had no afterimagery.

In a follow-up study less than a year later, reports of eidetic imagery generally coincided with the original data. Long-term follow-up studies of children with eidetic imagery are still needed, however, to chart the developmental aspects of this phenomenon.

Unlike images, *percepts* are evoked by actual physical stimuli. Not all individuals perceive vividly; and an individual's perception may vary, depending on his state of readiness and the strength of the stimulus. Similarily, two people may have different perceptions of the same object. For example, if a man and a woman are both shown a diamond pin and then asked to describe it, the woman might mention its hue, size, shape, or setting, whereas the man might have only a vague image of its shape.

EFFICIENT LEARNING

Learning is the chief survival tool of our species. It is not simply a process that we study in books; it is the process by which we study. Therefore, we are as interested in the variables that contribute to efficient learning as we are in the basic nature of learning. There are several such variables.

Knowledge of results

First of all, learning efficiency is increased when the subject has direct *knowledge of the results* of his performance in the learning situation. (We touched on this in paired-associate learning.) Knowledge of results, especially when favorable, reinforces learning and maintains interest. It tells the subject exactly how well he is doing—that he has developed a degree of competence in mastering the task at hand, that he has mastered the task, or that he needs to alter certain behaviors to perfect his mastery.

In motor and verbal learning, a quick report on the results of each trial will help the learner to adjust his behavior—to improve his performance on the next trial. But learning situations often do not provide directly observable results; the student, for example, must wait to receive his grade on an exam.

The value of feedback Thorndike (1932) tested two groups of blindfolded subjects on their ability to draw a line corresponding in length to a 4-inch piece of wood, which they could feel and manipulate at any time. Each subject drew 200 lines a day for 9 days. A correct response was one that came within two-tenths of an inch of the length of the wood. One group received feedback for 7 consecutive days followed by 2 days of no feedback. The other group received no feedback for the 9 consecutive days. Thorndike found that the no-feedback group never progressed beyond the first day. They were about 12 percent accurate. The feedback group, however, improved steadily during the 7 days of feedback, reaching a 60 percent level of accuracy. When feedback was eliminated for this group, the accuracy for line-drawing dropped to 30 percent. Still, it was shown that, given feedback, blindfolded subjects could learn to be more accurate than those not given feedback, even when the feedback was stopped at a later time.

Students usually learn more efficiently if graded tests or quizzes are returned to them immediately. However, immediate knowledge of results in school and other learning situations does not always produce superior learning and retention. In some recent experiments, feedback has been delayed for periods of time ranging from several seconds to several days. The results indicated that some forms of verbal learning may be unaffected or even improved by delays in feedback.

Meaningfulness

If the material to be learned is *meaningful* to the learner, the rate of learning is more rapid. The more meaningful the material, the fewer trials are necessary to learn it and the smaller the amount of variable behavior from trial to trial. A person learns faster, for example, if he is memorizing a poem rather than a list of nonsense syllables of similar length (Figure 7.6).

An individual will also learn faster if he is interested in the material to be learned. There is ample evidence that genuine relevance contributes significantly to faster learning; for example, high school students show a higher reading level on "relevant" material than on standard nonpersonal texts.

The significance of meaning in nonsense syllables
Nonsense syllables have no meaning. However, a nonsense syllable may suggest a meaningful association to the learner. Glaze (1928) used 15 subjects to rate the association value of more than 2,000 nonsense syllables. His findings enabled him to devise a scale of association values of nonsense syllables.

Because this study and others like it used a limited number of subjects, they have been heavily criticized. Archer (1960) used more than 300 subjects to reevaluate the meaningfulness of 2,480 possible nonsense syllables from established lists. The subjects were asked to express the meaningfulness of each syllable by stating whether the syllable was a word, sounded like a word, reminded them of a word, or could be used in a sentence. A high positive correlation was found between Archer's results and Glaze's.

To test the notion that more meaningful material is better retained, Underwood and Richardson (1956) devised several lists, each containing 10 nonsense syllables rated extremely meaningful according to Glaze. These researchers found that the more meaningful the material (even though nonsense syllables), the more effective learning became.

Amount of material

The *amount of material* that can be memorized depends on the length and type of material and its relation to the individual's memorization capability (or capacity). *Memory span* is the number of letters, numbers, or words that can be memorized in one trial. The average memory span is 7 or 8 characters (digits or letters). Although the time needed to memorize 10 char-

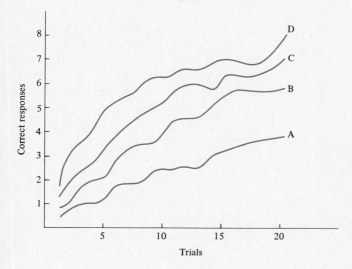

Figure 7.6   A graph showing the results of a test for learning of both nonsense and meaningful material. At A, nonsense material is used. As we progress from A to D, the material to be learned becomes more and more meaningful. Note that more of the meaningful material is retained. (After Underwood and Schulz, 1960)

acters is about double the time required to memorize 7 or 8, the jump from 10 to 13, for instance, is very slight. These wide variations in learning time indicate that the amount of information presented is a significant factor in learning. (Incidentally, it has been shown that we learn digit series more quickly than letters; see Figure 7.7.)

Distinctiveness of the material

Another factor that influences the rate of learning is the *distinctiveness of the material* to be learned, that is, those aspects that help an item to stand out—color, size, and other features that differentiate the item from others around it. We remember our first days at college very clearly, because the pattern of experiences was unlike any other. The unusual pattern is remembered much more clearly than the routine—how well do you remember dinner 5 nights ago? When we are learning new material, an unusual situation presents itself to us with emphasis, and we often respond by learning it immediately.

One theory suggests that an item stands out and is remembered because it is different from others nearby. An item grouped with similar ones, on the other hand, is remembered with difficulty, because the similarities cause interference and the learner becomes confused. This is known as *interference theory* and is based on a behaviorist view, which emphasizes interference among stimulus-response associations as the major impediment to learning.

Gestalt psychologists advance a different theory to account for the faster learning incurred by distinctive stimuli. They feel that every stimulus is perceived as a figure against a background, or field. In learning, the individual imposes his own pattern on the stimulus; similar items are perceived as the background for the distinctive item, which is thus learned first and remembered most vividly. At present, the interference theory has more research support than does the Gestalt theory.

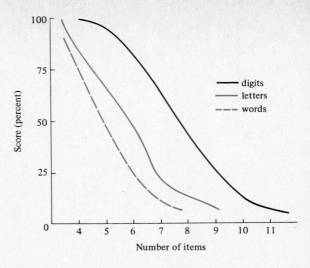

Figure 7.7　A learning curve showing the rate of learning of digits, letters, and words. Each subject was tested on digits, letters, and words that ranged between four and nine units each. The curves indicate the percentage of times that each set was memorized correctly. The larger sets were memorized correctly fewer times, and so received lower scores. Actually, these curves depict memory span; the easiest set to memorize consists of four units. (Adapted from Crannell and Parrish, 1957)

Distribution of practice

The length of a practice session and the distribution of rest periods are important variables in the learning process. Motor skill practice is more effective when it includes brief, wisely distributed rest periods; one's tennis will improve more after three 1-hour practice sessions than during one 3-hour session. Similarly, serial verbal learning benefits from *distributed practice* —a healthy practice-rest mixture. In paired-associate learning, the key variable seems to be the type of response required. If the task involves responses that are similar to each other, it is helpful to distribute the practice. It stands to reason that rest periods will help to extinguish interfering associations. The rest period allows the material to incubate before the next session.

Many factors contribute to the success or failure of distributed practice. The length and frequency of training periods, for example, must meet the needs of the particular subject. His performance and enthusiasm may be strongly influenced by frequent fresh starts. Or he may do poorly at the beginning of any activity and need extensive practice to reach a peak.

The material to be learned can impose restrictions, too. If the practice period is too short, the material may be artificially split into disjointed units that have little meaning for the subject. For classroom material to be retained by students, the practice period should be long enough for the teacher to present meaningful quantities of information—but not so much that it cannot be absorbed by the students. Psychologists tend to favor scheduling of frequent rest periods within the learning setting, especially in the teaching of motor skills.

The location of the rest periods must also be considered. If the surrounding environment offers distracting noises, social diversions, entertainment, and so on, students should probably not be allowed to leave the learning location for a lengthy rest period. The diversion may be so distracting that the student may lose track of his learning—and may even forget to return to the learning environment.

Whole versus part learning

The question of distribution of practice is closely related to the question of *whole learning* versus *part learning*—whether it is better to learn material as a complete unit or in parts. Whole learning is often the most efficient way to learn material, particularly for fast learners. Repeated use of the whole method improves the individual's facility with it. Short or highly meaningful material is easily memorized as a whole; if part learning is used, the continuity and sense of meaningful material can be lost.

The length of the material, however, may make it impossible to use the whole method. In such cases, the material should be broken into smaller but still meaningful parts, then memorized, part by part, and progressively recombined after each part is learned. This is called the *progressive part method*.

A special advantage of part learning is that it can be adjusted to the level of difficulty of each part; the learner can take longer to memorize the more difficult parts, less time to memorize the easier parts. But this method involves a risk of error in remembering the correct order of the separate parts and their connection. Also, the part method requires more time. When one tries to recall material learned by the part method, more interference may occur. Part learning may, in the long run, slow down overall learning. Part learning, however, is particularly valuable for motor skill learning. For example, a pianist must practice complex chords separately before he can put them together as a smooth-flowing musical composition.

Both part and whole learning are useful, depending on the situation, the learner, and the material to be learned. In general, whole learning is best for verbal learning of relatively short, highly meaningful material; part learning is best for verbal learning of lengthy, complex material and for most motor skill learning.

THE TRANSFER OF LEARNING

Learning experiences of the past have the ability to influence present learning. Thus, what we learn in one situation may affect other situations. This *transfer of learning* is an exceedingly important process. It is probably responsible for our ability to recognize objects, perceive relationships, and conceptualize the experiences we encounter throughout our lives. In addition, the transfer principle is in large part responsible for the enormous amount of knowledge we are able to acquire.

Types of transfer

We say that *positive transfer* has occurred when learning one task. A makes a second task B easier to learn. If, by learning task A first, a subject finds it more difficult to learn task B, then *negative transfer* has occurred.

The typical transfer-of-training experiment involves two groups: (1) an *experimental* group that learns task A and then task B; and (2) a *control* group that learns only task B (Figure 7.8). If positive transfer is operating, the experimental group will learn task B more easily than the control group. If negative transfer is operating, the experimental group will learn task B less easily than the control group. If the experimental group and the control group learn the material in task B equally well, then it may be said that the learning of material in task A had no effect on the learning of material in task B— *zero transfer* occurred.

Variables affecting transfer

Positive transfer usually occurs when two tasks require the same or a similar response to stimuli, even if the stimuli are different. Response generalization (discussed in Chapter 6) is involved. In the experiment described in Figure 7.8, positive transfer occurs between the two tasks because the responses are similar. The more similar the required responses, the stronger the positive-transfer effects will be.

Psychologists believe that training is positively transferred, because it is simpler for an individual to construct an association from an existing response than to construct a new association that uses both a new stimulus and a new response. Learning to drive a truck is easier if you already know how to drive a car. The stronger the original learning, of course, the stronger will be the effects of positive transfer.

The principles of positive transfer are apparent in learning foreign languages. You will always find a new language easier to learn if it is

Session	Experimental group	Control group
1	Learn A: JIF—LITTLE BIQ—DARK CAX—LARGE PER—FAST	Unrelated activity: (For example, series of authentic problems)
2	Learn B: JEF—SMALL BEQ—BLACK GOX—GREAT POR—QUICK	Learn B: JEF—SMALL BEQ—BLACK GOX—GREAT POR—QUICK

Figure 7.8   A typical experiment to test for the existence of transfer of training. Two groups are set up. One group is given task A to learn, while the other is given something unrelated to do. Then both groups are given task B to learn. The experimenter measures the learning of each group on task B. If there is positive transfer of training between task A and task B, the experimental group will learn task B faster.

closely related to one you already know; you can transfer more of what you have learned about the first language to the second.

Negative transfer

Negative transfer often occurs when the stimuli are similar but the response required for each stimulus is different. A previous association between stimulus and response interferes with learning the new association. For example, it is difficult to learn the binary number system that is based on the digits 1 and 0 when we have grown so accustomed to our familiar system based on ten digits. We know that $1 + 1 = 2$ (one plus one equals two) in our usual number system. But we have difficulty learning that $1 + 1 = 10$ (one plus one equals one zero) when we try to learn the binary system.

Stimulus-response variation and negative transfer
Numerous experiments have been conducted to determine the basis for negative transfer. One of the first, organized by Bruce (1933), called for the use of various combinations of paired-associates. Bruce

changed both syllables—the stimulus syllable alone, or the response syllable alone from the original set of nonsense syllables. When he changed the requirement to the learning of two new nonsense syllables (stimulus and response pair), he found a small measure of positive transfer, which he attributed to the practice of learning the original pair. When original responses were paired with new nonsense syllables, he found a large measure of positive transfer. However, when the learning requirement was a new response to an old stimulus, negative transfer occurred.

Since Gibson (1941) achieved similar results with both nonsense figures and nonsense syllables, it appears that negative transfer is not restricted to verbal learning.

Learning to learn

The amount of transfer between two tasks whose stimuli and responses are both different can be zero. But even where the contents of the tasks are quite different, similarity in the method of learning may produce positive transfer effects. These effects may stem from the phenomenon of *learning how to learn*. It is well known that student subjects in laboratory experiments improve their ability to master lists of nonsense syllables as they learn more lists. They learn to improve rote-learning skills.

Choosing the correct response The typical learning situation involves discrimination. For each problem in Harlow's (1949) experiment, the monkey was given a choice between two different stimuli. If he selected the correct stimulus, he was rewarded with food. If at first the monkey was rewarded for selecting the left stimulus, he would tend to choose the left stimulus the next time around (position preference). To force the monkey to respond to the specific reinforcing stimulus itself rather than to an irrelevant feature of the stimulus situation (position, for example), the problem was presented to the subject many times in different ways. When the subject consistently responded correctly, he was given the next discrimination problem.

On the first few tasks, the correct response was given only 50 percent of the time on the second trial (no more frequently than would be expected by chance). The number of correct responses on the second trial increased as more and more tasks were mastered until, after 300 tasks were mastered, the

correct response was given on the second trial 95 percent of the time. The subjects not only learned to master each problem but also learned to apply their initial experience to each new problem and to achieve progressively greater speed in reaching solutions.

Experiments have shown that learning to learn also occurs in lower animals. Figure 7.9 depicts a typical learning task as performed by Harry Harlow's monkeys. Harlow conducted more than 300 experiments with each monkey. As a result, the monkeys eventually were able to master new tasks by the second trial of each new task. In Harlow's terms, the monkeys had developed a *learning set*, an orientation toward learning a certain type of task (Harlow, 1949). Learning such an orientation is important when one considers the many different tasks that require similar or related procedures. Learning mathematics, for example, may enable you to transfer the learning set to such tasks as plotting the navigation course of a boat or a plane.

The effects of rest on the transfer of training Recent research indicates that the training experience of one animal can be transferred to another simply by injecting the second with some brain matter from the first. A significant finding of research in this area involves the effects of rest periods at varying times in the original training schedule. Golub, Masiarz, Villars, and McConnell (1970) trained 2- and 3-month-old food-deprived rats in a sequence that involved three steps: acquisition of a bar-press response to obtain food pellets; extinction training, during which the rats received no reward for bar-pressing; and reacquisition training, when regular reinforcement was resumed. Inserting a week's rest period into that sequence, however, greatly affected the training that was passed on to later rats, despite the fact that all trained rats were killed within minutes after their last reacquisition-training session. If the rest was inserted after the acquisition phase, the rats receiving the brain matter from the trained rats showed the expected acceleration in learning. But if the rest period was inserted after the extinction training, the recipient rats were less able to learn than the control rats injected with extract from untrained rats.

Apparently, the critical difference is that the

Figure 7.9   A typical Harlow experiment. The monkeys learn to discriminate the item that differs from the other two. (Harry F. Harlow, University of Wisconsin Primate Laboratory)

rest period allows time for the immediately preceding training to incubate; during this time, the chemical composition of the brain changes in such a way that the effects of the training can be transferred to another brain.

Transfer in education

The transfer principle was applied in earlier "classical" education, when courses were taught in a sequence believed to promote the positive transfer of basic learning techniques. It was thought that Latin and formal logic (the classical curriculum) should be taught first as basic disciplines, for mastering them would help students learn all subsequent material. This *formal discipline* theory of education held that initial training in certain disciplines laid the foundation for later learning. Although the benefits of the classical curriculum have been experimentally disproved and the system has been abandoned in the United States, it is still a foundation for formal learning in some European countries.

American educators today are concerned with educating the individual to make a positive transfer of learning to everyday life. They believe that if the schools can make the young confident that the complex problems of life are soluble, then the American education system is achieving a measure of success.

APPLICATIONS OF THE PRINCIPLES OF LEARNING

The principles of learning apply to every facet of life—at home, in school, at work, and, within these situations, to interpersonal relations. Here we will emphasize their relationship to education.

The following are eight generally accepted principles of learning, and some of their possible applications:

1 The learner learns from his own behavior. He should be prevented from learning incorrect responses at the outset.
2 Learning is most effective when the learner's correct responses are reinforced immediately. The feedback should be informative and rewarding whenever the response is correct. Because correct responses require positive reinforcement, it might seem that incorrect responses require

punishment. Although punishment may be effective if used prudently and cautiously, available data show that punishment may also inhibit learning. Even though punishment temporarily suppresses an incorrect response, the response may reappear when the punishment stops. Punishment is also emotionally disruptive.

3 The frequency of reinforcement will determine how well the response will be learned and retained. It should also be noted that the schedule or pattern of the reinforcements is as important as the number of times a reinforcement is used to maintain a learned response. This principle as applied to teaching is probably most effective when the learner receives continuous reinforcement at first and is gradually shifted to a partial reinforcement schedule.

4 Practice of a response in various settings increases both retention and transferability. Positive transfer must be encouraged, negative transfer discouraged. The mathematics teacher who gives his algebra students a variety of related algebra problems encourages positive transfer of the algebraic principles they have learned. If he were to try to teach his students the methods of calculus while teaching them algebra, negative transfer might result, for the students might confuse algebraic and calculus solutions.

5 Motivational conditions influence the effectiveness of positive reinforcement and play a key role in the level of performance. Motivated students learn more quickly and effectively than unmotivated students. The teacher who wishes to develop or increase his students' desire to learn needs to understand the incentives to learn and how they can be strengthened. (See Chapter 8 for a more complete discussion of motivation.) The following is a useful classification of common incentives and their rewards:

(a) *achievement motivation,* which is rewarded with success;

(b) *anxiety,* which leads to the avoidance of failure;

(c) *approval motivation,* which seeks the reward of approval in many forms;

(d) *curiosity,* which is rewarded with increased exposure to novel stimuli in the environment;

(e) *acquisitiveness,* for which the reward is some tangible material benefit.

Any or all of these rewards can be effective for the student. The value the student places on each reward—the degree to which each motivates him—can change from moment to moment. Nonetheless, certain rewards are likely to be more effective for certain types of people. Achievement and anxiety incentives are often found in the children of middle-class parents, who commonly set high goals for their offspring. The degree to which an individual seeks approval from others depends on personality factors and previous experiences; most people are motivated by this incentive. Curiosity, too, appears to be universal in the human character. Acquisitiveness depends directly on experience. Individuals who have owned and lost many material possessions are often very acquisitive.

6 Meaningful learning is more permanent and more transferable than rote learning. In applying this principle, a teacher should help the learner discover how the material relates to his own experiences. For example, the student who trains a pet dog or cat will be able to understand and use the principle of reinforcement more rapidly than the student who is simply told how the principal operates but does not have the experience of trying to keep his pet from ruining the carpet.

7 The learner's perception of the material determines how quickly and effectively he will learn. The way material is displayed by the teacher has a demonstrable bearing on what students will learn from it. Suppose that a third-grade teacher demonstrated the structure of sentences by putting several sentences on the blackboard, each exactly one line long and each ending with a period. In that case, the children might conclude that every *line* of writing should end with a period. They would learn what they perceived, and their perception would lead them astray. Teachers should be able to isolate the important stimuli and present them in a way that enables the learners to perceive them correctly, based on what they see and what they already know.

8 People learn more effectively when they learn at their own pace. Individuals differ widely in their ability to perceive relevant stimuli and in the time it takes them to respond and form associations. Even though a teacher may have too many tasks and too large a class to permit

each student to work independently, it is important for him to remember that an individual learns better when he sets his own pace. Programmed instruction uses the principle of self-paced learning (Figure 7.10).

Autonomous student behavior Brigham and Bushell (1972) argued that the typical elementary school classroom functions as a sometimes benevolent dictatorship in which authority rests with the teacher. They set up a classroom situation in which the students earned points, or tokens, for their work which could be exchanged for reinforcing activities. Measures were taken of the students' academic progress. Under one set of conditions, students worked and received tokens which could be traded for *their choice* of activities. Under the second condition, students worked and were given the *teacher's selection* of the same or similar activities. Then the *student-selected* reward procedure was reinstated. It was found that students progressed at a more rapid pace when they were able to select the consequences of their effort. The researchers suggested that because a token system

Figure 7.10   Guided discovery has been shown to be the most effective means of teaching. The student learns because he alone has figured out the solution. The instructor has subtly led him in the right direction. (Bruce Roberts— Rapho Guillumette)

Programmed instruction The importance of knowledge of results is demonstrated in a form of teaching called *programmed instruction.*

The term "programmed instruction" may be used to describe several teaching techniques, all of which have the following characteristics in common:

1 The material actively involves the student in the learning process.
2 The material provides the student with immediate knowledge of results.
3 The material is tested and revised until it demonstrably teaches what it is supposed to teach.

Programmed instruction is based on the principles of operant conditioning. Material is presented in steps (or frames), each of which consists of information, questions, and/or exercises, calling for a response from the learner. The frames follow each other so closely (in terms of the data presented and responses sought) that it is reasonably certain that the student will

make the correct responses throughout. After completing each frame, the student checks his answer with the answer given in the program. In this way, he receives immediate feedback on the success of his learning; if his answer is correct, he is positively reinforced. A program can be presented in book form, in a teaching machine, or even by means of a computer.

There are two principal types of programmed instruction: *linear* and *intrinsic* (or *branching*). Each represents a somewhat different teaching approach. A linear program breaks down the units of information as finely as possible, especially at the beginning of a program, and sequences them in such a way that the learner will respond correctly most of the time. Feedback is immediate and continuous. An intrinsic program, on the other hand, gives the student relatively little guidance, presenting the material in fairly large blocks of information. The student is given a *remedial step* (an additional unit of information) if he makes an error. If, however, he seems to understand the concept and answers several questions correctly, he may skip a block of material and move forward to a more advanced concept.

There are also differences in format between a linear and an intrinsic program. Linear programs usually seek *constructed* responses: the student must compose answers to questions, whether the answers are words, sentences, paragraphs, or diagrams. Intrinsic programs generally present a multiple-choice format in which the student selects the most likely answer. Figure 7.11 illustrates the differences between linear and intrinsic programs.

The relative effectiveness of linear and intrinsic programs depends on the subject matter and the capabilities of the students. Linear programs are more commonly used. They are easier to construct and quite effective in teaching basic skills and concepts—particularly to students who are not highly motivated or who are frightened by textbooks or the subject matter. Intrinsic programs, on the other hand, appear to be very well suited to teaching enrichment material to more mature, more highly motivated students.

Individual versus classroom and machine tutoring
Malpass, Gilmore, Hardy, and Williams (1965) successfully used programmed instruction to teach retarded children with IQs (intelligence quotients) of 50 to 80. Most were attending public school classes for the mentally retarded; some lived and received schooling in an institution. The children ranged in age from 10 to 16 years. Two different teaching machines were used: one was a multiple-choice apparatus, which produced an auditory and visual signal when the correct lever was pressed; and the other, a filmstrip, connected to a typewriter keyboard. Pressing the correct typewriter key caused the film to confirm the answer.

The children were divided into four groups: two groups were assigned to the machines; a third group was taught by conventional classroom methods; and a fourth group received individual instruction.

The results of individual tutoring were far superior to the results of classroom instruction. The children who were taught individually learned an average of more than 20 new words, while the classroom children learned an average of only 6 words. More important, both groups of children taught by programmed procedures learned as well as those given individual tutoring. In addition, the machine-taught children retained most of the words they had learned when they were tested 60 days later.

Opponents of programmed instruction maintain that it eliminates teachers and dehumanizes education. In practice, it does neither. A program is simply another teaching tool, effective if used properly, ineffective if used badly. The teacher who uses programmed instruction correctly continues to arrange the conditions of learning, to evaluate performance, to reward learning, and to offer review and practice.

Computer-assisted instruction   There is increasing interest in presenting programmed instruction by means of computers. Today's high-speed computers are well suited to provide the student with immediate knowledge of results and to keep an accurate account of the student's progress as he learns. Computers also allow the student to

6 Un

1. The prefix *un–* has several different meanings. If we
are uncomfortable we are not comfortable. If a box
is untouched it is——————touched.

                                    not

2. In many words we can, without changing the meaning,
substitute the word *not* for the negative prefix——.

                                    un–

3. If you are uncertain, you are——————certain.

                                    not

4. But what about *untie?* Is this a simple negative? Or a
reversal of verb action?

                                    a reversal of verb
action

5. In which of the following words is *un–* used to mean a
reversal of verb action?

    unaware
    unfasten
    unclean   unfasten

*Figure 7.11A   An example of linear
programming. (From James I. Brown,
Programmed vocabulary. New York:
Appleton-Century-Crofts, 1971)*

From page 58   55

Answer   Since $7 - 7 + y = 16 - 7$, we have $y = 9$.

    Did you get it correct? Remember that our justification for doing this is that
we are really subtracting the same amount (in this case, 7) from both sides of the
equation, which gives an equivalent equation.
    How do we solve equations for variables that are connected with other numbers
which are factors (multipliers) or divisors of that variable?
    Consider the relationship that exists between time, speed (or <u>rate</u>), and distance
(T, S and D). We know that distance equals time multiplied by speed, which gives
us the mathematical relationship

$$D = T \cdot S \text{ (or } TS)$$

    Suppose we have a problem in which we know distance and speed but wish to
solve for time. We must rewrite the equation in such a way that T (the unknown
factor) is by itself on one side of the equal sign, and that the two known values,
S and D, are on the other side.
    Remember that an axiom of algebra allows us to multiply or divide both sides
of an equation by the same number.

How would you accomplish the change you need?

    1. Multiply both sides by S.   60
    2. Divide both sides by S.   57
    3. Subtract S from both sides.   62

Turn to the page number corresponding to your answer.

*Figure 7.11B   An example of intrinsic
programming. (From Peter A. Selby
and Donald D. Frederick, Basic algebra I.
New York: Appleton-Century-Crofts,
1969)*

take alternative routes on his way to learning.

In some forms of computer-assisted instruction (CAI), the student is seated at a terminal that prints out a programmed sequence for him. The student responds to the presented material by typing his answers, and the computer then provides feedback and more information. If the student responds correctly, the computer proceeds to the next bit of instructional information. If the student's answer is incorrect, the computer may present additional information on the same material or new remedial information, or it may reroute the student on an easier path.

The flexibility of CAI is its major advantage. But its ultimate success depends on the way the computer is programmed, and the programming depends on our understanding of the learning process.

REMEMBERING

The process of *remembering* makes available to the individual something he has already learned. The learned material retained by the individual is retrieved. To study the process of remembering, psychologists have devised experimental situations that test *retention*, measuring the difference between what was originally learned and what is remembered. As we shall see, not all material stored in the brain can be remembered; many factors—such as how long ago the material was learned, the extent of interference, the strength of original learning, and the meaningfulness of original material—contribute to what is retained and what is forgotten.

Recall

Recall is the process of remembering learned associations, presumably without benefit of extra cues. This is the method whereby we remember material for use in essay tests, or recite a poem learned long ago, or drive a car after several years

of using buses and trains. The recall method of measuring retention characteristically involves a subject's reproduction of what he learned earlier. The most frequently used forms of testing for recall are based on the verbal learning situations devised by Ebbinghaus (1913). In these, the subject learns something completely new and unfamiliar to him (such as nonsense syllables); after a period of time away from the learning situation, he is required to reproduce what he learned earlier. No new stimuli are presented.

Word vividness in learning and recall   Words differ in many dimensions—for example, meaningfulness, pictorial vividness, and abstractness. How such differences affect our psychological processing of words has been the subject of considerable experimentation.

Tulving, McNulty, and Ozier (1965), for instance, found that vividness can help people learn and recall lists of words more easily. They asked people to rate equally familiar words for pictorial vividness and meaningfulness. Three lists of 16 words each were compiled, with each list consisting of words either high, moderate, or low in their vividness ratings. Other subjects then learned all three lists; order of presentation varied so that lists in the high, moderate, and low vividness categories came in a different sequence from subject to subject. As predicted, a recall test showed that subjects recalled highly vivid words better than those low in vividness, with recall of moderately vivid words falling between the two extremes.

Although the reason for this difference in learning is not actually known, it is thought that vividness (which is closely related to concreteness) allows words to be easily organized into large processing units (or chunks) so that less mental effort is required to learn the individual elements of the larger unit.

Recognition

Recognition is the flash of knowing that you have seen someone or something, or learned something before. It is the ability to look at several things and select the one that has been seen or learned before, as occurs in a multiple-choice test. Often less effort is required to remember by the recognition method than by recall. Usually, the association or memory connection is made instantly. Recognition is often a more sensitive measure of retention than recall; a test for recognition may turn up evidence of retained material even though a recall test does not indicate any. Like recall, memory by recognition can span many years of a person's life. For example, you might recognize a childhood friend if you pass him on the street; but if given only a name, you may not be able to recall who he was or what he looks like.

Recall stimuli

We have spoken of *recall* as remembering learned associations without benefit of cues, and we have observed that recall appears to occur in the absence of stimuli. But stimuli *are* present; we simply do not note them *overtly*. They may be external or internal. You may, for example, remember something from your childhood as you glance at someone who looks like a childhood friend, even though you are not overtly aware of the resemblance.

Recall can involve a chain of associations in which each thought produces the stimuli for the next. Some people, when trying to recall a name, do so by calling up a chain of events—associating events with names, and more events with more names, until the right name finally appears.

Recall is often produced by fragmentary stimuli. In such cases, some portion of a previously experienced stimulus pattern serves as a cue for remembering the whole pattern. Recall based on fragmentary cues is known as *redintegration*. While experimental attempts to show its existence are few, redintegrative recall has attracted a great deal of attention outside the laboratory. In fact, it is used most often in Freudian psychoanalysis, which emphasizes the recall of childhood experiences.

A form of redintegration is described by the French term *déjà vu*, which means "already seen." Individuals sometimes have the feeling that what they are experiencing has happened before. But, most likely, the feeling of *déjà vu* is merely a redintegration in which the same

stimulus or stimuli that occurred at another time elicits a pattern of remembering. The odor of some food not eaten since childhood, for example, may bring on the familiar feeling of having "been there before."

Relearning

A third method of measuring retention is *relearning* or the *savings method*. In this process, something previously learned is learned again. In relearning, the subject usually learns faster than he did the first time. This method is easy to use in experimental situations: the number of trials required to master the relearned material is compared to the number of trials it took to master the material originally. If the speed of learning, rather than the number of trials, is of primary interest, this too is measurable. The difference between the first learning and the second learning reflects the *savings* in trials or time. Savings can be specified as a percentage by means of the following equation:

$$\frac{\text{original trials} - \text{relearning trials}}{\text{original trials}} \times 100$$

Thus, if it took a subject six trials to learn a task the first time and four to learn it the second time, the savings is computed as

$$\frac{6-4}{6} \times 100, \quad \text{or } \frac{1}{3} \times 100, \quad \text{or } 33\frac{1}{3}$$

Relearning A most unusual account of the measurement of memory by relearning (or "saving") was reported by Burtt (1941). When his son was less than 2 years old, Burtt read the same Greek selections to him every day for 3 months. When the boy was 8, 14, and 18 years old, his father made him relearn these selections, in addition to other Greek selections. When the boy was 8, Burtt found that it took from 25 to 33 percent fewer trials to learn the material originally heard than to learn new Greek selections. Clearly, relearning is demonstrated here despite the unusual circumstances. At 14 years of age, however, relearning showed only about 8 percent savings, and by the time the boy was 18, no savings could be demonstrated.

Relearning is the most sensitive measure of retention over a long period of time. Recognition procedures are good at indicating retention immediately after the original learning, but their efficiency drops quickly thereafter. Recall is the least effective measure of retention, since it requires the reproduction of material without the benefit of overt cues.

Learning and retention

It is not surprising that well-learned material is retained better than poorly learned material. Consequently, all the variables we discussed in relation to more efficient learning have a bearing on retention, too. Meaningful material, for example, is much better remembered than meaningless material. Being easier to learn in the first place, the material is learned faster, and the learner can spend more time *overlearning* it—another factor that improves retention.

Effective distribution of practice during learning also improves retention. It is unusual to find instances in which cramming leads to better long-term retention. If a student intends to retain what he is learning, he might heed the advice of William James (1890), who felt that cramming does not allow many associations to develop.

Still another factor in retention is the speed at which the material is learned in the first place. Slow learners do not remember material better than fast learners—if we mean by fast learners those who typically can and do learn quickly. The fast learner retains more than the slow learner does, and he develops more durable associations for what he learns.

Two types of storage

Retention of facts and events requires an effective system for storing material for as long as one needs it. There is increasing evidence that memory involves at least two processes, or two types of *storage* systems. One storage system is thought to be short term, retaining new information briefly; and the other system is thought to be long term or permanent storage (Figure 7.12).

Short-term memory (STM) The system responsible for *short-term memory* has a limited capacity for stored material and a limitation on on the time of storage. No more than five to nine items can be stored at once, and for no more than 20 seconds. Information stored in STM is very vulnerable, for it is easily affected by interference. We all have had the experience of being told an address or telephone number, being distracted for a moment, and then forgetting what we were told.

Figure 7.12   Coding of short-term and long-term memory.

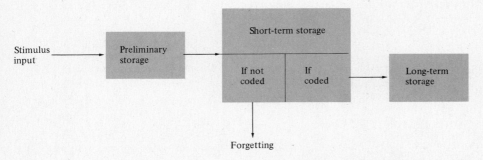

Short-term memory is tested in the laboratory by giving a subject several items to remember—usually meaningless series of digits, letters, or nonsense syllables—and following these with some other task that requires his concentration. He is next asked to repeat the items at various brief intervals of time. He is not given an opportunity to rehearse the items. While he can usually recall the items fairly well for the first few seconds, after approximately 12 seconds, recall becomes very poor. After 20 seconds it disappears entirely.

Two neural systems? If there are two memory systems, long-term (LTM) and short-term (STM), as some theorists propose, it is logical to assume two underlying neural systems, one for each type. This assumption was tested on laboratory rats by Kessner and Connor (1972). The rats were trained to bar-press for food when hungry. After they had learned this response well, they were given a strong shock to their feet during a bar-press session. Since foot shock typically causes rats to decrease the response that precedes it, a decrease in bar-pressing could normally be anticipated. However, following foot shock, an electrical impulse to the midbrain reticular formation was administered to one group to disrupt the memory process. These rats were then tested to see if they had retained the memory of the shock and consequently would press less frequently. Half were tested after 64 seconds to see if STM had been disrupted; the other half were tested after 24 hours to see whether or not LTM had been disrupted. The short-interval group forgot that they had received the foot shock. In contrast, the group tested after 24 hours remembered the shock. Another group of rats also received an impulse to the brain, but to a different brain structure, the hippocampus. In this group, the rats tested after 24 hours forgot the shock, but those tested after 64 seconds did not. Thus, it was concluded that STM processing may take place in the midbrain reticular formation, while LTM may involve the hippocampus; a separate neural system serves each of the two memory systems.

It has generally been assumed that a memory that is lost in STM would not get to LTM (as was found for the midbrain reticular formation group). The physiological psychologists who performed this experiment, however, are working on the idea that an item to be remembered enters into both STM and LTM and is processed independently in each through *parallel processing*.

Most studies have indicated that short-term memory retains information about seven items long when the items are presented all at once. Some subjects, however, can recall double and triple that number. To score well on long lists of items, the subject may break the lists down into smaller groups, each group containing no more than four or five items. He then works on remembering the order of the groups, which is usually not too difficult.

Some experts believe that short-term memory is stored by a *memory trace*, an as-yet hypothetical pathway that carries information through the nervous system. The trace fades very rapidly if the information is not used immediately or shifted to storage in the long-term system.

Long-term memory Long-term memories are those which are relatively permanent. That is, they are thought to be permanently available, even if they are not easily retrieved. Evidently, the ability to retrieve material in long-term storage depends on the cues that are provided. You may have stored someone's name in long-term storage but may be unable to recall it at the moment because enough relevant cues are not present or interfering cues are getting in the way.

The process by which short-term memories become long-term memories is still a mystery. Some psychologists believe it is a matter of coding, that the information in STM is organized into patterns that are transferred into LTM. There are many kinds of codes, individual and general. If you were trying to learn a list containing such words as "dog," "tire," "spoon," "mouse," "fork," and "horn," you would probably code them into animal words, eating utensils, and parts of automobiles; and then they could be transferred from STM to LTM.

An interesting and familiar form of memory coding involves the use of *mnemonic* devices (memorable phrases or associations that facilitate recall). "Thirty days hath September, April, June, and November . . ." is an example of a mnemonic device that many people use to remember the number of days in each month. The so-called memory experts improve memory by using a variety of mnemonic devices.

The most popular mnemonics involve the use of pictorial images. Some memory experts advise that if you wish to remember a person's name, associate his name with some distinctive feature of his appearance. If you are introduced to Mr. Benedict and you notice that he has a very pointed nose, you associate the pointed nose with the name Benedict. To recall the name at a later time, you form an image of the pointed nose, and this serves to evoke recall of the name. The key to this system is the identification of a truly distinctive feature; blue eyes or curly hair are not by themselves sufficiently distinctive to provide useful associations for pictorial images.

"Chaining" in memorization Memory experts have long recommended "chaining" unrelated words into narrative stories as a way of remembering the original list of words. Not until quite recently, however, was the everyday efficiency of this memory technique tested experimentally. Bower and Clark (1969) asked college subjects to learn 12 successive lists of 10 nouns. Each subject was instructed to integrate the words sequentially into some personally meaningful story; each subject set his own learning pace, repeating each list as soon as he had learned it, and then repeating all 12 lists (given the first word as a cue) at the end of the experimental session. In a control group, subjects did not chain the words, but each subject received the same amount of study time as a subject in the first group to whom he was matched; and each repeated the same lists in the same sequence as his match. Although memory immediately after study (immediate recall) was virtually identical and errorless for both groups, chaining subjects remembered seven times as many words in the final session (delayed recall) as did control subjects. Ruling out length of study time as a crucial factor in chaining effectiveness, the experimenters suggest that the complex organization imposed on the target words by embedding them in narrative stories somehow facilitates retention of even large amounts of material.

Another mnemonic device uses a system of places. The individual forms images of familiar places and then imagines placing the items or names to be remembered in those familiar places. If you have a list of names to remember, for example, you might think of a very familiar route you walk each day. Identify a number of familiar places you pass on this route, and place each name in turn at each one of the places. The route might be within your own home, beginning with your bedroom and terminating in the garage. If you were to use this route, you might put the first name to remember on your bed, the next one at the doorway from your room, the next one on the table in the upstairs hall beside your door, and so on. To recall the names, you think of the bed and then the associated name, then the doorway and its associated name, and so on down to the garage.

Consolidation theory The differences between long- and short-term memory have led some psychologists to adopt a *consolidation theory* of memory. This theory defines consolidation as a process by which the learned material (which causes changes in the nervous system) is carried by the memory trace and stored in the brain. This process requires a period of time to become operative, and so proof of its occurence may be a valid argument for learning by distributed practice. However, if disrupting or interfering events occur, the consolidation process will not be completed.

The consolidation theory is supported by clinical studies that show a head injury can result in a loss of immediate memory—memory of the events that occurred just before the injury. Systematic laboratory research with animals also supports the consolidation theory. Rats given brain shocks that cause convulsive reactions show memory loss for the learning immediately preceding the shocks.

Consolidation theory is also supported by research in neurology and physiological psychology. Patients who have had brain operations involving the hippocampus, a part of the limbic system (see Chapter 3), show little or no deficit in long-term memory. These patients, however, cannot consolidate what they learn; they seem unable to code short-term material for transfer to long-term storage. A typical patient cannot remember the special place he puts a tool every day. The disability is neither in the short-term nor long-term storage systems. It appears as a breakdown in the linkage between STM and LTM.

Retrograde amnesia In retrograde amnesia, the patient can remember events that happened long before he became amnesic, but he cannot remember events that happened just before that time. This condition seems to indicate that memory needs time to become consolidated.

Psychologists have been able to reproduce retrograde amnesia in rats by administering electroconvulsive shocks following their learning of a task. The more time that is allowed to lapse after learning occurs and before an electroconvulsive shock (ECS) is administered, the more time the memory has had to consolidate and the better learning is remembered. If the shock is administered immediately after learning, the task will be forgotten. By manipulating conditions under which electroconvulsive shock is administered, psychologists have been able to study different aspects of memory.

Lewis, Miller, and Misanin (1969) found that rats allowed time to consolidate their learning about an environment prior to the experiment did not forget their learning after an electroconvulsive shock was administered. In contrast, rats that were not familiar with the environment forgot most of their learning after receiving a shock.

FORGETTING

We cannot really separate remembering from forgetting. Retention, as noted earlier, is simply a measure of the learned material that we fail to forget; and to forget is simply not to remember. In this section we will concentrate on the eliminative or disruptive factors in remembering: interference, spontaneous decay of the memory trace, distortion of the memory trace, and emotional influences that may motivate an individual to forget something.

Multiple activities on the part of the learner may provide sources of interference with what is being learned. This causes forgetting. Interfering activity that occurs after the learned activity is called *retroactive inhibition*: the person's ability to recall is decreased (inhibited) in proportion to the amount of interference. If the interfering activity occurs *before* the learned activity, then the decrease is said to be due to *proactive inhibition*. In proactive inhibition, the individual is besieged by material he learned earlier at the same time that he attempts to remember his current learning activity; his associations become confused; and the interference causes him to forget parts of both activities.

Retroactive inhibition Retroactive inhibition is very common and much tested. In the standard experiment, one group of subjects learns a task, then learns another task, and finally is tested for retention of the first task. A second group learns the first task, *rests*, and then is tested for retention of this task. The extent of forgetting in the two groups is compared. Typically, the group that has to learn a second task forgets more of the first than does the group given only one task. The more similar the tasks, the less is retained. Figure 7.13 shows the design of a standard retroactive inhibition experiment.

Figure 7.13   An experimental model to study retroactive inhibition.

Experimental group	Control group
Learn Task A	Learn Task A
↓	↓
Learn Task B	Unrelated activity or rest
↓	↓
Test for retention of A	Test for retention of A

Psychologists have looked carefully at the type of *nonactivity* or rest period just mentioned. In any waking state, even at rest, stimuli are being received, some of which may trigger interfering associations. When the learning retention of awake resting groups is compared with that of resting groups that have slept, it has been found that the sleeping groups retained more of the learned task, probably because they acquired fewer interfering associations. The effects of the length of the sleeping period on retention have also been observed. Most such experiments show that during the first hour or two of sleep, some memory loss occurs, but after the second hour, little additional material is forgotten.

Proactive inhibition Proactive inhibition—the interference of associations from prior activities —can also be demonstrated in the laboratory. An experimental design for proactive inhibition is shown in Figure 7.14. Note the differences between the experiments in Figure 7.13 and Figure 7.14.

In the proactive inhibition experiment shown in Figure 7.14, task similarity is very important. If the two tasks require different responses and have similar stimuli, there will be considerable interference. The similarity between proactive inhibition and negative transfer is apparent. In negative transfer, the learning of A interferes with the *learning* of B; in proactive inhibition, the learning of A interferes with the *retention* of B.

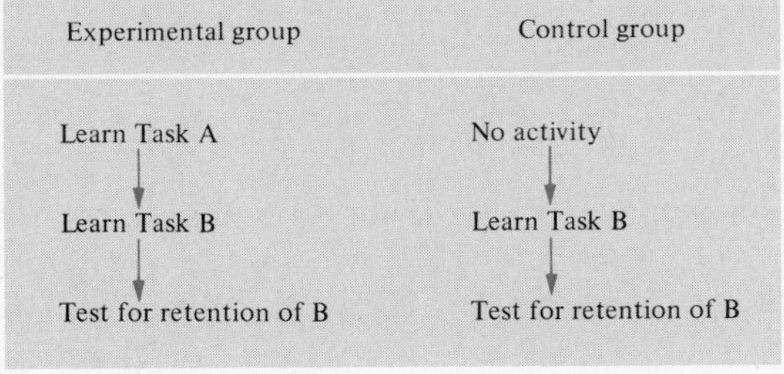

Other experiments with proactive inhibition show that the *number* of previously learned tasks influences forgetting: the more previously learned ·tasks there are, the more of the main task will be forgotten. This seems to imply that the more we learn, the easier it is for us to forget, a statement in which there is at least a grain of truth. An 8-year-old child can remember some things far better than a 16-year-old because the 8-year-old has less proactive inhibition. Many child geniuses seem less remarkable as they become, in fact, more knowledgeable, more full of experiences. (We should point out, however, that the more meaningful the material to be retained, the less the effect of proactive inhibition. An 8-year-old might remember a list of nonsense syllables markedly better than a 16-year-old, but the latter will learn and remember the rules of baseball better.)

Decay of the memory trace

Perhaps the oldest explanation of forgetting is that forgetting occurs when memories are not used. We mentioned earlier that what is stored in the brain is thought by some to be a *memory trace* that may disappear after prolonged disuse. The problem with this explanation is that some learning is retained for a lifetime, even though it may not be used for decades, and some is forgotten instantly. Elderly persons may, for instance, revert to a language they have not used since childhood. In a moment of crisis, a man may find himself making a response that he learned many years earlier and has not practiced since.

Figure 7.14   An experimental model to study proactive inhibition.

Experimental group	Control group
Learn Task A	No activity
↓	
Learn Task B	Learn Task B
↓	↓
Test for retention of B	Test for retention of B

What is forgetting? Does forgetting result from a failure to retrieve the appropriate memory, or is it result of decay or interference with the memory trace? Shiffrin (1970) sought an answer to this question by requiring subjects to learn a list of words, learn another list, and then recall the first list. Twenty lists consisting of either 5 or 20 words were used. Shiffrin attempted to determine whether the length of the lists being recalled affected the extent of the recall or whether the length of the intervening list affected the extent of recall of the first list.

Shiffrin found that the length of the list being recalled was the crucial variable. The length of the intervening list had no effect. These results support the view that retrieval failure is a more important variable in forgetting than decay or interference with the memory trace. The results also suggest that forgetting may be due to the way the individual searches his memory. Perhaps memory can be improved by varying the method of retrieval.

We know very little about the physiology of the hypothetical memory trace. Of what does it consist? Where is it stored? The decaying-trace idea continues to be of interest as a research problem. Has the trace really decayed, or is the memory stored so far back that it cannot be retrieved? Perhaps the memory can be restored by the presentation of the appropriate stimuli, cues currently lost to the individual's awareness.

Distortion of the memory trace

A viewpoint slightly at variance with the decaying-memory-trace idea is held by some psychologists, who suggest that forgetting is not simply decay of the trace but distortion as well. The passage of time may cause distortion in recalled memories, making them different from the experiences that were originally stored. Occasionally, if the passage of time is great enough, distortion may cause the recalled material to differ significantly from the original. We experience distortion when we recall that a friend, years ago, was good at playing the trumpet when, in fact, he was a tuba player.

Distortion of memory is real; those who theorize that the memory trace is distorted by time explain this distortion as a qualitative change in the memory process produced by spontaneous changes in the memory trace. It is also hypothesized that some experiences do not even require the passage of time to become distorted —that when they are first seen, they are "learned"

as distortions, with the result that the memory trace is inaccurate from the start.

In an interesting experiment on one type of memory distortion, known as *assimilation*, subjects are given word cues with which to identify incomplete visual stimuli; when different cues are spoken to different subjects, each subject tends to remember the stimulus as shaped like the object represented by the word cue. Thus, a circle shape can be presented to two subjects. If one is told it is a pie and another is told it is a face, each subject will re-create a shape related to the word he heard. The distortion is caused to a large extent by the verbal association to a picture—such as "face" or "pie." The word and the picture are assimilated and remembered as one. Figure 7.15 shows figures from one of the well-known experiments on this type of distortion.

Motivated forgetting

Another extremely important factor in forgetting is the individual's motive or desire to blot out certain things. There are many reasons why people repress certain memories; psychoanalysis is largely concerned with the exploration of this type of motivated forgetting. *Repression* (the burial in the unconscious of fear-arousing material) will be discussed in greater detail in Chapter 13; here we will concentrate on repression only as it relates directly to forgetting.

There is evidence to suggest that individuals repress memories or thoughts that are emotionally unpleasant or frightening. Repression often involves deep and powerful emotional and psychological problems with which the individual is afraid to cope. The individual represses memories to protect himself from the damaging consequences of their recollection.

In laboratory situations, experiments with repression have shown that individuals forget unpleasant experiences faster than pleasant ones. Learning situations that encourage the subject to relax and be comfortable have subsequently caused subjects to respond with greater retention

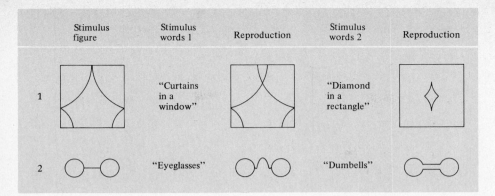

	Stimulus figure	Stimulus words 1	Reproduction	Stimulus words 2	Reproduction
1		"Curtains in a window"		"Diamond in a rectangle"	
2		"Eyeglasses"		"Dumbells"	

Figure 7.15   Carmichael, Hogan, and Walter (1932) showed 12 ambiguous figures to two groups of college students. The students were to reproduce each figure shortly after presentation. One of two stimulus words was presented with each ambiguous figure until all subjects reproduced 12 recognizable figures. It was found that, when the reproduced figures deviated from the original figures, they did so in the direction of the stimulus words that were presented with them. Thus, set may influence not only the way a subject remembers a stimulus, but also the way in which the stimulus is originally perceived. Two of the stimulus figures used by Carmichael and his colleagues are reproduced here.

of material. In these experiments, it has been noted that repression occurs in healthy individuals, just as it does in moderately or severely disturbed persons.

As we are motivated to repress some memories, so are we motivated to remember others. An interesting example of *motivated remembering* is the retention of uncompleted tasks. Experiments show that subjects who are given a certain number of tasks to perform and are allowed to complete some but not others, remember more uncompleted tasks than completed tasks. This effect, termed the *Zeigarnik effect* for its discoverer, usually occurs when the tasks are performed under relatively mild motivation. However, when the subjects are highly motivated to complete the tasks—for example, when they are told that the tasks are a measure of

ability—they remember more completed than uncompleted tasks. Under the high-motivation conditions, the Zeigarnik effect does not occur; the results are reversed.

THE PHYSIOLOGY OF LEARNING

Many psychologists and physiologists are working to discover how the learning process and the memory-storage process operate in the brain and nervous system. Although they have provided some interesting findings and speculations, these scientists are quick to point out that they do not yet have any answers. In this final section on learning, we will discuss three problems in the physiology of learning: (1) the role of the cerebral cortex; (2) the travels of memory between the hemisphere of the brain; and (3) the chemistry of learning and retention.

Role of the cerebral cortex

Since 1929, it has been known that learning does not depend on any one specific region of the cerebral cortex. In a series of experiments using rats as subjects, Karl Lashley (1929) showed that the destruction of tissue in any one part of the cortex had the same effect as destruction in any other part. Lashley's experiments proved, however, that when part of the cortex was destroyed, there was significant learning impairment; the greater the amount destroyed, the greater the learning impairment. Subsequent experiments have shown that although there may be some slight differences in the way some cortical areas affect learning, no single portion of the cortex plays a crucial role.

Most experiments on the cortex have involved tissue destruction. In them, animals with portions of the brain destroyed are compared with those whose brains are intact. Recently it has become possible to reverse that procedure and to study the learning abilities of animals

Figure 7.16   *Diagram of a split-brain experiment. In the first sequence, learning in one eye (the other was covered) could be transferred from one hemisphere to the other hemisphere. In the second sequence, the corpus callosum has been cut. Learning cannot be transferred from one hemisphere to the other.*

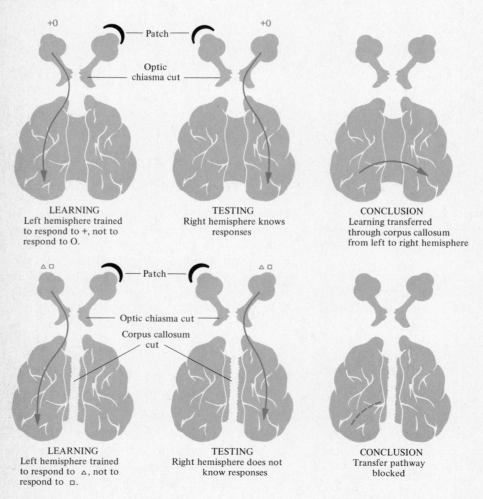

LEARNING
Left hemisphere trained to respond to +, not to respond to O.

TESTING
Right hemisphere knows responses

CONCLUSION
Learning transferred through corpus callosum from left to right hemisphere

LEARNING
Left hemisphere trained to respond to △, not to respond to □.

TESTING
Right hemisphere does not know responses

CONCLUSION
Transfer pathway blocked

who have been given more cortical tissue than is normal to their species. Early evidence from these experiments suggests that the "supplemented" animals may learn better than normal animals (Bresler and Bitterman, 1969).

The "split-brain" experiment

Application of the chemical potassium chloride to one hemisphere of an animal's brain anesthetizes that hemisphere without affecting the unanesthetized hemisphere. When the anesthetic wears off several hours later, any learning that occurred under the drug can be shown to have spread into the formerly sleeping hemisphere. For example, a rat trained to press a lever with his right paw while the right hemisphere is anesthetized can also press it with his left paw when the brain is deanesthetized.

In order to determine the location of such an exchange between hemispheres, psychologists have performed experiments in which they have cut the optic chiasma and/or the corpus callosum (the only two areas in which there is any exchange between the two halves of the brain). When the optic chiasma (the junction at the base of the brain where the optic nerve fibers cross) is cut, it is still possible for response patterns to be transferred from one hemisphere to the other. When the corpus callosum (the large bundle of nerve fibers that connects the two hemispheres) and optic chiasma are severed, such transfer between the two hemispheres can no longer take place. Figure 7.16 illustrates a split-brain experiment.

Chemistry of learning and retention

For some time, psychologists and physiologists have been trying to discover whether or not memory and forgetting are related to the biochemistry of the brain. Is memory the result of specific chemical changes in the brain? We do not have any direct answers to this question. But there is evidence that long-term memory may be impaired by the injection of certain chemi-

cally inhibiting drugs such as puromycin, an antibiotic. Goldfish trained to avoid a shock in their tank forget this response after puromycin is injected into their brains; they must be retrained to avoid the shock.

Transfer of the biochemistry of learning Braud and Braud (1972), in transfer-of-learning experiments with rats, found support for the view that the biochemistry of the brain is permanently altered by the learning process. Their rat subjects were taught to approach the larger of two circles in a Y maze. After the rats had learned the task, their brains were removed and ground into a solution. The solution was then injected into untrained rats. Without any training or reinforcement, these rats also approached the larger of two circles in a Y maze. The approach to a specific size of circle was not transferred, but rather the approach to the larger of two circles.

To demonstrate the relational nature of the transfer, the experimenters changed the size of the circles for the injected rats. Later, when the temporary effects of the injected solution had disappeared, the recipients were given rewards for approaching the larger of two circles. They mastered the task much more quickly than the original rats, indicating that they had benefited in some way from the transfer of the brain extract of the donors.

We have also observed that a number of chemicals appear to improve retention. One such chemical is the drug Metrazol, a nervous system stimulant. Mice trained to run through a maze show better retention after they have been injected with Metrazol. We do not know precisely how Metrazol facilitates retention, but we can expect vigorous research in this and related areas of study in the years to come.

The mysterious role of RNA in learning The most likely chemicals to play a role in the processes of learning are acetylcholine and RNA: *acetylcholine* (see Chapter 3) is believed to be involved in the transmission of nerve impulses across the synapse; *RNA* (ribonucleic acid) is a large molecule that acts as a messenger carrying the genetic code of the organism.

RNA research is both exciting and perplexing. It has been suggested that learning produces a change in RNA molecules (Hyden, 1969). After extracts of RNA from animals trained to perform a specific task were injected into untrained animals, the untrained animals behaved as if they had partially learned the task. The evidence is not always clear, however, and there is considerable controversy over how RNA might facilitate learning. One prominent investigator argues that it is unlikely that RNA acts on the brain, proposing instead that it produces "some secondary effect upon the liver or other structures and thereby stimulates the organism" to more active attempts to learn (Jarvik, 1972).

SUMMARY

In motor and verbal learning, feedback (knowledge of results) helps the learner adjust his responses and serves as positive reinforcement; conceptualization of the task also helps in motor learning.

Systematic study of verbal learning began with the research of Hermann Ebbinghaus, who used nonsense syllables in experiments to examine verbal learning.

Repetitive verbal learning is termed rote memorization. It may involve either serial memorization or paired-associate learning.

Imagery—internal sensory representation—is an aspect of the learning process emphasized by cognitive psychologists.

The rate of learning depends on meaningfulness, distinctiveness of material, distribution of practice, and amount of material to be learned.

Memory span depends on the amount and type of material to be memorized and the individual's capacity for memorization. The interference theory holds that similarities among items interfere with stimulus-response associations.

Learning may be affected by positive transfer or negative transfer.

When an animal learns how to learn, it acquires a learning set.

The formal discipline method of academic learning relies on the transfer principle.

There are eight principles of learning which produce more effective teaching techniques.

The two types of programmed instruction are linear and intrinsic.

Computer-assisted instruction (CAI) is being used increasingly to teach programmed material.

Remembering is a process that makes available something previously learned. Studies of retention test the amount of learned material that is remembered.

Learned associations can be remembered after the passage of time by recall. Redintegration is a form of recall based on fragmentary cues.

Recognition is remembering with the benefit of cues; it is often a more sensitive measure of retention than is recall.

Relearning is used as a measure of retention, for something once learned is usually relearned faster.

Memory is believed to involve at least two storage systems: short term, for retaining new information briefly, and long term, for permanent retention. Some scientists believe that short-term memory is stored by a memory trace. Consolidation is the process by which learned material is stored and organized in the brain after a period of time; it may be interrupted by disruptive factors.

Retroactive and proactive inhibition interfere with retention of learned material.

Forgetting has been studied in terms of the concepts of decay or distortion of a memory trace.

Repression is a form of motivated forgetting of painful or traumatic events.

One example of motivated remembering, known as the Zeigarnik effect, is the retention of more uncompleted than completed tasks. This effect is reversed under high-motivation conditions, when individuals remember more completed than uncompleted tasks.

The available evidence does not indicate that any single area of the cerebral cortex plays a crucial role in learning.

Learning may be transferred from one hemisphere of the brain to the other, unless the corpus callosum, which connects the two hemispheres, is severed.

SUGGESTED READINGS

Texts

Ausubel, D. P., & Robinson, F. G. *School learning: an introduction to educational psychology.* New York: Holt, Rinehart & Winston, 1969. An introductory text, organized and cross-referenced for would-be or practicing educators.

Barbizet, J. *Human memory and its pathology.* Saskatoon, Canada: Freeman, 1971. The nature and function of the human memory and various types of amnesia are explored. Excellent illustrations, glossary, and bibliography.

Bartlett, F. C. *Remembering.* New York: Cambridge University Press, 1932. Classic experimental study that deals with social as well as individual factors in remembering.

Gaito, J. *DNA complex and adaptive behavior.* Englewood Cliffs, N.J.: Prentice-Hall, 1971. Describes molecular events that are related to learning and memory. Final chapters survey literature concerned with biochemical mechanisms related to behavior.

Holtzman, W. H. (Ed.) *Computer-assisted instruction, testing and guidance.* New York: Harper & Row, 1970. A somewhat detailed but useful guide for the reader who wishes to acquire an overall appreciation of current CAI problems—psychological, social, educational, and technical.

Honig, W. K., & James, P. H. R. (Eds.) *Animal memory.* New York: Academic Press, 1971. Provides the layman with an overview of the field of memory and learning.

Kintsch, W. *Learning, memory, and conceptual processes.* New York: Wiley, 1970. An up-to-date, theoretically oriented introduction to human learning in terms of the new cognitive psychology.

Melton, A. W. (Ed.) *Categories of human learning.* New York: Academic Press, 1964. See chapters by Underwood (rote verbal learning) and Postman (short-term memory).

Miller, G. A. *Psychology: the science of mental life.* New York: Harper & Row, 1962. Chapters 10 and 11 give interesting discussions of recognition, identification, and other aspects of memory.

Norman, D. A. *Models of human memory.* New York: Academic Press, 1970. An examination of current research and theory in memory and information processing.

Postman, L. The present status of interference theory. In C. N. Cofer & B. S.

Musgrave (Eds.), *Verbal learning and verbal behavior.* New York: McGraw-Hill, 1961. Discussion of current research in interference theory.

Postman, L. Transfer, interference, and forgetting. In J. W. Kling and L. A. Riggs (Eds.), *Woodworth and Schlosberg's experimental psychology* (3rd ed.). New York: Holt, Rinehart & Winston, 1971. A brief but thorough introduction to these important issues in human learning research.

Slamecka, N. J. *Human learning and memory.* New York: Oxford University Press, 1967. Collection of articles on verbal learning and memory.

Popular books

Filloux, J. C. *Memory and forgetting.* Brief, interesting, and largely philosophical treatment; emphasizes contributions of French psychologists.

Goodwin, R., & Lewin, R. *New ways to greater word power.* Modern text on learning new words, utilizing feedback, positive reinforcement, distributed practice, part learning, meaningfulness, and material patterns for greater effectiveness.

Meems, M. *Studying and learning.* Application of learning and memory principles to tasks of the student.

Morrison, A., & McIntyre, D. *Schools and socialization.* An examination of how school processes—both in the classroom and behind the scenes—affect each child.

Weinland, J. D. *How to improve your memory.* Psychologically sound treatise on improving recall of names and factual material.

8

Motivation

Man has always been interested in the causes of his behavior. For many centuries he sought answers in animism. He speculated that some hidden spirit within man impelled him to act. As psychology developed and the study of man became more systematic, the animistic explanations were replaced by more objective analyses of the events that arouse action. The psychology of motivation concerns those events, the pushes and pulls that move us to action. It is the study of why individuals behave as they do, how the behavior is initiated, and how it is sustained.

We are constantly asking the question *why*. Why did Allen walk 5 miles, when the local bus goes directly to his destination? Why did Pam do so much better than George in biology? Why did Jill choose a career in medicine rather than in business? Questions of this sort reflect our interest in motivation. We are really asking for reasons that explain the behavior. We are not satisfied with such answers as, "Allen was motivated to walk rather than suffer the hot, crowded bus," or "Pam was more motivated to study than George." These answers fail to describe the motivation. Psychologists, therefore, prefer the question *How did it happen?* to *Why did it happen?* The question *how* leads us to the discovery of variables that activate, energize, and frequently direct behavior. Once we understand these variables, we can better explain how motivation influences behavior.

BASIC PSYCHOLOGICAL CONCEPTS OF MOTIVATION

It is often difficult to identify individual motivation by observing behavior. The same motivation may result in various types of behavior. The motivation for achievement, for example, may give rise to different actions: one person may study and work hard independently; another may seek outside help, cultivating people who will aid him in his efforts; another may

Figure 8.1   *Behavior is not always a true reflection of the individual's motivation.*

seek easy tasks to assure his success; and another may search for the most difficult tasks to prove his ability.

Conversely, dissimilar motivations may produce similar types of behavior. A group of students may choose a course in biblical literature for dissimilar motives: one student chooses the course because he is religious; another because he is interested in the Bible as literature; another because his girlfriend registered for it; and still another because he heard that the instructor is an easy grader. Obviously, there are numerous variables in motivation, and they result in similar or different forms of behavior.

Motivation may be overt (open) or covert (hidden). Figure 8.1 shows an amusing example in which an apparently covert motivation becomes overt. In fact, one is left to speculate about the man's real motivation for his action. Was it to practice putting or to irritate his wife? What the cartoon does make clear is that we are often unable to detect a person's motivation from his overt behavior. The person himself may

be unaware of the motivation behind his behavior. Through laboratory research and clinical observations, however, psychologists have been able to provide a framework for the analysis of motivation. This framework relies upon the concepts of *need* and *drive*.

Needs are derived from physiological (internal) or environmental (external) imbalances, and give rise to drives. At all times and in varying intensities, we all experience needs. The need for food is a physiological need. The need for social contact is an acquired environmental need. Our needs are most compelling when they are unfulfilled—when we are in a *state of deprivation*. We need food when we are hungry; we need social contact when we are lonely. During a state of deprivation, we suffer from an imbalance, and this makes us respond.

Drives are stimuli that arise from needs. If you have a need for food, you are stimulated to look for it by the hunger drive. A drive, or stimulus, to act or respond can come from various sources—physiological, social, intellectual, and so on. The words "drive" and "motive" are used synonymously. We will learn more about the concept of drive later in this chapter.

The four stages of motivation

The motivation process consists of four interlocking stages, beginning with a need and ending with responses that reduce or eliminate drive stimuli:

1 *Need stage*—A need is a condition of imbalance that arises when the individual is deprived of something that is required for his normal functioning. That thing may be as crucial as food, as important as love, or as trivial as the daily newspaper. A need may also be aroused by events that threaten the well-being of the individual, events such as painful stimuli.
2 *Drive stage*—Needs activate drives; drives are stimuli. If a person is thirsty (need), he will experience a thirst drive.
3 *Behavior stage*—Once the drive stage is activated, the individual is "forced" to behave. Drive stimuli energize the strength of behavior; a very thirsty animal will seek water more vigorously than will an animal that is only slightly thirsty. Drive stimuli also direct behavior by serving as eliciting stimuli or as discriminative stimuli. The stimulus pattern for thirst differs from the pattern for hunger. These characteristic patterns are important cues for appropriate behavior.
4 *Drive reduction stage*—The final stage of the motivation process is the drive reduction stage. While this stage usually involves the satisfaction of a need, in some situations drive stimuli may be reduced without satisfying the need. For example, taking an appetite-suppressing pill may reduce the drive stimuli associated with hunger, but the need for food remains. Events that reduce drives are usually reinforcers, but we need not think of reinforcement as being entirely dependent upon drive reduction.

The relationship between drive and need reduction is not always clear-cut. What satisfies a drive at one time for one person may not satisfy it at all other times for that person or for other people. Individual differences in learning and perception influence the results.

The presence of conflicting drives also influences our responses. A thirsty traveler may feel compelled, because of the strength of his need, to wander off the road to look for a drink. Another thirsty traveler may also have an important appointment to keep. If the conflicting drive (his appointment) is stronger than his thirst drive, he may continue on the road. Because many such conflicting drives usually exist simultaneously within an individual, every behavior is affected by the pull of conflicting drives. The degree of conflict will vary, and each individual will respond in his own unique way.

Drug addiction What makes drug addiction such a strong drive? Is the addict driven simply to reduce his need for drugs, or is he driven to obtain the pleasurable feeling he gets while under the influence of drugs?

Beach (1957) trained rats in a Y maze to run to a goal box on their right. He did this in two ways. One group of rats was first addicted to morphine. Later, when a rat showed symptoms of needing drugs, Beach placed the animal in the right-hand box and injected it with morphine. Thus, while in the right-hand box this rat experienced not only reduction of its need for drugs but also the pleasurable "high" created by the drugs.

Another group of rats was not put into the goal box until about 20 minutes after injection of morphine. Consequently, this group did not experience drive reduction in the box, but only the pleasurable feeling of being under drugs. After training, both groups, when run in the maze, chose the right box.

The rats were then kept away from drugs and the Y maze for 3 weeks. After this period, they were put into the maze. Those who had experienced drive reduction and pleasure in the right box ran to it; those who had experienced pleasure only did not run to it. Thus, drive reduction, accompanied by a pleasurable feeling in the box, had a stronger effect on behavior than pleasure in the box alone.

The study of drives and reinforcement is especially interesting because of the existence of a broad range of reinforcers, both positive and negative. A child motivated by a need for attention may seek a positive reinforcer, such as a gift or the privilege of accompanying his parents on a visit. Another child in need of attention may actually seek an aversive stimulus, such as a spanking or the loss of play privileges. The reinforcer that reduces a drive varies from person to person, and in the same person from one time to another. Reinforcers also may be replaced or substituted by other reinforcers.

MEASUREMENT OF DRIVES

Drives may be either unlearned or acquired. *Unlearned drives* (such as hunger and thirst) are rooted in the body's needs. Because they are usually easy to identify, psychologists began their studies of motivation by experimenting on unlearned drives. As a result, experimenters were able to formulate some basic principles of motivation and to apply these principles to the study of complex learned drives. *Acquired drives* are those learned by the individual (those that are not inborn) and involve the numerous social, economic, personal, and intellectual needs that motivate people to behave as they do.

Psychologists do not simply speculate about degrees of drive. They do not assume that a man making a sandwich for himself has a stronger drive for food than he had one hour ago when he was reading a newspaper. They do not state that a rat is hungrier one hour before it has eaten than it is 5 minutes after it has eaten, unless they can support such assertions. As scientists, they attempt to develop and use accurate and reliable measuring devices.

Drive itself is not measured; rather, manifestations of drive are measured, with observations as the basis for measurement. Four accepted observation techniques are used to measure the strength of a drive; they measure *general activity level*, *rate of performance*, *acceptance of punishment*, and *selection among goals*.

General activity level

The extent of a subject's drive may be determined by observation and measurement of its general activity level. The underlying assumption of this approach is that the conditions of the drive state increase the subject's overall activity.

Human activity is not always well defined and easily observed; hence, general activity level is better measured in animals. Rats are often placed for observation in special cages called *activity cages*. One type of activity cage has a sensitive floor that records the rat's running movements. Another type of commonly used activity cage is the running wheel. When the rat is restless, it runs in the wheel; the number of rotations around the wheel is a measure of the distance covered. Experiments have shown that if a rat is highly motivated—for instance, if it is deprived of food—it becomes agitated. The longer the animal is deprived of food, the faster and longer it runs and the more distance it covers. The conditions of the drive state are thus shown to increase the animal's overall activity.

Drive activates restlessness Suppose that it is now one hour before a final exam. You have completed your studying and you need to find something to do. Would you watch television or talk to a friend over a cup of coffee? You try the TV, but after a few minutes you find that you have got to get up, pace the floor, get something to eat, or try doing any number of things. This restlessness is caused by the high drive state you are in at the time; in fact, you may feel this restlessness any time that you are strongly motivated.

Rate of performance

Subjects increase their rate of performance if the performance has previously led to reward. In accordance with this assumption, a child who has been given certain rewards for cleaning up his room (such as praise from his parents or a wanted plaything) will tend to clean up his room again in order to continue receiving the same or similar rewards. This concept is demonstrated in a laboratory setting by using an experimental chamber (see Chapter 6) to test the rate of performance of a hungry rat. When the hungry rat presses the lever, food pellets drop into the food tray. The rat will continue pressing the lever until its hunger is satisfied. The hungrier the rat is, the more frequently it will press the lever. Figure 8.2 shows the lever-pressing activity of a hungry rat. We see from the graph that the rate of performance increased as drive increased.

The rate of lever-pressing is one of various tests used to measure drive. Another test shows, for example, that a hungry animal who has learned to find food at the end of a maze will start running sooner and faster to reach its goal even if, on some runs, no food is received.

Acceptance of punishment

The amount of punishment an organism is willing to accept in order to reach an established goal is a measure of the strength of the motivation. Strong drives generally enable the subject to accept a large amount of punishment, whereas weak drives may be temporarily overcome if punishment is administered as a prerequisite to reaching the goal. A child who dislikes school may fake a stomachache because he is motivated to stay home. However, his mother may force him to stay in his room all day, forbidding him to play outside or keep her company in the house. This punishment may be sufficient to overcome the child's motive to stay home; that is, he may dislike the punishment more than he dislikes his day at school. On the other hand, the punishment may not be severe enough to alter the child's behavior; confinement to his room may be less punishing to the child than spending the day in school. We can assume that the child will satisfy whichever drive is strongest —either the drive to avoid school or the drive to avert punishment.

Similarly, animals in the laboratory may be subjected to punishments that test the strength of their drive to seek food. After being conditioned to receive food at a certain place, the trained animals are shocked as they approach the food goal. The amount and number of

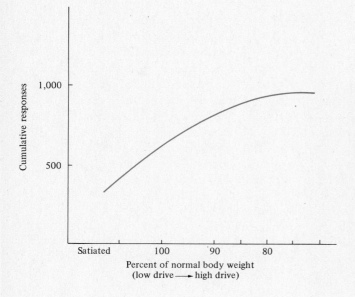

Figure 8.2 *The relationship between lever-pressing responses and the hunger drive. When the rat is satiated, its body weight is above normal, and its responses are few. As the rat continues to be deprived of food, its body weight is reduced to 80 percent or less of its normal weight. With this decreased body weight, the rat's hunger drive increases, and it makes more responses. Thus, high-drive rats make many more responses that do low-drive (satiated or slightly deprived) rats. (After Dinsmoor, 1952)*

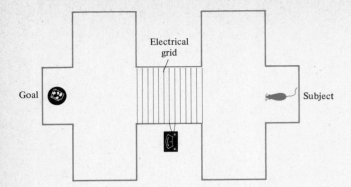

Figure 8.3   An obstruction box.

shocks they are willing to endure indicates the strength of their hunger. An *obstruction box*, a device for studying the acceptance of punishment, is shown in Figure 8.3.

Selection among goals

A fourth method of measuring drives is based on the assumption that a subject with several drives will select the goal associated with his dominant drive. Such behavior is common in everyday experience. A student may be motivated to study because he has an exam the next day, to sleep because he is tired, and to get a sandwich because he has had nothing to eat for hours. He will act on whichever drive is most pressing at the moment.

In nature, too, animals evidently behave by fulfilling their strongest motive before all others. The mother bear protects her cubs first and foremost; her maternal behavior dominates all other behavior.

In the laboratory, animals are easily motivated to select one goal from among several. Laboratory animals can be activated by hunger, thirst, and the desire to escape from discomfort. If the animals are provided with three clear goals —each one fulfilling a motive—the experimenter can determine by observation which motive is the strongest. The goal that best satisfies it will be chosen by the subject.

The selection method is not ordinarily used in measuring drive because it measures relative strengths of several drives and not the absolute strength of any one drive. With the selection method, the psychologist can find out which among several drives is dominant, that is, which directs behavior, but he cannot determine the degree to which that drive controls the particular behavior.

DRIVES ARISING FROM INTERNAL IMBALANCE

Certain unlearned drives are vital not only to man but to all organisms, regardless of their place on the evolutionary scale. These drives stem from needs whose satisfaction is essential to the survival of the individual and the species. The three most important and evident drives are hunger, thirst, and escape from pain. Even before birth, the fetus requires nourishment. Once born, the infant's primary needs are for food and drink. When he experiences painful stimulation, he responds to escape such stimuli and thus satisfy his need to reduce pain. If the infant's drives do not result in satisfaction of his needs, he dies.

Other drives may not be vital to the maintenance of an individual, but they are essential to the maintenance of the species. The sexual drive and the maternal drive are the obvious examples of drives that must be fulfilled if a species is to survive. These drives are not evident at birth but normally come into play at maturity without the necessity of learning.

Homeostasis

The concept of *homeostasis* applies to all drives that are essential to the individual's well-being. The body tends toward an optimal level of functioning, maintaining a normal state of balance between input and output. This maintenance of an overall physiological balance is homeostasis. The hunger and thirst needs, along with breathing, the elimination of waste, resting (including sleep), and waking are all part of the homeostatic system. When there is an imbalance, there is a need to restore balance; thus a drive arises. The specific need and drive depend on the nature of the imbalance.

Unfortunately, the homeostatic drive is not all powerful. People often ignore or overcome their homeostatic drives, even at the expense of their own well-being. The use of tobacco, alcohol, and drugs can so warp the homeostatic balance that the body craves these stimulants while ignoring vital bodily needs.

The homeostatic drive is also incapable of warning the body of other threats to its well-being. The impact of overexposure to radiation, the growth of cancerous tissues, the effect of sugar on an undiagnosed diabetic—these are not discovered until serious damage has resulted. In these situations, the homeostatic drive does not signal early enough.

Hunger

Hunger arises from the body's need for food, which is essential for growth, repair, maintenance of health, manufacture of energy, and other related vital functions.

The most obvious indications of the need for food are hunger pangs. Experiments have shown that hunger pangs are normally caused by contractions of the stomach muscles. In one experiment (Figure 8.4), a subject swallows a deflated balloon with a long, thin tube attached to it. Once in the stomach, the balloon is inflated until it touches the stomach walls. The inflated balloon is affected by stomach contractions: when the muscles contract, the balloon contracts and air is forced up the tube; when the muscles are at rest, no air is forced up the tube. The external end of the tube is attached to a pressurized measuring device that records the contractions as air-pressure changes. The subject is told to press a key whenever he feels a hunger pang. The tube and the key are each attached to a separate stylus that records its impulses on a revolving drum of paper. Whenever the *key-press* stylus rises, it is recording the subject's sensation of hunger; whenever the *tube* stylus rises, it is recording the released air caught by the stomach contractions. In test after test, the markings corresponded. Whenever the subject indicated he felt hungry, his stomach muscles were contracting.

From the preceding experiment, it might

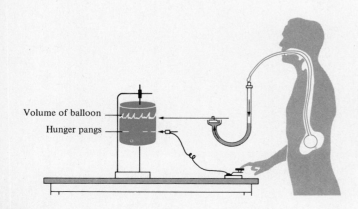

Volume of balloon
Hunger pangs

Figure 8.4 *The stomach-balloon apparatus is used to test and compare a subject's stomach contractions (shown by the volume of the balloon) to his hunger pangs.*

be assumed that the hunger drive is caused by stomach contractions. However, other observations and experiments have disproved this theory. Human beings whose stomachs are removed for medical reasons still feel hunger. Rats whose stomachs are removed in experimental situations still behave like hungry rats—restless and active, devouring food. They can still be conditioned by food rewards. The source of the hunger drive, then, is not the stomach alone.

Since hunger pangs are recognized only as indicators of hunger, it is necessary to determine the actual source of hunger. Only recently have psychologists come to agree on the physiological basis of the hunger drive. According to the prevailing theory, hunger is a stimulus brought about by a chemical imbalance in the composition of the blood. This imbalance activates the hypothalamus (see Chapter 3). As the hunger drive becomes more acute, the hypothalamus begins sending messages to the stomach muscles to contract and induce hunger pangs. If the stomach has been removed, the chemical imbalance still exists, and the hypothalamus somehow redirects its response to the stimulus. Other signs of hunger (manifested even with intact stomachs) are dizziness or light-headedness and general body activity. The theory that the hunger drive is induced by blood chemicals receives strong support from a test in which an animal that is not hungry appears to experience signs of hunger after receiving a blood transfusion from a hungry animal.

Controlled eating How does the body control food intake? Davis, Gallagher, and Ladove (1967) recently experimented with both hungry and well-fed rats to determine if there is a blood factor responsible for regulating the quantity of food eaten at one time.

One group of rats had continuous free access to a milk diet, whereas others were fed for only a half-hour once a day. Two days prior to the experimental day, a tubelike device was inserted under the skin of each rat, so that blood could be extracted and injected without the use of anesthesia. On the day of the experiment—just before the once-a-day eaters were to be fed—blood transfusions were given,

so that each rat had an even mixture of satiated (free-access) and hungry (once-a-day) blood. When the hungry rats were fed, they consumed only about 50 percent of their normal intake.

When the experimenters mixed the blood of two hungry rats—one, a once-a-day eater just before feeding; the other, a free-access eater deprived for a 24-hour period—they found that the food intake of the once-a-day eater did not decrease.

It seems that changes in the quantity or quality of certain blood-borne factors regulate the food intake of rats.

The hypothalamus and hunger As indicated in the preceding section and in Chapter 3, the hypothalamus plays an important part in the hunger drive. Two areas of the hypothalamus have been identified. One controls the "switching on," or excitation, of hunger; the other controls the "swtiching off," or inhibition, of hunger. Both centers can be artificially stimulated. If the "on" area is stimulated, the hunger drive is increased; if the "off" area is stimulated, the

Figure 8.5   When the excitatory center of a rat's hypothalamus is stimulated, the rat eats far more than he normally would. (Courtesy Neal E. Miller)

hunger drive is decreased. Figure 8.5 shows the results of an experiment that stimulated the excitation center of a rat's hypothalamus. As is evident, the rat became obese because it ate too much.

Although the hypothalamus appears to be the control center for the hunger drive, other areas of the brain function in connection with—and at times in substitution for—the hypothalamus. But the hypothalamus is clearly a major area of influence, and when it is destroyed, removed, or damaged it takes a while for other areas to take over its functions.

Hypothalamic norepinephrine Researchers know that the hypothalamus is integral to the regulation of the life rhythms found in many species. However, Margules, Lewis, Dragovich, and Margules (1972) discovered that the regulatory powers of the rat's hypothalamus are such that the same stimulus evokes opposite behaviors at two different times of day.

After measuring normal feeding activity in a group of male albino rats, the investigators performed surgery so that small quantities of norepinephrine (a drug known to affect feeding habits) could be applied directly to each rat's hypothalamus at will. Nighttime application of the drug, during those hours when rats usually eat most of their daily intake, produced marked reduction in both the amount of food consumed and in the effort expended to feed. On the other hand, daytime application, during those hours when rats normally eat least, produced significant increases in these same measures.

Just why the addition of this special drug should have such effects is as yet unknown. These investigators hypothesized that by upsetting the normal rhythm of the rat's natural hypothalamic norepinephrine, they somehow interfered with the animal's internal system for signaling its own states of hunger and satiety.

Hunger selection Hunger is not a blind drive satisfied by any nutrition. A carnivorous (meat-eating) animal may be very hungry, but it will not eat vegetable or grass foods even if meat is not available. Its system requires meat and cannot be satisfied by vegetables. Culture, too, affects diet. In some societies, most people are vegetarians and will not eat meat; and certain primitive tribes and religious sects impose dietary restrictions that do not allow free selection among foods. In learning his culture, man acquires tastes for specific foods. Different cultures have cultivated different tastes. Many Americans are repelled by snails as a food, while the French consider them a delicacy. Corn on the cob is a favorite American food, but in Scandinavia, corn is fed only to cattle and pigs and is considered unfit for human consumption. Man is so strongly influenced by his acquired personal and cultural tastes that he may reject a highly nutritional food yet glut himself with food that is valueless except for taste appeal.

Hunger balance To survive, human beings must eat the amount and kinds of food the body requires. Although we often choose pleasurable foods over more nutritional foods in amounts too large for our bodies to digest satisfactorily, in the long run we usually balance our diets quantitatively and qualitatively. Animals and human infants are less influenced than adult human beings by acquired taste. In experiments, rats, monkeys, and human infants left free to choose their diets from a relatively varied selection of foods tend to balance their diets. On a day-to-day basis, an animal might consume too much of one thing or not enough of another, but over an extended period of time it eats a balanced diet. Animals, including man, often crave foods that correct chemical imbalances in the body. Rats with a salt imbalance eat large quantities of salt until that need is satisfied. Perhaps some of the bizarre cravings of pregnant women arise from the body's need to adjust to unusual chemical changes caused by pregnancy. While the exact nature of this regulation of diet is not known, research has shown that the taste of food plays an important role. For example, rats whose taste buds have been cut do not choose a balanced diet.

Taste and the hypothalamus When an animal's hypothalamus is damaged, it is unable to regulate its food intake without help from taste cues. A normal animal does not need to rely on taste to regulate its food intake and body weight.

Teitelbaum (1964) reported a series of studies in which taste was bypassed in feeding. Using an implanted tube, the experimenter pumped liquid foods directly into a rat's stomach. When a normal rat is trained to press a lever that sends liquid food directly to its stomach, it quickly learns to press enough to maintain its normal food intake. It neither starves nor overeats. Although a rat with a damaged hypothalamus shows an excessive intake of food through the mouth, it does not press the lever for food delivered directly to the stomach; as a result, the rat starves. If, however, the same rat is given oral access to a sweet-tasting substance while the food is pumped into its stomach, it will press the lever for food. Thus, a rat with a damaged hypothalamus evidently needs to taste food in order to regulate its food intake.

Just as animals balance their diets, so do they tend to regulate the amount of food they eat. Somehow, animals know when they are satiated. Since we have already determined that the stomach is not the center of the hunger drive, we know that satiation is not merely a matter of stopping when the stomach is full. Recent research has shown that the satiation of the hunger drive is regulated by two factors: *taste sensitivity*, which occurs in the mouth during ingestion; and *postingestional sensitivity*, which is produced by signals from the bloodstream during digestion. These two processes operate independently: they may send their messages one after the other, reinforcing the feeling of satiation, or one may operate while the other does not. Taste sensitivity keeps track of the quantity of food chewed and swallowed. Postingestional sensitivity occurs when a message to cease eating is received by the stomach from the well-fed bloodstream. Tests have been conducted with animals who chewed and swallowed food that never reached the stomach but was instead detoured out of the body through an opening that had been cut into the passageway to the stomach. Even though the food never reached the stomach, the action of the animal's taste sensitivity caused it to behave as though it were fully fed.

Starvation Starvation is the extreme of food deprivation. An individual under extreme food deprivation is incapable of coping with most physical and social activities. He becomes

1 dizzy or light headed, experiencing a general decrease in bodily activity;
2 nauseated and unable to coordinate muscular activities;
3 apathetic and withdrawn from social relationships;
4 lacking in self-control, will power, and discipline;
5 lacking in drive for physical and sexual activities;
6 acutely aware of the hunger drive above all else.

Effects of starvation Normally, there are rigid limits to the frustration to which psychologists may subject human beings. One unique occasion for the observation of persons under conditions of extreme deprivation arose during World War II.

A total of 32 conscientious objectors volunteered to serve as "human guinea pigs" in a starvation experiment. For 24 weeks they lived on a famine diet, consisting mostly of turnips and cabbage. The diet, containing fewer than half the calories of a normal diet, produced a 25 percent weight loss in the men. Physiologists, physicians, and psychologists at the University of Minnesota observed them scientifically during the semi-starvation period, as well as for 12 weeks following. On some, there were follow-up studies for 12 months.

The subjects were healthy young men. Only those were accepted who were free from a history of disabling disease, including mental illness; had no physical handicaps; were able to get along well with others; were free from family responsibilities; and were willing to put aside personal concerns in the interest of the success of the experiment.

Yet hunger produced psychological and moral deterioration in these specially chosen persons. After 24 weeks of semi-starvation, personality tests showed the subjects to be more introverted, depressed, moody, impulsive, passive, tense, and suffering from feelings of inferiority. Their preoccupation with food made creative and coherent thinking almost impossible. Their social ties were loosened. Sex activity and interest subsided. They lost initiative, became irritable, took to nail biting, excessive smoking, coffee drinking, and gum chewing. They became careless of their personal appearance. Some took to stealing. Their sense of humor disappeared. They showed an increase in both neurotic and psychotic symptoms.*

Thirst

In some ways, thirst is a more physically compelling drive than hunger, for intense thirst often affects the individual more strongly and more obviously than does hunger. An individual can exist without food for longer periods than he can without water. When he has been deprived of water for a long time, his ability to function physically changes: he finds it difficult to breathe, his muscular movements are impaired, he feels queasy, and the sensation of dryness—the parched feeling in his mouth, throat, and tongue—becomes exceedingly painful.

Sensations from the mouth and throat play an important role in thirst, but these sensations are only part of the total thirst drive. We do not drink simply to keep our mouths and throats moist. A number of studies show that lack of water in the body's tissues is probably the basic condition for producing the thirst drive. When an individual is deprived of liquids, his tissues are insufficiently supplied with water, and he becomes thirsty. Any condition that upsets the water balance in the tissues will affect thirst. For example, when strong salt solutions are injected, the tissues will require more water in order to maintain the proper salt balance; this condition produces thirst.

Investigations of the role of the central nervous system have shown that the hypothalamus is involved in the regulation of thirst as well as hunger. Experiments with goats indicate that drinking may be elicited by electrical stimulation of the hypothalamus (Andersson and McCann, 1955); other experiments have found

*From Keys, A., Brozek, J., Henschel, A., Michelson, O., and Taylor, H. L. *The biology of human starvation.* Minneapolis: University of Minnesota Press. Copyright © 1950 by the University of Minnesota.

that the injection of a salt solution into the hypothalamus will motivate drinking. Injections of water into the hypothalamus will cause a thirsty animal to stop drinking and behave as if its thirst were satisfied (Miller, 1958).

Pain reduction

Whereas most drives impel us *toward* actions, the pain-reduction drive impels us *away* from actions that would be painful. All organisms seek to reduce pain and other aversive stimuli, such as excessive heat or cold, unbreathable air, fatigue, loud noises, bright lights, and foul odors.

Cultural reactions to pain Sternbach and Tursky (1965) conducted an experiment to determine how different cultures react to pain. They first interviewed and then tested elderly American (Yankee), Irish, Jewish, and Italian women. Yankee women took pain "in stride"; Irish women said one should "keep a tight upper lip" but "fear the worst"; the Jewish women seemed to be worried about the later implications of pain; and the Italians were concerned about the immediate reduction of pain.

Two tests were run. In the first, shocks applied to each woman's hands were gradually increased until the woman being tested said that she had had enough. In the second test, 30 shocks of equal intensity were applied 30 seconds apart, while recordings of the women's *Palmar skin potential* (the skin's reaction to electricity) were taken.

Results showed that in the first test the Italian women called a halt sooner than either the Yankee, Irish, or Jewish women. Although both the Jewish and Italian women were concerned about pain, this test showed how their similar concern stemmed from different attitudes.

The results of the physiological measures showed that the physiological response of the Yankees quickly habituates (decreases), whereas it remains high for the other three groups. This indicates a basic attitudinal difference between the Yankees and other groups. Whereas the former take pain in stride, the others are in one way or another concerned about it and always aware of it.

Pain-reduction is an especially interesting unlearned drive. In one sense it resembles a mere reflex action. For example, your body will recoil from the flame of a lit match brought close to your arm, even though you may not be aware of what stimulated your arm action. In another sense, many pain-reduction reactions, although they may seem to be automatic, are profoundly influenced by individual learning. People learn to tolerate or ignore certain uncomfortable stimuli while becoming especially responsive to others. A person who has grown up near a sulfur refinery will not even notice the odor that others find nauseating. A beekeeper may learn to ignore a bee sting, whereas a person who once became violently ill from a bee sting may scream with agony when stung again. Part of his pain is unlearned, while another part is due to past experience. (In Chapter 13 we will discuss the phenomenon of people who are preoccupied with pain and use their discomfiture, real and apparent, to satisfy other needs.)

The pain-reduction drive may not warn us of bodily damage until it is too late. It is not until the body feels pain—for example, until a tumor has grown large and is pressing against other tissues or organs—that the body is aware of the danger. In some cases, the warning may come too late for the damaging condition to be corrected.

Although most human beings seek to avoid pain, some individuals seem to enjoy the experience of pain. Instead of escaping pain, they seek its infliction on themselves (*masochism*) or on others (*sadism*). Both masochism and sadism have sexual overtones. Clinical cases of sadomasochistic behavior often show a link between sexual pleasure and pain. In such cases, the need-drive-satisfaction sequence is essentially sexual. These sadomasochistic individuals derive sexual satisfaction from the experience of pain.

Sex

The *sexual drive* is vital to the maintenance of all species. It is an unlearned drive dependent upon maturation. Unlike the hunger and thirst drives that are activated at birth, the sexual drive does not become overtly active until the organism has reached a relatively advanced stage of development. In human beings, the sexual drive is greatly influenced by social learning. According to Freud, sexual drives are present in the unconscious at birth. The child satisfies them by substitution—by sucking, excreting, and so on (see Chapter 2).

In mammals, the sexual drive is stimulated by the activity of the sex (gonadal) hormones. These are the same hormones responsible for secondary sex characteristics—body hair, voice change, and contouring of the body—in human beings. Thus, the hormones that make the body sexually mature also drive the body toward sexual behavior. However, the higher an organism is on the evolutionary scale, the less is its sexual behavior controlled by sex hormones, the more by learned, environmental factors.

Numerous experiments with sex hormones illustrate their importance in the sexual drive. Injection of the male sex hormones, *androgens*, into sexually immature or castrated male animals causes definite sexual behavior. Similarly, injection of female hormones, *estrogens*, into an immature or sterile female animal causes sexually active behavior.

In most species, the mature male requires little inducement to copulate; he is biologically ready to copulate at all times and needs only the willing female to provoke the drive. It has been shown in the study of rats that castrated males show sexual activity, while a female with her ovaries removed does not. Also, immature female animals do not and cannot engage in reproductive activities, whereas immature males commonly engage in sexual activities although they cannot attain sexual completion.

The reproductive cycle of female animals is called the *estrous cycle*. During estrus, commonly known as "heat," sex hormones are secreted that arouse the awareness of the male and produce in him an aggressive desire for copulation. Females in heat try to divert males from other interests, especially other females, in order to copulate. Females of certain species, such as dogs and cats, give off odors when they are sexually receptive. In other species, the roles are reversed; the males attract fertile females. For example, male frogs croak and male crickets chirp to let receptive females know of their presence.

Plasma testosterone and social environment Since plasma testosterone is an important physiological aspect of maleness, the intermittent rise and fall of the level of this crucial substance is a natural area for scientific study. Fluctuations in plasma testosterone level usually accompany dramatic changes in social behavior. One important question is whether changes in social environment cause the physiological fluctuations or whether testosterone changes cause the marked differences in social behavior.

Rose, Gordon, and Bernstein (1972) recently subjected four male rhesus monkeys to radical social-environmental manipulations in order to investigate this question. Plasma testosterone levels were first measured during 2-week periods of caged isolation. Soon after, each male was introduced into his own group of sexually receptive females. Along with the preponderance of aggressive and sexual activity shown by each male, there was a two- to threefold increase in plasma testosterone levels during this 2-week exposure. Subsequent periods of caged isolation then produced drops in plasma testosterone to prior baseline levels.

The experimenters then maneuvered a drastic change in each monkey's social environment—introducing him to a well-established (and therefore combative) group of 30 other males. Within minutes, each experimental monkey was the center of concerted attack from group members. Although "defeat" sessions were limited to 2 hours in order to prevent serious injury, plasma testosterone levels continued to drop well below baseline for several weeks. Subsequent reintroduction to new groups of receptive females, however, produced new upsurges in plasma testosterone levels, which matched or exceeded previously high levels.

Because each environmental manipulation was followed by significant physiological changes in the predicted direction, it seems reasonable to conclude that plasma testosterone fluctuations are in some way the result of changes in the social environment.

The human sexual drive In the human female, the estrous cycle is not so pronounced as it is in other species. She is receptive to sex at almost all times, as is the male. Her sexual drive, however, is somewhat affected by her menstrual cycle. It is at its weakest at the height of her menstrual period. It is at its strongest just prior to menstruation. The human female's reproductive system is most receptive to fertilization midway between menstrual periods.

In human beings, as perhaps in other animals, males and females do not reach sexual maturity and the height of reproductive capability at the same time. Surveys show that men reach their sexual peak at around 19 to 20 and that their sexual drive declines after that time. Women tend to maintain a longer and more consistent sexual drive, reaching a peak between 25 to 30 and declining at a later age than men.

At any age, sexual activity progresses through a very specific sequence of physiological events. Masters and Johnson (1966) identified this four-phase cycle of physiological activity. The beginning of sexual arousal is the *excitement phase*. This is followed by the *plateau phase*, at which time hormone activity plays a major role. Following the plateau is the *orgasm*, a brief phase during which muscular tensions are released. The final phase is the *resolution*, which is a return to the preexcitement level. There are individual differences in the length of time for each phase, with greater variability occurring in females than in males.

Although basically innate and biological in nature, our sexual drives have been restricted and rechanneled by environmental factors. Human beings are seldom able to "act out" their sexual drives as freely as their hunger and thirst drives. A man cannot sexually approach an appealing woman he sees on the street; customary patterns of courtship must be followed. And from early childhood we are told that certain sexual acts are acceptable while others are not. Thus, society places severe restrictions on when, where, and how we may act out our sexual drives.

Measurement of sexual responsiveness Fisher and Osofsky (1968) attempted to correlate objective physiological measurements with a woman's description of her sexual responsiveness and the quality of

In addition to, and in part because of, the restrictions of society, the expression of human sexuality is also greatly affected by psychological factors. Fantasy and vicarious sexual activity may play important roles in some aspects of sexual behavior. The combination of social and psychological restraints so affects the sexual drive that human beings often channel the sexual drive into acts unrelated to reproduction. For example, pornographic literature and X-rated movies enjoy great popularity because they enable the individual to act out his or her unsatisfied needs vicariously. In extreme cases, the peeping Tom or exhibitionist resorts to observing others or having others observe him performing a sexual act.

Homosexual behavior   The most prevalent form of deviation from normal sexual activity is homosexual behavior in which sexual acts are shared by two people of the same sex. Rarely is homosexuality caused by physiological abnormalities or even hormonal disturbances. Rather, it is believed to be the result of individual development and learning—perhaps due to a severe, domineering mother and a henpecked father, or an absent father and a mother trying to be both mother and father to a lonely child.

Many homosexuals function well in society; they do not behave according to the stereotyped patterns often associated with homosexuality. Frequently, people with homosexual relationships also engage in heterosexual activities. For example, men with latent homosexual tendencies frequently marry, have children, and live successfully within society's guidelines. But if the homosexual tendencies become manifest, the conflict of interests becomes obvious and the marriage may lose its foothold on permanence—not because of the husband's manifest feelings but because of the wife's inability to cope with this type of rivalry.

Kinsey's studies (Kinsey, Pomeroy, and Martin, 1948; Kinsey, Pomeroy, Martin, and Gebhard, 1953) have indicated that about 4 percent of the American population is homosexual. Furthermore, it has been estimated that one-third of the American male population has had at least one homosexual experience. Such experiences usually occur during adolescence, when the young boy is experimenting with his newly maturing sexual urges. In most learning situations, however, homosexual tendencies are rechanneled by the environment into socially acceptable activities.

The maternal drive

Closely associated with the sexual drive is the *maternal drive*, which is the need of females of many species to bear, nurture, and protect their young. The maternal drive is often spoken of as an instinctive behavior, for most mothers exhibit maternal behavior without training or previous experience. Among most animal species, females bear their young without assistance, provide for their nourishment, and protect them from danger.

Experiments with rats have shown that the maternal drive is motivated in part by hormonal stimulation. Of particular importance in mammals is the hormone *prolactin*, a pituitary secretion. The release of prolactin into the bloodstream stimulates the secretion of milk to nurse the newborn mammal. The presence of milk in the mammary glands provides a kind of cue or incentive for the mother to nurse her young. When prolactin is injected into nonpregnant mammals, maternal behavior, such as nest-building, is displayed. However, prolactin also lowers body temperature, indicating that the nest-building may be as much comfort-seeking as maternal behavior.

Human mothers are less impelled by the maternal drive than are other animal mothers. Many human mothers do not nurse their young. Some mothers turn over the care of their young to other people; others even abandon their young.

DRIVES TOWARD EXTERNAL STIMULATION

Man has the same basic physical needs as do all animals, but he has other needs as well. Man and at least some other primates experience drives toward external stimulation. Beyond his basic needs of hunger, thirst, and so on, man needs to interact with his environment, to sense and understand the objects and people around him. For example, an individual brought into a room containing unfamiliar objects has a need, a curiosity, to explore and probe them so as to become aware of their nature.

Some psychologists believe that human drives toward stimulation arise from the innate need to interact with the environment and thereby obtain stimulating experiences. Others argue that such drives are acquired as a result of learning. Although drives toward stimulation may not be essential for survival (we can exist without fulfilling them), they contribute to emotional health, a feeling of contentment, and the ability to adjust.

In this section we will discuss several specific drives toward stimulation: the curiosity drive; the affectional drive; the drive toward

self-actualization; and the unique need to experience a form of brain stimulation. We will then turn our attention to acquired drives in general.

Curiosity

Experimenters first observed the *curiosity drive* by accident. They noticed that animal subjects engage in considerable exploration and manipulation, particularly of unfamiliar stimuli. The animals exhibit the exploratory behavior without needing to be stimulated by physical deprivations such as hunger or thirst. Rats have been shown to learn a maze without receiving any overt reinforcement; the exploratory behavior is reinforcement enough.

City monkeys and curiosity In India, rhesus monkeys are found living in villages and cities as well as in the jungles. The city monkeys behave differently from their jungle relatives: they are much more interested in strange objects and will even handle such things as a human skeleton, which ordinarily evokes intense fear in monkeys. Singh (1968) compared the visual curiosity of city and jungle monkeys. He showed them various objects of increasing complexity, such as a set of blocks, a row of empty rat cages, and, most complex of all, a moving toy train. The blocks and the cages were equally interesting to both groups of monkeys. The city monkeys, however, spent much more time than the jungle monkeys looking at the moving train. Singh explains that because of their more extensive experiences, the city monkeys have developed more complex curiosity behavior and therefore show greater interest in the more complex stimulation of the toy train (Figure 8.6).

The curiosity drive is expressed in both exploratory and manipulative behavior. Exploratory behavior involves the need to know the environment by investigation and cautious manipulation. Manipulative behavior follows exploration; once the individual learns about his environment, he may find that he enjoys the simple act of manipulating a particular object, and he engages in manipulative behavior for its own sake. A monkey presented with a complicated-looking toy will first investigate it, looking,

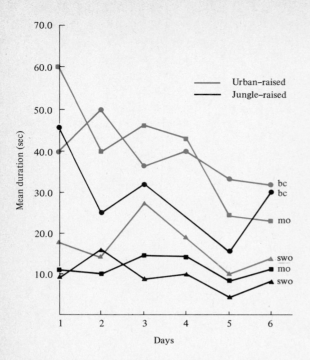

Figure 8.6 Mean duration of the visual responses of the jungle- and urban-raised monkeys to the three stimulus displays on six successive days. (From S. D. Singh, "Effect of Urban Environment on Visual Curiosity Behavior in Rhesus Monkeys," Psychonomic Science, 1968, pp. 83–84. Reprinted by permission)

touching, and moving it about. When he learns how to operate the toy, he may continue moving it about, for the sheer pleasure of manipulation.

Exploration We are all familiar with the restless pacing of animals in the zoo. Caged animals are not content to behave quietly and calmly. All animals seek to interact with their environments, even if they have no immediate needs to satisfy.

The initial reaction of an animal placed in an unfamiliar environment is called *habituation*; that is, it seeks to become accustomed to its unfamiliar surroundings and thus overcome its fear of the novel stimuli. After the animal becomes habituated, it often engages in exploratory behavior.

Man and other animals, particularly other primates, seem to seek information from their environment. This investigative-exploratory activity is both persistent and powerful. Young children use all their sense organs as they attempt to explore their surroundings. They look, feel, and often try to taste the objects they can reach. All healthy children seek variations in stimuli; they appear to be looking for the new, the unusual.

Monkeys, like human children, show a high degree of exploratory behavior. Experiments have shown that monkeys confined to a box will learn new responses when the reward for a correct response is the opportunity to look through a window (Butler, 1954). Apparently, under certain conditions, the curiosity drive is satisfied by visual stimulation.

Drives for new stimulation Beauchamp, Chapman, and Grebing (1967) predicted that, when given a choice, calves would approach a changed stimulus rather than a familiar one. On the first trial, each calf was allowed to explore the stem of a T maze. The arms of the T were blocked off by gates so that the calves could see them but could not enter either one. One arm was painted black and the other white. On trial 2, one of the arms was changed so that now they were either both black or both white, and the gates were removed so that the calf could enter the arm of its choice. The changed goal arm was entered more often than the unchanged goal arm. Inasmuch as the goal arms were identical in every other way, the animals were evidently attracted by the novelty of a different color.

Manipulation Curiosity is also expressed as a desire to manipulate objects in their environment for no apparent purpose other than the manipulation itself. Monkeys also manipulate any objects within their reach. Infant monkeys display this tendency even before they are old enough to eat solid foods. The manipulative activity of monkeys is strong enough to motivate

Figure 8.7 Monkeys learn manipulatory tasks for no extrinsic reinforcement. The tasks serve to satisfy their curiosity drive. (Harry F. Harlow, University of Wisconsin Primate Laboratory)

monkeys to solve mechanical problems. For example, as shown in Figure 8.7, rhesus monkeys will learn the solution to a mechanical, take-apart puzzle even though they receive no reward other than the opportunity to manipulate the puzzle (Harlow, Harlow, and Meyer, 1950). Evidently manipulation can be its own reward.

Curiosity and learning Some children exhibit more curiosity than others. If their curiosity is reinforced, they explore more of their environment. In this way, they constantly widen their range of learning experiences. A child that is not curious will suffer from a lack of sufficient and varied learning experiences (Figure 8.8).

Jean Piaget has applied the concept of the curiosity drive to his theory of cognitive development (see Chapter 2). He believes that, in the course of cognitive development, a succession of changes occurs in what he calls *schemata*, the organizing frameworks of thinking, planning, and problem-solving. Schemata change and increase in their complexity because the individual is driven by curiosity to know his environment.

According to Piaget, we have a drive to reconcile the unknown to our present level of knowledge, and this drive enlarges and expands our schemata in such a way that we seek to incorporate more and more environmental stimulation into increasingly more inclusive schemata. Motivation, is, for Piaget, a cognitive movement upward and outward; our horizons grow higher and wider as we continue to build on existing schemata. This theory of movement toward higher schemata, which places considerable emphasis on curiosity as a drive, is known as *equilibration*.

Affection

Throughout the world, children exhibit strong affection for their parents, who, in turn, display affection for their children. We show our affec-

Figure 8.8 Infants exhibit visual curiosity at a very early age. This 3-week old infant is content to watch and gurgle to her toys (faces are painted on the underside of the plastic pieces). (Betty Jane Shapiro)

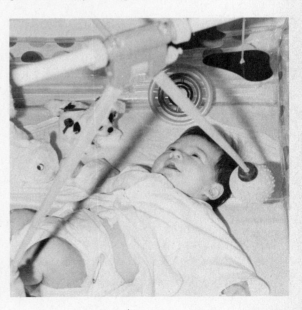

tion for our friends and the people we love and receive their affection in return. Although we all express and receive affection, it is difficult scientifically to define what we mean by the *affectional drive*. Perhaps affection is only an outward manifestation of other more basic drives: from mother to child, the maternal drive; from child to mother, the hunger drive; and between lovers, the sexual drive.

Until recently, many psychologists thought that children show affection for their parents because they recognize in them the satisfiers of such basic drives as hunger and thirst. However, as discussed more fully in Chapter 2, Harlow and his associates (Harlow, 1958; Harlow and Zimmerman, 1959; Harlow and Suomi, 1970; Harlow, Harlow, and Suomi, 1971) carried out a series of important and now famous experiments demonstrating that the basis for affectional behavior lies elsewhere. Harlow's monkeys very simply needed the warmth and comfort of a living body.

Self-actualization

Some psychologists, such as May (1953), Maslow (1954), Allport (1961), and Rogers (1963), have not been satisfied with human motivation theories emphasizing drives that reduce stimulation or lead to new stimulation. While they agree that the individual's first task is to fulfill his basic needs, they feel that man is further influenced by a more advanced and complex set of needs that enable him "to be positive, forward-moving, constructive" (Rogers, 1963). One of these is the need for *self-actualization*, an unlearned, uniquely human need to discover one's self and to fulfill one's potential (Maslow, 1954). The self-actualization concept (to be discussed further in Chapter 12) is found in the whole of human life, not merely in the individual drives that impel action. It is the drive that pushes man to make the most of his potential.

Although the concept of self-actualization is difficult to measure, these psychologists iden-

tify it as a heightened awareness of self. Persons identified as self-actualizing are considered healthy by the standards that Rogers, Maslow, and others have established. Self-actualizers are creative people; they understand themselves and the world around them, and so they go beyond the basic needs to a higher plateau of awareness.

In spite of the persuasive argument offered by the proponents of self-actualization theory, little is known about this drive (if indeed it is a drive). Considerable research must be done in order to identify and clarify the variables that enter into this type of motivation. It is not enough to say that a man is a self-actualizer; we need to know what produces this drive, how it may be measured, and what conditions change it.

The fully functioning person A key idea is Carl Roger's theory in his concept of the "fully functioning person." In a paper published in 1963, Rogers described what he means by fully functioning:

Here then is my theoretical model of the person who emerges from therapy—a person functioning freely in all the fullness of his organismic potentialities; a person who is dependable in being realistic, self-enhancing, socialized, and appropriate in his behavior; a creative person, whose specific formings of behavior are not easily predictable; a person who is ever-changing, ever-developing, always discovering himself and the newness in himself in each succeeding moment of time. This is the person who in an imperfect way actually emerges from the experience of safety and freedom in a therapeutic experience, and this is the person whom I have tried to describe for you in pure form.

Competence Closely related to the concept of self-actualization is the concept of *competence* developed by R. W. White (1959). White suggests that individuals are motivated by a desire to function as effectively as they can in their environment. A person has attained competence when he goes beyond the satisfaction of needs that are based on internal imbalance and has achieved a feeling that he can cope satisfactorily with his environment.

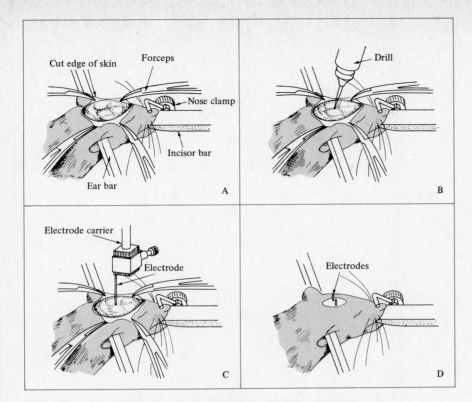

Figure 8.9   Implanting electrodes into the skull of a rat: (A) skull exposed; (B) holes drilled; (C) electrodes inserted; (D) electrodes in place, incision stitched up. (From Experimental neuropsychology by Benjamin L. Hart. W. H. Freeman and Co. Copyright © 1969.)

Intracranial stimulation

During the course of experimentation, psychologists discovered that they could motivate animals to engage in specific behavior by precisely stimulating particular areas of the animal's brain. The animal finds the stimulation pleasurable and seeks its repetition by performing any task that may be required. Rats, when left alone; learn to press levers, run mazes, and cross electrified grids when the only reinforcement is electrical stimulation of the forward portion of the hypothalamus, the rhinencephalon, and the limbic region of the brain (see Chapter 3). The reinforcing effects are evidently very powerful and have been demonstrated in a variety of animals. This technique is referred to as *intracranial stimulation* (ICS). The electrical stimulation is delivered by tiny electrodes carefully implanted in the animal's brain. The animal suffers no ill effects from the electrode implantation; he can function in a completely normal fashion with the electrodes in place. (Figure 8.9 depicts the surgical procedures used to implant the electrodes.) While this form of motivation appears to be unrelated to any of the known needs, it does resemble a kind of need for stimulation or perhaps something resembling a pleasure-seeking need (Olds and Milner, 1954; Olds, 1969).

Reinforcement from intracranial stimulation Olds (1958) showed that electrical self-stimulation of certain parts of the brain serves as a reinforcer. He noted that rats which normally press a bar only 25 times an hour when left alone will press it more than 200 times an hour, if pressing the bar is immediately followed by electrical stimulation of the rhinencephalon and parts of the hypothalamus. When the midbrain and certain parts of the thalamus and hypothalamus are stimulated, the rats either avoid the bar or press it very seldom.

To show the strength of the drive for brain stimulation, Olds allowed the rat to press a given bar only 3 times. The rat had to cross an electric grid to reach another bar, where he could again stimulate himself. Heat on the grid was constantly increased to see how much pain the rat was willing to endure for stimulation. Results showed that the rat was willing to endure twice as much pain to be stimulated as a rat who had not eaten for 24 hours would endure for food!

ACQUIRED DRIVES

Much human behavior is initiated and guided by complex drives that are only indirectly related to the basic unlearned drives of hunger, thirst, curiosity, and the like. We do not attend college because of biological or other internal imbalances, nor do we search for meaning, truth, or order in our lives because of a bodily need. Goals such as these are the result of the interplay of numerous unlearned and learned drives.

In this section we will explore some of man's acquired drives, those learned drives which are especially important to us and which arouse special kinds of behavior. Because human beings are not easily observable subjects, psychologists are not always able to classify these drives precisely, nor are they always able to measure the success of any one person in achieving his goal. Therefore, we must concentrate on what psychologists have learned about drives from the laboratory, from clinical observations, psychological testing, and observations of people in social situations.

The terms *learned*, *acquired*, and *derived* are used to describe those drives which depend initially on their association with other, more basic drives. Some psychologists use the term *secondary drives*, but this may be misleading because it may suggest that these drives are of secondary importance when, in fact, they are very important. An understanding of human behavior requires a thorough study of such learned drives as fear or anxiety, desire for approval, striving for achievement, aggression, and dependency.

Fear and anxiety

Conditioned *fear* is one of the most important and complex drives that we will study. Fear produces either escape or avoidance behavior—behavior that is aimed at reducing the fear stimulus in any degree possible. Fear becomes an acquired drive when a particular stimulus is associated with pain. A child who has felt the pain of a bee sting may run and hide at the mere mention of a bee. Many of the stimuli that elicit fear are conditioned stimuli; we relate the conditioned stimulus to an unconditioned one that previously produced pain or discomfort.

The strength of the conditioned fear drive is shown vividly in classical conditioning. If a neutral stimulus is associated time after time with a fear-provoking stimulus such as shock, then the previously neutral stimulus will become fear-producing when administered alone.

The acquisition of fear Miller (1948) set out to demonstrate that fear can be an acquired drive. To do so, he had to show that (1) when the drive is present, it causes random (trial-and-error) behavior; and (2) when the drive is reduced, this reduction reinforces the learning of the response immediately preceding reduction.

Miller constructed two adjoining compartments, one white and one black, with a door between them (Figure 8.10). Rats were placed in the boxes and allowed to roam freely; they showed no preference for either of the boxes. Then when shocks were administered to rats in the white box, these rats ran into the black box. After several such trials, the rats ran from the white box whether or not a shock was administered. They had learned to fear the white box.

The animals were then placed in the white box with the door closed. The door could be opened only if the rat rotated a wheel above the door. Each rat at first showed much random behavior, for example, scratching at the door, jumping up on it, rolling into it, and so forth. Then, quite by accident, he rotated the wheel and escaped into the black box. This was repeated until the rat learned to open the door by rotating the wheel. Later, the rat had no trouble learning to change his response from rotating a wheel to pressing a lever.

Thus, Miller showed that fear is an acquired drive, the reduction of which reinforces learning.

Many psychologists use the terms *conditioned* (or *learned*) *fear* and *anxiety* to mean one and the same thing. Others prefer to make a distinction, describing fear as a response to overt stimuli and anxiety as a state of fear

Figure 8.10   The shuttle box used by Miller to study acquired fear in rats. The left compartment was painted white; the right compartment, black. The door with horizontal black and white stripes drops down so that the rat can get from the white to the black compartment. (After Miller, 1948)

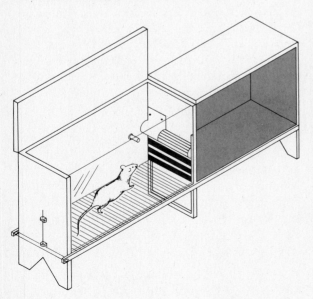

aroused by stimuli that are difficult for the person to identify. Thus, a person is said to be anxious when he experiences fear in the absence of any noticeable fear stimuli. A person may be anxious when he is afraid that he will fail next week's examination, that he will be late for an appointment, that his girlfriend's parents will not approve of him, or that he may be fatally ill. In all these examples, the fear-provoking stimuli are subjective; they are difficult to pin down by the observer, or by the person experiencing the anxiety. Contrast these fears with the fear provoked by flames, a dentist's drill, or deep water. The stimuli producing these fears are identifiable and can be escaped. Anxieties such as fear of failure are much more difficult to escape because the stimuli are not very clear.

Anxiety will be covered in greater detail in Chapter 9 (in the discussion of emotion) and in Chapter 13 (behavior pathology).

Social drives

Much of psychology is the study of individual behavior, and through it we realize that we are not isolated from other individuals. Our social environment—the people, places, things, institutions, ideals, and desires of others—greatly influences our own behavior. Philosophers may wonder if man rules society or if society rules man, but the psychologist tries to supplement theoretical speculation with scientific objectivity. In studying behavior, the psychologist isolates the social influences from the biological ones and hypothesizes general principles from his objective observations.

From the simplest social unit, the family, to the most complex social unit, the nation, we live in a world with others. Whether we want to or not, we become socially involved with family, friends, and colleagues. We may seek to please them, hurt them, love them, outdo them, rely on them, teach them. Our behavior is these broad areas is often socially motivated and, as we shall see, extremely complex.

There is no general agreement on the num-

LITTLE SPORT

By Rouson

Figure 8.11   *Approval may work wonders, especially if it comes from the right person. (Copyright, General Features Corporation. Reprinted with permission.)*

ber and nature of social drives. Many psychologists have compiled lists of social drives. Although most of these lists are useful, none is conclusive. In this section, we will cover some of the more common social drives.

Approval   From early childhood, we learn to associate *approval* with pleasant events. For example, the word "good" is often followed by other reinforcers, such as affection, food, or a toy. We also learn to associate disapproval with punishing stimuli, such as withdrawal of affection or a spanking that causes pain. What we learn in childhood is very frequently reinforced throughout our later years (Figure 8.11).

Social approval reinforces the responses of the individual who learns that pleasing others helps him to obtain further rewards. In other words, social approval is a signal; it tells us that we are behaving "correctly" in our search for some other reinforcer. If your professor nods at you after you ask an insightful question, his nod may be a signal to you that (1) he recognizes you; (2) he likes you; (3) he will remember you; (4) he thinks you are intelligent; (5) you will pass his course; (6) he wants you to develop the idea more fully. If your goal is to be graduated from college, then the professor's nod of approval is a cue that you are making progress toward that goal. In the business and professional world, social approval operates in much the same way. It may signal you that you are

about to land a good job, do something that others respect, or become influential in motivating others.

Verbal reinforcement Greenspoon (1955) showed that we can easily be conditioned to say a certain type of word if, for eample, our listener says "mmm-hmmm" each time we say that type of word. He asked his subjects to spend 50 minutes saying all the nouns that they could think of. Each time the subject said a plural noun (cows, houses, women) Greenspoon said "mmm-hmmm." After a while, the subjects were saying more plural nouns than anything else; they had unwittingly been conditioned.

A person may become so strongly conditioned to seek approval that approval becomes an end in itself. In such cases he is reinforced by signs of approval even when the approval does not lead to additional reinforcement. The idea that approval, or any other acquired drive, may become an independent reinforcer is known as the *functional autonomy of motives*. This concept was first proposed by Allport (1951), who observed that acquired motives (drives) may cease to depend on their original associations with other drives and come to function autonomously (independently). Approval is an acquired drive because it gets its drive characteristics from its original association with other reinforcers (such as affection, food, or a toy). However, we have noted that, as experiences with approval multiply, a person may come to seek approval without concern for its association with other reinforcers. Other drives can become functionally autonomous in the same manner. For example, a person may be motivated to seek money but then will not spend the money he obtains. This person has a drive to acquire money simply because money itself is reinforcing. The drive for money has become functionally autonomous.

Usually, social approval as a reinforcement is most successful in stimulating performances of persons who have been deprived of approval. In much the same way that food-deprived animals are reinforced by food, approval-deprived persons are reinforced by praise. A child who receives approval almost constantly is less likely to be motivated by it than one who has received approval and then is deprived of it.

Different cultures exhibit different forms of social approval. For example, people of the Italian culture use praise lavishly; they are quick to give praise, and when they do give it, they do so demonstratively. Other cultures, for example, the English, are slower to bestow praise and are more restrained in the way they express it. If an Englishmen says, "Well done," it may be high praise indeed.

Achievement The American way of life is typified by the *achievement drive*. We, as Americans, are proud of our competitive spirit (our need to achieve at a higher level than the next person). Here, the need to achieve is often stronger than the need for social approval.

The achievement drive was first observed as an experimental by-product. Psychologists, in studying other human drives, found that many individuals were driven to perform to their utmost even in noncompetitive situations. Based on this finding, these psychologists decided to study achievement as a separate and independent drive.

Achievement and success Is strong motivation half the battle to achieving success? To answer this question, McClelland (1955) made a study using a test of achievement motivation in which subjects were asked to write interpretive stories about pictures suggesting different work situations. The stories were then analyzed for content, with emphasis on achievement and success. Those subjects who had written many achievement ideas into their stories were considered to be "high achievers." The subjects were then given a number of verbal and mathematical tests to do. On all tests, the "high achievers" scored higher than the others. Thus, achievement motivation and success tend to go hand in hand, although the reasons for this correlation have not been scientifically demonstrated.

According to some studies, an individual's achievement drive is directly related to his early training. Researchers found that, in general, individuals with a high need for achievement were taught to be independent as children and were not allowed the comfort of close parental contact. Individuals with a generally low achievement need tended to recall themselves as dependent children and their parents as friendly, warm, and close. Similar studies have shown that parents—particularly mothers—who feel strongly that their children should become independent as early as possible, somehow transmit a need for achievement to their children.

It appears that children generally learn their achievement drive from their parents' attitudes. However, this is not always the case. Other factors also influence the child's development, and these factors may interrelate in such a way that children whose parents are warm and close may be independent or children of independent-thinking parents may be dependent. For example, an achievement-oriented parent may also have very definite, irrefutable opinions on many subjects. The child becomes fearful of contradicting the parent and is unable to express his own opinion or act independently of his parents.

It is probably to a child's advantage to develop independence early in life. If properly rewarded for his independent actions, the child will develop a sense of pride and pleasure in achievement. Of course, there are many degrees or levels of achieving; an individual who becomes overly motivated by an achievement drive may develop strong anxieties about his future success or failure, and may lose his perspective.

Aggression   To many psychologists, man is foremost an aggressive animal. And, because of the numerous historical examples of man's violence, many also regard his aggressive behavior as innate. For example, Freud argued that "the tendency to aggression is an innate, independent, instinctual disposition in man. . . ." Other investigators have asserted that our survival depends on our instinct for aggression (Lorenz, 1966). Ardrey (1966), a popular writer and a student of aggression, has further suggested that our instinct to defend our own territory (*territoriality*) is the basic source of aggression. However, the view that aggression is innate is not sufficiently documented. Many investigators prefer the position that aggression is learned.

Studies have indicated that frustration can lead to aggression (Dollard, Doob, Miller, Mowrer, and Sears, 1939). When prevented from satisfying a need, both man and lower animals increase the vigor of their behavior. They try to attack what they perceive to be the obstacle, the source of their frustration. The hungry dog may push open a door that is blocking him from food. The child whose toy is out of reach may scream or stamp his feet until he gets the toy. The professor whose class is noisy may shout or bang his fist on the desk until the class quiets down. Not all frustration necessarily leads to aggressive behavior, but an aggressive response will tend to persist or recur if it is reinforced.

Guns and anger elicit aggression Psychologists have tested the hypothesis that some aggressive responses may be impulsive reactions controlled by stimuli in the environment. Berkowitz and LePage (1967) showed that certain cues, such as guns, may elicit aggressive responses. They required a group of subjects to administer shocks to other subjects; some of the subjects who administered shocks did so while they were angry. The angered subjects had previously been shocked themselves. As might be expected, they gave more shocks than did those who were not angry. In addition, angry subjects who worked in a room with guns in full view gave more shocks than angry subjects who worked with only innocuous objects present. The guns, however had no perceptible effect on subjects who were not angry.

Although aggression is often a reaction to frustration, psychologists have noted considerable aggressive behavior in relatively unfrustrated children. In many cases this aggressive behavior is reinforced. Parents do not punish aggressive behavior every time it occurs; sometimes they actually admire it, considering it to be a sign of forcefulness or leadership. The children, in turn, do not consider aggression to be "bad"; often they enjoy it. Only when they grow older, when they are influenced more by the approval of their peers, do they realize the potential destructiveness of aggressive behavior.

The frequency and form of aggression shown by children depends in part on imitation. Children imitate adults and other children. When a child sees someone displaying aggression, he tends to imitate that person, particularly if the person he sees is someone significant such as a parent, sibling, or friend. Imitation of aggression is not confined to live models. Bandura, Ross, and Ross (1963) have shown that children will reproduce aggressive behavior that they have seen depicted in a motion picture.

Does experience modify aggression? Johnson, DeSisto, and Koenig (1972) tested rats in a variety of experimental situations to assess the effects of social and developmental experience on aggressive behavior toward other species.

In one experiment, rats raised communally proved to be less aggressive than rats raised alone. In a second experiment, each rat either was raised with a single frog or cockroach or was grouped with several other rats and raised with a group of frogs or cockroaches. This pairing of rats with nonaggressive species was an attempt to reduce aggression levels. However, neither aggression-reducing attempt truly succeeded. Rats raised communally continued to be aggressive, and rats exposed to other species during development often were more aggressive when confronted with a member of that species in the experimental test.

A third experiment assessed the effect of exposing nonaggressive rats from the previous experiments to killer rats demonstrating aggression against frogs in their cages. After the nonaggressive rats had spent 2 weeks watching one or two frog attacks per day, more than half of them became killers. Nonaggressive controls demonstrated much less aggression when simply given repeated opportunities to attack frogs. It appears that some aspects of the rats' aggressive behavior are modifiable by social and developmental experience, while others are not.

Dependency Dependency needs and the drives they evoke cover a rather broad area of human behavior. The clearest examples of dependency behavior are found in newborn infants and some very old people. Neither the infant nor the disabled older person can care for himself properly; each must depend on other human beings for survival. Dependency behavior, however, is not limited to the very young and the very old; it spans an individual's entire lifetime.

For infants, parents are objects that fulfill such basic drives as hunger and affection. The infant is completely dependent upon his parents for his well-being. As the child develops, he learns more and more to cope with his drives himself, but he still turns to his parents for assistance and advice. Eventually he finds satisfaction in an affiliation that is no longer a matter of total dependency. The child begins to generalize this satisfying relationship to other people. By the time he is an adolescent, his need to affiliate with other people, especially his peers, is stronger than dependency on his parents. When the young adult develops a close relationship that leads to a permanent affiliation, such as marriage, a certain degree of dependency returns. As a parent, he finds himself on the opposite side of the child-parent dependency relationship. Individuals, then, are affected by dependency throughout their lives.

Dependency rated by classmates Winder and Rau (1962) tested boys in the fourth, fifth, and sixth grades. The boys were to rate each other on aggression, dependency, withdrawal, depression, and likability. A "guess who?" test was used, that is, the children were given a list of items intended to describe a particular boy and were then required to name the boy who best fit the description. Thus, the boys themselves judged their classmates on the above characteristics. A boy voted by the majority to be dependent in one characteristic was judged dependent in other characteristics.

The parents of these children then filled out questionnaires regarding their attitudes toward each other, children, punishment, and so on.

It was found that too much punishment, demands for aggression, and restrictiveness all contributed to a child's characteristic behavior. Fathers who were concerned that their son behave like a he-man had predominantly aggressive children. Dependency, on the other hand, was brought on by a father who was lacking in confidence and a mother who reacted to the child's impulsive behavior with anxious overprotection.

Much dependency is learned through a process of operant conditioning. Dependent behavior either is reinforced or not reinforced. The schedule of reinforcement, in relation to the child's need, determines the amount of dependency a child will learn. Most parents tend to reward or punish their children occasionally. Because parents follow this variable-ratio schedule of reinforcement (see Chapter 6), learned dependency persists.

Cognitive dissonance Some psychologists believe that most people are affected by a need to balance their behavior with their beliefs (cognition). In other words, we try to be consistent in terms of what we believe and what we do. Frequently, we are unable to do this. The complex social world in which we live causes us to experience inconsistency more often than most of us like to admit. A well-known explanation of belief-behavior imbalance is the theory of *cognitive dissonance* (Festinger, 1957). Generally, if an individual is involved in a dissonant situation (a situation in which his drives are inconsistent with his beliefs), he experiences "psychological discomfort" and attempts to adjust his behavior or his beliefs so that they better coincide. For example, the information about the relationship between heart disease and overeating sets up dissonance in an obese person. He finds eating pleasurable, yet he is told that it is dangerous to his health. There is an imbalance, or dissonance, involving the pleasure he feels and the fear-provoking information. To reduce the dissonance, he can stop eating or he can refuse to believe the information about its danger. Another common example of cognitive dissonance involves the relationship between lung cancer and smoking. Festinger (1957) found that many smokers tend to reduce their dissonance by rejecting the information relating smoking to lung cancer. Heavy smokers are particularly prone to reject this information because the stronger the commitment to smoking, the stronger the dissonance.

End of the world "The world is coming to an end!" Many so-called prophets have made this prediction many times and in many different situations. Such people will continue to make this prediction and their followers will continue to believe them, even though their predictions are proven false.

In 1956, Festinger, Riecken, and Schachter infiltrated one such group. The group's prophetess said that she had received messages from flying saucers and that they had told her they were going to destroy the world because it was evil; only the group of believers would be saved because they were "good." When the prophesied day came and passed, the believers were confused; the world had not come to an end. However, the next morning the prophetess received a new message from the flying saucers congratulating the group for showing their faith and thus saving the world from doom.

This is a classic example of the theory of cognitive dissonance. People need balance. When reality did not agree with these persons' beliefs, they made an adjustment so that things made sense again. Dissonance may also explain why people who have lost relatives in a war continue to support that war. These people need to feel that the war is important. The knowledge that they had lost someone in a worthless cause would be unbearable.

*Figure 8.12   A three-dimensional model illustrating the relationship between motivation and the difficulty of a task. Rats were deprived of air by being restrained underwater for a varying number of seconds and were then permitted to escape by selecting the correct door. Optimum motivation for learning depended on the difficulty of the choice task. (After P. L. Broadhurst, Emotionality and the Yerkes-Dodson Law, J. Exp. Psychol., 1957, **54**, 345–352)*

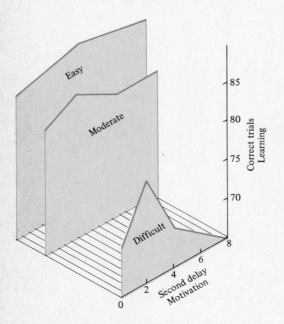

MOTIVATION AND AROUSAL

We have been discussing motivation in terms of specific types of drives. The problem of motivation may also be approached by considering the concept of *arousal*, the general level of drive. The concept of arousal allows us to think in terms of a central or general drive state on a continuum ranging from near zero to high levels of excitement. A sleeping person's arousal level is low: his nervous system is relatively inactive; his readiness to receive incoming stimuli is low, as is his readiness to respond. An excited person's arousal level is high: his nervous system is active, he is sensitive to a variety of stimuli, and he is prepared to respond.

We learned in Chapter 3 that most of our responses are processed through the central nerv-

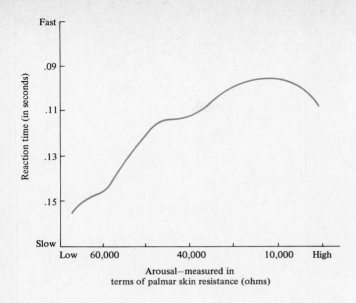

Figure 8.13   Arousal and speed of response. As arousal increases, speed of responding increases up to some optimum level of arousal. Beyond this optimum level, reaction time slows down. (After Freeman, 1940)

ous system, and that activity within the brain itself can be measured. We also know that the activity of parts of the body—in particular, that of the muscles—can be "read" by various electronic devices. The study of motivational arousal involves the relationship of readings from the central nervous system and the autonomic nervous system. Arousal is closely involved with the function of the reticular activating system of the brain (see Chapter 3).

In 1908, an experiment by Yerkes and Dodson suggested that behavioral efficiency is related to arousal and that efficiency is generally best when arousal is at some middle or intermediate level (Figure 8.12 shows the results of an experiment demonstrating what is now called the *Yerkes-Dodson law*). Such research shows that when arousal is very low, behavioral efficiency is low; the individual is insufficiently sensitive to stimuli and unprepared to respond effectively. When arousal is very high, behavioral efficiency may also be poor, because the individual is reacting to too many stimuli and is responding in an exaggerated or disorganized manner. Figure 8.13 graphically depicts one form of the relationship between arousal and efficiency.

Arousal and the reticular activatng system   Fuster (1958) showed that a general state of arousal, or "attention," was affected by stimulation of the reticular activating system in the brainstem. In other words, Fuster showed that stimulation of this area would increase an organism's general arousal state.

He first taught rhesus monkeys to discriminate between two objects, for example, a jar and a vase (Figure 8.14). If the monkey reached for the correct object, he was allowed to take the food reward that was placed under it. The objects were then illuminated for very short periods of time; the monkeys were expected to discriminate between them during this short period of illumination. The tests were run either under normal conditions or when the monkey's brainstem was electrically stimulated.

Results showed that the monkeys discriminated better (perceived better) when electrically stimulated. Fuster concluded that the reticular formation was a general activating system which, in this case, had aroused the "basic attentive behavior" of the monkeys—so that they perceived better.

Several leading psychologists, including Hebb (1955) and Malmo (1959), believe that the concept of arousal is more useful than the concept of different drives. Hebb and others have suggested the concept of an *optimal level*

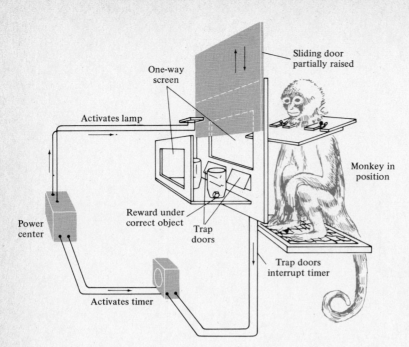

One-way
screen

Sliding door
partially raised

Activates lamp

Monkey in
position

Power
center

Reward under
correct object

Trap
doors

Trap doors
interrupt timer

Activates timer

Figure 8.14   Monkey discrimination
among tridimensional objects. See
abstract for a description of this
experiment. (After Fuster, 1958)

of arousal. According to this concept, a person who is insufficiently aroused tends to seek stimulation that will increase his level of arousal, whereas an individual who is excessively aroused seeks the means to reduce stimulation.

The specific symptoms and intensities of arousal vary, depending on the drive being aroused. When an individual is hungry, neural activity, heart rate, and blood pressure may be only slightly affected, whereas all the arousal systems may be greatly affected by the conditions of sexual arousal.

MOTIVATION AND LEARNING

Drives direct behavior and energize its strength. We know that drives direct behavior, because each drive has characteristic stimuli patterns: a thirsty person will act in certain ways and not in others. We also know that drives energize behavior, because we observe increased levels of activity: a thirsty person out for a stroll will act more vigorously upon seeing a drinking fountain than will a person who is not thirsty.

Both the energizing and the directing features of drives influence learning. A subject with a moderately high drive makes stronger responses and interacts with his environment more often than one with a corresponding but weaker drive.

Drive stimuli also serve as cues for the responses being learned. This effect has been demonstrated in experiments in which rats learn to go to one side of a maze when hungry and to a different side when thirsty. In much the same way, we learn to go to food when hungry and liquids when thirsty.

Conditioned fear or anxiety is often used in experiments designed to study the relationship between human drives and learning. These studies suggest that the effects of anxiety are complex and often depend on the type of learning task. Anxious subjects show faster classical conditioning than nonanxious subjects. But in complex learning situations, anxious subjects are slower than nonanxious subjects.

INCENTIVES:
REINFORCERS THAT MOTIVATE

The concept of *reinforcement* is essential to an analysis of motivation, as the last link in the chain of motivational events. The chain begins with a need, which is brought about by deprivation or by the presence of strong stimuli; the need produces a drive (or drives); the drive leads to behavior; and the behavior leads to reinforcement, often in the form of need reduction.

In discussing needs and drives, we have emphasized such needs as hunger, thirst, sex, affection, curiosity, and approval. Drives can result from many other stimuli and deprivations. For example, the deprivation of rest and sleep produces a strong drive to reduce fatigue. The deprivation of oxygen produces a drive to take in more oxygen. The deprivation of heat produces a drive to seek warmth, while too much heat produces a drive to reduce heat. A loud sound produces a drive to escape from the sound.

Reinforcement and motivation cannot be separated. But a reinforcer is effective only if the subject is motivated by that reinforcer. Food is not an effective reinforcer when the subject has been deprived of water; money is not effective when the subject has been deprived of affection. The deprived subject is reinforced by the object or event that has been withheld. If the subject is exposed to excessively painful stimuli, the termination of the stimuli is a negative reinforcement (see Chapter 6). Thus, an individual is motivated by a need when he is deprived of reinforcers (such as food or praise) or when he is presented with strong stimuli (loud noises or electric shocks) that he wishes to avoid.

Reinforcers that acquire motivating features in their own right are called *incentives*. For example, a person who is not hungry may be motivated to eat when he sees his favorite food displayed in a restaurant window. The food that usually serves as a powerful reinforcer is now acting as a drive producer.

Incentive motivation   You are at a baseball game. You are not hungry or thirsty, but then you look around and see that those near you are eating hot dogs coated with mustard and relish. The hot dogs look so good that you buy one.

This type of motivation was experimentally demonstrated by Ross and Ross (1949). Their subjects were dogs who had been allowed to eat until they were full (a dog was considered full when he had not licked his plate for 15 minutes). When a hungry dog was put into the same cage and allowed to eat, the "full" dog also began to eat, although he clearly was not hungry. In a control group, it was shown that if hungry dogs are not brought into the cage, the "full" dogs do not return to the food after the same amount of time has elapsed. The dogs' motivation for food was aroused by the other dogs' eating.

Advertisements are often based on the incentive principle. Suppose that you are watching television. A commercial for a soft drink appears on the screen and you suddenly develop a thirst for that or a similar drink, even though you were not thirsty before viewing the commercial. Because the drink has quenched your thirst in the past, you associate the drink with thirst; the drink becomes an incentive and arouses your thirst.

The incentive value of a reinforcer depends on the subject's previous experience with the reinforcer. A monkey that has learned to find a piece of banana under a bowl will continue to look under the bowl as long as a banana chunk appears there each time. If the monkey is shown, allowed to feel, or given a taste of the reinforcer before each learning trial, the incentive value of that reinforcer will be increased. Conversely, a substitute reinforcer will usually be much less effective than the original reinforcer. The monkey will show a marked reduction in performance if lettuce is suddenly substituted for the banana chunks.

Human beings also behave according to the incentive value of a reinforcer. For example, a child who has learned from previous experience that she will be allowed to play with her favorite toy after she has drunk her milk will down the milk quickly and happily. If she sees the toy while she is drinking her milk, she will probably drink even faster.

The incentive value of a reinforcer also depends on the size or amount of the reinforcer. The greater the reinforcer, the more effective it is as a motivator. Subjects are motivated more strongly by large incentives than by small ones. A whole banana is a more effective incentive than a piece of banana, and a $500 bonus certainly provides more incentive for the employee than does a $50 bonus.

Chimps and incentives Fletcher (1940) conducted a series of tests on chimpanzees to see whether or not they would work harder to obtain a larger reward.

To reach pieces of banana, the chimpanzee had to pull a steel cable to which the bananas were tied. The experimenter could make the cable more difficult or more easy to pull. Different amounts of bananas were put out in full view of the chimpanzee.

It was found that seeing greater amounts of bananas served as an incentive for pulling harder and harder on the cable.

THREE VIEWS OF MOTIVATION

Motivation, like learning, has been approached, viewed, and theorized about in a number of different ways. We will discuss three major viewpoints: behaviorist (largely S-R associationist), cognitive, and psychodynamic.

The behaviorist view The behaviorist views motivation in the same way that he views learning, that is, in terms of stimuli, responses, and reinforcers. An individual is motivated when

drive stimuli produced by needs impel and guide his responses. Behavior is directed by stimuli and reinforced by stimuli. The emphasis is on external variables, although there may be considerable interest in internal events that link stimuli and responses. When concepts such as need or drive are used, they are anchored to observables. Thus, a rat is said to be hungry when he is deprived of food; a child has a need for attention when he has been deprived of attention; a man is said to be afraid when he is exposed to a fearful stimulus and responds fearfully.

The cognitive view The cognitive approach to motivation emphasizes the idea of goals and goal-directed behavior. Behavior is seen as purposeful, and motivation as the tendency to move toward certain goals. Unlike the behaviorist, who adheres strictly to observable stimuli and responses, the cognitive psychologist emphasizes variables that are less directly observable—for example, concepts such as level of aspiration and success. The cognitive interpretation assumes that an individual aspires to a goal and that when he achieves his aspiration, he experiences satisfaction in his success. For example, the student who aspires to and obtains an A in a course is naturally pleased with the success his hard work has brought him.

The individual may or may not be aware of his *level of aspiration*. One individual may set goals for himself that are always attainable, but he may not recognize that he is limiting himself to easy goals. Another individual may set very difficult or even unattainable goals for himself. A person's level of aspiration in a given situation depends on his perception of the task, his abilities, and the possible consequences of success or failure. Previous success on a similar task usually leads to a raising of the level of aspiration, while failure lowers the level. However, this relationship is not so simple. People with generally high levels of aspiration may react to failure by raising their level of aspiration even higher. People with low self-opinions, who usually set low goals, will lower their goals even more after failure.

The individual's expectations of success or failure also combine with his perception of the value of success or the pain of failure. If he expects failure and perceives it as very painful, he will set a very low goal for himself; if he expects failure but is not afraid of it, he may set a higher goal. Thus, to describe success and failure requires a knowledge of the individual's private aspirations, expectations, and plans, as well as his overt behavior.

How one will be motivated to behave depends on a complex of variables. According to the cognitive viewpoint, stimuli do not direct a person's behavior; they set in motion processes that are influenced by his goals, expectations, and plans. The effects of a stimulus depend on how it is perceived. For example, a fear stimulus is not a fear stimulus until or unless it is perceived as such. The threat of a painful electric shock may be perceived as a challenge, an imminent danger, a joke, or some form of trickery. The motivating effects of such threats will depend on the individual's perception of the threat.

The psychodynamic view Freud's theory of human behavior is essentially a theory of motivation, in which all behavior is in part unconsciously motivated. But because behavior does not represent the unconscious drives directly, it is necessary to draw inferences from dreams, slips of the tongue, mistakes in memory, free association (a technique used in psychoanalytic therapy), and certain types of neurotic behavior.

Freud proposed that the true purpose of an individual's behavior was the satisfaction of his innate needs. Instincts are a part of these innate needs, and these instincts are the drives that impel and govern behavior. Two general groups of instincts are identified, the *life instincts* and the *death instincts*. The life instincts include the sexual drives and such life-mainte-

nance drives as hunger and thirst. The death instincts obviously include unconscious wishes to die, as well as outward and inward forms of aggression. (See Chapter 12 for a further discussion of Freudian psychodynamics.)

The three views contrasted A useful way to contrast the views of motivation just considered is to examine how each might analyze a particular motivation problem. Consider a 10-year-old student whose teacher says that, although he is bright, he is failing because "he is not motivated to learn."

The behaviorist would seek information about the classroom situation, including the approach of the teacher and the reinforcers she uses. He would also study the child's home environment, particularly the kind of emphasis the parents place on learning.

The cognitive psychologist would try to learn about the child's perception of and his expectations about school. He would be most interested in the child's goals and aspirations and the kinds of goals the school regards as important.

The psychodynamically oriented psychologist would interpret the child's problem in terms of conflict between his unconscious needs and school motivation. He might speculate that unconscious fear or hostility toward persons with authority was preventing the child from responding positively to his teacher. Or he might look for signs that unconscious hostility toward his parents resulted in his attempting to punish them by failing in school.

Although it may some day be possible to reconcile these three approaches, investigators continue to pursue their study of motivation within the framework they find most satisfactory. As more research is done and more data are accumulated, the most promising features of each of these approaches may in some way be combined.

SUMMARY

Needs are derived from physiological or environmental imbalances and give rise to
   drives. The individual's needs are produced by deprivation or excessive
   stimulation.
The motivation process consists of the need stage, the drive stage, the behavior
   stage, and drive-reduction stage.
Unlearned drives are rooted in the body's basic needs. Acquired drives are learned
   by the individual.
The strength of a drive is determined by measuring general activity level, acceptance
   of punishment, rate of performance of learned responses, and the selection
   among goals.
Homeostasis is the maintenance of an overall physiological balance.
Hunger pangs are produced by contractions of the muscles in the walls of the
   stomach.
The source of hunger is a chemical imbalance in the composition of the blood, which
   activates the hypothalamus to send messages to the muscles of the appropriate
   organs, causing them to contract or otherwise react. The hypothalamus is the
   major excitation and inhibition center for hunger.
Hunger selection, which is often altered in man by learning, occurs when the organism develops an appetite for foods containing those nutrients in which his body
   is deficient.
Satiation of the hunger drive is regulated by taste sensitivity in the mouth and
   postingestional sensitivity.
Thirst, like the hunger drive, is regulated by the hypothalamus. Thirst results primarily from a lack of water in the body's tissues.
Pain-reduction stems from the need of the organism to escape stimuli that cause
   discomfort and threaten tissue damage. Masochists seek the stimulation of pain,
   and sadists derive pleasure from inflicting pain on others.
The sexual drive is controlled in varying degrees by sex hormones.
The estrous cycle is the reproductive cycle of female animals. During estrus, often
   called heat, the female secretes the hormone estrogen.
Unlike drives in animals, human drives are influenced to a large degree by individual
   development and learning.
The maternal drive is innate in female animals and is in part a result of hormonal
   stimulation; of particular importance in this regard is the pituitary hormone
   prolactin. Many psychologists believe that the human maternal drive is primarily
   learned.
The drives toward environmental exploration and manipulation are forms of curiosity.
Piaget emphasizes the individual's curiosity to know his environment and in so
   doing expand his schemata.
The affectional drive appears to be based on an innate need that is not derived from
   other fundamental physiological drives.
Self-actualization is a concept describing a uniquely human drive toward fulfillment

of one's inner potential. The drive for competence is the desire to function as effectively as possible in the environment.

Intracranial stimulation of certain areas of the brain motivates animals to make responses that continue to provide such stimulation.

Conditioned *fear* becomes an acquired drive when a particular stimulus is associated with pain.

Anxiety is a state of fear roused by stimuli that are difficult for the person to identify.

Social drives—approval, achievement, aggression, and dependency—result from our contact and experience with other people.

Functional autonomy of motives describes the situation in which acquired drives become independent of their original associations.

Aggression often results from an accumulation of frustration experiences. In children, aggression may be an imitation of adult aggressive behavior or may result from the inconsistent use of punishment by parents.

Dependency may be learned through a process of operant conditioning.

When a person perceives discrepancies between an internal belief or attitude and his behavior, he experiences a state of imbalance known as cognitive dissonance. This imbalance may motivate the individual to reduce the discrepancy either by discarding the belief or by adjusting his behavior.

An individual's level of arousal or degree of physiological activity functions on a continuum—lowest during sleep, highest when the organism is excited.

Arousal level is related to behavior efficiency and seems to be controlled by the reticular activating system of the brain. According to the Yerkes-Dodson law, optimal level for most activities falls within a moderate range between the two extremes of very low or very high arousal.

The energizing and directing aspects of drives affect learning. The stronger the drive (up to some optimum level), the more responses the organisms will make and the more he will learn about his environment.

Drive stimuli also serve as cues for the responses being learned.

An incentive is a reinforcer that has acquired motivating properties, even in the absence of a need.

Behaviorists emphasize the external variables that impel a person to respond. They view all motivation in terms of stimuli, responses, and reinforcers.

Cognitive psychologists see behavior as purposeful and motivation as the tendency to move toward certain goals. Emphasis is on the level of aspiration and the effect of the individual's successes or failures on his behavior.

The psychodynamic theory of motivation is based on Freud's view that all behavior is in part unconsciously motivated to satisfy innate needs. Related to these innate needs are life instincts and death instincts.

SUGGESTED READINGS

Texts

Atkinson, J. W. *An introduction to motivation.* Princeton, N.J.: Van Nostrand, 1964. Critical review the historical development of fundamental concepts and their systematic integration into a theory of achievement motivation.

Bartoshuk, A. K. Motivation. In J. W. Kling & L. A. Riggs (Eds.), *Woodworth and*

Schlosberg's experimental psychology (3rd ed.). New York: Holt, Rinehart & Winston, 1971. A brief but thorough introduction to current methods, trends, and issues in motivation research.

Berlyne, D. E. *Conflict arousal and curiosity.* New York: McGraw-Hill, 1960. Discussion of the role of motivation in learning, with emphasis on the curiosity drive.

Birney, R. C., & Teevan, R. C. *Measuring human motivation.* Princeton, N.J: Van Nostrand, 1962. Reprint of a somewhat dated but nonetheless outstanding group of papers.

Brown, J. S. *The motivation of behavior.* New York: McGraw-Hill, 1961. Broad and clear formulation of the neobehaviorist position.

Cofer, C. N., & Appley, M. H. *Motivation: theory and research.* New York: Wiley, 1964. Comprehensive treatment of both animal and human motivation. An excellent reference book.

Hokanson, J. E. *The physiological basis of motivation.* New York: Wiley, 1969. Discussion of the bodily functions that affect motivation.

Kagan, J. *Understanding children: behavior, motives, and thought.* New York: Harcourt Brace Jovanovich, 1971. Motivation (and emotion) incorporated into cognitive theory in a very readable format designed for a sophisticated but non-science-oriented audience.

Moss, C. S. *Dreams, images, and fantasy: a semantic differential casebook.* Urbana: University of Illinois Press, 1970. An imaginative attempt to bring objectivity to the study of unconscious motivation and the resultant therapeutic technique.

Smith, C. P. (Ed.) *Achievement-related motives in children.* New York: Russell Sage Foundation, 1969. Sophisticated readings centered around the search for the origins and development of achievement motivation in children.

Popular books

Barker, W. *Brain storms: a study in human spontaneity.* Discussion of a new approach to the motivation of creative endeavors.

Lorenz, K. *On aggression.* A comparative study of the aggressive drive shared by men and animals.

Mayer, M. *Madison Avenue, U.S.A.* Discussion of the advertising industry and how it motivates behavior.

Ogilvy, D. *Confessions of an ad man.* Successful advertising man discusses his business career and the secrets of motivating consumers.

Storr, A. *The dynamics of creation.* An examination of the motivations behind creativity, with emphasis on interpretations that provide alternatives to the traditional Freudian viewpoint.

9
Emotion

Run up a flight of stairs: your heartbeat and breathing speed up and become more pronounced. Your viscera (internal organs) have increased their rate of activity to replace the oxygen you exhausted in running up the stairs. The visceral organs react to any physical change so as to maintain and regulate proper bodily functioning. Usually you are unaware of ongoing visceral activity; you become aware of it only when it is greatly increased.

Not all visceral activity occurs as a simple reflex reaction to physical changes in the body. You are walking down the street and a stranger with a knife grabs your arm. You look around for help, but no one seems to notice or care. You are on your own. Your heartbeat and breathing increase; you feel somewhat flushed and light-headed. These changes are brought about not by increased physical activity, but by a conditioned stimulus—your attacker. Your body is reacting to the fear you feel.

Emotion is behavior that is primarily influenced by *conditioned visceral responses*. Our viscera are always reacting; but in emotion, their reactions affect perception, learning, thinking, and virtually everything we do. In our example, your system may be so affected by the frightening event that you are unable to try to escape—you no longer find it possible to coordinate your normal muscular activities.

Sometimes we are unaware of the stimuli that cause us to react emotionally, and we cannot control our emotional reactions. A person may suddenly feel uncontrollably happy or sad without any apparent reason. Emotions depend even less on recognizable needs than do motives, and are less goal directed. They are frequently diffuse or disorganized reactions to barely perceptible or even imperceptible external or internal stimuli. But they are a major influence on behavior.

Arousal and emotion Schachter and Wheeler (1962), in studying the relationship between emotion and physiological arousal, separated subjects into three groups. The first group was given epinephrine, a solution that generally brings about a state of neurophysiological activity. The second group was given a placebo, a neutral solution that does not affect the normal physiological state. The third group was given the tranquilizer chlorpromazine, an autonomic blocking agent that inhibits neurophysiological activity. The subjects were then shown a slapstick comedy film. During the film their reactions were recorded; after the film they were asked to give an opinion about it. It was found that the epinephrine group laughed more and enjoyed the film more than either of the other groups. The chlorpromazine group laughed at and enjoyed the film least of the three groups. Thus, we may conclude that our emotional states and reactions depend on our general level of physiological arousal.

CHARACTERISTICS OF EMOTIONS

A good poker player must show no emotion or he will give away his hand. A peek at his cards or the money he has in relation to what he started with may provide a clue to the felt emotion, but his face never will. It is difficult to identify, isolate, and study individual emotions, for outward signs of emotion do not always reveal the emotion felt. Some people do not respond openly; their emotions are expressed inwardly. Others overrespond and may not behave according to expectation. Still others, for various reasons, pretend to respond in a particular way, overtly expressing emotional states they do not really feel. Because of these variables in observable reactions, the study of emotions must be approached with care. We must search out primary characteristics common to all emotional behavior and apply these characteristics to the study of some basic, typical emotions. Several characteristics have been identified as common, in varying degree, to all emotional behavior: emotion is *diffuse*, *persistent*, and *cumulative*.

Emotional diffusion

Suppose that you are about to drive through a busy intersection when suddenly another car comes speeding at you across the intersection.

Your neck muscles tighten; your head and trunk lurch forward; your stomach tightens into a knot. Your whole body reacts to the fear-inducing stimulus.

Emotional stimuli are able to affect the entire body by *emotional diffusion*. The impact is diffuse mainly because extreme visceral activity affects the reactions of the entire body. Once the visceral reactions are aroused in one organ, the muscles diffuse the impact rapidly to other organs. This diffusion intensifies the emotional response and makes it more difficult to control.

For each emotion, the body probably diffuses a different pattern of visceral functioning, and in different individuals the same emotion might be diffused differently. Similarly, an individual at different times might experience different bodily reactions to the same emotion.

Persistence of emotion

Closely related to the diffuse nature of emotion is the *persistence of emotion*. Once an emotional state has been aroused, it has a tendency to endure long after the immediate stimulus has disappeared. For example, when the other car has passed and you have stopped in time, you may realize almost immediately that you are safe and uninjured. Nevertheless, the effects of fear persist for a long time. The persistence of emotion is due in part to the structure and function of the smooth muscles of the visceral organs. The smooth muscles are not stimulated so quickly as the striated muscles; but once stimulated, smooth-muscle responses are persistent and slow to relax.

The persistent quality of emotional reactions often creates an attitude, a feeling, or a pervasive mood that lingers on through subsequent activities and reactions—long after the original stimulus has disappeared.

Cumulative nature of emotion

A third characteristic of emotional behavior is that it is *cumulative*. Anger causes more anger, joy tends to produce more joy, and so on. For example, if you argue with your parents in the morning, you may find yourself being angered by almost anything that occurs during the day.

Anger leads to more anger Kahn (1966) conducted tests to learn whether or not anger that is allowed expression will "cool off" faster than anger that is not expressed. Kahn's two groups of subjects were simply told that they were to have their pulse, heartbeat, and other readings taken for experimental purposes. The lab technician was extremely rude, constantly insulting each of the groups. The subjects could not respond to the insults because they were told that they had to remain quiet throughout the experiment.

When the rude technician left the room, Kahn came in and subtly encouraged one group of subjects to tell him of their treatment by the lab technician. He then promised that the technican would be reprimanded. Kahn did not allow the second group of subjects to express anger over the technician.

Afterward, while both groups were resting, readings were taken of the arousal state of the subjects' autonomic nervous systems. The subjects were also asked to express their feelings about the technician. Results showed that those subjects who had been allowed to express their anger showed more hostility toward the technician and more of the physiological symptoms usually associated with anger.

Kahn concluded that those who expressed anger and were told that the technician would be reprimanded may have developed guilt feelings. Like most people, they would ordinarily not want to be the cause of someone else's punishment, unless, of course, they were extremely angry with the technician. To escape this state of cognitive dissonance and justify their anger and the technician's punishment, these subjects became especially angry with the technician.

Those who were not allowed to express their anger, on the other hand, had to justify their passivity in the face of insults by telling themselves that the behavior of the technician was really not that bad.

The cumulative characteristic of emotional behavior can be explained in terms of *set*. As you will recall from Chapter 5, set is a *predisposition, a preparedness to respond*. The more frequently a stimulus is presented to an individual, the readier he is to respond to that stimulus.

A frequent result of set is *heightened* awareness. Because an individual is set to make a specific response, he will respond accordingly to external stimulation that ordinarily does not produce such a reaction. A person who is already angry might see provocation in almost anything another person does.

MOOD AND TEMPERAMENT

The terms *mood* and *temperament* are often used to describe general states of emotion. A mood is an emotional state that lasts longer and is less intense than the emotion itself. We experience moods of anger, depression, contentment, excitement, and so forth. Moods may be variable or persistent. A depressed mood may disappear in moments, or it may last for many days. Some individuals experience daily, weekly, or even seasonal variations in mood. Studies show that the evening and early morning may be low or "blue-mood" periods. For some people, spring and summer are cheerful periods, and winter brings on depressed moods.

Temperament is a persistent emotional reaction that types or characterizes a person. An individual who is frequently in an angry mood has an angry temperament; a typically cheerful person, a cheerful temperament. One whose moods change rapidly is said to be temperamental.

Several early philosophers believed that temperament is reflected in a person's appearance—his facial features, his posture, and the way he walks and talks. Some modern psychologists agree. A system for classifying temperament was proposed over 2,300 years ago by the Greek physician Hippocrates. He believed that there were four types of temperament: sanguine (cheerful), choleric (quick to anger), phlegmatic (calm), and melancholic (sad). Since Hippocrates, there have been many other classification schemes for temperament; the most recent are based on body types (see Chapter 12).

DEVELOPMENT OF EMOTIONS

Emotional behavior can be considered a response mechanism. As such, it can be studied within the framework used in Chapter 3 to study other response mechanisms. From earliest infancy, human beings display emotional responses. We will begin our examination of the overall pattern of emotional development by discussing how much of an infant's emotional behavior may be innate (inborn) and how much the product of early learning.

Role of heredity
in emotional development

Heredity does not specifically determine whether a person will have a gloomy or an exuberant temperament throughout his life. But insofar as it determines the individual level of visceral responses, heredity does predispose one toward fairly specific emotional tendencies. Psycholo-gists have further found that the closer the genetic similarity of two individuals, the more alike are the emotional responses. Studies of identical twins at an early age (before much learning can occur) reveal that, for those emotions that can be detected, the twins' emotional response patterns are very similar and sometimes even identical. As identical twins mature, their specific emotional response patterns become somewhat different, but the patterns remain within the framework of the inherited emotional tendencies.

Hereditary factors in emotional behavior Gottesman (1963) conducted a study of 68 pairs of twins. After the twins filled out various personality questionnaires, their personalities were judged by clinical assessment methods. The data then were correlated to determine which traits appeared most frequently in both members of the 68 pairs of twins. An analysis of these correlations by statistical methods showed that tendencies to be sober and serious as opposed to enthusiastic and happy-go-lucky, and shy and sensitive as opposed to adventurous, were gene dependent (hereditary). Thus, how intensely a person feels emotion and whether and in what manner he expresses his emotions seem to be in part genetically determined.

Figure 9.1   Bridges (1932) identified three stages in the emotional development of an infant. Delight is the third basic expression of a specific emotion. (DeLatour—dpi)

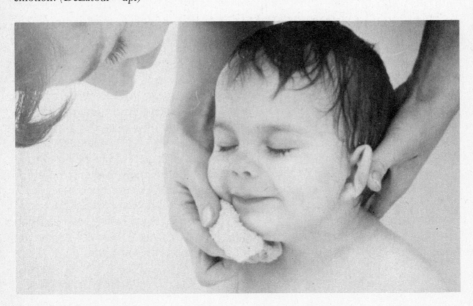

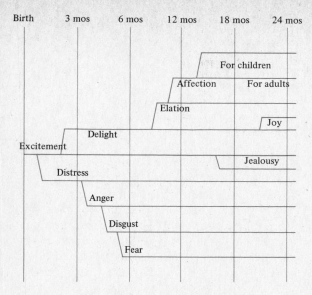

Figure 9.2   The development of emotional patterns in infants. (Adapted from Bridges, 1932)

Early learning factors

Besides the influence of inherited visceral response levels, early learning factors assist in determining an individual's basic emotional temperament. An infant who is colicky or suffers recurrent digestive acidity (gassiness) may overreact to other stimuli and develop a disgruntled temperament. Babies who are frequently held and fondled are more content than neglected babies. Some psychologists believe that breast-fed babies are more content than bottle-fed babies. If this is true, it may be due to the extra physical contact the breast-fed infants receive.

Maturation

The concept that maturation influences specific bodily functions, such as walking and talking, is easier to demonstrate than the idea that progressive emotional development depends on maturation. However, there is substantial evi-

dence to show that this is indeed the case. In this and the next section, we will point out that maturational and learning factors are so intricately interwoven that it is practically impossible to isolate one from the other and identify it as being wholly responsible for an emotional pattern. (We use the word "pattern" because it signifies the relatedness and general fluidity of emotions; for example, the emotion of fear is composed of factors that involve other emotions: anger, disgust, jealousy, and so on.)

The classic studies of the development of the infant's emotional pattern were conducted by Bridges in the early 1930s. Her evaluations are still accepted. Bridges believed that infants form a generalized pattern of emotion that becomes the basis for all future emotional behavior. At first, the infant varies only from a normal state of calm (usually sleeping) to one of *excitement*. By the time the infant is approximately 3 months old, he distinguishes between and responds to pleasant and unpleasant stimuli. Bodily discomfort, such as that caused by a wet diaper or hunger, brings forth the earliest unpleasant emotion, which is defined as *distress*; its complement, *delight*, is the earliest pleasant emotional behavior observed (Figure 9.1).

According to Bridges, behavior develops in a treelike fashion from the basic emotion of excitement (Figure 9.2). The infant's general state of excitement gives way to more specific responses as his perception of stimuli develops. Since sensory processes must mature before the infant can develop new emotional responses, emotional development is linked with perceptual maturation. The most active differentiation of emotional development occurs in childhood, not surprisingly, since the sensory systems make their greatest strides during childhood.

Studies of emotional behavior from infancy through old age have shown that emotional development follows a cyclical pattern directly related to the individual's maturational cycle. Beginning with infancy, the individual develops patterns of emotional differentiation that reach their height in early adulthood. As the adult grows older, the wealth of emotional patterns tends to diminish. Finally, in the very old, only the two basic emotions, delight and distress, remain. Delight subsides into a generalized feeling of contentment; distress becomes a more intensified experience of depression. Many very old people exhibit completely passive emotional behavior; they do not respond to stimuli that produce emotional reactions in younger persons.

Effects of learning on emotional behavior

Young children place no restrictions on their emotional reactions. They frequently cry, scream, become enraged, or otherwise freely express themselves. Furthermore, their overt emotional responses are more changeable than those of adults. But maturity and learning help them to understand and alter their emotional behavior. As soon as our sensory processes and response mechanisms are mature enough to respond, we begin to be influenced by and to learn from the world outside.

The effects of learning on emotional behavior have been seen in the study of fear in infants. Stimuli that evoke fear in older children or adults do not arouse fearful reactions in infants. Fears of animals, strange situations, darkness, and other specific objects, once believed innate in human beings, have been found to result from learning.

Much of the basic work in the study of fear was conducted by Watson and Rayner (1920). They first exposed a youngster to furry objects and observed no instinctive or innate fear-arousal pattern. They paired the furry object with a loud noise, a stimulus known to be innately fear producing. The youngster quickly was conditioned to fear furry objects.

As discussed in Chapter 6, it is easy to condition a human being or an animal to fear a previously neutral stimulus, but it is difficult to extinguish the conditioned fear. Such fear-conditioning experiences occur naturally in an infant's exploration of his environment. Many seemingly inexplicable fears of harmless stimuli can be traced back to accidental conditioning situations.

Parents often unknowingly condition their children to respond in certain ways. The young child quickly learns what his parents consider to be good and bad behavior, and he soon perceives that he can please his parents if he is good and displease them if he is bad. The reinforcing aspect of this parent-child learning situation is so strong that a parent's gestures, words, or facial expressions are often sufficient to arouse an emotion in the child. Words and gestures in themselves can become stimuli to trigger emotional behavior.

As children grow older, new situations tend to arouse new emotional responses. (Again, awareness of emotional stimuli is, in part, a result of the body's sensory maturation.) The child's response pattern becomes more highly structured because he has developed the ability to see relationships among stimuli and to classify the stimuli accordingly. He learns to control his emotions at about the same time that he learns to think conceptually; the development of intuitive thinking makes this possible (see Chapter 2).

Thus, while learning may restrict the expression of emotions, it may also help us to interpret emotions of others. We learn to recognize common cues of emotional reactions and to respond appropriately to them. Sadness may be evident in a frown; anxiety in a wringing of the hands. Such signs tell us that our friends are sad or anxious, and we attempt to cheer them or calm them as the occasion requires. We learn not only to interpret emotional cues but also to use them to communicate our own feelings.

When a child is able to anticipate emotional situations that lead to frustration of positive reinforcement, he develops a new emotion, worry. Worry is related to anxiety in that it is an anticipatory state; we worry about something that has not yet happened. Most of us continue to worry throughout our lifetimes—about grades, about the health of ourselves and others, about personal relationships, and so on.

The maturing child also begins to react to pressures from the external world. He learns to find pleasure in fulfilling his need for approval or praise. Through exposure to school, other children, and adults, the child develops *socially determined* emotional patterns. Most school-age children learn to restrain their infantile outbursts in the presence of their schoolmates, for such self-restraint usually brings social rewards. However, the same children may be unable to abandon such infantile behavior in the home. One reason for this inconsistency is that parents do not usually offer appropriate or meaningful alternatives. Many school environments channel the child's emotional energy into socially constructive goals, whereas the home environment may often fail to encourage the child to change his behavior patterns.

Parents should always try to arrange situations so that the child receives positive reinforcement when he exhibits desirable behavior. Punishment for undesirable behavior does not automatically lead to the adoption of appropriate behavior patterns. We cannot expect a child to "stumble into" and recognize a socially desirable emotion. The child must learn what is socially desirable by experiencing personal satisfaction in his response pattern. Many child psychologists are especially concerned with the proper direction of a child's emotional behavior, since pleasurable responses contribute to the development of the child's self-confidence and emotional stability.

Children learn kindness and compassion; so too can they learn hostility and selfishness. Psychologists have found that children are not innately prejudiced. The child learns hatred, distrust, and bigotry from those around him. As a character in *South Pacific* sang, "You've got to be taught to hate and fear. . . ." (See Chapter 15 for a more detailed discussion of prejudice.)

As the child reaches adolescence, his emotional behavior is more and more influenced by his role in society. Although he has learned to control his emotions to some extent, he wants to know why he must control them; that is, the adolescent seeks answers that he can accept. Adolescents face conflicts between what they experienced as children and what they experience in the present. The physiological changes that accompany adolescence are largely responsible for these conflicts. Physically capable of functioning as an adult, the adolescent is denied adult status. He is close to being an adult physically, but emotionally he may still be childlike, although he is often aware of the responsibilities of adulthood. His first task is to formulate his own personality, to relate himself to the world around him, a world whose shortcomings have become very clear to him. All things considered, the adolescent has a heavy burden to carry.

To complicate matters further, society demands sexual restraint from the adolescent, which creates an emotional crisis. The sexual drive, as well as the adolescent's curiosity about the body and about sex, is very strong. Because of the intensity of emotions aroused by these various dilemmas, and because of an inability to understand or cope with such emotions, the adolescent experiences many moods.

The mature adult is usually characterized as a person who is balanced emotionally so that he does not experience overwhelming personality frustrations. The adult is expected to provide strength as needed to his or her spouse, children, and parents. Adulthood is the time of life when individuals should be able to handle a wide range of emotional behavior. Of course, even adults can overcontrol or undercontrol their emotions. If an adult is at either end of the emotional continuum, or if he fluctuates easily from one end to the other, he has not learned how to live with his emotions. For example, a business executive who flies into a rage over a misplaced pair of scissors while calmly accepting a $50,000 loss in corporate revenue somehow suffers from emotional imbalance.

PHYSIOLOGY OF EMOTION

We have already noted that specific bodily changes occur during an emotional state. These changes, which are easily measured, are indicators of emotion.

Function of the brain in emotional response

Cerebral cortex The cerebral cortex of the brain appears to play an important role in the control of emotional behavior. Experimental animals whose cortexes are removed ("decorticate" dogs and cats) show emotional reactions, particularly rage and anger, when even the mildest stimuli are presented.

Hypothalamus Experiments have indicated that the activity of the hypothalamus regulates expression of emotion by the face and body posture. Impulses that come from the hypothalamus increase both smooth-muscle (involuntary) and skeletal-muscle (voluntary) activity. Impulses

Figure 9.3 Sham rage may be induced by passing an electrical current through the cat's brain. (Authenticated News International)

from the hypothalamus also determine the type of emotion experienced. If the impulses are from the posterior-sympathetic division, the emotion felt is excitement. If the impulses are from the anterior-parasympathetic division, the individual feels relaxed. The emotion felt by the individual is determined by the stimuli and the bodily responses they produce. Damage to the hypothalamus, as in the case of surgical lesions, dramatically affects the pattern and incidence of such emotions as rage. In the experimental laboratory, cats that were tame and friendly became perpetually hostile following surgery to produce lesions in the hypothalamus (Wheatley, 1944). This type of induced rage is referred to as *sham rage* (Figure 9.3). It is used by psychologists to study the physiological changes that take place in an enraged animal.

Role of the limbic and reticular activating systems

The study of emotion has led to interest in two systems within the central nervous system, the *limbic system* and the *reticular activating system*. We saw in Chapter 8 that electrical impulses to a part of the limbic system can serve as positive reinforcement. It has also been shown that electrical stimulation in another part of this system can arouse fear.

Because the reticular activating system is involved in individual arousal, many investigators feel that the system plays an important role in emotional excitement. Impulses from the reticular activating system are believed to travel to the limbic system, where they contribute to general emotional responsiveness. However, much research has yet to be completed before psychologists will be able to relate the limbic and the reticular activating systems accurately to emotional responses.

Drug-induced emotion Psychology has always been interested in the biochemical control of behavior, that is, how body chemistry affects behavior. Recently,

Table 9.1   Bodily experiences of fear in combat fliers[a]

Experience during combat missions	Total percent	Percent reporting "often"
A pounding heart and rapid pulse	86	30
Feeling that your muscles are very tense	83	30
Being easily irritated, angry, or "sore"	80	22
Dryness of the throat or mouth	80	30
"Nervous perspiration" or "cold sweat"	79	26
"Butterflies" in the stomach	76	23
Feeling of unreality, that this couldn't be happening to you	69	20
Having to urinate (pass water) very frequently	65	25
Trembling	64	11
Feeling confused or "rattled"	53	3
Feeling weak or faint	41	4
Right after a mission, not being able to remember details of what happened	39	5
Feeling sick to the stomach	38	5
Not being able to concentrate	35	3
Wetting or soiling your pants	5	1

[a]Adapted from Shaffer (1947).

hypersexuality, aggression, and behavior of a psychotic nature were induced in cats through the administration of a drug by Ferguson, Henriksen, Cohen, Mitchell, Barchas, and Dement (1970).

Following injections of the drug *p*-chlorophenylalanine, dramatic changes in behavior occurred. Hypersexuality was manifested by frequent and insistent mounting of one male cat by another, a type of sexuality rare in untreated animals. Extreme forms of aggression and rage also occurred, directed toward laboratory rats, other cats, and the laboratory technicians. A third category of behavioral change included restlessness, sniffing, extreme wariness, hissing and backing into a corner—all in the absence of any stimulus event. The cats often behaved as if they were hallucinating. Laboratory analysis showed changes in the chemical content of the cats' brains. When the drug injections were stopped, behavior returned to normal.

Bodily responses accompanying emotion

The individual is usually not aware of all the visceral responses that accompany his emotional state, although they are often widespread. Not all emotions arouse the body in the same way. For example, anger and fear bring about changes quite different from those produced by joy or contentment.

A list of typical fear responses was compiled from a survey of World War II combat fliers (Shaffer, 1947). The fliers were asked to report their feelings during each mission. Many of the symptoms of fear were physiological—tense muscles, nervous perspiration, trembling, and nausea, for example—whereas others involved such subjective states as confusion or forgetfulness. The bodily changes most often experienced by these fliers were internal; for example, the most frequently rated sensation was a pounding heart, a feeling familiar to most of us (waiting for an exam grade, escaping an accidental fall).

Data from the experiment, given in Table 9.1, became the basis for subsequent studies of fear symptoms. The specific identification of bodily changes by the fliers enabled researchers to devise physical tests to show specific bodily responses during various emotional states. The fact that these physiological changes last long enough to be adequately measured is due, as indicated in Chapter 8, to the smooth muscles that regulate the viscera. The bodily responses generally involve the association and integration of the glands, the skeletal muscle system, and the autonomic nervous system. All these systems are under the control of various parts of the central nervous system.

Galvanic skin reflex   Skin conducts electricity; under conditions of emotional arousal, certain areas of the skin, particularly the palm of the hand, show a pronounced increase in the level of electrical conductivity (conversely stated, a decrease in level of electrical resistance). Some physiologists believe that the level of conductivity increases because sweating (a response often associated with emotion) releases chemicals that coat the surface of the skin and make conductivity easier. Other physiologists believe that the change in electrical resistance is caused by a release of electricity that accompanies the contraction of the muscle cells controlling the sweat glands. Although these theories differ as to the exact source of the changes, they agree about the involvement of the sweat glands; all note that the sweat glands in the palm function only when stimulated by the sympathetic division of the autonomic nervous system, and since the sympathetic division operates under conditions of stress or arousal, the measurement of sweat gland activity may provide an index of emotional arousal. If a person is physically inactive and his body is not overheated, palmar sweating is probably due to emotional strain.

The *galvanic skin reflex* (GSR) is a measure of palmar sweat gland activity. The galvanic skin reflex is recorded by a device called a *galvanometer*, which measures the electrical resistance of the skin. GSR readings are imperfect, because they do not distinguish between the reasons for arousal. They do not, for example, distinguish between a person who is intellectually aroused by the topic of drug addiction and one who is actually a drug addict. Nevertheless, they may be a valuable aid in determining a subject's emotional involvement or detachment regarding particular stimuli.

GSR detects prejudice   Cooper (1959) conducted two sets of experiments to test the relationship between prejudice and GSR. In the first, his subjects were asked to rate 20 ethnic and national groups on a scale ranging from "like intensely" to "dislike intensely." The subjects then listened to statements that were unfavorable to their most liked group, favorable to their least liked group, and were either favorable or unfavorable to groups that they neither liked nor disliked. When the statements disagreed with their views about their best- and least-liked groups, GSR recordings showed high readings, but when neutral groups were mentioned, readings did not rise. Thus, the GSR was higher when a strong emotional attitude was touched upon.

It was believed that if a subject's GSR readings in reaction to statements about different ethnic groups could be obtained, his prejudices could be predicted. In the second set of experiments, the subjects first listened to statements about different groups. Based on GSR readings, predictions were then made about how the subjects would rate the different ethnic groups. If, for example, a subject showed a high GSR reading when a favorable statement was made regarding group A, it was predicted that he would give group A an unfavorable rating. The results bore out the hypothesis.

Circulatory system   The pounding heart experienced by a combat pilot in action (see Table 9.1) is one of the many detectable changes in the circulatory system. Our hearts pound under varying conditions of arousal—mild nervousness, as in apprehension or anxiety, love, fear, anger, sorrow, and rage. In each of these emotions, the increased pressure of blood passing through the heart causes the muscles of the chest to expand and contract in harmony with the heart; these constrictions of the chest wall cause the sensation of heartbeat. The pressure of the blood being pumped from the heart changes drastically under conditions of emotional stimulation. Scientists are able to measure this change of blood pressure by means of an instrument called a *sphygmomanometer*. This device is also used to test the functioning of the circulatory system.

A second detectable circulatory response to emotional arousal is the redistribution of blood to the parts of the body where blood is most needed. This distribution is made possible by the adrenal hormones that are secreted into the bloodstream and stimulate the blood cells to react properly to cope with the emotional emergency. These hormones also cause the blood pressure to increase.

Attack versus escape If two rats are placed together in a cage and shock is applied to their feet, the animals will attack each other. If shock is applied to the feet of an animal who is alone, persistent escape responses will take place. Williams and Eichelman (1971) investigated the changes in blood pressure that accompanied these two types of behavior. They found that fighting in reaction to shock was constantly followed by a fall in blood pressure. In contrast, there was a consistent rise in the blood pressure of the single rats who tried to escape. These results are similar to findings on humans who secrete different chemicals while engaging in different behavior: norepinephrine during aggression; epinephrine in avoidance states.

Besides this hormonal stimulation, there are other forms of glandular arousal of the circulatory system. Tell someone he is stupid, and watch him flush with anger. He is experiencing an emotional reaction in which the blood vessels near the surface of his skin dilate (enlarge), causing an increase in blood flow that appears as a flush. In order for the blood to reach the dilated areas, blood vessels in other parts of the body must contract at the same time that the involved vessels are expanding. Emotions of anger, love, and fear circulate more blood to the skin, thus sensitizing it and preparing it to respond quickly. Emotions of grief and sorrow operate in reverse; they distribute more blood internally to the viscera and leave the skin pale and slow to respond.

A third circulatory change in reaction to emotion involves changes in the chemical composition of the blood, brought about by hormones in the bloodstream. One easily detectable chemical change is an increase in blood sugar. Sugar, the source of internal energy, is released by activity in the endocrine glands. This increase in sugar level is thought to be necessary to stimulate responses in different parts of the body.

Respiration Emotional changes involve changes in respiration, but there is no simple identifiable pattern. Breathing often becomes faster to prepare the body for action, but gasping and labored breathing may also occur.

Pupil of the eye The pupil of the eye also reacts to emotional stimuli. The pupil dilates when the eye is focused on a pleasurable object; it contracts when it is focused on an unpleasurable object. Numerous tests have shown that an enlarged pupil signifies interest and that a contracted pupil signifies boredom.

The study of pupil size in relation to emotions is called *pupillometrics*. If an individual is shown several neutral photographs together with one photograph of a member of the opposite sex, the experimenter can usually tell when his subject is viewing the "special picture" by observing the predicted increase in the subject's pupil size. This method of recognizing an emotional state is significant, for pupillometrics may be used as a diagnostic method in treating behavior pathology. The psychologist can observe the patient's reaction to certain stimuli without requiring the patient to describe his reactions.

Gastrointestinal system The stomach and intestines may become tense or excited during emotional arousal. Gastrointestinal activity may take the form of mild fluttering (the so-called butterflies in the stomach), nausea, or disturbed gastrointestinal activity of the type that produces ulcers.

Fluttering or nausea may occur when the stomach's blood supply is suddenly decreased by the effect of emotional stimuli, as when the blood rushes from the stomach region to the skeletal muscles or to the head. Other emotional stimuli, such as fear and worry, overstimulate the secretion of stomach acids, which, over a long period of time, can lead to ulcers. Fear can also stop the flow of saliva, thus inducing the sensation of dryness in the mouth.

Experimental study of physiological processes

Several studies form the basis of our understanding of how the physiological processes work during emotional arousal. In most of these experiments, hormones are administered to subjects whose behavior is observed under various environmental conditions.

Ax (1953) performed a series of experiments to determine whether fear and anger elicit different physiological patterns of responses. The laboratory technicians produced anger by making derogatory remarks to the subjects during the course of the experiment. They provoked fear by acting clumsily and uncertainly while using the dangerous-looking electronic equipment.

Ax recorded pulse rate, heartbeat, GSR, respiration, hand and face skin temperature, and eyelid movements. Some of the response measurements for fear and anger did not differ significantly, but enough of them showed differences to suggest that fear and anger involve different physiological processes.

Fear-inducing events evoked changes in three response areas: respiration increased; palmar skin resistance (the electrical skin resistance of the palms of the hands, which varies constantly —low during arousal and high during relaxation) decreased; and muscular tension increased at certain points. A different pattern was recorded for anger: heart rate decreased; the number of GSRs increased; over-all muscular tension increased; and diastolic blood pressure (the measure of blood pressure when the heart valves are open and receiving blood) increased.

Upon close examination, Ax found that the pattern of fear resembled the pattern produced by the injection of the hormone adrenalin; the pattern of anger resembled the action produced by the injection of noradrenalin. Figure 9.4 summarizes Ax's experiment. In this connection, it is interesting that timid animals, such as rabbits, have an excess of adrenalin in their bloodstreams, whereas aggressive animals, such as lions, have an excess of noradrenalin.

Schachter and Singer (1962) devised an intricate experiment that combined hormonal activities with changes in the emotional setting. The hormone used was adrenalin. The emotional setting was provided by a *stooge*, a member of an investigative team who pretended to be a subject.

The subjects were divided into four groups. Group A was injected with adrenalin and told what reactions to expect. Group B was also injected with adrenalin but was misinformed as to its effects. Group C subjects were told that they were being injected with a mild and harmless fluid that would produce no side effects. Group D was also injected with a simple saline solution (that is, a *placebo*—a totally inactive substance) but not told what it was.

The four groups were further subdivided —half the subjects of each group were exposed to a stooge who acted angry and hostile, whereas the other half were presented with a "euphoric" stooge, who grinned, doodled, and flew paper airplanes.

The following results were obtained:

1 Subjects who knew what to expect from an adrenalin injection (group A) were not significantly affected by the situations designed to produce emotion; they felt little euphoria and no anger in the respective situations. They did, however, react normally to the adrenalin injection. They were affected by the hormone but not by the environment.
2 Subjects physiologically aroused by adrenalin, but misinformed or ignorant about its effects (groups B and C), reflected the emotion of the stooge in the euphoric situation; they were not tested in the anger situation. The emotional state was more pronounced in the euphoric situation than in the anger situation.
3 Subjects given the saline solution, a placebo

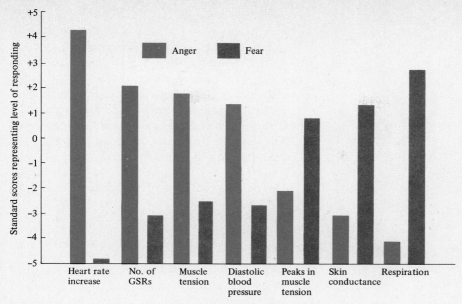

Figure 9.4   *Anger and fear show different physiological responses. Note that the units shown on the y axis are based on standard scores because different units of measurement were used for each type of response. The zero indicates the normal level of responding; the minus scores indicate below-normal levels and the plus scores indicate above-normal levels. (After Ax, 1953)*

(group D), showed no hormonal reactions and slight environmental reactions.

From this experiment we can conclude that physiological arousal for which subjects are unprepared sets the stage for them to react emotionally to external stimuli.

Psychosomatic effects

Another form of physiological process affecting emotional behavior is the *psychosomatic reaction*. Psychological stress, of which the individual himself is often unaware, may arouse emotional tension that affects the physiology of the body. People who undergo constant emotional tensions and who do not find adequate or acceptable means by which to reduce these tensions, may suffer bodily damage. Prolonged emotional arousal may be coupled with hormonal hyperactivity, severe muscular tension, disorganized digestive activity, and exaggerated heart and circulatory activity. The physiological mechanism for arousal primes the body for action; if no action results, then the body is overcharged and real physical damage can occur.

A stomach ulcer is a common psychosomatic disorder, as are high blood pressure, allergies, and obesity. Of course, many such illnesses are not completely psychosomatic; some disorders may be caused by a combination of emotional arousal and organic weakness. Emotional tension and stress can aggravate existing problems.

The executive monkey   Brady, Porter, Conrad, and Mason (1958) conducted an experiment to determine the cause of ulcers. Two monkeys were placed in seats from which they could not move (Figure 9.5). At regular intervals, an electric shock was delivered

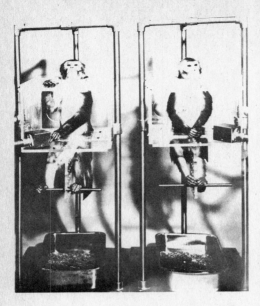

Figure 9.5   The executive monkey. The monkey on the right, who had control of the shock received by himself and the other monkey, developed an ulcer, whereas the monkey on the left did not. As the experiment shows, psychosomatic illnesses may develop from emotional stress. (U.S. Army Photograph)

physiological processes. The individual required to cope with strong stimuli or difficult situations is functioning under extreme stress, which arouses widespread bodily reactions. Hans Selye (1953, 1956), in extensive studies of the endocrine glands, identified a response pattern that occurs in extreme stress. This pattern, known as the *general-adaptation syndrome*, consists of three phases: the *alarm reaction, the stage of resistance,* and the *stage of exhaustion.*

1   *The alarm reaction*—The individual is momentarily immobilized (in a state of shock). This initial shock is followed by a rapid and intense mobilization of bodily resources, including a high degree of visceral and skeletal muscle activity.
2   *The stage of resistance*—During this period of recovery and restoration of balance, the individual adapts to the stress. Outwardly, resistance appears to be a quiet stage, but the endocrine glands, particularly the anterior pituitary and the adrenal cortex, are hard at work helping the individual to adapt to the stress.
3   *The stage of exhaustion*—If the stress continues and the individual is unable to maintain the resistance level, exhaustion occurs, and the alarm reaction is repeated. If stress is continued, serious injury or even death may occur.

to both. Within the reach of one monkey was a lever. If the monkey pressed the lever while the shock was being administered, he would stop the shock. Or, if he anticipated the shock and adjusted the lever in time, he would prevent the shock. The shock administered to both monkeys came from one source, and the lever-pressing monkey regulated the shock to the other monkey as well as to himself.

The monkey operating the lever, due to the constant state of alert it was in, was dubbed the "executive monkey."

After the experiment, it was observed that the executive monkey had developed an ulcer, whereas the other monkey had not. Since both monkeys had received the same shocks, the ulcer could not have been caused by physiological stress, but rather by the psychological stress of the executive, who had to forestall the shock.

The general-adaptation syndrome   Psychosomatic disorders result from the overreaction of

Performance under stress   Do people perform better or worse when under stress? Does the effectiveness of induced stress depend on the presence of some personality characteristic? These questions were examined by Martens and Landers (1970) in a study of subjects' motor performance under varying degrees of stress.

The experimenters used 90 junior high students divided into equal groups according to self-reported traits of high, moderate, or low anxiety. Each anxiety group was then randomly divided into groups subjected to high, moderate, or low states of experimental psychological stress. All subjects were asked to maneuver a metal ring along the length of an irregularly shaped metal bar without touching the bar with the ring. Under the low-stress condition, the experimenter attempted to put each subject at ease; in the moderate-stress condition, subjects were told they would be mildly shocked if their metal ring touched the inner bar too frequently; in the high-stress condition, subjects had electrodes attached to their foreheads and were told by a white-coated "doctor" that they would be painfully shocked for poor performance; moreover, they were placed next to an awesome-looking "shock machine."

Results supported the hypothesis that subjects generally make fewest errors when under moderate stress. Most errors, by far, were made by those under high stress. Subjects whose normal state was moderate anxiety appeared to perform best on this motor task, with low- and high-anxiety subjects performing at the same, lower level. No evidence was found to support the notion that the quality of performance depends on the interaction of the particular combination of induced stress level and the subject's customary anxiety level. (These findings remind us of the Yerkes-Dodson law discussed in Chapter 8.)

THEORIES OF EMOTION

Psychologists have not yet developed a single, comprehensive theory of emotional behavior. Several important theories exist, but none of them explains all aspects of emotion. These theories attempt to reconcile the existing evidence by explaining the feelings that accompany emotion, the behavior that results, and the physiological patterns that appear before, after, and during the emotional experience.

The James-Lange theory

The earliest formal theory of emotional behavior, now considered a classical approach to emotion, was formulated by two psychologists working separately and a few years apart, William James (an American) in 1889 and Carl Lange (a Dane) in 1885. The James-Lange theory holds that the sequence of an emotional experience is the reverse of what common sense would lead us to believe. We usually think that our emotional perception, or our feeling, occurs first, and that it stimulates our body to react. James and Lange proposed that the body reacts first, that it is the body's response that is our emotional perception. Thus, if we were confronted

by an enraged mob with guns, we would tremble and run away; the trembling and running away would make us feel the emotion of fear, not the other way around. The recognition of the emotion, our conscious feeling of fear, would be a result of our body's changes.

Many psychologists are skeptical of the James-Lange theory. They claim that each of the many emotions and the degrees of any one emotion could not possibly be created by a distinct bodily response. However, some psychologists still accept the basic concepts of the James-Lange theory.

The Cannon-Bard theory

The Cannon-Bard theory was developed because its authors felt that the existing theories of emotion, notably the James-Lange theory, did not explain emotion adequately. Walter B. Cannon originally proposed the idea in 1927, but the basic studies were performed by P. Bard in 1928. Cannon and Bard traced the path of emotion from stimulation through the full experience of emotional feeling. They concluded that the thalamic-hypothalamic region of the brain is the center for emotions and that the emotional experience and the bodily responses occur simultaneously because of the integrated functioning of the thalamus and hypothalamus.

According to the Cannon-Bard theory, nerve impulses travel the normal neural route to the cerebral cortex, except for one intervening step: an emotional impulse (from strong novel stimuli) passes through the thalamic region of the brain. As it passes through the thalamus, the emotional impulse splits, with part continuing straight to the cortex and part passing through to the hypothalamus, which, as we know, is an excitatory center (see Chapter 3). Presumably, the part of the impulse that travels through the hypothalamus is then also sent to the cortex, where the emotion is perceived and communicated to the muscles and internal organs.

The thalamus and hypothalamus, which are identified as "lower" centers of the brain, are therefore responsible for the excitation of both the cognitive and bodily response reactions to emotion-inducing stimuli. Many psychologists feel that the Cannon-Bard theory oversimplifies the problem by placing too much emphasis on the thalamic-hypothalamic region.

Activation theory

D. B. Lindsley (1951, 1957) proposed a theory of emotion to account for the extremes of the emotional continuum, calm and excitement. According to Lindsley, emotion-provoking stimuli activate the reticular activating system (RAS) in the brainstem, which sends volleys of impulses to the thalamus and the cortex, initiating emotional excitement. Only if the RAS is stimlated does the individual experience the extreme of excitement; if the RAS is at rest, calm prevails. Lindsley based his position on the observation that electrical stimulation of the RAS aroused activity in the cortex, neurally stimulating the organism.

In Lindsley's theory, emotional activation is similar, if not identical, to motivational arousal, and therefore they are difficult to distinguish. Under high activation of either type, the individual is prepared for action and geared to respond.

Perceptual-cognitive theory

Magda Arnold (1960) developed a theory of emotion which regards emotional activity as a response to a cognitive process, involving appraisal of a stimulus.

According to the Arnold theory, emotion involves a tendency to approach or avoid stimuli depending on how they are appraised. The sequence involves three connected stages: perception, appraisal, and emotion. The appraisal governs the emotion, and the emotion governs the resulting behavior. Each emotion governs a particular pattern of bodily response and thus sets the stage for specific forms of behavior.

Mind over matter How a person reacts emotionally to a situation is often affected by his cognitive appraisal of it. For example, in some potentially threatening emotional situations, it is possible to take a rational approach that may reduce the impact of the threat. In a series of experiments Lazarus, Averill, and Opton (1970) used an anxiety-inducing film to manipulate responses to stressful situations. The stressful movie, *Subincision,* which depicted crude genital operations among Australian aborigines, elicited widely varying responses from the subjects. Some reported being filled with strong emotions (the "sensitizers"), others reported intellectual interest in the film's cultural implications (the "intellectualizers"), and still others denied being emotionally affected (the "deniers"). Although they reported different feelings, measurements indicated that all had similar physiological reactions. Given no warning of the film's potential for arousing emotional stress, subjects apparently were unprepared to avail themselves of their habitual style of stress reduction.

With these three broad styles of emotional defense to guide them, the investigators used the same film with either new film soundtracks or new introductory statements to produce versions emphasizing either the movie's emotional trauma (*sensitization*), its intellectual implications (*intellectualization*), or content that would not trouble the viewer (*denial*). By the use of these manipulations, they produced both physiological and self-reported levels of emotional stress that were markedly different from those under control conditions: the "trauma" manipulation raised stress levels, whereas the "intellectualization" and "denial" manipulations reduced it. From this, it appears that a person's appraisal or interpretation of a potentially distressing event significantly affects the degree of immediate emotional disturbance he actually experiences.

MOTIVATIONAL EFFECTS OF EMOTION

We have already noted that emotional behavior and motivated behavior resemble each other so closely that the two are often grouped together. Certain types of motivated behavior give rise to emotional situations; for example, a cozy room, blazing fire, and hot cocoa give rise to pleasure or contentment. Emotions themselves may also serve as drives, or urges, that impel the individual to act. How many stories do you know (fictitious or otherwise) in which the emotion of love incites the lover to cross a continent, slay a rival, write a poem, and so on?

Moods or emotions that result in negative or escape behavior figure extensively in the current research on the relationship of motivation to emotion. Individuals are often driven by negative emotions, those generally associated with unpleasant or painful stimuli; behavior motivated by emotion often involves frustration, with the individual seeking satisfaction for thwarted needs. Frustration thus produces a drive that impels action. We will now examine some of the motives characteristic of frustration and conflict situations.

Frustration and conflict

We all learn early that some frustrations are inevitable. Few drives are consistently and fully satisfied. Human life has become so complex that we now have many complicated drives that are especially difficult to fulfill: acquired social drives toward approval, achievement, recognition, a sense of fulfillment, and numerous other personal goals.

The individual who is prevented from reaching a goal is frustrated. Persistent frustration leads to tension. A frustrated individual who cannot create or find a means to reduce his frustration may become deeply troubled. Most of us sense this in ourselves and attempt to seek a satisfactory substitute for frustrated goals. The individual's self-concept requires him to deal successfully with frustration.

Environmental frustration Environmental frustration is caused by any external object or event that prevents us from obtaining needed reinforcement. A door that will not open, a rainstorm that interferes with a day's outing, a stern

and arbitrary teacher—all are causes of environmental frustration.

Frustration and regression Barker, Dembo, and Lewin (1943), in their experiments with children, tested and verified the hypothesis that environmental frustration may lead to regression. Each child was placed alone in a room that contained a large selection of toys. However, the availability of toys differed. Sometimes the child was allowed to play with all the available toys in the room. At other times, the more attractive toys were placed behind a wire gate. The child could see the toys, but he was unable to reach them; as a result, he suffered frustration.

The experimenter observed the children's play activities in both situations, noting whether their behavior was constructive or nonconstructive. For example, merely picking up a toy and examining it was considered nonconstructive (or not creative) behavior. Pulling up the ladder of a big fire truck and using it as a runway for smaller cars or airplanes was seen as constructive behavior.

Children showed much more constructive behavior when in the free play situation than in the frustrating situation. Thus, the experimenters concluded that children regressed to a less mature form of behavior when they were frustrated.

Personal frustration Limitations of an individual's personality, physiology, or intelligence often contribute to personal frustration. For example, a girl may want desperately to become an airline stewardess but may discover that she is too tall. An individual who is personally frustrated is often one who aspires to a level above and beyond his capabilities. Most realistic people, however, learn early in life that not every goal is attainable.

Conflict frustration The largest category of frustration involves conflicting attitudes toward a goal-directed activity and is known as *conflict frustration*. There are four types of conflict situations:

(1) *Approach-approach conflict* arises when two pleasurable or desirable goals are within an individual's reach and he must choose one over the

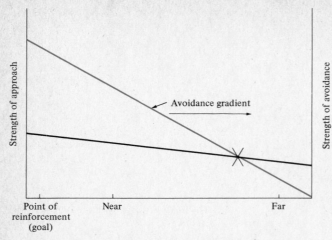

Figure 9.6   Graph of an approach-avoidance conflict. At **X**, the point of conflict, the approach tendency and the avoidance tendency are equal.

other. We may remember as a child being offered chocolate layer cake or strawberry short-cake for dessert; this is an approach-approach conflict—although, of course, a mild one. One goal is frustrated simply because the other is selected. Conflicts of this type are often easily resolved. Once a choice is made, positive reinforcement takes over.

(2) *Approach-avoidance conflict* occurs if both positive and negative feelings are associated with a goal. In such a conflict, an individual is drawn to a goal by one attractive element and simultaneously repelled by a less attractive element (Figure 9.6). For example, a student may wish to become a surgeon, but he is repelled by the sight of blood. This type of conflict is difficult to resolve. It is best resolved by allowing the approach tendency to overcome the avoidance tendency—either by emphasizing the positive features of the goal or by reducing the negative features. The student might resolve his conflict by seeking more information about the study of medicine and becoming so enthusiastic that he forgets his fear of the sight of blood. Or, more likely, he may make an effort, perhaps with professional help, to extinguish his fear of the sight of blood. Psychologists often use the term *am-*

bivalence to label the conflict of a person caught in an approach-avoidance conflict. When the individual wants both to obtain and reject the same goal, we say he is ambivalent toward it.

(3) *Double approach-avoidance conflict* arises when the individual is confronted by a conflict situation that involves two goals, each with an approach-avoidance conflict of its own. Many college students experience this type of conflict in deciding whether to enter the business world or to "drop out." Both situations have positive and negative aspects. Conflicts of this type are resolved in the same way as approach-avoidance conflicts.

(4) *Avoidance-avoidance conflict* occurs when someone is caught between two equally undesirable or fear-evoking goals. For example, a student must choose between physics and chemistry, though he is afraid to take either course. This type of conflict may produce tension until the conflict is resolved. For example, the student may take a summer course in geology, and thereby escape the chemistry or physics requirement. Although the escape solution is often not the best one for the individual, he is sometimes driven to it by the intensity of the conflict.

person raised in China may display anger by a wide-eyed look, and a Japanese may show regret by a smile.

THE LANGUAGE OF EMOTIONAL EXPRESSION

In 1872, Charles Darwin proposed a theory of emotional expression in which he identified three principles. *The principle of serviceable habits* suggested that the expression of a particular emotion began as a serviceable habit that had survival value for the species. For example, the facial expression of anger was probably assumed as a warning against an enemy.

The principle of antithesis suggested that gestures and posture associated with one emotion occur in an opposite manner for the opposite emotion. For example, an angry horse puts its ears back and swishes its tail, but in displaying friendship, the horse does the opposite—it moves its ears forward and keeps its tail still.

The principle of direct action of the nervous system suggested that many emotional actions and expressions simply result from excessive neural reaction, as occurs when we are terrified and tremble.

In 1971, Izard, while stating that "Darwin was correct in seeing a functional aspect in facial expressions . . . ," proposed his own view of emotional expression. Izard suggests that we all have certain basic emotional experiences and these experiences produce certain common expressions and labels about emotion that have universal meaning. According to Izard, little difference was found among subjects from different cultures who were asked to match pictures of facial expressions with descriptions of the fundamental emotions. Although agreement was high for identification of facial expressions, it was poor when emotions were depicted by such physical acts as handclapping or clenching of fists. These instrumental acts apparently are more culture bound than is the expression of emotion by facial expressions. Nevertheless, facial expressions may, on occasion, reveal cultural differences. A

The universality of facial expressions The reasons for facial display of emotions may vary widely in different cultures, but there is evidence of substantial cross-cultural similarity in how various basic emotions are expressed facially. Ekman, Sorenson, and Friesen (1969), for example, tested members of several literate and preliterate societies to determine the degree to which they agreed in their interpretations of facial emotions.

The experimenters selected 30 photographs of Caucasian adults and children, each clearly expressing a single strong emotion. Native college students in the United States, Brazil, and Japan were shown each picture for 20 seconds, then asked to state which of six listed emotions was displayed by each face. From 63 to 93 percent of the responses, depending on the picture shown, agreed with the predicted response, regardless of the subjects' cultural background. With only one exception, a majority of each culture's observers made the predicted response to each of the 30 picture stimuli.

Among the Borneo and New Guiana (preliterate) societies sampled, there were considerably fewer responses that agreed with the predicted ones, but the experimenters attributed this largely to language barriers and task unfamiliarity. Despite these hindrances, there was considerable cross-cultural recognition of happiness, fear, and anger among the preliterates, and moderate agreement on the disgust, surprise, and sadness photographs. Similar results were obtained when photos of Melanesian faces were used in a later study of one of the New Guinea populations.

The experimenters regard their findings as supportive of the Darwinian notion that facial expressions of emotions are of evolutionary origin.

Emotions can be communicated by means other than gestures and facial expressions. The human voice is an exceptionally provocative communicator of emotion. Tone, loudness, and speed of speaking all can act as signals of the communicator's emotional state. Loud and rapid speaking can convey excitement; subdued and lethargic speaking may reveal depression. We convey much more than words when we speak.

The arts—music, poetry, painting, and so on—can vividly portray emotions, although we require continued exposure to the fine arts before we can fully recognize and appreciate what is being expressed. Even then, great works of art may remain puzzling. Many great artists not only effectively portray universal emotions but also reveal their personal emotions in their works. We can learn a great deal about these men through their art. The emotions expressed by many musical compositions do not need lyrics, titles, or interpretations to explain them. Great music is itself an expressive language without words.

SUMMARY

Emotion is behavior that is primarily influenced by conditioned visceral responses; important characteristics common to all emotional behavior are its diffuse, persistent, and cumulative nature.

An emotional state that lasts a long time is termed a mood. Temperament is a persistent emotional reaction that types or characterizes a person.

Some general classifications of emotion are joy, sorrow, anger, fear, love, and hate.

Both anger and fear readily lend themselves to stimulus generalization.

Emotional development is influenced by heredity, maturation, and learning.

The infant first exhibits excitement, which later differentiates into delight and distress.

The manner in which we express emotions results from learning.

Worry is the anticipation of frustrating emotional situations.

Bodily, or visceral, changes involved in emotion are regulated by the autonomic nervous system, the endocrine glands, and the central nervous system (particularly the hypothalamus and cerebral cortex). Both the limbic and reticular activating systems play an important role in emotional expression.

Changes in galvanic skin reflex, circulation, gastrointestinal activity, respiration, and pupil size are all physiological components of emotion.

Motivational and emotional arousal states are very similar.

Psychosomatic illnesses originate from or are aggravated by severe emotional stress.

The stages of Selye's general-adaptation syndrome are the alarm reaction, the stage of resistance, and the stage of exhaustion.

Some theories of emotion are the James-Lange theory, the Cannon-Bard theory, Lindsley's activation theory, and perceptual-cognitive theories.

Emotions themselves may function as drives.

The three major sources of frustration are obstacles in the environment, personal limitations, and conflict.

Conflict, the most common cause of frustration, usually takes one of the following forms: approach-approach; approach-avoidance, double approach-avoidance; and avoidance-avoidance.

Charles Darwin suggested that the expression of human emotions had survival value for the species; that gestures that convey an emotion occur in opposite forms for opposite emotions; and that emotional behavior results from excessive neural action.

Izard found that most cultures have the common tendency to associate certain facial expressions with certain emotions, whereas bodily gestures to indicate emotions tend to differ from culture to culture.

SUGGESTED READINGS

Texts

Arnold, M. B. (Ed.) *The nature of emotion.* Baltimore: Penguin, 1971. Introduction to the theoretical and empirical issues of current interest.

Buss, A. H. *The psychology of aggression.* New York: Wiley, 1961. A useful reference work that includes a good discussion of ways to investigate aggression in the laboratory.

Cannon, W. B. *Bodily changes in pain, hunger, fear and rage.* New York: Appleton-Century-Crofts, 1929. Classic description of bodily changes that occur during emotional states.

Darwin, C. *The expression of the emotions in man and animals.* Chicago: University of Chicago Press, 1965. Reprint of this classic (published in 1872), with a new introduction by Konrad Lorenz.

Davitz, J. R. *The language of emotion.* New York: Academic Press, 1969. An extensive categorization—based on empirical findings—of the experiences associated with fifty emotions.

Eron, L. D., Walder, L. O., & Lefkowitz, M. M. *Learning of aggression in children.* Boston: Little, Brown, 1971. An insightful account of the methods and reasons for studying the relationship between children's aggression and their parents' behavior at home.

Kurzweil, A. E. *Anxiety and education.* New York: Barnes & Noble, 1968. Discussion of the effects of anxiety on the educative process.

May, R. *The meaning of anxiety.* New York: Ronald Press, 1950. Perceptive analysis of the trends in Western civilzation that make anxiety so important to our way of life.

Plutchik, R. *The emotions: facts, theories, and a new model.* New York: Random House, 1962. Review of theoretical positions, and the formulation of a multi-dimensional theory.

Rappaport, D. *Emotions and memory* (5th ed.). New York: International Universities Press, 1971. Analysis of the effects of emotion and emotional conflicts on memory.

Spielberger, C. D. (Ed.) *Anxiety and behavior.* New York: Academic Press, 1966. Collection of useful and informative papers.

Switzer, D. D. *The dynamics of grief.* Nashville, Tenn.: Abingdon, 1970. An overview of this neglected psychological topic.

Popular books

Grier, W. H., & Cobbs, R. M. *Black rage.* Discussion of the special emotional problems of blacks in American society.

Kahn, S. *The psychology of love.* Popular discussion of the psychology of this emotion.

Toch, H. *Violent men: an inquiry into the psychology of violence.* Discussion of the emotional origins of violence.

10

Language, thinking, problem-solving, and creativity

Man's superior development of language, thinking, and problem-solving distinguishes him from all other forms of life. These three important characteristics of human behavior interact: language is used in thinking; thinking is used in problem-solving; problem-solving generates new thinking; thinking and problem-solving contribute to the acquisition of more language. All three functions depend on sensation, perception, maturation, and learning, and all are influenced by motivation and emotion.

Language uses words as symbols for thinking and problem-solving. A *symbol* is anything that stands for something else. Language is symbolic in that words represent and substitute for aspects of experience. The use of symbols is central to human communication. Besides words, man communicates symbolically by other means, such as sign language, Morse code, shorthand, and written languages, which use gestures or graphic symbols to represent words or ideas. If you have taken a course in shorthand, you will immediately know what ∩ means. Try to figure it out from its grammatical context here. If you cannot, see the parenthetical sentence in the last line of the next paragraph.

Language is the most important and complex form of human symbolic communication. Behind every word is an idea, a concept for which the word stands. To all English-speaking people, "table" immediately brings to mind the characteristics of an object with a flat top surface and four legs. The word "table" merely represents or symbolizes the object. (∩ means "this.")

Although language is complex, we have all acquired it and use it without too much concern for its complexity or for the difficulties of language learning. Once we understand how ideas are formed, organized, and expressed, however, we will be better able to appreciate how profoundly our actions are affected by language, thinking, and problem-solving.

Language enables us to organize our experiences, recall past experiences, and imagine the future. It tells us about our environment-related behavior. Language makes possible problem-solving and creative thinking. As a system of communication, language is used to share concepts and ideas, as well as to convey the meaning of new experiences and perceptions.

FUNCTIONS OF LANGUAGE

Language serves man as a means of communication in two ways: among individuals (*intercommunication*), and within the individual (*intracommunication*). We use language in thinking as well as in verbal communication.

Communication among individuals relies on their acceptance of the same meanings of words and related symbols. Recent research has shown that differences among societies are often reflected in differences in their languages. Later in this chapter we will discuss this subject more fully.

Among people who speak the same language, the meaning of words may change, often creating an obstruction to communication. To be easily understood by another person, you need to employ words, phrases, and gestures that conform to his experience.

Psychologists once believed that such aspects of language study as the structural concerns of linguists were unrelated to their own discipline and too technical for practical application. This attitude has changed, and a new field of study, *psycholinguistics*, has developed. Psycholinguistics is the study of language acquisition and use. Psychologists are especially concerned with language as a stimulus that induces behavior; language can directly stimulate a particular response pattern, and it plays a crucial role in learning and thinking.

He'd rather talk than eat Language is a crucial part of man's behavior. Language is so important to man that his vocal apparatus appears to have evolved to the point where talking is anatomically favored over eating and breathing.

Lieberman and Crelin (1971) point out that man's vocal apparatus has evolved from a primitive ape-like form to its present anatomical arrangement with a wider and deeper pharynx, shorter jaw, and finely controlled vocal chords. They maintain that these evolutionary changes benefit man's vocal ability but make him less efficient in chewing, swallowing, and breathing.

STRUCTURE OF LANGUAGE

There are numerous languages other than the spoken and written language of words. All utilize signs and rules to represent objects or ideas, and you use many in your everyday living. You could not drive a car safely without understanding the language of traffic signs and lights. You could not play a game of cards unless you understood the marking on each card and its meaning in the game being played. For example, the ace of spades has different meanings to players of poker, bridge, and solitaire. There are some forms of language that have a distinct advantage over word languages in that they are universally understood. Musicians can all read the same musical score regardless of nationality; the symbolic language of mathematics is understood throughout the world. Figure 10.1 illustrates only a few of many different types of languages that have been evolved by man.

This chapter concentrates on spoken and written word language. Words offer the largest single system of symbols. (The English language alone consists of more than half a million words.) Words enhance the perception of sensory stimuli; they introduce variety and distinction into the individual's existence. The experience of learning words and of learning spoken language affects every aspect of a person's mental development and therefore his behavior.

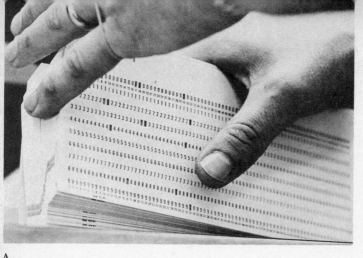

A

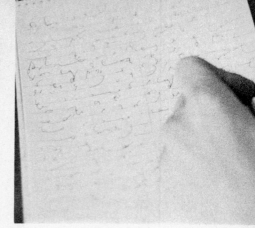

C

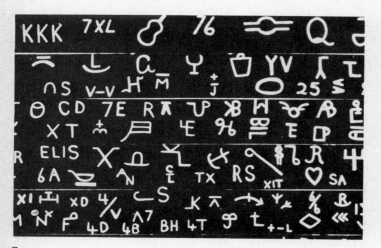

B

D

Figure 10.1   Some examples of sign languages that enable people to communicate. (A and B) Jan Lukas—Rapho Guillumette; (C) Beckwith Studios; (D) The Granger Collection.

Phonemes and morphemes

Every language is composed of two basic units, phonemes and morphemes. A *phoneme* is a class of sounds which speakers of a language identify as being linguistically similar. For example, the sound of /t/ in "take" and the sound of /t/ in "steak" are not exactly the same, but speakers of English identify these two sounds as linguistically similar. In English, then, the two sounds belong to the same phoneme. The English language has a total of 45 phonemes. The sounds of /b/ in "bay," /th/ in "think," and /i/ in "pit" are all phonemes. Other languages have different numbers of basic sound. The simplest language has 15 phonemes; the most complex, 85.

Recognizing phonemes "Vright, Zbroad, Vgtory." When you look at these combinations, you may at first think that they are either a foreign language or incorrect English. Once you are aware that they are typographical errors in English, you can guess what the words were meant to be.

/Vr/, /vg/, and /zb/ are not acceptable pho-

Language, thinking, problem-solving, and creativity   **266**

neme combinations in the English language. When phonemes are correctly combined in our language, they give it form and structure. In addition, the correct combination of phonemes seems to give even meaningless nonsense words some quality that makes them easier to remember.

Brown and Hildum (1956) learned that subjects found it easier to memorize and remember nonsense words that include correct phoneme combinations (for example, "phareves," "stroop," "skile") than nonsense words that did not include correct phoneme combinations ("zbax," "xrop," "gtbil"). Since both sets of words were meaningless, it is evident that correct phoneme combinations contribute a property to words (perhaps familiarity) that makes them easier to remember.

In English, certain phonemes are used more frequently than others; approximately nine phonemes comprise more than half the sounds we make in daily conversation. Consonant phonemes are used far more frequently than vowel phonemes. This is reflected in our alphabet, which contains slightly more than five times as many symbols for consonant sounds as for vowel sounds. Usually, English words begin with consonant phonemes, and of these initial-consonant words, slightly more than half begin with one of the five most frequent initial-consonant sounds.

Phonemes are not combined randomly; the number of English phoneme combinations is limited. No phoneme can appear with every other phoneme. For example, no English word begins with the phoneme combination /ng/; in English this combination of sounds occurs only at the end of a word. Yet the Bantu languages of Africa begin many words with the /ng/ phoneme combination.

Phonemes and learning to read American children often experience great difficulty in learning to read. Rozin, Poritsky, and Sotsky (1971) believed that this might be due to the inconsistencies between the spelling and the pronunciation of many English words. They gave lessons in Chinese to second-grade Philadelphia children who were failing reading. The children were taught the English meanings of 30 Chinese characters, including those for "mother," "house,"

"you," "see," "buy," "want," "big," "red," and "this."

The children who had not mastered English in one and a half years of schooling were able to read a Chinese sentence in the first ten minutes of tutoring. They learned five more new words within the next four minutes. In an average of four hours, they were able to read a story and understand it.

While phonemes are linguistically significant units of sound, morphemes are linguistically significant units of meaning. A *morpheme* is the smallest unit of language that has recognizable meaning. A morpheme should not be confused with a word. While many words are single morphemes, others are composed of several morphemes by combining prefixes, roots, and suffixes. For example, the word "joy" has one morpheme, but if we add the suffix "ful," the resulting word "joyful" is composed of two morphemes—the root meaning "joy" and the suffix meaning "full of." The word "berry," in contrast, is a single morpheme. Neither "ber" nor "ry" is linguistically meaningful.

Syntax

In any language, words are not combined randomly; they follow some kind of ordered pattern or structure. The way in which elements of language are combined into phrases, clauses, and sentences so as to convey meaning is called *syntax*. In some languages the rules of syntax are quite flexible; in English they are fairly rigid. A child may recognize the words "horse," "Tom," "rode," but he will not perceive meaning in a sequence of these words unless they are ordered according to our rules of syntax. He finds meaning in the sentence "Tom rode the horse," but, like any of us, he would be mystified by "Tom the rode horse."

In English, then, the order of words is crucial to the meaning of the sentence. A sequence of words such as "crumb ant big the carried the" is not a sentence, for it does not convey meaning. For this sequence to become meaningful, it must be reorganized so that the verb-object relationships are clear. The sequences "the big ant carried the crumb" or "the ant carried the big crumb" or "the crumb carried the big ant" are all meaningful because they conform to our rules of syntax. They tell us what is occurring—what is being done to what, or who is doing something to what.

If words were selected at random from the dictionary and strung together as a "sentence," we would be unable to attach a meaning to this jumble. A "sentence" constructed of random words is called a *zero-order approximation* of an English sentence. Several gradations have been devised between such word concoctions and structured sentences as a way to illustrate the development of word sequences from meaningless to meaningful language. A *first-order approximation* is a body of text that contains single words occurring at about the same frequency as they appear in normal use of the English language. A *second-order approximation* shows two words appearing together at a rate of frequency similar to the rate at which they are found in pairs in standard English. As the order progresses, we find words occurring in triple sequence, quadruple sequence, and so on to higher orders of approximation to spoken English. The higher the order, the easier it is to convey meaning. Table 10.1 presents a sample of approximations to normal English ranging from zero-order to fourth-order.

DEVELOPMENT AND ACQUISITION OF LANGUAGE

Speech mechanisms in human beings mature during the fetal stage and are ready for use at birth. Sound patterns begin to develop from the moment the neonate utters his first cries. The babbling sounds characteristic of infancy serve as exercises that train the muscles of the vocal cords, tongue, lips, and jaw for future use. As noted in Chapter 2, such babbling sounds may cover the entire range of vocal pronuncia-

tions and include sounds that are basic to other languages but may never be used in the language later learned by the infant. The infant's sound-making ability is soon restricted to those sounds that occur in his native tongue. He imitates his parents, who not only serve as models but positively reinforce the correct responses of their children.

Making babies babble To what extent can adult vocal stimulation modify infant babbling? Dodd (1972) investigated this question by exposing infants to short periods of vocal, social-vocal and normal social stimulation to see which, if any, infant vocalizations were changed.

After recording baseline measures of amounts and types of vocalization, the experimenter exposed her 9- to 12-month-old subjects either to a prerecorded tape of repetitions of various consonant plus vowel phonemes (vocal), to these same phonemes babbled by the experimenter while each subject was engaged in "frolic play" on her lap (social-vocal), or to normal playful interaction with an adult using only standard grammatical sentences. All experimental "treatments" lasted approximately 15 minutes. Postexperimental recorded measures were then obtained immediately and analyzed for length, frequency, variation of consonant and vowel, and total number of utterances.

Only the social-vocal experimental treatment had any significant effects, and those were limited to the frequency and length of consonant utterances. Interestingly, the types of consonants vocalized by the infants were unaffected, even though repetitions of 14 distinct consonant phonemes were used during the experimental stimulation. The investigator reasoned that the relative lack of effect on infants' phoneme repertoires may indicate that adult vocalization has a very limited influence on the prelinguistic babbling of infants.

By the time the infant is approximately 6 months old, he is able to reproduce several English phonemes. At about 9 months, he is sometimes able to repeat a few words. His vocabulary development is slow at first, but it soon gains speed. By about 15 to 18 months of age, the child's rate of word acquisition is remarkable. It has been estimated that the number of different morphemes known by an average child

Table 10.1   Word-order approximations[a]

Order	Example
Zero-order (words chosen at random from a dictionary)	Combat callous irritability migrates depraved temporal prolix alas pillory nautical
First-order (words chosen independently but with their probability of occurrence proportional to their frequency of occurrence in large samples of normal English text)	Day to is for they have proposed I the it materials of are its go studies the our of the following not over situation if the greater
Second-order (words chosen and paired in such a way that the frequency of appearance of each word is proportional to its frequency in following the word with which it is paired in large samples of meaningful English text)	Goes down here is not large feet are the happy days and so what is dead weight that many were constructed the channel was
Fourth-order (words chosen in such a way that the probability with which each word appears is proportional to the frequency with which it follows the three words preceding it in large samples of normal English text)	We are going to see him is not correct to chuckle loudly and depart for home

[a]After Miller (1951).

in the first grade is 7,500 (Carroll, 1964). This suggests that the child learns, on the average, four new morphemes a day from the age of 1 to 6 years.

Grammar

The acquisition of grammar (the rules of morphology and syntax) is a source of considerable controversy in psychology and linguistics. At one time it was generally agreed that a child learns to speak properly because his parents correct his errors and insist upon correct usage. Recent research contradicts this assumption. Brown and Hanlon (1970) found little indication that parents correct the grammatical errors of their children. More often the mother and father simply ignore the mistakes.

There is evidence that children begin to talk by using a kind of abbreviated speech often referred to as *telegraphic speech.* They use single words or pairs of words to convey the meaning of an entire sentence. A child may say "Cookie" to indicate that he wants one. He may say "All gone egg" to indicate that he has finished eating his egg. Table 10.2 shows a number of telegraphic or two-word sentences used by a child from age 19 to 22 months (Braine, 1963).

The sentences in Table 10.2 contain two kinds of words. Words such as "see," "do," "my," "bye-bye," and so forth are *pivot* words. Words such as "boy," "sock," "it," "mommy," "daddy," and so forth are *open* words. The open words appear alone or in combination with pivot words. They refer to concrete objects or events. The pivot words, on the other hand, are more

Table 10.2   Two-word sentences recorded from the vocalizations of a young-ster from age 19 to 22 months[a]

See boy	My mommy	Night-night office	All-gone shoe
See sock	My daddy	Night-night boat	All-gone vitamins
See hot	My milk		All-gone egg
		Pretty boat	All-gone lettuce
Do it	Bye-bye plane	Pretty fan	All-gone watch
Push it	Bye-bye man		
Close it	Bye-bye hot	More taxi	
Buzz it		More melon	

[a]From Braine (1963).

abstract. A pivot word such as "see" indicates that something is visible; "my" indicates possession; "pretty" indicates desirability; and "all-gone" indicates disappearance. Concrete open words are acquired more readily than the more abstract pivot words.

Theories of grammar acquisition

Language displays a high degree of regularity because of its grammatical structure. The question of how grammatical structure is developed, however, remains largely unanswered, although a number of explanations and opinions have been offered. The various viewpoints can be grouped into two broad categories—one emphasizing learning; the other, the concept of innate biological capacities.

Language in chimps Man's ability to communicate verbally and conceptually has long been considered a primary adaptive achievement. Yet there is a great deal we do not know about how children learn language. We do not know whether certain linguistic principles are innate or learned, or whether other species have any potential for abstract communication. In their search for information in the field of linguistics, scientists have been using chimpanzees in experiments involving conceptual ability and gesturing. The chimpanzee is considered an excellent subject because of its relatively high intelligence, its similarity to the human child in behavior, and its fondness for human contact, a trait that facilitates experimental handling (Gardner and Gardner, 1969).

Experimental studies of language in chimps are particularly interesting. David Premack's experiments (1971) have touched on the very nature of language itself, while the studies of the Gardners have explored the possibilities of nonvocal communication. Premack was primarily interested in determining how successfully chimps can be taught to use linguistic concepts, ranging from simple words to naming and classifying objects, to complex "if-then" sentences. The chimp Sarah was first conditioned to associate plastic symbols with objects; for example, a piece of blue plastic meant "apple." Through repitition and a series of rewards, Sarah was taught to master not only single words but combinations of four elements representing words, each in its proper syntactical order (Figure 10.2). The ability to use the correct symbols to form "Mary give apple Sarah" won the chimp an apple.

Sarah also showed a marked ability to answer questions of "same or different," a step on the way to the general classification of objects. She displayed little difficulty in transferring her knowledge of the training symbols to unfamiliar but similar objects. Sarah was able, with the proper training, to apply the concept of "red" to both apples and cherries. Though she had some difficulty with the concept "is," even changes in syntax did not prevent her from comprehending.

The most significant finding of this experiment was that Sarah seemed to understand the linguistic principle that symbols stand for actual things—in effect, the concept of words. Premack concluded that there is probably an innate ability to symbolize in higher vertebrates that facilitates the learning of language.

Figure 10.2 (A) Sentences spelled out in Sarah's plastic symbols. The chimp had to get each element in the proper sequence to be rewarded. (B) Tests devised to teach chimpanzees the names of objects. Both positive and negative examples are used. (David Premack)

A

"Apple" is the name of apple.

"Banana" is not the name of apple.

B

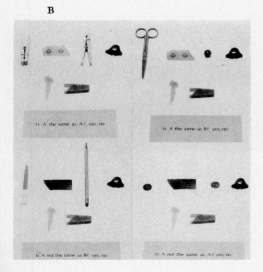

Is A the same as A? yes no

Is A the same as B? yes no

Is A not the same as B? yes no

Is A not the same as A? yes no

The Gardners (1969) relied on the ability of their chimp Washoe to learn gestures from the American sign language of the deaf. This method was used because chimpanzees lack the ability to vocalize but are extremely adept in the use of their hands. Many methods of training were used, including the encouragement of random gestures and imitation of the trainers' gestures.

This training enabled Washoe to learn 30 signals in 22 months, and the rate of learning became more rapid as time passed. As in the Premack study, the Gardners found their chimp subject capable of transferring to similar objects the signs for the objects used in teaching her. By the end of 22 months, Washoe was connecting two or three gestures to form phrases that she had not been taught (Figure 10.3).

Experimental work with chimps is currently being pursued at various research centers around the world (Goodall, 1971).

Learning The emphasis on learning as the primary source of grammar acquisition is based on the analysis of language according to the principles of classical and operant conditioning. Staats (1968), adopting the position of Skinner, suggests that the child learns words by the process of differential reinforcement. He is reinforced for pronouncing an approximation of a word, and, by successive approximations and reinforcement, he learns to pronounce it correctly. He is also reinforced for using words appropriately. Thus, he learns to say "water" when he sees or wants water, "dog" when he sees a dog, "rain" when it is raining, and so on.

Staats also suggests that word meanings are acquired through a form of classical conditioning. A word is meaningless until it has been paired with some other stimulus that elicits a particular response. The word "cookie" acquires meaning when it is associated with actual cookies; and the word "dog" becomes meaningful when paired with live dogs or pictures of dogs.

According to the learning view, basic sentence structures are acquired when the child imitates those around him and is reinforced for making correct grammatical responses. Basic grammatical habits become established because certain sequences of words are conditioned. This

Figure 10.3 *(A) Washoe uses signs to name objects, for example, "sweet" identifies the lollipop. (B) Washoe seriously contemplates the woolen cap she is asked to identify as "hat." (Beatrice T. Gardner and R. Allen Gardner) (C) Lana answers a question of researcher Timothy Gill on a computer console at Yerkes Primate Research Center, Atlanta. The researcher, outside the room, asks Lana a question by pressing the symbols on his console for the words "What name of this." He also holds up a candy. (D) The chimp answers by pressing symbols "M&M name of this." She is rewarded with the candy. (The New York Times)*

A

B

C

D

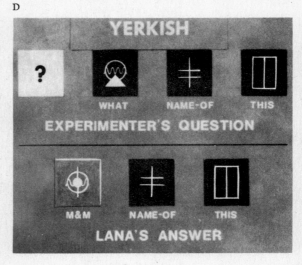

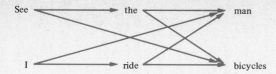

Figure 10.4   *Some learned privileges of occurrence.*

conditioning results in certain allowable word sequences (Brown & Berko, 1960). For example, nouns can follow articles such as "the" or "a" and can occur as the objects or subjects of verbs. Only certain types of words can be connected to certain other types of words: adjectives are not connected to verbs; verbs are not connected to other verbs. Figure 10.4 provides an illustration of the types of interconnections that are allowable in a series of words. The figure shows that certain interconnections are not permissible. For example, "Ride I bicycle" may be understandable, but it is not grammatically permissible because the verb "ride" does not usually have the privilege of preceding the pronoun "I." The sentence "The see man" is neither understandable nor permissible. Telegraphic sentences such as "See bicycle" and "I man" are permissible although not representative of good adult grammar.

Innate capacities   The view that language behavior is determined by innate underlying structures is also finding considerable support (Chomsky, 1967, 1968; McNeil, 1966, 1970). It is argued that the fundamental structure of language is universal and as such is based on the innate capacities of the human being.

The emphasis on underlying structure and innate capacity has been fostered by the writings of Noam Chomsky (1968). According to Chomsky's observations, all normal persons share a basic knowledge which he calls *language competence.* Thus, we hear a sentence for the first time, and without knowing what all the words mean, we recognize it as a sentence and perceive

that it has some meaning. A good example of this is the first stanza of Lewis Carroll's "Jabberwocky" (1872). Youngsters who hear the poem, with its wonderful nonsense words, are able to derive meaning from it:

'Twas brillig and the slithy toves
    Did gyre and gimble in the wabe;
All mimsy were the borogroves,
    And the Mome raths outgrabe.

Chomsky maintains that every sentence has both a *surface structure* and a *deep structure.* The surface structure is what we see or hear. The deep structure involves the fundamental grammatical relationships, for example, between nouns and verbs. It also involves the intended meaning—the thought that the surface-structure sentence is trying to convey. The relationship between deep and surface structures may be seen in the following sentences:

1 Tom rode the horse.
2 The horse was ridden by Tom.

The surface structure of these two sentences is different, but their deep structure is the same. One is an active sentence and the other is a passive sentence; the underlying noun-verb relationships, however, convey the same meaning.

According to Chomsky, the child learns to use *transformational rules* to convert deep structures into the specific surface structures of the language used in his culture. By means of these transformational rules, "Tom rode the horse," for instance, may be transformed into "The horse was ridden by Tom," but not into "Tom was ridden by the horse" or "Tom ridden the horse." Chomsky suggests that we know how to use these rules in the same way we know how to tie our shoes or ride a bicycle or walk; although we usually cannot state the rules, we use them effectively.

The deep structures of sentences are said to be universal, but the surface structures are specific to each language. It has been observed that children between the ages of 18 months and 2 years who live in various parts of the world, and whose parents speak different languages, form sentences that are grammatically similar (Brown, 1973). Youngsters at this age seem to speak deep structure. As they acquire transformational rules, their surface-structure language appears, and with it various learned differences in language.

Meaning

We recognize that a child has acquired the meaning of a word when he responds to it in some understandable manner or uses it in a calculated way. Parents are delighted when their child first says "dada," even though the child is unaware of any meaning in his utterance. It is just a pleasant sound in his random babbling. But this particular sound is reinforced by parental praise, encouragement, and repetition. The child keeps repeating "dada" because of his parents' favorable reaction. Eventually, he learns that the word is positively reinforced primarily when his father comes into view. Finally, perhaps after several weeks, the child learns that "dada" means his father. He has acquired the *meaning* of a word.

The meaning of words is directly related to their order, or *sequence*. The body of text in which words appear is the *context*. Meaning and context are so closely interrelated that one implies the other. To define words precisely, it is necessary to know the context in which they are actually used.

Words may acquire various meanings. When a word has more than one meaning, its appropriate meaning will depend on the context in which it is used. Table 10.3 lists 15 meanings of the word "fast."

Because a word may acquire multiple meanings, word usage changes and old words often take on meanings that are very different from the original one. Most of us understand, "Cool it. We have the bread. Let's split." In

Table 10.3 The many meanings of the word "fast"[a]
A person is *fast* when he can run rapidly.
But he is also *fast* when he is tied down and cannot run at all.
And colors are *fast* when they do not run.
One is *fast* when he moves in bad company.
But this is not the same thing as playing *fast* and loose.
A racetrack is *fast* when it is in excellent running condition.
A friend is *fast* when he is loyal.
A watch is *fast* when it is ahead of time.
To be *fast* asleep is to be deep in sleep.
To be *fast by* is to be near.
To *fast* is to refrain from eating.
A *fast* may be a period of noneating or a mooring line for a ship.
Camera film is *fast* when it is sensitive (to light).
But bacteria are *fast* when they are insensitive (to antiseptics).

[a]After W. V. Haney, *Communication patterns and incidents*, p. 48. Homewood, Ill.: Richard D. Irwin, 1960.

1940, these remarks did not have the same colloquial meaning, and there are probably many people over 40 today who do not understand them.

Words acquire different meanings in different regions. Few people outside New York City know what a "chocolate egg cream" is (a chocolate soda made with soda water and chocolate syrup, containing neither eggs nor cream). In Massachusetts, a "tonic" is a soda, and in the Midwest, a soda is a "pop." If you stopped at an ice cream counter in Boston, just 40 miles from Providence, Rhode Island, and asked for a "coffee cabinet," the clerk probably would not know what you were talking about. But in Providence a soda jerk would know immediately that you wanted a coffee milk shake with coffee ice cream.

Special interests, as well as geography, can be a source of special vocabularies. For instance, members of the same professional or vocational group tend to develop their own private language, called a *jargon*, in which they communicate with each other. There is also the special vocabulary of sports. A nonfan would certainly be confused by the following jargon-filled conversation between two football fans: "That red dogging certainly psyched our scrambler." "Yes, but he still got us close enough for the toe to split their uprights three times." Jargon may arise to save time in communicating, but ultimately it serves a kind of reinforcing function; the users of the jargon feel special because they are part of an "in-group" that uses terms outsiders do not understand.

Denotative and connotative meaning When words represent objects, events, or relationships, they *denote* the things for which they stand. The word "school," for example, denotes a set of stimuli with particular objective characteristics. The *denotative* meaning of the word "school" refers to the objectively identifiable set of stimuli.

Words may also carry additional meaning attached to particular conditioning experiences. A word such as "school" may remind some individuals of negative or uncomfortable experiences and therefore has acquired emotional connotations. The *connotative* meaning is the evaluative or emotional responses that a word elicits in addition to its denotative meaning. Connotative meanings frequently obscure or confuse communication, because the connotative features of a word depend upon individual experiences. Words such as "Democrat," "Republican," "Communist," "sex," "drugs," and so forth tend to evoke a wide variety of connotations.

Language and the social environment

Regardless of which theory of language development we espouse, we need to recognize that language is largely a social process. We learn language in settings where people play the major role. Their words become our words, and their manner of speech becomes our manner of speech. In today's world the number and variety of people who influence our language learning is very large. We read and hear the words of many different persons, view television, watch movies, and in general are exposed to a wide variety of people. These experiences extend the range of our language proficiency.

We speak, read, write, and listen because those around us do so. Our social environment shapes our language by providing models for us to imitate and reinforcement when we make the appropriate language responses. We learn language as a means of communicating; consequently, we learn to report what we see, hear, feel, and so on, in an orderly way, so that what we say will be understood. We learn to be consistent in the use of words, for unless we are consistent, we will not be understood. Also, the people we come into contact with reinforce our use of language as a substitute for impulsive action. We learn to stop and think, and in that way to avoid serious mistakes in action.

"Newspeak" George Orwell, in his famous science fiction novel of *1984*, describes a dictatorship that takes over the minds and souls of the people, devising a new language called "Newspeak":

The purpose of Newspeak was not only to provide a medium of expression for the world-view and mental habits proper to the devotees of Ingsoc, but to make all other modes of thought impossible. It was intended that when Newspeak had been adopted once and for all and Oldspeak forgotten, a heretical thought—that is, a thought diverging from the principles of Ingsoc—should be literally unthinkable, at least so far as thought is dependent on words. Its vocabulary was so constructed as to give exact and often very subtle expression to every meaning that a Party member could properly wish to express, while excluding all other meanings and also the possibility of arriving at them by indirect methods. This was done partly by the invention of new words, but chiefly by eliminating undesirable words and by stripping such words as remained of unorthodox meanings, and so far as possible, of all secondary meanings whatever. To give a single example. The word *free* still existed in Newspeak, but it could only be used in such statements as "This dog is free

from lice" or "This field is free from weeds."
It could not be used in its old sense of "politically free," or "intellectually free," since political and intellectual freedom no longer existed
even as concepts, and were therefore of necessity nameless.

THINKING

Thinking, because so much of it is hidden
from objective observation, is one of the most
interesting and difficult areas studied by psychologists. We are all curious about thought processes, at times trying to be spectators of our own
thought processes. Self-observation, however, is
difficult and unreliable. We cannot hold our
thoughts still while we observe them because
so much of our own thinking is a free-flowing,
spontaneous form of inner communication—
communication that we carry on with ourselves.

While much of our thinking is personal
and involves such seemingly nondirected activities as daydreaming, even more of our thinking
is provoked by the environment around us and
directed toward specific purposes. This kind of
thinking is referred to as *reasoning*.

Although the thinking process is not overt,
many psychologists consider it a form of behavior. Thinking deals with the symbolic level of
experience, be it ongoing, re-created, or imagined
experience. Most psychologists believe that individuals are constantly thinking; even when they
are not influenced by immediate, specific stimuli, they are formulating ideas, symbols, and
representations of events. In this respect, thinking transcends the simple stimulus-response pattern characteristic of most behavior patterns.

In this section, instead of offering elaborate definitions of types of thinking, we shall
concentrate on the relationship between language and thinking, as well as the learning principles involved in concept formation, an area
in which psychologists have made many discoveries.

As we have noted, language plays an important
role in thinking. More than any other symbolic
system, thinking involves *verbal manipulation*.

Although most of our ideas are formulated
with the use of words, some thinking evidently
occurs without their use. Many scientists, especially mathematicians, claim to think without
words, using scientific notations instead. Some
persons are convinced that they create thoughts
without words even though they cannot describe
the process. Einstein once said that he dealt
directly with images in his thinking, not words.

Obviously, some simple thought processes
can be completed without words. Animals engage in behavior that apparently requires thinking or some similar process that does not involve
the use of words. A monkey can learn a sequence
in which he finds food under a box at his right
(R) or a box at his left (L), even when the sequence is as complex as RR LL RR LL RR. To
do this the monkey has to have some system
for keeping track of his last response, since he
must make two responses to the left (or to the
right) before switching.

Before the onset of speech, human beings,
too, carry on simple thought processes. Children
usually do not learn to organize their thoughts
until they are about 3½ years old; generally, they
are not able to give verbal descriptions until they
are nearly 5 years old. Once they reach this stage
of development, however, nearly all their thinking is in verbal terms.

The language used in thinking that we do
not voice is called *silent thinking*. In silent
thinking, we adopt our own language shorthand;
we abbreviate forms and skip transitional and
logical sequences. In silent thinking, we are apparently quite able to deal with incomplete and
otherwise vague language. Our silent language
shorthand differs greatly from the language we
use to communicate with others. However, often
when we speak to others (friends, relatives) with
whom we have common experiences, we are able

to transfer much of our silent thinking shorthand directly into a kind of verbal shorthand. Husbands and wives, brothers and sisters, best friends, and so on communicate in this way easily and naturally. With outsiders and strangers, our communicative language becomes much more formal.

According to the *motor theory of thinking*, we, in effect, talk to ourselves physically. Although we usually do not vocalize our thoughts, we do make covert vocal responses while we are thinking. Our speech muscles are active when we are thinking. Supporting this theory, studies have shown that when electrodes are placed on the tongues of relaxed subjects, no muscular activity is detected. When the subject is asked to think of a poem or a prose passage, his tongue muscles show activity, even though he is not actually speaking.

This motor theory also applies to muscular activity in other parts of the body. In experiments in which electrodes are attached to arm muscles, subjects display excessive muscular activity in their wired arm when asked to think that they are lifting that arm. When asked to imagine that their nonwired arm is being raised, the wired arm shows no muscular activity. Thus, if thought relates to a bodily function, the muscles of that organ become active. (Try thinking of the word "bubble" with your mouth open.)

Images are important to the thinking process. Their interaction with words enables the thinker to construct ideas. When a problem has to be thought out, it generally involves some combination of these two factors. Occasionally, the individual who is exceptionally good at creating images may find that talent overpowers his ability to tackle other problems. As valuable as imagery may be, when it dominates the thinking process to excess it may interfere with abstract and original ideas.

Does thinking ever occur without images? Some psychologists believe that imageless thought is possible, but there is no conclusive proof. Proponents of the *theory of imageless thought* believe that thinking can occur on a subconscious level, and that some thinking is controlled automatically by an individual's state of readiness. There is some evidence that we may sometimes think without images, but whether our thoughts are determined by preexisting images or mechanical responses is still debatable.

Learning of concepts

The most common form of thinking involves the formation of *concepts*, enabling the individual to classify his experiences. A concept is an abstraction of an aspect of a group of objects or events common to each object or event. An assortment of objects such as a glass of water, a bottle of wine, and a container of milk may be grouped together by the concept of "liquid"— a characteristic common to all the objects. Should a loaf of bread be added, the concept "liquid" would no longer be appropriate. A new concept would be required; in this case, the objects might be reorganized as "things to eat or drink."

An integral part of the learning process is thinking in terms of concepts. Concepts may be concrete or abstract; any object may belong to more than one concept. Thus, a loaf of bread on a table with the liquids mentioned earlier belongs to the concept "food," but a loaf of bread on a table with a shoe box and a block of wood belongs to the concept "rectangular." A poster for peace and a poster for war are each part of the concept of "posters," although they propagandize opposing concepts.

Children begin the process of concept formation with relatively concrete notions. It is not always easy to judge whether a child has successfully formed a concept. However, we assume that if a child is able to select and identify objects correctly, then he has mastered the particular concept being tested. According to Jean Piaget, the ability to form concepts occurs in stages. Piaget's stages of cognitive development (see Chapter 2) were developed from his observations of children.

Piaget was able to determine that infants cannot conceptualize movement or spatial position. He found that an infant does not possess the ability to distinguish among objects that require organization according to the concept of distance. The child will reach for, grasp, and perceive objects in his visual field as if they were all the same distance away. A very young child cannot recognize that a toy in one position can be moved to another position and still be the same toy. He sees no relationship between objects with the same characteristics.

To develop concepts, children must learn to discriminate among the abstract qualities of an object. For example, when the parent says "bottle" and simultaneously touches or points to the bottle, the child learns to associate the object (the bottle) with the word. This association not only helps him learn the word but also starts him toward learning the concept. If the child is repeatedly presented with objects that bear the same label, he soon learns the concept, even though each object may be slightly different from the others. Give the child a round-necked bottle, a square-necked bottle, a tall bottle, and a short bottle, and he will eventually learn that all these slightly different objects belong to the concept "bottle."

The child's earliest concepts result from visual experiences. As the child matures, he learns to distinguish among more abstract properties. Thus, daffodils and tulips may at first be the only flowers he recognizes, but as his experiences expand, he will also call gardenias flowers. A child's maturational schedule thus greatly determines his ability to perceive and identify concepts, but once he understands some basic concepts, he is able to learn new ones rather rapidly.

As an individual's ability to conceptualize increases, he becomes less dependent upon strictly perceptual experiences to stimulate his thought processes. Eventually, when he can "see" beyond his own perception of an object, his ability to think conceptually has fully matured. As might be expected, this ability results from the individual's increased experiences. Thus, young children who have had the advantage of a great variety of sensory stimuli frequently exhibit this higher level of thinking despite their age. Especially in mathematical learning, some children have no problem understanding higher-level concepts. Mathematics provides a vivid illustration of concept formation through the use of abstraction.

Disordered thinking

The words we use and the structure of our language play an important role in what we think and how we think. Grossly misusing words or treating them as if they were real objects and events and not merely symbolic representations of objects and events is symptomatic of disordered thinking. Consider the following excerpt from the diary of a patient in a psychiatric hospital. The patient, at the time he wrote the diary, was a 30-year-old high school teacher who was hospitalized when his behavior became too disorganized for him to function properly. The section shown here provides an example of disordered thinking. (More excerpts from this diary will be presented in Chapter 13.)

Friday, September 12: I arose early. Today, Dad, my sister, and I went to town to the Veterans' Hospital. I had an appointment with a psychiatrist. I was rather interested in the trip as it offered some possibility of finding out what was wrong with me and effecting a cure. On the way my mind started playing tricks with words and sentences; i.e., I don't think I need to see a psychiatrist. I don't think; I need to see a psychiatrist. My stars! I don't think. I need to see a psychiatrist. I don't seem to be thinking too well this morning. I'll try to think this through again and think my way out. I'll change the wording. I think I don't need to see a psychiatrist. Good. I think. I don't need to see a psychiatrist. Obviously, I think I'm all right. I think. I'm all right. I'll check that first idea again about seeing the psychiatrist. If I leave out the negative, then there should be the opposite meaning. So, here goes: I think I need to see a psychiatrist. I think; I need to see a psychiatrist. I think. I need to see a psychiatrist. Horrors! Regardless of whether I think or whether I don't, I need to see a psychiatrist. I'm tired of thinking. I suppose there is something wrong with me. I am not getting things very straight. Trying to think doesn't seem to help.

By treating words as real objects or events, this patient indicates that he has lost his grasp of reality. He no longer understands himself or his environment; he cannot "see" beyond the words themselves.

PROBLEM-SOLVING

Psychologists regard thinking as a process that enables the individual to find solutions to problems by means of his past experience and learning. Problem-solving is usually defined as an advanced stage of thinking arising out of the individual's need to seek a solution to a situation that he has never before encountered. Once a problem arising from a new situation is solved, the individual transfers this learning experience to his repertoire of everyday thinking. It will never again be a problem of the magnitude that it was at the time it first occurred.

Benefits of the cradle gym The ability to solve problems is rooted in early experiences, according to Dennenberg, Woodcock, and Rosenberg (1968), who tested the effect of environment in infancy on later problem-solving behavior. Their subjects were rats who were placed in either an enriched environment or the usual impoverished environment of the laboratory cage. The enriched environment included food scattered on the floor and toys such as a block, a can, a ramp, and a running wheel. The impoverished environment contained nothing but a food container and a water bottle. The experiment started at birth. Some rats lived in the enriched environment from birth until they were weaned; some lived in the enriched environment after weaning until they were 50 days old; some lived in the enriched environment from birth until they were

50 days old; and some were never exposed to the enriched environment. After all training was completed, an interval of a year was allowed to elapse. This period is almost one-half the life expectancy of the rat. The rats were then tested on a series of problem-solving mazes.

Results showed that the rats that lived in the enriched environment either before or after weaning made fewer errors in solving the problems than did the rats raised in bare cages. And subjects that lived in the enriched environments both before and after weaning did best of all—particularly when compared to subjects who had enrichment only prior to weaning. The authors concluded that early enrichment brings about permanent improvement in ability. Moreover, enrichment is most effective when the nervous system has been given a little time to develop after birth. Publicity given to this finding, and to others like it, may account for the rise in the use of mobiles and toys where infants in cribs can see and touch them.

Trial and error

One method of solving a problem is by trying all the seemingly appropriate solutions one by one until the correct solution appears. This *trial-and-error method* can be used to solve the simpler problems, those that do not really involve thinking. For example, a landlord gives you the keys to a new house, complete with several entrances, a garage door, porch doors, and inside locking doors. You have the chain of keys in your hand as you approach the front door. The immediate problem is to find the key that opens the front door. With no other idea and no clues as to the correct key, you randomly slip each key into each lock. Thus, you are using trial-and-error behavior to find the correct solution to your problem. At each door you will be faced with the same problem, finding the correct key, until only one door and one key are left.

Trial and error may also be conducted *covertly.* That is, you think through the possible solutions and then apply your *covert* solution to *overt* behavior. Suppose that you cannot find your set of keys. Instead of searching the house for them, you can think about where you might have placed them. In such a case, your thinking or visualizing is equal to, and perhaps superior to, the method of overt trial and error. We often save time and energy in problem-solving by utilizing covert behavior.

Gap-filling

Thinking entails a series of successive responses; when we think, our responses (ideas) often rush ahead and leave gaps between them. For example, when we think through a problem—such as how to get to Anita's house now that the main road to her town is closed—we usually examine alternate solutions in large-scale terms without worrying about details. We might recall that Highway 46 goes to her town. When we decide to take that route, we may then have to fill in the gap between our point of departure and Highway 46, and so on.

Sir Frederick Bartlett, a distinguished English psychologist, regarded gap-filling as an important tool in efficient thinking. He pointed out that intelligent people are able to use a minimum amount of information to develop a sequence of ideas leading to the solution of a problem. Some typical examples of the type of gap-filling problems used by Bartlett (1958) are shown in Figure 10.5A. (You will find the solutions to these problems in Fig. 10.5B.)

Processes that influence problem-solving

Many processes are involved in problem-solving. They all influence the individual on his way to a solution. Each individual is influenced by his own previous experience as well as by the language he uses.

It is difficult to assess the role of prior experience in a particular problem-solving situation. We know that prior experience can help the individual solve a new problem through positive transfer of training. However, prior experience may also hinder his ability to solve a problem by preventing a fresh, imaginative, and immediate solution.

Language, also an important influence, interacts in problem-solving much as it does in the process of thinking. It affects our ability to understand a problem and to think through a solution to that problem.

In this section we will describe the basic problem-solving processes. Then we will discuss the concept of a *decision tree*, the factors of *habit* and *set* (prior experience), and language as they influence problem-solving.

Steps in problem-solving Most people are not aware of how they deal with problems, probably because they concentrate, rather, on the specific details of the problem before them. It appears that the problem-solver functions on two levels of thought—the general process on one level, and the actual problem on another. The difference between the two levels is a matter of degree rather than kind.

Effects of a frontal lobectomy Researchers have long disagreed about the extent to which man's frontal lobes are responsible for intelligent behavior, thinking, and problem-solving. Milner (1964) recently clarified this issue, however, with her reports of impaired performance after operations for the removal of damaged frontal-lobe tissue. (The operation is termed a "frontal lobectomy.")

Milner's subjects were patients she could test both before and after their operations. Her control subjects, also tested pre- and postoperatively, underwent surgery for lesions in other parts of the brain. Each subject was given the Wisconsin Card-Sorting Test, which requires that cards be sorted according to the form, color, or number of objects pictured. Since the sorting problem changes periodically—and suddenly—throughout the test, subjects must continually reestablish appropriate strategies after a problem shift with a minimum of cues: after a shift, the subject is told only that each response guided by his old strategy is "wrong," and he must then vary his strategy until he is told he is "right."

While the postoperative error rate was somewhat reduced for control subjects (presumably because of practice at the task), frontal lobectomy subjects showed much higher error rates than the controls. Analysis of the data revealed that these new errors came almost entirely from subjects' preservation of old, no longer appropriate response strategies after the experimenter indicated a shift in the problem. Although subjects were often able to verbalize their recognition of the need for some new strategy, they frequently persevered in their "wrong" responses despite the experimenter's continued feedback. Consequently, the investigator reasoned that frontal lesions do not affect intelligence as much as they affect the individual's ability to shift his problem-solving strategies to meet constantly changing environmental demands.

The amount of data now available on the seemingly automatic function of problem-solving is sufficient to offer a meaningful description of the steps involved. These steps should provide clues to your own methods of problem-solving. Wallas (1926) emphasized the processes of creating ideas that contribute to the solution of a problem, identifying four steps toward reaching the solution to a problem.

1 *Preparation*—When faced with a problem, an individual must first study it and recognize its elements. The *stage of preparation* consists, first of familiarizing oneself with the problem and then assuming an exploratory attitude to allow different ideas to emerge. Many possible solutions are considered and rejected until only a few possible solutions remain.

2 *Incubation*—The *incubation stage* is characterized by inactivity. The individual has narrowed the solution down to a few possibilities, and he now allows his thoughts to rest. He is not aware of the incubation stage as he progresses toward a solution. Some psychologists assert that sleep is a period of incubation, a

Figure 10.5A   Gap-filling problems.

A   Look at the terminal words and fill in the gap in any way that you think is indicated.

A, By, Cow,   Horrible

B   From the words shown below complete the vertical arrangement indicated by the two words "Erase" and "Fate." Take "Erase" as the middle word in the column. Not all the words shown need be used.

A, Gate, No, Duty, In, Cat, Bo, Ear, O, Travel, Erase, Bath, Get, Ho, Fate

Erase
Fate

view supported by the claims of many scientists that they arrived at important theories by allowing their ideas to incubate during sleep. The mathematician René Descartes claimed, for example, that he developed some important ideas while dreaming. Many scientists and writers keep a pad of paper by their bedside. Sleep is certainly not the only incubating activity; other behavior unrelated to active problem-solving can also serve as a medium for so-called unconscious thinking.

3 *Illumination*—The sudden realization of a solution or the ability to renew pursuit of the problem after incubation is known as *illumination*. Illumination is similar to insight. Individuals are often confident that they have solved their problem during the illumination stage.

4 *Verification*—During the fourth and last stage in problem-solving, the solution is checked and tested. This step is considered critical by scientists, who rely on tests to verify their insights. In other situations, a solution may be verified either by an actual test or by logical argument. In mathematics, a proof is the symbolic verification of the theorem. In everyday life, most of us put our solutions to the test simply by seeing if they do what we want them to do.

The decision tree In solving a problem, we often move from a general understanding of what must be done to a general solution and finally to a specific solution. This pattern, known as the *decision tree*, was defined by the German psychologist K. Duncker. His experiment with University of Berlin students is now a classic, contributing much to the understanding of problem-solving.

Duncker required his students to solve a medical problem that he had devised. (Figure 10.6 schematizes the original diagram used by Duncker.) The problem: A human patient had a stomach tumor that could not be removed by surgery. Radiation rays could definitely destroy the tumor, if applied at an extremely high intensity. However, the intense radiation would destroy the healthy tissues in the path of the rays as well as the unaffected tissue surrounding the tumor itself. What course of action could be taken to treat this patient?

Duncker had his students think aloud so that he could follow their approaches to a solution. After observing the thinking processes of his students, he created the decision tree. Figure 10.7 shows Duncker's description of the three stages of solution: general, functional, and specific. The tree structure shows growth from the original problem (how to kill the tumor by radiation without destroying healthy tissue), which serves the function of a trunk from which all other solutions branch off. The first level of solutions, the general solutions, spring from the problem itself and serve as a basis for the functional solutions that arise from them. As depicted in Figure 10.7, more than one functional solution can arise from a general solution. Each

Figure 10.5B   Solutions to the gap-filling problems in Figure 10.5A

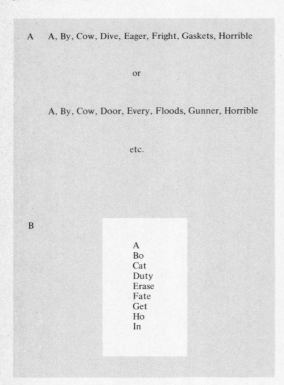

A   A, By, Cow, Dive, Eager, Fright, Gaskets, Horrible

or

A, By, Cow, Door, Every, Floods, Gunner, Horrible

etc.

B

A
Bo
Cat
Duty
Erase
Fate
Get
Ho
In

Figure 10.6 *Schematic of Duncker's presentation to his students. The radiation machine is represented by the figure at the left. The stomach tumor is indicated within the shape representing the body. Rays emitted from the machine will follow a straight path, as indicated by the arrow.*

functional solution gives rise to a specific solution that is an application of the functional solution. Duncker's students examined their specific solutions one by one. Those that were impractical or impossible were dismissed. Finally a specific solution was reached that appeared to solve the problem.

The stages of a decision tree are used to organize problem-solving. When solving a problem, we do not usually note each stage as we pass through it, even though we do go through each stage.

Habit, set, and functional fixedness Through the course of his experience, the individual ac-

quires *habits* that continually interplay with his behavior. We have already noted that past learning and one's set to respond are generally helpful to learning. However, in problem-solving, habitual behavior and set may tend to interfere rather than help.

Our habits allow us to function efficiently in most routine circumstances. But in problem-solving, we are not confronted with routine circumstances. The novel situation demands a novel solution.

Consider the problem of hammering a nail into a delicate painted surface. You have only a large hammer at hand. Your problem is to obtain a smaller hammer, so you postpone hammering the nail until you have had a chance to go to the hardware store. Had habit not been so strong, you would have been able to solve the problem by any of several acceptable methods: placing a wooden block against the head of the nail so that the hammer hits the wood and the wood hits the nail; placing a cloth around the hammer head; using the heel of a shoe instead of a hammer; or using any one of a number of other tools.

Closely related to the influence of habit is the influence of set, which was discussed earlier

Figure 10.7 *Duncker's decision tree, showing the stages of solution, from general to functional to specific.*

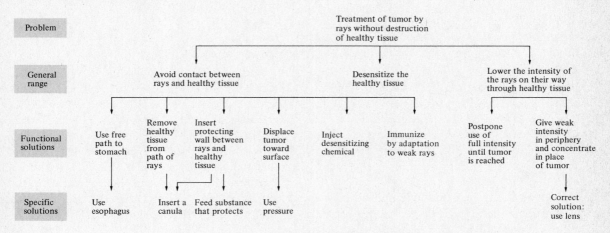

(Chapter 5). Set is the way that an individual is primed, or made ready, to receive a particular stimulus. If someone hands you a textbook, you expect to open it and find printed pages; you are set to find the usual kind of type and illustrations. However, you might discover that it is full of blank pages of different colors. Because you were set to expect one thing and something else appeared, you must readjust your perceptions; you must decide how to respond to this new object.

Functional fixedness is another aspect of habit and set. This process prevents an individual from realizing that a familiar object may have uses other than those already known to him. The individual behaves as if the object has only one use, the one he knows. For example, suppose you move into a new apartment and need something to hide a window. You do not have any curtains, but you have sheets, towels, a blanket, many cartons, and some posters. If you are thinking only in terms of curtains for a window, your functional fixedness may prevent you from arriving at a solution to your immediate problem. If you are less fixed in your thinking, you might choose to hang one of the posters over the window, covering the glass and giving you privacy.

Role of language in problem-solving The individual confronted by a problem often does not realize that some relatively simple rules of language can help him to reach a solution. He is aware that he uses language in his thinking, but he may not be aware of how he uses language to reason out his activities and to relate elements of a problem consistently and intelligently. Reason is a characteristic of logic, although logic is far more than an exercise in reasoning. *Logic* is a formal discipline that applies simple rules to reasoning. Language used in logic is often symbolic. The construction of a sentence is, to the logician, a way of recognizing truth (reality) from untruth (fallacy).

Logical thinking, if properly and conscientiously applied to everyday situations, can prove helpful in solving problems. Logic enables the perplexed individual to test his reasoning, to judge for himself whether or not he has arrived at an acceptable solution.

Traditionally, logical thinking is explained in terms of syllogisms. A syllogism is a logical sequence that derives a truth from a relationship between a major and a minor premise. Thus, we may say:

1 All birds fly.
2 A sparrow is a bird.
3 Therefore, a sparrow flies.

The conclusion (A sparrow flies) follows logically from the major premise (All birds fly) and the minor premise (A sparrow is a bird). Assuming that our major premise is correct, the conclusion is true. In logic, a conclusion that stems from a false major premise is untrue factually, although it is reached by a sound procedure of reasoning. Thus, conclusions can be true and sound or untrue and sound (logically). For example, we may syllogize the following:

1 All animals that live in water are fish.
2 The porpoise lives in water.
3 Therefore, the porpoise is a fish.

This conclusion is untrue; porpoises are mammals. The logic is sound, but the major premise (item 1) is untrue.

CREATIVE THINKING

Outstanding examples of creative thinking may be expected to come from the works of recognized artists and scientists. Today's psychologists, however, are concerned with creativity in the average person. Creativity is no longer thought of as a gift or luck or simply a characteristic of intelligence. Psychologists have taken the creative process into their laboratories for study.

Creativity, intelligence, and social traits Wallach and Kogan (1967) devised a battery of creativity tests for children to determine the number and originality of associations the child could make to several concepts: for instance, round things, possible uses for shoes. Answers given by a child were considered original (for example, "to catch a mouse in" for the shoe problem) only if they were not bizarre.

Creativity scores were compared with IQ scores in such a way that subjects could be classified as high on both measures, high on one and low on the other, or low on both. The analysis of personality traits associated with these four classifications revealed interesting sex differences. Girls showed significant variations in their social relationships and self-confidence among the four classification groups: the high creativity, high-intelligence group was most self-assured, socially active and popular, and interested in schoolwork; high-creativity, low-intelligence girls tended to be the least confident, least social, and most hesitant; high-intelligence, low-creativity girls were usually self-assured, achievement oriented, popular (but somewhat socially backward), and least disruptive; and, surprisingly, the group low in both intelligence and creativity exhibited more confidence, assertiveness, and sociability than did their high-creativity, low-intelligence peers.

Boys, however, showed the most noteworthy differences in their cognitive activity: boys high in creativity exhibited considerable flexibility in problem-solving; the intelligent but noncreative boys seemed restricted to more traditional, less flexible responses; and the group low in both traits seemed restricted to simple responses based on low-level associations. Interestingly, high-intelligence, low-creativity girls showed a sort of intellectual rigidity similar to that of their male counterparts.

The Wallach and Kogan study thus distinguished between measures of creativity and intelligence, while showing the variety of personality traits correlated with various combinations of creativity and intelligence.

Problem-finding

A creative person is usually willing to take chances. He is a source of new ideas. He finds new problems, suggests new lines of approach, and is eager to probe what others have not seen. There are relatively few such people. Most people are practical; they want to know what to do and how to find the expected, rather than the unexpected. The problem-finder takes pleasure in coping with the unexpected; he is curious about the unknown.

Problem-finding entails inventiveness. The problem-finder is not willing to limit himself to the application of other peoples' findings. In his desire for new ideas, he goes beyond what he sees. Many scientists are problem-finders. Mackworth (1965) states, "Good scientists have to be careful conservatives and wild radicals almost at the same time." While problem-solving requires the careful, systematic examination of possible alternatives, problem-finding is always inventive. It stems from the recognition that new approaches are needed and is therefore typically more demanding of originality than problem-solving. The problem-finder wrestles more with ideas than with data from experiments.

The twin traits of imagination and imitation Is a person born with an imagination? Or does he develop it? Sarbin and Juhasz (1970) argue that the ability to imagine is a developmental product of the child's skills in imitation and role-taking. Imagination, by their definition, is a kind of internalized imitation occurring without the presence of any tangible model.

To test their theory, they set out to show that subjects who were skillful at imitating a model as well as in acting out an assigned role would also do well at solving a set of problems requiring imagination. One problem required the subject to taste (or taste and smell, or touch) two unfamiliar substances and pick from a choice of five others one that represented a combination of the qualities of the first two. Another problem required subjects to imagine painting and dissecting a cube and to give information about the painted areas of the resulting pieces. In yet another type of problem, subjects were blindfolded and asked to feel an abstract-shaped wooden tile; when the blindfolds were removed, they were told to pick this tile—without touching—from a set of four similarly shaped tiles.

As the investigators predicted, performance on these imagination tasks was positively correlated with skills in imitation and role-taking. This correlation, they argue, supports the view that the development of imagination heightens man's ability to act *as if* he were actually experiencing sensations relevant to various situations.

A. Guilford, 1954

　Alternate Use:
　　Name as many uses as you can think of for a chair, a shoe, a spoon.

B. Flanagan Ingenuity Test, 1957

　Finding "Ingenious" Solutions:
　Find a solution by completing the last sentence:
　"A hostess for a children's party wanted to serve ice cream in an
　interesting manner, and she decided to make a clown for each child.
　She placed a ball of ice cream to represent the clown's head on a
　round cookie that served for a collar, and on top of this she inserted
　a _____ ."

C. Torrance, 1962

　Product Improvement:
　　Child is asked to list the "cleverest, most interesting" and unusual
　　ways he can think of changing some object, such as a stuffed animal,
　　to make it more fun to play with.

　Just Suppose:
　　Child is asked to guess what would happen in certain unusual situations.
　　For example, "Just suppose clouds had strings attached to them, which
　　hang down to earth. What would happen?"

D. Getzels and Jackson, 1962

　Word Association:
　　Child is asked to write as many associations as he can to each word in a
　　list of words.

Figure 10.8　Samples from various types of creativity tests.

Creative people

Many psychologists believe that creativity is an aspect of personality. Although creative individuals tend to be intelligent (as defined by IQ rating), the most intelligent people are not necessarily the most creative. Based on extensive testing, the following attributes have been found to be characteristic of the creative person:

1 *Independence*—Nonconforming and individualistic, in the sense that the person tends to ignore group opinion if his own differs.
2 *Flexibility*—Does not view the world in terms of only one principle.
3 *Impulsiveness*—Takes chances.
4 *Preference for unstructured, complex experiences*— Searches for the unusual.
5 *Sense of humor*—Appreciates "lighter" thoughts.
6 *Strong motivation*—Strong drives.

Figure 10.8 presents examples from various creativity tests.

　　Based on comparative studies, creative individuals do not appear to be any more disturbed or emotionally unstable than other individuals. They are freer and less confined by conventional thinking than noncreative persons, and they often are more concerned with personal and philosophical values than with material success.

Is the poet's vision programmed?　Can a poet take individual credit for his poems? B. F. Skinner (1972) argues that he cannot. Like a mother having a baby or a chicken laying an egg, a poet merely delivers a product of his genetic and environmental histories. According to Skinner, the poet's most personal contribution to his work is his stringing together the bits and pieces of language that occur to him during the writing process. In essence, he simply serves as a place for the process of poetry writing to happen. The exploration and discovery that go into the writing process are, according to Skinner, simply reworked products of the past—and the poet can never be totally aware of how his actions are tied to his history.

　　Skinner asserts that this view does not deny the uniqueness of man, for only man can write poetry. What it does threaten is the traditional belief that creativity is something mysterious. Efforts to preserve the mystery and myth of creativity, he argues, only deny man the opportunity to plan the kind of environment in which creative acts such as writing a poem would flourish more abundantly.

SUMMARY

Language and thinking are symbolic processes, and both are used in problem-solving.
The major functions of language are intercommunication and intracommunication.
Psycholinguistics is the study of the acquisition and use of language.
Phonemes are the basic units of sound, and morphemes are linguistically significant units of meaning.
Words strung together at random without meaning are called zero-order approximation of an English sentence.
Syntax orders words into meaningful sequences, enabling us to communicate in sentences.
Speech in all languages develops from the universal babbling sounds of infants.
Children begin to talk by using abbreviated speech, known as telegraphic speech.
Current views on language acquisition emphasize either learning or biological factors.
The meaning of words depends on their sequence and context.
The denotative meaning of a word refers to an objectively identifiable set of stimuli.
The connotative meaning is the evaluative or emotional response elicited by a word.
Social environment shapes language by providing models for imitation and reinforcement for appropriate responses.
Thinking is a form of behavior involving the covert manipulation of symbols, concepts, and images.
Reasoning is thinking that is directed toward a specific purpose.
Silent thinking refers to communication within the individual.
According to the motor theory of thinking, muscular activity occurs in specific parts of the body at the same time that thought processes related to those particular body regions occur.
Images and words foster ideas.
The theory of imageless thought states that thinking can take place in the absence of imagery on a subconscious level.
A concept is an abstraction of an aspect of a group of objects or events that is common to each of those objects or events.
Disordered thinking is sometimes the result of a language disturbance in which the individual reacts to words as if they were objects rather than symbols.
Problem-solving is an advanced stage of thinking; it usually involves a situation with which the individual has had no previous experience.
The individual may solve problems by overt or covert trial and error or by gap-filling techniques.
Wallas identified four steps in the problem-solving process; preparation, incubation, illumination, and verification.
Duncker's decision tree shows three stages of problem-solving: general, functional, and specific.
Habit, set, or functional fixedness may block problem-solving.
Logical thinking is a form of reasoning that involves sequentially structured phrases called syllogisms.
Creative thinking is characterized by problem-finding, the discovery of novel relationships that results in new inventions or artistic creations.

SUGGESTED READINGS

Texts

Bar-Adon, A., & Leopold, W. F. (Eds.) *Child language: a book of readings.* Englewood Cliffs, N.J.: Prentice-Hall, 1971. An excellent historical introduction to the various theories, methods, and research interests within the field of child language development.

Berlyne, D. E. *Structure and direction in thinking.* New York: Wiley, 1965. Systematic analysis of thinking and its relation to other forms of behavior.

Britton, J. *Language and learning.* Coral Gables, Fla.: University of Miami Press, 1971. Traces the development of language from infancy to adolescence. Good as supplementary reading.

Broadbent, D. E. *Decision and stress.* New York: Academic Press, 1971. An eminent psychologist updates his own thinking on cybernetic approaches to human information processing.

Carroll, J. B. *Language and thought.* Englewood Cliffs, N.J.: Prentice-Hall, 1964. Brief but comprehensive treatment of language behavior.

Cole, M., Gay, J., Glick, J. A., & Sharp, D. W. *The cultural context of learning and thinking.* New York: Basic Books, 1971. A cross-cultural examination of thinking and problem-solving in a search for universal cognitive processes.

Duncan, C. P. *Thinking: current experimental studies.* Philadelphia: Lippincott, 1967. Collection of some of the best articles available; covers the range of experimental studies.

Hayakawa, S. I. *Language in thought and action* (3rd ed.). New York: Harcourt Brace Jovanovich, 1972. Treatment of thinking and communication in terms of semantics; interestingly and simply written.

Humphrey, G. *Thinking: an introduction to its experimental psychology.* New York: Wiley, 1951. Scholarly treatment of classical work on problem-solving and theoretical views of thinking.

Mandler, J. M., & Mandler, G. *Thinking: from association to Gestalt.* New York: Wiley, 1964. Collection of some classical papers.

Markel, N. W. (Ed.) *Psycholinguistics: an introduction to the study of speech and personality.* Homewood, Ill.: Dorsey, 1969. Introduction to the subject.

McGuigan, F. J. *Thinking: studies of covert language processes.* New York: Appleton-Century-Crofts, 1966. Excellent collection of papers dealing with theory and research.

Mussen, P. H. (Ed.) *Carmichael's manual of child psychology* (3rd ed.). New York: Wiley, 1970. Chapters 8 through 19 provide a thorough review of research, trends, and issues in all areas of cognitive development—conceptual, perceptual, linguistic, and creative.

Parry, J. *The psychology of human communication.* New York: American Elsevier, 1968. Discussion of the theory of communication as it applies to human behavior and experience.

Piaget, J. *The language and thought of the child.* New York: Meridian, 1955.

(Originally published in 1926.) Piaget's theories of thinking and problem-solving. A classic.

Ray, W. S. *The experimental psychology of original thinking.* New York: Macmillan, 1967. Introduction to methods and principles involved in the study of creative thinking.

Richard, A. *Mental imagery.* New York: Springer, 1969. Discussion of imagery in thinking.

Slobin, D. I. *Psycholinguistics.* Glenview, Ill.: Foresman, 1972. A lively, readable introduction to the psychology of language.

Wallach, M. A., & Kogan, N. *Modes of thinking in young children.* New York: Holt, 1965. A comprehensive study of the creativity-intelligence distinction.

Williams, F. (Ed.) *Language and poverty.* Chicago: Markham, 1971. A nontechnical survey of the issues involved in evaluating the nonstandard English characteristics of poverty subcultures.

Popular books

Brown, D. V., & MacDonald, P. *Learning begins at home: a stimulus for a child's I.Q.* On stimulating the thinking processes of children.

Brown, R. *Words and things.* Interestingly written survey of work on language and related topics.

DeBono, E. *New think: the use of lateral thinking in the generation of new ideas.* Description of a method of stimulating creative problem-solving.

Fichtelius, K., & Sjolander, S. *Smarter than man.* An absorbing argument for man's inferior intelligence adaptation as compared with the intellectual capacities of whales and dolphins.

Ghiselin, B. (Ed.) *The creative process.* Thirty-eight of this century's most brilliant men and women explain their ideas and experiences of creativity.

Hawkins, G. S., & White, J. B. *Stonehenge decoded.* A fascinating excursion into prehistoric thinking, using the problem-solvers of modern technology—computers.

Lewis, M. M. *How children learn to speak.* Traces the development of speech.

Thompson, R. *The psychology of thinking.* Survey of work on thinking in animals and humans.

Wyatt, G. L. *Language learning and communications disorders in children.* Discussion of language and thinking problems in children.

11

Testing intelligence and ability

The psychologist does not guess at a child's intelligence, an airline pilot's emotional fitness for his job, or the aptitudes of an adolescent asking for career guidance. Because he cannot let his biases intrude on an evaluation, he endeavors to base his judgments on scientific measurements. Test scores are a form of measurement, and the professional has at his command a variety of systematic testing procedures. Devised by psychologists, such tests are now essential tools in clinics, schools, industry, and government.

Every child amasses a record of classroom test scores. The scores tell teachers how well he has learned a particular subject. He may also be required to take a different kind of test, one to evaluate his intelligence so that he can be placed in a proper class or be given special attention if he needs it. Later, when he applies for a job or for college admission, he is also required to produce evidence of how well he can perform. To this end, systematically developed, standardized tests, designed as a measure by which to compare many persons in many situations, have become an important source of information.

EVALUATING TESTING DEVICES

People do not behave according to fixed patterns; their thinking, motivation, and physical condition may vary from one measurement to the next. A good testing device must therefore deal with the problem of variability. Above all, it must have the confidence of the psychologist. It must be demonstrably *reliable*, *valid*, *objective*, and *standardized*. These four characteristics of a good test are interdependent.

Reliability

For a test to be useful, it must be *reliable*. A test is reliable if it produces the same or similar measurements time after time for the same qualities. In other words, its measurements must be repeatable. A test is unreliable if it produces widely differing results for no reason. For example, if every time you stepped on your bathroom scale it recorded a different weight, you would know that something was wrong. Such a scale could hardly be called a reliable measuring instrument.

To check the reliability of a test, psychologists measure more than once; they give the test on at least two separate occasions and then compare the sets of scores. This procedure is referred to as *test-retest reliability*. Where specific questions are asked, it is usual to administer parallel forms of the test on the two occasions.

Figure 11.1 presents a scatter diagram (see Chapter 1) showing the results of a reliability check on the Stanford-Binet test of intelligence (to be discussed in a later section). Form M and an alternate, Form L, were administered a few days apart to a sample of 7-year-olds. The correlation of $+.91$ that was obtained indicates that the test has high reliability. However, we can see that the correspondence is not perfect; some shifts in scores do occur. These shifts are found most often among very high scores. For example, of the four scores in the 125 to 129 range on Form M, one shifted to the 145–149 range on Form L; one was in the 130–134 range on L; one was in the 120–124 range on L; and one was in the 115–119 range on L. The test appears to be most reliable for the low and middle ranges of scores.

Another check of a test's reliability is the *split-half method of reliability*. In this method, the score for one half of a test is compared with the score for the other half. For example, the score for the odd-numbered questions may be compared with the score for the even-numbered questions to determine whether the test is internally reliable.

Validity

The usefulness of any measuring instrument depends on how well the instrument measures what it is intended to measure, that is, on the *validity* of the device. At the beginning of any testing situation, the scientist must ask himself the purpose of his testing procedures; he must have a clear understanding of what he is measuring, how he is measuring it, and why he is measuring it. He must be sure that his measuring device is actually measuring what he has set out to measure. If a scientist devised a test to measure color perception but the subjects' reactions were influenced more by the shape of the objects than by their color, he would not have a valid test of color perception. In determining validity, we evaluate the relationship of the purpose of a measuring device to its actual use.

The validity of a new test can be determined by comparing its results with those obtained by another test already recognized as valid for measuring the same or similar factors. The established test serves as the *criterion*—the standard against which the validity of the new test is compared.

The type of test used depends on the characteristic being studied. A test to detect ability in accounting would differ from a test for writing ability. In some cases, a test cannot be adjudged valid until the subjects have fulfilled their predicted behavior. If a new test for accounting ability predicts that certain subjects will become superior accountants, the experimenter will not know whether the predictions are valid until the subjects enter this career and prove their ability. Of course, after several tested groups have carried out the prediction, the test may be regarded as valid. It may then be accepted as a useful measuring instrument.

The validity of a device that measures thinking and problem-solving ability is extremely difficult to assess. To develop valid tests for these abilities, we need to establish meaningful definitions of thinking and problem-solving. Only then do we have a target at which to aim the test. It is sometimes necessary to use a ranking system to measure thinking and problem-solving. For example, a group of persons presented with a number of problems might be ranked on the basis of the ease with which they solved the

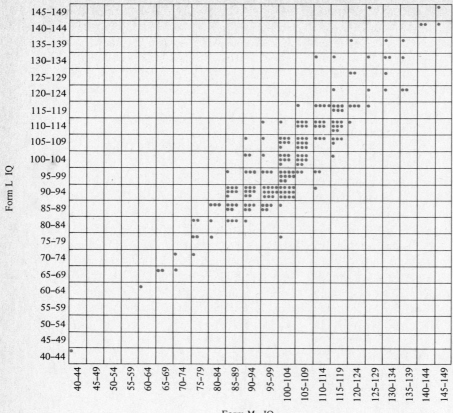

Figure 11.1   IQs obtained by 7-year-olds when tested successively on two forms of the Stanford-Binet. (From Terman, L. M., and Merrill, M. A., Measuring intelligence. Boston: Houghton Mifflin Company, 1937.)

problems. This ranking would be compared with the test scores and, if the test were valid, the individual with a high test score would also be ranked high in problem-solving. Table 11.1 presents the hypothetical results of two problem-solving tasks, Test X and Test Y. Compare each individual's test score with his rank in a separate problem-solving task, and then decide which test is more valid.

Objectivity

Certain types of tests involve judgment as a method of scoring. In such cases, the experimenter must be *objective*; he must be careful not to allow his personal biases to influence the scoring of subjects. If scoring a test involves personal judgments, the participation of more than one trained scorer is required to insure objectivity.

Standardization

In psychological testing, it is important to have a *standardization group*, a group that serves as a reference against which we may compare any

Table 11.1 The hypothetical results from two problem-solving tests: which test is more valid— X or Y? [a, b]

Test X		Test Y	
Test scores	Problem-solving ranks	Test scores	Problem-solving ranks
61	2	53	7
48	5	94	3
32	7	81	5
91	1	45	6
86	3	68	1
29	8	27	8
66	6	73	2
75	4	35	4

[a]Test X is more valid because the test scores correlate (correspond) better than those of Y with problem-solving ranks.

[b]Note that 1 indicates the highest rank.

individual's score. For example, in measuring intelligence, a large representative group of children is tested; their scores are then used to establish a set of *norms* (standards). When a child is tested thereafter, his score is compared with these norms. The norms allow us to make comparisons such as "He is above the average," or "He is in the upper 10 percent."

Once the validity, reliability, objectivity, and standardization of a test have been determined, psychologists can compare its results with the results of other tests or with other measures of behavior.

USE OF TESTS

Tests are being used with increasing frequency and in more varied situations. Most employers screen applicants by testing them for particular skills. Tests are generally classified according to their use: *prediction, diagnosis,* or *research.*

Prediction Tests are commonly used to *predict* an individual's future behavior—his performance in school, on a job, or in some other kind of specific activity. The individual results of these tests are often compared. College administrators and employers, for example, are interested in finding individuals who are likely to succeed; therefore, they often base their decisions on a comparison of scores, using tests designed to predict future preformance in a particular area.

Diagnosis Psychologists often use *diagnostic* tests to uncover psychological problems. Although a diagnostic test can also be used to predict an individual's performance in relation to some standard, it is not usually used for this purpose; in such cases, predictive tests are used. Diagnostic tests attempt to find causative factors. With proper diagnosis, an individual can recognize the factors that caused his difficulties and work toward overcoming them.

Research Tests are used for *research* purposes to help the experimenter identify and describe behavior. As experimental techniques become more complex, psychologists are constantly devising new tests. Tests used for research must be carefully validated. A valid test to measure anxiety, for example, is useful in behavior studies to determine the various effects of anxiety on other behavior.

MEASUREMENT OF INTELLIGENCE

Intelligence testing has generated more interest, both professional and nonprofessional, than most other areas of psychology. The testing of intelligence originated with two Frenchmen, Alfred Binet, a psychologist, and Theodore Simon, a physician, who were doing a research study on feeble-minded children attending the public schools early in this century. The French government had asked Binet and Simon to find some way to identify children who could not learn by ordinary methods. It had become obvious that not only the slow learners but their more capable classmates were not learning efficiently. Binet and Simon felt that a valid measure of intelligence needed to be found so that children could be separated according to intelligence.

The Binet tests

Binet and Simon began by attempting to identify differences between "bright" and "dull" children. They tried a variety of measurements, including tasks involving moral judgment, sensory discrimination, and suggestibility; they even tried handwriting analysis and palm reading. Soon discovering they were on the wrong track, Binet and Simon decided to develop tests of intellectual activity, such as judgment, reasoning, attention, vocabulary, and memory.

In 1905 Binet and Simon published a tentative intelligence scale. It consisted of 30 tests arranged in increasing order of difficulty. The level of difficulty was established by comparing the test performance of 50 normal children aged 3 to 11 with the performance of a group of children known to be mentally retarded. The easiest tests involved such tasks as repeating simple comments and imitating gestures; the moderately difficult tests included describing the objects in a picture or repeating sentences with as many as 15 words after a single hearing. The most difficult test involved such tasks as stating the similarities between two familiar objects and distinguishing between abstract terms.

Binet and Simon revised their scale in 1908 by adding some new tests and eliminating others. They grouped the tests into age levels by determining the normal age at which children passed the various tests. For example, tests normally passed by 3-year-olds were placed in the 3-year age level, tests normally passed by 4-year-olds were placed in the 4-year age level, and

so on up to age 13. Scores on the tests were expressed in terms of *mental age*. If a 10-year-old passed only those tests up to and including the 8-year level, he would have a mental age of 8.

Revisions of the Binet tests

In 1916, L. M. Terman, a psychologist at Stanford University, prepared the first major revision of the Binet tests, called the *Stanford-Binet Test*. Terman, like Binet, classified the data according to mental age rather than chronological age. To have a measure that could be interpreted regardless of the individual's age, William Stern suggested a simple ratio formula referred to as the intelligence quotient (IQ). The formula is the ratio of mental age (MA) to chronological age (CA), with the fraction multiplied by 100 to eliminate decimals. The formula is

$$IQ = \frac{MA}{CA} \times 100$$

Thus, if a 5-year-old passes all the tests up to and including the 7-year level, his mental age is 7. The *mental age* is then divided by the *chronological* (actual) age, and the quotient is multiplied by 100 to obtain the IQ. In this case, the IQ is 140 ([7 ÷ 5] × 100).

By means of the IQ, psychologists have established an arbitrary scale of intelligence: an IQ score of 100 is "average intelligence"; an IQ over 140 is "gifted"; an IQ of 70 is "borderline"; and an IQ below 70 may indicate mental retardation. Although scores and definitions are important, much depends on the meaningful interpretation of the test results and on the test itself.

Studies performed with the Stanford-Binet test showed that intelligence is distributed on a normal curve (Figure 11.2), and that it is impossible to define any sharp break between levels of intelligence. Figure 11.3 presents some typical problems from the revised Binet tests. Note that the ages specified are chronological ages.

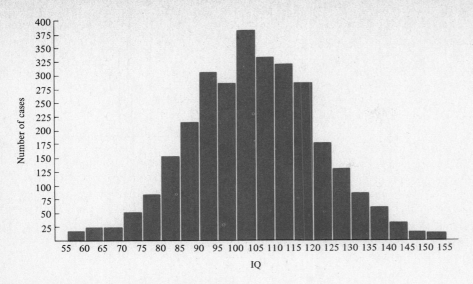

Figure 11.2   Frequency distribution of IQs on Form L of the Stanford-Binet test, ages 2½ to 18. (From McNemar, Q., The revision of the Stanford-Binet Scale. Boston: Houghton Mifflin Company, 1942)

Figure 11.3   Examples of the type of problems used in a Binet test.

TWO-AND-A-HALF-YEAR LEVEL

Identifies object by use
    Subject is shown a card depicting 6 small objects
"Show me the one that we drink out of; show me. . ."
    Three out of 6 for credit

Identifies parts of the body
    Subject is shown a large paper doll
"Show me the dolly's hair; show me. . ."
    Six out of 6 for credit

Names objects
    Subject is shown 5 small objects
"What is this?"
    Five out of 5 for credit

SIX-YEAR LEVEL

Defines orange, envelope
completes "An inch is. . .; mile is. . ."
Gives examiner 9 block

TWELVE-YEAR LEVEL

Defines skill, juggler
Defines constant, courage
Completes "The streams are dry. . ."
Finds absurdity in a picture

The Stanford-Binet test (the original Binet test as revised by Terman) was further revised in 1937 (see Terman and Merrill, 1959). Two alternate versions of the test were prepared so that those persons who needed to be tested more than once would not become familiar with the problems.

Even more important, this revision was designed to correct the definition of mental age in adults. Materials were added to test the intelligence of adults, even though at the time most psychologists speculated that few adults grow in mental capacity beyond the age of 16. The 1937 revision also included materials for testing preschool children, including those as young as 2½ years of age.

It was found, however, that the IQ scales of the 1937 Stanford-Binet tests did not permit valid comparisons of test scores of individuals at different ages. In 1960, the tests were revised a third time; this time, Terman and Merrill improved the scoring techniques so that IQs could be compared at all age levels. The IQ in the 1960 revision of the Stanford-Binet is a *standard score* computed from a set of preestablished tables. In these tables the average IQ is defined as 100 and the standard deviation of the IQs is 16. The 1960 Stanford-Binet IQ is no longer a ratio; it is simply a score showing the individual's standing in relationship to others. Thus, the average IQ score of 100 is higher than 50 percent of all test scores. A score of 116 is one that is higher than 84 percent of all scores; a score of 132 is higher than 98 percent of all scores; and a score of 84 is higher than only 16 percent of the total (Terman and Merrill, 1960).

A defect of the Stanford-Binet tests is that they emphasize verbal skills; that is, they rely on understanding of words and verbal communications. As a result, children whose ability to communicate verbally is limited by psychological or environmental factors often score low on these tests. Children with auditory or visual defects also do not score well, so that the tests fail to reflect their true capabilities. Children whose families speak a foreign language have difficulty with the tests, as do those whose verbal development has been neglected, which is often the case when parents are ill, absent, or themselves limited verbally.

Raven's progressive matrices test Developed in the late 1930s, this popular test measures the ability to perceive and utilize abstract relationships. Persons taking the test are instructed to select the one design that completes the pattern in a number of two-dimensional analogy problems.

Because the directions are simple and the range of problems presented can be very large, the content and format of this test are highly flexible. Raven Matrices can, for instance, be used in schools to screen students for special courses or to identify those with good reasoning abilities but poor educational background. Outside the classroom, the test has also been widely used in personnel selection. During World War II, the Raven Matrices test was adopted as the principal test for military classification in Great Britain, but this single-ability measurement proved less satisfactory than tests tapping a variety of abilities. In situations for which it is suitable, however, the Matrices have the advantage of being relatively uninfluenced by past educational attainments: the test is a good measure of abstract reasoning.

The validity of the Raven Matrices test is supported by its correlations with other tests that measure (either exclusively or in part) abstract reasoning—for example, most of the popular IQ tests. The popularity of the test's format is shown by the number of versions developed all over the world for use with a wide variety of testing populations.

The performance IQ Test

Performance tests, including shape and pattern puzzles and picture completion puzzles, were created to circumvent the problems raised by the emphasis on verbal skills in the Stanford-Binet tests. Administered nonverbally and requiring no verbal response, these performance tests provide a measure of mental age and thus of IQ. Also, because the tests are not in written or spoken form, children are apparently more at ease when taking them. Adults, too, can be given performance tests. Figure 11.4 is an example of a performance test.

The Wechsler tests

An American psychologist, David Wechsler, developed an intelligence test comprised of two separate scales, a verbal scale and a performance scale. The first form of the Wechsler test, known as the Wechsler-Bellevue Intelligence Scale, was published in 1939. This test was replaced in 1955 by a revised version, the Wechsler Adult Intelligence Scale (WAIS). Table 11.2 shows the

Table 11.2   The subtests of the Wechsler Adult Intelligence Scale[a]

Verbal	Performance
General information	Picture completion
General comprehension	Block design
Arithmetic	Picture arrangement
Similarities	Object assembly
Vocabulary	Digit symbol
Digit span	

[a]From Wechsler (1955).

Figure 11.4   To account for the effect of environmental differences on intelligence tests, performance tests were devised. The child must determine how many of the small blocks fit into each column. (Raimondo Borea)

eleven subtests, six verbal and five performance, that comprise the WAIS.

The Wechsler Intelligence Scale for Children (WISC) was published in 1949. It is essentially a revision of the original Wechsler-Bellevue test; while consisting of the same types of subtests as the adult test, it uses coding or maze tests in place of the digit-symbol test of the adult scale, and digit span is a supplementary test to be used if time permits. The subtest items were designed to accommodate the age range of 2 to 16 years.

In both the WAIS and the WISC, IQ measures are derived as in the 1960 revision of the Stanford-Binet. The IQ score is assigned by comparing the subject's test score with the scores of other individuals in the standardization group of the same age. The Wechsler IQs are based on a normal distribution with an average of 100 and a standard deviation of 15. For example, a subject who obtains an IQ of 115 has a score that exceeds those of 84 percent of the standardization group.

Both Wechsler tests have a high correlation with the Stanford-Binet. The WAIS and the WISC show correlations of around .80 with the Stanford-Binet, but it should be noted that correlations of the Wechsler verbal scales to the Stanford-Binet are higher than those of the Wechsler performance scales. These differences are not surprising considering that the Stanford-Binet tends to be heavily weighted with items requiring verbal ability.

What intelligence tests measure

Intelligence tests measure ability at the time of testing. There is no evidence that they measure an inborn capacity. Performance depends on earlier experiences and possibly innate factors, but the test scores merely describe an individual's performance relative to that of others tested. Table 11.3 lists a classification of IQ scores based on data from the Stanford-Binet test.

The relationship between intelligence test scores and school achievement is usually quite high. Many studies have indicated that intelligence test scores predict fairly well for groups of individuals, but it is important to realize that great discrepancies are possible between individual IQ scores and school performance; a youngster with an IQ of 125 may be a poor student, while one with an IQ of 105 may do quite well.

The intelligence tests currently used in the United States are generally based on the assumption that all children have had experiences that

Table 11.3   Classification of IQ scores based on data from the Stanford-Binet test[a]

IQ range	Percentage of population (approximate)	Classification
140 and above	1.3	Gifted
130–139	3.1 ⎫	Superior
120–129	8.2 ⎭	
110–119	18.1	High average
90–109	46.5	Average
80–89	14.5	Low average
70–79	5.6	Borderline
Below 70	2.6	Mentally retarded

[a]After Terman and Merrill (1959).

are, in fact, common only to the urban middle-class culture. The experiences of blacks, chicanos, American Indians, and foreign-born children are not well represented. Consequently, most standard tests do not serve as a basis for comparing children from a wide variety of backgrounds. Some children are at a disadvantage because their early experiences have not been like those of the standardization sample. A youngster who has not seen many books or has not played with alphabet blocks is likely to obtain lower scores on the verbal subtests simply because he has not had opportunities to become familiar with printed verbal material.

An unbiased intelligence test Intelligence tests should contain no cultural bias, for when a test is culturally biased, it measures only the intelligence of that culture or social class. For example, it would be unfair to ask an Eskimo a question such as "If you wanted to go from New York City to London, England, which method of transportation would get you there fastest: (1) boat; (2) plane; (3) car?" He does not know these cities, and he is not familiar with the modes of transportation. They are not part of his culture. Therefore such questions should not be used to test his intelligence.

Davis and Eells (1953) constructed a test, known as the Davis-Eells games, that they felt was valid, at least across socioeconomic levels in the United States. The test was constructed so that no child, regardless of social background or place of residence, would have difficulty in answering any question due to lack of experience or concepts presented in the question. According to Davis and Eells, their test may be said to measure "intelligence," not "knowledge."

Performance on an intellectual task, whether an intelligence test or some aspect of schoolwork, will vary with the individual's environment and his early learning experiences. Before comparing children on the basis of intelligence-test performance, we must first be sure that the groups or individuals have had equal opportunities.

Intelligence test scores are also influenced by personality and emotion. A child who is shy with adults, lacks confidence, and becomes rattled in new situations will do poorly on a test although he may be quite intelligent. Some youngsters are very cautious or self-critical and may tend to say they do not know an answer if they are not completely certain; others will take a chance on the answer. In such cases, differences in scores may be largely a function of personality.

Careful interpretation of intelligence test scores requires a consideration of all factors that may affect the child at the time of testing—for example, his previous experiences, his attitude toward tests and school, and the standardization group to which he is being compared. Even when all factors are considered, test scores should be treated with caution. No matter how carefully obtained, a score does not do justice to the breadth of an individual's behavior. It is at best a limited description of the individual's capablities that may be useful when considered with other data that describe the person.

What makes IQ vary? The Declaration of Independence says, "All men are created equal." Yet from experience we know that some seem to be more equal than others. Social scientists for years have maintained that intellectual differences that exist between people are not present at birth; they are, rather, a product of each person's unique environment. Head Start programs have been instituted by our government to provide preschool ghetto children with an environment more similar to that of middle-class children; these early learning programs are intended to help deprived children compete scholastically with socially advantaged children. The underlying philosophy of this program is that if the disadvantaged child's ghetto environment is modified, that child will learn just as much as other children will.

In February 1969, Arthur R. Jensen, a psychologist at the University of California, published an article entitled "How much can we boost IQ and scholastic achievement?" In this article Jensen asks, "What makes the IQ vary from one individual to another? What can change it? By what amount?" His answers produced a storm, for he concluded that the individual's IQ level, or at least his potential IQ level, is genetically determined at birth. According to Jensen, although a good environment and education can raise a person's IQ, it cannot raise it above a genetically determined peak. Jensen also notes that blacks as a group score low on tests involving abstract reasoning and problem-solving, whereas whites and Orientals score comparatively high on such tests. Jensen holds that this is an inherited trait and that it will not be changed by exposure to culture. He points out that individual blacks may excel in those traits, but they are the exception rather than the rule. In addition, Jensen emphasizes that no one trait is intrinsically more important than any other trait; intelligence has become important because of the values placed on it by middle-class white society. According to Jensen, the fact that blacks did not perform well on these tests does not mean that they do not possess other, equally important traits that are not possessed by whites.

This position, of course, brought on a barrage of criticism. But Jensen refused to budge from his position, stating that it was based on scientific fact. Jensen based his position on:

1 *Data from studies on siblings and twins*—These show that twins have more similar IQ scores than the rest of the population, even when they are reared apart in different environments. This points to a genetic basis for intelligence.
2 *The fact that blacks on the average score lower than whites on intelligence tests*, even when the two groups are from the same social class.

The many criticisms leveled at Jensen from all quarters of the academic field point to the many available studies that show that an improved environment raises IQ scores in children, that many black youngsters suffer from malnutrition (which affects performance), that IQ tests are culturally biased, and that the meaning of these tests is ambiguous. Many social scientists have since ceased to support the use of IQ tests.

One of the more apparent flaws in Jensen's findings may be seen in his admission that IQ-score differences between whites and blacks do not become apparent until the upper grades in school. Jensen, in answer to this, proposes that there are two types of intelligence: (1) basic intelligence, which is equal for all races; and (2) higher intelligence, which is found more among whites than blacks. However, it seems that his data do not require this conclusion. We have already seen that different child-rearing practices will encourage different types of intelligence development in children. Is it not possible that different home environments and cultural traditions of blacks and whites, rather than inheritance, are responsible for the difference in IQ scores?

HEREDITY AND INTELLIGENCE

How nature and nurture interact to determine intelligence is of central interest to educators and parents, as well as scientists. Many experiments have been reported that attempt to explain the genetic basis of intelligence. In studies of twins, the influence of environment and heredity on intelligence can be observed.

Effect of heredity and environment on intelligence

Understanding the genetics of the family makes it possible to study the influence of heredity and environment on intelligence. Studies—particularly studies of genetically related individuals—have pointed out that the two factors tend to interact in highly significant ways.

Measuring infant intelligence Psychologists have long searched for the true nature of infant intelligence. Can we somehow measure infant IQ so as to predict later intellectual capacities? Lewis and McGurk (1972) argue that we cannot.

Their sample of infants was tested at regular intervals during their first 24 months. Subjects were administered the several tests which comprise the Bayley Mental Development Index (MDI) along with an accepted measure of object permanence at 3, 6, 9, 12, 18, and 24 months of age. In addition at 24 months all infants were tested for elementary verbal abilities—language comprehension and ability to name or describe various pictures

Once all scores were obtained, the investigators examined patterns of correlations between scores, on the premise that high correlations would allow performance on one of the correlated variables to predict performance on the other. As expected, however, virtually none of the sets of scores correlated well with any of the others from one age to another. In effect, neither the MDI nor the object permanence scores at one age predicted performance on the same type of measure at a later age; nor did scores on any one measure predict performance on any of the other measures (except for some moderate predictive power in the new instances when two tests were measuring similar specific abilities).

Lewis and McGurk conclude that infant intelligence is not the same sort of general ability one finds in adults. Instead it is probably a set of relatively discrete abilities which undergo a series of qualitative changes throughout infancy. Conseqently, anyone who tries to use a general intelligence measure to assess the adequacy of infant educational programs is simply trying to measure with a nonexistent yardstick.

As stated earlier (Chapter 2), inherited similarities are found to be strongest between identical twins, less strong between fraternal twins, and less still between ordinary siblings. The strength of these relationships is measured by the *correlation coefficient* (see Chapter 1).

Table 11.4 presents the correlation coefficients for the intelligence test scores for several groups of family members. The findings result from a number of studies of the relationships between heredity, environment, and intelligence.

The material in the table may be summarized as follows:

1 There is a high positive relationship between the intelligence test scores of identical twins. The relationship is less apparent when the twins are raised apart (in different homes), but it is still high.
2 Test scores for fraternal twins show a fairly high

Table 11.4 Correlation of IQ test scores among genetic relatives and family groups

Family relationship	Correlation coefficients	
Identical twins	.92[a]	.92[c]
Identical twins (raised apart)[a]	.73[a]	.86[c]
Fraternal twins (of same sex)[a]	.63[b]	.53[c]
Siblings[b]	.51[b]	
Parents and their children[d]	.60[d]	
Parents and adopted children[d]		
Father and child	.19[d]	
Mother and child	.24[d]	
Unrelated children reared together[d]	.28[e]	

[a]From Newman, Freeman, and Holzinger (1937).
[b]From Burt and Howard (1956).
[c]From Freeman, Holzinger, and Mitchell (1928).
[d]From Leahy (1935).
[e]From Burt (1966).

positive relationship, but it is less apparent than that shown by identical twins.
3 Siblings raised in the same home show slightly lower intelligence test score relationships than do fraternal twins.
4 There is a fairly high positive relationship between intelligence test scores of parents and any of their children raised by them. There is little relationship between the scores of adopted children and those of their foster parents.

We can see that high positive correlations in intelligence test scores tend to occur where there is the most genetic similarity. These findings suggest that the *heritability* of intelligence is high. Heritability refers to the proportion of a characteristic that is controlled by genetic variables. When we say that intelligence has high heritability, we are saying that a large proportion of intelligence comes from genetic factors.

Inheritance of intelligence Four decades of twin studies have consistently found from 70 to 80 percent of general intelligence level to be of genetic origin. Less settled, however, is the question of whether that large genetic factor applies only to the general ability called "intelligence"; only to the several specific abilities inherent in the subtests by which "intelligence" is usually measured (like vocabulary, mathematics); or to both general intelligence and its component abilities.

Nichols (1965) reports one major attempt to answer these intriguing questions. On the 1962 National Merit Scholarship examinations, students were asked whether or not they were twins. Extensive follow-up investigation turned up 42 sets of fraternal twins and 82 sets of identical twins, all with closely matched environmental backgrounds.

Test scores for these 124 sets of twins were then analyzed for intertwin correlations on both composite score and scores on all five subtests. In line with previous studies, more than 70 percent of the composite score was statistically shown to be of genetic origin. In addition, the average heritability rating for the separate subtests was about 75 percent. It seems, therefore, that the high heritability of general intelligence is probably a function of the hereditary determination of many very specific abilities, and that the composite, general-intelligence score simply reflects the repeated application of these abilities.

Despite such impressive evidence for the influence of heredity on intelligence, environment plays a crucial role, as a number of studies have shown. A recent report prepared by Skeels (1966), for example, indicates that a group of children who were diagnosed as mentally retarded were able to become self-sufficient and to function normally in other respects after they were given special attention in foster homes. Skeels's findings were based on a study group of 13 children. Their average age was 19.4 months, and their average IQ was 64.3 with a range of 35 to 89. (Average IQ for a population of 100 is 100, with a normal range of 85 to 115.) The children were considered unsuited for adoption because they were believed to be mentally retarded and, in some cases, imbecilic. However, 11 of the 13 children were placed in adoptive homes, where they experienced mother-child relationships and where they were encouraged to learn to do things for themselves.

Skeels contrasted this study group with another group of 12 children of approximately the same background, drawn from the same orphanage. Those in the second group were not adopted. They had an average age of 16.6 months and were basically brighter than the study group.

(The average IQ of the brighter group was 86.7, with a range of 81 to 103, except for two children who had IQs of 71 and 50.) The brighter group did not receive any extra stimulation at the orphanage.

After 2 years, Skeels retested both groups for intellectual development. He found that the first study group showed increased intellectual development, whereas the group in the orphanage—despite their early superiority—showed decreased intellectual development. The 1966 follow-up study showed that the original 13 children had all become self-supporting, whereas those that remained from the second group never developed the skills to become economically independent. Without parental stimulation, some of these children simply graduated from the orphanage to a home for the feeble-minded; none of them was able to do more than the most menial tasks.

Jensen (1968) claims that Skeels's evidence does not necessarily contradict a genetic theory of intelligence. According to Jensen, the orphanage children may have inherited normal intelligence, which, through extreme cultural deprivation, was depressed.

Genetics and mental retardation The development of normal intellectual functions depends on the development of the nervous system. Defects in nervous system development may result from genetic variables. Such defects may involve the anatomy or the biochemistry of nerve tissue.

Genetically produced biochemical defects are usually recessive and often involve some enzyme deficiency. Phenylketonuria (PKU) is an example of a genetically determined form of mental retardation. In PKU, the lack of enzyme (phenylalanine hydroxylase) results in excessive levels of phenylalanine in the blood, and this leads to defects in brain metabolism and ultimately to mental retardation (Mitoma, Auld, and Udenfriend, 1957). This form of retardation may be diagnosed by testing for the presence of phenylpyruvic acid in the urine. Children who carry the recessive gene can be identified and treated by a special diet that is low in phenylalanine. Some states in fact require that all newborn infants be tested immediately after birth for the presence of execessive phenylalanine.

PSYCHOMETRIC THEORIES
OF INTELLIGENCE

When Binet and Simon set out to develop an intelligence test, they assumed that intelligence is "a fundamental faculty. . . . This faculty is judgment, otherwise called good sense, practical sense, initiative. . . ." (1905). The test they developed was based on the idea that intelligence is a single unitary factor. In contradiction, Charles Spearman, an English psychologist, viewed intelligence as a general factor plus a number of independent factors (Spearman, 1904).

According to Spearman, any task involves not only the general factor of intelligence but specific factors for particular skills required by the task. He reached this conclusion after observing that many different test items correlated with each other, indicating the involvement of some common factor. He then assumed that some general mental capacity, which he termed g, was the basis for the intercorrelations. Further observation led Spearman to conclude that the specific factors were not necessarily independent of one another and that there could be overlap among them. He referred to such overlap as a group factor.

Factor analysis

Spearman's formulation led to factor analysis, a statistical procedure for analyzing intercorrelations of tests. A factor analysis begins with a study of correlations of test scores to determine what, if anything, different tests might indicate in common.

Suppose that we have given four tests to a group of students and have computed the correlations of the scores for each test with the scores for every other test. Table 11.5 shows a hypothetical group of intercorrelations for our four tests. We find in the table two fairly high correlations—one between tests A and B, and one between tests C and D. We assume that these correlations indicate an overlap of abilities measured by the correlated tests. The overlap in A and B and the overlap in C and D suggest that the same underlying factor or ability operates in both tests A and B and that another underlying factor or ability accounts for the performance in tests C and D.

The factor analyst looks for the areas of overlap among tests and then seeks to identify the common factor or factors that account for the overlap. When overlap, in the form of a correlation, is discovered, the assumption is that a certain factor is responsible. Steps are then taken to discover how influential this factor is in each of the correlated tests.

The investigator thus seeks to determine the correlation of the factor to the tests in which it is believed to be influential. This correlation, known as factor loading, is found by comparing the scores of each of the tests containing the factor with the scores for a number of test items that represent the factor in question. For example, in determining the loading of a factor such as verbal comprehension in a vocabulary test, we would compare the particular test score with scores of a variety of verbal comprehension items and other similar tests. Often reference tests, regarded as a pure measure of the given factor, are used in determining the factor loading.

The loading of a particular factor in a particular test indicates the extent to which the factor accounts for the test score. For example, L. L. Thurstone and T. G. Thurstone found that

Table 11.5	Hypothetical correlations among four tests		
Tests	B	C	D
A	.68	.08	.12
B	—	.05	.18
C	—	—	.62

Table 11.6 Factor loadings based on a factor analysis of 21 tests[a]

Tests	Perceptual speed I	Numerical ability II	Word fluency III	Verbal comprehension IV	Spatial visualization V	Memory VI	Reasoning VII
1 Identical numbers	.42	.40	.05	—.02	—.07	—.06	—.06
2 Faces	.45	.17	—.06	.04	.20	.05	.02
3 Mirror reading	.36	.09	.19	—.02	.05	—.01	.09
4 First names	—.02	.09	.20	.00	.05	.53	.10
5 Figure recognition	.20	—.10	.02	—.02	.10	.31	.07
6 Word-number	.02	.13	—.03	.00	.01	.58	—.04
7 Sentences	.00	.01	—.03	.66	—.08	—.05	.13
8 Vocabulary	—.01	.02	.05	.66	—.04	.02	.02
9 Completion	—.01	.00	—.01	.67	.15	.00	—.01
10 First letters	.12	—.03	.63	.03	—.02	.00	—.00
11 Four-letter words	—.02	—.05	.61	—.01	.08	—.01	.04
12 Suffixes	.04	.03	.45	.18	—.03	.03	—.08
13 Flags	—.04	.05	.03	—.01	.68	.00	.01
14 Figures	.02	—.06	.01	—.02	.76	—.02	—.02
15 Cards	.07	—.03	—.03	.03	.72	.02	—.03
16 Addition	.01	.64	—.02	.01	.05	.01	—.02
17 Multiplication	.01	.67	.01	—.03	—.05	.02	.02
18 Three-higher	—.05	.38	—.01	.06	.20	—.05	.16
19 Letter series	—.03	.03	.03	.02	.00	.02	.53
20 Pedigrees	.02	—.05	—.03	.22	—.03	.05	.44
21 Letter grouping	.06	.06	.13	—.04	.01	—.06	.42

[a]From Thurstone, L. L., and Thurstone, T.G. Factorial studies of intelligence. *Psychometric Monographs*. Chicago: University of Chicago Press, 1941. All rights reserved. Published by permission.

their tests of sentences, vocabulary, and completion had high factor loadings for the factor of verbal comprehension; and their tests of mirror readings, identical numbers, and faces had high factor loadings for the factor of perceptual speed. Table 11.6 displays a factor matrix of factor loadings for 21 tests from the Thurstone and Thurstone battery of tests.

The Thurstone factors

Thurstone sought to develop a multiple-factor theory of intelligence based on his belief that the complex process called intelligence is a composite of simpler processes.

In 1938 he administered a series of 56 tests to a large group of students. By factor analysis, he found six major factors. A later study showed seven predominant factors, and these were referred to as the *primary mental abilities*. As shown in Table 11.6, the seven factors are the following:

1 *Perceptual speed* (P)—The discrimination and identification of visual details.
2 *Numerical ability* (N)—Often referred to as the *number factor*, it involves arithmetic computational skills.
3 *Word fluency* (W)—The ability to think of words rapidly.

4 *Verbal comprehension* (V)—Involves the meaning and use of words. V and W are different. Selecting the correct synonym for a word among several choices involves V; quickly naming several synonyms involves W.
5 *Spatial visualization* (S)—The ability to deal with relationships among visual forms.
6 *Memory* (M)—Involves memory for words, numbers, symbols, and designs.
7 *Reasoning* (R)—The ability to discover a rule when given several instances where it applies.

Thurstone's list of primary mental abilities is a useful classification system, but it does not adequately represent the complexity of intelligence. It has been shown that the factors are not independent of one another. There are general intercorrelations among the seven factors, suggesting that some general ability factor may be involved.

The Guilford model

J. P. Guilford (1957, 1967) constructed a theoretical model for the structure of human intellect as a means of organizing the results of his own factor analyses and those of others. Using this *structure of intellect* model, he identified three ways of classifying mental abilities—according to *operation*, *content*, and *product*. Figure 11.5 is a graphic representation of the model; it describes the five types of mental operations, four types of content, and six types of product. The mental operations are the following:

1 *Evaluation*—deciding how appropriate or significant an idea is;
2 *Convergent thinking*—sorting out information to arrive at the correct solution to a problem;
3 *Divergent thinking*—using information to discover a variety of ideas or solutions to a problem;
4 *Memory*—retention of information;
5 *Cognition*—the possession of information in the sense of recognizing and rediscovering it in new contexts.

Within each of the five mental operations, tasks can be classified by their contents:

1 *Figural*—directly perceived objects or events;
2 *Symbolic*—letters, numbers, etc.;
3 *Semantic*—verbal meanings;
4 *Behavioral*—social situations.

The kinds of responses the individual can make are classified according to the six products:

1 *Units of information*—identifying single units such as numbers, letters, words, etc.;
2 *Classes*—identifying and sorting units according to their common characteristics;
3 *Relations*—discovering relations among things;
4 *Systems*—organizing things into patterns;
5 *Transformation*—transforming patterns;
6 *Implications*—using foresight in planning and selecting a course of action.

Guilford's model calls for 120 factors, since there are 5 × 4 × 6 possible combinations of operations, contents, and products. Evidence for 77

Figure 11.5   Guilford's structure of intellect. The cube contains 120 elements, each of which functions in three dimensions: content, operation, and product. (Guilford, 1961)

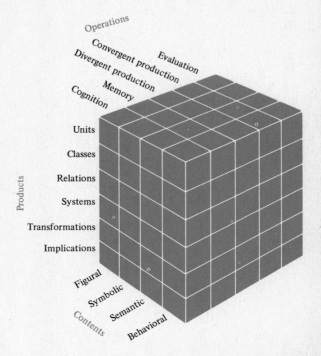

of the factors has been found by means of new tests designed in accordance with the model (Guilford, 1967).

The Guilford structure-of-intellect model has generated important research on the subject of intelligence. When he proposed a distinction between *convergent* and *divergent* thinking, Guilford set the stage for systematic comparisons between conventional and creative intelligence. Before Guilford's distinction, most intelligence tests consisted of questions and problems for which there was only one correct answer. Such questions do not elicit information about originality and creativity. Guilford's approach to testing includes items designed to elicit many kinds of answers, a method that allows some measure of originality to be demonstrated. A typical item asks the child to name unusual uses for a common object such as a newspaper. The child who answers, "Roll it up to make a tunnel for a pet hamster," or "Tear it up and stuff it into a pillow case to make a mattress for a dog," scores high on divergent thinking.

DEVELOPMENTAL CHANGES IN INTELLIGENCE

Does intelligence change with age? At what age is intelligence development completed? According to Tyler (1965), both questions must be answered with the qualification, "That depends."

Intelligence changes with age, but the kind and degree of change depends on the age range and environmental influences. Children's intelligence-test scores change as they mature and learn. Human development, particularly intellectual development, is not independent of the environment: there is continuous interaction.

It has been shown that children whose parents are well educated are more likely to show increases in IQ than decreases (Tyler, 1965).

Boys' IQs tend to increase more often than girls' IQs; and children rated high on traits such as independence and competitiveness show greater IQ increases than children rated low on these traits (Sontag, Baker, and Nelson, 1958).

These findings suggest that intellectual growth is accelerated in the children of well-educated parents who provide a home environment that favors intellectual development, and that both boys and girls who seek to know their environment tend to develop faster intellectually than children who are passive and dependent.

It was once thought that intelligence development was completed by the age of 16. Careful research has shown, however, that intelligence-test scores may increase past the age of 21 for individuals who continue their formal education. No single upper limit has, in fact, been identified. People who continue to seek knowledge tend to show intellectual growth, even though as adults they may not perform as well as they did as children on tests that require speed of performance.

Decline of intelligence

Because there is growth in intelligence and because it parallels biological development in general, intelligence may also be expected to decline at some time. The evidence suggests that while decline does occur, it is not a unitary or general decline. Some abilities decline before others during the aging process.

Scores on verbal intelligence tests remain relatively stable during adulthood, into late middle age, with little or no decline in verbal abilities and vocabulary or the use of previously learned information. Tests involving dexterity or quick solutions to new problems, however, do show decline, beginning around age 35. The greatest differences between young and elderly adults occur on problem-solving tests that present novel problems (Reed and Reitan, 1963). Little difference occurs, however, on tests of stored information.

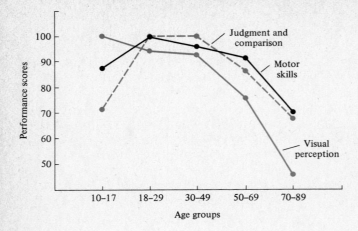

Figure 11.6   Average performance of different age groups on special abilities tests. (From Miles, W. R., "Age and human ability," Psychological Review, 1933, *40*, 99–123)

Fluid and crystallized intelligence Some studies show that intelligence decreases with age, while others confirm exactly the opposite trend. Horn and Cattell (1967) explain these differences by calling attention to the distinction between "fluid" and "crystallized" intelligence.

Fluid intelligence is comprised of abilities centering around concept formation and attainment, reasoning, and abstraction—abilities relatively free of cultural exposure and education. Crystallized intelligence, on the other hand, requires substantial use of reasoning processes based on the verbal and arithmetic abilities one acquires from exposure to education and life in general. Although there may be several other factors involved in the usual measures of intelligence, these two are said by Horn and Cattell to be the only factors which measure "pure" intelligence.

After dividing their subjects into five age groupings—early adolescence, late adolescence, twenties, thirties, and older—Horn and Cattell administered measures of fluid intelligence and crystallized intelligence, controlling for all other relevant variables (like sex or education level). Comparison of mean scores in each age group revealed that fluid intelligence declined systematically with age while crystallized intelligence increased systematically.

The decline of special abilities is of particular importance when questions about the employability of older people arise. Figure 11.6 shows the rate of decline of three types of abilities—judgment and comparison, motor skills,

and visual perception. Motor skills do not mature until the individual is between 18 and 29 years, and such skills do not show substantial declines until age 50 or beyond. Judgment skills also mature during the 18- to 29-year period, and these skills hold up well until at least age 50. Visual perception matures the earliest (10–17) and declines the earliest. By age 50, visual perception skills are well below their peak.

Studies dealing with the decline of intelligence indicate that older persons become slower at some tasks but often compensate by utilizing their previous experience, which often makes them more able than their younger colleagues. Because they have encountered certain situations before, they are often better at solving related problems than are less experienced individuals.

THE EXCEPTIONAL CHILD

Intelligence testing has called attention to the variety and extremes of human ability. Some children are exceptionally able in school, and others, because of disabilities, have exceptional difficulty in school. The term "exceptional child" has come to be used to include the two extremes—the mentally retarded child and the gifted child.

Mentally retarded children

An IQ below 70 is regarded as an indication of some form of mental retardation. There are a number of classification systems of mental retardation. Most agree that persons with IQs of 55 to 70 are retarded but can be taught simple reading and writing; those with IQs from 35 to 55 can be trained to perform simple tasks and take care of their personal hygiene; those with IQs below 35 are usually wholly untrainable.

The National Association for Retarded Children estimates that about 3 percent of the population is retarded. However, mental retardation is no longer regarded as a hopeless impairment. The very fact that today we use the term "retardation" in place of "feeblemindedness" and "mental deficiency" indicates optimism. The emphasis today is on training retarded youngsters rather than relegating them to custodial institutional care.

The causes of mental retardation are a major research concern in both medicine and psychology. Two primary areas of causation have been identified: One is medical, including genetic and congenital factors that may result in physical deficits that contribute to faulty intellectual development. The other is environmental, as, for example, when early deprivation of stimulation holds back a child's normal intellectual development. Genetic factors and defects that occur during pregnancy or at birth are believed to account for severe retardation. Environmental conditions are suspected as a cause of relatively mild retardation.

Gifted children

Less than 2 percent of the population is intellectually gifted. Contrary to popular belief, gifted persons tend to be stronger and more vigorous than the average person. A genius is very often the opposite of the timid, 99-pound weakling of popular mythology.

Much of our information about gifted children comes from a large-scale study involving 1,000 preschool and elementary school children and 300 high-school students with IQs of 140 or above (Burks, Jensen, and Terman, 1930; Terman and Oden, 1947). This study showed that the parents of gifted children were better educated than those of nongifted children. Fathers of the gifted were preponderantly in the professions and in business: 31 percent of the fathers were in one of the professions; 50 percent were semiprofessionals or businessmen; 12 percent were skilled laborers; and 7 percent were semiskilled or unskilled workers.

The gifted children were generally superior to the normal population in developmental and physical characteristics. They were, on the average, taller, heavier, and better developed than other children. They walked and talked at an earlier age, and were healthier than other children. Approximately 85 percent of them skipped at least one grade. They were avid readers and scored high in all subject-matter areas.

Table 11.7 compares the ratings on personality traits of a group of gifted and a group of nongifted children. The two groups were similar in social traits such as fondness for groups and popularity, but the gifted children had higher teacher ratings on traits reflecting intellectual activity, such as desire to know and general intelligence, and on traits reflecting motivation, such as perseverance, conscientiousness, and desire to excel.

The key question is what happened to the gifted children when they grew up. A study following the performance of these children through school (Burks, Jensen, and Terman, 1930) showed that the gifted children maintained their academic superiority. A later follow-up (Terman and Oden, 1947) showed that the gifted group as a whole had achieved more success than comparable nongifted groups. About 90 percent had

Table 11.7 Teachers' ratings of gifted and comparison children for various traits[a,b]

"Traits"	Gifted		Control	
	Boys	Girls	Boys	Girls
Common sense	4.2	4.1	6.2	5.9
Conscientiousness	4.8	4.0	6.2	5.4
Desire to excel	4.2	3.6	6.1	5.6
Desire to know	3.5	3.9	6.3	6.2
Fondness for groups	6.2	5.6	6.1	5.9
Freedom from vanity	5.9	5.4	6.1	5.6
General intelligence	3.1	3.1	6.4	6.2
Leadership	6.3	5.8	7.2	7.0
Originality	4.4	4.5	6.8	6.9
Perseverance	4.4	4.1	6.4	6.1
Popularity	6.4	5.7	6.5	6.2
Sympathy	5.8	5.2	6.3	5.7

[a]From Miles, C. C. Gifted children. In L. Carmichael (Ed.), *Manual of child psychology* (2nd ed.). New York: Wiley, 1954.
[b]The smaller the number the higher the rating.

attended college and more than two-thirds had graduated. Approximately 71 percent of the gifted men were in one of the professions or in managerial positions in business as compared with 14 percent of a comparable group of non-gifted males. The percentage of gifted women in the professions and in business was much less. (It should be noted here that 1947 was long before the women's liberation movement.) Some of the gifted failed in college; some were unsuccessful vocationally; and some had adjustment problems. But the proportion of failures was well below that found in a sample of the general population.

In the most recent follow-up study, Oden (1968) reports that 133 was the average IQ of a large sample of children who each had a parent from the original gifted group. The average of 133 does not mean that all the children had high IQs. Some were low and some were in the gifted range, but, on the whole, their scores were much higher than those of the general population at large.

Figure 11.7 In this test of manual dexterity, the subject must move the electrical bar in line with the triangle. Each movement away from the outline of the triangle is recorded on the device attached to it. (Lafayette Instrument Co.)

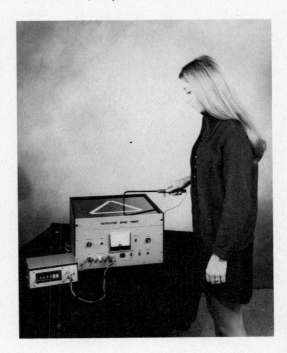

ACHIEVEMENT
AND APTITUDE TESTING

Ability tests that measure what an individual is able to do under certain standardized conditions are usually referred to as *achievement* tests or *trade* tests. Ability tests designed to predict the potential for future achievement are called *aptitude* tests. Since to predict an individual's potential skill, we must consider his achievement, the difference between these two types of tests is really one of emphasis. Any test measures what the individual can do at the moment; but aptitude tests are especially designed to be predictive instruments, and achievement tests, to

evaluate the effects of past instruction. Aptitude tests may be used to put together a *profile* of an individual—a description of the overall individual.

Some recent improved methods of aptitude testing are based on experimental data concerned with the specific interests of separately tested occupational groups—the things they like, dislike, and are indifferent to. Experimenters found that, for one reason or another, individuals who enter certain fields tend to have similar interests. Whether this is the influence of the field itself (since the individuals tested were already established in that field) or whether these interests are related to the inherent special aptitudes of individuals who select a particular field is not now known. However, it has been shown that persons in certain occupational groups have common likes and dislikes. *Interest tests* are seldom used alone to predict future behavior, but they

Figure 11.8   *Relationship between pilot aptitude scores and successful completion of pilot training. The higher the aptitude test score was, the more successful was the pilot in completing his training course.*
"Psychological activities in Training Command AAF." (Psychological Bulletin, 1945, **42**, 46)

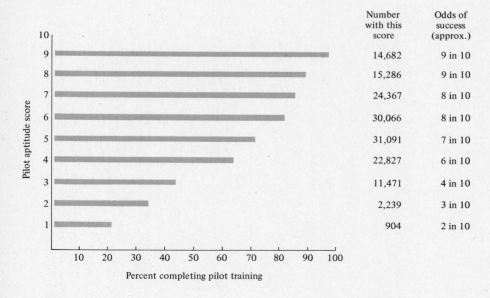

Pilot aptitude score	Number with this score	Odds of success (approx.)
9	14,682	9 in 10
8	15,286	9 in 10
7	24,367	8 in 10
6	30,066	8 in 10
5	31,091	7 in 10
4	22,827	6 in 10
3	11,471	4 in 10
2	2,239	3 in 10
1	904	2 in 10

Percent completing pilot training

are helpful when used in conjunction with other types of tests. Correlations found between the interests of college students and their later interests and occupations have been high enough to suggest a strong relationship between interests and occupation.

Effective means of describing *psychomotor* abilities, such as dexterity, strength, and coordination, have improved vocational testing (Figure 11.7). Much of the testing information in this area has come from the armed forces, which have tested large numbers of men through the years. Using psychomotor testing, they have been able to find individuals for jobs requiring manual dexterity and coordination. Figure 11.8 shows the relationship between scores on a pilot aptitude test and successful completion of pilot training.

The *trade test*, essentially an achievement test, measures an applicant's skills in his line of work. Such tests have been standardized for many common manual occupations and are a useful way to distinguish levels of occupational accomplishment (see Stead and Shartle, 1940).

SUMMARY

To be useful, a test must be reliable, valid, objective, and standardized.

Tests are used for prediction, diagnosis, and research.

Alfred Binet and Theodore Simon designed the first formal intelligence test for schoolchildren using the concepts of mental age (MA) and chronological age (CA). The test procedure was later revised by L. M. Terman, who, following an idea of Stern's, used the intelligence quotient, or IQ ($[MA/CA] \times 100$).

Performance IQ tests consist mainly of motor or perceptual test items.

The Wechsler Intelligence Scale for Children (WISC) and the Wechsler Adult Intelligence Scale (WAIS) are individually administered intelligence tests with both verbal and performance items.

Intelligence tests measure ability at the time of testing compared with that of others tested. Because other factors influence test performance, intelligence test scores must be considered in conjunction with other data.

According to Spearman's two-factor theory, intelligence consists of an overall general factor and specific factors.

Factor analysis is a statistical procedure for analyzing intercorrelations of tests. Factor loading is the correlation between a factor and the tests in which it is believed to be influential.

The Thurstone seven-factor theory of intelligence consists of specific factors such as verbal comprehension, numerical ability, and perceptual speed.

Guilford's structure of intellect is a theoretical model consisting of 120 factors of intelligence. Each factor is divided into three main components—content, operation, and product.

Intelligence changes with age, depending on the age range and environmental influences.

How nature and nurture interact is a central question in the study of intelligence.

Studies have shown a positive relationship between heredity and intelligence test scores. Environmental deprivation or enhancement also has an effect on intelligence test score.

Some intelligence abilities decline before others. Verbal abilities hold up better than skills requiring dexterity or speed.

Mental retardation is indicated by an IQ below 70; it may be either medical (genetic or congenital) or environmental in origin. About 3 percent of the population is retarded.

Intellectually gifted persons (with IQs above 140) make up less than 2 percent of the population.

Aptitude and achievement tests are both tests of ability. An aptitude test attempts to measure what a person can learn to do if given the proper training. An achievement test measures what an individual has learned to do as the result of previous training and experience.

Interest tests are based on the finding that individuals in the same occupation share similar interests.

Vocational testing has been aided by the use of effective means of describing such psychomotor abilities as dexterity, strength, and coordination.

Trade tests measure skills in a specific kind of work.

SUGGESTED READINGS

Texts

Anastasi, A. *Psychological testing.* New York: Macmillan, 1968. Comprehensive coverage of tests and their uses.

Burdock, E. I., & Hadest, A. S. *Structural clinical interviews (SCI).* New York: Springer, 1969. Detailed discussion of the evaluation of such interviews.

Cronbach, L. J. *Essentials of psychological testing* (2nd ed.). New York: Harper & Row, 1960. Highly readable surveys of tests and testing.

Dustin D. S. *How psychologists do research: the example of anxiety.* Englewood Cliffs, N.J.: Prentice-Hall, 1969. Discussion of psychological measurement in a specific area.

Environment, heredity, and intelligence. Cambridge, Mass.: Harvard Educational Review, 1969. Reprint Series No. 2. A controversial study of IQ and the genetic-environmental question.

Getting, T. *Exercises in psychological testing.* New York: Harper & Row, 1969. Some applications of psychological measurement.

Helmstadter, G. C. *Principles of psychological measurement.* New York: Appleton-Century-Crofts, 1964. Introduction to the basic principles of psychological measurement.

Horst, P. *Personality: measurement of dimensions.* San Francisco: Jossey-Bass, 1968. Survey of personality assessment techniques.

Savage, R. D. *Psychometric assessment of the individual child.* Baltimore: Penguin, 1968. Application of psychological assessment to individual children.

Schoeninger, D. W., & Insko, C. A. *Introductory statistics for the behavioral sciences.* Boston: Allyn & Bacon, 1971. A lucid but very elementary (presupposing almost no ability in mathematics) introduction to the statistical methods used in psychological experimentation.

Stodola, Q., & Stordahl, K. *Basic education tests and measurements.* Chicago: Science Research Associates, 1967. Discussion of the procedures of assessment in education.

Thorndike, R. L., & Hagen, E. *Measurement and evaluation in psychology and education.* New York: Wiley, 1955. Very useful guide to tests and their practical uses.

Popular books

Lehman, P. R. *Tests and measurements in music.* Application of scientific measurement to musical ability.

Porteus, S. D. *A psychologist of sorts: the autobiography and publications of the inventor of the Porteus Maze Test.* An interesting personal document which includes Porteus's methods of psychological assessment.

Rich J., *Interviewing children and adolescents.* Discussion of special interviewing techniques.

Weisberger, L. A. *Psychological assessment of candidates for a religious order.* Interesting example of psychological assessment in action.

12
Personality

No one person is *exactly* the same as any other. Look around you—whether you are at home with your parents or in school with your friends. Consider your friends. One is stimulated by learning of any kind; another adores a good gab session; a third likes to dance. They may be different heights and weights, with brown, blond, or red hair, but all may equally enjoy a good movie or a ride in the country. The varied physical and psychological (learned) characteristics of each individual combine to form his or her unique personality.

Personality is the term we use when we refer to the organized system of behavior patterns, attitudes, and values that characterize a given individual and account for his particular manner of functioning. Personality psychology is the study of each person's characteristics as they make him different from others and consistent within himself (Mischel, 1968). Like other areas of psychology, personality study deals with characteristics common to all men; unlike these other fields, it places its emphasis on individual variation (Lazarus, 1971).

Because the factors that contribute to the total personality are many and complex, it is difficult to formulate general principles that apply to all people. Nevertheless, psychologists have uncovered certain similarities and consistencies that enable them to explain, predict, and sometimes therapeutically influence the individual's behavior.

Faced with the enormous complexity of personality, psychologists have sought to organize their data in a variety of ways. Some have classified persons into type categories; some have attempted to identify traits, particularly persistent ways of responding; and some have proposed theories to explain the development and functions of human personality (Table 12.1).

Most psychologists, whether they adhere to one approach or another, discuss personality in terms of traits. A *trait* is a particular and persistent feature of an individual's personality—a characteristic that can be measured and observed.

Table 12.1   Major figures in the study of personality

Type	Trait	Psychodynamic approach	Self-actualization approach	Behavioral approach
Sheldon	Allport	Freud	Rogers	Dollard and Miller
Jung	Cattell	Adler	Maslow	Skinner
		Jung	May	
		Horney		
		Fromm		
		Sullivan		
		Erikson		

TYPING THE INDIVIDUAL

The earliest personality theories involved the study of *typology*—the tendency of certain traits to occur together. In typing, each group of traits forms a different category, and each individual fits into one of these specific categories, based on the pattern of traits in his personality.

Type theories base their classification on general aspects of human behavior or appearance. There are many different type theories; we shall examine only some of the more comprehensive ones.

A chemical typology: temperament

Personality theory is not unique to our times. As early as 400 B.C., Hippocrates (known to us as the Father of Medicine) was interested in classifying personalities and in learning how each type behaves. Hippocrates believed that each individual's temperament (or way of behaving) was controlled by his bodily condition or type. Specifically, he believed that there were four basic body fluids, called *humors*, and that if a person possessed an excess of any one of the four, this excess would cause him to act in a certain way. Table 12.2 shows the relationship between humor and temperament. Although modern medicine and psychology reject Hippocrates' theory, the idea of a physical basis to temperament remains as the foundation for new chemical typology theories.

Some modern theorists have developed a chemical typology based on the hormones secreted by the endocrine glands (see Chapter 3). Studies have shown that the endocrine glands are not the same size and weight in every individual; the larger a gland, the greater the secretion of its particular hormone. Thus, according to these psychologists, because each hormone activates different bodily functions, and because

Table 12.2   Hippocrates' proposed relationship between humors and temperaments

Humor	Temperament	Characteristics
Blood	Sanguine	Warm, happy, optimistic
Yellow bile	Choleric	High-strung, easily angered, passionate
Phlegm	Phlegmatic	Slow-moving, apathetic
Black bile	Melancholic	Depressed, sad, romantic

these activities relate to our emotional feelings, each person is temperamentally affected most by the hormone secreted by his largest glands. For example, a person with extra-large adrenal glands will probably be more excitable and nervous than most people. Endocrine typologists therefore conclude that differences in hormone secretions account for our unique temperaments.

While studies in endocrine typology provide some interesting and useful information, psychologists do not yet know enough about hormone activity to frame an all-encompassing personality theory based on endocrine typology.

Hormones and sexual behavior Current evidence indicates that individual differences in hormonal activity, resulting either from genetic or early environmental influences, can contribute to long-term differences in personality and behavior patterns. Levine (1966) began with the premise that adult sexual activity in rats depends on a process of sex-related brain differentiation that takes place during a critical period soon after each rat's birth. He found that variations in hormonal levels of very young rats caused marked differences in later sexual behavior. Levine theorized that the brains of developing male mammals are essentially female until some critical period of sex-related changes. During this period, hormonal activity, mainly of testosterone, directs cellular differentiation in accordance with the organism's morphology. Normal testosterone levels cause the brain to develop normal male characteristics. Should hormonal activity during that critical period be abnormal, then the brain will develop abnormally with respect to the determination of subsequent sexual activity.

As would be predicted by this theory, young female rats injected with testosterone not only failed to develop normal female sexual behavior in adulthood but also failed to develop normal ovaries regularly. Young castrated males showed signs of female physiology and female behavioral receptivity in adulthood.

Thus, according to Levine, early hormonal activity alters the central nervous system in various ways, which later affect brain organization and behavior. That such chemical influences may also apply to complex aspects of man's personality seems a reasonable hypothesis for a new generation of study.

Endocrine typology is not the only body-chemistry theory of personality. There are many others, most concentrating on the reactions of the parasympathetic and sympathetic divisions of the autonomic nervous system (see Chapter 3)—the nerves and ganglia that activate or calm internal body organs. Because the parasympathetic and sympathetic divisions function in opposition to each other, advocates of such theories believe that only one of these divisions plays a dominant role in an individual's personality. Certain people are more prone to sympathetic-controlled temperament; others to parasympathetic-controlled temperament. For example, a person who tends to be fearful is thought to have a sympathetic-controlled temperament; the sympathetic division accelerates heartbeat, which is an organic manifestation of fear. Various test results show that such a relationship exists, but the physiological processes involved are still largely unknown.

A physical typology: body type

Other type theories associate personality with the external structure of the body, the physique. These theories may have evolved from the common belief that individuals of a certain physique possess certain personality traits in common; a fat man is typically described as jolly and a skinny man as serious.

According to one theory, proposed by Ernest Kretschmer in 1936 on the basis of his observations of psychiatric patients, body types are divided into three categories:

1 *asthenic* (tall and thin);
2 *pyknic* (short and plump);
3 *athletic* (muscular).

Kretschmer described the asthenic type as introverted and withdrawn; the pyknic type as emotional and outgoing; and the athletic type as somewhere between the other two.

W. H. Sheldon (1942), an American psychologist, believed that Kretschmer's typology was too rigid. He substituted a system of body typing known as *somatotyping*, in which each individual is classified according to the degree to which his body build reflects certain physical characteristics (somatotypes). The three somatotypes (shown in Figure 12.1) are as follows:

1 *endomorphy* (fleshy);
2 *mesomorphy* (muscular);
3 *ectomorphy* (thin, fine-boned).

Sheldon correlated the somatotypes with personality characteristics.

Sheldon's procedures and conclusions have been widely criticized. Many psychologists believe that he was not truly objective in his judgments, because he did both the somatotyping and the observations of personality himself. To test Sheldon's objectivity, some researchers repeated his procedures in similar situations; A. B. Hood (1963), for example, tested 10,000 male college freshmen and found that the relationship between somatotype and personality was insignificant. Psychologists have thus labeled Sheldon's experiment contaminated (biased), since it is quite possible that his prior knowledge of physique ratings affected his later observations of personality.

A behavior typology: psychological characteristics

A popular and influential psychological type theory is the introvert-extravert classification established by Carl Jung, the Swiss psychoanalyst. Jung suggested that most people were either predominantly *introverted* (shy, withdrawn, interested in their own subjective cognitions and ideals, unsociable) or predominantly *extraverted* (realistic, conventional, sociable, and generally aggressive). The individual's life experiences strengthened or weakened these tendencies, so

Figure 12.1   *Sheldon's somatotypes and their personality traits.*

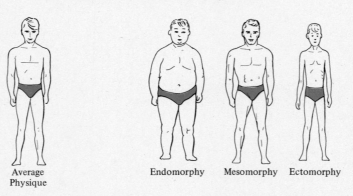

PHYSIQUE	TEMPERAMENT	PERSONALITY TRAITS
Endomorphy	Visceratonia	Relaxed stance, seeks physical comfort, friendly, seeks others when troubled, slow to react, deep sleep
Mesomorphy	Somatotonia	Definite stance, seeks physical adventure, restless, needs activity when troubled, aggressive, competitive, general noisiness.
Ectomorphy	Cerebrotonia	Rigid and controlled stance, socially inhibited, quick to react, seeks to be alone when troubled, poor sleep habits, thus, constant fatigue.

that one or the other became the predominant and conscious form of behavior, while the opposing tendency was banished to the unconscious.

Jung based this theory of personality upon clinical observation. In testing his theory on numerous patients, he was able to classify each patient as one personality type or the other. More recent tests, however, have shown that total introverts and extraverts are rare extremes. Most individuals in a normal population are *ambiverts*, that is, they alternate between introversion and extraversion. Using Guilford's 120 factors of intelligence (see Chapter 11), psychologists have been able to separate five factors on a continuum of introversion-extraversion. These five factors are

1 *depression;*
2 *social introversion* (inability to interact with others);
3 *thinking introversion* (tendency to be quiet, reflective);
4 *tendency to swings of mood;*
5 *happy-go-lucky disposition.*

CLASSIFICATION OF TRAITS

In typology, individuals are classified into groups and characterized by group traits. Trait studies, however, are concerned with individuals and the traits that each possesses. While typology assumes that all the individuals classified in a group possess similar traits, trait theories describe particular traits and the degree to which each appears in a given individual.

Psychologists who use the trait approach often describe personality in terms of *trait profiles* (Figure 12.2), which graphically depict the kind and degree of traits displayed by an individual as determined by a personality questionnaire. Psychologists who use trait techniques for compiling personality profiles must assess each trait separately and then draw a composite that accurately describes the individual.

Avoiding observer bias Experimenters who work with trait profiles need to be wary of the problem of bias. For example, since identical twins are expected to have similar personalities, experimenters may tend to observe such similarities, whether or not they exist. Freedman and Keller (1963) sought to avoid this problem by studying identical twins when they were only one year; because at that age a child's characteristics are not yet fully developed and overt, the experimenters could not distinguish one twin from the other. The study tested emotional, physical and psychological aspects of the twins' behavior. Detailed records were kept, and at the end of the year, trait profiles were compiled for each subject. The twins were then identified and their separate records were compared. It was found that the records were remarkably alike in every aspect tested, far more than those for fraternal twins.

Trait profiles must necessarily be relatively brief, but they are useful only if they are based on complete lists of traits. There are literally thousands of traits, and psychologists have attempted to identify all of them. In one study, 17,953 individual traits were identified (Allport and Odbert, 1936).

Obviously, working with a list of 17,953 traits would present an enormous problem to a psychologist. To make the list workable, he would need to condense it while endeavoring to encompass the essential traits in the complete list.

Cattell

Raymond B. Cattell was one of the first psychologists to attempt to reduce Allport and Odbert's list of 17,953 traits to a more workable length. In 1946, sampling from different populations, he first eliminated all the infrequently occurring traits. Then, by using the method of factor analysis (see Chapter 11), he found that certain traits, such as boldness, independence, and toughness, are often clustered in the same person; that is, they have a high correlation. He combined all the clustered traits under inclusive headings to produce a list of *surface traits*—traits that are

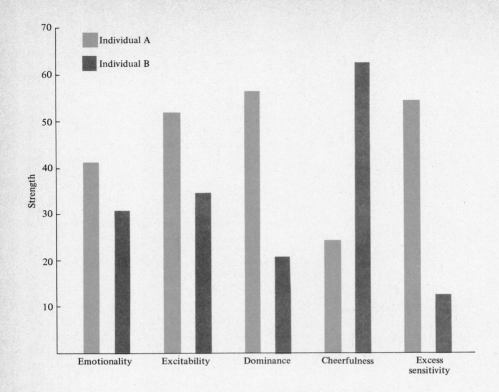

Figure 12.2 A comparison of two trait profiles. The measurement of the strength of the traits is based on scores from a personality questionnaire. The 5 traits are from a longer list of 16 traits.

readily observable in the behavior of the person. For example, boldness, independence, toughness, and so on might be grouped under the surface trait *autonomy.*

Cattell then condensed this list of surface traits. Rather than have a relatively long list of surface traits, such as emotionality, reserve, egotism, and modesty, he classified clusters of opposites, such as emotionality versus reserve, or egotism versus modesty. These trait clusters were rated as to similarity by a group of subjects. The resulting correlations between pairs were submitted to a factor analysis that revealed what Cattell calls the *source traits* of personality. These source traits are the deeper underlying traits responsible for the surface personality. Typical source traits are dominance versus sub-

missiveness and ego strength versus proneness to neuroticism.

Factor analysis of personality Cattell, Blewett, and Beloff (1955) studied the inheritance of personality by means of their multivariance analysis method (an extension of factor analysis), using 104 identical twins, 64 fraternal twins, 182 siblings reared together, and 540 children from the general population. All subjects answered the Junior Personality Questionnaire test, which measures 12 personality factors.

A statistical analysis of the correlations from a number of studies suggested to them that some factors—for example, tender-mindedness, general neuroticism, and bodily anxiety—were determined predominantly by environment. Other factors, such as the drives to conform and to dominate, were about equally determined by heredity and environment. General intelligence and emotionality versus absence of emotion were determined primarily by heredity.

Other factor analysis studies prompted by Allport and Odbert's 17,953 traits did not arrive at the same source traits as did Cattell's. But the differences are differences in emphasis rather than in substance.

Guilford

J. P. Guilford (1959) classified all traits or personality factors as either motivational or temperament. The *motivational traits* (called hermetic by Guilford) involve needs, attitudes, and interests. For example, aggressiveness, endurance, orderliness, liberalism, and vocational and cultural interests are considered motivational traits. The *temperament traits* involve general, emotional, and social behavior. General behavior includes such trait dimensions as confidence versus feelings of inferiority and impulsiveness versus deliberateness. Among emotional traits are cheer-

fulness versus depression and nervousness versus composure. Social traits include such factors as ascendance versus timidity and social initiative versus passivity.

Eysenck

Another approach to trait theory has been taken by H. J. Eysenck, an English psychologist who made extensive use of psychological testing and the method of factor analysis (Eysenck, 1960). Eysenck suggested that personality can be described in terms of two major dimensions: emotional stability–neuroticism and introversion–extraversion. An individual's pattern of traits defines his place on each of these two dimensions. For example, a person who scores high on the traits of talkativeness and sociability might be identified as being high on the stability and extraversion dimensions. One who scores high on passivity and thoughtfulness might also rate high on the stability dimension, although he also rates high on the introversion dimension. Figure 12.3 provides an illustration of Eysenck's two-dimensional model.

Figure 12.3   Eysenck's two-dimensional model. (From H. J. Eysenck and S. B. G. Eysenck, The Eysenck Personality Inventory. London: University Press, Ltd., 1963.)

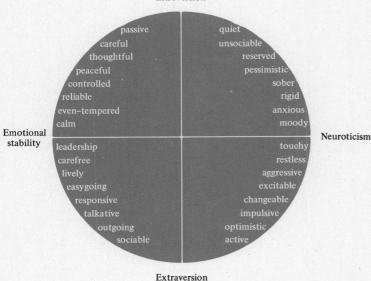

PERSONALITY DEVELOPMENT

The concepts of type or trait are only a beginning. They help to describe personality, but we also need to know where these traits and types come from, how they develop, and what processes influence their devlopment. In this section we shall discuss the variables that influence the formation and development of personality—heredity, experience, and culture. The individual's total personality results from the interaction of these three sets of variables.

Influence of heredity

The most effective technique for measuring the influence of heredity on personality development has been the testing and comparison of subjects with the same heredity but different environments. For such studies, psychologists have relied largely upon analysis of identical twins raised apart.

Twins raised together, usually dressed alike and expected to be alike, are obviously very much influenced by their mutual environment, so that it is hardly surprising to find that their personalities are similar. However, studies have shown that personality similarities in identical twins are so striking that they must be due to more than environmental factors. Reared separately, identical twins do not ordinarily have the same role expectations imposed upon them and are not expected to be mirror images of each other; nevertheless, they develop remarkably similar personalities. Such studies strongly suggest that heredity is a major influence in personality formation.

Genetic components of personality Schoenfeldt (1968), using questionnaire data from several hundred sets of same-sex twins, determined that there do seem to be personality traits of substantial genetic origin. (As in other twin studies, "heritability" reflects the difference between degree of similarity of fraternal twins and degree of similarity of identical twins.) Schoenfeldt's most striking finding was that heritability is much more important a factor for females than for males. Females, for instance, showed significant heritability of various needs and motivations: sociability, impulsiveness, leadership, scholasticism, activity level, and conformity needs (given roughly in order of heritability strength). In contrast, males only showed significant heritability patterns in certain interest areas: business, outdoors, and cultural interests. Cultural interests was the only one of the 11 independent personality factors evaluated which reflected significant heritability for both sexes.

These findings indicate that females are exposed to much narrower environmental stimuli than are males. Thus, the female's inherited characteristics are less obscured by learning and experience. Because the male is customarily allowed more variation and nonconformity in his personal needs and activities, his inherited characteristics are by adulthood more fully integrated with his learning and experience.

Studies have also found that certain characteristics of personality are more prone to genetic transmission than others. For example, there is some evidence that the introversion–extraversion dimension is influenced by various hereditary factors.

Many psychologists interested in the genetic influence on personality subscribe to an interaction position in which environmental variables are also given important emphasis. They believe that a child does not inherit introversion or extraversion, aggressiveness or submissiveness, as such; he inherits a physical characteristic which influences his environment and is in turn influenced by his environment. This is the dynamic interaction described in Chapter 2. A child may inherit a physiological makeup that leads him to be overactive. This overactivity puts him more in touch with his environment than is an underactive child. If he is very overactive, he may cause his environment to react negatively. His parents may attempt to restrain and punish him to make him limit his activity. He, in turn, may become increasingly aggressive as a reaction to these restraints. The aggressiveness itself, then, is not an inherited trait, but the result of a genetic tendency to overactivity.

Influence of experience on personality

Although a child's heredity may predispose him to respond to new experiences in certain ways, as determined by his level of maturation and temperamental tendencies, his responses are altered considerably by contact with parents, playmates, relatives, and others. For example, children develop emotional responsiveness only through observing the effects of their responses on others.

The importance of emotional relationships early in life is documented by studies of children raised in orphanages. In such environments, the infant may receive a proper diet and be properly cared for, but he does not ordinarily receive sufficient affection or genuine emotional warmth from orphanage personnel. Most institutions cannot provide the infant with parental closeness and usually fail to offer the kind of emotional environment needed to develop a warmly responsive personality.

Effect of genetic and environmental factors on personality The relative effects of genetic and environmental factors on personality have been of continual interest to researchers in all areas of psychology. In a recent study, Freedman (1965) produced a number of films of same-sex infant twins to determine whether important behavioral differences could be noted between identical and fraternal twins.

The infants were filmed separately—but in the same situations in their homes—over a period of several months. All films taken of each twin were then combined on separate reels, so that specific behaviors could be rated by independent groups of judges using the Bayley Infant Behavior Profile.

While many behavioral characteristics were found to be significantly more similar between identical than fraternal twins, two were particularly interesting. These were positive social orientation and fear of strangers. For example, identical twins from 1 to 5 months old engaged in much more similar patterns of social smiling than did fraternal twins;

similarly, identical twins older than 5 months showed much more similar patterns of fearfulness toward the investigator than did their counterparts. Freedman suggests that these apparently genotypic differences in infant behaviors are extremely important because of what they imply about pleasure or fear of others in the adult personality.

Juel-Nielsen (1965), using an older subject population, investigated behavioral similarities of identical Danish twins reared apart from infancy or very early childhood. In a series of interviews and projective personality measures, he discovered almost as many differences as similarities in behavior. For example, their manner of interacting with others, their interests, and their choices of mates were quite different. They also tended to differ in ambition, aggressiveness, and emotional control, as well as in matters of taste and dress. On the other hand, the twins exhibited remarkably similar expressive movements: gestures, facial expressions, tone of voice, gait, carriage, and laughter. A number of striking similarities were also noted in complaints of a psychosomatic type.

In recent years, however, the generality of this statement has been called into question by researchers who have studied the kibbutz, a special type of collective farm or commune in Israel. Because the adults must concentrate their efforts on the farm's productivity, all the children are reared from birth in a communal institution by special teachers. But the children receive the same love and attention normally provided by parents. Thus, it seems that the crucial variable is not the institution but the treatment received in the institution. (Kibbutz parents do spend time with their children every day, however.)

Most psychologists believe that the mother, because she spends the most time with the child, has the best opportunity to influence his personality and subsequent behavior. Mothers themselves generally agree upon what makes a "good" child, but they tend to disagree on just how to raise one.

Every aspect of child-rearing has been debated, starting with whether to breast-feed or bottle-feed. When bottle feeding was first introduced, mothers were skeptical of it, regarding it as too mechanical and dehumanized. Eventually, bottle feeding became an accepted and even preferred method, especially by mothers who insisted upon a well-defined, well-regulated system of child-rearing (the behavioristic approach). For example, the bottle (stimulus) could be presented at exact hours in exact amounts with the exact nutritional content known, and each time it would evoke the same response from the infant. More recently, many mothers have rejected the regulated approach to infant feeding, moving from a scheduled system to a permissive, feeding-on-demand approach, and from bottle feeding to breast feeding. Today there are enthusiastic proponents of both methods of infant feeding.

Isolation in Guatemala Does early deprivation necessarily doom a child to a life of failure? Although many psychologists currently hold to the early-deprivation notion, Kagan (1973) has reported a new sense of optimism resulting from data collected in a remote Guatemalan village. Because the village mothers believe that diseases can be prevented only if their children are shielded from the natural elements and the gaze of certain people, the infants are kept completely isolated during their first 2 years. Although mothers provide body contact and nurturance to their young during these years, there is almost no social interaction. Consequently, these infants and toddlers are not only quiet and fearful, but also retarded, relative to normal middle-class American children. Such developmental milestones as object constancy, stranger anxiety, and early language are all delayed by many months or even a year or more.

By contrast, however, the 11-year-olds of this same village were normally active, alert, and gay. In intellectual tasks requiring reasoning, memory, inference, deduction, and perception, these preadolescents showed every sign of having fully recovered from what Kagan assumes was the "ghostlike" infancy he observed in the village infants. Thus, he concluded that early deprivation does not doom a child to social and intellectual retardation as long as the child has several years of childhood exposure to a normally supportive and challenging environment.

Many mothers prefer breast feeding because they believe it creates a warmer, more affectionate relationship for the infant. Psychol-
ogists, however, have concluded that more important than the feeding method is the manner in which the infant is held and treated during the feeding. Breast feeding by itself does not assure a comfortable environment. If the mother feels insecure or uncomfortable about breast feeding, the baby will sense the agitation and become disturbed. If, using either feeding method, the parent merely holds the child, never fondling him, she may be setting the basis for the child's development into an unresponsive individual. Parents who do not show affection fail to create the warm, emotionally positive environment necessary for healthy personality adjustment outside the home.

Similarly, the way that parents handle weaning, toilet training, and other routine practices of child-rearing greatly affects the infant's personality formation. If parents are responsive, consistent, and understanding, the child can develop the healthy attitudes and confident self-image that lead to a well-adjusted personality. If the child learns from his parents that he is an individual and an important part of his family, if he has a secure home atmosphere, if he is given the right to say no as well as yes, he is being helped to develop into a mature individual who can cope with life's many problems and frustrations.

If parents create an insecure home—if they are inconsistent in their behavior toward him, hateful toward each other, or distrustful of the world—the child will acquire many fears. Unfortunately, a child can sense when he is not wanted or not respected long before he is able to label such feelings.

Although we know a great deal about the influence of childhood experience on personality, we do not yet have any theory of child-rearing that can guarantee the development of a healthy and happy child. Some parents try the authoritarian approach, others the permissive approach, and still others compromise between the two. But many a bewildered parent has, to his own heartbreak, raised a happy child and a disturbed child side by side using the same methods. No one approach has proved to be consistently successful with all children.

Child-raising, like other activities, is subject to changing fashion, and has been defined and redefined by pediatricians, parents, and (more recently) psychologists. At one time, child experts cautioned parents to be strict and explicit in establishing rules of behavior. But most psychologists found that a strict upbringing tended to make children mild, unaggressive, and conforming. Sometimes these children were inhibited in their responses and fearful of unfamiliar or unstructured situations. But sometimes their exposure to family discipline led to an admirable discipline in study, art, or physical achievement; sometimes it led them to react against the parental system with the creative energy and insight we call reform. A child raised in a strict home, like all children, depends on the understanding and consistent love of his parents. In the last analysis, his adjustment may depend on the way he is treated within the system that the family has established.

Many child experts today advocate the more permissive family—the family in which each member participates in family decisions as befits his age and maturity. Children raised in a permissive family tend to be curious, fearless, socially aggressive, and generally nonconforming. Furthermore, they may be more at ease in a world in which social restrictions outside the home are becoming somewhat relaxed, at least on an observable level. But, again, it is the emotional climate of the family that is critical. If the parents' permissiveness simply reflects a half-hearted revolt against their own upbringing, or if it reflects a lack of values altogether, the child may be subject to ambiguous and confusing behavior; thus, he may distrust parents and other authorities and try to manipulate people. If, on the other hand, the parents' permissive attitude represents a confirmed belief in living with a minimum of anxiety and restriction and the opportunity for each member of the family to express himself fully, they communicate such attitudes to a very fortunate child.

Permissive attitudes and child-rearing Does a parent's permissive attitude affect the social behavior of his child? Lorber (1971) found that permissive home atmospheres were correlated with socially exploitative and domineering peer behavior among a sample of suburban seventh-graders.

Defining exploitative-domineering peer behavior as "social relations involving the use of one's peers for one's advantage and their control and manipulation for one's self-serving purposes," the investigator asked teachers to identify pupils who exhibited criteria behavior such as "Makes friends do things for him instead of doing them himself," or "Turns individuals against each other to suit his own desires." On the basis of these teacher ratings, Lorber classified students as high, moderate, or low social exploiters.

The subjects' parents were asked to respond to questionnaires inquiring about such things as children's privileges, liberties, and freedom of decision. When questionnaire responses were rated and matched with students' social exploitation ratings, a direct correlation of scores was found: the higher the social exploitation rating, the higher the parents' permissiveness rating tended to be. The investigator concluded that permissive upbringing may not generally encourage optimum socialization and social adjustment.

Influence of culture on personality

Behavior can be transferred from parent to child, because children are especially prone to imitate behavior that they see acted out by those who are closest to them. They indiscriminately copy good and bad behavior, without realizing why. *Imitative behavior* is an integral part of growing up. When the boy models himself after his father and the girl after her mother, they are absorbing the attitudes and related personality traits of their models.

Parents encourage imitation by responding with approval and pleasure when the child behaves as they do. This response reinforces the child's imitative behavior. Many cultural and ethical attitudes are transferred from parent to child in this manner (Figure 12.4).

Hostile and aggressive behavior is as readily imitated as friendly and nonaggressive behavior.

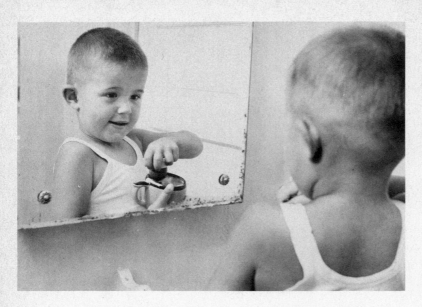

Figure 12.4   *Boys imitate their fathers and girls imitate their mothers.*
This sex-typing helps the child to develop a sense of his or her sex role.
(Robert J. Smith—Black Star; Jan Lukas—Rapho Guillumette)

It may be punished or encouraged, depending on how the parent views his own hostile behavior. Children imitate adults, whether or not the adult's behavior is socially acceptable; they are incapable of discriminating between appropriate and inappropriate behaviors.

Although sexual personality does not appear until adolescence, children learn their *sex roles* at an early age (see Chapter 2). They are prepared for adolescence through the process of *sex-typing*. Girls are taught to play with dolls, to sew, to help with housework, and even to respond in a flirtatious way to male attention. Boys are taught aggressive games, rewarded for "being like Dad," and encouraged to be straightforward and individualistic.

As we can see, environmental factors that shape personality are closely linked to the cultural standards upheld by the child's models. Each culture has its own standards of conduct, which are the society's model for acceptable behavior and preferred personality traits. Religious groups, ethnic groups, communities, and even social groups or club organizations are examples of environmental agencies that have a cultural influence on the individual. Because most adults are affiliated with one or more such cultural groups, they tend to raise their children according to the values set by the groups and by the overall culture.

Cultural values Because of differences in life-styles and cultural histories, people develop varying conceptions of good and bad and tend to value different things.

Britton, Britton, and Fisher (1969) compared 9- and 10-year-old Finnish and American children's perceptions of moral and emotional behavior. Results showed that Finnish children seem to view personal achievement as good and personal failure as bad more than American children do. The Finnish answered questions about "best and worst thing that could happen" and "good and bad thing to do" in terms of personal achievement. The American children, on the other hand, seemed to value personal comfort and pleasure more.

Finnish children named their parents or adults in general as those who would be pleased or displeased with their behavior. Americans more often named the recipient of their activity or themselves.

The authors attribute these differences to the fact that Finnish children take a very difficult exam in the fifth grade; the exam determines their academic and vocational future, and so probably sharpens the meaning of personal achievement and failure. Also, Finnish families are more tightly knit and strongly defend their right to privacy. At best, their interaction with strangers is cool. For this reason, Finnish children expect that approval and disapproval will come from their parents. American children reflect their pleasure-seeking, socializing culture in their answers. Culture, then, influences our perceptions.

The findings of anthropologists and social psychologists show that personality tendencies are strongly influenced by the individual's culture. This fact must be considered when establishing a system of values and a scale of norms for the interpretation of personality; any assessment of motives or traits, abilities or interests must consider cultural expectations. For example, a United States citizen who fought his way to the top of a large corporation, stepping on a few toes on the way, might be described as "industrious" or "a clever businessman," while in Latin America a person with the same tendencies might be negatively labeled "competitive," "unfriendly," and "impolite" (see Table 12.3).

The influence of culture is cumulative, life-long, and multidimensional. No single childhood impression ever produces a particular personality trait in the adult. For an adult personality to be shaped by a childhood experience (1) the experience must be continued or prolonged by a series of reinforcing events, and (2) the cultural environment responsible for the original experience must be maintained and reexperienced.

PERSONALITY THEORIES

Personality theory as we know it today was first conceived by clinicians—psychologists who work with the day-to-day problems of their patients. Because each of the major theorists had his own methods of dealing with patients, they have given us several different theories of personality.

Clinical psychologists disagree over the variables that contribute to an individual's personality. One clinician may say that a child whose toilet training is severe will develop an overwhelming compulsion for orderliness and cleanliness during his adult years. Another might say that the severity of toilet training is largely irrelevant and that many other variables con-

Table 12.3 Culturally desirable and undesirable traits in the United States and in Latin America

	United States	Latin America
Desirable traits	Industrious Ambitious Aggressive Individualistic Innovative Practical Punctual	Fatalistic Cooperative Respect tradition Accept things as they are Accept group goals
Undesirable traits	Passive Dependent Bound to tradition Lazy	Competitive Individualistic Preoccupied with time Desire to change things

tribute to the development of compulsive behavior.

Because clinical theories are based largely on personal observation and experience and are subject to individual bias, behaviorally oriented psychologists argue that personality theory needs to be clarified by an experimental approach. They believe laboratory techniques should be used to analyze the theories, thereby eliminating individual bias.

This chapter is organized from a historical perspective. The clinical approaches of psychoanalysis, which first appeared at the beginning of the century, are concerned with the unconscious conflicts within the individual's personality. Self-actualization theories, which were first presented in the 1950s and 1960s, deal with the individual's internal desire to fulfill his potentialities. The experimentalists' behavioral theories, which were developed fairly recently, concentrate on the analysis of responses to determine what evokes and maintains them.

Psychoanalytic theories

The earliest psychoanalytic theories were based on clinical observations of disturbed people, because their conflicts were more pronounced than those of most individuals and, therefore, more apparent. Since the psychoanalyst could use his method of psychotherapy to identify many of these conflicts, he naturally tried to fit his observations into a comprehensive theory that would apply to the general population.

Psychoanalysts view personality as the end result of the many forces acting within the individual. The unit of study in psychoanalytic theory is thus the life history of a person.

In this section, we will consider seven different psychoanalytic theories of personality. The first and foremost of these theories was developed by Sigmund Freud. Although there have been departures from many of his original concepts, Freud remains a major source of important ideas on personality formation.

Sigmund Freud Freud's early thinking was strongly influenced by his clinical observations. For example, Miss Elizabeth von R. was a patient who suffered from pains in her legs and an inability to walk properly. No organic basis could be found for her illness. Freud deduced that there were conflicting emotional forces within her and that these forces strongly affected her personality and, hence, her behavior. From his investigation of patients such as Miss von R., he developed his theory that most emotional problems stem from conflicting emotional forces within each individual—specifically, between the patient's conscious self and his unconscious sexual desires—and that these conflicts could be uncovered through what we know as psychoanalysis.

Freud believed that such conflicts arise in all human beings, not only in disturbed patients, and that individuals become emotionally disturbed only when the conflict cannot be resolved. For example, after many sessions with Miss von R., Freud concluded that her inability to walk resulted from a conflict related to her unconscious sexual attraction to her brother-in-law. While her unconscious desires drew her to him, her conscious self was repelled by the attraction. The intensity of the emotional crisis affected her deeply, and she unconsciously sought escape through her illness.

Psychic determinism In one of his earliest books, *The Psychopathology of Everyday Life* (1901), Freud argued that all behavior is determined. Everything a person says or does has meaning, although the meaning may be buried in the person's unconscious. Freud paid special attention to errors of memory and slips of the tongue, for he felt that one could learn much about an individual's unconscious by analyzing his errors and slips.

A Freudian might interpret a forgotten appointment as indicating that the person unconsciously did not want to keep the appointment. And a slip of the tongue such as the following would be ripe for interpretation: A state senator was addressing a meeting of candidates for public office when he made the following statement: "What are the qualifications for public office? Well, first of all a man has to recognize that he's a public serpent."

Psychoanalysis is not only a method for treating the disturbed personality; it is also a theory of personality that deals with the structure and development of the individual as a unique being. In Chapter 14, we will discuss Freud's psychoanalytic theories as applied to psychoanalytic treatment of disturbed personalities, but here we will concentrate on Freud's theory of personality, which has profoundly affected contemporary thought.

As discussed briefly in Chapter 2, Freud concentrated on the study of motivational forces that he felt existed in all human beings. He divided personality into three parts: the *id*, the *ego*, and the *superego*. The id is the reservoir of basic instinctual urges, psychic forces that the individual feels but usually does not recognize and cannot always satisfy. These urges are known as the libido. Channeled through the id, the libido is essentially sexual energy that expresses itself through various responses in the course of the individual's development and is the source of all motivational energy. The id operates according to the *pleasure principle*, whereby immediate satisfaction is sought regardless of the consequences.

Freud identified the ego as the process that functions to satisfy the id's urges. The ego is rational, and it directs and uses libidinal energy within the framework of socially acceptable and well-regulated behavior. In other words, the ego acts as a mediator between the demands of reality and the irrational demands of the id. The ego operates according to the *reality principle*, whereby immediate satisfaction is postponed in order that a greater degree of satisfaction may be gained at a later, more appropriate time.

If personality were composed of only the id and the ego, the individual would be able to satisfy his unconscious urges without difficulty. The ego would function as the servant to the id,

realistically responding to its every demand. Because this was evidently not the case, Freud concluded that the impulses of the id are controlled by some other force. He suggested that the ego must be responsible to some structure that imposes morality and inhibition on an individual's behavior. He called this part of the personality the superego, and described it as some libidinal energy that implements the restraints and percepts imposed upon the individual by society in general and by parents in particular. (The superego in this role has often been equated with what has been known as the "conscience.")

Freud: the analysis of dreams Freud is well known for his use of dream analysis to bring unconscious motives into the open. In *A General Introduction to Psychoanalysis* (1916), he wrote:

The number of things which are represented symbolically in dreams is not great. The human body as a whole, parents, children, brothers and sisters, birth, death, nakedness—and one thing more. The only typical, that is to say, regularly occurring, representation of the human form as a whole is that of a house, as was recognized by Scherner, who even wanted to attribute to this symbol an overwhelming significance which is not really due to it. People have dreams of climbing down in front of a house, with feelings sometimes of pleasure and sometimes of dread. When the walls are quite smooth, the house means a man; when there are ledges and balconies which can be caught hold of, a woman. Parents appear in dreams as emperor and empress, king and queen, or other exalted personages; in this respect the dream attitude is highly dutiful. Children and brothers and sisters are less tenderly treated, being symbolized by little animals or vermin. Birth is almost invariably represented by some reference to water: either we are falling into water or clambering out of it, saving someone from it or being saved by them, i.e., the relation between mother and child is symbolized.

The ego is constantly caught between the impulses of the id and the controls of the superego. When the superego blocks the ego from carrying out the demands of the id, the id can usually find a substitute for its demands. The displaced or substituted drives of the id appear in various forms of behavior.

Freud's structure of personality explains conflict as the unconscious struggle among instinctual urges. The conflict of id, ego, and superego gives rise to *anxiety*, which, according to Freud, causes the intervention of defense mechanisms, the appearance of illness, and the enactment of disturbed behaviors (see Chapter 13). Freud sought to free his patients from anxiety by making them aware of the motivational forces within them; he developed the method of psychoanalysis specifically for this therapeutic purpose.

Closely tied to Freud's theory of personality structure is his psychoanalytic theory of personality development. Freud's theory delineates five different stages in the life of the growing child. Because Freud believed that the id impulses were sexual in nature, he termed the various stages, *psychosexual stages*. Each stage represents a need for a different type of bodily gratification. In order for the individual to develop into a whole, well-functioning human being, he must successfully pass through each of the stages:

1 *The oral stage*—During the first year of life, the libido's pleasure-seeking is centered on oral gratification. As noted in Chapter 2, the infant seeks psychosexual satisfaction by stimulation to his mouth in the form of sucking. Freud believed that if oral gratification is frustrated or unfulfilled at this stage, the adult personality may develop traits that characterize an *oral fixation*, for example, greed, dependence, overabundant speech or chatter, chewing, smoking, and a general desire to seek oral activities.

2 *The anal stage*—During the second and third years of life, the libido forces are centered on anal gratification. This is the time when the infant is toilet-trained and when much of his activity is anal-centered. Satisfaction of the id's impulses during the anal stage can be achieved by the child's learning to control his eliminative functions with pride and not with shame. If the child's libido is not satisfied at the anal stage, he may develop an *anal fixation* later in life. Anal fixation produces certain distinct personality traits, such as stinginess, possessiveness, punctuality and excessive precision in organization, and sadism (desire to hurt others).

3 *The phallic stage*—Children between the ages of 3 and 5, said Freud, are dominated by unconscious impulses of genital curiosity. This period is known as the *phallic stage*, because here the child first becomes aware of his sexual organs as sources of pleasure and also becomes sexually attracted to the parent of the opposite sex. The son seeks affection from his mother, the daughter from her father. This period is also called the *Oedipal stage*, so named after the legend of Oedipus, who unknowingly killed his father and married his mother.

The phallic stage marks the child's entrance into heterosexual roles. The child resolves his Oedipus complex by sublimating his sexual feelings and *identifying* with his father in the case of a boy, or with her mother in the case of a girl. By identifying with a parent, the child takes on the standards of the parent and thus those of the culture. These standards become incorporated within the child as his superego. A failure of an individual to resolve the Oedipus complex may result in later personality defects. As an adult, such a person may be unable to distinguish or accept an adult sexual role (he is "in love with his mother," his wife complains); or he may show a tendency toward homosexuality (he feels guilty over wanting his mother, and so fearfully rejects all women because they might make him feel that way).

4 *The latency period*—The period of *latency* occurs from about 5 to the beginning of adolescence. No dynamic conflicts occur during this time. It is a time of social and intellectual development as encouraged by the early school years. Freud concluded that no basic personality changes occur during this time.

5 *The genital stage*—When the individual

reaches puberty, his id directs itself toward adult sexuality and psychological maturity, and this *genital stage*, according to Freud, is the ultimate conflict that the individual must face. His success will be determined to a large extent by the ability he gained earlier to fulfill his needs in the oral, anal, and phallic stages. Freud believed that if the individual is unable to resolve the first three psychosexual stages, then he will be unable to channel his libido into the outlets that allow him to function in a mature way.

Although recent personality theorists have rejected Freud's analysis of the sexual urge as man's fundamental drive, no other theorist has ever aroused as much public interst as Freud has. Although all of Freud's views are not fully accepted today, his influence is still felt.

Alfred Adler Adler, a student of Freud, owed much to Freud's early observations on the relationship between illness and psychological conflicts. But, like many of the post-Freudians, Adler felt that personality was determined by social drives, rather than by the basic physical urges that Freud had described. Adler's unique contribution to personality theory lay in his perception of man as a being who harbors *feelings of inferiority*—feelings that, according to the Adlerian concept, direct the development of personality and behavior in general.

As a physician, Adler had noted the remarkable ability of the body to work around any diseased or damaged part: if one organ failed to function efficiently, other organs worked overtime. Adler translated this phenomenon into psychological terms and proposed that the individual developed (or overdeveloped) certain personality qualities to enable him to *compensate* for his feelings of physical or intellectual inferiority.

Adler believed that feelings of inferiority are normal in children, who, after all, are totally dependent and cannot compete with adults in most endeavors. To compensate for this normal inferiority, the child strives for attainable social goals—for praise, attention, respect, and so on. Adler termed this lifelong striving for superiority the "will to power." If frequently frustrated in this striving, the individual becomes overanxious and exhibits what Adler called the *inferiority complex*.

Adler: traits displayed in sleep In analyzing personality, Adler paid careful attention to a person's "style" of behavior. In 1930, he wrote:

When we see a person sleeping upon the back, stretched out like a soldier at attention, it is a sign that he wishes to appear as great as possible. One who lies curled up like a hedge-hog with the sheet drawn over his head is not likely to be a striving or courageous character. . . . A person who sleeps on his stomach betrays stubbornness and negativity.

For Adler, the uniqueness of personality lies in the distinctly personal ways in which each individual strives to overcome his feelings of inferiority. The well-adjusted person strives toward realistic goals, developing strengths that will compensate for his inferiorities. The maladjusted person may overcompensate by overdeveloping such qualities as aggressiveness or industry, by developing a disorder that serves as an excuse for failure, by setting unrealistic goals, and by other means of compensation.

Carl Jung For many years Jung was a close friend and great admirer of Freud. However, the two men eventually came to very different conclusions about essential human conflicts. The friendship was dissolved and all collaboration between them ceased.

The Jungian and Freudian theories of personality differ in several ways. Jung disagreed with Freud that human development was strongly affected by libidinal (sexual) urges. Jung also disagreed that the individual's personality was shaped and defined at a very early age. Jung argued that personality is as much affected by the individual's future goals as by his present experiences (internal and external).

Jung's theory of personality is purposive, for it allows for each individual's continued striving toward a future goal—the *unified self*. By uniting all aspects of his personality, solving all conflicts in a mature and well-adjusted pattern of purposive behavior, the unified individual is able to control his own life. Abnormal personality results when the pressures that exert themselves on the individual are imbalanced and the individual is no longer master of his destiny.

Jung also differs from Freud in his concept of the unconscious. Freud's concept of the unconscious includes only the one person's experiences. Jung divides the unconscious into two parts: an individual's *personal unconscious*; and his *collective* or *racial unconscious*, which extends beyond the structure of any one individual's experiences to the experiences of his race. A person's collective unconscious includes his accumulation of cultural symbols, called *archetypes*. Archetypes—the mother archetype, for example—are universal, because they are part of everyone's mental life. The individual's attitude toward a particular archetype is predetermined. Although these attitudes are unconscious, they give rise to universal behaviors, for example, mother love.

Jung: the collective unconscious Jung placed great emphasis on mythology, for he felt that mythological themes reflect the collective unconscious of all men. In 1926 he wrote:

Freud has shown in a brief essay how Leonardo da Vinci was influenced in his later life by the fact that he had two mothers. The fact of the two mothers, or of a double origin, was real in Leonardo's case, but it has also played a role in the lives of other artists, as in that of Benevenuto Cellini who in phantasy devised such an origin for himself. In general, it is a mythological theme, and many heroes are endowed by legend with two mothers. The phantasy does not come from the actual fact that the heroes have two mothers, but is a generally disseminated "primordial image" belonging to the secrets of the common mental history of humanity, and not to the field of personal memory.

Karen Horney Another psychodynamic theory of personality was proposed by Karen Horney, who, like Adler, emphasized social conflict (between the individual and his environment) over personal (internal) conflict, as proposed by Freud. According to Horney, the individual in conflict with or frustrated by his environment develops a *basic anxiety* with which he must cope. Everyone encounters such frustrations, and everyone has basic anxieties. The first time a child's comfort and security are threatened, that child develops a basic anxiety, and the manner in which he satisfies his anxieties becomes a part of his personality. Horney termed the need to adjust to basic anxiety a *neurotic need* and held that everyone has such neurotic needs.

Horney: basic anxiety Horney (1945) believed that the origin of neurotic conflict could be found in the child's basic anxiety, which she defined as

. . . the feeling a child has of being isolated and helpless in a potentially hostile world. A wide range of adverse factors in the environment can produce this insecurity in a child: direct or indirect domination, indifference, erratic behavior, lack of respect for the child's individual needs, lack of real guidance, disparaging attitudes, too much admiration or the absence of it, lack of reliable warmth, having to take sides in parental disagreements, too much or too little responsibility, over-protection, isolation from other children, injustice, discrimination, unkept promises, hostile atmosphere, and so on and so on.

Neurotic needs that develop from basic anxieties usually play dominant roles during the individual's childhood. Children are almost entirely dependent upon their parents, and when their parents are inconsistent in their praise and punishment, children become anxious and need to adjust their behavior to satisfy the anxiety. For example, a child in need of affection may prance about and show off in front of his parents and relatives; his parents may sometimes praise him for his adorable antics and other times scold him for "pestering the grownups." The child develops a basic anxiety over his behavior and thus seeks a more consistent way to obtain affection. He pouts and acts sullen and his parents repeatedly provide the affection or concern he is seeking. This sullenness may become a permanent part of his personality. The need for affection is not the only neurotic need specified by Horney; power, achievement, approval, self-sufficiency, and prestige are also neurotic needs that develop from the individual's basic anxieties over his environment. Only when a neurotic need is satisfied maladjustively does the person become a neurotic individual.

Harry Stack Sullivan In the early 1950s, Sullivan proposed that personality as a uniquely individual characteristic did not exist. Sullivan defined personality as a social product, a need for interpersonal relations. He believed that every human being constantly seeks to satisfy a need for interpersonal relationships, and that this need is reflected in the individual's behavior.

Since social events follow a general pattern in every individual's development, Sullivan applied this pattern to his theory that personality develops as a result of the regular stages of interactions between the individual and the significant other people in his life. It should be pointed out that his stages of social significance are common only to our own society. Sullivan did not attempt to impose his theory on other cultural systems, for the same sequence of interactive relationships would probably not occur in other cultures. Each interpersonal event influences the development of certain personality characteristics, even though these characteristics may not appear overtly at the same time that the event is experienced. Therefore, according to Sullivan, our personalities are constantly emerging, constantly being stimulated by the variety of interpersonal events that we experience.

Erich Fromm Like Adler, Horney, and Sullivan before him, Fromm is concerned with the conflict between man and his environment. However, Fromm stresses man's constant search for an identity, his need to overcome the conditions imposed on him by his social environment. (In his term "social environment," Fromm includes many facets of life—social, political, industrial, philosophical, and so on.) He says that human beings must seek to fulfill their basic needs within the framework of this social environment and that five basic needs arise because of conditions in society: *relatedness, rootedness, identity, transcendence,* and *orientation.*

According to Fromm, today's society leaves man free to do as he pleases. Whether he succeeds or fails, is loved or is not loved, whatever he does or whatever is done to him, man has the freedom to direct his own life. This freedom, on the other hand, tends to isolate individuals. Because of the loneliness and fear caused by isolation, people tend to seek an escape from their freedom, to regain admission into the social order, and to structure society in a way that will give them security. The individual needs to carve a niche for himself in society and to remain there unharmed and safe from the risks and fears of freedom and complete individuality. If society accepts the individual's chosen place in society (that is, if man conforms successfully), then society has given him the identity he needs. By giving the individual an identity, and therefore a relatedness and rootedness, society solves man's need to escape from freedom (Fromm, 1941, 1955).

Fromm believes that if individuals cooperate to form a better society, they will be able to satisfy their needs for transcendence as well as for a productive, loving orientation.

Erik Erikson Erikson's theory of personality is based in part on psychoanalysis but extends beyond Freud's biologically determined psychosexual stages. Erikson speaks of a series of *psychosocial* stages that govern the entire life of the individual, not simply his preadult years.

Erikson further differs from Freud in that he does not utilize the concepts of the id and the superego. However, he does accept Freud's concept of the ego and its functions as the source of the behavior that characterizes the individual's adjustments, decisions, beliefs, and attitudes. To Erikson, the ego acts as the executive of the personality.

In the course of development, the human being passes through eight stages, and at each stage he faces a psychosocial crisis (see Chapter 2). The psychosocial dilemmas are based on real-life adjustments made necessary by the social and cultural environment into which the individual is born. The eight stages are not rigid, however; if the individual fails to resolve any of the psychosocial conflicts at the appropriate time, he may yet resolve it in some later period of his life, when the time is right for him.

The concept of *identity* plays a key role in Erikson's theory. Through the process of identity *formation*, the individual integrates his personality, developing personal maturity. He *identifies* with significant people around him. From these various models, the individual unconsciously selects certain characteristics and forms a unique, unified, and well-functioning identity. For example, a woman who is concerned about her appearance may sit for hours in front of a mirror, fixing her hair and makeup. Her husband is the strong, silent type. Their son spends most of his childhood with his mother and father, and so he is very aware of their distinctive personalities. Although the son has to form his own identity (or personality), he can do so only by integrating the personalities of those around him—he takes his father's silence and his mother's vanity and becomes outwardly shy and retiring and inwardly vain and conceited.

This integration characteristically occurs during adolescence, for it is then that the individual establishes a psychosocial personality for himself. For Erikson, the actual integration process is the crucial stage in achieving an independent identity. If integration is resolved, the individual is free to progress into adulthood with an awareness of who he is and a consistent commitment to his own identity. If integration is not resolved, the individual undergoes role *diffusion* and suffers a poorly integrated personality.

Erikson: ego identification Erikson (1963) describes his concept of identity as follows:

The growing child must, at every step, derive a vitalizing sense of reality from the awareness that his individual way of mastering experience (his Ego synthesis) is a successful variant of a group identity and is in accord with its space-time and life plan. . . . Ego identity gains real strength only from . . . recognition of real accomplishment—i.e., of achievement that has meaning in its culture.

Erikson's theory of personality attempts to cover the complete development of the individual, from birth to death. He takes into account the individual's effect on the environment as well as the environment's effect on the individual.

Theories emphasizing self-actualization

Self-actualization theories maintain that an individual is motivated by the constant need to expand his own frontiers, to be as much of a person as he can, and to realize his full potential. The basic unit of study in these theories is the individual's self-perception and his perception of the environment.

Carl Rogers Perhaps because of his experience as a therapist, Carl Rogers conceives of personality in terms of the individual's perception of himself, his self-concept. Rogers noted that all people exist in a framework of interpersonal relationships between their inner world, known as the *organism*, and their total realm of experience, known as the *phenomenal field*. He views behavior in terms of the individual's perception of these elements. Rogers further assumes that part of the phenomenal field forms the *self-concept*, that is, the individual's view of himself as a result of the interaction of the organism and the phenomenal field. The individual strives to maintain a constant self-concept. He regulates his behavior, accepting, rejecting, or deliberately misinterpreting perceptions and relationships in order to maintain this self-concept. If an experience is consistent with his self-image, then the experience is a vivid perception, according to Rogers, and is admitted and maintained at the conscious level. Experiences that never reach the level of consciousness are those that threaten the self-image; these experiences may even be totally ignored by the self.

Rogers also believes in the existence of an *ideal self*, which represents the goals and aims of the individual. The human being wants most to attain his ideal self—to be actualized. Behavior pathology occurs when the individual is unable, through fear, to become that self or to solve and understand his own experiences.

Rogers: fully functioning person Rogers's (1963) view of the "fully functioning person" is summarized, in part, as follows:

He is able to live fully in and with each and all of his feelings and reactions. He is making use of all his organic equipment to sense, as accurately as possible, the existential situation within and without. He is using all of the data his nervous system can thus supply, using it in awareness, but recognizing that his total organism may be, and often is, wiser than his awareness.

He is able to experience all of his feelings and is afraid of none of his feelings; he is his own sifter of evidence, but is open to evidence from all sources; he is completely engaged in the process of being and becoming himself; and thus discovers that he is soundly and realistically social; he lives completely in this moment, but learns that this is the soundest living for all time. He is a fully functioning organism, and because of the awareness of himself which flows freely in and through his experience, he is a fully functioning person.

Abraham Maslow Most modern personality theories, psychoanalytic as well as self-actualizing, are based on the observation of disturbed personalities. Abraham Maslow, however, based his theory on the study of normal personalities. Essentially, Maslow's theory states that, although every individual is striving for self-actualization, it is difficult to reach the ideal self because of external factors that interfere with this striving. These factors confront the individual at different stages during his life; they may at some point block the individual from progressing toward the fulfillment of higher-level needs. For example, the person who is afraid to express his thoughts and feelings is denied the fulfillment of expressing himself openly. He cannot progress to a more advanced stage of interpersonal relations until he is able to overcome this fear.

Maslow defined man's strivings in terms of a *hierarchy of needs*. The earliest needs are for physiological comfort. These are followed by safety needs (a drive toward security and organization). Satisfaction of these needs in turn leads to needs for love, esteem, self-actualization, knowledge; and, finally, there is an aesthetic need. The highest form of satisfaction is termed by Maslow a *peak experience*; it involves a sense of complete fulfillment, an experience like that of the great artist Michelangelo when he completed the Sistine Chapel. Peak experiences are not limited to self-actualizing individuals. Anyone can have such an experience, but they occur more frequently among self-actualizers.

Maslow arrived at his concept of the self-actualizing individual by interviewing many individuals or examining their biographies. Among them were Albert Einstein, William James, Abraham Lincoln, and Eleanor Roosevelt, all of whom were regarded by Maslow as self-actualizing individuals. He then drew up a list of the characteristics typical of such persons:

1 are clear in their perceptions of reality and able to accept the ambiguities in their environment;
2 are self-accepting and accepting of others—experience little or no guilt or anxiety about themselves;
3 are fanciful thinkers and spontaneous behavers, but not totally unconventional;

4 are not self-centered, but rather problem-centered;

5 are able to be objective about life and often search for privacy;

6 behave independently, but are not deliberately rebellious;

7 enjoy life;

8 have experienced powerful and ecstatic, even mystical, events—moments when they appear to be on the brink of something new;

9 are socially involved and identify sympathetically with the human race;

10 can have deep interpersonal experiences, but usually only with a few people;

11 respect all people—are democratic in their attitudes toward others;

12 know the difference between means and ends and are not annoyed by having to endure the means to arrive at the ends;

13 have a philosophical sense of humor, spontaneity, and play—lack hostility toward others in their humor;

14 are uniquely creative, that is, uniquely capable of problem-finding;

15 do not allow the culture to control them.

Personality of the creative individual Is there a personality profile for creativity? Recent work by Cross, Cattell, and Butcher (1967) indicates that certain personality dimensions characterize not only a variety of creative artists but also many persons eminent for their creativity in scientific research.

The investigators chose more than 60 artists—teachers, professional painters, and students—who had given "clear evidence of unusual talent" in drawing and painting. A group of nonartists was then matched with the experimental group for length of professional experience, age, sex, and educational background. A smaller, third group of craft students was also chosen to test the hypothesis that their creativity profile would be about midway between that of the artists and that of the controls.

All subjects were given tests to measure aspects of general personality characteristics such as extraversion, anxiety, sensitivity, experimentation, moral concern, and intelligence. Results showed many very clear differences between artists and controls, as well as between the artists and previously established norms for the American population. Artists were, for instance, more assertive, more self-sufficient, less emotionally stable, more casual about self-control, more imaginatively experimental, and less bound by social conventions. As predicted, the profile of the craft students was between that of the artists and the controls on almost every factor.

Since many of these same characteristics—particularly the self-sufficiency, imaginativeness, and relative emotional instability—have also been found in previous tests of eminent American research scientists, the evidence clearly suggests that creative people may share similar personality characteristics.

The interest in concepts such as self-actualization and ideal self corresponds with the upsurge of interest in Eastern philosophy and mysticism. There is much fascination today with various practices of meditation such as those based on *yoga* or *Zen*. These practices aim at altering states of awareness so that the individual can "expand his consciousness" and get closer to his self or arrive "at the source of the thought" (Mahesh Yogi, 1969).

It is difficult at this time to evaluate these practices and their aims. They are of interest to psychologists, but their principles and techniques are hard to pin down because of their subjective characteristics.

Behavioral theories

The behavioral approach to personality is based on the psychology of learning studied in Chapter 6. The behavioral psychologist believes that personality characteristics are learned in much the same manner that other things are learned, and that personality can be studied by analyzing the stimulus, response, and reinforcement variables. In short, the basic unit of study is the individual's specific responses to stimuli, and these responses enable the behaviorist to predict future responses.

John Dollard and Neal Miller According to Dollard and Miller (1950), personality is acquired (learned) in the normal course of development through the processes of classical and operant conditioning. That is, personality is simply a form of behavior. Dollard and Miller maintain that the individual is driven, or motivated, by physiological and learned needs. If these needs are properly satisfied, the individual learns how to satisfy other similar needs in the same general way.

Thus the individual learns a personality trait in the same way that he learns an operant response. He makes a response to reduce a drive, and if the response reduces that drive, then in the future similar responses will occur. Since the response was successful in the past, it will probably be successful in the future. The individual thus learns those responses that enable him to produce reinforcing stimuli. In developing a personality trait, the individual acquires responses that were previously reinforced. Responses that were not reinforced are extinguished. Personality is thus affected by the individual's social environment. When the individual makes a particular response, his parents (or others) can reinforce the learning situation by words of approval, smiles, gestures, or any of the individual's previously conditioned reinforcers.

The reinforcements that shape personality may be positive or negative. A child may acquire seclusiveness or shyness as a pattern of behavior by constantly making escape responses. He may initially seek to escape the nagging and threats of a very severe and demanding parent. These escape responses may take the form of removing himself from the parent's presence whenever he can. Aversive experience with other adults—for example, teachers—may lead to a generalization reaction in which other people become conditioned negative reinforcers. Each time he escapes from the presence of people, he is negatively reinforced. The transition from escape to avoidance is a common one, because avoidance prevents the occurrence of the aversive stimuli. When avoidance of people becomes habitual, we say the person is seclusive or shy.

Dollard and Miller: human drives Dollard and Miller (1950) emphasize the role of drives and drive reduction in human behavior, but unlike Freud they pay special attention to learned or acquired drives. They write:

The helpless, naked, human infant is born with primary drives such as hunger, thirst and reactions to pain and cold. He does not have, however, many of the motives that distinguish the adult as a member of a particular tribe, nation, social class, occupation or profession. Many extremely important drives, such as the desire for money, the ambition to become an artist or a scholar, and particular fears and guilts are learned during socialization.

At present only a modest beginning has been made in the experimental study of learned drives and rewards. The work has a long way to go before it bridges completely the gap between the fundamental biological drives and the wonderfully complex web of socially learned motives that determine adult human behavior. The facts that have been learned, however, are extremely important for an understanding of normal and abnormal personality and of psychotherapy.

Dollard and Miller constructed their theory in order to explain the conflicts common to maladjusted personalities. The neurotic's symptoms are learned patterns of responses that generally appear during childhood. The child is confused when on one occasion his parents spank him for taking a new toy apart and at another time smile approvingly at him because they find his curiosity appealing. Parents frequently cause confusion in their children by positively reinforcing rough or aggressive behavior or snobbish or cruel attitudes on one occasion and then punishing the same behavior on another occasion. The child may often be unable to understand his parents' interpretation of his behavior. The child's confusion results in conflict and, if the parents continue to evaluate the reward and punishment values inconsistently, the child may learn such neurotic types of behavior as hysteria, phobias, and other maladjustive mechanisms for defending his own perceptions (see Chapter 13).

According to Dollard and Miller, it is the culture, as interpreted by the parents, that is responsible for the personality behavior learned by the child. Four childhood learning situations are most likely to arouse neurotic conflicts: handling and feeding; toilet training; early training about sex; and training to teach the child to control anger and aggression.

Experimental analysis of behavior   Psychologists whose fundamental interest is the experimental analysis of behavior do not make a distinction between personality and behavior. B. F. Skinner, for example, argues that an individual's personality consists of the responses he makes. An analysis of an individual's personality entails a systematic description of the stimuli to which he responds, his responses, and the reinforcers that maintain his responses. The entire analysis is descriptive and specific. It does not assume general traits or underlying processes, and unlike Dollard and Miller's approach, it makes no reference to such concepts as needs and drives.

For example, an individual is said to be aggressive because he emits aggressive responses. That same individual may be aggressive in one situation and not in another. "The pious church-goer on Sunday may become an aggressive, unscrupulous businessman on Monday" (Skinner, 1953). His piety is reinforced on Sunday by his family and friends and perhaps by himself, and his aggressiveness may be reinforced during the week each time he succeeds in outdoing his competitors. Thus, behavior depends upon the specific stimulus context in which the behavior is occurring.

Skinner: stimuli and responses   Skinner (1967b) asserts that answers to questions about personality can be found in an analysis of behavior. In discussing psychotic behavior, he wrote:

We look inside the organism for a simpler system, in which the causes of behavior are less complex than the actual hereditary and environmental events and in which the behavior of a personality is more meaningful and orderly than the day-to-day activity of the organism. . . . But the simplification achieved by such a practice is, of course, illusory, for it follows only from the fact that a one-to-one correspondence between inner and outer events has not been demanded. It is just this lack of correspondence which makes such an inner system unsuitable in the experimental analysis of behavior. . . . If the behavior we observe simply expresses the functioning of a personality, the personality cannot be simpler than the behavior.

ASSESSMENT OF PERSONALITY

As with the theory of personality, personality assessment may be approached from several different directions, depending on the needs and orientation of the tester. For example, the personality characteristics a factory manager looks for in hiring an assembly-line worker are different from those sought by a school administrator who hires a teacher, or an airline executive who is looking for a pilot. The needs of the situation affect the choice of measurement used.

Questionnaires

A test of personality constructed to elicit straightforward answers to ready-made questions is known as a *personality inventory* or *questionnaire*. Questionnaires are usually designed to provide a score that may be compared with the scores of other individuals. They may be designed to measure general adjustment, which depends on multiple factors of personality, or to measure the positive and negative aspects of a single characteristic. The validity of a test is based on the test's correlation with observable predetermined criteria, such as objective ratings of the characteristic in question. Because the researchers are able to identify which questions are answered a certain way by individuals with certain known characteristics, the validity of the test can be determined.

Unlike intelligence tests, personality questionnaires require subjective answers. Subjects, however, do not always tell the truth. Their answers may be influenced by their attitudes and desires. Psychologists realize that many individuals can "see into" personality questionnaires

I enjoy social gatherings just to be with people.

There's no use in doing things for people; you only find that you get it in the neck in the long run.

I doubt whether I would make a good leader.

I think I would like the work of a school teacher.   I like school.

I often feel as if the world was just passing me by.

Sometimes I think of things too bad to talk about.

The average person is not able to appreciate art and music very well.

I was a slow learner in school.

Most people make friends because friends are likely to be useful to them.

Figure 12.5   A sample from the California Psychological Inventory test of personality. The subject is asked to answer true or false to 480 questions similar to those shown here. (Reproduced by special permission from the California Psychological Inventory by Harrison G. Gough, Copyright 1956, published by Consulting Psychologists Press Inc.)

because they respond in ways that show that they understand the implication of particular questions. However, because psychologists are aware of how their subjects behave, they have created "key" items that help to reveal inconsistencies and inaccuracies in a particular subject's pattern of responses. By checking the answers to these key questions, the investigators can pick out many of the false answers.

There are numerous questionnaires in use to test various aspects of personality. Some questionnaires seek to identify positive aspects of personality, such as assertiveness or confidence in oneself. Other questionnaires seek to identify individuals who have personality problems. Whether the questionnaire is designed to uncover positive attitudes or problem areas, its findings must be confirmed by additional evidence. Here we will look closely at three of the most widely used questionnaires.

California Psychological Inventory (CPI)   This test covers a total of 18 scales of positive personality characteristics, including responsibility, tolerance, and sociability. It has 480 questions, each requiring a true or false answer. (A sample of the CPI is shown in Figure 12.5.) Each question measures one of the 18 personality characteristics. Since the scorer knows which question relates to which factor, scoring is not difficult.

The number of questions devoted to each of the 18 different personality scales varies according to the complexity of the characteristic. In scoring the CPI, each of the 18 scales is given a separate rating. However, an individual's behavior is assessed as a whole instead of as a series of separate scores. In this way, the response of a subject on one of the scales is integrally related to his responses on the other scales.

Edwards Personal Preference Schedule (EPPS)   The EPPS attempts to measure an individual's interests or attitudes. In compiling his test, Edwards used a list of 15 essential human needs drawn from a list prepared by H. A. Murray (1938). For each question, the subject must make a choice between two sentences, each describing a different need. Thus, the subject is forced to make a choice between two needs. The *forced-choice technique* is designed to minimize falsification by a subject who is tryng to look good; many of the choices are equally negative. Figure 12.6 shows statements similar to those found in the EPPS. There are 210 paired sentences, which allows each of the 15 needs to be paired with every other need on the list.

Minnesota Multiphasic Personality Inventory (MMPI)   The MMPI was designed as an aid in diagnosing pathological (disturbed) behavior.

Figure 12.6   Examples of the types of items used in the Edwards Personal Preference Schedule. The subject must choose one statement in each pair.

The subject is asked to respond to 550 statements. He may answer "true," "false," or "no reply." The "no reply" category makes the subject feel that he is not forced to answer if he does not wish to. Each statement is worded to suggest a personal opinion, that is, the sentences are constructed in the first person singular.

The subject who repeatedly answers "no reply" on the MMPI test is saying that these qualitative characteristics do not apply to him. The examiner interprets this category as easily as the other two; it is informative to know that a subject is indecisive or evasive. If too many statements are put into this category, however, the subject's overall score cannot be based on the standardization correlations. Failure to respond may be one indication of certain characteristics of personality, but excessive failure to respond may be an indication that the individual is uncooperative, and his results should not be compared with the scores of the others who take the test. The MMPI also contains a method of recognizing inconsistent or false answers, but this method is difficult to use effectively. Figure 12.7 compares the personality profile of a normal adult male on the MMPI with that of a psychotic adult male.

Projective tests

Projective tests are based on a concept of measurement different from that of questionnaires. Whereas questionnaires are structured to elicit responses that characterize particular personality traits, projective tests try to call upon the total personality. Projective tests compel the individual to base his responses on his own perceptions.

In most projective testing situations, the subject is on a one-to-one basis with the examiner. However, certain variations of projective testing procedures do utilize groups. There are no "yes-no" answers. The responses are as unstructured as the stimuli themselves. The subjects must interpret or project themselves into the stimuli. Some psychologists believe that by forcing the subject to use his own imagination in responding to the stimulus, they make him reveal unconscious factors that influence his personality. Perhaps the greatest advantage of projective tests is that the subject does not know exactly what is expected of him. It is therefore unlikely that he can falsify his answers.

Rorschach test   A frequently used projective test is the Rorschach test. It consists of 10 symmetrical inkblots in shades of gray or black or in color. Figure 12.8 shows an ink blot similar to those found in the Rorschach test.

Figure 12.7   The personality profiles of a normal adult male and a psychotic adult male. The psychotic person shows "higher" scores on those personality traits that are symptomatic of his disorder [After H. G. Gough, Minnesota Multiphasic Personality Inventory. In A. Weider (Ed.), Contributions toward medical psychology, Vol. 2, pp. 545–567. New York: Ronald Press, 1953]

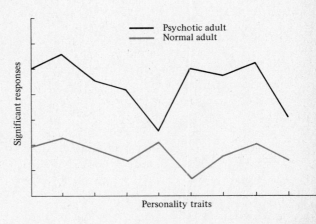

There are no correct answers to the Rorschach test. None of the inkblots represents a specific object. The subject is asked to describe what he sees when he looks at the inkblot; the examiner transcribes his remarks verbatim. There is no time limit and no special position for looking at any of the cards.

Because the Rorschach test is subject to individual interpretations, the examiner must be thoroughly trained to score it in an unbiased and scientific manner. He must understand that because different aspects of the subject's perceptions are interpreted in terms of personality characteristics, the subject's statements of what he sees are important. The determinants of his percepts—form, color, movement, and so on—play an important role in the examiner's interpretation of the subject's personality. The examiner also notes whether or not the individual responds to a large detail of the blot, the entire blot, or a small part of it.

The determinants given here are merely representative. In actual scoring, many more categories are of interest to the examiner.

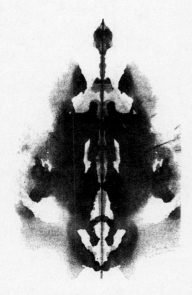

Figure 12.8   A sample inkblot. (Fundamental Photographs from The Granger Collection)

Rorschach shows cultural differences Bleuler and Bleuler (1935) and Cook (1942) conducted studies of Rorschach readings across two cultures, European and Moroccan. They believed that if most members of a culture show the same traits, cross-cultural personality studies should tell us something about each culture under study.

The studies found that Moroccans show more fine-detail responses than do Europeans. Thus, looking at the inkblot outline shown here (Figure 12.9), Europeans would most often describe it as "two women talking," whereas a typical Moroccan might interpret the tiny irregularities at the top of the blot (see arrow) as "a row of riflemen opposed by a row of warriors."

Figure 12.9   See text.

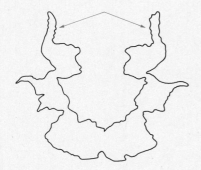

Thematic Apperception Test (TAT)   The TAT uses a set of pictures, each designed to serve as a stimulus for the telling of a story. The subject is shown one picture at a time and asked to build a story, a theme, around what he sees. Usually, the subject is encouraged to invent a background, or a past, for the characters shown and then a future. The TAT series also ingeniously includes a completely blank card, for which the subject is asked to create his own story. Figure 12.10 reproduces one of the TAT pictures.

Often a subject's narratives will reveal his problems. As in the Rorschach tests, the examiner's skill is extremely important, for he must

Figure 12.10   A sample picture from the Thematic Apperception Test of Personality. Note the possibilities for dramatic storytelling. (Harvard University Press)

Clinical psychologists rely heavily on interview procedures for their observations of personality. The interview is also used by the layman whenever he is faced with the task of assessing personality. In employment interviews and college interviews, the individual's personality characteristics are analyzed by the interviewer to determine whether or not these characteristics conform to the interviewer's idea of acceptability. The interview, although it may be casual, is an anxiety-arousing situation because the person interviewed is aware that he is being assessed.

Interviews may be either nonstandardized (loose or informal) or standardized (structured or formal); neither is a very successful method of personality assessment. In a standardized procedure, the interviewer organizes his important questions and may not digress from them. Such procedures may be too rigid; the interviewer cannot be flexible if he has to concentrate on covering the items on his list. The unstructured interview, on the other hand, is a more active conversation between the interviewer and the interviewee. The interviewee can be encouraged to ask questions; often these questions reveal certain aspects of his personality. At the same time, the interviewer must be aware of his own attitudes, since these might interfere with his objective evaluation. Some of these attitudes are listed here:

be able to pick out vital clues to the subject's personality. After the pictures in the TAT series are shown to the subject, the trained observer can identify recurrent themes. The more recurrent a particular theme, the more likely that the subject is bothered by this problem. Of course, problems are not always what they seem; the responses require careful interpretation.

The use of projective tests   Clinical psychologists find both the Rorschach inkblots and the TAT pictures useful despite the fact that research studies show the tests to be of questionable reliability and validity. Projective tests are seldom the sole basis on which clinicians evaluate a personality. The diagnoses obtained from them often lead to other testing measures to corroborate identification of the problem. Projective tests are recognized as useful instruments for securing as much information about a person as possible before offering a total assessment of his personality (see also Kinget, 1952).

1 Stereotyping—Preexisting judgments of an individual because of his race, religion, occupation, or other distinguishing nonpersonality characteristics. Laymen fall into the trap of stereotyping an individual more easily than do professional counselors.

2 Insensitivity—Failure to recognize places in the interview when the interviewee is evasive or when he is too eager to talk about something. Lack of sensitivity may arise when the interviewer is trying to substantiate a fixed idea or hypothesis.

3 Halo effect—The experimenter's personal taste

can influence his objective observation of the individual. The interviewer may regard someone favorably simply because of his name, his body build, his hair color, and so forth. Or the interviewer may be impressed with the interviewee's opinions simply because they concur with his own.

Behavior samples

Individuals may be systematically observed by means of *behavior samples* or *situational tests*. Situational tests for identifying personality characteristics may involve any real-life setting. Here we deal with the structured situation, in which the individual is observed naturally but is given a task that has been planned beforehand by the observers. In this type of behavioral sample, an individual is placed in the kind of situation that he would have to face in the future. If a man is to be judged as to his future ability as a schoolteacher, then his behavior in such a situation can be predicted if, in the course of the testing, he is asked to conduct a class for several days. The way that he handles himself can be observed as an indication of his on-the-job performance level. If a man does well with no prior experience, it is probable that he will improve with experience.

The degree to which behavior samples have been valid is controversial. No really substantial data exists as to the validity of the behavior sample as a testing device.

An interesting behavior sampling project was conducted by the United States Office of Strategic Services (OSS) during World War II. At that time, the OSS was the intelligence branch of the federal government responsible for infiltration and sabotage behind enemy lines. It had to recruit men who could withstand frustrations, physical strain, and emotional stress. The OSS candidates were constantly tested without their knowledge. As part of their training, these men were asked to do jobs for which inadequate time was allowed, or they were assigned personnel who were deliberately incompetent. The recruits were then observed to determine how well they performed in the face of frustration and how they reacted to insurmountable difficulties. Since all the agents selected went to foreign countries, and during wartime it was impossible to keep track of them, the OSS was not able to test the validity of its behavior samples. Some correlations were attempted, but the range was so broad as to invalidate the findings.

As you can see, the analysis and measurement of personality is one of the most difficult areas of psychological study. Individuals are simultaneously unique and consistent, and it is the psychologist's task, through various forms of observation, to determine the variables involved in personality traits and to predict future behavior from these variables. As psychology grows as a science, it will be better able to identify the many different variables.

SUMMARY

The term personality refers to the organized system of behavior patterns, attitudes, and values that characterize a given individual and account for his particular manner of functioning in the environment.

A trait is a particular and persistent feature that is repeatedly expressed in an individual's behavior or appearance. Types are clusters of traits that seem to form a pattern that may be used to classify an individual.

Hippocrates used a physiological typology to explain differences in personality. More sophisticated biochemical typologies are based on the influence of hormones or the relative dominance of either the sympathetic or parasympathetic division of the autonomic nervous system.

Kretschmer developed a physical typology based on body structure. Sheldon later developed a more flexible typology called somatotyping.

Jung hypothesized that individuals may be classified in terms of introversion or extraversion. However, most people are ambiverts.

By using factor analysis, Cattell identified surface traits and source traits.

Guilford classified traits as motivational and temperamental.

Eysenck sees personality in two dimensions: emotional stability–neuroticism and introversion–extraversion.

Heredity, learning, and cultural influences combine to shape personality.

Sex-typing helps a child to develop his sexual identity in terms of the society in which he lives.

Most personality theories derive from clinical observation. The clinical approach may be further divided into psychoanalytic theories and self-actualization theories.

Psychoanalysis is both a theory of personality development and a method of treatment. According to Freud, personality is composed of the id, the ego, and the superego. The libido is essentially sexual energy.

In Freud's theory of personality development, the child passes through five psychosexual stages on his way to maturity—oral, anal, phallic, latent, and genital.

Adler stressed social drives, which are based on the child's feelings of inferiority in a world of adults.

Jung's theory of analytical psychology emphasizes the importance of purposive behavior toward future goals and the development of the unified self. Jung also broadened Freud's concept of the unconscious to include a collective or racial unconscious as well as a personal unconscious.

According to Karen Horney, the central factor in personality conflict is basic anxiety, which results in neurotic needs.

Sullivan viewed personality as the result of recurrent interactions of the individual with the significant people in his life.

Fromm's theory of personality is based on modern man's need to escape from freedom; man's five basic needs are relatedness, rootedness, identity, orientation, and transcendence.

Erikson defines eight psychosocial stages, each presenting a conflict that must be resolved at some time during the individual's life.

In his self-actualization theory, Rogers stresses the development and maintenance of the self-concept and the attempt to achieve the ideal self.

Maslow's theory of self-actualization is based on his study of emotionally healthy, rather than disturbed, individuals. Maslow believes that each person develops according to a hierarchy of needs.

According to behavoral theories of personality, personality patterns are the result of learned responses to environmental stimuli.

Skinner is an experimentalist who believes that personality is explained in terms of stimuli, responses, and reinforcement.

Among personality inventories or questionnaires are the California Psychological Inventory (CPI), the Edwards Personal Preference Schedule (EPPS), and the Minneosta Multiphasic Personality Inventory (MMPI).

Projective tests include the Rorschach inkblot tests and the Thematic Apperception Test (TAT).

The interview may be biased by stereotyping, insensitivity, or the halo effect.

Behavior samples or situational tests are observation techniques aimed at predicting future behavior in real-life situations by observing individuals in simulated test situations.

SUGGESTED READINGS

Texts

Adorno, T. W., Frenkel-Brunswik, E., & Levinson, D. J. *The authoritarian personality*. New York: Norton, 1969. Analysis of this particular type of personality.

Allport, G. W. *Pattern and growth in personality*. New York: Holt, Rinehart & Winston, 1961. Revision and extension of Allport's famous work on personality (1937).

Bales, R. F. *Personality and interpersonal behavior*. New York: Holt, Rinehart & Winston, 1970. Study of the interaction between personalities.

Ferguson, L. R. *Personality development*. Belmont, Calif.: Brooks/Cole, 1970. A very readable developmental account of personality (infancy through adolescence), drawing in several theoretical backgrounds.

Greenacre, P. *Trauma, growth and personality*. New York: International Universities Press, 1969. Discussion of personality in the context of psychoanalysis.

Hall, C. S., & Lindzey, G. *Theories of personality* (2nd ed.). New York: Wiley, 1970. Excellent, comprehensive review of the major theories.

Horst, P. *Personality: measurement of dimensions*. San Francisco: Jossey-Ross, 1968. Survey of personality assessment techniques.

Janis, I. L., Mahl, G. F., Kagan, J., & Holt, R. R. *Personality: dynamics, development and assessment*. New York: Harcourt Brace Jovanovich, 1969. Comprehensive discussion of all aspects of contemporary research in personality.

Lundin, R. W. *Personality: a behavioral analysis*. New York: Macmillan, 1969. Behavioristic approach to personality.

Maddi, S. R. *Personality theories: a comparative assessment*. Homewood, Ill.: Dorsey, 1969. A good comparative analysis of the different theories.

Sarason, I. G. (Ed.) *Psychoanalysis and the study of behavior*. New York: Van Nostrand, 1965. Papers that discuss Freud's place in general psychology and the contribution of his work to diverse fields in social science and psychology.

Sarason, I. G. (Ed.) *Contemporary research in personality*. New York: Van Nostrand, 1969. A well-planned survey of the interests and methods of contemporary personality researchers.

Popular Books

Alschuler, R. N., & Hattwick, L. B. W. *Paintings and personality: a study of young children*. Interpreting the personalities of children through art.

Bawden, N. *Anna apparent*. The story of a woman who has tried all her life to be all things to all people at the expense of her own self-image.

Berne, E. *What do you say after you say hello?* A popular essay on the ways one writes and rewrites—often with the help of a therapist—one's own life script.

Fromm, E. *The art of loving.* A popular book about Fromm's self-actualizing theories of personality, specifically applied to the relationship between a man and a woman.

Fromm, E. *Escape from freedom.* Fromm's theories of personality-shaping by societies.

Gotesky, R. *Personality: the need for liberty and rights.* The effects of the social system in shaping personality.

Grey, A. (Ed.) *Class and personality in society.* Collection of articles on the power of social and economic factors in shaping personality.

Hough, R. *Captain Bligh and Mr. Christian.* A thoroughly researched description of two very interesting historical personalities, the captain and first officer of *H.M.S. Bounty.*

Lewis, E. C. *Developing woman's potential.* Discussion of ways to improve the opportunities for women in our society, based on the dynamic theory of personality.

13

Behavior pathology

People who are obviously disturbed—the man who shouts at no one in particular in a public place, the well-dressed woman who sits on the curb talking to herself—upset us momentarily, very much as the sight of a man without fingers or a crippled child upsets us. The emotional response is not so much to the trouble that distinguishes the victim as to his essential sameness with ourselves; our momentary identification suggests that it is within the range of human experience to live without fingers or to rave or mutter irrationally. What others experience, we suspect, is in some way within the range of our own experience. We want to know more about it. For much the same reason, we study disturbed behavior; we expect to acquire information relevant to our understanding of ourselves.

Another reason for the study of *behavior pathology*—maladjusted, abnormal, or disturbed behavior—is that it enables us to better appreciate the real needs of the people we encounter from day to day. The braggart, met with scorn, becomes even more boastful. The insecure girl clings too tightly to her man, only to be rejected; made more insecure, she is likely to cling more to the next man. The young man with feelings of inferiority chooses a wife who can in no way challenge him, only to become ashamed of his choice and again be overwhelmed by inferiority. In countless instances, the individual supposes that certain behaviors will help him adjust, but in fact they contribute to his defeat by the environment. Each of us is part of someone else's environment, and at times we unwittingly stimulate a maladaptive behavior in others. An understanding of maladjustive behavior—however preliminary—may prevent us from doing this. Sensitive to the needs of the braggart, we can try to make him feel less insecure, which might make him a more interesting conversationalist, even a friend.

Behavior pathology is a condition that prevents an individual from functioning effectively within his society. Psychologists view poor adjustments to stimuli as evidences of possible pathology. Because we all exhibit such behavior occasionally, the psychologist must somehow recognize the difference between occasional eccentric actions as part of normal human behavior and the same acts as evidence of pathology. He must be able to distinguish between normal absentmindedness in one individual, for instance, and pathological absentmindedness in another.

BEHAVIOR PATHOLOGY AND ABNORMALITY

Because overt behavior is frequently misleading and because society's standards change, it is often extremely difficult to distinguish between the normal and the abnormal. Although we can identify highly abnormal behavior, it is difficult to identify pathology in an individual who deviates occasionally from society's expectations. The line between normal and abnormal, exceedingly fine, differs in different societies. What is seen as abnormal in one society may be normal in another. For example, Ruth Benedict (1934) has described the Kwakiutl, an Indian culture of the Pacific Northwest Coast, in which acts of aggression are considered normal in everyday social relationships. In our own culture, these "normal" Indian people would be regarded as pathologically violent. In this chapter we shall see that pathological behavior is not always unusual behavior—and that the individual who behaves abnormally does not always do so consistently.

Who is sane? Neither behavior pathology nor normal behavior is easily identified. Suppose you had to prove you were "normal." Could you do so?"

Rosenhan (1973) has shown that there are few standards to distinguish sanity from insanity in mental hospitals. In his study, eight sane volunteers (three psychologists, a psychiatrist, a pediatrician, a painter, a housewife, and a graduate student) admitted themselves as patients to various psychiatric hospitals. Three were women; five were men. The volunteers gained admission to the hospitals on the pretext that they were hearing voices.

Once admitted as patients to a psychiatric ward, the pseudopatients dropped their feigned symptoms and behaved normally. Although they showed no signs of behavior pathology, the volunteers were never detected as sane. Each was diagnosed on admission as schizophrenic and each was eventually discharged with the diagnosis of schizophrenia "in remission" (temporarily lessened). Often other patients recognized that the newcomers were not insane, but the hospital staff did not.

Rosenhan points out that the psychiatric hospital is a special environment in which behavior can easily be misunderstood. It is assumed that the patients must be insane because they are there, and they continue to be regarded as insane because the hospital setting distorts the impression given by patients. With so much odd behavior going on, almost all patient behavior seems odd. Such environments, instead of being therapeutic, may retard therapy.

In this chapter we shall discuss the ways people behave when they are unable to adjust to their environment. First, we shall discuss *defense mechanisms*—the psychological maneuvers we all employ in reaction to frustration and anxiety—and later, the unusual kinds of behavior that are the special misfortune of the emotionally disturbed.

DEFENSE MECHANISMS

Man lives with frustration: his car will not start; he loses a game; he does not get the promotion he has worked for. The daily list is endless. At an early age, we learn that our own shortcomings, as well as an environment that is not always friendly, may block attainment of our goals. Our reactions to the frustrations we encounter at almost every level of existence can help us adjust to such shortcomings and obstacles. But as frustrations accumulate and become increasingly difficult to resolve directly, we may react to defend ourselves against the feelings that accompany frustration. Instead of coping with the causes of frustration, we may seek ways to reduce the discomfort frustrations produces. We may also defend ourselves in the same way against the tension that accompanies fear and intense anger. These reactions are known as *defense mechanisms*—they are employed as protective devices to distort or escape reality.

We all use defense mechanisms to adjust our behavior in frustrating situations. In anticipating a potentially frustrating situation, most of us tell ourselves that we are not really interested in achieving certain goals. Consequently, if we do not satisfy these goals, we are not too disappointed. Defense mechanisms are not abnormal. They are classified as pathological only when they cause an individual to lose touch with reality or become ineffectual in his workaday activities.

We consider two types of defense mechanisms—*escape techniques* and *compromise techniques*. Aggression is sometimes included in discussions of defense mechanisms because it is often a reaction to frustration or anxiety. However, aggressive behavior usually represents a direct attack on the source of frustration or anxiety and in this respect differs from the escape and compromise techniques (see Chapter 9).

Escape techniques

The escape techniques—*repression, fantasy* and *regression*—enable man to escape or avoid situations that generate anxiety.

Repression   A common defense mechanism is withdrawal from a frustrating or anxiety-arousing situation. *Repression* is one of several forms of withdrawal. The concept of repression was introduced by Freud to identify the process of preventing unconscious anxiety-producing thoughts from becoming conscious and interfering with the individual's efforts to cope with everyday living. The last time you went to the dentist, perhaps you suffered considerable pain and were uncomfortable for hours. Your next appointment was a week later—but you "forgot" to go.

You may have repressed the appointment date and, in doing so, were less anxious.

Unlike *suppression*, which is the conscious checking of thoughts or feelings, repression is the unconscious, although active, withdrawal of certain painful or self-injurious thoughts or feelings. Repression is meant to reduce anxiety, as distinguished from normal forgetting, which is unrelated to anxiety. The similarity between repression and normal forgetting conceals from the frustrated individual the realization that he does not want to remember certain experiences. Their similarity also may make it difficult for the therapist to distinguish between generally unimportant situations that a patient has forgotten and those that he has repressed. Through free association, hypnosis, and similar techniques, the therapist attempts to bring forth the repressed thoughts and identify those that the patient must recognize and understand.

According to psychoanalytic theory, unless severe repressions are treated, the individual is in danger of losing control of himself. He tends to repress not only the painful event but everything associated with it. In addition, he may develop defenses that bury his repressed memories still further. Keeping the repressed memories from intruding on the conscious level requires great psychological exertion and may in fact mobilize all the patient's energy, leaving him tired, nervous, and unproductive. As long as the patient remains in this state of defensive "forgetfulness," he will retreat from reality and seek a new reality in his maladaptive personal adjustment. This is not to say that all repression is maladaptive; whether or not it is depends on how deep the repression is and how frightened the individual is of a confrontation with his conflicts and frustrations.

The most extreme form of repression is *amnesia* (loss of memory). There are varying degrees of amnesia, depending on the individual and the causative situation. For example, in the case of a visit to the dentist, the person may "forget" the location of the office, the time of the appointment, and even the dentist's name.

Where a major operation is involved, the fearful person might forget not only external details but also the illness itself.

Some amnesia is biological rather than psychological in origin, for amnesia may be caused by damage to the brain tissue in the memory area. The symptoms of biologically based amnesia are sometimes similar to those of repression-produced amnesia, so that it may be difficult to distinguish one form from the other. Both medical and psychological examinations may sometimes be necessary to determine the cause of amnesiac withdrawal.

Fantasy The individual frustrated by reality may escape from that reality into a world of *fantasy*, where he is no longer disturbed by his frustration. Because he cannot cope with the conditions of reality, he resorts to fantasies, using them to reduce his anxieties and satisfy his needs.

The fantasy world may be entered at many different levels, the most common of them being daydreaming. *Daydreaming* is a defense we have all used at some time. It occurs with greatest frequency during adolescence when we are often most apprehensive about our unfulfilled roles as human beings. However, adults also may fantasize desirable (but unrealistic) solutions to their problems.

Individuals who are unable to adjust their aspirations to reality may withdraw completely into a fantasy world. When this happens, the individual becomes increasingly dependent upon his fantasy solutions and less able to deal with his frustrations. Ultimately, he may be unable to distinguish the real from the unreal, manifesting behavior pathology (Figure 13.1).

Regression The individual may escape from frustrating or anxiety-provoking situations by returning to earlier or more primitive forms of behavior. A common example is the wife who is unable to adjust to the adult demands of marriage and returns to her parents' home to assume the familiar and safe role of daughter instead of the difficult role of wife.

Figure 13.1   *The individual uses fantasy as a defense mechanism that will enable him to escape from the reality with which he cannot cope. (Syd Greenberg—dpi)*

Regressive behavior is common among children. A child upset by the presence of a new sibling may revert to such earlier forms of behavior as thumb-sucking or bed-wetting, or he may seek attention in other ways that were successful when he was younger.

Some psychologists believe that hypochondriacs exhibit a form of regression, because the hypochondriac uses illness to seek help from others—depending on others in much the same way that a child depends on his parents. Believing that he is ill makes it easier for an adult to regress to a dependent relationship.

Regression may be accompanied by *stereotypy*, in which a particular pattern of behavior, such as thumb-sucking, is relied upon so heavily that the individual becomes blindly repetitive and so inflexible that he cannot meet the demands of his environment. Stereotyped behavior may result from severe frustration, and the persistence of such behavior makes it more difficult for the individual to cope with frustration.

Compromise techniques

The compromise techniques—*rationalization, projection, sublimation, reaction formation,* and *compensation*—enable the individual to cope with anxiety-arousing situations. The means of coping usually involves changing the situation in some way.

Rationalization A person may defend himself and his own inadequacies by finding "logical" excuses or arguments for his behavior. By placing the blame on someone or something else, for example, he avoids risking a loss of self-esteem and social approval. This kind of reasoned excuse is known as *rationalization*.

Since we are often reluctant to admit to our failures, we may rationalize by believing that they are unworthy of our attention. When we treat others badly, we may rationalize that they deserve it; if we cannot maintain good grades in college, we may rationalize that the students who get good grades are only "grinds" who spend all their time at their books; if we are turned down for a job, we may rationalize that we did not want it anyway. As a rule, such types of rationalization are normal ways of coping with frustration. However, when used to excess, they may be symptomatic of a severe behavior disorder and may cause unrealistic action. For example, a man might regularly beat his wife, rationalizing that his wife's unspoken thoughts justify this behavior.

Projection A person who attributes his own undesirable qualities to others is exhibiting a defense mechanism known as *projection*. By repressing awareness of his own undesirable characteristics and projecting them onto others, the individual alleviates his feelings of inadequacy or guilt and avoids recognition of certain of his own deep feelings, such as hostility, jealousy, or forbidden love.

Projection is said to be an unconscious response. Preferring not to see undesirable traits in ourselves, we accuse others of possessing these traits instead. We may have uncharitable thoughts toward others but, rather than admit them, we believe that others are unkind or unscrupulous. It is much simpler and far less anxiety-provoking to project our undesirable thoughts or traits onto others than to face up to them.

Projection often seems to be a form of misperception based on set or faulty discrimination (see Chapter 5). The hostile person may be set to recognize hostility, and therefore he tends to perceive all stimuli as hostile. A person with strong feelings of guilt may be so preoccupied with these feelings that almost anything he sees or hears reminds him of his guilt. For example, he may perceive a smile as a sign that the smiling person knows his secret.

Sublimation As noted earlier, some defense mechanisms serve neither to block nor to avoid a frustrating situation; instead, they provide an indirect solution to frustration. According to Freud, *sublimation* is the establishment of a secondary goal that an individual can satisfy in place of a primary goal that is either socially unacceptable or physically impossible. Realizing that his attempts to attain the primary goal will meet frustration, the individual redirects his behavior toward an alternate goal, one that he can fulfill without feeling guilty or inadequate.

Psychoanalytic theory suggests that we sublimate behavior when we fear social disapproval, particularly in relation to our sexual urges. We cannot always satisfy our sexual urges directly, for they are controlled by the social conscience we develop in childhood. We therefore seek sublimated ways of satisfying these urges, finding them in such activities as sports, dancing, painting, and writing. Although our activities are not always direct representations of sublimated urges, sublimation may have a subtle influence even on a choice of career or occupation.

Sublimation is a compromise reaction; the compromise may be necessary and the rewards real. Nevertheless, too much sublimation may ultimately threaten an individual's self-esteem.

If an individual cannot accept the compromise reaction, his frustration will grow more intense. Or he may be unable to judge his own level of competence accurately and sublimate at a level far too low to relieve his frustrations even partially.

Sublimation of an urge According to psychoanlysis, socially disapproved drives may find expression through sublimation. Alpert (1949) reports such a case: Peter, a bright 11-year-old, was very nervous and was having trouble in school. His problem manifested itself in two ways: (1) he had a generally short attention span; and (2) he listed his worst subjects as his favorite subjects. He declared that music was his most important subject and that science and sculpture were his hobbies, although he did not do particularly well in these areas. These facts, which were brought out during therapy, together with several other facts, were part of a very definite pattern.

Peter's mother was a concert pianist, his father an eminent scientist, and his mother's most ardent admirer, a sculptor. Knowing these facts, the therapist felt that Peter might be sublimating his Oedipal conflict by translating his incestuous urges into activities admired by his mother—science, sculpting, and music.

According to the psychoanalytic interpretation, the Oedipal conflict was sublimated to socially acceptable behavior. Peter's nervousness indicated, however, that his sublimation was not entirely successful.

Reaction formation Another defense mechanism, closely related to sublimation, is *reaction formation*. It occurs when an individual protects himself from a repressed feeling by developing an active belief in some diametrically opposed cause. Perhaps the individual is unconsciously afraid of his drives and defends his self-esteem by pursuing an overt behavior that he knows is socially acceptable and guilt free. If, for instance, a man is ashamed of his frequent and intense sexual thoughts, he might develop a reaction formation involving the adoption of puritanical beliefs; he might, for example, devote himself wholeheartedly to fighting pornography. This is a *negative reaction formation*. A *positive reaction formation* may involve the exaggeration of socially acceptable behavior. Thus, some people are referred to as *too* nice or *too* considerate; guilt feelings for their repressed hostility push them to exaggerate the opposite behavior.

A positive reaction formation may conceal deep hostility or negative feeling. A young woman who neglects her own life and future to care for her elderly mother may develop an overindulgent attitude toward her mother to appease her guilt and hide her hatred for the mother who forced her into this situation. Parents of an unwanted child may be overattentive and overprotective because of guilt feelings for not wanting the child.

A reaction formation is often deep-rooted and difficult to uncover. On occasion, it may be helpful rather than harmful, as when it acts as a redirecting force to prevent undesirable behavior. In other cases, the redirection may be injurious to the individual as well as those around him

Reaction formation attention Rubenstein (1959), a psychiatrist, relates the case of a woman who had felt as a girl that she was being neglected by family and friends. As a result, she developed a strong need for attention. However, as a woman, she showed sadistic tendencies that disguised her attention seeking. For example, she once noticed that her daughter was making numerous Easter baskets. The daughter had emptied the pantry of all candies, cookies, and nuts, and had talked her younger brothers and sisters into giving her their toys. When the mother expressed anger, the child announced that she was making the baskets for poor people in the hospital. This calmed the mother, and she told her daughter that she should have come to her to discuss her needs, because she could have helped her. When the child continued working on her own without enlisting her mother's help, the mother found a pretext to give her a severe scolding (the child refused to lend her brother a pen), and sent her to her room.

The mother's anger was really provoked by the fact that the child had ignored her. The mother needed attention, and her moralistic wrath was a reaction formation to this need, which she had refused to recognize.

Compensation When human beings are frustrated by failure or loss of self-esteem occasioned by their inadequate performance in a particular activity, they will tend to seek a new goal, one they are sure that they can reach. Often this goal will be closely related to the original goal; for example, a man who dreams of becoming a great author may establish a career in advertising copy-writing—the higher goal is not achievable, so his desire for it is rechanneled to an occupation in which he can reach a higher performance level. This is *compensation*, a counterbalancing mechanism that permits the individual to achieve success. Like sublimation, it allows the person to substitute one goal for another. Unlike sublimation, it results from experience of failure. (You will recall that sublimation is caused by the expectation of failure or the anxiety over socially disapproved activities.)

Some psychologists (Alfred Adler, for example) believe that compensation underlies most significant achievements. Knowing what he cannot do, the individual pursues what he can do, hiding his real or imagined weaknesses from others. Compensation can be beneficial to an individual and to those around him. A shy businessman, for exmple, compensates for his shyness by being extremely efficient and hard-working; the student who has no athletic ability becomes a member of the debating team or the newspaper staff; the overweight person attracts people with his humor and friendliness.

The individual who overcompensates, however, may be rejected because he becomes too assertive—because he forces his friendship and humor. His feelings of inferiority become stronger and deeper; as this happens, he tries harder to find acceptance by overcompensating for his weakness. Overcompensation becomes a source of annoyance and a cause for disapproval. An overcompensating individual may be called a "show-off," a "loudmouth," or "obnoxious."

Compensating for feelings of inferiority Shaffer and Shoben (1956) describe the case of James, a thin, meek-looking 12-year-old boy. Although James did not participate in active sports, concentrating instead on indoor games, he tended to bully boys younger than himself. Consequently, James was considered a disciplinary problem in school, and his teachers condemned him as a "tough guy."

Close analysis of the case revealed that the boy's home situation had prevented him from becoming "manly." His father, a salesman, was never home; James thus had no paternal model to imitate. His overprotective mother discouraged him from sports or rough-and-tumble play with boys his own age, since he had once been seriously hurt while engaging in such activities. James also felt anxious about taking part in such activities, and this anxiety, combined with his physical frailness, gave him inferiority feelings about his "manliness." To compensate for these feelings, he bullied smaller boys. Overcoming smaller boys was a substitute for proof of true physical capabilities. When his teachers called James a "tough guy," they were unknowingly rewarding him.

NEUROSES

Defense mechanisms are exhibited at one time or another by almost everyone. *Neuroses*, on the other hand, are less common, longer lasting, and more incapacitating than defense mechanisms.

The term "neurosis" does not refer to a hard and fast category of behavior pathology. It is merely a general term used to refer to maladjustments that are usually characterized by attempts to escape from anxiety or to cope with anxiety by using defense mechanisms in exaggerated ways.

It is often difficult to pinpoint the difference between a defense mechanism and a neurosis. A man may regress to a state of extreme dependency upon his wife and yet still be a productive wage earner and loving father. If his regression should make him unable to function, he might be referred for professional help, at which stage his neurosis might be detected.

In the following sections we will outline and describe the four general categories of neurosis (depicted in Figure 13.2): *anxiety reactions, obsessive-compulsive reactions, phobias,* and *hysteria.*

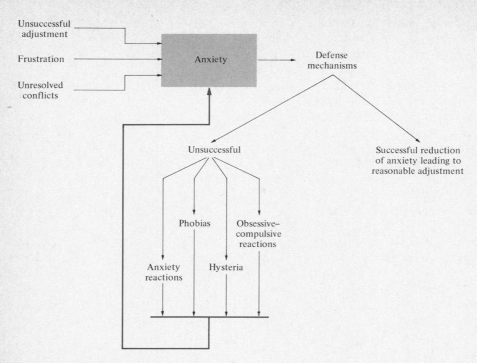

Figure 13.2   *The neurotic cycle.*

ANXIETY REACTIONS

When the stress of daily living becomes too great for the individual to bear and he can no longer solve his internal or external conflicts, his anxieties adversely affect his overt behavior. An individual whose anxieties control his behavior is said to be suffering from an anxiety neurosis. His behavior is technically defined as an *anxiety reaction.* Because he is overwhelmed by fears and anxieties, the anxiety neurotic develops a pattern of maladaptive responses, the most pervasive of which is overall physical and emotional tension. Anxiety reactions can incapacitate an individual; fears overwhelm him, dominating his waking and sleeping hours to the eventual exclusion of all else.

An anxiety neurosis, especially, does not develop suddenly but usually over an extended period of time. In fact, most anxiety neuroses probably originate in childhood.

Anxiety in childhood

Children learn anxiety reactions all too easily. Psychologists believe that parents often condition their children to develop anxieties—for example, by punishing them when they try to satisfy their needs (particularly their sexual needs); by frightening them with fearful tales and strong statements designed to discourage undesirable behavior; by setting goals far too high for them to attain; or by repeatedly showing displeasure at their overall behavior. If the parents' behavior is not understood by the child, he begins to feel that his needs are wrong or immoral and that he is a failure in the eyes of his parents. Parents who are too strict with their children and do not allow room for occasional failures are actually encouraging their anxieties and apprehensions.

The child, especially the young child, seeks to please his parents. When his parents are displeased, the child may assume it is because he has failed in some way and he may expect to be punished. Parents trying to teach the child to distinguish between correct and incorrect behavior may make the mistake of punishing him too severely, too often, and for too many things (including behavior caused by natural desires). As a result, the child becomes anxious about everything he does. He feels that he is somehow different from everyone else—that he is "bad"—and that he may lose the security of his parents' love. He does not consciously know why he fears certain things. By the time he is old enough to understand his fears (and perhaps resolve them), he may be so permanently conditioned that his attempts to be free of anxiety are stymied. An anxious person often looks for someone or something to cling to. If he has not found security in his early years, he may believe that none is possible, and continue to react anxiously.

The case of Ellen M. A 7-year-old girl, Ellen M., was referred to a child guidance clinic because she was a behavior problem in school and at home. She was frequently disruptive in school, and at home her temper tantrums were becoming increasingly violent. Ellen's mother reported that scolding and spanking did not seem to reduce her tantrums. Her mother was perplexed because earlier she had felt that Ellen was a "quiet" child who did not need much attention. According to the mother, there had been a period when Ellen had frequent nightmares and was afraid to go to sleep. But these nightmares became less frequent when "we decided to ignore them because we knew she'd outgrow that stage."

Therapy revealed that Ellen was a fearful, dependent child who was shy rather than simply quiet, and who was able to gain her parents' attention only when she misbehaved. When her nightmares were ignored, Ellen apparently discovered that the best way to get attention was to misbehave; and when Ellen was afraid or anxious, this is how she sought attention. Attention accompanied by punishment was better than no attention at all.

Anxieties generally are well established before adolescence, and at that time they begin to exert new pressures. Children are often taught that sex and the human body are embarrassing, dirty, or sinful; this teaching may be reflected in the adolescent's guilt feelings about sex. Also, children are sometimes taught that a meaningful disagreement with the parent is forbidden; this teaching may be reflected in adolescent anxieties over identity. Anxiety that is easily conditioned during childhood seems to grow stronger as the child grows older. It is extremely difficult to extinguish.

Anxiety reactions take many forms. Some children may overcome the stress and tension of anxiety symptoms, while others generate conflicts so severe that their behavior becomes totally maladaptive. Still others resolve their conflicts during childhood only to find the same inexplicable fears and continuous tensions recurring later in life. Let us examine some conditions in the development of an anxiety reaction.

Conditions of anxiety

Many everyday situations arouse anxieties in the individual who suffers from undefined fears. These situations may be merely uncomfortable for a normal person, but for the highly anxious they are unbearable. A lost library card, a stopped-up sink, a sarcastic remark can be conditions of crisis in the life of an anxiety-driven person. The following conditions are particularly disturbing to him:

1 If placed in a situation from which escape is impossible, he becomes severely disturbed. He will try to avoid such a situation, and if unsuccessful in doing so, may develop physical symptoms of illness, such as nausea and diarrhea, as manifestations of his anxiety. The depth and powers of his terrors and their control over him are formidable indeed: he fears not one but many situations. To make matters worse, this type of anxiety leads to all sorts of social deceptions. The anxious person may, for example, refuse an invitation that involves a long automobile ride on the grounds that he gets carsick or is afraid of being unable to get to a

bathroom. Or he may avoid the theater on the grounds that he "hates crowds." He feels guilty and inferior for making excuses for himself, and he suspects that others find him odd.

2 The anxious individual is terrified of any situation in which he can perceive even the remotest possibility of personal failure. As mentioned earlier, people sometimes develop personality disorders as a result of earlier childhood punishment. After repeated and severe punishment, the threat of punishment can become so great that it produces more fear than the punishment warrants. Transferring such threat-related anxieties into adult life, the individual may respond anxiously to situations that merely hint at possible failure. He may avoid any sort of dating confrontation. Or he may approach unavoidable trials (like the job interview) with such nervousness that his fear of failure is inevitably realized.

3 The individual becomes anxious when separated from his sources of support. The most obvious example is the child who is lost while out with his mother; serious physical symptoms, such as uncontrollable crying, trembling, and immobilizing fright, may result. Loss of a parent, separation from one or both parents, breakup of the family, and even separation from a close friend leave the person in a state of anxiety greatly exceeding that of the normal person. Ordinarily, the anxious person relies for support upon an unbelievable number of objects and conditions. This is why he becomes upset over such things as the disappearance of a favorite waitress (whom he invariably patronizes); the presence of a house guest (who disrupts a familiar room); or the loss of a favorite umbrella—one of the many things that he uses to characterize himself to himself. The anxious person sometimes seems inflexible in his behavior, precisely because he depends on so many external things for his support and because he cannot be separated from these props.

Chronic anxiety reactions

Let us examine a fully developed anxiety disorder that involves the total functioning of the individual, namely, the *chronic anxiety reaction.*

In this condition, the entire body is in a constant state of tension; this general state of disturbance causes improper adjustive behavior and exaggerated responses. The anxiety reactions include all aspects of functioning, from internal organic disturbances and skeletal muscle tension to an inability to concentrate. All the symptoms of fear are present, even when nothing is happening to the individual to really justify fear.

The variety and severity of the symptoms of chronic anxiety seriously affect the individual's daily life. Continued fatigue and tensions lead him to reject social activities in favor of isolation and to avoid outside contacts that would worsen his "illness." As a patient, the anxiety neurotic must be treated carefully. The patient generally appears unable to accept the true reasons for his condition. He appears to be dominated by his own physical symptoms, which prove to him that he must be suffering from an organic illness. He avoids confrontation with his real situation.

The following is a case history of an individual with typical anxiety reactions:

The patient was a 32-year-old American oil geologist who lived abroad for many years and was unmarried. He was referred by his company for diagnosis because of numerous ailments that made him believe he was insane. For 5 or 6 years, he had been suffering from intermittent attacks of dizziness, blurred vision, weakness, and an unsteady gait, for which no satisfactory explanation had been found by his medical examiners. For 3 years he had been bothered by almost constant nervous tension, irritability, increased sex pace with incomplete satisfaction, inability to relax, poor sleep, and frequent troubled or terrifying dreams. His neck seemed always strained and he frequently rubbed it and made rotary head movements to relieve the pull. For about a year the patient had been so restless that he could scarcely sit or stand still in the daytime or lie still at night. He walked so vigorously that he tired everyone else out and himself too. As long as he kept on the move, he felt in reasonably good spirits, but he was intolerant of delay and opposition no matter from what or whom it came. The moment he let up in overt activity, his symptoms increased, his legs ached, he felt "jumpy," and he could get no satisfaction unless he drove himself on to further activity, even though he felt worn out. He began to rely more and more on whisky to steady him during the day and on barbiturates to get him to sleep at night.

One day, about 8 months before his referral for diagnosis, while the patient was dressing to go out for an evening's entertainment, he felt something in his head suddenly snap, everything around him looked unnatural, and he seemed to be about to faint. He lay down on his bed for a long time, his heart pounding and his breathing labored, while the thought kept recurring, "I'm dying, I'm dying." Eventually he managed to sit up, weak and shaky, to drink about a pint of whisky and take a double dose of sedative, after which he slept through the evening and the night following this, the patient had frequent recurrences of anxiety attacks that consisted of "queer head sensations," weakness, sweating, coarse tremor, palpitation, and the conviction that something terrible was happening to him. He had only one repetition of the snapping in his head, but he dreaded its return more than anything else. He stated that, from the time of the first snapping to the present, he had never regained his previous ability to think clearly, concentrate, or remember.*

Anxiety attack

Usually, the individual suffering from chronic anxiety reactions also experiences *acute anxiety attacks* in which all the symptoms appear, overwhelming him with a feeling of emotional dread, so that he responds as if he were intensely frightened. Most anxiety attacks occur when the individual feels overpowered by the stress of life. The individual suffers from acute physical dis-

comfort, often climaxed by his belief that he is suffering from a heart attack and that he will die or that some physical disaster is about to occur. He may faint, or feel numb, or become chilled or flushed; he may vomit and lose bladder and sphincter control; his pulse becomes rapid and irregular; he perspires, his mouth becomes dry, his face flushes, his pupils dilate, and he may experience severe pain in the chest region. Violent though this attack may be, it soon subsides. But acute anxiety attacks can occur as frequently as two or three times a day. The following is an example of a case history of an individual who has been suffering from acute anxiety attacks.

The patient, a twenty-nine-year old married stenographer, was referred [to a psychiatrist] by an internist after his examinations failed to reveal signs of organ pathology [physical damage or defects in the heart]. She complained of sudden attacks which first made their appearance a year earlier and a few hours after she had been reprimanded by her employer. It was toward the end of a hot, tiring day during which she had been more than usually annoyed by the petty, domineering manner of her immediate superior, a female secretary. "My heart suddenly stopped. Then it came up in my throat and turned over and quivered so fast you couldn't count it. I had a pain in my chest and down my arm. I was like in a tight vise; I couldn't breathe. It seemed like I was going to die." She was given a week's vacation, which she extended to a month by using her accumulated sick-leave. Three months after her return to work, she had another attack, and during the month immediately preceding her referral she had been having one every three or four days. The chief etiological factor seemed to be her conflict over having to go on working to help a husband whom she loved but who, she was beginning to recognize, was dependent and incompetent. She said, "I guess I'll just have to go on working like this till I die."†

*Adapted with permission from Norman Cameron, *Psychology of behavior disorders: a biosocial interpretation*, pp. 251–252. Boston: Houghton Mifflin, 1947.

†From Cameron, *op. cit.*, pp. 255–256.

OBSESSIVE-COMPULSIVE REACTIONS

Another type of pathological behavior is diagnosed as *obsessive-compulsive reaction*. An obsession is a persistent, habitual, involuntary thought that dominates the individual's thoughts. The individual is thereby blocked from productive and adjustive behavior. A compulsion is the irrational act that usually results from obsessive thoughts. The person who has an obsession that apples may be poisoned by insecticides might compulsively wash each apple before eating it, even though he knows the apple was thoroughly washed earlier. Usually, obsessive thoughts and compulsive behavior occur together, but there are infrequent instances when one occurs without the other.

Most of us have probably experienced a mild obsession at some time or another. The man who repeatedly looks at his watch may be obsessed with time, and the woman who is afraid that something will happen to her mother if she does not call her every day is obsessed with disturbing thoughts of disaster. Individuals who whistle whenever they are alone are giving way to a compulsive urge. Persons who are aware of their obsessive-compulsive reactions usually agree that their behavior may be silly, but they tend to continue it all the same.

When, however, the individual's obsessive-compulsive reaction interferes with his normal functioning, we may say that he is suffering from a neurosis. The obsession can become so severe that all his thoughts revolve around it. An individual who has obsessive thoughts of death and suicide may be so disabled that he can think of nothing else and can do nothing at all.

Compulsive behavior often assumes a ritualistic character. The function of the ritual appears to be the establishment by the compulsive individual of an orderly climate in which he can function to his own satisfaction without being overwhelmed by his repressed anxieties.

Obsessive-compulsive reactions .are often accompanied by considerable anxiety. The anxiety may be momentarily checked by the obsession or the compulsion, but it quickly returns to motivate additional obsessive or compulsive activity. The cycle is usually *anxiety—obsessive thinking or compulsive activity—relief from anxiety—return of anxiety*, and so forth. Let us examine one case in which an individual's obsessive-compulsive behavior was heightened by a threat to his job security. The individual in this case acted in a repetitious, compulsive pattern that eventually interfered with his normal functioning.

A young man, with a background of mild childhood and adolescent compulsions, accepted an offer of employment as a bank teller because bank officials said that if he proved satisfactory the bank would make his future secure. His vision of secure future, however, turned out to be a mirage. He soon found himself obliged to count and recount money, check and recheck, always doubting his results and day by day getting more anxious, until finally it became utterly impossible for him to keep up with his work. He grew afraid that others would notice his repetitive and often furtive behavior and misinterpret it as an indication of criminal behavior. After work he was unable to relax or to gain restful sleep, because of frightening imaginations and dreams that he had slipped up somewhere and would be disgraced or imprisoned. He was referred for psychiatric consultation by the family physician in his home town.*

The following is an illustration of a more severe case of an obsessive-compulsive disorder. Here, ritual behavior led to bizarre actions that the individual could not understand. It was easier for her to endure her neurotic behavior than to suffer the anxieties of breaking it. Note the uncontrollable spreading of this behavior.

*From Cameron, op. cit., pp. 282–283.

A young unmarried woman developed an irresistible need to think of a different person with each separate act she performed in a given series, until she finally reached a point at which gainful employment and marriage were both out of her reach. This magical practice began originally as a technique of distraction from sex preoccupations, which had induced severe anxiety reactions in the patient as she walked each morning to work. She established a rule that each step on or off the curb at a corner must be accompanied by the thought of some adult she knew, the adult must be a different one for each step on or off the curb, and she must have one clearly ready in her imagining ahead of time. If she thought of the same person twice on the same street something terrible might happen. The provisions of her ritual made a frequent change of street convenient and this obliged her to start to work earlier and to shun company, both because talking interfered with preparation for the curb crises, and because her changes of course were hard to justify to someone else.†

†From Cameron, op. cit., p. 296.

PHOBIAS

Some individuals have irrational fears of specific objects or situations and will do anything to escape from the source of that fear. Phobias, or phobic reactions, are intense feelings of anxiety that become attached to objects or situations that the individual imagines as the cause of his anxiety. Often, simply by associating an object with a previously experienced fearful situation, the individual becomes conditioned to fear the object as much as he feared the original situation. Feelings of inadequacy and inferiority may also induce generalized phobias in an individual; such a person might fear being alone, being with too many people, becoming sick, being stared at, having sexual relations, and so on.

A phobia may cause the individual to panic. For example, a man who panics when he has to walk alone at night will do anything to avoid walking alone at night, no matter what the consequences. During psychotherapy, he might remember an incident from his childhood when he wandered off into the night and was lost for several hours. From that time on, he had unconsciously felt compelled to go indoors whenever he was alone outside at nightfall.

Phobias may also be the result of repressed conflicts. The individual affected by such a phobia will avoid places or situations that might bring the conflict into the open. The exact nature of the phobic reaction may be symbolic, which makes the individual's repressed impulses difficult to identify. Some of the common phobic disturbances are *claustrophobia* (fear of closed places or being shut in), *acrophobia* (fear of high places), *ochlophobia* (fear of crowds), *zoophobia* (fear of animals), *nyctophobia* (fear of the dark), and *pathophobia* (fear of disease).

HYSTERIA

Hysterical reactions arise from deep motivational conflicts from which the individual seeks to escape. There are two types of hysteria —dissociative reaction and conversion hysteria; both illustrate the process of repression in an advanced stage, and both are extremely incapacitating. Patients with this kind of pathology are not difficult to diagnose, but the true extent of the disorder is often well hidden, and intensive treatment is usually necessary.

Dissociative reactions

A *dissociative reaction* is a form of hysteria that typically involves the repression of thoughts or experiences with which the individual cannot cope. He dissociates any thoughts or situations that would cause him pain or harm. Mild dis-

Figure 13.3   *The dancing mania that appeared in Italy during the thirteenth century is an example of a dissociative hysteria. It was believed that people inflicted with the disorder were stung by the tarantula, which caused them to run suddenly into the streets and dance wildly. The cause turned out to be a need to overcome the feeling of sinning against the church, which had outlawed the people's wild, orgiastic dances. By attributing their dancing to the tarantula bite, the people could repress their feelings of guilt.* (From The epidemiology of mental disease by Ernest Gruenberg. Copyright © 1954 by Scientific American, Inc. All rights reserved.)

sociations are relatively harmless, since the repressed thoughts are not strong enough to conflict with the conscious personality. However, the dissociative reaction tends to grow as the individual becomes more troubled and seeks an outlet for his repressions (Figure 13.3). The following are forms of dissociation.

Amnesia   The individual tends to forget all ideas and experiences associated with an unpleasant situation. In such cases of repression (as opposed to biologically caused amnesia) the individual may forget his name and other personal information about himself, or he may forget certain personal experiences. Therapeutic techniques, such as hypnosis, are used to bring the forgotten material to a level of awareness.

Some individuals develop temporary amnesia, repressing painful situations long enough to carry them beyond a particular situation with which they feel they cannot cope. Generally, the troubled person escapes from the situation by running from it; then he develops temporary amnesia, referred to as a *fugue*, to explain his flight. A fugue generally comes to an end, and the individual regains his memory. But he does not remember what happened to him during the fugue and cannot explain why he fled.

A case of dissociative reaction   Thomas S. was a 22-year-old graduate student in biology. A serious student, he had made a favorable impression on his professors. However, 2 months before he was to complete his Ph.D. dissertation and take his oral examination, he disappeared from the university. After 3 days, his parents received a telephone call from him from a city hundreds of miles from the school. Thomas had found himself wandering about the city not knowing how or why he had arrived there. His parents arranged for him to be placed under the care of a physician there until they arrived. When they reached the city, they found him in good spirits. However, he had no memory of the 4 days between the time he departed from the university and the day he found himself wandering around the city.

He returned to the university, where a psychiatric examination indicated that the pressure and tensions generated by work on his dissertation and his anticipation of his upcoming oral exam had produced a dissociative reaction, causing him to flee from the scene of his difficulties. He was given supportive psychological counseling and successfully completed his dissertation and degree.

Multiple personality When an individual's conflicts are so severe that he cannot cope with them by direct repression, he may develop one or more additional, separate personalities to account for his repressed motives. Only one personality can function at the conscious level at one time; at intervals, another personality takes over. It is possible for none of the personalities to be aware of the others. Sometimes, however, the dissociated personalities are aware of the original personality, but the first personality is not aware of the dissociation. Multiple personality is often confused with schizophrenia because both result in a drastic change in personality. However, they are very different. Multiple personality is the maintenance of two or more personalities at the same time. In schizophrenia, as will be seen, the person usually breaks from reality by withdrawing into himself.

One of the best-known examples of a multiple personality is described in the book *The Three Faces of Eve*. Eve White was not aware of her second personality; she only knew that she was troubled by blackouts, blinding headaches, and what appeared to be frequent amnesia. It was later discovered through therapy that when Eve White suffered a blackout, her second personality, Eve Black, emerged as her conscious personality. During therapy, Jane, a third personality, appeared; she was a more sensible, less fearful woman than either Eve White or Eve Black. As therapy progressed, Jane came to control the other two personalities. The analyst learned during therapy that as a child Eve White had been forced to kiss her dead grand-mother. During one dramatic session, Eve White was shown the cause of her disturbance; her multiple personalities disappeared, and a new, mature personality, Evelyn, emerged.

The causes of dissociation are difficult to determine. It usually arises from a traumatic emotional conflict, which leads to a very deep level of repression.

Conversion hysteria

The term *conversion hysteria* was originated by Freud to denote patients with psychological disorders who manifested all the symptoms of a physical illness. In such cases, the patient's frustration and internal conflicts are converted into a physical malfunction. This physical "illness" conveniently allows the individual to justify to himself or to others his inability to cope with any situation that he cannot handle at a conscious level. The patient seems to be suffering from an organic illness, but there is no organic basis for the symptoms. Freud believed that hysterical symptoms are often directly related to some aspect of the individual's problem. For example, a woman who fears sexual intercourse may suffer from paralysis of the legs.

A case of conversion hysteria   Martha N., a 31-year-old unmarried nurse, found that, after recovering from a mild case of laryngitis, she was unable to talk above a whisper. No organic reason could be found for her disability. She suffered no pain, but no matter how she tried, she could not talk aloud. Her physician examined her thoroughly and referred her to specialists, who could find no medical reason for her difficulty. After many consultations, her physician decided to send her for psychiatric help because he was convinced that her disability had an underlying emotional cause.

Martha was a cooperative but unmotivated patient and seemed untroubled by her difficulty. She managed to communicate by whispering and writing notes. After four therapy sessions, Martha consented to be interviewed while under the influence of sodium pentothal. (Sodium pentothal is a sedative drug that may be used to induce a state of semiconsciousness; under its influence, the person becomes very relaxed and is often able to talk about problems that he would not ordinarily be willing to discuss. See Chapter 14.)

During this interview, Martha provided much information about herself. She had been having an affair with a married man. Some months before her illness, her lover had decided to end the affair because he was worried that his wife might learn about it. Martha reacted violently to her lover's decision. She flew into a rage that led to a coughing spell in which she thought she was choking to death. Her lover came to her assistance and, in a moment of compassion, promised that they would continue to see each other. Shortly after this scene, however, he stopped phoning and made it plain in a letter that they would not meet again. Martha appeared to accept the termination of the affair until she became ill with laryngitis, the organic manifestation of her conversion reaction.

Following the pentothal interview, Martha began treatment on a regular basis. After 3 months of therapeutic consultations, she regained the use of her voice and returned to her job as a nurse.

Conversion hysteria may first affect one part of the body and then transfer to another part. This happens when the individual is afraid that his psychological problem is becoming apparent. In conversion hysteria, the type of illness depends on the nature of the conflict and, of course, on the individual involved. The point is that the hysterical symptoms allow the individual to resolve his frustration without feeling the stronger pain of conflict; the symptoms are so effective that the illness is usually extended far beyond the time it would take an actual physical illness to abate. It may take a therapist months or years to help rid the individual of his hysterical symptoms, depending on the therapist's ability to uncover the individual's conflicts and enable him to understand them. Under hypnotic treatment, conversion hysteria has been known to disappear entirely—the man who cannot move his arm is able to lift it, the woman who cannot walk suddenly does so, and so on.

Unlike other neurotic reactions, conversion hysteria is seldom accompanied by anxiety. The individual's symptoms may be very serious, as in the case of a paralysis, or they may be relatively mild, as in the case of hysterical fatigue; but serious or mild, the individual is often indifferent to the illness. This indifference, referred to as *la belle indifference*, evidently results from the reduction of anxiety that occurs when the illness seems to eliminate the individual's problem.

PSYCHOSES

Thus far we have been dealing with behavior generally termed neurotic. The individual may become so incapacitated by neuroses that he can no longer function in an everyday environment. But the neurotic wants to cope with his environment and tries to do so. A *psychotic* does not seek adjustment to the world in the same way. Rather, he adjusts the world to himself. In doing so, he creates a personal world markedly different from the world experienced by most of us. For this reason, we say that the psychotic has lost touch with reality.

For example, a psychotic may find it excruciating to be at the mercy of random events—perhaps because during childhood he was excessively and inconsistently punished, or because loved ones disappeared inexplicably. So that he will not be surprised by an unexpected hurt, he may create a world in which terrible things always happen and are invariably expected. Or he may restructure the world so that it is entirely within his control. In such a case, the psychotic believes his own explanations of events; he feels responsible for the deaths of great figures and the state of current events, as well as innumerable incidents that affect him personally.

In contrast to the psychotic, the neurotic who fears punishment and the loss of loved ones might defend himself by clinging unduly to those close to him or by shunning close relationships altogether. He might avoid all situations that hint of failure or else seek the strongest possible position, so that he can afford

Table 13.1   Major differences between neurotic and psychotic behavior[a]

Neurotic patient

Is in touch with reality, but sometimes unable to cope with frustration
No significant personality changes
Symptom may be overpowering, but patient neither hallucinates nor shows delusions
Is oriented to his environment
Frequently understands the nature and implications of his behavior
Psychotherapy or behavior modification is the prescribed treatment
Seldom requires hospital care

Psychotic patient

Loses touch with reality
May show marked personality changes
May be delusional and may experience hallucinations
May be disoriented as to time, place, or person
Often does not understand the nature of his own behavior
Drugs and other medical therapies often required along with psychotherapy or behavior modification
Usually requires institutional care

[a]Adapted from Louis P. Thorpe, Barney Katz, and Robert T. Lewis, *The psychology of abnormal behavior—A dynamic approach* (2nd ed.). Copyright © 1961. The Ronald Press Company, New York.

to ignore criticism and disapproval. However self-defeating his defenses, the neurotic uses them to contend with the environment. The psychotic often will not contend at all.

The psychotic patient may be so disoriented that he loses contact with reality. False beliefs in the form of delusions interfere with his ability to adjust to his environment. He may feel that others are always talking about him (*delusion of reference*), or are out to interfere with his activities and harm him (*delusion of persecution*), or are trying to control him (*delusion of influence*), or that he is really a president or a king (*delusion of grandeur*). Often he feels "unreal"; sometimes he adopts another identity. Hallucinations—perceptions in the absence of appropriate stimulation of sense organs —confuse him.

Although psychoses are extreme personality disorders, they do not necessarily prevent the patient from having normal, lucid states. Table 13.1 provides guidelines to some of the major differences between neurotic and psychotic behavior.

In diagnosing various psychotic ailments, psychologists have realized that psychotic reactions may be either *organic* (now known as *chronic brain disorders*) or *functional*. Individuals with organic psychotic disorders (brain damage, for example) can be helped only to the extent that the individual's organic malfunction can be alleviated. Functional psychotic reactions do not seem to be caused by any organic malfunction. However, recent research has indicated that some psychoses hitherto regarded as functional may be due to organic disorders of a biochemical nature; in other words, the body chemistry causes a certain brain reaction to occur, which, in turn, brings about psychotic behavior. However, the evidence is inconclusive, and it is also speculated that the psychotic state may cause the biochemical condition (rather than the reverse). Later on, we will discuss psychoses known to result from physical conditions.

PARANOID REACTIONS

Various paranoid reactions constitute one category of psychotic behavior. Although *paranoid psychosis* is abnormal behavior, it is often difficult to identify the symptoms in even the most paranoid individuals. Generally, these individuals apply apparently logical thinking to their normal behavior and even to their paranoid reactions. They seem reasonably well adjusted, except when involved in a situation that stimulates their paranoid behavior. The most obvious symptoms of paranoia are the individual's delusions, and these can be either grandiose or suspicious or both. The patient believes that he is what his delusions tell him he is. His behavior otherwise is rather orderly and consistent. The individual suffering from delusions of persecution often becomes suspicious and mysterious, as if he suspects that everyone is seeking a way to destroy him. Usually he has a basis for this perception—

he was raised in a destructive or conspiratorial family, he had early experiences that impressed upon him his membership in a hated race, and so on. If his tendency to see persecution in everyone and everything is understandable in terms of his past but unrealistic in terms of his present situation, we may say that he is psychotic.

The delusional system of the paranoid psychotic encompasses almost the total range of his perceptions. Paranoid delusions often take the form of delusions of reference, in which the patient believes others are watching him or interfering with his activities. He sees threat and potential danger in other people; because he himself is basically aggressive, he projects this aggression onto others. Without realizing it, he seems to be saying in his behavior, "I do not trust them, so they do not trust me. I am angry, so they must be angry." The reverse is also true: a paranoid personality will find reasons to blame himself for the genuinely hostile attitudes others show toward him. One patient who felt that disaster followed him everywhere felt equally strongly that he caused any real disaster he heard about. To prove that he brought about such

Table 13.2   Some major schizophrenic symptoms

Symptom	Description
Emotional disorders	Apathetic; is emotionally flat; makes inappropriate emotional responses
Contact with reality	Does not interact with people; loses all interest in his environment
Fantasy	Responds to his own private fantasies; engages in strange mannerisms: disoriented as to space and time
Disorders of perception	Believes others are trying to control him; has delusions (for example, believes other are persecuting him or that he is the President); has hallucinations (for example, hears voices)
Disorders of thinking	Makes inconsistent and illogical statements; intellectual capability weakens; gives bizarre associations
Lack of "self"	Feels he is too bad or immoral to be a real person; may feel that he has been punished with death and that a part of him (his exterior or interior) is dead

disasters, he developed complex and quite irrational links between his behavior and the disasters—blaming some trivial action of his own for an airplane crash 50 miles away, for example.

A case of paranoid reaction Martin W., unmarried and 42 years of age, was referred to a Veterans' Administration hospital following a suicide attempt. Upon admission to the hospital, he was severely disturbed. He maintained a fixed delusional system in which he was the object of a wide-ranging plot; he felt that everyone he knew was "out to get him," and that he was the subject of an intensive search by the FBI, which was rounding up all the "sex perverts." He know that the FBI was after him because he frequently saw an automobile pass in front of his house. This automobile, he said, had "significant" license plates. When asked what he meant by "significant," he replied that the plates contained a number 62 followed by an I. He then pointed out that F was the sixth letter of the alphabet and B the second letter and then, of course, there was the I. He also claimed that his boss was aware of his sexual perversions and kept teasing him secretly. When asked how he knew this, he pointed out that each week his payroll slip carried the letters Pb rather than Pd, meaning "paid." he said Pb must mean "perverted boy."

During a 6-month stay in the hospital, Martin developed a good therapeutic relationship with the psychologist and his delusional system gradually became weaker. When discharged from the hospital, he still showed some mild delusional activity but was generally more relaxed and better able to cope with his problems. The hospital authorities felt that there was no danger of another suicide attempt.

Paranoid reactions are very difficult to treat. The paranoiac's suspicion and hostility usually make him an uncooperative patient; few paranoiacs respond very well to psychotherapy.

SCHIZOPHRENIA

Approximately half of all psychotic disorders are diagnosed as *schizophrenia*, a term that comes from the Greek words meaning split (*schiz*) of the mind (*phrenia*). Schizophrenia refers to the separation of an individual's psyche from his behavior. Although in essence each case of schizophrenia is different from all others, a group of symptoms tends to appear in varying degree in all schizophrenic disorders. These are withdrawal from reality, distorted or disturbed contact with reality, regressive behavior, erratic thought, inconsistent emotional or affective relationships, hallucinations, delusions, and deterioration of physical condition. Although the symptoms of schizophrenia are usually recognizable, locating the causes and developing successful treatments still present tremendous difficulties. Table 13.2 shows the major schizophrenic symptoms.

The traditional schizophrenic classification —*simple*, *hebephrenic*, *catatonic*, and *paranoid* —are not very satisfactory on at least two counts. First, since the symptoms of schizophrenia can be symptomatic of more than one classification, we cannot be certain that identification of symptoms will enable us to diagnose the disorder. Second, the traditional classes do not take into account the fact that many schizophrenic patients undergo symptomatic alterations during the course of their illness. Thus, a diagnosis of clinical symptoms may have to be modified later because the symptoms change. Table 13.3 presents the traditional schizophrenic classifications for the four major types of schizophrenia. Note that many of the symptoms are closely interrelated.

Some psychologists now classify schizophrenic conditions as being one of two types: *process schizophrenia* or *reactive schizophrenia*. The categorization depends on what happened in the patient's personality adjustment before the diagnosis. Process schizophrenia occurs in individuals whose personalities have undergone a progressive process of increasingly severe maladaptive behavior. If the schizophrenic deterioration has been gradual, the prognosis (prediction for recovery) is very poor (Figure 13.4). Process schizophrenics are usually protected for many years by their families. (Typically, maladjustment is prevalent in such families.)

Table 13.3   Traditional schizophrenic classification

Type	Symptoms
Simple	Withdraws from reality; passive and apathetic
Hebephrenic	Childish, foolish, and bizarre thoughts and feelings; hallucinations are common
Catatonic	Deep preoccupation resulting in periods of muscular rigidity (the catatonic stupor); responses are negative and contrary to what is called for; often aggressive; is delusional and may hallucinate
Paranoid	Illogical delusions predominate; suspicious and hostile; thinking is disorganized

The second category, reactive schizophrenia, occurs in individuals whose schizophrenic behavior is triggered by a traumatic experience or by adolescence, but whose earlier personality and level of adjustment could be termed adequate. Thus, the reactive schizophrenic is one who suffers a sudden personality collapse. Clinical psychologists believe that the chances for

recovery of the reactive group are good, for in such cases psychotherapeutic techniques can be used effectively (see Chapter 14).

However useful this two-category theory may be, it still leaves many unanswered questions. No physical determinant has been found to be present in process schizophrenics that is not present in reactive schizophrenics, and there is no definite way to distinguish organically between the two forms of the disorder. Some studies have shown, however, that reactive schizophrenics are more physiologically and emotionally alert in their responses to various stimuli—because the reactive schizophrenic's stressful situa-

Figure 13.4   The schizophrenic withdraws from reality. The therapist may gain insight into the source of the patient's problems through analysis of paintings such as this one. (Walt Sanders— Black Star)

tion is generally recent and his emotional and physiological response mechanisms are still intact.

A clue to physiological differences in schizophrenics Investigators have observed that paranoid and nonparanoid schizophrenics react differently to sensory stimulation. The paranoid schizophrenic, who is constantly scanning his environment, suffers from an inability to focus attention. The nonparanoid schizophrenic, in contrast, seems to tune out strong stimuli while keenly attending to moderate and weak stimulation. It has also been observed that tranquilizers, commonly used in the treatment of emotional disturbances, tend to modify sensory sensitivity.

Using these facts as a basis for their experiments, Rappaport, Silverman, Hopkins, and Hall (1971) made predictions about the sensory acuity of schizophrenics treated with tranquilizers. They reasoned that the drug would cause paranoid schizophrenics to focus attention, thereby experiencing increased sensory acuity. The drug would make nonparanoid schizophrenics experience less interest in weak simulation, thereby decreasing sensitivity.

The experimenters used a signal-detection task to test their predictions. The subjects were required to press a microswitch each time they heard a tone that was presented against a background of noise. Tranquilized nonparanoid schizophrenics showed lowered ability to recognize the tone, while tranquilized paranoid schizophrenics showed an increase in recognition ability. Thus, the drug appears to have an opposite effect on the two types of schizophrenics. From this, it is surmised that the underlying physiology of the two disorders probably differs.

Causes of schizophrenia

The causes of schizophrenia, like the causes of other psychotic disorders, have not yet been conclusively identified. We surmise that heredity is a factor because it has been shown that the schizophrenic individual is likely to have brothers, sisters, parents, or other relatives who are also schizophrenics. (We will return to the genetics of behavior pathology later in this chapter.) Many psychologists believe that the genetic inheritance probably includes a biochemical predisposition that creates schizophrenia when coupled with a maladaptive family situation.

The unhealthy family relationship is per-

haps the pivotal factor. Typically, the schizophrenic is raised in an atmosphere of emotional confusion. Family members behave inconsistently, communicate through double meanings, misinterpret each other's thoughts, and so on. Frequently, there is hostility between parents—hostility that may be undeclared or disguised by the appearance of normalcy. The child does not know what is real and what is unreal. Because he is (like all young children) completely dependent upon his parents, he must believe in them. Yet what they say often has no relation to how they behave.

Usually the child will believe adult family members. Consequently, he will disbelieve or deny his own thoughts. For example, a child who is told that mother loves him and "does everything for him" will believe this, even if the mother is working directly against him. The cost of this belief—so necessary to his childhood survival—is high. In order to believe, the child may assume that any conflicting thoughts he may have are not really his, that they belong to an alien person inside him. It is not difficult to see why the child becomes confused about his identity, why he develops behaviors to help him exist in an unreal world, and why he is able to believe preposterous things about himself and his environment.

Case histories of schizophrenics have yielded a great variety of data about the causes of the disorder. No one cause can be assigned. It seems clear, however, that the schizophrenic is somehow induced to behave consistently in a way that reflects demands originating outside the self. When he begins to assert his own demands, he feels in danger of losing his other self; he becomes confused and breaks with reality.

Schizophrenia and culture Harry Stack Sullivan, the noted psychiatrist once observed, "Schizophrenia is not a disease but a way of life." Sullivan believed that schizophrenia is too widespread and takes on too many forms to be attributed to any one kind of adjustment problem; he suggested that schizophrenia is related to the individual's way of life and the makeup of the social system of which he is a part.

The role that cultural and social forces play in the development of schizophrenia is evident when we look at the normal life-styles of various groups and relate these styles to the form taken by schizophrenia in people of each culture.

Opler (1957) studied Italian and Irish schizophrenics who were patients in a New York hospital. First, however, he studied the neighborhoods from which they came. He found that Italian homes were dominated by an authoritarian father, that the children were allowed to express their emotions freely, and that little or no guilt was attached to sex. On the other hand, Irish homes were dominated by the mother, emotional expression was suppressed, and sexual desires were considered sinful.

Opler's examination showed that Irish patients had more fantasy delusions (due to repressed emotions) and more guilt feelings about sex (due to the attitude that sex was sinful). They all revealed homosexual tendencies, but none became overt homosexuals (homosexuality was a sin). The Irish were also afraid of women (representing the domineering mother), low in self-esteem, quiet, and withdrawn.

The Italian patients were hostile toward male figures (representing their authoritarian fathers), loud and boisterous (expressing emotions freely), had no fantasies or guilt feelings about sex, and many became overt homosexuals (because they were not sexually inhibited).

This study indicates that understanding of a schizophrenic's culture offers insight into the causes and manifestations of his illness.

The onset of schizophrenia is marked by a general confusion that leads to failures in perception and thought. The following example of paranoid schizophrenia illustrates the delusional thinking of the schizophrenic. You may recall from Chapter 10 the case of the disturbed teacher who manipulated words to satisfy his delusions of reality. Here are some facts about this patient, along with other sections of the diary he kept during his hospitalization.

Arthur T., age 30, was a high school teacher with a master's degree. He was admitted to a psychiatric hospital at the request of his parents, with whom he lived. They reported that his behavior had become increasingly "strange." His conversation did not make sense,[1] and he spent most of his time in his room talking to himself. Upon admission, he was found to be disorganized but not violent. He was cooperative, knew that he was being hospitalized, and had some understanding of the reasons why. His case is, in part, described by his diary.

Monday, January 8 I arose early. Today, Dad, my sister, and I went to town to the Veterans' Hospital.

I objected to signing a paper to the effect that I would accept any treatment that the hospital would recommend. "Any" covered a lot of territory. The doctor had a very pretty assistant whom he introduced as his social worker. When I get to feeling better, I'd like to get better acquainted. I was given another paper to sign when I changed from street clothes to hospital pajamas and a bath robe. This time I objected even more strenuously. I wanted to read and study it first. At last I signed. I had already signed the first paper and was caught in the net.

Presently I was conducted to the admitting ward of the hospital. I felt disgraced and felt that I had disgraced the family and friends. I probably would have wept if I could have shed tears. The nurse asked what my difficulty was. I remarked that I seemed to be going crazy, or something, I guess. She laughed and said something that sounded like, "We're all crazy down here." She measured my height and weight. She said that my height was six feet. That was an inch more than I thought. Perhaps my memory is beginning to fail me.[2] Perhaps they are going to make a new man out of me.[3] They will perhaps use an illusion technique. Maybe I won't even know myself when I come out.[4]

---

[1] His parents were referring to the fact that his sentences were frequently disjointed. For example, he would say, "It looks like rain today. I think I'll buy a new shirt. Have you seen my dictionary?"

[2] Indicates his strong feelings of self-doubt.

[3] Reflects his delusion of influence: he feels he may be controlled or manipulated by outside forces.

[4] Many psychotics experience confusion about their own identities and feel that they are becoming someone else. In this patient's case it may also be wishful thinking.

The nurse then took my blood pressure and pulse. She gave me what I thought might be a sexy look. I guess she did that to learn what would happen to my pulse. I don't care much what she finds out. Maybe she thinks I'm impotent or a pervert, I don't know.[5] Maybe she'll be right.

Soon the nurse called an attendant. This white uniformed man took me through a locked wire door, down a long hall to the Day Room and the sleeping room. The men were sitting around talking. Some were smoking. The attendant brought me a blue jacket and trousers to put on.

Presently the pretty social worker came through the room on an errand. She smiled. I don't know whether it was meant for me or not. I thought it might be. At any rate I was glad she smiled. It indicated that everything seemed to be all right with her. Perhaps, eventually, everything would be all right with me, too.[6]

In just a short time another doctor came and took me to his office for an examination. He asked me a lot of questions. I did a lot of talking, I guess. I'm glad to have the chance to get some of these doubts, fears, and ideas off my chest. It was time for dinner and he walked with me back to the ward.

In the evening we all went to the dining room for supper. We sat at a table with a "reserved" sign on it. I wonder why we have a special table. I wonder what is wrong with all the other men at this table. Perhaps the staff is observing us to discover the kind and degree of our insanity.[7] After supper the group lined up again with an attendant in front and one behind. We went to the recreation hall and saw a movie. After the movie, we all plodded back to the ward where we watched television for a while.

Bedtime! Here I am in a hospital under the care of a psychiatrist. There must be some things that I don't know or else I must have much of what I do know twisted up pretty badly. I guess perhaps I have been rather contrary, stubborn, and independent. In general, I think that I need to learn to trust and have faith that God works through people. This is a pretty good idea that Dad mentioned. When (Sister) left this morning she told me to do what I was told and to cooperate. Maybe I have been uncooperative sometimes. I believe she has a fine idea.

I need help. One just can't solve all of his own problems. He can't live in a world by himself.[8] I must learn to trust these people and have confidence in them and believe what they tell me. Actually there isn't much other choice. Isaiah 1:19 and 20 says, "If ye be willing and obedient, ye shall eat the good of the land: But if ye refuse and rebel, ye shall be devoured with the sword: for the mouth of the Lord hath spoken it."

Saturday, January 13 I didn't sleep very good last night. One reason I am locked in this ward is to make me want out. By depriving me of my freedom, I can have a chance to make up my mind what I want to do when I get out. I want to go to work and get married. Perhaps I'll be released from here soon, since I have decided what I want to do. I am surely in a mess. I came in here on Friday. Jesus was crucified on Friday and arose on the first day of the week—perhaps I can get out of here on the first day of the week—that will be Sunday tomorrow—but if I do that I will be like Jesus—but he was perfect and I am not perfect—perhaps I am in Hell now.[9] If I tell the staff that I think I'm all right they may let me out because that would be a good reason for not keeping anybody: I think. I'm all right. I am caught in a web, it seems. It is a known fact that insane people think they think that they are all right. It seems that things are getting more and more tangled up.[10]

[5] An example of projection.
[6] He attaches important personal meaning to inconsequential events.
[7] Delusion of reference: he feels people are watching him.
[8] Indication of insight: he recognizes his withdrawal from reality.
[9] Good example of word play and the use of symbols (for example, Friday—Jesus—first day of the week—perfect—hell).
[10] He is aware in part of his own confused thinking.

In the morning we went to breakfast. That "reserved" sign bothered me. Which side of it should I sit on? Perhaps one side is for those people who show tendencies toward sexual perversion. The other side might be for those who are just plain losing their minds. No matter which side I sit on, it is the wrong side.[11] After breakfast we went down to the gymnasium to stay a while. A very energetic man asked us to come and play volleyball. Sometimes, when he served, he would yell something about a weak spot and then serve the ball to me. I guess everybody must know that I have a weak mind by now. He knows my name—now that I think of it, the attendants and the nurses seem to know my name. They probably wouldn't have learned so quickly unless I was unusual in some respect. Perhaps I have some unusual type of insanity or sex perversion.[12]

We returned to the ward and again all sat down. I still had the feeling that someone was observing my every move. I became afraid of saying anything to anybody. I sometimes suspect that only a part of these men have anything wrong with them. I soon decided that I couldn't tell which ones were ill and which ones weren't. Some of these people are, in all probability, all right, and are just putting on an act so that they can see what I will do under certain conditions.[13] I had difficulty trying to decide where to sit for fear of sitting down by the wrong person. If I choose to sit by an insane person, I probably would be classed as insane. I can see no one acts perfectly normal. Neither can I see anyone who is abnormal. The ones who seem a little peculiar may be just acting that way but are really all right. In fact they may be part of the hospital staff.

Dinnertime. I went back to my tray and noticed that I had somehow gotten my dessert on the front part of the tray. Things just were hopeless. I seemed to be doing nearly everything backwards. If I were doing things all right, why was I in the hospital? If I were in the hospital for observation, if the attendants or the patients saw me with my dessert on the tray backwards, they would know that I needed attention. More troubles! I forgot my glass or straw for the milk container. If I went back for either, that would be observed and I would get another *black mark* for loss of memory.[14] I decided just to drink the milk out of the container. Now I realize that that was the worst thing to have done. I surely was going from bad to worse.

After the meal we went back to the ward. We sat for a while. I had the feeling that I was sitting in the wrong place. The attendant looked at his watch. I got up and moved. Someone said, "Here they come!" Through the door came in single file a group of people. Some of the women had on blue and yellow uniforms. Some were wearing ordinary street clothes. A man, wearing an American Legion hat, brought up the rear. They passed out cards and we played bingo. I was nearly out of my wits. These people must be people from some other ward for mental patients. They are probably trustees, and, in addition, are suffering from delusions of grandeur.[15] The women are given a uniform and the men a hat. It makes them feel important. All these people may be on the staff and are here in disguise, to have a better chance to observe us. That man with the hat who called out the bingo numbers is probably a doctor. The woman who looked the craziest of the bunch passed out the bingo cards. She gave each of us two. Smart people do only one thing at a time. In order to prove that I was not insane, I stuck one card under the chair and used only one card. She also passed out slips of paper on which were numbers. This was for the door prize. I had no idea what one group of crazy people would give as a door prize to another group of crazy people. I didn't want to take any chance and

[11]Extreme projection resulting in a delusion.
[12]His use of the term "insanity" does not reflect insight; he is simply saying that he is confused and powerless to help himself.
[13]Again—his delusional belief that he is being watched and tested.

[14]Every insignificant detail gets woven into his delusional system.
[15]Projection with a glimpse of his sense of humor.

so gave my slip of paper to the patient next to me. Afterwards I wasn't so sure that I did the right thing. If the people were part of the staff of the hospital, the door[16] prize might be the door, the open door, a way out, and freedom. I was wrong, as far as the door prize was concerned, on both counts. The prize was an extra package of cigarettes.

I didn't cover the "free" space in the middle of the card. I sure didn't intend to block my own free[16] space in anything. I couldn't concentrate very well on this game. I didn't much want to win anyhow. Somehow or other, I have a feeling that if one wins he will in the long run lose. I don't know what is going on around here. Until I can get things figured out, I think I'll try to remain in the background.

Finally, they all filed out in sort of mechanical fashion. I don't like this business. This noon, I crossed the room, the attendant looked at his watch, and those people filed into the room. It seems as though things are timed to the minute and that I am the controlling factor.[17] I have had about enough of this. I am going to try to figure a way to get out of here. That is probably the way of treatment, anyhow. In the past, I have occasionally had ideas of being somehow abnormal. By staying here for awhile, one soon gets so confused that he wants to get with normal people and is never coaxed back into anything resembling a mental hospital again.

The flowers on the end of each row of tables in the dining room didn't help my morale any. I had a vague feeling that they had something to do with dying.[18] I was reluctant to inquire about them for fear that my suspicions would be confirmed, and I would then have an item to worry about for sure. When it was time to eat, I began to wonder if I was in the right place. I asked the attendant if I had any certain place to eat. I was still perturbed over that "reserved"

sign. Since, apparently, either side was the wrong place to sit, I thought, I should ask the attendant where to sit. He said that any place would be all right. That wasn't a bit comforting. If sitting on either side of that sign was the wrong group, then, obviously, if a person had a choice of two things, and they were both wrong, then the choice, although wrong, would still be all right since that was the only thing that could be done. The staff are very intelligent people. They know or concluded that I sometimes feel that, no matter what I do, it is wrong. They are trying to teach me that, no matter what I do, sometimes, even if it is wrong, it is still all right. I think that I will be able to leave soon, perhaps. Only a reasonably intelligent person could have figured what it is that they are trying to do.

After supper, we all went to the recreation hall for the movie. Before the picture started, I wandered into the lounge. It was in semi-darkness so that the patients could watch the television program. My unhappy frame of mind was not made any happier by noting the baskets of flowers sitting about the room. The half-light gave a deathly pallor, I thought, to the faces in the room. I had thoughts concerning the death of some of these people and of what it might be. Perhaps it might be soon and these flowers are some kind of indication of who might die next and when.[19] One of the attendants saw me and winked. I wonder what he thinks or was thinking. I don't especially want to know. The news might have something unpleasant in it for me. I decided to get out of the lounge. Several things in that movie seem to apply to me.

I surely do not care for the loud talking and laughing of some of these men. Neither do I like cursing and filthy language. I wonder if some of these people are of a homosexual nature or whether they just do a lot of filthy, disgusting talking. One patient disgusted me. He seemed to me to be an expert at doubletalk. I could find nothing in his general behavior or speech which indicated

[16]Words such as "door" and "free" take on powerful symbolic meaning for him.
[17]In his delusional system he is either the controlled or the controller.
[18]Again—his symbolism.

[19]Symbolism.

that he had anything but indecent thoughts to convey in phrases and sentences with double meaning.[20]

Monday, January 2 Some days, some very unusual things occur. This morning, I asked for a pair of scissors to trim my finger-nails. The nurse said that she would try to find me a pair. In just a few minutes, another nurse called my name and said that she wanted to see me. After ascertaining that I had not eaten, she took me to another room where there were some other patients. She took a needle and gave me a shot in the arm. She said that she was giving me some insulin. I had a suspicion that it was water that she was giving me in the arm. I don't think that there is anything wrong with me, anyhow. If insulin is supposed to produce a reaction, probably the same reaction could be produced by describing the kind of reaction expected and then giving us an injection of water. Our imaginations could then produce the reaction. After the injection, my suspicions were almost confirmed. An attendant brought us glasses of chipped ice to eat. He said that it was to go with the treatment. Since ice is water, it is easy to see how he was trying to be subtle and tell us that the fluid in the needle was water.[21] I surely was amused at the clever stunt that was being pulled on us. After chuckling, I felt better. I don't feel nervous. Salt shakers were also provided. In the shaker were little solid objects that resembled seeds. They were probably bird seed. When I was a youngster, I had heard of putting salt on a rabbit's tail to catch him. This time, there was bird seed in the salt shaker. We patients were the "birds." Several of the chairs in the room were yellow, about the color of a canary. These chairs helped confirm my suspicions. I wouldn't sit on them nor the red ones either.[22]

Tonight as we were leaving the television room, there was an advertisement concerning tea kettles. One tea kettle was shown whistling. Birds also chirp and whistle. Is it possible that the tea kettle company and the television company are working with this hospital? There must be some relationship between the insulin, water, bird seed in the salt shaker, and the whistling tea kettle.[23]

This evening, I overheard one patient mention to another that someone had laughed today. He hadn't seen him laugh before. I wonder if they are referring to me. I don't believe I have laughed since I came in here until today when I saw the funny angle to this insulin treatment.

Tuesday, January 23 This morning, we had "insulin" treatment here again. I don't know whether things are getting better or worse. The doors on this ward swing in. "They swing outward never." I wonder if this is also some sort of sign that we are advancing to a permanent place in the hospital. On the other ward, the doors swing outward. Unless there is some significance, why do the doors swing "out" on one ward and "in" on the other.[24]

This morning, I decided to miss the appointment with the psychologist. I think that it is a waste of time to talk with him. He isn't learning from me.[25] He has more training than I have in psychology. I can't teach him anything new. I can't learn by doing all the talking. If I work in the laundry, the time spent there will be useful in doing work. However, I had only worked in the laundry about ten minutes when the psychologist called for me and said that he wanted to see me. He said that the staff wanted me to have these

---

[20]His perplexity is real, for he is evidently referring to another psychotic patient whose conversation is incoherent.
[21]He attaches personal meaning to everything; his associations run freely and he responds to them as if they mirrored reality.
[22]Again—his personal associations support his delusions.

[23]Something as trivial as a whistling tea kettle arouses in him the suspicion that the hospital, the tea kettle company, and the television company are plotting against him. The bringing together of such details is typical of paranoid thinking.
[24]Again—he gives meaning to everything, and the meaning has special significance for him.
[25]His reference here is to the nondirective form of therapy he was undergoing.

conferences. They think that they are important. It seems to me that, whenever I try to think for myself any more, I either come out with the wrong answers or at least several people consider that my answers are wrong.

I wonder if the staff is disagreeing with me to teach me that my own ideas are often wrong or at least that people will not always agree with me regardless of whether I am right or wrong.

Treatment

A large percentage of the people now in mental institutions are schizophrenics, but hospitals and clinics have lagged in developing satisfactory methods of treatment, and the rate of complete recovery is low. Most hospital programs concentrate on treatments to help socialize the schizophrenics. Many are treated with drugs to improve their contact with the environment. Once the schizophrenic realizes that someone cares about him, he may exhibit an interest in recovering. Consequently, the establishment of an understanding relationship between doctor and patient is of primary importance. Until better methods of therapy evolve, the therapist's chief approach to the schizophrenic is to try any way he can to reach him in his private world and help him return to the real world.

Childhood schizophrenia

Young children sometimes display schizophrenic-like reactions, the most common being *autism* (withdrawal). There is considerable disagreement about the diagnosis of childhood schizophrenia, but most practitioners agree that children may develop autistic reactions that render them helpless. Such children are almost totally unable to form relationships with other people, including parents and other children. Often autistic children engage in bizarre motor behavior, whirling around or monotonously repeating gestures. They are sometimes so oblivious to their immediate environment that an uninformed observer might conclude they were blind or deaf.

The human machine The psychiatrist Bruno Bettelheim (1959) described a young patient, Joey, a boy who saw himself as a machine. Joey felt that he needed electrical power to help him live, and machinery to aid him in eating, defecating, and sleeping. For a long time after he entered the hospital, Joey did not speak to anyone. When his "machine" was turned off, he just sat there quietly, as though he did not exist. When investigating Joey's background, Bettelheim found that Joey had been largely ignored by his parents. He was an unwanted and unloved baby. For example, when he cried, as most babies do, his parents would not comfort him or satisfy his needs; they would simply leave him alone. His toilet training was strict and conducted at a very early age.

Joey retreated into a world of machines, where he could not be reached or hurt by human feelings. Gradually, through patience and human understanding, he began to act like a human being. In an essay that he wrote after he had made good progress toward recovery, Joey declared, "Feelings are more important than anything under the sun."

MANIC AND DEPRESSIVE REACTIONS

Some individuals display extreme swings in mood from depression to excitement or from excitement to depression. The excited mood is often accompanied by very disorganized, boisterous, and even aggressive behavior and is referred to as *manic behavior. Depressed* reactions are characterized by overwhelming feelings of sadness and futility. We speak of a *manic-depressive reaction* when an individual displays both extremes of mood.

The depressed patient may be very withdrawn and so preoccupied with his hopelessness that he stops eating and reacting to his surroundings. Some depressed patients are very anxious and agitated. They exhibit restlessness and their anguish is often expressed in crying and in declarations of worthlessness. But sometimes depression is concealed from the outsider. A smiling, friendly appearance may hide feelings of inadequacy and futility.

Suicidal behavior. Depression plays an important role in the development of suicidal behavior. The feelings of futility experienced by the depressive or his obsessive guilt may set the stage for his decision to die. At least 25 percent of patients hospitalized for depression show some form of suicidal behavior, either as thoughts, threats, or actual attempts (Mendels, 1970).

It has been suggested (Farberow and Schneidman, 1965) that suicidal behavior is the distressed person's way of telling others that he is suffering and needs their help. In most cases, the suicide threat is a warning designed to gain attention. Nonetheless, it is a real warning that the individual is contemplating his own death. Even though he does nothing to carry out the threat, the threat itself is significant and usually reflects some form of serious distress.

The majority of patients with manic reactions have a history of depression. Manic reactions follow increased feelings of anxiety, usually arising from an episode of deep depression. The manic outburst is not to be confused with joy. The patient may appear elated, but his excitement is more a desperate effort to escape from depression than a manifestation of genuine pleasure. The patient's apparent gaiety is exaggerated. His delusions—"I am the emperor" or "I am the smartest person in school"—appear to be a defense against feelings of low worth.

Manic patients appear to have unlimited energy. They have difficulty sleeping and may be too excited to eat; because they are so active, they are often physically destructive, particularly if frustrated.

George H. was a 21-year-old college student referred for hospitalization by the health service of his college after he was brought in by his roommate, who reported that George had not only stopped eating and talking, but no longer did anything. The roommate reported that, for the preceding 3 days, George had simply sat on his bed staring at the walls, answering questions with a nod of the head and an occasional word, but no more.

For a period of 8 weeks following his hospital admission, George showed little or no change. He was a cooperative patient, but did no more than eat and sleep when told to do so.

A sodium pentothal interview revealed that George had been an active and outgoing student, but that his relationships with girls had been unsatisfactory. He spoke at length about a girl he liked very much and who he had hoped would be his girlfriend. He had made an attempt to visit her and was surprised and hurt by the way she greeted him. She told him that he had no business coming to her home and that he should leave immediately. It was shortly after this incident that the roommate reported George's depression.

After 3 months of hospitalization, during which George progressed very little, his parents asked that he be released so that they could take him home and care for him there. The hospital authorities agreed and no more was heard from George until 6 months after his release. He returned to the hospital looking like a totally different person. Gone were the stooped shoulders and the slow, downcast manner; instead there appeared a fast-talking young man with cheeks flushed and eyes sparkling. He had come to the hospital to tell the doctors how "well he was," but it was apparent that he was highly excited and irrational. His speech was so rapid as to be incoherent and he was unable to stop talking. He claimed he had had "a revelation" showing him that he was better than most people and that there were "great things for him to do." Since it was clear that he was in a *manic* state, with the consent of his parents, he was again hospitalized. For 4 months he was most uncooperative, assaultive, noisy, and generally disruptive, requiring sedation and constant attention. Gradually the manic mood diminished until he was in a less excited state. He appeared in good control of himself and was therefore discharged. Two years later he was readmitted after another extreme manic episode. This time, the hospitalization lasted 2 years. When discharged, he had presumably been restored to a functional level.

Treatment Individuals suffering from manic and depressive reactions usually respond to treatment. Various new drugs have been developed that reduce manic behavior. Other drugs help to raise the depressive out of his melancholic mood, at least temporarily.

Electroconvulsive therapy (ECT), described in Chapter 14, has been effective in the treatment of depression. This form of treatment, like drug therapy, temporarily changes the way the patient feels, but it does not get to the conditions that produced the depression in the first place.

PSYCHOSOMATIC DISORDERS

An individual's emotional state often plays a key role in organic (*somatic*) disorders. This type of bodily disturbance is known as a *psychosomatic disorder*, or a psychophysiological disorder. The various psychosomatic disorders—ulcers, certain forms of high blood pressure, migraine headaches, asthmatic reactions, and skin allergies—are thought to be due wholly or in part to long-term tension.

The visceral organs play a key role in emotional behavior and, when they undergo prolonged, exaggerated activity, damage may result. The damage is real; unlike hysteric conversions, psychosomatic reactions involve noticeable organic damage.

While it is known that prolonged stress or tension causes psychosomatic disorders, it is not always clear why, under similar stress conditions, one individual develops a particular type of symptom and another a different symptom, or no symptom at all. Numerous attempts have been made to induce psychosomatic disorders in animals. (Monkeys have been used in most such experiments, and their reactions have contributed to the psychologist's understanding of the physiology of human emotion.) In each experiment, however, no two animals responded in exactly the same way. Some animals developed ulcers, for example, whereas others in the same experiment remained normal. A similar degree of stress was used to produce disturbance in all the animals tested, yet some became more emotionally tense and agitated than others.

Although significant numbers of animals have been known to develop psychosomatic disorders, each animal seems to have his own system of emotional balances that enables him to cope with stress-provoking situations in his own way. As in human personality, this system is thought to depend on the individual's past experiences, his genetic disposition, and his general psychological state. In the well-known "executive monkey" study (see Chapter 9), emotional stress affected one monkey so severely that he died of an ulcerous condition, whereas other monkeys in the same study did not develop ulcers.

Stress and psychosomatic neuroses Lacey, Bateman, and Van Lehn (1953) tested to determine whether stressful situations always produce the same symptoms of psychosomatic disorders in the same persons. That is, under stress, do people show the same specific autonomic response from situation to situation? Subjects were tested under four different stress situations: (1) the subjects were instructed to do mathematics problems; (2) they had to take quick, deep breaths; (3) they had to try to remember as quickly as possible all words beginning with the letter *w*; (4) each subject's foot was suddenly immersed in ice-cold water. During these stress situations, measurements were taken of each subject's palmar skin potential (indicative of activity of the sweat glands) and heart rate.

Although the responses of most subjects to different stress situations varied, the pattern of autonomic response for a subject generally remained the same. Thus, a subject who showed a greater change in heart rate than in palmar skin potential under one situation also showed a greater change in heart rate under all stress situations.

According to some psychologists, psychosomatic reactions are learned as responses to recurring specific stimuli. When an individual cannot cope with a situation, he may become so tense that he responds by means of a bodily disturbance. Headaches, backaches, high blood pressure, asthma, and skin eruptions are frequently reactions to otherwise overly emotional situations. A psychosomatic reaction may serve the same purpose as, for example, a conversion hysteria (discussed earlier). If a psychosomatic reaction works to solve the individual's emotional dilemma, this response becomes learned and is repeated each time the individual faces a similar situation.

Psychologists have recently examined the connection between the amount of stress an individual experiences and the type and intensity of psychosomatic disorder that may occur as a response. A group of experimenters gave numerical values to stress situations, in a system called *life change units* (LCUs). All common anxiety-producing and tension-producing situations were assigned a life change unit value; for example, marriage was assigned 50 LCUs; receiving a traffic ticket was valued at 11 LCUs; and death of a husband or wife was valued at 100 LCUs, the highest stress value in the scale (the lowest LCU value was 11). Individuals were asked to complete a questionnaire aimed at determining their recent life changes. After the questionnaire was completed, each life change indicated was assigned a numerical value from the LCU scale. Health, for example, was an item on the questionnaire. The experimenters found that when LCU values equaled more than 150 points in a 2-year period, a *life crisis* would occur and this would affect the individual's health. The emotional stress of a life crisis led to conditions of ill health.

Tension and stress do more than cause illness; they can affect the treatment of individuals suffering from normal (nonpsychosomatic) physical illnesses. Physicians have found that even though a disorder arises from strictly physical causes, treatment may be impaired by the emotional attitude of the patient. The patient who believes he is hopelessly ill may actually become unresponsive to treatment, whereas the patient who believes he will get well does so even though

his chances look very poor. There is reason to believe that heart disease can be accentuated by conditions of emotional tension, and that intense stress damages parts of the circulatory system as well as other organs.

CHARACTER DISORDERS

A *character disorder* is a relatively habitual way of responding that is integral to the individual's behavior. Although character disorders are pathological, they are not classified as either neuroses or psychoses. They are classed as *sociopathic*, that is, directed against the social system in which the individual is required to function. The sociopath is not usually motivated by anxiety and stress or by a need to escape or to create a behavioral shield to protect himself. Instead, the sociopath is frequently self-centered and entirely amoral. He cares little for the laws or customs of his society. The three types of character disorders that we shall consider are the *antisocial reaction*, *alcoholism*, and *drug addiction*.

Antisocial reaction

One of the most severe and most persistent character disorders is known as the *psychopathic* (or *antisocial*) personality. The psychopath lacks a moral conscience; he is not law-abiding. Although he understands the consequences of amoral or unlawful acts, he is not concerned about them. His selfish and impulsive behavior is meant only to satisfy his own needs. He shows little or no feeling for others and therefore does not function effectively in a world whose members habitually depend on one another to survive.

According to psychoanalytic theory, the psychopath's antisocial reactions originate during childhood, when he fails to develop a superego —the restrictive, moral aspect of a personality (see Chapter 12). The child who does not develop a superego is one who has been unable to resolve his Oedipal conflict. All psychologists, whether or not they adhere to the psychoanalytic theory, agree that the parent-child relationship, as evidenced by parental love responses, is necessary for a child to develop a moral conscience and the ability to cope with his emotions. Without an adult to stand as a model for proper social and moral behavior, the child does not develop normally. Psychopathic behavior develops when the child learns that there is nothing to lose by behaving antisocially, since he does not have his parents' love and acceptance in the first place. He seldom feels anxious, he has no fear of frustration, and he feels little or no guilt. For the psychopath, the social rewards that affect the behavior of most of us are inconsequential. It is difficult to treat psychopathic behavior because by the time the psychopath is identified, his antisocial reactions are deeply embedded in his personality.

Rejection as a cause of psychopathy Most, if not all, psychopaths experienced rejection in childhood. But all rejected children do not develop psychopathic personalities. Additional variables are evidently involved.

McCord and McCord (1964), after reviewing most of the available information on psychopathy, described three apparent causal patterns in the development of psychopathic behavior. They found that:

1 severe rejection alone can produce psychopathy;
2 mild rejection in combination with damage to the brain (possibily the hypothalamus) can cause psychopathy;
3 rejection without any evidence of brain damage can cause psychopathy if the child's environment fosters such behavior; for example, psychopathy may occur if one of the parents is psychopathic, if discipline is erratic and excessively punitive, or if there is a total absence of adult supervision.

Addictive reactions

The term "addiction" originally meant physiological craving and dependence, but today it also includes psychological dependence. A person is said to be addicted to alcohol, for example, when he uses alcohol compulsively to relieve feelings of frustration or anxiety.

Alcoholism Addiction to alcohol is one of the most common medical and social problems in the United States. There are estimated to be at least 5 million alcoholics in this country. Alcoholics are in constant need of alcohol to help them escape the frustrations and emotional disturbances of their everyday existence. Even after treatment, many alcoholics return to alcohol.

This type of addiction generally acquires so great a hold on the individual that alcohol dominates his life. More often than not, his career, his family ties, and his self-respect deteriorate. Long-term alcoholics may suffer severe bodily disintegration—even brain damage—which results in death.

Types of alcoholism A fine, often indistinguishable line exists between a "social drinker" and an "alcoholic." Although it is generally difficult to classify people according to degrees of alcoholism, investigators continue to attempt such categorization.

Jellinek (1960) describes four patterns of drinking behavior, which he labels Alpha, Beta, Gamma, and Delta alcoholism. The Alpha alcoholic drinks to alleviate bodily or emotional pain. He does not drink at the times or places that society has set aside for drinking, and he generally does not lose the ability to abstain. His drinking, however, hurts his interpersonal relationships.

Beta alcoholism is characterized by physical complications, such as gastritis or cirrhosis of the liver, nutritional damage, and a shortened life span. The Beta alcoholic is not necessarily addicted to alcohol.

The Gamma and Delta alcoholics develop an increased tolerance for alcohol, and this makes it necessary for them to drink more and more before the alcohol has any effect. Their craving for alcohol is physically based, and they are unable to control these cravings and the behavior that results from them.

Socially, Delta and Gamma alcoholics suffer a complete breakdown of relationships with friends and family. These two types of alcoholics differ in that the Delta alcoholic never abstains from drinking, while the Gamma alcoholic drinks intermittently. Delta alcoholism is prevalent in wine-drinking countries such as France, and Gamma alcoholism is found in Canada and the United States.

Alcoholism seems to be influenced by heredity, although developmental factors must also be considered. Individuals may drink heavily, for example, when alcohol enables them to express repressed sexual and aggressive feelings. Some psychoanalysts explain alcohol addiction as the individual's nonresolution of the oral stage of psychosexual development (see Chapter 12).

Alcoholics are often dependent, anxious, and fearful of life's frustrations. Such fears and anxieties must be resolved before a cure can be effected. Treatment must begin, however, by breaking the addiction. Alcohol addiction is hardest to treat in individuals who have long histories of drinking. Recent alcoholics who still possess the desire to be cured can be successfully treated.

A new type of chemical treatment of alcoholism is based on the theory that alcohol addiction is brought about by a nutritional deficiency. According to this theory, alcohol provides the nutrients that certain individuals need but cannot obtain adequately from food sources. Experiments have shown that some rats, when deprived of certain vitamins (the B complex vitamins), will drink alcohol rather than water when dishes of both liquids are placed in their cages. Given the B complex vitamins, these rats will no longer need alcohol.

In similar studies with human subjects, alcoholics have been supplied with vitamin pills in an attempt to reduce their need for alcohol. The results are promising and may provide the means for reducing physical dependence on alcohol. Subjects who have consistently taken the vitamins as directed have lost their desire for alcohol; some subjects have been totally cured of alcoholism. These vitamin treatments are not used alone, however; psychotherapeutic methods are employed to supplement them.

Some alcoholics voluntarily participate in the Alcoholics Anonymous program. As a type of group therapy (see Chapter 14), Alcoholics Anonymous has helped large numbers of alcoholics by making them realize that others want to help them and that others have shared the same experiences.

Drug addiction The drug addict is uncontrollably driven to drugs, and the addiction intensifies over time, sometimes leading to death from overdose. The narcotic addict is physiologically dependent upon the drugs, and his needs must be satisfied regularly or he may become extremely ill. The drug-induced state varies from reverie and drowsiness to euphoria and excitement, depending on the kind of drug used. Most drug addicts begin taking drugs as a means of escape or to find relief from feelings of futility or boredom.

Most of the drugs that are physiologically addictive are opium derivatives, such as morphine and heroin. Marijuana, obtained from the leaves of the hemp plant, does not appear to be addictive. Hashish, derived from the syrup of the hemp plant, also appears nonaddictive. Psychologists have found, however, that continued use of hashish may result in neural disintegration affecting certain thinking processes, speech, perception or orientation, and memory.

Drug addicts in the United States are subject to imprisonment or fine for selling or possessing a drug. In addition, because the addict's "habit" demands that he take as many as two or more doses a day, and because drugs are so expensive, the addict may feel forced to steal or commit other crimes to raise money to support his habit. He often steals because his addiction prevents him from working at a regular job.

The treatment and cure of drug addiction is not a simple matter. Most therapists recommend extensive psychotherapy after the habit is medically broken. One successful approach to drug addiction treatment is, like Alcoholics Anonymous, neither clinical nor professional. To give confidence to the ex-addict in his readjustment to society, addicts live in a community or family structure that includes other addicts and ex-addicts. Synanon, the original movement, was founded in 1958. The Synanon group, which is a privately run organization, sponsors rehabilitative therapy, using former addicts as therapists. The assumption is made that no one is better qualified than the ex-addict to understand the problems of addicts.

DISORDERS FROM DAMAGE TO THE CENTRAL NERVOUS SYSTEM

Behavior pathology may be related to damage to the central nervous system. The psychotic disturbances that result are often similar to the psychological maladjustments we have described. Diagnosis of a central nervous system disorder may be difficult because of this similarity of symptoms. Central nervous system disorders are sometimes called *organic psychoses* or *chronic brain disorders* and result from infections of brain cells and tissues, tumors, physical injuries to the head, and blood, hormonal, and nutritional deficiencies.

Senile psychosis

The most common organic disorder is *senile psychosis*, the behavior of old persons caused by aging of the brain. This damage is frequently permanent and may lead to incomplete or defective memory, disorientation, disorganization, and delusions, in addition to damage to the peripheral nervous system.

The brain degenerates because it no longer receives enough oxygen or nourishment to maintain its function. The blood supply is blocked from reaching certain brain cells by the accumulation of fatty deposits along the small blood channels. These fatty deposits increase in size until they entirely fill the channel and thus stop circulation. This condition is known medically as cerebral arteriosclerosis. The behavior symp-

toms depend, of course, on which areas of the brain are damaged. Frequently, the behavior symptoms are so extreme that the individual must be hospitalized or placed in the care of a full-time nurse.

General paresis

Before penicillin was used to treat syphilis, as many as 15 percent of the patients admitted to psychiatric hospitals were suffering from a psychosis produced by this disease. *General paresis* is an inflammation of the brain that develops as a result of a long-term syphilitic infection. Many of the behavioral symptoms are similar to senile psychosis, but loss of control of the fine muscles of the tongue and lips is also highly characteristic. The patient has difficulty with pronunciation and gradually his speech and thinking become confused. Delusions and hallucinations are common and, unless treatment is undertaken, death occurs.

With the introduction of penicillin, the percentage of paretics in the psychiatric hospitals has dropped to less than 2 percent of the total hospital population.

Alcoholic psychosis

Chronic alcoholism of long duration may result in damage to the central nervous system and ultimately in psychosis. The damage is not directly due to alcohol; it is the result of a vitamin deficiency that comes from improper diet. Alcoholics typically eat irregularly, and their diet is often insufficiently supplied with proteins, minerals, and vitamins.

A disorder commonly associated with long-term alcoholism is *delirium tremens*, or "DTs." It occurs in heavy drinkers who have been alcoholics for many years. It usually appears after a prolonged period of heavy drinking and during the time when the individual is "sobering up." Delirium tremens includes trembling and muscular weakness, convulsions (in some cases), and frightening hallucinations of a visual, auditory, or tactile nature. The individual sees or feels bugs, lizards, or snakes crawling on him. Objects in the room take on the appearance of grotesque creatures; sounds become voices.

The delirium episode may last as long as a week, and unless the patient is carefully attended and treated, there is danger of death. Treatment consists of massive doses of vitamins, particularly vitamin B complex. Recently, it has been found that certain drugs, such as chlorpromazine and Librium, are effective in reducing the intensity of the symptoms.

Another possible disorder resulting from alcoholism is *Korsakoff's psychosis*, which is marked by progressive loss of memory. As the patient's memory becomes poorer, he tends to fill in memory gaps by inventing or improvising. This process of filling memory gaps is known as *confabulation*, and is seen in other forms of brain damage as well.

GENETICS OF BEHAVIOR PATHOLOGY

The view that psychotic behavior runs in families is as old and as controversial as the view that intelligence is inherited. Many people probably still feel that they have a "skeleton in their closet" if some member of their family has a history of behavior pathology.

This view is based more on folklore than on fact, and its prevalence served to retard efforts to develop treatment methods. When psychology and psychiatry began to develop new attitudes toward the diagnosis and treatment of behavior pathology, the heredity view fell from favor, but factual evidence was lacking. The same lack flaws the newer environmental view, which is based as much on opinion as the older heredity view.

There is now a renewal of interest in the genetics of behavior pathology. The new interest is based on more objective and more critical

grounds than the old view. The results of numerous studies suggest that a predisposition toward certain psychoses does seem to be inherited. A predisposition does not in itself cause a disorder; it sets the stage for a disorder. Thus, the genetic factors must be considered with respect to environmental variables.

Genetic study of schizophrenia

The psychosis that has received the most attention from the standpoint of genetics is schizophrenia. Studies of genetic influence in schizophrenia resemble studies of intelligence in that their basic data come from comparisons between twins. In studying schizophrenia, investigators apply a measure of *concordance*; they determine the percentage of twin pairs in which both twins develop schizophrenia. If a characteristic is genetically transmitted, one would expect 100 percent concordance in identical twins, for they carry the same genes. For example, in physical characteristics that are known to be genetically transmitted, such as hair and eye color, the concordance percentage in identical twins is 100.

Table 13.4 presents a summary of concordance percentages for a number of twin studies of schizophrenia. This table shows that the concordance percentages for identical twins are relatively high but are less than 100 percent, often much less. The concordance percentages for identical twins is, however, always greater than for fraternal twins. Findings such as these lend support to the view that there is a genetic component to schizophrenia. But the findings also suggest that nongenetic variables play a significant role, since the disorder in one identical twin often fails to occur in the other identical twin.

Slater (1968) has summarized the findings of various investigators who studied a total of 16 identical-twin pairs raised apart. His summary indicates that in 10 of the 16 pairs, where one twin developed schizophrenia the other twin also developed the disorder. This represents a concordance percentage of 62.5, providing additional support for a genetic view of schizophrenia. Fig-

Table 13.4 Concordance percentages in twin studies of schizophrenia[a]

Study[b]	Source	Identical		Fraternal	
		Number of pairs	Concordance (%)	Number of pairs	Concordance (%)
Luxenburger (1928, 1934)	Germany	17–27	33–76.5	48	2.1
Rosenoff et al. (1934)	United States and Canada	41	61.0	101	10.0
Essen-Moller (1941)	Sweden	7–11	14–71	24	8.3–17
Kallman (1946)	New York	174	69–86.2	517	10.0–14.5
Slater (1953)	England	37	65–74.7	115	11.3–14.4
Inouye (1961)	Japan	55	36–60	17	6.0–12.0
Tieman (1963, 1968)	Finland	16	0–6	21	4.8
Gottesman and Shields (1966)	England	24	41.7	33	9.1
Kringlen (1967)	Norway	55	25–38	172	8.0–10.0
Fischer (1968)	Denmark	16	19–56	34	6.0–15.0
Hoffer et al (1968)	U.S. veterans	80	15.5	145	4.4

[a]After Rosenthal (1971).
[b]References to the studies shown are found in the Rosenthal text.

ure 13.5 graphs the relationship between degree of genetic similarity and schizophrenia.

The evidence suggesting that genetic variables are involved in schizophrenia is compelling, but the fact remains that the concordance percentages are not close to 100 percent. More research is needed to clarify the precise nature of the genetic involvement and to identify the inherited characteristics that may predispose a person to become schizophrenic.

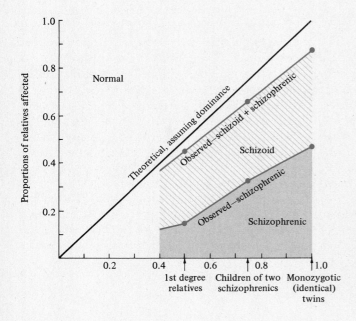

Figure 13.5   Observed and expected proportion of schizoids and schizophrenics. (From Leonard L. Heston, "The Genetics of Schizophrenic and Schizoid Disease." Science, January 16, 1970, **167,** 253. Copyright © 1970 by the American Association for the Advancement of Science.)

A genetic marker In studying the genetic transmission of behavioral characteristics, investigators seek the actual anatomical or physiological variables affected by particular genes. Such biological variables are known as *genetic markers*. They indicate the specific effects of a gene or group of genes.

Genetic study of schizophrenia has been hampered by the failure to find genetic markers. However, a recent exploratory study involving identical twins has pointed up a possible genetic marker for schizophrenia (Wyatt, Murphy, Belmaker, Cohen, Donnelly, and Pollin, 1973). The study showed that monoamine oxidase (MAO), an enzyme found in the body that exerts an influence on the transmission of nerve impulses, is implicated in schizophrenia—and that MAO activity may be a possible genetic marker.

A promising avenue of research is offered by Mednick and Schulsinger (1968), who have found that the children of schizophrenic mothers show different autonomic responses from the children of nonschizophrenic mothers. Such findings suggest that the inherited features of schizophrenia may occur in the form of certain neural or endocrine defects that set the stage for the disorder. It is this kind of research that may someday unravel the mystery and put the genetic and environmental aspects in proper perspective.

Genetic study of manic-depressive disorders

Fewer studies have been made of the genetics of manic-depressive disorders than of schizophrenia. However, the available evidence suggests a genetic influence in manic-depressive psychosis. Concordance percentages for identical twins range from 50 percent to as high as 92.6 percent, and for fraternal twins from 0 to 38.5 percent (Rosenthal, 1971).

The genetic research has uncovered support for the view that two distinct types of manic-depressive psychosis exist—one in which both depression and mania occur, and one in which only depression (or in rare cases only mania) occurs—and that these different types show similar concordance percentages. One study has shown that among 138 cases in which both depression and mania occur, 58 of the patients' relatives developed depression and mania, while only 3 relatives developed depression or mania alone (Perris, 1966). The same study showed that in 139 cases in which only depression occurred, 44 of the patients' relatives developed depression, whereas only 2 relatives developed mania and depression.

Future of behavior genetics

An examination of the relationship of heredity and environment to behavior indicates that it is impossible to hold one of these elements constant while manipulating the other, although in the future this may be done by actually modifying genes. Research in behavior genetics is also making it clear that it is unreasonable to assume that a given type of behavior is determined simply by a combination of heredity and environment. It is now apparent that a consideration of either factor apart from the other is unrealistic; they constantly interact. Particular genes may simply establish potentials for particular types of behavior; the child who carries the gene or genes predisposing him to schizophrenia may or may not develop schizoid behavior depending on his learning experiences and frustrations.

Evidence indicating that genetic variables are involved in behavior does not warrant the conclusion that environmental manipulations cannot modify such genetic predispositions. Heritability need not be considered incompatible with *teachability*. It would be scientifically incorrect and socially irresponsible to conclude on the basis of current research that tendencies toward behavior pathology are not modifiable. (In Chapter 14 we consider this further.)

SUMMARY

Defense mechanisms are ways of coping with or escaping from anxiety.

Defense mechanisms may be divided into two groups. The first involves the escape techniques of repression, fantasy, and regression.

The second group involves the compromise techniques of rationalization, projection, sublimation, reaction formation, and compensation.

Neuroses are maladjustments characterized by attempts to escape from or cope with anxiety by exaggerated use of defense mechanisms. The individual's behavior prevents him from functioning adequately in society.

The general category of neurosis includes anxiety reactions, obsessive-compulsive behavior, phobias, and hysteria.

Chronic anxiety reactions consist of vague fears of impending disaster, constant emotional and physical tension, fatigue, inability to concentrate, and so on. A chronic state of tension may build into an acute anxiety attack.

In obsessive-compulsive reactions, a persistent, habitual thought (obsession) dominates the neurotic's thoughts and often leads to urges to perform apparently meaningless, ritualistic acts (compulsions).

Phobias are excessive fears of specific objects or environments in the absence of any real danger.

The two types of hysteria are dissociative reactions and conversion hysteria.

A dissociative reaction is loss of contact with, or repression or compartmentalization of, specific areas of conflict. It may take the form of amnesia or multiple personality.

Conversion hysteria is characterized by the appearance of physical symptoms for which there is no organic basis. It is often accompanied by *la belle indifference*.

Organic psychoses are those that stem from a known physiological cause.

Functional psychoses are those that have no apparent physiological causes; the pathological patterns of behavior are believed to be the end result of responses to severe psychological conflict.

The most obvious symptoms of paranoia or paranoid reaction are the individual's delusions—of grandeur, persecution, influence, or reference.

Schizophrenia is characterized by delusions, hallucinations, withdrawal from reality, regressive behavior, erratic thought, inconsistent emotional or affective relationships, and deterioration of physical condition.

Process schizophrenia and reactive schizophrenia are new classifications that some clinicians prefer in place of the familiar categories of simple, hebephrenic, catatonic, and paranoid.

Childhood schizophrenia is frequently characterized by autistic behavior.

Manic-depressive reactions are characterized by extreme swings in mood from depression to excitement or from excitement to depression.

Psychosomatic disorders are physical illnesses caused or aggravated by psychological stress.

Character disorders are well-established reactions that are often antisocial.

Alcoholism and drug addiction are generally methods of escape from conflict.

Organic psychoses or chronic brain disorders result from actual damage to brain tissue.

Senile psychosis is caused by the deterioration of the brain due to aging. Symptoms include loss of short-term memory, inattention, disorganized thinking, and delusions.

Prolonged, untreated syphilis may result in a psychosis known as general paresis.

An alcoholic who is sobering up after a prolonged period of heavy drinking may develop a temporary psychosis known as delirium tremens.

Alcoholic psychosis is caused by a vitamin deficiency that results from the inadequate diet of the typical alcoholic. Prolonged alcoholism may eventually result in Korsakoff's psychosis, which involves gradual memory loss and confabulation (filling in memory gaps by inventing fictional tales.).

A tendency toward certain psychoses seems to be inherited, but their appearance probably depends on environmental variables.

The heritability of schizophrenia, the psychosis of greatest interest to geneticists, is studied by determining the percentage of twin pairs in which both twins develop schizophrenia; that is, a measure of concordance is applied.

Recent evidence suggests a genetic influence in manic-depressive psychoses.

The available evidence suggests that it is unwarranted to conclude that environment cannot change genetic predispositions.

SUGGESTED READINGS

Texts

Barber, B. *Drugs and sanity.* New York: Russell Sage Foundation, 1967. Text on drugs.

Buss, A. *Theories of schizophrenia.* New York: Atherton, 1969. Excellent text on modern theories of schizophrenia.

Coleman, J. C. *Abnormal psychology and modern life* (3rd ed.). Chicago: Scott, Foresman, 1964. Comprehensive survey of personality, behavior, and intellectual disorders, with emphasis on causative factors and problems of mental health.

Freeman, T. *Psychopathology of the psychoses.* New York: International Universities Press, 1969. Discussion of the more extreme forms of behavior pathology.

Gottesman, I. I., & Shields, J. *Schizophrenia and genetics: twin study vantage point.* New York: Academic Press, 1972. Thorough and objective development of a model for the etiology of schizophrenia, based on a particular twin study.

Hare, R. D. *Psychopathology: theory and research.* New York: Wiley, 1970. A very brief but thorough introduction to many facets of psychopathology, including assessment, physiological correlates, and behavior modification.

Holms, D. S. *Reviews of research in behavior pathology.* New York: Wiley, 1968. Empirical research on behavior pathology in case-study form.

Jones, S. *Drugs and alcohol.* New York: Harper & Row, 1970. Discussion of drug addiction and alcoholism.

London, P., & Rosenhan, D. (Eds.) *Foundations of abnormal psychology.* New York: Holt, 1968. Discussion of the background and substance of several behavioral deviations.

Maher, B. *Introduction to research in psychopathology.* New York: McGraw-Hill, 1969. Specifically directed at the undergraduate who wants some background before reading primary source materials in the journals.

Mendels, J. *Concepts of depression.* New York: Wiley, 1970. Review of depressive and manic reactions.

Millon, T. *Modern psychopathology.* Philadelphia: Saunders, 1969. Good recent survey of the field.

Mussen, P. H. (Ed) *Carmichael's manual of child psychology* (3rd ed.). New York: Wiley, 1970. Chapters 27–29 provide a comprehensive overview of recent research and current issues in mental retardation, behavior disorders, and childhood psychosis.

Rachman, S. *Phobias: their nature and control.* Springfield, Ill.: Thomas, 1968. Complete discussion of this form of pathology.

Sarason, I. G. *Abnormal psychology: the problem of maladaptive behavior.* New York: Appleton-Century-Crofts, 1972. An excellent basic text in the study of psychopathology.

Schultz, C. G., & Kilgalen, R. K. *Case studies of schizophrenia.* New York: Basic Books, 1970. Group of case studies.

Szasz, T. S. *The manufacture of madness.* New York: Delta, 1970. A scholarly, controversial comparison of the belief in witchcraft (and the persecution of witches) to the belief in mental illness (and the persecution of mental patients).

Thompson, T., & Pickens, R. (Eds.) *Stimulus properties of drugs.* New York: Appleton-Century-Crofts, 1971. Twelve papers dealing with the response-eliciting, discriminative, and behavior-reinforcing properties of drugs.

Ullman, L. P., & Krasner, L. *A psychological approach to abnormal behavior.* Englewood Cliffs, N.J.: Prentice-Hall, 1969. Comprehensive text from the behavioral point of view.

Weinberg, S. K. (Ed.) *The sociology of mental disorders: analysis and readings in psychiatric sociology.* Chicago: Aldin, 1967. Treatment of social factors and processes that contribute to behavior pathology.

Popular books

Ellis, A. *How to live with a neurotic.* Discusses the symptomatology of defense mechanisms and anxiety reactions.

Freeman, L. *The cry for love: understanding and overcoming human depression.* Discussion of causes and countermeasures for depression.

Greene, H. *I never promised you a rose garden.* A 16-year-old girl's thoughts and experiences in a mental institution.

Kesey, K. *One flew over the cuckoo's nest.* People and practices in a mental institution are described from an "inside" view.

Langer, W. *The mind of Adolf Hitler.* A psychoanalyst's secret World War II military report on Hitler's sociopathic character.

Roth, Lillian. *I'll cry tomorrow.* The autobiography of a potentially great singer who almost destroyed herself with alcohol.

Rycroft, C. *Anxiety and neurosis.* Popular treatment of these behavior pathologies.

Stearns, J. *The seekers.* Discussion of the drug subculture.

Thigpen, C. H., & Cleckley, H. M. *Three faces of Eve.* Description of the classic case of multiple personality.

Tryon, T. *The other.* A journey into the troubled consciousness of a schizophrenic.

14
Therapy

Everyone at some time may provide therapeutic help to someone else. Chances are that you have often helped a friend to relax or feel better momentarily. Yet you would probably feel completely helpless with a severely disturbed person —a person who could not hear you because of his inner "voices," who could not trust you because he saw danger in your outstretched hand.

The professional therapist, however, has special ways of reaching the psychotic patient— even one who is emotionally deadened or physically locked in a catatonic state. He is also trained to treat the adjustment problems of the mildly disturbed in ways that will lead to permanent behavioral changes. In this chapter we shall discuss the kinds of therapy that are effective in treating disturbed people. We shall emphasize the differences among the major types of treatment. In some forms of therapy, the patient is helped to understand the psychological origin and meaning of his problems and to apply this insight to their solution. In other forms, the patient is taught new kinds of behavior to replace the pathological behavior that made him unhappy or ineffectual. In still other forms, the patient is first treated medically, so that his overt symptoms of behavior pathology are reduced or eliminated; psychotherapeutic treatment may proceed from that point.

BACKGROUND OF PSYCHOTHERAPY

The term *psychotherapy* embraces a number of different techniques for the treatment of personality and behavior disorders; psychotherapeutic methods of treatment are essentially psychological in approach (rather than pharmacological or physicomedical). Although psychology has only recently been systematized as a science, the problems of behavior pathology were recognized and treated even in ancient times. The Bible shows evidence of this—in the therapeutic relationship of David and King Saul, for instance, after the king became mentally disturbed: "an evil spirit from the Lord tormented him" (1 Samuel 16:14). In ancient times, what we now call a psychological disorder was thought to be an evil spirit that had entered the body and taken possession of it. The Greeks, Hebrews, Egyptians, and Chinese all developed methods of treating the individual who was thus "possessed" (no longer himself); incantations and prayer, magic, music, herb medicines, starvation, burning, beating, and condemnation to death are characteristic of the major treatments devised by the ancients to rid the body of evil spirits.

Behavior pathology was blamed on evil spirits for many centuries thereafter, as evidenced by the witch hunts of the Middle Ages. In fact, not until the early twentieth century did people begin to understand the meaning of behavior pathology and treat the emotionally disturbed in a more realistic and humane manner. If such understanding did exist prior to the twentieth century, it was certainly not reflected in the treatment of disturbed persons. "Asylums" were dirty, dark, and otherwise unpleasant, and patients were beaten, poorly fed, left to writhe in their own excrement, and often chained.

Some improvement in conditions in mental institutions was initiated in France in 1792. Philippe Pinel, the director of a mental hospital in Paris, had the chains removed from all the patients, demonstrating that patients could and should be treated as "sick" people and not as dangerous animals. Pinel helped somewhat to make the mental hospital more humanitarian, but not until a century later did a movement toward real improvement take place. Clifford Beers, an American who had suffered through 3 years of confinement in mental hospitals, published his experiences in *A Mind That Found Itself* (1908) and awakened the public to the horrible conditions in these institutions. Beers actively sought the public's help in changing the hospitals. He was one of the founders of the National Committee for Mental Hygiene, which set the stage for the development of the mental health movement in the United States and elsewhere (Figure 14.1).

Public awareness helped change mental hospitals from crude and often cruel custodial institutions to more humane, well-intentioned establishments, but the concept of treatment as such did not take hold until the end of World War II, stimulated in part by the needs of war veterans, many of whom turned to Veterans' Administration hospitals and clinics for help in readjusting psychologically to civilian life. For the first time, funds became available to train and hire skilled personnel and to concentrate on diagnosis and treatment rather than simple custodial care. The decade from 1946 to 1956 saw a tremendous upsurge of interest in psychiatry and clinical psychology, and many more professional therapists were added to hospital and clinic staffs. But the demand then, as today, was greater than the supply.

The public's attitude toward behavior pathology has changed dramatically in the last 30 years. People no longer hide the fact that they have sought psychiatric or psychological help. Discussion of psychological problems has become commonplace. It is now recognized that many effective and successful people sometimes need psychological assistance from a therapist. In fact, it is estimated that one out of ten persons in the United States at some time in his life seeks some form of psychiatric or psychological help, and one out of every four persons experiences a need for such help, even though he does not actively seek it.

PSYCHOTHERAPISTS

Behavior pathology may be treated in different ways by various kinds of therapists with varying titles, backgrounds, and legal status. In some parts of the United States today, the state licenses practitioners and demands that they fulfill certain academic requirements. In some

Figure 14.1   Until Clifford Beers and others like him were able to institute more humane treatment of the disturbed person, such people were jailed, chained, beaten, and generally treated as "freaks" of nature. (The Bettmann Archive)

states, full medical and resident training is mandatory; in others, no restrictions exist, and anyone can call himself a "psychologist."

Broadly speaking, psychotherapists may be classified as follows:

1 The *clinical psychologist* is trained in psychological methods but does not have a medical degree. Generally, he has earned a Ph.D. Since one of his prime functions is to devise, administer, and evaluate psychological tests, he usually works in a hospital, a school, a prison, or other places where testing is done. To practice psychotherapy, he should have a Ph.D. and have completed a specified period of internship. Many clinical psychologists are involved in the study or application of the principles of behavior modification.

2 The *psychiatrist* is a qualified, licensed physician who did his postgraduate work and residency in psychiatry. As a medical specialist, the psychiatrist can prescribe and administer medicines, drugs, and electroconvulsive shock therapy, and can perform surgery. In other words, he may administer any kind of therapy, psychological or medical, that he deems necessary.

3 The *psychoanalyst* differs from other psychotherapists in that he practices according to a psychoanalytic theory of personality. Many psychoanalysts are psychiatrists, but some are clinical psychologists. In this connection, it is interesting to note that Freud believed that medical training was not necessary for psychoanalysts. All psychoanalysts must themselves be psychoanalyzed, however.

4 The *psychiatric social worker* usually has earned the degree of master of social work (a postgraduate degree) and has been trained to gather information helpful to the psychiatrist in prescribing treatment. He is responsible for interviewing the disturbed patient, talking to his family, friends, and acquaintances in the community, and uncovering cultural and economic factors

pertinent to the case. Since many disturbed patients need special help in securing jobs, finding a place to live apart from their families, and obtaining welfare support, the psychiatric social worker often represents the patient in his dealings with social agencies. Psychiatric social workers may also work in the education system as counselors.

5 Nurses and *mental health aides* are being given increasing responsibility for therapy in hospital settings. In some institutions, *psychiatric nurses* are trained to carry out behavior modification techniques under the supervision of psychiatrists or clinical psychologists. *Mental health counselors* have been trained to assist in clinics and, in some cases, to work with severely disturbed children.

We shall now examine the most commonly used psychotherapeutic methods: psychoanalysis, therapies based on self-actualization, directive therapy, group therapy, play therapy, and behavior modification. Each aims at improving the individual's response to himself and his surroundings. The duration of treatment, the length and frequency of sessions, the type of treatment used, and the number of individuals involved in each session depend on the individual who needs treatment and the type of therapy used. In every method, psychotherapy is based on some form of personal interaction.

Poll of therapists Scientists and laymen alike tend to place labels on clinical psychologists and psychoanalysts. Thus, one therapist might be called "dynamically oriented," and another, a "behaviorist." While such labels may often be useful in describing a therapist's opinions and biases on psychological issues, should all psychologists be stereotyped in this fashion?

Wagner (1970), a psychologist interested in this question, sent a questionnaire to 300 clinical psychologists asking them to give their opinions on "learning and deviant behavior" and to state their own theoretical orientation or label.

Although most of those who answered labeled themselves as "dynamically oriented" (psychoanalytically inclined), their opinions tended to favor the nondynamic approaches (as is evident in the answers to the sample questions below). It would seem that most clinical psychologists (and, for that matter, other psychologists), regardless of what they may call themselves, tend to be guided by facts and experimental evidence rather than group or personal biases.

Sample questions and answers:
1 Do you *believe* that the symptoms or deviant behaviors of most psychotics are learned? (62 percent yes)
2 Does the *evidence* tend to support the belief that #1 is true? (55 percent yes)
3 Do you *believe* that the symptoms or deviant behaviors of neurotics are learned? (89 percent yes)
4 Do you *believe* that the symptoms or deviant behaviors of personality disorders are learned? (88 percent yes)
5 Does the evidence tend to support the belief that #3 and #4 are true? (75 percent yes)
6 Is psychoanalysis the treatment of choice for neurotics? (63 percent no)
7 Are psychosis and neurosis best conceptualized as analogous to physical illness? (86 percent no)

PSYCHOANALYSIS

Psychoanalysis was first proposed as a formal method of treatment by Sigmund Freud. Freud's psychoanalytic theory of personality (see Chapter 12) is at the core of this form of therapy.

Psychoanalytic therapy involves intensive sessions between a psychoanalyst and his patient. These sessions are usually scheduled for at least once a week and are often continued over a long period of time (2 or 3 years, on the average). In the sessions, the psychoanalyst attempts to help the individual to become aware of his unconscious urges and conflicts, that is, to uncover the source of his conflicts and his motives for repressing them. Freud held that unconscious drives, which originate in the id, are sexual in nature and cannot be fully expressed because the ego and superego force the individual to repress them. Although many psychoanalysts no longer adhere strictly to this belief, they agree that repressed conflicts and unconsciously stored frustrations are the causes of psychological maladjustment, and that these conflicts can be resolved only when the individual becomes aware of their existence and can "work them through" successfully. The analyst therefore concentrates on helping the individual to become aware of the unconscious causes of his anxieties. Solutions are thought to depend on the individual's ability to understand and rechannel his repressed ideas, feelings, and urges.

Although a psychoanalyst "conducts" the session, he stays in the background. The couch has become a familiar symbol of psychoanalytic therapy, but it is important only to the mood or the attitude that the psychoanalyst wishes to establish. The patient often does not face the analyst but relaxes on the couch or chair, letting his thoughts wander. He is free to talk about anything he wishes, to introduce or ignore ideas that come to him. The psychoanalyst guides the conversation, but he does not specifically direct the patient's comments.

In some cases, the therapeutic situation itself creates anxieties. The individual may resist conversation, he may mistrust or fear the analyst, or he may expect miraculous "cures." Many psychoanalysts believe in explaining the general therapeutic approach to their patients, emphasizing that the individual cannot be expected to respond to therapy immediately. In the early stages of the development of psychoanalytic therapy, considerable emphasis was placed on the release of emotional expression, a process known as *catharsis*. However, Freud soon discovered that it was not enough for patients to undergo catharsis; he recognized that they needed to develop *insight*, an understanding of the unconscious roots of their problems. A patient gains insight only when he has been able to face his basic conflicts and cope with them in reality.

There are four fundamental psychoanalytic techniques: free association, dream analysis, the analysis of resistances, and the analysis of transference.

Free association

In psychoanalytic therapy, the patient is encouraged to respond freely, abandoning his conscious inhibitions and verbalizing all his ideas. This technique is known as *free association*. To free associate, the patient must refrain from "editing" or organizing his thoughts as he might if speaking with friends or business acquaintances. It is difficult to abandon organized thought for free association, and at first the patient may feel that some of his conscious ideas are insignificant or silly, or too intimate to reveal. But properly encouraged, the patient will cooperate, making free association a very useful tool for the psychoanalyst.

Free association may eventually bring to light the patient's hidden motives and repressed thoughts. From time to time, the psychoanalyst interprets and asks questions. By this method he hopes to make the patient recognize these hidden motives himself. These motives may be so deeply buried that they appear only in symbolic thoughts or words. The analyst must wait until he is able to interpret the symbolism before he can convey its meaning to his patient.

Dream analysis

Freud spoke of the analysis of dreams as the "royal road" to the unconscious (1914). Psychoanalysts believe that a person's unconscious motives are often played out in his dreams. These unconscious thoughts may be obvious or they may be disguised. As in free association, it is up to the analyst to interpret the patient's symbolism and to make the patient aware of its meaning. Most analysts do not have a fixed set of interpretations to particular dream symbols; the symbols are created by the individual and are pertinent to his unique frame of reference. Some symbols, however, are usually interpreted in fixed ways. For example, many Freudians regard such objects as sticks, poles, trees, knives, guns, pencils, and hammers as male sexual symbols, and boxes, jars, bottles, pockets, rooms, and doorways as female sexual symbols.

The psychoanalyst must be able to uncover the *latent content* of the dream, based on his knowledge of its *manifest content*. The manifest content is the remembered portion of the dream, the actual sequence of events in the dream as recalled by the patient after he wakes up. The latent content refers to the unpleasant or painful unconscious thoughts that are expressed in disguised form in the manifest content. The patient's conscious statements may give the analyst clues to the dream's hidden meaning.

Resistance

If you have ever been reluctant to enter a discussion because you were afraid that you might reveal something about yourself, you can well understand the fears suffered by a patient asked to expose his spontaneous thoughts to the psychoanalyst. Patients commonly refuse to reveal thoughts that they consider insignificant, foolish, or taboo. This *resistance* is significant in psychoanalysis, for it gives the analyst clues to his patient's repressions. Thoughts that are "forgotten" or that the patient will not reveal to himself or to his analyst are believed to be related to his unconscious conflicts. As the analyst moves closer to uncovering these repressed thoughts, the patient may become extremely apprehensive of his sessions with the analyst; he may forget his appointment completely or be late for his session. Such behavior indicates to the psychoanalyst that he may be getting close to an area of repression.

The psychoanalyst tries to make his patient aware of his resistance, since it may be a shield for the basic unconscious feelings that underlie his problem. It is difficult for the analyst to treat a person whose resistance is deeply imbedded in his unconscious. Yet, before any progress can be made, the individual must be able to associate freely, without resisting.

Transference

All psychoanalysts realize that their patients come to regard them as other than a doctor; they may see the psychoanalyst as a love object, a parent, a close friend, or perhaps as an object of hatred, fear, or envy. When this happens, the patient is said to be unconsciously transferring to the analyst his feelings from an earlier relationship.

In *transference* the patient is essentially attempting to repeat or reestablish the earlier relationships, one which he may have repeated unhappily in other relationships throughout his life. Obviously the analyst cannot allow the patient to become too emotionally involved with him. But he can use transference to understand the patient's problems and to help the patient gain insight into the nature of the earlier relationship with the person the analyst has come to symbolize.

The father image Sigmund Freud, the founder of psychoanalysis, tells of a patient who transferred his feelings toward his father to the analyst so completely that his own overt actions reflected his attitude toward his father. For example, the patient was afraid to be near Freud because he feared that Freud would hit him just as his father had done. In describing this case, Freud (1909) wrote:

While he talked like this, he would get up from the sofa and roam about the room—a habit which he explained at first as being due to delicacy of feeling: he could not bring himself, he said, to utter such horrible things while he was lying there so comfortably. But soon he himself found a more cogent explanation, namely, that he was avoiding my proximity for fear of my giving him a beating.

If he stayed on the sofa and behaved like someone in desperate terror trying to save himself from castigations of terrific violence. . . . He recalled that his father had had a passionate temper, and sometimes in his violence had not known where to stop.

The patient was reenacting with Freud the pattern of the relationship he had with his father.

As transference appears in the patient's dreams and free associations, the analyst determines whether it is an authority figure, a father figure, a love figure, or another kind of figure that stands out in the patient's unconscious. If, for example, a patient is hostile to the analyst and has given him information that would suggest that the analyst has become a father figure, the analyst can relate the patient's hostility to his father. At the appropriate moment—invariably a distressing one—the analyst interprets the transference, thereby modifying his relationship to the patient and enabling the patient to respond more realistically to both his present conflicts and his deep-seated ones.

THERAPIES BASED ON SELF-ACTUALIZATION

In most therapies based on self-actualization, the client or patient is free to direct the course of each session. Because the client can talk about anything that interests him, the therapist's role here is very different from that of the psychoanalyst. The therapist accepts whatever the patient has to say and speaks only to rephrase and clarify thoughts expressed by him.

Client-centered therapy

As opposed to psychoanalysis, *client-centered* therapy is more concerned with the client's current problems than with his childhood experiences. Because the therapist neither initiates nor controls the conversation, this method is also known as *nondirective psychotherapy*.

Client-centered therapy was first developed by Carl Rogers (1951), who believed that anyone (under proper direction) can solve his own problems of adjustment. But the individual must want to help himself, or treatment will be futile. If at any time the client wishes to end a particular session or discontinue treatment altogether,

the therapist does not try to dissuade him. It is believed that those who do remain in therapy gain self-confidence because they are allowed to "lead" the session without being contradicted or judged by the therapist. The sessions are paced at a rate set by the client, for the therapist does not force, prescribe, or interrupt the client's progress. When a patient is not immediately able to "open up," the psychotherapist and his client may sit in silence for a full session. Eventually the motivated individual begins to talk and progress can be made.

Client-centered therapy has been used successfully with children and groups, and with individuals who have been sufficiently motivated to examine their problems. From his experiences with this type of therapy, Rogers developed the *self-actualization theory of personality* (discussed in Chapter 12).

Finding oneself Axline (1966), in *Dibs: In Search of Self*, describes how Dibs "found himself" through client-centered (play) therapy.

Before therapy, Dibs talked to nobody, and in school he was totally unresponsive to his teachers' approaches. He would usually hide under the table during class periods. As a result, his teachers believed that he was probably mentally retarded.

Therapy sessions were completely nondirective. Dibs interacted—talked and played—when and for as long as he wanted; he was never forced to continue a conversation, even though the topic might be of importance for therapy. Dibs slowly and painfully found himself—an extremely gifted child.

Following is an excerpt from Dr. Axline's first session with Dibs:

As we entered the room I said, "We'll spend an hour together here in the playroom. You can see the toys and the materials we have. You decide what you would like to do."

I waited. We had an hour to spend in this room. There was no urgency to get anything done. To play or not to play. To talk, or to be silent. In here it would make no difference.

Slowly, one by one, he picked up each piece of furniture [in the doll house]. As he did, he muttered the name of the objects with a questioning, halting inflection. His voice was flat and low. . . .

Each time he named an object I made an attempt to communicate my recognition of his spoken word. I would say, "Yes. That is a bed," or, "I think it is a dresser," or "It does look like a rabbit." I tried to keep my response brief, in line with what he said, and with enough vibration to avoid monotony.

Then he sat down on the floor facing the doll house. He stared at it in silence for a long time. I didn't prod him on. . . . I wanted him to take the initiative in building up this relationship. Too often, this is done for a child by some eager adult.

He clasped his hands tightly together against his chest and said over and over again, "No lock doors. No lock doors. No lock doors." His voice took on a note of desperate urgency. "Dibs no like locked doors," he said. There was a sob in his voice.

I said to him, "You don't like the doors to be locked."

Dibs seemed to crumple. His voice became a husky whisper. "Dibs no like walls around him."

Obviously, he had had some unhappy experiences with closed doors. I recognized the feelings he expressed. Then he began to take the dolls out of the house where he had placed them. He took out the mother and father dolls. "Go store! Go store!" he said "Go away to the store. Go away!"

Existential therapy

Existential therapy has been prominent in Europe for many years but has only recently attracted attention in the United States. It is more a therapeutic attitude than a system of therapy, for it is based on the view that a person's sense of being is the fundamental problem and that it either enables him to become what he wishes or hinders his progress. The task of the existential therapist is to assist rather than guide or direct the patient. This kind of therapist lets the patient lead the discussion but takes a more active role than the nondirective therapist. Existential therapists, such as May (1960), feel that a person is capable of denying his self-actualization potential, and this is one reason why the therapist must play an active role.

Existential therapy is a flexible, somewhat intuitive approach. It is subject to criticism by those more scientifically-oriented practioners who feel it is too loose and ill-defined to be a comprehensive system of psychotherapy.

DIRECTIVE THERAPY

Some psychotherapists adopt a flexible or eclectic approach to treating the disturbed personality, one in which the therapist is free to use any technique that seems right for his patient and in which he plays an active, directing role. Such techniques are often referred to as directive therapy.

In directive therapy, the therapist first decides on a course of action whereby the patient can be reconditioned or can relearn adaptive behavior in an active way. Essentially, the therapist identifies the problem and prescribes activities that will enable the disturbed individual to readjust his personality. The therapist believes that planned action serves to eliminate hours of aimless pursuit and leads the individual to a solution quickly and efficiently.

Directive therapists are usually concerned with the individual's overt behavior, not with his unconscious or symbolic thoughts. Since overt behavior reflects the individual's problem, the directive therapist treats overt behavior in the belief that, as behavior changes, personality changes. For individuals with multiple problems, the directive approach will, if necessary, prescribe a behavior appropriate to each problem. In a sense, then, the individual is helped to reeducate himself.

In addition to observing overt behavior, the directive therapist studies the individual's personal history, his ability, achievement, and projective tests, and general clinical description. The causes of the individual's maladjusted response pattern are considered in the analysis of the behavior and the patient is encouraged to recognize them. Once the patient understands the nature of his difficulties, the therapist begins the second half of his treatment—the active relearning (reconditioning) of the appropriate adaptive response patterns. The therapist needs to prescribe a behavior that will not bore the individual or otherwise prevent him from correcting the problem. For example, the man who is afraid to behave decisively for fear of ridicule may be encouraged to lead group therapy sessions.

GROUP THERAPY

Sorrow, disappointment, and failure are personal but universal feelings. Because they are personal, we tend to keep them to ourselves; because they are universal, we ought to share them with others who can lend insight and understanding. The woman who faces divorce may gain sympathy and sound advice from others who understand her psychological dilemma. And the man who cannot relate to others may learn to do so in a situation free from the usual social threats. *Group therapy* gives the individual a chance to submit his thoughts, his problems, his entire self-image to the understanding of his peers. By doing this and listening to others in his group, the individual may find a personal solution or may learn to adjust his values to society's values as defined by his group.

The group functions as a small society—discussing, objecting, helping each member to reorient himself. It is assumed that once an individual can "work through" his psychological disturbances in the presence of and in interaction with the group, he will be able to face the larger society with confidence.

Most groups are kept small to assure that each member's identity will not be submerged. Usually a group is composed of people with similar types of maladjustment. This similarity enables the members to recognize their own problems in others. Members are usually not grouped by age or by sex.

During the session the therapist remains in the background. He generally allows members of the group to explore areas of conversation on their own; if necessary, he will contribute to group discussion. He does not interject value judgments but allows each member to establish his own values in accordance with the personality changes brought about by the group process.

Many persons in group therapy are in individual therapy as well. They explore themselves in depth during the individual sessions and interact with other people during the group session.

It is often difficult for individuals to adjust to group therapy. The first group sessions are slow. The members do not know each other, and they are usually anxious about expressing themselves freely in the presence of others. To break down interpersonal barriers, members may be encouraged to touch each other, as is done in *encounter groups*, a form of expressive group interaction that emphasizes the importance of feelings in interpersonal relations. The usual procedure is to avoid focusing on specific problems during the early meetings of the group. Interpretive remarks are made only after the group members are able to express themselves freely and accept the other members of the group. And, in the process, as many as 25 to 30 percent of group enrollees ordinarily drop out. Those who benefit most from group therapy seem to be the mildly or moderately disturbed; although group sessions are regularly conducted in mental hospitals, many of the severely disturbed cannot begin to relate to others or express themselves in a group.

Various nonprofessional forms of group therapy have been found effective. Organized groups such as Synanon for drug addicts, Weight Watchers for the overweight, and Alcoholics Anonymous for problem drinkers have been especially effective with specialized problems of adjustment. By sharing experiences, the members of the group assist each other with their common problem.

Many therapeutic groups are organized by

such formal institutions as hospitals, clinics, prisons, and schools. It is extremely important, for example, to reorient prisoners about to be released who will have to function in a society that will treat them as outcasts. Individuals who have been institutionalized for behavioral disturbances are generally placed in group therapy prior to release. In both cases, the inmates are helped to become familiar with the types of interpersonal communications they will have to establish in normal life (see Chapter 15).

Psychodrama

In a special form of group therapy known as *psychodrama* (Moreno, 1946), a patient enacts scenes from his own life to express the deepseated feelings that he has been unable to express in real-life situations. In acting out an episode from his own life, the patient undergoes an expansion of reality that includes the thoughts, feelings, and fantasies that he was unable to display in the real situations. The dramatization of certain situations also gives the patient a chance to try out new methods of coping. Temporarily secure from external reality, he may be able to develop behavior better suited to coping with reality.

One of the techniques of psychodrama, called *role reversal*, enables the patient to assume a new role and interact with another person playing the role of the patient himself. A patient may reenact an argument with his father, playing first his father and then himself. A reversal of roles broadens the patient's understanding of how others react to him. He may want to introduce a current problem, so that by acting out one or two solutions he may come to understand the choices open to him. Or he may simply reenact a troublesome past experience. If the patient's past responses to a situation are the source of anxiety, he or his therapist may suggest a psychodrama that re-creates such an experience. This method of expression enables him to learn appropriate response patterns.

Psychodrama may also help the patient face a future situation. Situations can be designed that require the patient to act out a role that he knows will be particularly disturbing to him. Some patients may fear meeting new people or applying for a job. They may wish to act out an encounter to ease their anxiety about the situation. Again, the patient can play either himself or a person who is the source of his anxiety, thereby obtaining practice in how to handle himself in a difficult situation.

PLAY THERAPY

Play therapy is a special psychotherapy technique for young children. The disturbed child is brought into a playroom—a room filled with toys and other play materials; he is allowed to choose freely from among the dolls, crayons, paints, clay, and other playthings available to him. In his play, the child may reveal emotional conflicts and insecurities. For example, the child who likes to hit or break toys but who is usually scolded for such behavior is put in a play situation in which he can relieve his hostilities without fear of punishment. The child who feels insecure may simply curl up in a corner with a baby bottle. Many therapists have found that the atmosphere of the play therapeutic situation helps the child express negative feelings he would ordinarily not express.

Some forms of play therapy emphasize an atmosphere of acceptance and permissiveness similar to that of client-centered therapy. Axline (1947) suggests that the child in therapy should see himself as the central figure in a free, permissive situation which allows him to express his feelings openly through play and perhaps verbally as well. As the child plays, the therapist talks to him about his feelings as reflected in his actions. By clarifying attitudes in this way, the therapist helps the child understand his own feelings and gives him assurance that someone else understands him. Through treatment, even relatively young children can attain a certain degree of insight into their own behavior.

Some play therapists emphasize the principle of catharsis. Levy (1939) used a technique that encourages the child to release pent-up feelings and desires that he has been afraid to express. Feelings such as aggression toward his parents or other members of his family are, according to Levy, eliminated or reduced in intensity as they are released in the nonpunitive, doll-play situation.

Play therapy may also be directive. Some therapists use doll-play to instruct children in better-adjusted forms of behavior. Instead of telling the child what to do, the therapist or the child tells the doll what to do.

BEHAVIOR MODIFICATION

Behavior modification differs from most methods of psychotherapeutic treatment for, as the term implies, the therapist who uses this approach seeks to change, adjust, or modify the disturbed individual's behavior. Advocates of behavior modification believe that the maladjusted personality results from maladjusted behavior and that this behavior was learned by the individual. This learning may have been accidental or planned: unknowingly or knowingly, the individual may have been conditioned to respond in a certain way that later prevented him from adjusting to society.

The behavior-modification approach is an extension of the psychology of learning, for many of the principles of the learning process (see Chapter 6) are used in the therapeutic modification of behavior. Treatment is based on the idea that, if abnormalities are improper responses, an individual can be taught proper responses to replace them; that is, maladaptive behavior can be unlearned. The behavior therapist's aim is to eliminate inappropriate responses and substitute adjustive responses. He

begins with the principles of learning and then develops therapy suited to the individual. He is not concerned with unconscious motivations, conflicts, repressions, or dynamic personality struggles; he deals with overt behavior.

Release versus suppression Which is better, to permit aggressive behavior, or to punish aggressive behavior and reward suppression of aggression? The answer depends on whether one adheres to psychoanalytic or to behavior-modification principles. Psychoanalysts believe that a patient should be allowed to release his pent-up emotions and project them outward, whereas many behavoral-modification proponents believe that a patient should be rewarded for suppressing his aggressive feelings.

Nelsen (1969), in an effort to determine which theoretical viewpoint was correct, placed his subjects in a game situation. Subjects were told that they were being tested to determine the workings of cooperation, that they could win the game only if they cooperated with their partners. Each subject's partner was in collaboration with the experimenter, so that when the subject tried to cooperate, his partner consistently failed to cooperate, and was, in addition, arrogant and obnoxious.

After the game was over, the experimenter told each subject that he had expected a higher degree of cooperation. Individual interviews were then conducted. Some subjects were allowed to express their opinions freely and were reinforced for showing anger or criticizing their partners.

The remaining subjects were told to make allowances for their uncooperative partners and were reinforced for all positive remarks about their partners. All subjects were tested on their ability to remember and their general hostility, and then were asked to rate themselves on aggression. Results showed that the group whose members were encouraged to express themselves described themselves as more hostile than did the group that suppressed the outward display of feeling; the "expression" group also performed poorly on the memory tests. Thus, a state of high anxiety or aggression was indicated in the "expression" group.

It would seem, then, that the expression of aggression is less effective than reinforcement of nonaggressive behavior in reducing aggression.

The behavior therapist seeks to identify specific stimulus-response associations learned by the patient in the past. He does this primarily by carefully observing the patient's behavior; after an investigation of the patient's past associations and present behavior, the therapist sets up a program to break the old associations by introducing reinforcement for new, more adaptive responses and by eliminating reinforcement for the old, maladaptive responses.

Behavior modification is an obvious challenge to the more conventional methods of psychotherapy. The traditional therapies focus on the interaction between the therapist and the patient, whereas behavior therapy concentrates on the processes of learning. Behavior modification is derived from experimental principles, whereas psychotherapy, as noted earlier, is not a laboratory science. Although these groups generally oppose each other's methods, their differences will probably be reconciled as each group recognizes the values of the other's work. A reconciliation may take some time, however, for behavior modification is a fairly new approach, still limited to use in controlled situations where the therapist can alter the environment as he sees fit.

Systematic desensitization

Because the principles of learning can be generalized and applied in many different ways to behavior pathology, behavior therapists have gradually expanded their techniques to deal not only with neurotic fears and anxieties but with other maladaptive symptoms.

In applying the principles of learning, the therapist actually *counterconditions* the individual; that is, he extinguishes certain conditioned responses and conditions the client to make new responses. If a client has been conditioned to stay away from high places and becomes anxious each time he goes above the fourth floor, the therapist reinforces him for voluntarily climbing up to the eighth floor. In other words, the client is conditioned by strengthening responses in opposition to his "incorrect" responses. This technique is known as *reciprocal inhibition* and has been used successfully in therapeutic situations.

Reciprocal inhibition was first tested with animals who were conditioned to develop symptoms of anxiety when presented with certain stimuli. The most important work in this area was done by Joseph Wolpe (1958), who applied his observations of animals to human behavior.

Wolpe conditioned his animals to become anxious when a specific stimulus was presented. The animals learned not only to fear the stimulus but also the place in which it was administered. In fact, their anxiety was so great that it interfered with many of their normal functions. For example, they could not eat when in or near the apparatus associated with the unpleasant stimulus. They had developed a form of neurosis.

Since Wolpe assumed that the animals would normally eat when hungry (and not anxious), he fed each animal some distance from the anxiety-provoking place. The purpose was to eliminate the anxiety by gradually reintroducing the anxiety-provoking stimuli at the time the animal was eating well. This was done by slowly moving the animal's feeding place closer and closer to the source of anxiety. Eventually, he was able to get the animal to eat in the very place its anxiety response was provoked. By that time, the animal was able to eat without behaving anxiously; that is, its anxiety response was eliminated by the stronger reciprocal inhibiting response of eating. The key to reciprocal inhibition is thus to provide a strong response incompatible with the neurotic response.

To apply his theory to human beings, Wolpe used relaxation, rather than eating, to counter anxiety, because relaxation is a response incompatible with anxiety, and, in human beings, a more useful counterresponse. Wolpe hypothesized that if he trained a patient to relax, he could introduce him to non-anxiety-provoking situations and move that patient gradually toward adjustment to a more fearful situation. If conditioning was strong enough, the patient's fearful or anxious responses would gradually be eliminated. Because this technique depends on the relative success of each confrontation between relaxation and ever-stronger anxiety-provoking situations, it is known as *systematic desensitization.*

Wolpe's sequence depends on each patient's case history. First, he interviews a patient to determine the patient's ability to cope with various anxiety-producing experiences. On the basis of this interview, Wolpe next compiles a list, which he calls the *anxiety hierarchy*, on which he ranks situations from least anxiety producing to most anxiety producing. He then uses these stimuli to desensitize the patient's anxiety. However, before the stimuli can be introduced, the patient must be relaxed; this relaxation is sometimes accomplished through hypnosis. Under hypnosis the patient responds to the therapist's suggestion to relax and maintains this relaxed state through therapy. While the patient is relaxed, he is asked to visualize each item on the anxiety hierarchy, beginning with the least anxiety-producing item. If any item disturbs his relaxation, the session ends temporarily. As long as the patient remains undisturbed, each succeeding item on the anxiety hierarchy is presented. The patient continues to relax; anxiety-producing situations no longer produce anxiety; and eventually, the original maladaptive response is overcome. Thereafter, under normal conditions, the patient will be relaxed in situations that formerly produced fear or anxiety.

Drug-induced relaxation Drugs may be used to assist patients who have difficulty learning to relax during the desensitization process. Friedman (1966) showed that Breital (mexohexitone sodium) produces deep relaxation without interfering with a patient's ability to visualize anxiety-evoking items.

The use of such a drug can reduce the number of desensitization sessions needed. Instead of going through a long anxiety-hierarchy list, the patient under the influence of the drug deals with only the high-anxiety item. The dosage of the drug is gradually decreased until the patient no longer feels anxious while visualizing the anxiety-producing item or when actually in its presence.

Aversion therapy is a variation of counterconditioning. A form of this therapy has been used to condition alcoholics to avoid alcohol. The alcoholic is treated with drugs that in combination with alcohol bring on nausea. He is then shown and made to smell alcohol. When the alcohol is repeatedly associated with the state of nausea, the patient becomes repulsed by the previously pleasant stimulus (alcohol). Eventually, the mere presence of alcohol without the drug induces nausea. Since the alcoholic's problem probably lies deeper than his taste for alcohol, the therapist must do more than modify the behavior of drinking. He may, for example, seek to modify some aspects of the alcoholic's interpersonal relations, helping him to learn to enjoy the company of others without the support of liquor.

Therapy using principles of operant conditioning

Knowing that classical conditioning (Wolpe's technique) can be used to treat behavior disorders, we may assume that operant conditioning can also be used for this purpose. The use of the principles of reinforcement has become a major therapeutic technique in modifying pathological behavior. By this means, the individual learns to respond in a certain way if he finds that his response will lead to positive reinforcement (see Chapter 6.)

In using operant conditioning to modify behavior, the therapist arranges contingencies of reinforcement designed to increase the frequency of desirable behavior while reducing the frequency of undesirable or pathological behavior. Isaacs, Thomas, and Goldiamond (1960) used such a procedure to treat a schizophrenic patient who had not talked for 19 years. They found that chewing gum was effective in reinforcing the patient. They then arranged for him to receive a stick of gum as a reward for making responses that approximated communication. He was successively reinforced for following the gum with his eyes, for moving his lips, for uttering some sound, for specific words, and finally only when he answered questions by talking. When his nonverbal attempts to communicate were no longer reinforced, he replaced them with verbal responses.

Therapists have used positive reinforcement to treat many different types and degrees of maladaptive behavior, from the relatively minor problem of disorderly conduct in a classroom to the very difficult problem of the behavior of an institutionalized psychotic with violent tendencies.

Proper reinforcement Wolf, Risley, and Mees (1964) reported the case of Dicky, a 3½-year-old boy brought to them for treatment. At the slightest provocation, the child would throw a long, wild temper tantrum. During these tantrums, Dicky bit and slapped himself, tore his hair, kicked, and screamed. He also refused to wear glasses, which he needed in order to see properly.

The principles of operant conditioning were used to treat both problems. Each time Dicky started a tantrum, he was placed in his room and the door was locked. When he stopped, he was let out. Gradually the tantrums became shorter. Within a few months, the tantrums stopped altogether. This combination of mild punishment and negative reinforcement was effective in getting Dicky to stop throwing tantrums.

The problem of the glasses was approached not through punishment but with food. Rather than punish Dicky for not wearing his glasses, the doctors rewarded him with food each time he put his glasses close to his head. Finally, one day when Dicky was very hungry, a plate of ice cream was used as the reward. Dicky put his glasses on correctly to get the reward and continued to wear them from that day on.

Token economies The principle of reinforcement can be used effectively in large-scale institutional programs of psychological rehabilitation. The general procedure is to establish a set of desirable responses, such as making one's bed, shaving or dressing oneself, and participating in the activities of the institution. Patients learn that they will be rewarded each time they make a desirable response. Many different types of rewards are possible—for example, food (candy, gum, ice cream) or cigarettes. When the patients learn to trust the therapists, tokens are used as conditioned reinforcers. The patient learns that a token is desirable because it can earn or buy him some pleasing object or activity; the patient with a token is free to decide how to spend it. Each objective or activity is worth a different number of tokens: one token might buy the patient a pack of cigarettes; three tokens, a chance to see a movie or read a book. An entire economy is thus established, much like the economy of the outside world. By establishing a *token economy*, the therapist simulates a real-world atmosphere and enables the patient to practice real-world activities.

The token economy is one of the most successful behavior-modification treatments thus far established. It has been used in hospitals with mildly disturbed individuals, state institutions, Veterans' Administration hospitals, schools with classes of retarded children, delinquents, and culturally disadvantaged youths, and in noninstitutional situations, including the home. Reinforcement by the token-reward system is always for performance of any one of a group of previously identified desirable behaviors. Starting with rather simple rewards, a token-reinforcement program may eventually be extended to allow patients to spend hours or days out of the institutional environment, even permitting them to leave for an extended period of time, perhaps permanently.

Many patients are at first reluctant to participate in such a program. In such cases, the individual's behavior is *shaped* (see Chapter 6) by means of a series of successive approximations to the desirable behavior. For example, an uncooperative patient may be given a token if he asks a question about the token program or shows a slight degree of interest in it, or he may be given one token for cleaning a portion of his room when five tokens would be given for a completely clean room that passes daily inspection. The desire for tokens grows quickly. As patients become bored or as they become expert in earning tokens for a particular set of responses, the responses can be changed. The program can be used until a patient is ready to be released from the hospital.

Tokens and adjustive behavior Ayllon and Azrin (1968) described a token economy established in a hospital as a system for rehabilitation of psychotics. Patients who had not worked for more than 3 years (although they had been asked to) were given jobs off the ward. They washed dishes, did their laundry, and helped the attendants with various tasks; in return, they received tokens for their work. In exchange for the tokens, patients could "buy" lunches, preferred rooms, a leave from the ward, and recreational opportunities.

The system was very successful in helping patients to function on a normal level. During a week when patients were given tokens but were told that they did not have to work for them, no work was done. Thus, the tokens played an important role in maintaining adjustive behavior.

The token economy allows the patient to participate in an aspect of the outside environment without being subject to the fears and anxieties of that environment. As patients improve, they create fewer custodial chores for hospital attendants, who can then spend more time with the patients in interpersonal relationships that also contribute to the patients' sense of achievement and self-confidence. It is hoped in all token programs that social acceptance will come to replace the token as the reinforcement.

Modeling

Another new and important method of behavior modification is *modeling*, or imitation; this procedure works particularly well with children, but it need not be limited to them. Under appropriate circumstances, anyone who has acquired the skill of imitating others may acquire new responses by observing someone else make these responses. Bandura (1965) argues that modeling can accelerate behavior therapy and should be used wherever possible to establish new responses. He suggests, however, that modeling procedures and operant conditioning be regarded as complementary methods: modeling helps to develop new responses; reinforcement maintains them.

The following study clearly illustrates the effectiveness of modeling as a technique of mod-

ification. A group of subjects were to be cured of a fear they held in common, a pronounced snake phobia. They were not institutionalized patients, nor were they psychotherapeutic patients. They were otherwise well-adjusted individuals who volunteered in the hope that their snake phobia could be cured.

The 32 volunteers were divided into four groups; the experimenters treated each of the four groups in a different way:

1 Group I was counterconditioned by the techniques of systematic desensitization, which we discussed earlier.
2 Group II was exposed to a film depicting adults and children playing with snakes.
3 Group III watched a live model, the therapist, playing with a snake; first the group watched through a glass (one-way mirror), and then the group watched while standing or sitting in the same room with the therapist and the snake. Gradually, they were encouraged to imitate the snake-handling behavior of the model, first by touching the snake and then by handling the snake as the model did.
4 Group IV received no treatment.

Prior to the tests, and after the experimental sessions were completed, each of the four groups was asked to handle a snake. There were 10 sessions for each of the first three groups (the experimental groups), and no sessions for Group IV (the control group). Results clearly showed that each subject in Group III (the modeling group) was able to complete the task of sitting in a chair, hands at his sides, while a snake crawled on him for a period of seconds. Neither Group I nor Group II volunteers showed such marked improvement, but they were considerably less fearful than the control group, Group IV.

As a further test of the effectiveness of the modeling procedure, Groups I and II were then trained in the same way as Group III. The experimenters found that the live-model treatment enabled these subjects to overcome their fear of snakes to the extent that they were able to complete the post-treatment task.

OTHER PSYCHOTHERAPIES

A wide variety of theories of psychotherapy compete for attention. Claims and counterclaims proliferate, and no single point of view or set of procedures is supported by all or even most psychotherapists. None has sufficient objective or long-term evidence to support it above all others.

Some therapists are willing to adopt combinations of various ideas and methods. Others tend to rely on a particular theory or viewpoint.

Hypnotherapy

Hypnosis, or *hypnotherapy,* is regarded by some as a quick, efficient method of reaching the unconscious when other methods fail or when the therapist needs to uncover additional information. However, psychotherapists recommend that hypnosis not be used alone, for several reasons: (1) not all individuals can respond to the use of hypnosis; (2) hypnosis does not provide a permanent adjustment or cure; (3) there is danger that the patient will become excessively dependent upon the therapist. Some psychotherapists claim that hypnotic treatments can alter or correct a behavior disorder only to the extent that the overt symptoms can be manipulated; the actual psychological difficulty is rarely relieved by hypnotic treatment, and the behavioral disorder is likely to appear in the form of a new and different symptom, which will require treatment at some future time.

Although hypnotic techniques are easily performed, hypnosis in the hands of amateurs is extremely dangerous. Unless the hypnotist is a trained therapist, the individual may be improperly or incompetently hypnotized, which can cause disturbances that may affect his posthypnotic adjustment.

Essentially, hypnosis is a trancelike state. The hypnotized person is open to almost any suggestion (he can be made to bark like a dog, for instance). Once the subject has been put into a deep hypnotic state, the therapist may use two techniques to examine the patient's behavior pathology: *suggestion* and *regression.*

Release of pent-up aggression Servicemen assigned to wartime combat often develop symptoms that originate from a traumatic event. The symptoms are often eliminated as soon as the psychologist is able to work back to that event.

Marcuse (1959) relates the case of a seaman who had developed an uncontrollable arm motion. The sailor first exhibited this symptom shortly after his ship was sunk. Under hypnosis, he was made to relive the sinking of his ship. He recalled that he was blown on deck during an air attack and, in a rage, had looked for a machine gun in order to fire back at the enemy but had failed to find one. The doctor noticed that his arm motion was precisely the kind he would have made in firing a machine gun. By means of hypnosis, he was able to reenact the scene and to fire a gun in order to release his pent-up aggressive emotions. When the patient came out of the hypnotic state, he was no longer making the involuntary arm movement.

Posthypnotic suggestion Under hypnosis, a patient will believe much of what is suggested. A therapist may suggest to the hypnotized patient that he is relaxed and free of anxiety. Or, he may use posthypnotic suggestion to eliminate the patient's maladaptive symptoms and substitute other, less maladaptive ones; upon awakening, the subject's symptoms will be gone and he will respond or behave as his therapist has suggested. Posthypnotic suggestion may be especially helpful in treating such mild disorders as nailbiting, smoking, twitching, excessive blinking, scratching, and hiccups, but it is not usually effective for more severe behavioral problems.

Hypnotic regression While under hypnosis, the patient may be asked to remember material from his past as a means of recalling suppressed conflicts. Recall can be systematized by a technique known as *hypnotic regression.* Some patients can be helped to remember things further and further into their past by a step-by-step process of regressing through time. On occasion, a patient may relive his past experiences so accurately that his handwriting or speech also regresses to the period being recalled. Repressed unconscious conflicts may also be brought to the surface, often with great emotionality, as the patient relives the psychological dilemmas that led to his maladjustments.

FUTURE OF PSYCHOTHERAPIES

Differences over the relative effectiveness of the various psychotherapies will continue until more data are available to support or refute the claims. We will probably see an increasing emphasis on objective research to determine the scope and limitations of specific therapies. Therapy research is difficult and very time-consuming, however. The traditional experimental situation using a control group is not always possible, nor is it always appropriate. Efforts to compare patients undergoing a particular therapy (experimental group) with patients who need therapy but are not receiving it (control group) present ethical as well as technical problems. If two people need help, it is not easy to give therapy to one and not the other. In some forms of therapy research, the patient is his own control: comparisons are made of his behavior and the feelings and attitudes he reports before, during, and after therapy. But such reports are not always a reliable basis for generalization. We need to consider the wide variety of individual differences in patients. All hysterics are not alike, nor are compulsives or anxious individuals similar enough to be lumped together into one category.

Research also requires that we specify the goals of therapy and the criteria of therapeutic effectiveness. There is disagreement, particularly between psychoanalysts and behavior modifiers, about what constitutes successful therapy. The behavior modifier considers his efforts successful when his patient can once again function effectively—return to his job, tolerate his nagging wife (or husband), study efficiently, feel comfortable in the company of the opposite sex, and so on. The psychoanalyst agrees that these outward signs are important but believes that even more important are indications (not always overt) that the patient has resolved his unconscious conflicts, has gained insight into his own personality, and can use his psychic energy to cope with his environment instead of wasting it on defense mechanisms.

Until therapists adopt the same criteria, they will have difficulty resolving their other differences. To reach this goal, better communication is needed among the advocates of the various psychotherapies and theories (Table 14.1).

MEDICALLY BASED THERAPIES

Many forms of medical therapy have developed accidentally or by trial-and-error procedures. *Insulin-coma treatment* was discovered quite by accident when a schizophrenic patient who was being treated for diabetes slipped into a deep coma following an overdose of insulin. When he came out of the coma, he was found to have lost many of his schizophrenic symptoms. In the insulin-coma treatment that was subsequently developed, patients were given large doses of insulin to reduce their blood sugar level and induce a coma in which brain metabolism was slowed. Insulin-coma treatment is no longer used, for it is undependable and dangerous.

Shock therapy

Electroshock or *electroconvulsive therapy* is an offshoot of the insulin method in that it involves a brief period of unconsciousness following the induction of a convulsion. The convulsion is produced by passing an electric current across the frontal portion of the cerebral cortex for a frac-

Table 14.1   Comparison of three major therapies

Psychoanalysis (based on psychoanalytic theories)	Client-centered (based on self-actualization)	Behavior modification (based on learning theories)
Utilizes free association	Nondirective	Directive
Interprets dreams	Noninterpretive	Deals with overt behavior
Probes the unconscious	Concerned with the present	
Utilizes transference		Utilizes principles of conditioning
Concerned with patient's past		Concerned with the present

tion of a second. The current is delivered by means of electrodes attached to the patient's forehead. Electroshock therapy has been found most effective for patients suffering from depression. On occasion, the results of such therapy are quite dramatic, and the patient shows rapid recovery. In most cases, electroshock therapy is effective only when used in conjunction with some form of psychotherapy.

Psychopharmacology

The study and treatment of behavior pathology by chemical means—that is, with drugs—is known as *psychopharmacology*. For many years, psychologists have been interested in the effects of drugs on behavior. The first drugs used in the treatment of behavior pathology were those of the sedative (sleep-inducing) type. Chloral hydrate, a mild sleep-inducing drug, has been in medical use since 1875; and phenobarbital has been prescribed for anxiety reactions since 1912. Not until the early 1950s, however, did drugs come into widespread psychiatric use. Table 14.2 summarizes the major drugs in use today.

Antipsychotic drugs   The first drugs used extensively in the treatment and management of psychoses were *reserpine* and *chlorpromazine*. Reserpine is extracted from *Rauwolfia serpentina*, a root long recognized for its calming effects by Hindu physicians in India. The drug's ability to reduce anxiety was observed in the United States in 1953 (Wilkens and Judson, 1953). In 1954, following extensive tests, Kline reported that reserpine had a quieting effect on disturbed psychotics. The drug has been shown to promote emotional control and personality integration, to decrease inhibition, and to increase responsiveness. But it is unpredictable, affecting patients in varying degrees or not at all.

Chlorpromazine is more widely used and appears to have fewer side effects. Derived from phenothiazine, it was first used as an antihistamine. In early tests, chlorpromazine was observed to have calming or tranquilizing effects. More extensive studies showed it effective in quieting agitated and excited patients. Subsequent findings showed that chlorpromazine and the other antipsychotic drugs in Table 14.2 help to decrease delusional behavior in schizophrenics. Patients who are treated with these drugs have fewer hallucinations and seem to respond better to psychotherapy than those who do not receive drug treatment.

The effect of antipsychotic drugs varies from very slight to very pronounced. Even when the drugs are effective, patients sometimes relapse into psychotic behavior when drug treatment is discontinued. Generally, these drugs do not "cure" the patient; they merely reduce the severity of the psychotic symptoms.

Table 14.2 Major psychopharmacological drugs in current use[a]

Type	Generic name	Some common trade names
Antipsychotic drugs (major tranquilizers)	phenothiazines:	
	chlorpromazine	Thorazine
	trifluopromazine	Vesprin
	thioridazine	Mellaril
	carphenazine	Proketazine
	acetophenazine	Tindal
	thiopropazate	Dartal
	trifluoperazine	Stelazine
	butaperazine	Repoise
	fluphenazine	Prolixin, Permitil
	piperacetazine	Quide
	prochlorperazine	Trilafon
	butyrophenones:	
	haloperidol	Haldol
	thioxanthenes:	
	chlorprothixene	Taractan
	thiothixene	Navane
Antianxiety drugs (minor tranquilizers)	chlordiazepoxide	Librium
	chlorazepate diopotassium	Tranxene
	diazepam	Valium
	doxepin	Sinequan
	hydroxyzine hydrochloride	Atarax
	hydroxyzine pamoate	Vistaril
	meprobamate	Miltown, Equanil
	oxazepam	Serax
	tybamate	Solacen, Tybatran
Barbiturates	phenobarbital	many manufacturers
	pentobarbital	Nembutal (and others)
	secobarbital	Seconal
	thiopental	Pentothal
Antidepressants	imipramine	Tofranil
	iproniazid	Marsalid
	amitriptyline	Elavil
	desipramine	Norpramin, Pertofrane
	nortriptyline	Aventyl
	protriptyline	Vivactil
	tranylcypromine	Parnate
	phenelzine	Nardil
	isocarboxazid	Marplan
Antimanic drugs	lithium carbonate	Lithomate, Lithane
	rubidium[b]	
Psychomotor stimulants	amphetamine sulfate	Benzedrine
	d-amphetamine sulfate	Dexedrine
	methamphetamine hydrochloride	Methedrine
Psychotomimetic drugs (may imitate psychotic reactions)	d-lysergic acid diethylamide	LSD
	3,4,5-trimethoxphenyl-ethylamine	mescaline
	N-allynormorphine	Nalorphine, Nalline

[a]Compiled from various sources, including Kline and Davis (1973).
[b]Chemical element still in experimental stage; not for therapeutic use.

Patients who regularly receive antipsychotic drugs must be carefully observed, for these drugs can have serious side effects—for example, low blood pressure, blurred vision, allergic reactions, and nausea.

Antianxiety drugs For many years the most popular *antianxiety drugs* were the barbiturates (see Table 14.2), but the introduction of meprobamate in 1954 (Berger, 1954) set the stage for a variety of new antianxiety drugs, as shown in Table 14.2. It has been suggested that the effect of the antianxiety drugs is quite different from that of the antipsychotic drugs. All the antianxiety drugs—the so-called minor tranquilizers—tend to have a sedative effect; but such drugs as meprobamate (Miltown), chlordiazepoxide (Librium), diazepam (Valium), and oxazepam (Serax) produce less drowsiness than the barbiturates.

Unlike the antipsychotic drugs, the antianxiety drugs usually have little direct effect on schizophrenic patients (Kline and Davis, 1973). They can, however, be useful in treatment. As the patient's symptoms of anxiety are reduced, he becomes more responsive to other forms of therapy and feels more confident that he can deal with his problems. The drugs do not rid the patient of his anxieties, but they can help him reach a point where he can cope with the frustrations and conflicts that make him anxious.

Antidepressive drugs Drugs such as imipramine and iproniazid, used in treatment of severe depression, have been found useful in making patients more responsive and more interested in solving their problems. It is interesting that such psychomotor stimulants as amphetamines (see Table 14.2) are unsuitable for treating depressions. Their effect is short-lived, and after the drug has worn off, the depression is frequently more intense than before.

Antimanic drugs Studies indicate that lithium carbonate is effective in treating the manic episodes of manic-depressive psychosis (Milner, Ruffin, and McGinnis, 1971). The drug has little or no effect, however, on schizophrenic reactions or paranoiac disorders. Lithium carbonate has some effect on depressions that follow manic episodes, although it is not useful in treating any other kind of depressive state. Taken on a regular basis, it can also help to prevent future manic-depressive episodes (Kline and Davis, 1973).

Psychotomimetic drugs Drugs such as *d*-lysergic acid diethylamide (LSD) have been found to produce reactions that mimic psychoses. LSD first came to the attention of psychiatrists in the early 1950s when it was found to be related to a chemical substance found in the brain. Experiments with LSD revealed that it had dramatic and complex effects, often producing psychotic-like behavior (Figure 14.2). A few psychotherapists have used the drug as a way to view the patient with his defenses removed and to allow the patient to experience momentary personality changes. The effects of psychotomimetic or psychedelic drugs, however, vary widely: every test shows a slightly different result.

The therapeutic use of psychotomimetic drugs is highly controversial. Some psychologists claim that they are too dangerous to be used even experimentally, whereas others believe that much can be learned, particularly about psychotic behavior, by carefully controlled research with these drugs. In a recent poll of psychologists and laymen who subscribe to a popular psychology journal, 36 percent of those questioned refused to give an absolute yes or no opinion about the use of psychedelic drugs as compared to tranquilizers. But they did agree that because not enough is known about these drugs, their use might be dangerous in an uncontrolled situation.

LSD Cohen (1960) and Cohen and Ditman (1963) studied the effects and after effects of LSD on patients undergoing psychotherapy as well as on experimental subjects.

In the 1960 study, Cohen concluded that com-

Figure 14.2   Persons under the influence of LSD
often exhibit psychotic-like behavior. In these
drawings, done as part of a projective test,
three individuals reveal various forms of mental
disturbance: (A) depressive; (B) manic; (C) schizoid.

A

B

C

plications were more likely to occur in patients undergoing psychotherapy than in experimental subjects.
He described the LSD experience as very dramatic
and found that although subsequent physical disturbances might be attributed to the drug exposure,
it was more likely that the drug would not cause
such disturbances. Most of the subjects did not become addicted to LSD. However, there were a few
cases in which psychological disturbances, such as
suicidal tendencies or prolonged psychotic reactions, developed.

The 1963 study reviewed cases of patients
who had been prescribed LSD in treatments. In some
patients LSD was shown to have caused: (1) prolonged hallucinations (it seems that the drug released
repressed conflicts that patients, most of whom were
disturbed, could not handle); (2) depressive reactions
due to fear; (3) abandonment of all social responsibilities; and (4) paranoid reactions. Cohen and Ditman
suggested that LSD can be beneficial in therapy, but
cautioned against its indiscriminate use.

Research   Many other psychotherapeutic drugs
remain in the experimental stage because investigators are not certain that they have controlled
all the variables. A typical drug experiment involves two groups, both suffering the same disorder at the same level of intensity: one group
is injected with the drug, and the other is given
a placebo (salt solution injection or pill). A flaw
of this procedure is that its outcome may be
influenced by the expectations of the experimenter. Anticipating that those given the drugs
will improve, while those in the control group
will not, an experimenter may easily perceive
what he expects to find.

The experimenter's first concern, therefore,
is to make his tests as objective as possible. To
do this, he employs a technique known as the
double-blind method, whereby neither the experimenter nor the patient knows who has been
given the drug and who the placebo. The experimenter can then objectively record each patient's
improvement. As for the patients, they do not
know whether they have taken the drug or a
placebo, and thus they do not show improvement simply because they expect the drug to
work.

Narcoanalysis

As noted, drugs are sometimes administered as aids to psychotherapy. In *narcoanalysis*, or *narcotherapy*, the individual who appears to be repressing emotional anxieties is injected with a trance-inducing drug (sodium amytal or sodium pentothal) and in a half-awake stage is able to recall emotionally charged experiences which he could not otherwise remember. He responds readily to suggestion and will answer questions and remember material that he cannot handle when completely conscious. However, because the patient is as much asleep as awake, he drifts in and out of reality; he may fantasize and dream portions of his reactions. Yet, even dreams and fantasies give the therapist symbols to work with. When the therapist interprets these symbols, based on his knowledge of the patient and the situation, he may, as in dream and free-association analysis, be able to understand the patient's repressed conflicts. Later, the therapist can help the patient to overcome these conflicts.

The effects of narcoanalysis are most dramatic in the treatment of hysteric reactions (see the example in Chapter 13). Guilt feelings and repressed hostilities can be so intense that an otherwise normal individual may become paralyzed, deaf, or speechless, or he may forget his past. Such critical turning points may happen, for example, to the combat soldier who for the first time sees the face of the enemy he has to kill, or to the man who has survived a fire while those with him were killed or maimed. Such behavior pathologies are usually short-term when the individual is placed under the care of a therapist immediately following the appearance of his illness. If other methods of therapy fail, one session of narcoanalysis may enable the therapist to suggest modes of action that the patient will remember upon awakening. This technique is similar to the posthypnotic suggestion procedure discussed earlier.

If the patient has been ill for a relatively long period of time, or if he is not suffering from a hysteric reaction, he will probably gain very little from only one session of narcoanalysis. The therapist then must devise other methods of probing and searching for information. In such cases, narcoanalysis might be used in combination with a program of other psychotherapeutic methods to enable the patient to improve his adjustment on a more permanent basis.

SUMMARY

Philippe Pinel and Clifford Beers were instrumental in the movement toward more humane treatment of disturbed persons.

Psychotherapists generally have specialized training in either psychiatry, clinical psychology, psychoanalysis, or psychiatric social work.

In psychoanalysis, the therapist's aim is to help the patient to work through his conflicts and to gain insight.

Psychoanalytic techniques include free association and the analysis of dreams, resistance, and transference.

In client-centered or nondirective therapy, the therapist accepts, restates, and clarifies the spontaneous expressions of the patient.

Existential therapy concentrates on the patient's "sense of being."

In directive therapy, the therapist actively intervenes in the life of the patient by
    helping him to plan a course of action or life-style and by prescribing or teaching
    him more effective patterns of behavior.
In group therapy, several patients meet with a therapist to work through their
    problems together.
Psychodrama is a form of group psychotherapy in which the patient
    acts out situations from his own life. Role playing is often used in psychodrama.
In play therapy, the therapist encourages the child to express his feelings through
    play activity.
Behavior modification or behavior therapy, based on the principles of classical and/or
    operant conditioning, views behavior pathology as a system of learned maladap-
    tive responses.
In the behavior therapy method of systematic desensitization or reciprocal inhibi-
    tion, anxiety-evoking stimuli are paired with stimuli that evoke responses
    incompatible with the anxiety response.
The principle of reinforcement has been used to develop token economies.
Modeling is a form of behavior modification in which the individual learns to change
    his maladaptive responses to more adaptive ones by imitating the behavior of
    other persons.
Hypnosis is a trancelike state that the hypnotist induces in the subject through the
    process of suggestion. Hypnotherapy may be used to put the patient in a state of
    deep relaxation and to rid him of such habits as nail-biting and
    twitching. Therapists may also use hypnotic regression to help the patient recall
    significant past experiences.
In electroshock therapy, convulsions and brief unconsciousness are produced in the
    the patient by passing an electric current through the frontal lobes of his brain.
    Insulin-coma shock treatment is no longer used because it is unsafe.
Psychopharmacology is the study and treatment of behavior pathology with chem-
    ical substances such as antipsychotic, antianxiety, antidepressive, antimanic,
    and psychotomimetic drugs.
In narcotherapy, the patient is injected with a drug such as sodium amytal or sodium
    pentothal to produce a semiwakeful state in which he may be able to recall
    emotionally charged experiences he could not otherwise remember.

SUGGESTED READINGS

Texts

Ayllon, T., & Azrin, N. *The token economy: a motivational system for therapy and
    rehabilitation.* New York: Appleton-Century-Crofts, 1968. Discussion of a
    therapeutic system based on token reinforcement.
Bandura, A. *Principles of behavior modification.* New York: Holt, Rinehart &
    Winston, 1969. Comprehensive text covering the entire field of behavior
    modification.
Bordin, E. J. *Psychological counseling.* New York: Appleton-Century-Crofts, 1968.
    Practical discussion of counseling.

Bry, A. *Inside psychotherapy*. New York: Basic Books, 1972. Nine clinicians explain the various psychological approaches (Jungian, Frommian, behavioral therapy, etc.) they use to deal with their clients' problems.

Eron, L. D., & Callahan, R. (Eds.) *The relation of theory to practice in psychotherapy*. Chicago: Aldine, 1969. Describes significant, varied problems to show the current state of the art.

Ford, D. H., & Urban, H. B. *Systems of psychotherapy: a comparative study*. New York: Wiley, 1963. Explanation of basic propositions of major approaches to psychotherapy and development of an integrated picture of their fundamental similarities and differences.

Freud, A. D., *Difficulties in the path of psychoanalysis: a confrontation of past with present viewpoints*. New York: International Universities Press, 1969. Historical analysis of the development of psychoanalysis.

Gardiner, H. (Ed.) *The wolf man: By the wolf man*. New York: Basic Books, 1971. Recollections of Freudian psychoanalysis by Freud's most legendary patient.

Greenwald, H. (Ed.) *Active psychotherapy*. New York: Atherton, 1967. Sampling of therapeutic techniques that are goal-oriented toward increased insights, decreased anxiety, and so on.

Hadfield, J. A. *Introduction to psychotherapy: its history and modern schools*. New York: Atherton, 1967. Discussion of modern techniques such as psychodrama, hypnotherapy, marriage therapy.

Kanfer, F. H. *Learning foundations of behavior therapy*. New York: Wiley, 1971. Well-documented and well-written work showing how learning principles enter into behavior.

Klein, D. F., & Davis, J. M. *Diagnosis and drug treatment of psychiatric disorders*. Baltimore: Johns Hopkins Press, 1969. Introduction to chemotherapy.

Martin, D. G. *Introduction to psychotherapy*. Belmont, Calif.: Brooks/Cole, 1971. A readable introduction to nearly a dozen different methodologies of psychotherapy.

Ruitenbeck, H. M. *Group therapy today: styles, methods and techniques*. New York: Atherton, 1969. Comprehensive discussion of group therapy.

Schneidman, E. S., Farberow, N. L., & Litman, R. E. *The psychology of suicide*. New York: Science House, 1970. A compendious selection of readings ranging from the theoretical aspects of all death-wish phenomena to the assessment and prevention of suicide attempts.

Spence, D. P. (Ed.) *The broad scope of psychoanalysis: selected papers of Leopold Bellak*. New York: International Universities Press, 1969. An attempt to rewrite psychoanalytic theory so that it can be tested experimentally.

Popular books

Beech, H. R. *Changing man's behavior*. Philosophical discussion of the nature of psychotherapy and behavior modification.

Coulson, W. R. *Groups, gimmicks, and instant gurus*. An examination of encounter groups, their distortions, and their assets.

Emplan, Ruth. *Psychiatry and the community in the nineteenth century*. History of institutional psychiatry and its community involvement.

Krumboltz, J. D., & Krumboltz, H. B. *Changing children's behavior*. A popularized presentation of behavior modification principles and techniques as they can be applied to children's behavior.

Laing, R. D. *The politics of experience.* A prominent British psychiatrist attempts to look at psychosis from the patient's "inside" viewpoint. Note especially Chapter 7, a moving account of a "ten-day voyage" (psychotic episode).

Leifer, R. *In the name of mental health: the social function of psychiatry.* Achievements of psychiatry in terms of our society's welfare.

Shepard, M., & Lee, M. *Games analysts play.* Highly critical commentary on psychiatric and psychoanalytic practice.

Viscott, D. S. *The making of a psychiatrist.* A well-constructed description of 3 years of psychiatric residency.

15

Psychology and society

Psychology—the study of human behavior—is largely concerned with individuals. In most research situations, subjects are individually tested, and in therapeutic sessions, patients are treated for their individual psychological problems. But people do not function in a vacuum; their behavior is affected by many interrelated circumstances involving interpersonal relationships. These relationships are the main interest of *social psychology*.

Almost everything we do is influenced by others, by their attitudes and beliefs as well as by their overt actions. However, merely knowing that people influence one another does not enable us to predict how they will affect one another. To make such predictions, we must be able to answer three questions: (1) What is the relationship between the individual performing the action and the other people present? (2) Under what circumstances is he performing the activity? (3) What are his attitudes and the attitudes of the others toward the activity?

The effects of people on each other are termed the *differential effects* of social situations. This term implies that there is a *difference* between an individual's behavior when he performs an activity alone and when he performs the same activity in the presence of others. Differential effects are universal. They are at the core of social psychology—as well as sociology, anthropology, political science, business management, and industrial relations.

The rise of modern science in the last half of the nineteenth century affected traditional attitudes to the study of man. Recognizing the profound effects of environment, the science of human psychology grew out of a new awareness that adversity hindered individual development. The traditional belief that the character of individuals and their social backgrounds were unrelated was supplanted by the realization that our actions are influenced by people around us. Psychologists began to recognize the need to examine man's behavior in the context of social situations in order to draw valid conclusions about his nature.

This new interest in behavior in its social setting led to extensive research of *small group* interaction. The pioneering work of C. H. Cooley (1922) and G. H. Mead (1934) in studies of human *socialization* (the process by which people learn socially acceptable behavior) and the individual's relationship to various types of groups inspired research psychologists to investigate small group behavior in almost every facet of human life. Groups that have proved productive for psychological research have been found in schools, in business, in the military, and in psychotherapy.

GROUP INFLUENCES ON BEHAVIOR

Groups are important in that they establish standards of behavior. The early kindergartner learns how to act and react in the setting of his classroom and begins to change from a highly individualized infant into a socialized child. The transformation continues with each new group that the child joins, and eventually he is able to think and act freely in many different groups.

Group norms

To understand the influence of groups on individual behavior, we must first study *group norms*—the standards of behavior set by the group. Norms (*social norms*, as they are sometimes called) are the products of the social relations shared by the members of the group. Norms refer to expected behavior, or ideal behavior. The norm does not specify the *only* way of acting or behaving, but rather a range of acceptable and unacceptable behavior. We can thus say that a norm is a scale that defines a *latitude of acceptance* and a *latitude of rejection* of behavior in relation to the members of the group.

An example of a group norm of contemporary Americans is in standards of dress. In 1965 the miniskirt was greeted with raised eyebrows, but gradually it became an accepted group norm, even among fashionable women in the older generation. With women's liberation, bras and girdles, as inhibitors of free movement, were rejected by large numbers of young women, a phenomenon to which the general public soon grew accustomed. However, the norm has not changed to the extent that nudity in public places is permitted, though even this has been challenged in the recent "streaking" fad. It is interesting to note that while today's styles are less inhibiting, they are also reminiscent of the 1920s.

Not all kinds of behavior are regulated by norms. Norms may be obscured, especially in times of rapid social change, and members of a group may be confused about the appropriate behavior in certain situations.

Group pressure

Group norms can exert tremendous pressure on the behavior of the individual. The influence of the group may be so great that in certain situations it causes the individual to act contrary to the way he would act if he were alone. In a crowd, a meek man may be swept up in the emotion of the moment and display aggression. When a person finds himself in a situation that has no definite or apparent structure, he depends heavily on the group for norms of behavior.

Effect of group pressure on individual judgments The tendency to conform to group pressures and to seek group acceptance is so strong that in certain situations individuals modify or even reverse their prior judgments.

Laboratory experiments have repeatedly shown that group pressure can cause individuals to modify their judgments. As early as 1924, Allport showed that group pressures were strong enough to influence individual judgments, even when the group was composed of people who were complete strangers to the subject. Allport's subjects tended to give more moderate answers to questions when others were present, indicating that they were less confident of their own opinions when with others. Very often a person's first experience with drugs or alcohol occurs under pressure to conform to the group. He may know of the dangers of drugs, but in the context of the group he can be persuaded to try them.

Most experiments conducted to study group pressure and individual judgments have called for perceptual decisions. For example, subjects might be asked, "How far are these two points from each other?" But it should be remembered that real-life situations are far more complex and involve many more kinds of decisions than it is possible to create in the psychology laboratory. Such subtle factors as the composition of the group or majority as well as the relationship of the individual to the group play important parts in determining the effects of group pressure on individual judgments. Although behavioral trends are outlined by laboratory findings, we must be careful in applying results from the laboratory to real-life situations.

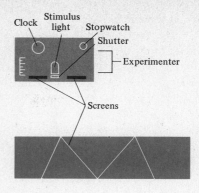

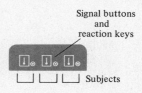

The autokinetic effect and norms Sherif (1936) used the *autokinetic* phenomenon to demonstrate the influence of group norms on individual behavior. The autokinetic phenomenon is an illusion of movement. The experimental subject is seated in a dark room and informed that a small light will come on some distance away from him. The light remains on for a new minutes and then is turned off. The subject then is asked to indicate how far the light moved. Actually, the light does not move at all; it simply appears to move. Figure 15.1 diagrams an experiment on the autokinetic phenomenon.

Sherif found that an individual alone quickly establishes a pattern of responding when he is presented with the phenomenon. The subject's judgments about the movement of the light begin to fall within a specific range. In other words, each individual establishes his own norm.

After a group of subjects had established individual norms, Sherif put them together and asked them to make their judgments aloud. After a period of time, their judgments tended to move toward a common group opinion. A social norm had been established.

Finally, after the group norm was established, Sherif broke up the group and once again asked individuals to make their judgments alone. The effect

of social pressure was evident in these last results. Instead of returning to their individual norms or establishing new individual norms, the subjects continued to adhere to the social norm established in the group. The pressure of the group was great, even though most individuals were not consciously aware that the judgments had been altered by their membership in the group.

Conformity and personality factors Two reasons are generally offered for individual conformity to group pressure. First is the desire for social approval and a fear of social censure if one does not go along with the group. These feelings are so strong that they compel many persons to seek social approval from any available group, even from complete strangers. Second, people tend to place more faith in the group's judgment than in their own, particularly if the situation is unfamiliar or ambiguous. In this context, a person will compare his behavior with the group's. If he finds that the group's standards are very different from his own, he will assume that the group, not he, is correct and will therefore modify his behavior accordingly.

Conformity experiments have found that many individuals are not susceptible to group pressures. The degree to which the individual habitually conforms seems to be related to his personality. A series of personality studies (Crutchfield, 1955) designed to separate conformers from nonconformers revealed that nonconformers (male, in these studies) scored high in the following areas: (1) intelligence; (2) originality in thought processes and problem solving; (3) ego strength or ability to cope under stress; (4) self-confidence and absence of feelings of anxiety and inferiority; (5) tolerant social attitudes, acceptance of responsibility, and freedom from disturbed and dependent interpersonal relationships.

There is, however, another type of nonconformist—the person who tries deliberately to be different, who resists group pressure because of his hostility toward others or because he has a need to rebel. He may change his judgments merely to be different from the group consensus: if the group says yes, he says no. This type of nonconformist is not the "true" independent just described, for a true independent resists group consensus to conform because he has confidence in his own ability to make accurate judgments.

The drive for uniformity The theory of social comparisons contends that people have a drive to evaluate their own opinions and abilities and that the only source of evaluation is often a comparison with others and not some objective standard. To this end, they compare themselves with someone similar to themselves in opinion and ability rather than to someone who is unlike themselves in these respects. On the basis of their theory, Festinger (1957) put forward several interesting hypotheses related to the nature of conformity. First, self-evaluation will be more stable when comparison is made with a similar individual. Second, comparison with a "somewhat different" person will produce tendencies to change one's evaluation so it is less different. Third, a person will be less attracted to situations in which others present are divergent from him than to those in which others are similar to him. And fourth, the existence of an outstanding opinion or ability discrepancy in a group will lead to action to reduce the discrepancy.

Personality factors are significant in understanding an individual's tendency to conform, but they are not the sole influence on conformity. Influences may vary according to the type of stimuli, the individual's perception of the group and his particular place in it, his expectations about the consequences of conformity and nonconformity, and the strength of his convictions.

Reasons for conformity to group pressures We have discussed some of the generally accepted reasons for individual conformity (group approval, reliance on the group's judgments), but the sources of conformity are, in fact, more complex, requiring deeper investigation.

Two psychologists (Deutsch and Gerard, 1955) have determined that the individual conforms because of distinct types of pressure: *informational social influence* and *normative group influence.*

When we feel pressured to accept another person's view of reality, we are acting under informational social influence. Such influence is felt when an individual goes through a process of social comparison and changes his behavior (conforms) in accordance with group pressure.

Then, too, we are often placed in situations that demand judgments, commitments, or actions. There may be insufficient time to make an adequate evaluation, or the environment may fail to provide us with an objective or logical basis for forming conclusions. In such ambiguous situations, where the individual may need answers to unfamiliar questions and problems or is placed in a setting removed from his everyday experience, he is often under pressure to accept the solutions of others. The degree to which he is influenced by informational social influence will depend on the ambiguity or the difficulty of the situation.

Normative group influence is the pressure

we feel to conform to the expectations of others. A teenager wants to join a club and is told that he must "prove himself." He submits to the tests of the group, hoping to win the members' approval. After acceptance, he knows that the group expects him to behave in a certain way and, if he wants to continue as a member of that group, he modifies his behavior to suit these requirements.

Normative group influence Milgram (1964) investigated the operation of normative group influence. His subjects were told that the purpose of the experiment in which they were participating was to determine the effects of punishment on learning in a collective teaching situation. In each situation, the subject was designated as one of three teachers to test a learner in a verbal-learning task. The other two and the learner were confederates of the experimenter.

The subject was told to administer an electric shock to the learner each time he made an error, and the teachers were to decide on the strength of the shock. The teacher-confederates had previously decided on a 15-volt increase after each mistake. The teacher-subject was expected to administer the shock by depressing a lever.

The shock generator was actually a fake device, but the learner-confederate, who deliberately made 30 errors in the series of 40 trials, feigned increasing discomfort as the strength of the shocks was increased; he also protested the experimental situation. After the shocks supposedly reached the level of 120 volts, the learner pretended to feel pain; he cried and screamed and finally refused to go on with the learning task.

Despite the learner's protests, the subjects continued to go along with the decisions of the other teachers to repeat the shocks. Of the 40 experimental subjects, 27 administered shocks above the 150-volt level, even though the learner complained of a heart condition. Seven subjects went as high as 450 volts.

A group of 40 control subjects received the same instructions. However, each subject had to make his own decision about the amount of shock. There were no group expectations and no group standards. In this group, only two subjects continued to administer shocks greater than 150 volts.

Milgram's study dramatically shows the enormous influence of normative group pressure. Because experimental subjects wanted to win the approval of the other teachers, they continued to abide by their suggestions, even though they seemed to be causing harm to another individual.

Group problem-solving

Social psychology is concerned with the group's influence not only on the behavior of individuals but also on the performance of the group itself. A group activity that is relatively easy to study in the laboratory situation is problem-solving.

It is commonly believed that a group can solve a problem more effectively than can separate individuals. The time-worn axiom "Two heads are better than one" is rooted in our culture's folk wisdom and is supported by the large number of social institutions that rely on group, rather than individual, problem-solving, so that many commissions and committees are continually being designated to find answers to social problems.

Some social psychologists maintain that the performance of a group is more efficient than that of its individual members. In one study (Barnlund, 1959) subjects were given verbal tests individually and as part of the group. They solved problems faster and more correctly when they worked together as a group. As a group, they were able to discard wrong answers quicker through discussion. The group, however, could do no better than its most capable member.

But there is evidence that people do not always work more effectively as a group. In certain situations, groups may hinder the development of solutions, as when members waste time arguing fruitlessly.

Variables in group effectiveness

Groups vary in their attainment of goals. In every kind of organization, from the family to the larger culture, groups differ in their effectiveness. The fate of the group can have an enormous effect on individual fortunes. It is therefore necessary to understand what makes a group succeed—or fail.

Group composition The composition of a group is an important factor in its effectiveness. A combination of individuals gives the group its character, just as the group helps give a self-image to the individual.

In the study of productive group composition, the psychologist attempts to determine the degree of similarity among group members that will insure optimum group performance and the most satisfaction to individuals. Some complicated group tasks appear to be completed more efficiently if group members have diverse abilities. One member might be more proficient in a specific task and can handle it more productively while detecting another's errors in a related job. There is always a danger, however, that the group will fail if group members are too dissimilar. Individual differences may cause disagreements on crucial decisions, methods of operation, and other important matters. The group may become partially or totally ineffective.

Homogeneous versus nonhomogeneous groups Hoffman (1959) studied group composition and group effectiveness. First, he administered a personality test to a group of college students and, on the basis of their test scores, divided them into four groups. Two groups were homogeneous (members had similar scores on the personality test), and two were nonhomogeneous (members had widely varying scores on the test). Each group was told to attack the following hypothetical problem as a unit: The group was to imagine itself a team of soldiers attempting to return to its own lines without leaving a trail for the enemy to follow. Their truck had to cross a heavily mined road. They had various scrap materials at hand to assist them in crossing the road. They were to determine a way of crossing the road quickly and safely without leaving any traces of their passage.

The nonhomogeneous groups produced not only a greater number of solutions but also more efficient answers. It is significant, however, that when asked to indicate their degree of satisfaction with group solutions, the members of the nonhomogeneous groups were less satisfied than the members of the homogeneous groups despite the fact that they had produced objectively better solutions to the problem. This lack of satisfaction suggested that the nonhomogeneous groups were more effective because they were willing to look harder for good solutions; on the other hand, it also indicated that the group members might have had trouble agreeing on which plan to use in a real solution.

Studies have shown that nonhomogeneous groups produce more creative, more effective, and more numerous solutions to complex problems. Homogeneous groups are most effective for tasks that require a great deal of cooperation—where each person acts as a separate yet indispensable link. Football squads, basketball teams, military units, teams of scientists guiding astronauts, and similar kinds of groups must be homogeneous to carry out their task in the most effective way.

Homogeneity, however, presents its own problems. Although a homogeneous group is one whose members think and act in similar ways, one slow member may hamper the effectiveness of the entire group. In addition, a group of like-minded people may not be sufficiently critical of each other and may thus arrive too hastily at a solution. In a nonhomogeneous group, there is likely to be more criticism of suggestions and more thorough discussion in the course of which alternative suggestions may be proposed.

Figure 15.2   Two communication patterns. Which one is more effective?

Pattern A:
1. "George, that last play failed badly. Have you any ideas as to what may have gone wrong?"
   (Assume an answer from George)
2. "Well, you may be right, but it may have failed because of the way they shifted their defense. What did their middle linebacker do?"
   (Assume an answer)
3. "Yes, he moved to his left, but he also dropped back. Perhaps the move to the left threw you off. What will you do the next time he drops back like that?"
   (Assume an answer)
4. "I agree. A screen pass will do nicely . . ."

Pattern B:
1. "George, that last play failed badly because of the way they shifted their defense. Did you notice the shift?"
   (Assume an answer from George)
2. "You did not seem to see the middle linebacker dropping back. Perhaps his move to the left threw you off."
   (Assume an answer)
3. "The next time he drops back like that you ought to use a screen pass. Don't you agree?"

Pattern A is likely to be more effective because it involves both the communicator and the recipient in an exchange of information.

Organization and communication patterns In a group, the easiest thing to do about a problem is to talk about it. The success with which solutions and ideas are communicated bears directly upon the overall performance of the group.

To perform successfully, we rely on feedback from others. *Feedback* is information received by the individual that tells him how well he is doing on a task. Without adequate information, he is unable to adjust his performance properly. The communication patterns of a group determine the amount of feedback that each member receives in any group task. Several experimenters have sought to identify the kinds of communication patterns that provide maximum feedback for individual members. In general, the best patterns involve a give-and-take situation in which the individuals may freely ask questions of each other. Figure 15.2 shows two types of communication from a football coach to his quarterback. Which one is more likely to be effective?

Risk-taking in groups

Which makes more conservative decisions, the individual or the group? Are individuals more willing than groups to take risks? Questions such as these have opened up an avenue of research that has helped shed light on group behavior.

Research shows that a group typically makes decisions that are less conservative and riskier than the decisions made by its individual members. This tendency of a group to opt for riskier decisions has been called the *risky shift* (Wallach, Kogan, and Bem, 1962).

Consider, as an example, a group of several persons trying to decide what to advise a friend who has to choose between taking a new job and staying in his present one. The new job includes good chances for advancement in status and salary, but the risk of failure is also present. The old job is secure with no real danger of failure but also not much opportunity for advancement. Under such circumstances, the group will usually decide to advise taking the new job, even though the members of the group may be unwilling to make such a decision for their friend individually.

The shift by groups toward riskier decisions has been explained as a means of diffusing responsibility within groups (Wallach, Kogan, and Bem, 1964). Responsibility for the decision is spread out among the members; no individual need accept personal responsibility if the decision results in failure. Another explanation is that shifts tend to occur when risk-taking in the task or situation is culturally valued but group members, as individuals, are concerned that their inclinations may be too risky. Group discussion serves to assure such members that their judgments are correct (Brown, 1965; Vidmar, 1970).

Deindividuation by groups The individual member of a large group may become "submerged" in the group. Festinger, Pepitone, and Newcomb (1951) have described this effect as *deindividuation*, a situation in which individuals do not feel that they are individuals. The group takes precedence over the individuality of its members.

Deindividuation is often accompanied by a lowering of the usual inner restraints that people apply to their own behavior. The deindividuated person feels anonymous and consequently acts as if he need not accept responsibility for his action. Since others in the group feel the same anonymity, they tend to reinforce irresponsibility.

Zimbardo (1969) has shown that deindividuation can be studied in a laboratory setting. He compared aggression in anonymous subjects with aggression in individuals whose identity was emphasized. The anonymous, or deindividuated, subjects displayed more aggression and their aggression seemed to increase each time they repeated an aggressive act (shocking their victims).

NATURE OF ATTITUDES

Although influenced by the social environment, we remain unique individuals. We absorb the teachings of others, developing behavior that combines, alters, and sometimes dismisses what others have taught us. Thus, each of us accumulates a specific collection of *attitudes* that make us all different from one another in our particulars as well as remarkably alike in our generalized outlooks.

What, exactly, is an attitude? We will start with a general definition and build upon it: *an attitude is a tendency or predisposition to respond in a specific manner to particular stimuli (including people, objects, and situations).*

Not all tendencies to respond or behave in certain ways can be regarded as attitudes, however (Figure 15.3). Additional criteria are necessary. Sherif and Sherif (1956) suggested five characteristics of attitudes that we can use to amplify our basic definition:

1 Attitudes are learned. This characteristic distinguishes attitudes from inborn predispositions,

such as physiological drives. Hunger, for example, is a physiological drive—but the type of food an individual seeks is based on social learning. Thus, a preference for meat over fish is an attitude.

2 Attitudes are reasonably long lasting. Although attitudes can change, like all learned responses they seldom fluctuate from moment to moment. The individual who has the attitude that he must appear at work correctly dressed will groom himself even on a morning when he feels groggy and out of sorts. His attitude dominates his mood.

3 Attitudes are directed toward specific referents (stimuli). They are found in response to specific stimuli that the individual can identify readily.

4 Attitudes can be held toward persons, objects, groups, institutions, ideas, and processes. The stimuli that elicit an attitude can be just about anything—liver, college kids, politicians, moon flights.

5 Attitudes are based, at least in part, on drives. This characteristic distinguishes attitudes from predispositions that are merely well-established habits. The predisposition to open a door with the right hand, for example, is merely a well-learned habit, whereas predispositions to respond in specific ways toward a particular religion often involves drives and, hence, are attitudes.

Figure 15.3   *Overt behavior is not always a good indication of an attitude.*

VISIT

Verbalized attitudes Subtle verbal expressions often reveal our feelings about a person or object. Mehrabian (1966) describes how our choice of words allows others to know more than we intend to say. In general, Mehrabian's principle is that the cooler and more formal our verbal description of our interaction with a person or object, the more distant is our actual interaction with that person or object. For example, if you say, "He and I live in the same room," you are showing a cooler attitude toward the person than if you were to say, "He is my roommate." In the same way, describing someone as "a girl I know" implies less proximity than "my girlfriend"; "my wife's sister" is more distant than "my sister-in-law." Also, "my mother-in-law" implies a greater immediacy, for better or for worse, than does "my wife's mother."

Mehrabian calls this an "immediacy scale" and contends that the less immediate our stated verbal relationship with a person or object, the more negative our feelings toward that person or object.

Beliefs and opinions

Although the terms "attitude," "belief," and "opinion" are often used interchangeably, psychologists make distinctions among them, A *belief* may be loosely defined as the acceptance of a statement or proposition as a fact or a truth. A belief does not necessarily predispose an individual to act in a particular way, because it does not necessarily make him "for" or "against." To believe, for example, that English tradition fostered American democracy does not require taking action based on that belief.

Opinions are even less well defined. Some psychologists hold that an opinion is a weakly held belief. As such, opinions may frequently change with changing circumstances. A voter who has observed a number of administrations may be of the opinion that, on the whole, Republicans have sounder financial programs. But if a Democrat succeeds in effecting major budget control, this voter may change his opinion.

MEASUREMENT OF ATTITUDES

An understanding of human attitudes is very useful to psychologists in predicting individual behavior. It is equally useful to social and political leaders who study the attitudes, opinions, and beliefs of groups in order to formulate policies their followers will accept. In each instance, although the *prevalence* of an attitude or attitudes is important, the *intensity* of an attitude is at least as significant. If we do not know the strength of an attitude, we cannot predict its influence.

Attitude scales

One of the devices used to measure attitudes is the *attitude scale*. A psychologist uses an attitude scale to assign a numerical score that indicates the strength of a particular attitude held by the individual being tested. To determine the range of public opinion on a given subject, individual numerical attitude ratings are compared.

The Thurstone scale   One of the earliest and best known attitude scales, developed by L. L. Thurstone (Thurstone and Chave, 1929), can be used to measure attitudes on any topic. The procedures followed in constructing and administering a Thurstone scale are described below.

1 *Choosing and defining an issue*—The investigator begins by deciding the kinds of attitudes he wants to measure. For example, he may decide to measure attitudes toward religion, or war, or morality.
2 *Collecting relevant statements*—The investigator then accumulates as many statements relevant to his topic as possible. The statements must be clear, simple, and unambiguous. Here are two sample statements chosen from a measurement of attitudes toward war: "War is the best way to preserve a nation's honor"; "All nations should disarm immediately."
3 *Presenting the statements to judges*—The investigator gives his list of relevant statements to a large group of judges, preferably more than 100. Each judge sorts the statements into 11 piles, based on the attitude he feels is expressed by each statement. Attitudes may range from extremely favorable to extremely unfavorable, on a numerical scale from 1 to 11.
4 *Selecting a group of statements*—Next, the investigator selects a limited number of the statements (usually 20) that most of the judges rated similarly on the numerical scale. A median rating of the scale value for each of the selected statements is prepared.
5 *Administering the scale*—Once the statements have been selected, the investigator presents them to the group or groups that he wishes to study. Respondents are asked to check each statement they agree with.
6 *Scoring the results*—To score each individual's responses, the investigator may either average the scale values of the items checked or select the individual's median score. This procedure provides him with a numerical score that indi-

cates how positive or negative the respondent's attitude toward the issue is.

Social distance Triandis and Triandis (1966), in an attempt to standardize the study of attitudes toward other people, used Thurstone's method to construct a "social distance" scale.

This scale consisted of 11 statements, each indicating a different degree of social distance. The scale was constructed as follows: A large number of statements were rated by judges. "I would marry this person" indicated 0 social distance and "I would kill this person" indicated 100 social distance. Intermediate statements were rated, and each was assigned a social distance value from 0 to 100.

Once the scale was developed, subjects were presented with the names of people and asked to check the statement that most closely expressed their feelings toward each person.

The use of these statement scales allows experimenters to quantify each subject's social distance relative to a particular person. In this manner, social distance and cultural norms can be studied and compared within a society and between societies.

The Likert scale Another frequently used attitude scale is that created by R. Likert (1932). It, too, involves the choice of an issue and the collection of a large number of relevant statements, but it differs from the Thurstone scale in that the first, large list of statements is judged differently. A judge in a Likert scale study is instructed to indicate how he feels about each statement by reacting in one of the following ways: strongly approve; approve; undecided; disapprove; strongly disapprove. Items that are frequently correlated by the judges (for example, two items consistently marked "strongly approve" by the judges) are retained; infrequently correlated statements are discarded. This system of evaluation has two advantages: it makes the discard of nonessential statements easier, and statements that remain tend to be grouped in clusters. The clusters permit accurate measurement of individual attitudes. When, for example, Likert constructed a scale to measure attitudes toward America's involvement in foreign wars, the statement-evaluating process left him with two distinct statement clusters. One

dealt with problems related to imperialism, the other with internationalism—two words that, for most Americans, have highly loaded negative and positive connotations, respectively.

Polling

The United States is the most polled nation in the world. Polls measure the intentions of the electorate, the consumer, the business executive, the television watcher, the student, the religionist, the suburbanite, and the inner-city citizen. Polls are so common and so well publicized that they actively influence responses, as suggested in the effect of the Gallup and Roper polls on the Dewey-Truman presidential contest in 1948. (It is widely believed that the polls, which showed Dewey a substantial winner, combined with Truman's "give-'em-hell" campaigning, produced a wave of public support for Truman—and brought out the vote that carried him into office.)

Polls differ significantly from attitude scales in that they are usually used to measure the attitudes of entire populations (for example, all Americans, all college students, all the residents of Sandusky, Ohio, all women between 18 and 25), rather than those of smaller groups. The pollster cannot ordinarily reach an entire population, however. To conduct an effective poll, he must do two things: develop a satisfactory *representative sample* to poll for predictive evidence of the attitudes of the population under study, and devise a question or set of questions that elicit the actual attitudes of the polled sample.

Polls and questions Because the group surveyed is almost invariably large, the poll taker usually has little time to spend with each individual polled. His questions must be precise. He should eliminate questions that respondents cannot answer because they lack information and that most will not answer because the answers are embarrassing or damaging. The pollster should also avoid questions that bias the response. "You're in favor of freedom of speech, aren't you?" is a question with a built-in bias. Because people frequently try to win the poll taker's approval by saying what they think he wants to hear, it is essential that questions place the poll taker in a completely neutral position.

A biased poll   In 1948 *The Reader's Digest* conducted a poll to determine the outcome of the forthcoming presidential election. It asked its 13 million or so subscribers to send in a ballot indicating who they were going to vote for as president of the United States. The results were overwhelmingly in favor of Thomas E. Dewey. To everyone's astonishment, Harry Truman was elected.

Where did the magazine go wrong? Did its readers send in their true preferences? The readers certainly did, and had voting privileges been confined to *Reader's Digest* subscribers only, Dewey would no doubt have won. However, the subscribers were not representative of the whole population. All other voters were not the middle-class working people represented by *Reader's Digest* subscribers. In short, the sample was biased.

FORMATION OF ATTITUDES

Polls and scales are designed to measure existing attitudes. These measures do not, however, reveal how attitudes are formed. Attitudes are learned, usually in a social context; we tend to adopt the attitudes of the people with whom we are in close association. Within our own groups, we are rewarded for expressing attitudes acceptable to the group. Many of our attitudes are acquired ready-made, as when we imitate the attitudes of others, but some depend on our personalities and our experiences as individuals.

Group influences

Our attitudes are significantly influenced by membership in groups. It has been suggested that the similarity of attitudes among the members of closely knit groups may be explained in four ways (Krech, Crutchfield, and Ballachey, 1962):

1 The group exerts pressure on members to conform.
2 People seek groups whose attitudes are congenial to their own.
3 All group members are exposed to the same information.
4 A new member takes on the group's attitudes in order to be accepted by the group.

The small groups to which we have the most direct relationship, such as family and friends, exert the most influence. But even such broad or abstract groups as the culture or social class play key roles.

Culture   Culture exerts a constant and powerful influence on the individual. Culture is the context in which the individual perceives his social relationships—the mass of traditions and customs, obligations and values that define his world.

The *cross-cultural method*, which compares aspects of two or more different cultures, has been used to determine the prevalence of particular attitudes in a culture. Resulting data has indicated that societies vary in certain patterns of attitudes and that such patterns are reflected in individual attitudes. Societal tendencies are just that—tendencies—and the cross-cultural method can tell us only of *average* differences and similarities between societies.

Study of feminism   Brotman and Senter (1968) conducted a cross-cultural study to determine the attitudes of people of various cultures toward feminism.

Unmarried and married males and females in a number of countries filled out attitude scales on feminism. These scales yielded the following rank ordering from low (anti) to high (pro) on feminism: Moroccan male, American male (in USA), French male, German female, German male, French female, American female (in Europe), English male, English female, American male (in Europe), American female (in USA).

The influence of a culture on attitudes can also be studied by comparing the attitudes of the various subgroups and social classes within that culture. Many studies, particularly in the United States, have uncovered attitude differences that directly reflect differences in educational, economic, and religious backgrounds. Among them, for example, have been studies indicating that those in the upper socioeconomic classes tend to hold liberal views with regard to foreign affairs and civil liberties and conservative views with regard to economic issues, whereas the attitudes of those in the lower socioeconomic classes tend to be exactly the reverse. Prediction of attitude on the basis of social class membership is becoming more and more difficult, however. The college population, particularly, tends to hold social beliefs grounded in intellectual and moral commitment rather than economic considerations.

Family The family has always been the most important social group. It is the earliest agency of socialization; the attitudes it instills in the individual are generally the most enduring. Within the family, parents exert the most influence on the child. Themselves products of their culture, they present cultural attitudes and practices to the child. But parents are individuals as well as participants in a culture. The cultural attitudes they present are those they have accepted or modified through their own experience. Since parental influence is constant during the child's early formative years, his attitudes and beliefs almost always reflect some aspect of his parents' attitudes and beliefs, even after he has grown up.

The process of *identification* plays an important part in the transmission of attitudes in a family. A child, for example, tends to identify with a parent and in so doing he incorporates many of the parent's attitudes, particularly moral attitudes.

Both parents may be identification models, but one parent is usually more dominant than the other. In most families, the male child tends to identify with the father and the female child with the mother. But the identification pattern is not always that simple, for a dominating parent may be the identification model for both boys

and girls. An affectionate and attentive parent tends to be a significant model (Bandura, 1962; Mussen and Parker, 1965). Psychoanalytic theory suggests, however, that identification may come from fear or envy of a parent. In describing the Oedipus complex, Freud (1910) asserted that young boys at a certain stage of development (phallic stage) are sexually attracted to their mothers and thus fear their fathers. They resolve this problem by identifying with the father in order to be more like him.

Politics and family Are political activists on college campuses really rebels? Are they rebelling against the political ideals and parties of their parents? Westby and Braungart (1966) compared the backgrounds of students on a university campus belonging, respectively, to either a far-right or a far-left student group. They found that the political views of these students could best be understood in terms of their backgrounds.

Students on the right generally came from lower-income working-class families, whereas those on the left came from a more affluent and higher social class. The researchers suggested that those of lower class and income status joined rightist groups because they felt insecure in their social position. Thus, they conformed to the accepted modes of society in a quest for security; as Richard Hofstadter has put it, "conformity is a way of guaranteeing and manifesting respectability among those who are not sure that they are respectable enough." The more secure higher classes could afford to deviate from the norm without threat to their feeling of "respectability." The actions of young people in joining either the political left or the right may thus be seen not as a rebellion but as ways of acting out the class consciousness of their respective parents.

Also, when the students' parents were asked to give their political party affiliation, 68 percent of the parents of "leftist" students were affiliated with either the Democratic or Socialist parties; only 29 percent of the parents of "rightist" students were so affiliated. Seventy-one percent of the "rightist" parents, as opposed to 32 percent of the "leftist" parents, identified with the Republican party. It seems clear, then, that a student's political views are very often a direct reflection of his parents' views.

Persons with very strict and punitive moral codes often acquire them through identification with a harsh or punitive parent. This form of identification is called *identification with the aggressor*. According to Anna Freud (1937), it is a process by which a fearful child takes on the aggressive characteristics of the threatening person and thereby resolves his own fear by becoming like that person.

In some cases, the family induces attitudes in children that are in opposition to those held by the family. A child may revolt against the strict discipline of his parents and thereby reject their attitudes. If his parents hold conservative views, he may tend toward very radical views; if they advocate capital punishment, he will denounce it; if they favor birth control, he will be against it.

The peer group The individual's peer group consists of his friends and acquaintances—the people he sees as social equals. As the child grows, he spends more and more time with his peers. They exert an ever-increasing influence on his attitudes, for he relies on his peers for social approval, advice, companionship, and entertainment. Gradually, the peer group becomes the most important group shaping the way he thinks and acts.

In one well-known study, a social psychologist (Newcomb, 1943) investigated the influence of peers on individuals' attitudes. His subjects were a group of girls who attended Bennington College in the mid-1930s. Most came from the middle or upper socioeconomic class and originally held conservative political and economic views typical of their class. Under the influence of the college community, however, many strongly supported the policies of the liberal New Deal.

Not every girl modified her views to the same degree, of course. It is interesting to note that the girls whose attitudes became most liberal were regarded by their peers as being highly involved in the college community. Conversely, the girls who remained essentially conservative despite the increasing liberalism of their peer group tended to participate least in the life of the community. Attitudes do not become changed in isolation. To be affected by the attitudes of the group, the individual must interact with the group.

Attitudes and personality

The individual personality is the filter through which the influence of others must pass. The acceptance of attitudes, whatever their source, depends on the individual's motivation at the moment and his personality characteristics of long standing.

Early studies sought to determine whether certain attitudes are associated with given personality traits. One study (Dexter, 1939) measured attitudes of women students toward political and social issues. The students were divided into radical, moderate, and conservative groups, according to their replies to certain questions. Using the scores on personality tests taken by the students, the investigator found that the radical students tended to be more introverted, more self-sufficient, and more dominant than the conservative and the moderate students. He concluded that the personality traits of introversion, self-sufficiency, and dominance in women inclined them toward the adoption of unconventional beliefs and attitudes.

Individuals often acquire attitudes that are consonant with their personalities. While attitudes usually reflect an individual's personality, they are not always predictable. Human behavior is very complex; there are too many interacting variables to rely on a single set of formulas. While it may be true that many political conservatives show such personality traits as lack of self-awareness and poor self-confidence (McClosky, 1958), there are many other conservatives whose personalities show considerable self-awareness and a high degree of self-confidence. As a result of certain experiences, an individual may acquire attitudes that seem to contradict one another or to contradict his personality.

PREJUDICE

A *prejudice* is a fixed attitude toward a person or group of people. It is an irrational judgment based not on facts but on emotion. The word "prejudice" commonly is used to indicate a negative judgment; it suggests hostility toward another person, group, or object. However, it may also refer to a positive judgment, a prejudice toward only tall basketball players, for example. In this section we will examine prejudice in its most destructive form: the hatred of individuals because they belong to certain groups. We will discuss how individuals acquire prejudiced attitudes, the social supports they find for their prejudices, and the destructive effects of prejudice.

Formation of prejudice

Prejudice is an attitude produced, like other attitudes, by social learning and personality variables. Psychologists believe that the best way to eliminate prejudice is to keep prejudiced attitudes from being acquired in the first place. Therefore, they are deeply interested in the origins of prejudice.

Beginning of prejudice Prejudice can begin simply with a child's realization that some people seem different from himself and his family. It has been shown that white children between the ages of 2 and 6 may regard dark-colored dolls as different from white dolls and therefore undesirable (Ammons, 1906). When such misperceptions are supported by parental attitudes, the seeds of prejudice are planted.

Attitude transfer, in which a prejudiced person influences the development of prejudice in someone else, is very common. But whether or not persons who come into contact with a prejudiced individual acquire his prejudices depends on the influence of the transmitter of prejudice.

Since children's attitudes are largely shaped by their parents, it is not surprising that a high positive correlation exists between parents' and children's prejudices. Unfortunately, prejudiced parents often train their children to be prejudiced, impressing upon them the notion that a certain group is inferior. The children learn that to gain parental approval they must behave as their parents do toward members of this group. The children are given specific reasons for disliking the group, with the parents themselves acting as models of hate for the children to imitate.

Children also develop prejudices from contact with prejudiced teachers and other adults, from their friends, and from misunderstandings resulting from carelessly presented information. Prejudice among children can be likened to a contagious disease; it is easy to acquire, and it spreads rapidly.

Occasionally, prejudice results when an individual has a bad experience with a member of a particular group and generalizes his feelings toward the individual to all members of the group. Usually, however, people do not develop a prejudice against a whole group because of a single unpleasant or painful contact. But when an individual is insecure and defensive, he may respond to a negative experience with prejudice as a way of dealing with his own feelings of inadequacy.

Changing social attitudes A method of changing the racial attitudes of schoolchildren was reported by Litcher and Johnson (1969). Two groups of second-graders in an overwhelmingly white Midwestern city (black population under 100) were tested for their racial attitudes toward blacks. One group used a second-grade reader with all white characters, while the other group used a multiethnic reader. The two readers were basically alike. However, the multiethnic reader contained pictures of black people. Also, the black characters in the multiethnic reader were depicted in a way that was diametrically opposed to the stereotype black; they were shown as middle class, hard-working, nicely dressed, and so on.

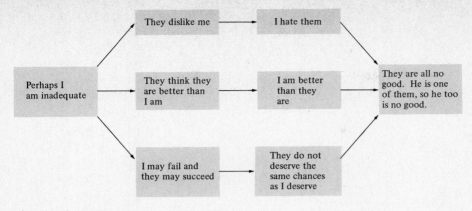

Figure 15.4   *Prejudice emerges from self-doubts, projection, and defense.*

It was expected that "ready contact" with unstereotyped blacks would substantially eliminate the children's stereotypes and much of the prejudice toward blacks. The results confirmed the investigators' expectations. The children using the multi-ethnic readers showed a greater decrease in prejudice on postexperimental tests than did those using the regular reader. Schools, then, can do a great deal toward preventing or eradicating prejudice.

Projection

Investigators frequently find that the bigot needs his prejudices because they provide him with an outlet for hostility, aggression, and feelings of inadequacy. He copes with his self-doubts by *projecting* negative feelings about himself onto a group other than his own and then defending his own position. Rational appeals to the person whose prejudices serve a defensive function invariably fail and may sometimes serve to increase prejudice. In such cases, the cognitive dissonance caused by a presentation of factual data is reduced by a vehement rejection of the facts and a passionate defensive clinging to the prejudiced attitudes. Figure 15.4 depicts one course for the development of a prejudice.

Projection and prejudice According to Mussen's 1950 study on prejudice, children who are high in prejudice also feel more hostility toward their par-

ents. Adorno, Frenkel-Brunswick, Levinson, and Sanford (1950) have shown that those who are high in prejudice report a harsh and threatening home discipline and see their parents as being forbidding and distant:

Family relationships are characterized by fearful subservience to the demands of the parents and by an early suppression of impulses not acceptable to them.

Because children are not able to express their suppressed impulses in relation to their parents or anyone resembling their parents, they project their impulses onto those most unlike their parents, that is, onto persons in groups different from their own. Thus, in such cases prejudice is a projection of the impulses the child dares not express directly.

The prejudiced person, often driven by self-doubt and feelings of inadequacy, uses his prejudice to construct a social hierarchy in which the objects of his hatred are at the bottom and he is near the top. In this way, he creates an identifiable group of people to whom he *always* feels superior. Regardless of how the world may evaluate or ignore him, he can reinforce his worth with the assumption that he was born superior to a great many people. An individual's prejudices will tend to expand; the wider his net, the more people to whom he will be able to feel superior.

Displaced aggression and scapegoating Prejudices also take root because they provide an outlet for aggressive responses that cannot be carried out directly. If a person feels hostile and frustrated because he cannot obtain the things he wants—or if the cause of his frustration is a person of superior status or a situation he cannot control—he will look around for a substitute on which to vent his rage with impunity. The substitute action is called *displaced aggression*. Displaced aggression usually is directed at people who cannot retaliate.

In one study (Miller and Bugelski, 1948) boys at a summer camp were subjects in a test of the power of displaced aggression. The boys were frustrated by not being permitted to see a movie that had been promised to them. Their attitudes toward two minority groups (Mexican and Japanese) were measured before and after the frustration. The boys showed considerably more prejudice after the frustration than before the movie was withdrawn.

The use of displaced aggression in such a situation is called *scapegoating*. A minority group usually becomes the scapegoat for the prejudiced individual's feelings of frustration and aggression. The scapegoat receives the hostility felt by the prejudiced individual, who tells himself that all his failures are the fault of the scapegoat. Adolf Hitler managed to convince his followers that Germany's social and economic ills were the fault of "international Jewry," and the millions of Jews murdered in concentration camps by the Nazis thus became the most tragic victims of scapegoating of our time.

Maintaining prejudiced attitudes An individual with a prejudice uses it in his everyday life, along with his other attitudes. But unlike other attitudes, prejudice requires constant support, since it is essentially irrational and frequently contradicted by reality. So the individual must evaluate all his experiences in the dim, distorting light of his prejudice. Because his prejudice constantly affects his perceptions, the prejudiced response continues to grow stronger.

An individual maintains his prejudices by constantly finding "evidence" to support them and discarding any information that runs counter to them. He perceives only those things about the target group that support his prejudices. What he really wants is a consistent, comfortable view of life—and he will not accept anything that is inconsistent with the patterns he perceives.

Personality characteristics in prejudice

Personality variables play an important role in the formation of prejudices. Various studies tend to support the proposition that certain personality characteristics *predispose* people toward prejudices. One large-scale study by Adorno and associates (1950) identified a group of people who exhibit a tendency to glorify groups to which they belong and to display hostility toward groups to which they do not belong. This attitudinal pattern is called *ethnocentrism*. From this and other studies, we can draw a composite portrait of a typical ethnocentric personality.

1 *He is moralistic.* He rigidly defends his society's conventions. In the United States, he would, for example, probably be a staunch advocate of the idea that sex should never be discussed in the presence of children.
2 *He is authoritarian.* Because he believes that the world is essentially hostile and dangerous, he seeks security in the form of a strong ruler. He desires a definite social hierarchy in which each individual knows his place.
3 *He oversimplifies his intepersonal relationships.* People are all good or all evil, 100 percent right or wrong.
4 *He projects any socially disapproved tendencies he may have onto others.* If, for example, he has a desire to steal, he may very well feel that all members of a group he dislikes are thieves.
5 *He tends to support current political and economic policies.* His desire for clear lines of authority in the social order leads him to prefer very conservative views, although a conservative point of view does not necessarily indicate that an individual is ethnocentric.

Oversimplified relationships Adorno, Frenkel-Brunswick, Levinson, and Sanford (1950) found that prejudiced people are very rigid in their attitudes and their perceptions of people and things. They tend to attribute good traits only to themselves and their parents and friends, and to rationalize their faults as being very minor or harmless. They also tend to make blanket condemnations of others for even the slightest fault. For example, a highly prejudiced person may describe women as either "pure" or "unpure," or "good" or "bad"; he will not qualify his opinions.

The following are descriptions given by a highly prejudiced individual of (1) his mother and (2) members of a minority group:

1 *Most terrific person in the world* to me. (Q. Any shortcomings?) Well I don't really think she has any, except may be too wound up in her home, and didn't take interest in social affairs . . . *I truthfully can't say she has any shortcomings.*
2 The majority are ignorant, close to animals as anything else. I mean *dumb* animals.

Such prejudiced persons have a low tolerance for ambiguity. They see things as either good or bad, big or little, high or low; they seem unable to perceive the middle ground.

Effects of prejudice

Prejudice is one of the oldest and most serious problems of mankind. If enough people in a society share a set of prejudices, they can create social conditions that appear to provide objective evidence for their prejudice. An example of this can be found in our own society. Consistent denial of educational opportunities has severely handicapped blacks in America, so that when they take intelligence tests designed by whites for whites, their lower scores support a common white prejudice that the black is inherently less intelligent. The vicious and self-perpetuating nature of this system is obvious. In one form or another, it has been repeated many times, in many places.

Prejudiced people avoid the groups they dislike. They also work hard to persuade others that any contact with members of such groups is dangerous and unhealthy. The histories of almost all ghettos, past and present, are incredible records of pogrom and massacre, abuse and extermination, segregation and degradation.

Eliminating prejudice

Can prejudice ever be eliminated on a mass scale? Is it possible to eliminate the influence of prejudiced groups on attitude formation? Can prejudiced responses be extinguished? In theory, such goals are within the realm of possibility—we often know what must be done. But knowing is not the same as doing. If we are to eliminate or reduce individual or group prejudice, we must take the following measures:

1 Work to prevent primary groups from teaching prejudice to children. More adults must become aware that prejudices are harmful influences on personality.
2 Communicate accurate information about different groups to people who appear to be prejudiced, even though this is difficult because their prejudice may make them distort such information and reject it.
3 Provide, whenever possible, positive reinforcement for any evidences of unprejudiced behavior, and seek to eliminate reinforcement for the display of prejudice. This approach must be used carefully because it may produce conflict in the individual, and to reduce the conflict, the individual may give up his unprejudiced behavior rather than his prejudice.
4 Increase contacts beween groups. This is probably the most workable method of eliminating prejudice.

The authoritarian Martin and Westie (1959) used a scale to organize the results of interviews that elicited subjects' prejudices. The subjects were then classified as either "tolerant" or "prejudiced" and were administered a battery of personality tests to see whether the tests would differentiate between tolerant and prejudiced attitudes. They did.

Prejudiced individuals were shown to be more nationalistic, intolerant of ambiguity, and superstitious. They had a more suspicious, competitive, "jungle" attitude toward life and the people around them (exemplified by such statements as "If a person doesn't look out for himself, nobody else will") and, perhaps most significantly, had a higher score on the F scale, which measures the authoritarian personality. The measure includes such statements as "What youth needs most is strict discipline, rugged determination, and the will to fight for family and country." People who agree with this line of thought tend to be more authoritarian and generally more prejudiced.

ATTITUDE CHANGE

Attitudes usually are based on a person's accumulated experiences rather than on any single situation. Although not easily changed, attitudes are not *necessarily* permanent. An attitude can be modified, discarded, or replaced—usually in response to new information. Many things can cause an individual to change his attitudes. In this section, we will be concerned with three particularly important ways: persuasion, membership in a new group, and increased familiarity with the object of the attitude.

Persuasion

Individuals sometimes change their attitudes because they have been *persuaded* by information received from others. Persuasion requires a *communicator, a message,* and an *audience* (even if the audience consists of only one person). Let us summarize the findings of various studies in this area (see, for example, Bochner and Insko, 1966).

The communicator The degree of attitude change possible in an audience depends largely on its evaluation of the source of the communication.

1 When the audience regards the communicator as credible, there will be a greater immediate change in attitude than if they regard him as untrustworthy. In time, however, people tend to forget the source of a message and remember only the message. This phenomenon is sometimes referred to as the *sleeper effect*. In the long run, it does not appear to matter greatly, for example, whether the communicator in a television commercial appears to be a doctor (more credible) or a housewife (less credible); people will (or will not) purchase the product solely on the basis of the message.

2 If the audience perceives that the communicator has attitudes similar to its own, the communicator will be more successful. The politician who persuades voters that he is a "man of the people" takes advantage of this fact. Moreover, if the audience knows *in advance* that the communicator thinks as they do, he will be even more successful in persuading them to accept some particular point or points. This has been shown to hold true regardless of the content of the persuasive message.

Fear-arousing communication Berkowitz and Cottingham (1960) exposed groups of students to taped lectures on the importance of safety belts in cars. The students were separated into two groups; each group heard a slightly different lecture.

One lecture was impersonal, factual, and relied heavily on statistics to bring home its point. The lecture was only minimally fear-arousing.

The second lecture, although it included basically the same arguments, was delivered on a more personal and emotional pitch. The lecturer used slides which depicted gruesome car accidents that were considered highly frightening.

A month before the experiment, both groups of subjects had filled out a questionnaire on various issues, including safety belts. The opinions expressed at that time were compared to those expressed on a questionnaire answered after listening to the lecture. The experimenters were thus able to determine whether opinion change had occurred and by how much. Results showed that the fear-producing lecture had produced more opinion change than the dry, statistical one.

Propaganda A special type of persuasion involves the use of propaganda, an attempt to influence the attitudes of others by means of the "hard sell," emotional appeals, and sometimes misinformation. Propaganda seeks attitude change in a definite direction. In this it differs from education, which we define as a process for developing an individual's ability to think critically and to form independent conclusions. Propaganda may be used in an attempt to persuade individuals to abandon reasoned behavior in favor of irrationality. Propaganda, then, is a powerful weapon in the hands of demagogues—disseminators of the "big lie."

RESISTANCE TO ATTITUDE CHANGE

Some attitudes can be changed only with great difficulty or not at all. And some individuals resist attitude changes much more vigorously than do others. Against the unending barrage of propaganda, what processes serve to preserve individual attitudes? We can identify three: *selective perception*; *avoidance* (of information that is likely to change an attitude); and *group support* (social pressure to maintain existing attitudes).

Selective perception

The sum of an individual's attitudes is his view of the world. The world may seem to him warm and accepting, hostile and rejecting, or something in between these poles. When he has a new experience or receives new information, he tends to emphasize only the aspects of the experience or of the data that fit his world view. Suppose an individual believes that the members of a certain group are dirty by nature. When he sees members of that group, he will look at their appearance to find evidence that will confirm his belief. Finding no dirt will not weaken his belief; finding dirt will strengthen it. His prejudice dictates what he pays attention to, what he perceives. This is *selective perception*, and it causes resistance to attitude change because it reinforces and strengthens existing attitudes. Selective perception is encouraged by the ambiguity of most social experiences—any experience involving others can usually be interpreted in a variety of ways.

Perceptual vigilance Cantril (1957), citing some observations of Allport, showed that a person looking at two different pictures in a stereoscopic slide sees only the face that contains features that are most significant to him. When a South African Zulu looked at a European face paired with an Indian face, and a Negro face paired with an Indian face, he tended in each instance to see only the Indian face. The Zulu, who is often prejudiced against Indians because they pose an economic threat to him, exhibited perceptual vigilance: he saw the type of face that worried him most.

Avoidance

An individual is always on the lookout for evidence that confirms his attitudes. But information that contradicts his attitudes tends to make him uncomfortable. He actively avoids such information whenever he can. The *avoidance* technique is sometimes called the *ostrich phenomenon*. A liberal ostrich often refuses to read *The National Review*; a conservative ostrich ignores *The New Republic*.

To ignore or discount information, it is not necessary to avoid the experience. Have you ever been part of a "captive audience," where you had no choice but to remain while the speaker offered views contradictory to your own? Later, when asked about the speech, you may have found yourself replying with perfect candor, "I don't know. Didn't hear a word the man said."

Group support

The individual's membership in social groups can produce strong resistance to change in his attitudes. Going along with the group is usually comfortable and safe, but displaying attitudes that run counter to group norms can disrupt the group's social patterns, leading to group criticism of the disrupting individual.

Because the members of a group tend to

pool all information that supports group attitudes, and because the group provides social support, group affiliations stabilize an individual's attitudes.

COMMUNITY PSYCHOLOGY

Community psychology is concerned with the individual and his relationship to the community. Actually we belong to many communities at once: we relate to others through our family, school, work, church, and, in a less direct way, through politics, the legal system, the market place, social agencies, and the other institutions of society. Thus we see that the scope of community psychology is very wide.

As our society grows more urban, it acquires more community organizations of increasing importance. The older, more established agencies now find themselves under pressure to adapt to a rapidly changing urban society with new social expectations; they must be able to satisfy the changing needs of the people they serve if they are to influence society as a whole. Schools, welfare and social aid organizations, churches, and the police are being made aware that they must modify or discard old approaches and institute dramatically different ones. The local minister may thus conduct a youth seminar on drugs; the welfare agency may support an able-bodied adult who leaves a dead-end job to pursue a college education. New as well as established programs call for psychologists who can assist community organizations to deal effectively with their clients and can help them with problems of staffing, personnel training, and program development and implementation.

Because it is widely recognized that solutions to many kinds of community problems rely on the same basic principles and techniques, general training programs are being developed for psychologists in all areas of specialization. Such training has its basis in clinical as well as social psychology, since in many cases the skills used by a clinical psychologist in treating a single patient are those needed by community psychologists to counsel community agencies effectively.

The nonprofessional in community psychology

Paralleling psychology's involvement in community problems has been the development of the role of nonprofessionals in applied psychology. Lobey (1970) describes the movement of nonprofessionals into the mental health field as "the nonprofessional revolution." Beginning with programs in which college students served as aides and companions to patients in mental hospitals (Gruver, 1971), the movement now includes programs in which college students serve as play therapists and as companion-counselors for delinquents or school dropouts or for other students in need of friendly counsel. Even high school students have been tried out as "help agents" with hospitalized adolescents (Walker, Wolpin, and Fellows, 1967).

Housewives seeking ways to use their leisure time productively have also become involved in a variety of nonprofessional services. For example, as mental health counselors, they have proved to be very useful as therapeutic aides. In a similar vein, parents have been trained to carry out certain therapeutic programs with their own children. This, however, is often a difficult role for a parent, who cannot be expected to be objective and dispassionate in dealing with his or her own child. Parental therapy stands its best chance of success when the parents use methods of behavior modification and do not attempt to engage in the kind of relationship therapy used by psychoanalysts.

The behavior modification movement promises an important place for trained nonprofessionals in community psychology; it employs techniques that can be used successfully by nonprofessionals under the supervision of professionals. The role of the nonprofessional is not limited to the mental hospital or clinic. Community-based rehabilitation centers, such as the Residential Youth Center (Goldenberg, 1971), have been designed to help young men and women in the inner city. According to Goldenberg, the center is based on the concept that the problems of poor people are most effectively treated in their own neighborhood by people like themselves. The Residential Youth Center is thus staffed by individuals who have been helped by the center. It has been shown that the center is effective in aiding adolescents who are not usually helped by the standard mental health services (Cowen, 1973).

COMMUNITY MENTAL HEALTH

A primary concern of community psychology today is the promotion of *mental health* for all segments of society. Different groups in the general population have different problems, and treatment and prevention programs need to be tailored to the specific needs of each group. For example, a program involving residents of a slum neighborhood might help clients cope with drug usage, hunger, overcrowding, poverty, and crime. A suburban program, on the other hand, might help clients with problems of apathy, alienation, and alcoholism. Regardless of which problems are involved, all psychologists engaged in community mental health have the same goal: the successful prevention of behavior pathology or, when necessary, its treatment.

In general, Americans have given growing support to the effort of community psychologists. Over the last several decades, the public has become increasingly aware of the problem of behavior pathology in the community. It has been widely noted that one out of every four hospital beds in the United States is occupied by a person suffering from some form of behavior pathology. Almost everyone feels the pressures of our fast-moving society, and many of us have sought

help through psychological counseling and know others who have done the same. Public concern over community mental health has manifested itself in increased government support for research in behavior pathology and treatment. Medical doctors, psychologists, social workers, and other specialists have seen the need to cooperate with one another. Community psychologists have played an important part in this movement by conducting studies and setting up programs to promote public mental health.

Nationwide problems Gurin, Veroff, and Feld (1960) conducted a nationwide survey to determine the incidence of psychological problems in the general population and in subgroups within the population. Some of their findings were somewhat unexpected:

1 More than half the married Americans admitted that they felt inadequate as husbands or wives and less than half considered their marriages "very happy."
2 Nearly 25 percent of the Americans questioned admitted that they had felt on the verge of a nervous breakdown at some point in their adult lives, often because of tensions connected with their jobs.
3 More college-educated people suffered from anxiety symptoms than did those with less education.
4 The most common worry among Americans, regardless of age, group and background was financial insecurity.

Prevention

Community mental health is concerned with more than the treatment and rehabilitation of persons who are psychologically ill. It is also concerned with the prevention of behavior pathology. Workers in the mental health field engage in two types of preventative action: *primary prevention*, which aims at structuring life experiences, helping people to cope with life's problems so that behavior pathology may be averted; and *secondary prevention*, which attempts to identify and treat minor psychological disturbances before they become serious problems.

Primary prevention of behavior pathology has a larger, more ambitious scope than secondary prevention. Essentially, primary prevention aims at forestalling psychological trouble. Ideally, the psychologist reaches children during the formative years and helps them build resistance to stress that will later enable them to deal with frustration, anxiety, and fear. Thus, a community psychologist working in community mental health might practice primary prevention by advising parents and teachers on child-rearing problems or by setting up discussion and encounter groups to educate young people and parents on drug abuse and its causes.

The mental hospital

What happens when primary and secondary prevention fail? Or when primary and secondary prevention programs do not exist at all? People with minor problems may eventually solve them on their own; others may continue to make marginal adjustments to life situations, never really coming to grips with their difficulties, never really feeling content. Still others may finally reach a point where their problems seem to overwhelm them. Because they can no longer cope with life in the larger community, they seek help in the smaller community of the mental hospital.

The old image of the mental hospital is forbidding: a fortress-like building with barred windows, the patients confined to wards where they wander aimlessly or sit for hours staring, interacting only very infrequently with a therapist, if at all.

Many problems of the old-style "asylums" are common to all institutions that segregate their populations from contact with the outside community. Institutionalization of the mentally ill forces them to enter an unreal world, organized around totally different principles than the larger society that they have just left.

The therapeutic community

Community mental health workers no longer view the mental hospital as a last resort, a place to put the seriously disturbed for their own good and the good of the larger society. They view it, rather, as a *therapeutic community,* a place where people beset by uncontrollable anxieties can gradually be helped to deal with life in society. The concept of the therapeutic community holds that the disturbed patient, like the normal person, requires a community in which to live and interact with others. In the therapeutic community, the patient can be helped in many ways other than in regularly scheduled, formal therapy sessions. The patient's entire environment must be therapeutic if he is to improve his adjustment.

Environmental therapy The goal of *environmental therapy* in the therapeutic community is to better the patient's chances of recovery by preventing him from losing social contact. Staff members of the therapeutic community establish programs to provide hospitalized patients with normal social experiences to reduce their social disabilities.

Short-term therapy According to Sadock, Newman, and Normand (1968), short-term community group therapy programs are usually very effective. Even people of the lowest economic level, who are often not motivated to undergo psychotherapy, have been helped by this type of program. The group support that the individual receives helps him even more than the presence of the therapist, who often is seen by members of the group as an outside authority figure.

In one case, group therapy sessions were held once a week. The individuals received treatment within their own community and with fellow community leaders. When they found that others with whom they could identify had problems similar to their own, they felt less apprehension and were able to face their problems more realistically.

Patients' families are encouraged to visit frequently and to take the patients on outings. In another approach, groups of patients are taken off hospital grounds by staff members to attend community functions where they may interact with other members of society. Frequently, volunteers come to the hospital to spend time with patients. All these measures are designed to keep the patients aware that there are communities outside their protective hospital setting and that they are still part of those communities, to which they will eventually return as full participants.

Today, more and more institutions are incorporating the ideas of the therapeutic community and are turning away from the inhuman and largely custodial care of the patient characteristic of society's response to him up until now. Some hospital programs have gone beyond the limits of the usual measures to maintain a strong link between the disturbed patient and the community outside. These programs are structured so that the patient remains in the outside community for part of the day, and spends another part of his day in the therapeutic setting. Examples of such programs are the *day hospital*, where the patient lives at home and comes to the hospital during the day to participate in therapy programs; the *night hospital*, where the patient may hold a job, go to school, or perform some other normal daytime function, but returns to the hospital at night; and the *outpatient clinic*, where the patient merely comes to the hospital at regularly scheduled times for his therapy.

The halfway house This increasing recognition that therapy must prepare patients to cope with their environment outside a hospital setting has led to the establishment of a number of *halfway houses* for patients to live in after their release from the hospital (Raush and Raush, 1968). Such houses are designed to ease the transition from hospital to community. While their operations differ, they are usually run by ex-patients whose job it is to help fellow patients adjust to life outside.

The aged

Many old people feel useless and alienated. At a time in their lives when they find it difficult to adapt to change, old people face a variety of new experiences: retirement, loss of physical vigor, the deaths of contemporaries. Because these are difficult psychological problems, and because an increasing number of Americans survive well into old age, the problems of the aged have become an important concern for community mental health agencies.

Community mental health programs can help the elderly overcome their feelings of social uselessness. First, such programs can teach the public that total loss of ability does not necessarily accompany old age and that the aged can make a contribution to the community. Second, they can offer ways to keep the elderly usefully employed.

Here, then, is another area of community life where mental health workers can help. In programs to counsel the aged and their families, they can bring old people closer to the life of the community. Through public education, they can change the traditional image of old age, thereby helping to create more humanitarian attitudes toward elderly people.

CRIME PREVENTION AND TREATMENT OF OFFENDERS

The alarming increase in crime in the United States over the past decade has given rise to new concern over the role of our penal institutions (prisons, houses of detention or correction, reform schools). The *penal system* is the community instrument that deals with the criminal offender and with the prevention of crime within the community. All branches of the penal system—the police, the courts, and the prisons—have recently come under close scrutiny, for it has become clear that many of the traditional approaches to treatment of the criminal offender are not successful. In this section we will examine the penal system as part of community mental health. We will discuss problems of the penal system and the role psychology can play in improving the community's response to the offender.

Over and over, in cities and towns through-

Figure 15.5 *Prisoners are isolated not only from the community in which they lived, but also frequently from each other. (Cornell Capa— Magnum)*

out the United States, similar scenes are enacted: a taxi driver is robbed and shot; a young secretary returns home after work to find her apartment rifled and valuables missing; an old man is mugged and beaten for the five dollars in his wallet. With luck, the offender is apprehended, brought to a local police precinct, booked, and brought before a judge soon after his arrest. He is usually young, in his late teens or early twenties, poor, and very often addicted to drugs. Usually, he cannot afford the expense of a lawyer; he is defended by an attorney supplied by the state, who often does not have time to speak to him until a few minutes before the hearing. What happens to him if he is found guilty depends greatly on the gravity of his offense, his prior record, whether or not he is a drug addict, his age, and other factors. If he is a first offender —if he has no record—he may be released on probation; that is, he may be allowed to live at home, while reporting regularly to a supervising officer. If he has a record and if his offense is a serious one, he will probably be sent to prison.

Unfortunately, the prison system has many

of the worst features of the old-style mental hospital. There is no true community within the prison walls to replace the outside communities the inmates have lost. Perhaps more unfortunate, however, is that little or no effort is made to prepare the inmate for a successful resumption of life when his prison term is over (Figure 15.5).

Few prisons provide psychological diagnosis or treatment for prisoners; little attempt is made to prepare convicted criminals for the traumatic transition to prison life or to help them solve their problems once they are there. Attempts at rehabilitation are usually confined to work programs; in the few states in which education or other training programs have been instituted in prisons, such programs have been among the first to suffer budget cuts. Incarceration in the United States is at best custodial and at worst punitive.

Offenders who have served part of a prison sentence and are considered ready to resume life in society are often released on *parole*. The parole system frees the prisoner under controlled conditions and is designed to ease the transition between the prison community and society. However, parole officers are often overburdened, and rules are frequently too strict and unrealistic.

The successful parolee Gough, Wenk, and Rozynko (1965) administered personality tests to prisoners who were about to be paroled and reviewed their past records to find variables upon which to predict whether or not a given parolee would break his parole. They also conducted a follow-up study of those who had been paroled.

Results indicated that the prisoner's previous criminal record was the most reliable single indicator of the success or failure of parole. The earlier in life that a criminal embarked on his career, and the longer his criminal career, the less chance there was for his success as a parolee. However, the record is a better predictor when considered together with the prisoner's present personality structure. The successful parolee, according to Gough and his colleagues, "is a person who is conscientious and moderate, not in any way flamboyant and perhaps even unduly subdued." The unsuccessful parolee tends to be a "more narcissistic, restless under-controlled individual, too sure of himself and too quick to take offense when blocked or criticized."

The ex-convict on parole is at a greater disadvantage than the offender on probation in one important respect—he has been to prison and has a record. Society treats the ex-convict thoughtlessly and cruelly. The hostile attitudes he encounters make it nearly impossible for him to find rewarding work or understanding friends. A society that should go out of its way to smooth the path for released prisoners often forces them back into old patterns of behavior and old associations that lead to further criminal activities—and another trip to prison. A truly effective parole program depends not only on changes in parole procedures but also on a change in public attitudes.

Specialized treatment

Certain groups of offenders have special problems that preclude the usual prison treatment. For example, *drug addicts* and *juveniles* need specialized treatment as a means of preventing them from returning to criminal activity when they are released.

Drug addicts   The drug adict is a major offender in every urban area in this country. Drug addicts commit burglaries, muggings, and robberies as a means of supplying themselves with heroin or other drugs to support their habits. While many addicts engage in criminal activities for the sole purpose of obtaining money to purchase drugs, recent evidence indicates that some addicts may have a predilection for criminal behavior.

Addiction and crime   A study of the relationship between drug addiction and crime by Lukoff, Quatrone, and Hayim (1973) supports earlier findings that deviance and criminality often precede addiction. Moreover, the addict becomes part of a drug-crime culture that causes an increase in his criminal activities, which he may often continue after treatment.

The study was based on the lives of over 400 addicts in a methadone program administered by the Addiction Research and Training Corporation in the Bedford-Stuyvesant section of Brooklyn, New York. It found that patients who become involved in crime early in life are likely to become addicts at an early age. Of the addicts under study, 37.5 percent were arrested before becoming addicted; after addiction, the percentage rose to 83, with the sharpest increases in three areas; drug charges, property charges, and forgery charges. After entering methadone treatment, patients as a group displayed a gradual decrease in criminality, but significantly less marked than the decreases reported in earlier studies of methadone programs. The explanation given for this is that pioneer methodane programs were highly selective in admitting addicts for treatment, choosing those who appeared to be "rehabilitation prone," whereas the ARTC program, an unusually large one, includes many hard-core addicts with long criminal records.

A growing number of people recognize that the drug addict must be treated as a patient rather than a criminal. Although by law drug addicts must be imprisoned, they receive special treatment in prison. Addicted prisoners are separated from the rest of the inmate population and remanded to treatment centers where dependency on drugs is eliminated. Addicts are treated in one of two ways: they are either deprived of drugs immediately in order to remove both physiological and psychological dependency as rapidly as possible, or they receive a less harmful substance in place of the drug and the drug itself is gradually withdrawn.

There are several problems in the treatment of the addicted prisoner. Most important is the absence of motivation to stop using drugs. Prisoners are forced to withdraw from drug usage; they do not ordinarily do so on their own. The months or years spent in a special drug treatment program are often only "dry spells" for the addict; when he finishes his term, he returns to his old environment and the temptation of drugs.

Closely related to lack of motivation is a lack of effective counseling programs to support the drug user and motivate him during treatment. Most compulsory drug rehabilitation programs have a very poor record of achievement; an extremely high percentage of "graduates" of this type of program return to drug use and, eventually, to the cycle of arrest, imprisonment, release, and rearrest.

The best answer to both problems has come from outside the prison system. The concept of the therapeutic community has been successfully applied to the problem of drug addiction. Therapeutic communities are sometimes organized by former addicts, sometimes by mental health workers. Residents in these communities are usually self-referred; they are sufficiently motivated to stop drug use to have entered a drug program on their own. Treatment is based on many hours of group or individual counseling, and each member of the therapeutic community receives as much attention as possible. The therapeutic community offers the encouragement and positive reinforcement needed by the addict to overcome his habit. Whereas compulsory drug programs address themselves chiefly to the physical aspects of addiction, the therapeutic communities concentrate on the underlying causes of addiction.

Juvenile offenders The penal system also recognizes the need for specialized treatment of juvenile offenders. Society realizes that it cannot mete out the same punishment to a 14-year-old youngster as to an adult. Yet, while special juvenile courts, prisons, and reformatories have been set up, the same basic processes of probation, imprisonment, and parole are applied to the young delinquent as to the adult offender. Naturally, the same faults of the adult system plague the juvenile penal system.

The 14-year-old boy or girl who is arrested for shoplifting often comes from a chaotic home in which affection and trust are virtually nonexistent. There is frequently a history of disciplinary problems in school. The neighborhood idol may be the local drug dealer.

Such offenders are usually sentenced to a reformatory for about 6 months. In the reformatory they meet others like themselves and form friendships. They learn new ways to shoplift and not get caught, or how to use drugs. When they leave the reformatory 6 months later, they are usually 6 months farther along the road to a criminal future.

In this context it is easy to see that imprisonment of the juvenile offender is not an answer by itself. Although prospects for rehabilitation are probably much better with the young person, treatment of young offenders does not depend on the individual's capacities and limitations, but on the type of crime committed. At present, programs for the rehabilitation of juvenile offenders fail to respond sufficiently to the particular problems of the individual.

Rehabilitation The greatest challenge to the prison reformer is the *negative psychological atmosphere* of prisons. Inmates live in a strange and unnatural environment. They are deprived of normal companionship of the opposite sex, which puts a severe strain on their family relations and encourages homosexuality. The prison itself is an isolated community of offenders. Like any other community, it develops its own norms and rules of behavior which may be contrary to desirable patterns of behavior of communities outside.

Prison rehabilitation programs require the active cooperation of prison personnel. Unfortunately, many officials prefer to keep inmates locked in their cells because they are easier to manage this way. The problem of *idleness* within prisons is great and its influence demoralizing. Inmates soon learn to do as little as possible, and their repertoire of social responses may diminish, as is true of disturbed patients. Vigorous programs are needed to overcome the apathy that the present system produces among prisoners.

Despite the glaring faults of our penal system, there are certain encouraging developments. For instance, in some places new concepts of sentencing have been developed and applied. The *indeterminate-length sentence*, in which the offender receives a sentence of indefinite length —2 to 4 years, for example—allows greater flexibility in designing rehabilitation programs for the individual. An even newer idea is that of the *weekend sentence*, or non-working-hours sentence. Under this program, an offender serves his sentence in parts: he maintains a job in the community and returns to prison during his non-working hours until his sentence is completed. Although there is the risk that the offender will not return for his weekend in prison, experience has shown that this does not happen very often. Such a program allows the offender to maintain contact with his own community; it eliminates the usual strain of a prison sentence on family life and permits the offender to remain self-supporting. This last aspect of the weekend sentence program has a very practical advantage; it makes it unnecessary for the taxpayer to support either the offender in jail or his family because he cannot earn a living.

Violence

Violence has clearly become a problem of major social importance. Urban crime and violence has become a political issue as well as a social problem. Personal violence involving one individual against another seems to be increasing, and organized violence involving group against group is today overshadowing the quality of human life.

Movie violence It has been argued that observing violence enables people to express their own aggression vicariously and thus reduces aggressive urges. This catharsis theory of aggression reduction was discussed as long ago as 350 B.C. in the writings of Aristotle.

Research by modern psychologists calls the catharsis view into question. Berkowitz (1968) found that observing violence tends to increase rather than decrease aggression in the observer.

Such findings are regarded as highly pertinent to the kind of movies and TV programs shown to the public. Even a conservative interpretation suggests that violence in our society is not likely to be reduced while it is perpetuated on TV and movie screens.

Two recent reports of gang violence (Thompson, 1966; Bychowski, 1968) provide a view of how the group known as Hell's Angels became an angry, defiant gang. The gang members were, for the most part, frustrated individuals who bore grudges against society. The individual anger and resentment grew collectively into hatred for all those in authority and everyone who accepted the law and order required by society.

Group violence tends to be self-perpetuating. In the case of the Hell's Angels, each act of defiance or violence performed by the gang further inflamed society against them and society's reaction, in turn, strengthened the gang's hostility. Prevention of group violence is more manageable than treatment. Once group violence gets under way, it snowballs and is difficult to halt except by punitive means.

HUMAN RELATIONS TRAINING

By analyzing the human relations in a community, developing ideas on how they can be improved, and devising programs to implement these ideas, the psychologist works to improve human relations within the community. Human relations may be improved by teaching people skills that facilitate effective and satisfying interaction with others. Many techniques are used in *human relations training*, but we will discuss only three: the case method, sensitivity training, and role playing.

The case method

Groups that have problems with interpersonal relationships may be trained through the *case method*. In this technique, each person is instructed to analyze a fictitious case involving a group with problems similar to those of his own group. For instance, boys who create disciplinary problems in school might work with cases that depict the problems of young draftees in responding to authority. When the members of the community begin to discuss possible solutions, they simultaneously work out solutions to their own problems and engage in a human relations experience that aids their understanding. It is hoped that the solutions worked out in the case analysis will be transferred to the daily operations of the group.

Sensitivity training

Another group technique, *sensitivity training*, is perhaps the most popular approach to human relations training today. A less structured technique than the case method, sensitivity training can be organized in various ways. Basically, the procedure involves a small group of people who meet to discuss their problems and interpersonal feelings in an atmosphere of complete candor. The group may be composed of members of the same community or of people who are unacquainted. Group members spend a short time together in an isolated place, with a minimum of outside interference. The group leader uses various techniques to encourage honest interaction among members. The ultimate goal of the training is to increase each participant's self-awareness and insight into the behavior and attitudes of others. This, in turn, promotes acceptance of self and others and improves interpersonal relationships.

Role playing

An excellent method for getting people to understand the reactions and feelings of others is through *role playing*; the enactment of the roles of other community members. Usually a case is first presented on film, or through verbal or written instructions, or in a dramatized presentation using a prepared script. For example, for a group of teachers, the case might involve young Mexican-American students who feel that the faculty members of their high school lack understanding and appreciation of their cultural heritage and treat them with bias. After hearing the case, group participants assume various roles: one plays a student leader, one a teacher, another a school superintendent, and so forth. Keeping within limits set by instructions, participants act out the situation, fully involving themselves so that they feel as their characters might feel. Here again, it is hoped that the insights gained will be used in the larger community.

ENVIRONMENTAL PSYCHOLOGY

The influence of the environment on man has long concerned psychologists, but not until recently has psychology entered into the study of man's interaction with his environment. Too often, when we speak of intervention in nature, we think of large-scale events, such as the building of dams to change the course of rivers or the destruction of forests to make way for highways and homes. But intervention that changes ecological balances also occurs through small-scale events, as when a person drives his automobile to work and thereby, in a small way, contributes to the poisoning of the air that he and everyone else breathes.

Psychologists sensitive to environmental problems recognize that they involve the psychology of individuals as well as of governments and large organizations. They feel that individuals must be made aware of the long-range consequences of their daily actions, which, when multiplied, result in drastic environmental changes.

Merely preaching about ecological problems is clearly not effective. What is needed are programs of education designed to inform and to change old attitudes. What reinforcers can be found to compete with the powerful reinforcers of immediate personal satisfaction? In his controversial book *Beyond Freedom and Dignity* (1971), B. F. Skinner eloquently argues that the time has come to replace some of our old reinforcers with survival of the culture as a primary goal. Skinner argues that "the good of a culture must, in some way, be made to be a source of genuine reinforcement for the individual."

The population problem

The threat of overpopulation is part of the environmental problem. It has been estimated that the population of the earth is increasing at a rate that will double the number of people every 35 to 40 years. In 1960 there were approximately 3 billion people in the world and it is expected that by 2000 there will be close to 6 billion. While 1973 estimates indicate that the United States has reached zero population growth, researchers warn that this is not a stable situation. Subsequent generations may reverse the trend, creating a new baby boom larger than that in the 1940s. And most other nations of the world are far from achieving zero population growth; the earth's population continues to multiply. Food supplies are being seriously depleted. At the present time, North America and Western Europe are the only areas of the world that can supply their people with an adequate daily protein requirement. Unless the problems of overpopulation are met, what will the situation be like in the year 2000?

The psychological pressures of overcrowding are already producing serious breakdowns in social organizations. Overcrowding is particularly serious in the cities, where it has been shown that population density is correlated with crime (Schmitt, 1957).

A population crisis may not be far off, but no clear way to cope with it is at hand. Government control of the birthrate is unlikely, and moral suasion does not seem to have much effect. Perhaps answers lie in some combination of population planning and environmental engineering. This is a problem that goes beyond psychology and into the political arena (Esser, 1971).

Designing a community

Man has mastered his environment in many ways, but he has only begun to cope with the problems caused by mankind itself. Our understanding of technology and the physical sciences grows at a rapid rate, while our social problems increase and human relations deteriorate. But many community psychologists look forward to the day when what is known about behavior and human relations can be applied to designing a better, more rewarding community than the one we now have.

B. F. Skinner is the most outspoken advocate of the view that we can succesfully manipulate the social environment to produce a new and better culture. Skinner asks, "Why should the design of a culture be left largely to accident? Is it not possible to change the social environment deliberately so that the human product will meet more acceptable specifications?" He explores this possibility in his novel *Walden Two*, which takes place in a community based on the principle of positive reinforcement. The community is organized around the basic ideas of behavioral engineering: behavior is controlled by its consequences, and the most effective consequence is positive reinforcement. There is no punishment in *Walden Two*, but there is discipline; children are taught self-control by the use of positive reinforcement. The reinforcers are socially, not personally, determined and are based on the well-being of the community. According to Skinner (1953), "The culture . . . determines the extent to which the members of the group are preoccupied with food or sex or with escape from minor aversive stimulation in the search for 'comfort.' "

Many people rebel at the idea of "controlling" man from the outside, however. Skinner's views regarding the engineering of a culture are opposed by a number of psychologists as well as nonpsychologists. Carl Rogers feels that Skinner does not take into account the self-actualizing drives of man, and that he places too much emphasis on external control, rather than internal, personal control (Rogers and Skinner, 1956). Rogers has not attempted to design a culture, but he has indicated that the task should be the "subjective personal choice" of individuals. For Rogers, a culture will thrive to the extent that it focuses on man as a "process of becoming" and provides him with the opportunity to pursue "internally chosen goals." His behavior should be self-directed rather than controlled from the outside. Free man, says Rogers, and he will find the best way. Control him, and he will cease to be creative. It is interesting to speculate about what a Rogerian utopia would be like.

The fact that Skinner and Rogers disagree about the means of improving communities and societies should not distract us from their agreement that change is necessary and the fact that neither is afraid of social experiment. It is certainly too soon to determine whether Rogers or Skinner is correct, or whether neither is correct. It is not too soon, however, to suggest that there is need of more social experimentation if the quality of human life is to be improved.

SUMMARY

Social psychology deals with the influences of society and culture on the individual and the effects of individuals or groups on other individuals or groups.

A group is an aggregate of individuals who have a relatively extended relationship governed by a mutually shared set of goals, activities, and standards of behavior.

Group norms are the expected standards of behavior set by a group for its members. They cover latitudes of acceptance and latitudes of rejection.

Differences in susceptibility to group pressure may be attributed to differences in personality.

There is contradictory evidence as to whether or not group problem-solving is more effective than individual problem-solving. The communication patterns of a group often determine its success. The risky shift refers to the tendency of groups to make riskier decisions than individuals do.

Attitudes are learned and enduring predispositions to respond in a specific manner to particular stimuli. Either the Thurstone or Likert attitude scales may be used to measure the strength of an attitude.

Polling is used to measure attitudes and opinions of large numbers or groups of people. Polls are conducted using representative samples of the group in question. Two types of questions generally used in polls are fixed-alternative questions and open-ended questions.

The culture as a whole and the peer groups and family to which the individual belongs are largely responsible for the shaping of attitudes.

The cross-cultural method may be used to compare attitudes of people of different cultures toward the same issue.

Culture refers to the pattern of norms that a society establishes and passes on to each succeeding generation.

An individual tends to acquire attitudes consonant with his personality.

Prejudice refers to prejudgment based on emotion. Prejudices grow out of social learning and personality variables.

Prejudices are often reflections of frustrated needs for superiority or aggressive feelings. If the individual's aggression is displaced onto a minority group that cannot retaliate, his behavior is called scapegoating.

Ethnocentric individuals often display prejudice. They are often moralistic, authoritarian, and conservative.

Prejudice may be eliminated by preventing primary groups from teaching prejudices to children; reinforcing nonprejudiced behavior, while eliminating support for prejudiced attitudes and activities; giving objective facts about minority groups; and providing contact between groups.

The deliberate attempt to manipulate attitudes for specific predefined goals is called propaganda.

Selective perception and avoidance of information cause resistance to attitude change.

Attitude change may be explained by one of the consistency theories—balance, congruity, or dissonance.

Community psychology is concerned with the individual and his relationship to the various communities in which he holds membership. The nonprofessional aide is beginning to play an important role in community psychology.

Primary prevention is designed to help people cope with life's stresses in order to prevent psychological problems. Secondary prevention is aimed at the early detection and treatment of behavior pathology.

Community psychologists are most concerned with the promotion of mental health, that is, with the prevention and treatment of behavior pathology.

The modern mental hospital is conceived of as a therapeutic community.

Environmental therapy, by providing many socially stimulating activities, attempts to keep the patient in a mental hospital from withdrawing from human contact into an imaginary world.

Some mental hospitals allow patients to live in part time while spending some time in their own communities.

Community mental health is also concerned with problems of the aged.

The present penal system is based on the systems of probation, imprisonment, and parole. Effective rehabilitation programs are rare.

The penal system provides specialized treatment for drug addicts and juvenile offenders.

Two recent reforms in sentencing are the indeterminate-length sentence and the weekend sentence.

Crime prevention may best be achieved by changing the social environment which promotes criminality.

Some methods of human relations training are the case method, sensitivity training, and role playing.

Environmental problems, including overpopulation, are now a concern of community psychologists, who see them as related to questions of individual responsibility.

Some psychologists advocate designing communities so as to improve the quality of human life. The form that such new communities would take is still subject to debate.

SUGGESTED READINGS

Texts

Baughman, E. E. *Black Americans: a psychological analysis.* New York: Academic Press, 1971. A brief, informal look at various cognitive and personality aspects of our black subculture.

Blackwell, R. D., Engle, J. F., & Kollat, D. T. *Cases in consumer behavior.* New York:

Holt, Rinehart and Winston, 1969. For students interested in the behavioral aspects of marketing.

Britt, S. H. *Consumer behavior in theory and in action*. New York: Wiley, 1970. An inclusive selection of readings regarding recent research and theorizing in this growing field of inquiry.

Burgess, R. L., & Bushell, D., Jr. *Behavioral sociology: the experimental analysis of social process*. New York: Columbia University Press, 1969. Discussion of a closely related discipline.

Cartwright, Z. *Group dynamics, research and theory* (3rd ed.). New York: Harper & Row, 1970. Textbook on group dynamics. Includes a representative collection of experimental studies on intragroup processes and group properties.

Collins, B. E., & Guetzkow, H. A. *Social psychology of group processes and decision making*. New York: Wiley, 1964. Comprehensive study of group interaction.

Dean, D. G. *Dynamic issues in social psychology*. New York: Random House, 1969. Analysis and measurement of basic concepts in social psychology.

Deutsch, M., & Krauss, R. M. *Theories in social psychology*. New York: Basic Books, 1965. A comprehensive—and comprehensible—discussion of various theoretical perspectives and the role of theory in social psychology.

Fawcett, J. T. *Psychology and population: behavioral research issues in fertility and family planning*. New York: The Population Council, 1970. A relatively sophisticated introduction to the important and intriguing areas of psychological research in the quest for multidisciplinary answers to questions of diverse population behaviors.

Glass, D. C., & Singer, J. E. *Urban stress*. New York: Academic Press, 1972. An interesting investigation of the psychological price urban dwellers pay for their adaptation to noise and social stress.

Hare, A. P., Borgatta, E. F., & Bales, R. F. (Eds.) *Small groups: studies in social interaction* (rev. ed.). New York: Knopf, 1965. Historical and theoretical articles covering many topics, including the individual as a component of group interaction and the group as a system.

Kiesler, C. A. *The psychology of commitment*. New York: Academic Press, 1971. A serious account of empirical evidence for the effect of commitment on attitude change, resistance to persuasion, and adverse reactions to persuasive attack.

Kohn, M. L. *Class and conformity, a study in values*. Homewood, Ill.: Dorsey, 1969. Detailed discussion of this special cultural phenomenon.

Lewin, K. *Field theory in social psychology*. New York: Harper & Row, 1951. A classic collection of interesting papers on group dynamics.

Lindgren, H. C. *An introduction to social psychology*. New York: Wiley, 1969. Recent textbook on the subject.

Lucas, R. A. *Men in crisis: study of a mine disaster*. New York: Basic Books, 1969. Social psychology in action; describes an intragroup relationship for a period of time.

Malpass, L. F. (Ed.) *Social behavior: a program for self-instruction*. New York: McGraw-Hill, 1967. A programmed text dealing with major topics in sociology and social psychology.

McDavid, J. W., & Harari, H. *Social psychology: individuals, groups, societies*. New York: Harper & Row, 1968. Statement of the current status of social psychology.

McGinnes, E. *Social behavior: a functional analysis.* Boston: Houghton Mifflin, 1970. Discussion of social behavior in terms of what it accomplishes.

Mehrabian, A. *Tactics of social influence.* Englewood Cliffs, N.J.: Prentice-Hall, 1970. Discussion of how individuals operate in the social structure.

Shaw, M. E., & Constanzo, P. R. *Theories of social psychology.* New York: McGraw-Hill, 1970. Discussion of some of the major theories of social psychology.

Shore, Milton F., & Mannino, F. V. (Eds.) *Mental health and the community: problems, programs, and strategies.* New York: Behavioral Publication, 1969. Eleven views of how to translate community mental health concepts into action programs.

Smith, M. A. *Social psychology and human values: selected essays.* Chicago: Aldine, 1969. Relationships between this social science and the humanistic tradition.

Weschler, H. *Social psychology and mental health.* New York: Holt, Rinehart & Winston, 1970. Discussion of social psychology and behavior pathology.

White, R. K., & Lippitt, R. *Autocracy and democracy.* Westport, Conn.: Greenwood Press, 1972. Discussion of social change in terms of "social climate."

Popular books

Benedict, R. *Patterns of culture.* Three cultures are examined by a noted anthropologist.

Bradbury, W. C. *Mass behavior in battle and captivity: the Communist soldier in the Korean War.* Extensive study of a different culture in action and under stress.

Cantril, H. *The psychology of social movements.* Studies of mass movements, aimed at clarifying their psychological aspects.

Davis, J. H. *Group performance.* Nontechnical examination of group effectiveness at various tasks.

Feur, L. S. *The conflict of generations: the character and signifiance of student movements.* Social psychology applied to students.

Goldenson, R. M. *Mysteries of the mind.* A case-history investigation of mass-psychology phenomena through the last several centuries.

Hall, E. T. *The hidden dimension.* Discussion of cultural differences and how they affect perception, motivation, emotional behavior, and other aspects of life.

Hoffer, E. *The true believer.* Nontechnical study of the fanatic follower.

Janis, I. L. *Victims of groupthink.* A psychological study of the possibilities and hazards of group decision-making at the foreign-policy level.

May, R. *Power and innocence.* A social-psychological analysis which finds violence the dire social consequence of minority humiliation, debasement, and institutional impotence.

Mead, M. *Coming of age in Samoa.* Discussion of the cultural aspects of maturity in another society.

Melville, K. *Communes in the counter culture.* An examination of present trends and future possibilities within communal life-styles.

Bibliography

Adler, A. *Problems of neurosis.* New York: Cosmopolitan Books, 1930.

Adorno, T. W., Frenkel-Brunswick, E., Levinson, D. J., & Sanford, R. N. *The authoritarian personality.* New York: Harper, 1950.

Adrian, E. D. Olfactory discrimination. *Année Psychologique,* 1951, **50**, 107–113.

Allport, F. H. The influence of the group upon association and thought. *Journal of Experimental Psychology,* 1920, **3**, 159–182.

Allport, F. H. *Social psychology.* Boston: Houghton Mifflin, 1924.

Allport, G. W. *Personality.* London: Constable, 1951.

Allport, G. W. *The nature of prejudice.* Reading, Mass.: Addison-Wesley, 1954.

Allport, G. W. *Personality and social encounter.* Boston: Beacon Press, 1960.

Allport, G. W. *Pattern and growth in personality.* New York: Holt, Rinehart and Winston, 1961.

Allport, G .W. (Ed.) *William James/Psychology: The briefer course,* pp. 161–162. New York: Harper Torchbooks, 1961.

Allport, G. W., & Odbert, H. S. Trait names, a psycholexical study. *Psychological Monographs,* 1936, **47** (Whole No. 211).

Alpert, A. Sublimation and sexualization: a case report. In A. Freud, H. Hartman, & E. Kris (Eds.), *The psychoanalytic study of the child,* Vol. 3, pp. 271–278. New York: International Universities Press, 1949.

Ammons, R. B. Reactions in a projective doll play interview of white males two to six years of age to difference in skin color and facial features. *Journal of Genetic Psychology,* 1960, **76**, 323–341.

Andersson, B., & McCann, S. M. A further study of polydipsia evoked by hypothalamic stimulation in the goat. *Acta Physiologica Scandinavia,* 1955, **33**, 333–346.

Archer, E. J. A. re-evaluation of the meaningfulness of all possible CVC trigrams. *Psychological Monographs,* 1960, **74**.

Ardrey, R. *The territorial imperative.* New York: Atheneum, 1966.

Arnold, M. B. *Emotion and personality,* Vol. 1: *Psychological aspects.* New York: Columbia University Press, 1960.

Asch, S. Opinions and social pressure. *Scientific American,* 1955, **193**(5), 31–35.

Aschoff, J. Circadian rhythms in man. *Science,* 1965, **148**, 1427–1432.

Ax, A. F. The physiological differentiation of fear and anger. *Psychosomatic Medicine,* 1953, **15**, 433–442.

Axline, V. M. *Play therapy.* Boston: Houghton Mifflin, 1947.

Axline, V. M. *Dibs: in search of self.* Boston: Houghton Mifflin, 1966.

Ayllon, T., & Azrin, N. *The token economy, a motivational system for therapy and rehabilitation,* pp. 219–271. New York: Appleton-Century-Crofts, 1968.

Bandura, A. Social learning through imitation. In M. R. Jones (Ed.), *Nebraska symposium on motivation,* pp. 211–269. Lincoln: University of Nebraska Press, 1962.

Bandura, A. Behavioral modification through modeling procedures. In L. Krasner & L. P. Ullman (Eds.), *Research in behavior modification,* pp. 310–340. New York: Holt, Rinehart and Winston, 1965.

Bandura, A., Ross, D., & Ross, S. A. Imitation of film-mediated aggressive models. *Journal of Abnormal and Social Psychology,* 1963, **66**, 3–11.

Barber, T. X. *Hypnosis: a scientific approach.* New York: Van Nostrand Reinhold, 1969.

Barker, R. G., Dembo, T., & Lewin, K. An experiment with young children. In R. G. Barker, I. S. Kounin, & H. F. Wright (Eds.), *Child behavior and development,* pp. 441–458. New York: McGraw-Hill, 1943.

Barnlund, D. C. A comparative study of individual, majority, and group judgment. *Journal of Abnormal and Social Psychology,* 1959, **58**, 55–66.

Barron, F., Jarvik, M., & Bunnell, S., Jr. The hallucinogenic drugs. *Scientific American,* 1964, **210**(4), 29–37.

Bartlett, F. *Thinking: an experimental and social study.* London: Allen & Unwin, 1958.

Bass, M. J., & Hull, C. L. Irradiation of a tactile conditioned reflex in man. *Journal of Comparative and Physiological Psychology,* 1934, **17**, 47–65.

Beach, H. D. Morphine addiction in rats. *Canadian Journal of Psychology,* 1957, **11**, 104–112.

Beauchamp, K. L., Chapman, A., & Grebing, C. Response by the calf to stimulus change. *Psychonomic Science,* 1967, **9**, 125–126.

Beers, C. *A mind that found itself.* New York: Longmans Green, 1908.

Benedict, R. Anthropology and the abnormal. *Journal of General Psychology,* 1934, **10**, 59–82.

Berger, T. M. The pharmacological properties of 2-methyl-2n-propyl-1,3-propanediol dicarbonate (Miltown), a new interneuronal blocking agent. *Journal of Pharmacology and Experimental Therapy,* 1954, **112**, 413–423.

Berkowitz, L. *Roots of aggression: a reexamination of the frustration-aggression hypothesis.* Menlo Park, Calif.: Atherton, 1968.

Berkowitz, L. Anti-semitism and the displacement of aggression. *Journal of Abnormal and Social Psychology,* 1969, **59**, 182–187.

Berkowitz, L., & Cottingham, D. R. The interest value and relevance of fear arousing communications. *Journal of Abnormal and Social Psychology,* 1960, **60**, 37–43.

Berkowitz, L., & LePage, A. Weapons as aggression-eliciting stimuli. *Journal of Personality and Social Psychology,* 1967, **7**(2), 202–207.

Bettelheim, B. Joey: a mechanical boy. *Scientific American,* 1959, **200**(3), 117–127.

Bigge, M. L. *Learning theories for teachers.* New York: Harper & Row, 1964.

Binet, A., & Simon, S. Méthodes nouvelles pour le diagnostic scientifique des états inférieurs de l'intelligence. *L'année psychologique,* 1905, 163–191.

Birney, R. C., & Teevan, R. C. (Eds.) *Instinct.* Princeton, N.J.: Van Nostrand, 1961.

Bleuler, M., & Bleuler, R. Rorschach ink-blot tests and social psychology. *Character and Personality,* 1935, **4**, 99–114.

Bochner, S., & Insko, C. A. Communicator discrepancy, source credibility and opinion change. *Journal of Personality and Social Psychology,* 1966, **4**, 614–621.

Boring, E. G. *A history of experimental psychology* (2nd ed.). New York: Appleton-Century-Crofts, 1950.

Boring, E. G., Langfield, H. S., & Weld, H. P. (Eds.) *Foundations of psychology.* New York: Wiley, 1948.

Bower, G. H., & Clark, M. C. Narrative stories as mediators for serial learning. *Psychonomic Science,* 1969, **14**, 181–182.

Bower, T. G. R., Broughton, J. M., & Moore, M. K. Demonstration of intention in the reaching behavior of neonate humans. *Nature,* 1970, **228**, 679–681.

Brady, J. V., Porter, R. W., Conrad, D. G., & Mason, J. W. Avoidance behavior and the development of gastroduodenal ulcers. *Journal of Experimental Analysis of Behavior,* 1958, **1**, 69–73.

Braine, M. D. S. The ontogeny of English phrase structure: the first phrase. *Language,* 1963, **39**, 1–13.

Braud, D. S., & Braud, W. G. Biochemical transfer of relational responding (transposition). *Science,* 1972, **176**, 942–944.

Braud, W. G. Extinction in goldfish: facilitation by intercranial injection of RNA from brains of extinguished donors. *Science,* 1970, **168**, 1234–1236.

Bresler, D. E., & Bitterman, M. E. Learning in fish with transplanted brain tissue. *Science,* 1969, **163**, 590–592.

Bridges, K. M. B. Emotional development in eary infancy. *Child Development,* 1932, **3**, 324–334, 340.

Brigham, T. A., & Bushell, D., Jr. Notes on autonomous environments: students selected versus teacher selected rewards. *Background Paper, Behavior Analysis Program.* Lawrence: University of Kansas Press, 1972.

Britton, J. H., Britton, J. O., & Fisher, C. F. Perception of children's moral and emotional behavior: a comparison of Finnish and American children. *Human Development,* 1969, **12**, 55–63.

Broadhurst, P. L. Emotionality and the Yerkes-Dodson law. *Journal of Experimental Psychology,* 1957, **54**, 345–352.

Brotman, J., & Senter, R. J. Attitudes toward feminism in different national student groups. *Journal of Social Psychology,* 1968, **76**, 137–138.

Brown, R. *Social psychology.* New York: Free Press, 1965.

Brown, R. W. The development of the first language in the human species. *American Psychologist*, 1973, **28** (February), 97–106.

Brown, R. W., & Berko, J. Word association and the acquisition of grammar. *Child Development*, 1960, **31**, 1–14.

Brown, R. W., & Hanlon, C. Derivational complexity and order of acquisition in child speech. In J. R. Hayes (Ed.), *Cognition and the development of language*. New York: Wiley, 1970.

Brown, R. W., & Hildum, D. Expectancy and the identification of syllables. *Language*, 1956, **32**, 411–419.

Bruce, R. W. Conditions of transfer training. *Journal of Experimental Psychology*, 1933, **16**, 343–361.

Brunswick, E. *Perception and the representative design of psychological experiments*. Berkeley: University of California Press, 1956.

Burke, R. J., & Maier, N. R. F. Attempts to predict success on an insight problem. *Psychological Reports*, 1965, **17**, 303–310.

Burks, B. S., Jensen, D. W., & Terman, L. M. *Genetic studies of genius*, Vol. 3: *The promise of youth: follow-up studies of a thousand gifted children*. Stanford, Calif.: Stanford University Press, 1930.

Burt, C. The genetic determination of differences in intelligence: a study of monozygotic twins reared together and apart. *British Journal of Psychology*, 1966, **57**, 137–153.

Burt, C., & Howard, M. The multiple factorial theory of inheritance and its application to intelligence. *British Journal of Statistical Psychology*, 1956, **9**, 95–131.

Burtt, H. E. An experimental study of early childhood memory. *Journal of Psychology*, 1941, **58**, 435–439.

Butler, R. A. Discrimination learning by rhesus monkeys to visual-exploration motivation. *Journal of Comparative and Physiological Psychology*, 1953, **46**, 95–98.

Butler, R. A. Curiosity in monkeys. *Scientific American*, February 1954.

Bychowski, G. *Evil in man: The anatomy of hate and violence*. New York: Grune & Stratton, 1968.

Cantril, H. Perception and interpersonal relations. *American Journal of Psychiatry*, 1957, **114**, 119–126.

Carmichael, L. A further study of the development of behavior in vertebrates experimentally removed from the influence of environmental stimulation. *Psychological Review*, 1927, **34**, 34–47.

Carmichael, L. Hogan, H. P., & Walter, A. A. An experimental study of the effect of language on the reproduction of visually perceived form. *Journal of Experimental Psychology*, 1932, **5**, 73–86.

Carroll, J. B. *Language and thought*. Englewood Cliffs, N.J.: Prentice-Hall, 1964.

Carroll, L. *Through the looking glass*. New York: Macmillan, 1872.

Cartwright, D., & Zander, A. *Group dynamics research and theory*, pp. 45–48. New York: Harper & Row, 1968.

Cattell, R. B. *Description and measurement of personality*. Yonkers, N.Y.: World Book, 1946.

Cattell, R. B., Blewett, D. B., & Beloff, J. R. The inheritance of personality. *American Journal of Human Genetics*, 1955, **7**, 122–146.

Chomsky, N. The formal nature of language. In E. H. Lenneberg (Ed.), *Biological foundation of language*. New York: Wiley, 1967.

Chomsky, N. *Language and mind*. New York: Harcourt Brace Jovanovich, 1968.

Christie, R., & Geis, F. L. (Eds.) *Studies in Machiavellianism*. New York: Academic Press, 1970.

Clark, W. E. Anatomical basis of colour vision. *Nature (London)*, 1940, **146**, 558–559.

Cohen, D. Magnetoencephalography: detection of the brain's electrical activity with a superconducting magnetometer. *Science*, 1972, **175**, 664–666.

Cohen, J. *Complex learning*, p. 50. Chicago: Rand McNally, 1969a.

Cohen, J. *Sensation and perception in vision*. Chicago: Rand McNally, 1969b.

Cohen, S. Lysergic acid diethylamide: side effects and complications. *Journal of Nervous and Mental Disorders*, 1960, **130** (January), 30–40.

Cohen, S., & Ditman, K. S. Prolonged adverse reactions to lysergic acid diethylamide. *Archives of General Psychiatry*, 1963, **8**, 475–480.

Cook, T. H. The application of the Rorschach test to a Samoan group. *Rorschach Research Exchange*, 1942, **6**, 51–60.

Cooley, D. H. *Human nature and the social order*. New York: Scribner's, 1922.

Cooper, C. J. Some relationships between paired-associate learning and foreign language aptitude. *Journal of Educational Psychology*, 1964, **55**(3), 132–138.

Cooper, J. B. Emotion in prejudice. *Science*, 1959, **130**, 314–318.

Cottrell, N. B. Performance in the presence of other human beings: mere presence, audience, and affiliation affects. In E. C. Simmel, R. A. Hoppe, & G. A. Milton (Eds.), *Social facilitation and imitative behavior*. Boston: Allyn & Bacon, 1968.

Cowen, E. L. Social and community interventions. In P. H. Mussen, & M. R. Rosenzweig (Eds.), *Annual Review of Psychology*. Palo Alto, Calif.: Annual Reviews, 1973.

Cowles, J. T. Food-tokens as incentives for learning by chimpanzees. *Comparative Psychological Monographs*, 1937, **14**, 71.

Crannell, C. W., & Parrish, W. M. A comparison of immediate memory span for digits, letters, and words. *Journal of Psychology*, 1957, **44**, 319–327.

Crick, F. H. The genetic code. *Scientific American*, 1962, **207**, 66–74.

Cronbach, L. J. *Essentials of psychological testing* (2nd ed.), p. 249. New York: Harper & Row, 1960.

Cross, P. G., Cattell, R. B., & Butcher, H. J. The personality pattern of creative artists. *British Journal of Educational Psychology*, 1967, **37**, 292–299.

Crutchfield, R. S. Conformity and character. *American Psychologist*, 1955, **10**, 191–198.

Darnell, C. D., & Bourne, L. E., Jr. Effects of age, verbal ability, and pretraining with component concepts on the performance of children in a bidimensional task. *Journal of Educational Psychology*, 1970, **61**, 66–71.

Darwin, C. *The expression of emotion in man and animals*. London: Murray, 1872.

Davis, A., & Eells, K. *Davis Eells Games*. Yonkers, N.Y.: World Book, 1953.

Davis, J. D., Gallagher, R. L., & Ladove, R. Food intake controlled by a blood factor. *Science*, 1967, **156**, 1247–1248.

Day, E. J. The development of language in twins: I. A comparison of twins and single children. *Child Development*, 1932, **3**, 179–199.

Deese, J. *General psychology*. Boston: Allyn & Bacon, 1967.

Dement, W., & Kleitman, N. Cyclic variations in EEG during sleep and their relations to eye movements, body motility and dreaming. *Electroencephalography and Clinical Neurophysiology*, 1957, **9**, 673–690.

Dennenberg, V. H., Woodcock, J. M., & Rosenberg, K. M. Longterm effects of preweaning and postweaning free-environment experience on rats' problem solving behavior. *Journal of Comparative and Physiological Psychology*, 1968, **66**, 533–535.

Dethier, V. G., & Stellar, E. *Animal behavior* (3rd ed.). Englewood Cliffs, N.J.: Prentice-Hall, 1970.

Deutsch, M. An experimental study of the effects of cooperation and competition upon group process. *Human Relations*, 1949, **2**, 199–232.

Deutsch, M., & Collins, M. E. *Interracial housing: a psychological evaluation of a social experiment*. Minneapolis: University of Minnesota Press, 1951.

Deutsch, M., & Gerard, H. A study of normative and informational social influences upon individual judgment. *Journal of Abnormal and Social Psychology*, 1955, **51**, 629–636.

DeValois, R. L., & Jacobs, G. H. Primate color vision. *Science*, 1968, **162**, 533–540.

DeVries, R. Conservation of generic identity in the years three to six. (Doctoral thesis, University of Chicago.) Chicago: University of Chicago Microfilms, 1967.

Dexter, E. S. Personality traits related to conservatism and radicalism. *Character and Personality*, 1939, **7**, 230–237.

Diamond, I. T., & Ness, W. D. Ablation of temporal cortex and discrimination of auditory patterns. *Journal of Neurophysiology*, 1957, **20**, 300–315.

Dinsmoor, J. A. The effect of hunger on discriminated responding. *Journal of Abnormal Psychology*, 1952, **47**, 67–72.

Dodd, B. J. Effects of social and vocal stimulation on infant babbling. *Developmental Psychology*, 1972, **7**, 80–83.

Dollard, J., Doob, L., Miller, N., Mowrer, O., & Sears, R. *Frustration and aggression*. New Haven: Yale University Press, 1939.

Dollard, J., & Miller N. E. *Personality and psychotherapy*. New York: McGraw-Hill, 1950.

Duane, T. D., & Behrendt, T. Extrasensory electroencephalographic induction between identical twins. *Science*, 1965, **150**, 367.

Duncker, K. On problem solving. *Psychological Monographs* (No. 270). Washington, D.C.: American Psychological Association, 1945.

Ebbinghaus, H. *Memory* (1885). Trans. by H. A. Ruger and C. E. Bussenius. New York: Teachers College Press, 1913.

Edson, L. Brain damage: use of the mind's spare tire. *The New York Times*, May 7, 1972, p. 16.

Ehrhardt, A. A. & Money, J. Progestin-induced hermaphroditism: IQ and psychosexual identity in a study of ten girls. *The Journal of Sex Research*, 1967, **3**, 83–100.

Eimas, P. D., Siqueland, E. R., Jusczyk, P., & Vigorito, J. Speech perception in infants. *Science*, 1971, **171**, 303–306.

Ekman, P., Sorenson, E. R., & Friesen, W. J. Pan-cultural elements in facial displays of emotion. *Science*, 1969, **164**, 86–88.

Ellis, A. Outcome of employing three techniques of psychotherapy. *Journal of Clinical Psychology*, 1957, **13**, 344–350.

Ellis, A. Rational psychotherapy and individual psychology. *Journal of Individual Psychology*, 1957, **13**, 38–44.

Engsberg, L. A., Hansen, G., Welker, R. L., & Thomas, D. R. Acquisition of key-pecking via autoshaping as a function of prior experience: "learned laziness"? *Science*, 1972, **178**, 1002–1004.

Erikson, E. H. *Childhood and society* (rev. ed.). New York: Norton, 1963.

Esser, A. H. (Ed.) *Behavior and environment: use of space by animals and men.* New York: Plenum Press, 1971.

Evans, C. R., & Marsden, R. P. A study of the effects of perfect retinal stabilization on some well-known visual illusions, using the after-image as a method of compensating for eye movements. *British Journal of Physiological Optics*, 1966, **23**, 242–248.

Ewert, J. P. Untersuchungen über die Anteik zentralnervöser Aktione an der Taxisspezifischen Ermüdung beim Beutefang der Erdkröte *(Bufo bufo L.). Zeitschrift für Vergleichende Physiologie,* 1967, **57**, 263–298.

Eysenck, H. J. *The structure of human personality* (2nd ed.). London: Methuen, 1960.

Fantz, R. L. The origin of form perception. *Scientific American*, 1961, **204**, 66–72.

Farberow, N. L., & Schneidman, E. S. *The cry for help.* New York: McGraw-Hill, 1965.

Fechner, G. *Elements of psychophysics* (1860). Trans. by H. E. Adler. New York: Holt, Rinehart & Winston, 1966.

Ferguson, J., Henriksen, S., Cohen, H., Mitchell, G., Barchas, J., & Dement, W. "Hypersexuality" and behavioral changes in cats caused by administration of *p*-chlorophenylalanine. *Science*, 1970, **168**, 499–501.

Ferster, C. B., & Skinner, B. F. *Schedules of reinforcement.* New York: Appleton-Century-Crofts, 1957.

Festinger, L. *A theory of cognitive dissonance.* Evanston, Ill.: Row Petersen, 1957.

Festinger, L., & Carlsmith, J. M. Cognitive consequences of forced compliance. *Journal of Abnormal and Social Psychology*, 1959, **58**, 203–210.

Festinger, L., Pepitone, C., & Newcomb, T. M. Some consequences of deindividuation in a group. *Journal of Abnormal and Social Psychology*, 1952, **47**, 382–389.

Festinger, L., Riecken, H. W., & Schachter, S. *When prophecy fails.* Minneapolis: University of Minnesota Press, 1956.

Fisher, S., & Osofsky, H. Sexual responsiveness in women, physiological correlates. *Psychology Reports*, 1968, **22**, 215–226.

Fitzwater, M. E., & Reisman, M. N. Comparison of forward, simultaneous, backward, and pseudo conditioning. *Journal of Experimental Psychology*, 1952, **44**, 211–214.

Flavell, J. H. *The developmental psychology of Jean Piaget.* Princeton, N.J.: Van Nostrand, 1963.

Fletcher, F. M. Effects of quantitative variation of food incentive on the performance of physical work by chimpanzees. *Comparative Psychology Monographs*, 1940, **16**(3, Serial No. 82), 1–46.

Foulkes, D., & Vogel, G. Mental activity at sleep onset. *Journal of Abnormal Psychology*, 1965, **70**, 231–243.

Fowler, M. J., Sullivan, M. J., & Ekstrand, B. R. Sleep and memory. *Science*, 1973, **179**, 302–304.

Freedman, D. An ethological approach to the genetical study of human behavior. In S. G. Vandenberg (Ed.), *Methods and goals in human behavior genetics.* New York: Academic Press, 1965.

Freedman, D. G., & Keller, B. Inheritance of behavior in infants. *Science*, 1963, **140**, 196–198.

Freedman, T. L., & Sears, D. D. Warning, distraction and resistance to influence. *Journal of Personality and Social Psychology*, 1965, **1**, 262–266.

Freeman, F. N., Holzinger, K. J., & Mitchell, B. C. The influence of environment on the intelligence, school achievement, and conduct of foster children. *27th Yearbook, National Society for the Study of Education*, Part I, 1928, 102–217.

Freeman, G. L. The relationship between performance level and bodily activity level. *Journal of Experimental Psychology*, 1940, **26**, 606.

Frenkel-Brunswick, E. Intolerance of ambiguity as an emotional perceptual personality variable. *Journal of Personality*, 1949, **18**, 108–143.

Freud, A. *The ego and the mechanisms of defense.* Trans. by C. Baines. London: Hogarth Press, 1937.

Freud, S. *The psychopathology of everyday life.* New York: Macmillan, 1914. (First German edition, 1901.)

Freud, S. *A general introduction to psychoanalysis.* Garden City, N.Y.: Permabooks, 1953. (First German edition, 1916.)

Freud, S. *The problem of anxiety.* New York: Norton, 1926.

Freud, S. *Civilization and its discontents*, p. 102. London: Hogarth, 1930.

Freud, S. Notes upon a case of obsessional neurosis, 1909. In S. Freud, *The standard edition of the complete psychological works*, Vol. 11. London: Hogarth Press, 1955.

Freud, S. *The standard edition of the complete psychological works*, Vol. 10 (J. Strachey, A. Freud, A. Strachey, & A. Tyson, Eds.), trans. by J. Strachey. London: Hogarth Press, 1955.

Freud, S. A special type of choice of object made by men, 1910. In S. Freud, *The standard edition of the complete psychological works*, Vol. 11. London: Hogarth Press, 1955.

Friedman, D. A. A new technique for systematic desensitization of phobic symptoms. *Behaviour Research and Therapy*, 1966, **4**, 139–140.

Fromm, E. *Escape from freedom.* New York: Holt, 1941.

Fromm, E. *The sane society.* New York: Holt, 1955.

Fuhrer, M. J., & Baer, P. E. Differential classical conditioning: verbalization of stimulus contingencies. *Science*, 1965, **150**, 1479–1481.

Funkenstein, D. H. The physiology of fear and anger. *Scientific American*, 1955, **192**(5), 74–80.

Fuster, J. M. Effects of stimulation of brain stem on tachistoscopic perception. *Science*, 1958, **127**, 150.

Galanter, E. Contemporary psychophysics. In *New directions in psychology*, Vol. I, pp. 89–156. New York: Holt, Rinehart and Winston, 1962.

Gardner, R. A., & Gardner, B. T. Teaching sign language to a chimpanzee. *Science*, 1969, **165**, 664–672.

Gazzaniga, M. S. One brain—two minds? *American Scientist*, 1972, **60**, 311.

Gazzaniga, M. S., & Sperry, R. W. Language after section of the cerebral commissures. *Brain*, 1967, **90**, 131–148.

Gendlin, E. T. Psychotherapy and community psychology. *Psychotherapy: Research and Practice*, 1968, **5**(2), 67–72.

Gibson, E. J. Retroactive inhibition as a function of degree of generalization between tasks. *Journal of Experimental Psychology*, 1941, **28**, 93–115.

Gibson, E. J., & Walk, R. D. The effect of prolonged exposure to visually presented patterns on learning to discriminate them. *Journal of Comparative and Physiological Psychology*, 1956, **49**, 239–242.

Gibson, J. J. The reproduction of visually perceived forms. *Journal of Experimental Psychology*, 1929, **12**, 1–39.

Gibson, J. J. *The senses considered as perceptual systems.* Boston: Houghton Mifflin, 1966.

Gil, D. G. *Violence against children: physical child abuse in the United States.* Cambridge, Mass.: Harvard University Press, 1970.

Girden, E., & Culler, E. Conditioned responses in curarized striate muscles in dogs. *Journal of Comparative Psychology*, 1937, **24**, 261–274.

Glaser, D. *The effectiveness of a prison and parole system.* Indianapolis: Bobbs-Merrill, 1964.

Glaze, J. A. The association value of nonsense syllables. *Journal of Genetic Psychology*, 1928, **35**, 255–267.

Glueck, S., & Glueck, E. Potential juvenile delinquents can be identified: what next? *British Journal of Criminology*, 1964, **4**, 215–226.

Goddard, H. H. *The Kallikak family.* New York: Macmillan, 1912.

Goldenberg, I. I. The residential youth center: problems of theory and research in the creation of a community based rehabilitative setting. In M. J. Feldman (Ed.), *Studies in psychotherapy and behavior change. No. 2: Theory and research in community mental health.* Buffalo: State University of New York Press, 1971.

Golub, A. M., Masiarz, F. R., Villars, T., & McConnell, J. V. Incubation effects in behavior induction in rats. *Science*, 1970, **168**, 392–395.

Goodall, J. *In the shadow of man.* Boston: Houghton Mifflin, 1971.

Goodwin, E. W. Powell, D. B., Haskel, H., & Stern, J. Alcohol and recall: effects of drug state in man. *Science*, 1969, **163**, 1358–1360.

Gottesman, I. I. Heritability of personality: a demonstration. *Psychological Monographs*, 1963, **77**(9), 1–21.

Gottlieb, G. *Development of species identification in birds*. Chicago: University of Chicago Press, 1971.

Gough, H. G. Minnesota Multiphasic Personality Inventory. In A. Weider (Ed.), *Contributions towards medical psychology*, pp. 545–567. New York: Ronald Press, 1953.

Gough, H. G. *California Psychological Inventory*. New York: Consulting Psychologists Press, 1956.

Gough, H. G., Wenk, E. A., & Rozynko, V. V. Parole outcome as predicted from the CPI, the MMPI, and a Base Expectancy Table. *Journal of Abnormal Psychology*, 1965, **70**, 432–441.

Goy, R. W. Early hormonal influence on the development of sexual and sex related behavior. In F. O. Schmitt (Ed.), *The neurosciences*. New York: Rockefeller University Press, 1970.

Gray, J. A. B., & Sato, M. Properties of the receptor potential in pacinian corpuscles. *Journal of Physiology*, 1953, **122**, 610–636.

Green, D. M., & Swets, J. A. *Signal detection theory and psychophysics*. New York: Wiley, 1966.

Greenspoon, J. The reinforcing effect of two spoken sounds on the frequency of two responses. *American Journal of Psychology*, 1955, **68**, 409–416.

Grinspoon, L. Marijuana. *Scientific American*, 1969, **221**(6), 17–25.

Gruver, G. G. College students as therapeutic agents. *Psychological Bulletin*, 1971, **76**, 111–127.

Guilford, J. P. A revised structure of intellect. *Report from the psychology laboratory*, No. 19. Los Angeles: University of Southern California Press, 1957.

Guilford, J. P. *Personality*. New York: McGraw-Hill, 1959.

Guilford, J. P. Factorial angles to psychology. *Psychological Review*, 1961, **68**, 1–20.

Guilford, J. P. *The nature of human intelligence*. New York: McGraw-Hill, 1967.

Gurin, G., Veroff, T., & Feld, S. *Americans view their mental health: a nationwide interview survey*. New York: Basic Books, 1960.

Guthrie, E. R. *The psychology of learning*. New York: Holt, 1935.

Haber, R. N., & Haber, R. B. Eidetic imagery: I. Frequency. *Perceptual and Motor Skills*, 1964, **19**, 131–138.

Hall, K. R. L., & DeVore, I. Baboon social behavior. In I. DeVore (Ed.), *Primate behavior*, pp. 53–110. New York: Holt, Rinehart and Winston, 1965.

Hamson, T. L. Determinants of psychosexual orientation. In F. A. Beach (Ed.), *Sex and behavior*, p. 119. New York: Wiley, 1965.

Harlow, H. F. The formation of learning sets. *Psychological Review*, 1949, **56**, 51–65.

Harlow, H. F. The nature of love. *American Psychologist*, 1958, **13**, 673–685.

Harlow, H. F. The affectional systems. In H. F. Harlow, J. L. McGaugh, and R.

F. Thompson (Eds.), *Psychology*, pp. 42–71. San Francisco: Albion Press, 1970.

Harlow, H. F., Harlow, M. K., & Meyer, D. R. Learning motivated by manipulation drive. *Journal of Experimental Psychology*, 1950, **40**, 228–234.

Harlow, H. F., Harlow, M. K., & Suomi, S. J. From thought to therapy: lessons from a primate laboratory. *American Scientist*, 1971, **59**, 538–549.

Harlow, H. F., & Suomi, S. J. The nature of love—simplified. *American Psychologist*, 1970, **25**, 161–168.

Harlow, H. F., & Zimmerman, R. R. Affectional responses in the infant monkey. *Science*, 1959, **130**, 421–423.

Harris, C. S. Perceptual adaptation to inverted, reversed and displaced vision. *Psychological Review*, 1965, **72**, 419–444.

Hart, B. L. *Experimental neuropsychology*. San Francisco: Freeman, 1969.

Havens, B. Investigation of activity patterns and adjustment in an aging population. *American Gerontologist*, 1968, **8**, 201–206.

Hebb, D. O. Drives and the C.N.S. (conceptual nervous system). *Psychological Review*, 1955, **62**, 243–254.

Hebb, D. O. *The organization of behavior*, 2nd ed., pp. 18, 28, 31. New York: Wiley, 1961. (First edition, 1949.)

Hebb, D. O. *Textbook of psychology*, 3rd ed. Philadelphia: Saunders, 1972.

Hecht, S. Vision. VI. The nature of the photoreceptor process. In C. Murchison (Ed.), *A handbook of general experimental psychology*. Worcester, Mass.: Clark University Press, 1934.

Heider, F. Attitudes and cognitive organization. *Journal of Psychology*, 1946, **21**, 107–112.

Heider, F. *The psychology of interpersonal relations*. New York: Wiley, 1958.

Helson, H. Current trends and issues in adaptation-level theory. *American Psychologist*, 1964, **19**, 26–38.

Hernández-Péon, R., Scherer, H., & Touret, M. Modification of electric activity in the cochlear nucleus during "attention" in unanesthetized cats. *Science*, 1956, **123**, 371–372.

Hess, E. H. Imprinting. *Science*, 1959, **130**, 133–141.

Hoffman, L. R. Homogeneity of membership personality and its effect on group problem-solving. *Journal of Abnormal and Social Psychology*, 1959, **58**, 27–32.

Hoffman, L. R., & Maier, N. R. F. Sex differences, sex composition, and group problem solving. *Journal of Abnormal and Social Psychology*, 1961, **63**, 453–456.

Holland, J., & Skinner, B. F. *The analysis of behavior*. New York: McGraw-Hill, 1961.

Homme, L. E. Contiguity theory and contingency management. *Psychology Record*, 1966, **16**, 233–241.

Homme, L. E., De Baca, P. E., Devine, J. V., Steinhorst, R., & Rickert, E. J. Use of the Premack principle in controlling the behavior of nursery school children. *Journal of Experimental Analysis of Behavior*, 1963, **6**, 544.

Honzik, M. P. Personality consistency and change: some comments on papers by Boyley, MacFarlane, Mors, Kagan and Murphy. *Vita Humana*, 1964, **7**, 139–142.

Hood, A. B. A study of the relationship between physique and personality variables, measured by the MMPI. *Journal of Personality*, 1963, **31**, 97–107.

Horn, J. L., & Cattell, R. B. Age differences in fluid and crystallized intelligence. *Acta Psychologica*, 1967, **26**, 107–129.

Horney, K. *The neurotic personality of our time*. New York: Norton, 1937.

Horney, K. *Our inner conflicts*, p. 41. New York: Norton, 1945.

Hovland, C. I. The generalization of conditioned responses: IV. The effects of varying amounts of reinforcement upon the degrees of generalization of conditioned responses. *Journal of Experimental Psychology*, 1937, **21**, 261–276.

Hovland, C. I. Reconciling conflicting results derived from experimental and survey studies of attitude change. *American Psychologist*, 1959, **14**, 8–17.

Hubel, D. H., & Wiesel, T. N. Receptive fields, binocular interaction and functional architecture in the cat's visual cortex. *Journal of Physiology (London)*, 1962, **160**, 106–154.

Hull, C. L. Quantitative aspects of the evolution of concepts. *Psychology Monographs*, 1920, **28**(Whole No. 123).

Hull, C. L. *Principles of behavior*. New York: Appleton-Century-Crofts, 1943.

Hull, C. L. *Essentials of behavior*. New Haven: Yale University Press, 1951.

Hull, R. F. C. *From the life and work of C. G. Jung*. New York: Harper & Row, 1971.

Hyden, H. Biochemical aspects of learning and memory. In K. Pribram (Ed.), *On the biology of learning*. New York: Harcourt Brace Jovanovich, 1969.

Isaacs, W., Thomas J., & Goldiamond, J. Application of operant conditioning to reinstate verbal behavior in psychotics. *Journal of Speech and Hearing Disorders*, 1960, **25**, 8–12.

Ittelson, W., & Kilpatrick, F. Experiments in perception. *Scientific American*, 1952, **185**, 50–55.

Izard, C. *The face of emotion*. New York: Appleton-Century-Crofts, 1971.

James, W. *The principles of psychology*, 2 vols. New York: Holt, 1890.

Jarvik, M. E. Effects of chemical and physical treatments on learning and memory. *Annual Review of Psychology*, 1972, **23**, 457–486.

Jellinek, E. M. *The disease concept of alcoholism*. New Haven, Conn.: Hillhouse Press, 1960.

Jensen, A. R. Estimation of the limits of heritability of traits by comparison on monozygotic and dizygotic twins. *National Academy of Science*, 1967, **58**, 149–156.

Jensen, A. R. Social class, race and genetics: implications for education. *American Educational Research Journal*, 1968, **5**, 1–42.

Jensen, A. R. How much can we boost IQ and scholastic achievement? *Harvard Educational Review*, 1969, **39**, 1–123.

Jewkes, J., Sawers, D., and Stillerman, R. *The sources of invention*, pp. 338–339, 381–383. New York: St. Martin's Press, 1961.

Johnson, R. N. *Aggression in man and animals*. Philadelphia: Saunders, 1972.

Johnson, R. N., DeSisto, M. J., Jr., & Koenig, A. B. Social and developmental experience and interspecific aggression in rats. *Journal of Comparative and Physiological Psychology*, 1972, **79**, 237–242.

Jones, H. A. The galvanic skin reflex in infancy. *Child Development*, 1930, **1**, 106.

Juel-Nielsen, N. *Individual and environment*. Copenhagen: Munskgaard, 1965.

Jung, C. G. *Two essays in analytical psychology*. London: Balliere, Tindall, 1926.

Kagan, J. A conversation with Jerome Kagan. *Saturday Review of Education*, 1973, **1**(3), 41–43.

Kahn, M. The physiology of catharsis. *Journal of Personality and Social Psychology*, 1966, **3**, 278–286.

Kellogg, W. N., & Kellogg, L. A. *The ape and the child*. New York: McGraw-Hill, 1933.

Kessner, R. P., & Connor, H. S. Independence of short- and long-term memory: a neural system analysis. *Science*, 1972, **176**, 432–434.

Keys, A., Brozek, J. Henschel, A., Michelsen, O., & Taylor, H. L. *The biology of human starvation*, Vol. 2. Minneapolis: University of Minnesota Press, 1950.

Kimble, G. A. (Ed.) *Hilgard and Marquis' conditioning and learning*. New York: Appleton-Century-Crofts, 1961.

Kinget, G. M. *The drawing-completion test*. New York: Grune & Stratton, 1952.

Kingsley, R. C., & Hall, V. C. Training conservation through the use of learning sets. *Child Development*, 1967, **38**, 1111–1126.

Kinsey, A. C., Pomeroy, W. B., and Martin, C. E. *Sexual behavior in the human male*. Philadelphia: Saunders, 1948.

Kinsey, A. C., Pomeroy, W. B., Martin, C. E., and Gebhard, P. H. *Sexual behavior in the human female*. Philadelphia: Saunders, 1953.

Kline, N. S. Use of *Rauwolfia serpentina* in neuropsychiatric conditions. *Annals of New York Academy of Science*, 1954, **59**, 107–132.

Kline, N. S., & Davis, J. M. Psychotropic drugs. *American Journal of Nursing*, 1973, **73**, 54–62.

Köhler, W. *The mentality of apes*. New York: Harcourt, 1925.

Köhler, W. *Gestalt psychology*. New York: Liveright, 1929.

Köhler, W. Gestalt psychology. *Psychologische Forschung*, 1967, **31**, 18–30.

Koeppel, J. C., & Raffeto, A. M. Response and associative learning as a function of warmup. *Psychonomic Science*, 1969, **14**, 59–61.

Kohler, I. The formation and transformation of the perceptual world. Trans. by H. Fiss. *Psychological Issues*, 1964, **3**(4), 1–173.

Kooker, E. W., & Bellamy, R. Q. Some psychometric differences between graduates and dropouts. *Psychology*, 1969, **6**, 65–70.

Krech, D., Crutchfield, R. S., & Ballachey, E. G. *Individual in society: a textbook of social psychology*. New York: McGraw-Hill, 1962.

Kretschmer, E. *Physique and character*. New York: Harcourt, 1936. (Original German edition, 1921.)

Lacey, J. I., Batemen, D. E., & Van Lehn, R. Automatic response specificity: an experimental study. *Psychosomatic Medicine*, 1953, **15**, 8–21.

Lacey, J. I., & Van Lehn, R. Differential emphasis in somatic response to stress. *Psychosomatic Medicine*, 1952, **14**, 71–81.

Lang, P. J., & Lazovic, A. D. Experimental desensitization of a phobia. *Journal of Abnormal and Social Psychology*, 1963, **66**(6), 519–525.

Lashley, K. S. *Brain mechanisms and intelligence*. Chicago: University of Chicago Press, 1929.

Lazarus, R. S. *Personality*. Englewood Cliffs, N.J.: Prentice-Hall, 1971.

Lazarus, R. S., Averill, J. R., & Opton, E. M., Jr. Towards a cognitive theory of emotion. In M. Arnold (Ed.), *Feelings and emotions*. New York: Academic Press, 1970.

Leahy, A. M. Nature-nurture and intelligence. *Genetic Psychology Monographs*, 1935, **17**, 235–308.

Leavitt, H. J., & Mueller, R. A. H. Some effects of feedback on communication. *Human Relations*, 1951, **4**, 401–410.

Lehrman, D. S. The physiological basis of parental feeding behavior in the ringdove (*Streptopelia risoria*). *Behavior*, 1955, **7**, 241–286.

Lehrman, D. S. *Hormonal regulation of parental behavior in birds and infrahuman mammals in sex and internal secretions* (William C. Young, Ed.). Baltimore: Williams & Wilkins, 1961.

Levine, S. Sex differences in the brain. *Scientific American*, 1966, **214**, 84–90.

Levy, D. Release therapy. *American Journal of Orthopsychiatry*, 1939, **9**, 713–736.

Lewin, K. Field theory and learning. In *National Society for the Study of Education, 41st Yearbook: The psychology of learning*, Part II, pp. 215–242, 1942.

Lewin, K., Lippitt, R., & White, R. K. Patterns of aggressive behavior in experimentally created social climates. *Journal of Social Psychology*, 1939, **10**, 271–299.

Lewis D. J., Miller, R. R., & Misanin, J. R. Selective amnesia in rats produced by electroconvulsive shock. *Journal of Comparative and Physiological Psychology*, 1969, **69**, 136–140.

Lewis, M., & McGurk, H. Evaluation of infant intelligence. *Science*, 1972, **178**, 1174–1177.

Lewy, A. J., & Seiden, L. S. Operant behavior changes norepinephrine metabolism in rat brain. *Science*, 1972, **175**, 454–455.

Lieberman, P., & Crelin, E. S. On the speech of Neanderthal man. *Linguistic Inquiry*, 1971, **2**, 203–222.

Likert, R. A. Technique for the measurement of attitudes. *Archives of Psychology*, 1932, **22** (Whole No. 140).

Lindgren, H. C., & Byrne, D. *Psychology: an introduction to the study of human behavior*. New York: Wiley, 1961.

Lindsley, D. B. Electroencephalographs. In J. McV. Hunt (Ed.), *Personality and the behavior disorders*, Chap. 33. New York: Ronald Press, 1944.

Lindsley, D. B. Emotion. In S. S. Stevens (Ed.), *Handbook of experimental psychology*. New York: Wiley, 1951.

Lindsley, D. B. Psychophysiology and motivation. In M. R. Jones (Ed.), *Nebraska symposium on motivation*. Lincoln: University of Nebraska Press, 1957.

Lindzey, G. Some remarks concerning incest, the incest taboo, and psychoanalytic theory. *American Psychologist*, 1967, **22**, 1051–1059.

Litcher, J. H., & Johnson, D. W. Changes in attitudes toward Negroes of white elementary school students after use of multi-ethnic reader. *Journal of Educational Psychology*, 1969, **60**, 148–152.

Lloyd, K. E., & Garlington, W. K. Weekly variations in performance on a token economy psychiatric ward. *Behavior Research and Therapy*, 1968, **6**, 407–410.

Lobey, F. *The nonprofessional revolution in mental health*. New York: Columbia University Press, 1970.

Locke, J. *An essay concerning human understanding: in four books*, Book II. London, 1690.

Lorber, N. M. Permissive home environment and exploitative-domineering preadolescent peer behavior. *Psychology*, 1971, **8**(1), 12–15.

Lorenz, K. *On aggression*. New York: Harcourt Brace Jovanovich, 1966.

Lukoff, I. F., Quatrone, D., & Hayim, G. J. *Heroin use and crime in a methadone maintenance program: interim report*. Washington, D.C.: U.S. Department of Justice, 1973.

Luria, A. R. The functional organization of the brain. *Scientific American*, 1970, **222**(3), 66–78.

Lutenberg, H., Rawson, R. A., & Bath, K. Reinforcement of competing behavior during extinction. *Science*, 1970, **169**, 301–303.

McCarthy, D. Language development in children. In L. Carmichael (Ed.), *Manual of child psychology* (2nd ed.), p. 523. New York: Wiley, 1954.

McClelland, D. C. *Studies in motivation*. New York: Appleton-Century-Crofts, 1955.

McClosky, H. Conservatism and personality. *American Political Science Review*, 1958, **42**, 27–45.

Maccoby, E. The meaning of being female. *Contemporary Psychology*, 1972, **17**, 369–372.

McCord, W., & McCord, J. *The psychopath: an essay on the criminal mind*. Princeton, N.J.: Van Nostrand, 1964.

McGeoch, J. A., & Irion, A. L. *The psychology of human learning* (2nd ed.). New York: Longmans, Green, 1952.

McGlashan, T. H., Evans, F. J., and Orne, M. T. The nature of hypnotic analgesia and placebo response to experimental pain. *Psychosomatic Medicine*, 1969, **31**, 227–246.

McGuire, W. J. A. syllogistic analysis of cognitive relationships. In C. I. Hovland & I. L. Janis (Eds.), *Attitude organization and change*. New Haven: Yale University Press, 1960.

Mackworth, N. H. Originality. *American Psychologist*, 1965, **20**, 51–66.

Mackworth, N. H. Visual noise causes tunnel vision. *Psychonomic Science*, 1965, **3**(2), 67–68.

McNeil, D. Developmental psycholinguistics. In F. Smith & G. A. Miller (Eds.), *The genesis of language: a psycholinguistic approach*, pp. 15–84. Cambridge, Mass.: MIT Press, 1966.

McNeil, D. Language development in children. In P. Mussen (Ed.), *Handbook of child psychology* (3rd ed.). New York: Wiley, 1970.

McNemar, Q. *The revision of the Stanford-Binet scale.* Boston: Houghton Mifflin, 1942.

MacNichol, E. F., Jr. Three-pigment color vision. *Scientific American,* 1964, **211,** 48–56.

Mahesh Yogi, M. *Maharishi Mahesh Yogi on the Bhagavadagita: a Zen translation and commentary.* Baltimore: Penguin, 1969.

Malmo, R. B. Activation: a neurophysiologic dimension. *Psychological Review,* 1959, **66,** 367–386.

Malmo, R. B., Wallerstein, H., & Shagass, C. Headache proneness and mechanisms of motor conflict in psychiatric patients. *Journal of Personality,* 1953, **22,** 163–187.

Malpass, L. F., Gilmore, A. S., Hardy, M. W., & Williams, C. F. Programmed instruction for retarded children. In J. S. Roucek (Ed.), *Programmed teaching: A symposium on automation in education.* New York: Philosophical Library, 1965.

Marcuse, F. L. *Hypnosis—fact and fiction.* Baltimore: Penguin Books, 1959.

Margules, D. L., Lewis, M. J., Dragovich, J. A., & Margules, A. S. Hypothalamic norepinephrine: circadian rhythms and the control of feeding behavior. *Science,* 1972, **178,** 640–642.

Martens, R., & Landers, D. M. Motor performance under stress: a test of the inverted-U hypothesis. *Journal of Personality and Social Psychology,* 1970, **16,** 129–137.

Martin, J. G., & Westie, F. R. The tolerant personality. *American Sociological Review,* 1959, **24,** 521–528.

Masica, D. N., Money, J., & Ehrhardt, A. A. Fetal feminization and female gender identity in the testicular feminizing syndrome of androgen insensitivity. *Archives of Sexual Behavior,* 1971, **1,** 131–142.

Maslow, A. H. *Motivation and personality.* New York: Harper & Row, 1954.

Maslow, A. H., & Mintz, N. L. Effects of esthetic surroundings. I. Initial effects of three esthetic conditions upon perceiving "energy" and "well-being" in faces. *Journal of Psychology,* 1956, **41,** 247–254.

Masters, W. H., & Johnson, V. E. *Human sexual response.* Boston: Little, Brown, 1966.

May, R. *Man's search for himself.* New York: Norton, 1953.

May, R. *Existential psychology.* New York: Random House, 1960.

Mead, G. H. *Mind, self and society.* Chicago: University of Chicago Press, 1934.

Mead, M. *Growing up in New Guinea.* New York: Apollo, 1962.

Meade, R., & Whittaker, J. A cross-cultural study of authoritarianism. *Journal of Social Psychology,* 1967, **72,** 3–7.

Mech, V. E. Factors influencing routine performance under noise: I. The influence of set. *Journal of Psychology,* 1953, **35,** 283–298.

Mednick, S. A. *Learning.* Englewood Cliffs, N.J.: Prentice-Hall, 1964.

Mednick, S. A., & Schulsinger, F. Some premorbid characteristics related to breakdown in children with schizophrenic mothers. In D. Rosenthal & S. S. Kety (Eds.), *The transmission of schizophrenia,*

pp. 267–291. New York: Pergamon Press, 1968.

Mehrabian, A. Immediacy: an indicator of attitudes in linguistic communication. *Journal of Personality,* 1966, **34,** 26–34.

Melzack, R., & Scott, T. H. The effects of early experience on the response to pain. *Journal of Comparative and Physiological Psychology,* 1957, **50,** 155–161.

Mendels, F. *Concepts of depression.* New York: Wiley, 1970.

Miles, C. C. Gifted children. In L. Carmichael (Ed.), *Manual of child psychology* (2nd ed.). New York: Wiley, 1954.

Milgram, S. Group pressure and action against a person. *Journal of Abnormal and Social Psychology,* 1964, **69,** 137–143.

Mill, J. Analysis of the phenomenon of the human mind (1829). In W. Dennis (Ed.), *Readings in the history of psychology.* New York: Appleton-Century-Crofts, 1948.

Miller, G. A. *Language and communication,* pp. 84–85. New York: McGraw-Hill, 1951.

Miller, N. E. Studies of fear as an acquirable drive: I. Fear as motivation and fear-reduction as reinforcement in the learning of new responses. *Journal of Experimental Psychology,* 1948, **38,** 89–101.

Miller, N. E. Central stimulation and other new approaches to motivation and reward. *American Psychologist,* 1958, **13,** 100–108.

Miller, N. E., & Banuazizi, A. Instrumental learning by curarized rats of a specific visceral response, intestinal or cardiac. *Journal of Comparative and Physiological Psychology,* 1968, **65**(1), 1–7.

Miller, N. E., & Bugelski, R. Minor studies of aggression: II. The influence of frustration imposed by the in-group on attitudes expressed toward out-groups. *Journal of Psychology,* 1948, **25,** 437–442.

Milner, B. Some effects of frontal lobectomy in man. In J. M. Warren & K. Akert (Eds.), *The frontal granular cortex and behavior.* New York: McGraw-Hill, 1964.

Milner, G. C., Ruffin, W. C., & McGinnis, N. H. Lithium carbonate: is it successful? *Psychosomatics,* 1971, **12,** 321–325.

Minnick, R. S., Marden, C. J., & Arieti, S. The effects of sex hormones on the copulatory behavior of senile white rats. *Science,* 1946, **103,** 749–750.

Mischel, W. *Personality and assessment.* New York: Wiley, 1968.

Mitoma, C., Auld, R. M., & Udenfriend, S. On the nature of the enzymatic defect in phenylpyruvic oligophrenia. *Proceedings of the Society for Experimental Biology and Medicine,* 1957, **94,** 634–635.

Moore, O. K. *The automated responsive environment.* New Haven: Yale University Press, 1962.

Moreno, J. L. *Psychodrama.* New York: Beacon House, 1946.

Morris, L. W., & Siebert, R. M. Effects of anxiety on timed and untimed intelligence tests: another look. *Journal of Consulting and Clinical Psychology,* 1969, **33,** 240–244.

Mundy-Castle, A. C. Electrophysiological correlates of intelligence. *Journal of Personality,* 1958, **26,** 184–199.

Munn, N. L. *The evolution and growth of human behavior.* Boston: Houghton Mifflin, 1955.

Murray, H. A. *Explorations in personality.* New York: Oxford University Press, 1938.

Mussen, P. H. Some personality and social factors related to changes in children's attitudes toward Negroes. *Journal of Abnormal and Social Psychology,* 1950, **45,** 423–441.

Mussen, P. H., & Parker, A. L. Mother nurturance and girls' incidental imitative learning. *Journal of Personality and Social Psychology,* 1965, **2,** 94–97.

Myers, R. E. Interocular transfer of pattern discrimination in cats, following section of crossed optic fibers. *Journal of Comparative and Physiological Psychology,* 1955, **48,** 470–473.

Myers, R. E. Function of corpus callosum in interocular transfer. *Brain,* 1956, **79,** 358–369.

Neisser, U. *Cognitive psychology.* New York: Appleton-Century-Crofts, 1967.

Neisser, V. A. Paradigm shift in psychology. *Science,* 1972, **176,** 628–630.

Nelsen, E. A. Social reinforcement for expression versus suppression of expression. *Merrill-Palmer Quarterly of Behavior and Development,* 1969, **15**(3), 259–278.

Newcomb, T. M. *Personality and social change.* New York: Holt, 1943.

Newman, H. H., Freeman, F. N., & Holzinger, K. J. *Twins: a study of heredity and environment.* Chicago: University of Chicago Press, 1937.

Nichols, R. C. The National Merit twin study. In S. G. Vandenberg (Ed.), *Methods and goals in human behavior genetics.* New York: Academic Press, 1965.

O'Connell, D. N., Shor, R. E., & Orne, M. T. *Hypnotic age regression: an empirical and methodological analysis.* Philadelphia: Philadelphia Unit for Experimental Psychiatry, 1968.

Oden, M. H. The fulfillment of promise: 40-year follow-up of the Terman gifted group. *Genetic Psychology Monographs,* 1968, **77,** 3–93.

Olds, J. Self-stimulation of the brain. *Science,* 1958, **127,** 315–324.

Olds, J. The central nervous system and the reinforcement of behavior. *American Psychologist,* 1969, **24,** 114–132.

Olds, J., & Milner, P. Positive reinforcement produced by electrical stimulation of septal area and other regions of the rat brain. *Journal of Comparative and Physiological Psychology,* 1954, **47,** 419–427.

Opler, M. K. Schizophrenia and culture. *Scientific American,* 1957, **197**(2), 103–104.

Orne, M. T. The nature of hypnosis: Artifact and essence. *Journal of Abnormal and Social Psychology,* 1959, **58,** 277–299.

Orne, M. T. On the social psychology of the psychological experiment: with particular reference to demand characteristics and their implications. *American Psychologist,* 1962, **17,** 776–783.

Orne, M. T., Sheehan, P. W., & Evans, F. J. The occurrence of posthypnotic behavior outside the experimental setting. *Journal of Personality and Social Psychology,* 1968, **9,** 189–196.

Orwell, G. *1984.* New York: Harcourt, 1949.

Oster, G. Phosphenes. *Scientific American*, 1970, **222**(2), 82–87.

Paivio, A. *Imagery and verbal processes*. New York: Holt, Rinehart and Winston, 1971.

Pavlov, I. P. *Conditioned reflexes*. Trans. by G. V. Anrep. New York: Oxford University Press, 1927.

Penfield, W., & Roberts, L. *Speech and brain mechanisms*. Princeton: Princeton University Press, 1959.

Perris, C. A Study of bipolar (manic-depressive) and unipolar recurrent depressive psychoses. *Acta Psychiatrica Scandinavia*, 1966, **42**(Suppl.), 194.

Piaget, J. *The language and thought of a child*. New York: World, 1969.

Poulton, E. L. Listening to overlapping calls. *Journal of Experimental Psychology*, 1956, **52**, 334–339.

Premack, D. Toward empirical behavior laws: I. Positive reinforcement. *Psychological Review*, 1959, **66**, 219–233.

Premack, D. Reinforcement theory. In D. Levine (Ed.), *Nebraska symposium on motivation*. Lincoln: University of Nebraska Press, 1965.

Premack, D. Language in chimpanzees? *Science*, 1971, **172**, 808–822.

President's Commission on Law Enforcement and Administration of Justice. *The challenge of crime in a free society*. Washington, D.C.: U.S. Government Printing Office, 1967.

Rappaport, M., Silverman, J., Hopkins, H. J., & Hall, K. Phenothiazine effects on auditory signal detection in paranoid and nonparanoid schizophrenics. *Science*, 1971, **174**, 723–725.

Ratliff, F. *Mach bands: Quantitative studies of neural networks in the retina*. San Francisco: Holden-Day, 1965.

Raush, H. L., & Raush, C. L. *The halfway house movement: a search for sanity*. New York: Appleton-Century-Crofts, 1968.

Ray, V. F. Human color perception and behavior response. *Transactions of New York Academy of Sciences*, 1953, **16**, 98–104.

Reed, H. B., & Reitan, R. M. Changes in psychological test performance associated with the normal aging process. *Journal of Gerontology*, 1963, **18**, 271–274.

Restle, F. Moon illusion explained on the basis of relative size. *Science*, 1970, **167**, 1092–1096.

Riesen, A. H. Arrested vision. *Scientific American*, 1950, **183**, 16–19.

Riesen, A. H. Stimulation as a requirement for growth and function in behavioral development. In D. W. Fiske & S. R. Maddi (Eds.), *Functions of varied experience*, pp. 57–80. Homewood, Ill.: Dorsey Press, 1961.

Rock, I. *The nature of perceptual adaptation*, pp. 15–77. New York: Basic Books, 1966.

Roffwarg, H. P., Dement, W. C., Muzio, J. N., & Fuher, C. Dream imagery: relation to rapid eye movements of sleep. *Archives of General Psychology*, 1962, **7**, 235–258.

Roffwarg, H. P., Muzio, J. N., & Dement, W. C. Ontogenetic development of the human sleep-dream cycle. *Science*, 1966, **152**, 604–619.

Rogers, C. R. *Client-centered therapy*. Boston: Houghton Mifflin, 1951.

Rogers, C. R. *On becoming a person: a therapist's view of psychotherapy*. Boston: Houghton Mifflin, 1961.

Rogers, C. R. The concept of the fully functioning person. *Psychotherapy*, 1963, **1**, 17–26.

Rogers, C. R., & Skinner, B. F. Some issues concerning the control of human behavior. *Science*, 1956, **124**, 1057–1066.

Rose, R. M., Gordon, T. P., & Bernstein, I. S. Plasma testosterone levels in the male rhesus: Influences of sexual and social stimuli. *Science*, 1972, **178**, 643–645.

Rosenblatt, J. S. Nonhormonal basis of maternal behavior in the rat. *Science*, 1967, **156**, 1512–1514.

Rosenhan, D. L. On being sane in insane places. *Science*, 1973, **179**, 250–258.

Rosenthal, D. *Genetics of psychopathology*. New York: McGraw-Hill, 1971.

Rosenthal, D., & Kety, S. S. (Eds.) *The transmission of schizophrenia*. New York: Pergamon Press, 1968.

Ross, S., & Ross, J. G. Social facilitation of feeding behavior in dogs: II. Feeding after satiation. *Journal of Genetic Psychology*, 1949, **74**, 293–304.

Rozin, P., Poritsky, S., & Sotsky, R. American children with reading problems can easily learn to read English represented by Chinese characters. *Science*, 1971, **171**, 1264–1267.

Rubenstein, B. O. The problem of interlocking systems of mother and child. In M. Levitt (Ed.), *Readings in psychoanalytic psychology*, Chapter 26. New York: Appleton-Century-Crofts, 1959.

Sackett, J. B. Monkeys reared in isolation with pictures as visual input: evidence for an innate releasing mechanism. *Science*, 1966, **154**, 1470–1473.

Sadock, B., Newman, L., & Normand, W. C. Short-term group psychotherapy in a psychiatric walk-in clinic. *American Journal of Orthopsychiatry*, 1968, **38**, 724–732.

Sarbin, T. R., & Juhasz, J. B. Toward a theory of imagination. *Journal of Personality*, 1970, **38**, 52–76.

Schachter, S., & Singer, J. E. Cognitive, social and physiological determinants of emotional states. *Psychological Review*, 1962, **69**, 379–399.

Schachter, S., & Wheeler, L. Epinephrine, chlorpromazine, and amusement. *Journal of Abnormal and Social Psychology*, 1962, **65**, 121–218.

Schapiro, S., Salas, M., & Vukovich, K. Hormonal effects on ontogeny of swimming ability in the rat: assessment of central nervous system development. *Science*, 1970, **168**, 147–150.

Schmitt, R. Density, delinquency, and crime in Honolulu. *Sociology and Social Research*, 1957, **41**, 274.

Schoenfeldt, L. F. The hereditary components of the project TALENT two-day test battery. *Measurement in Evaluation and Guidance*, 1968, **1**, 130–140.

Schwartz, A., Rosenberg, D., & Brackbill, Y. Analysis of the components of social reinforcement of infant vocalization. *Psychonomic Science*, 1970, **20**, 323–325.

Schwartz, G. Voluntary control of human cardiovascular integration and differentiation through feedback and reward. *Science*, 1972, **175**, 90–93.

Sears, R. R. Relation of aggressiveness to punitiveness of the home. *American Psychologist*, 1951, **6**, 476–483.

Sears, R. R. Relation of early socialization experiences to aggression in middle childhood. *Journal of Abnormal and Social Psychology*, 1961, **63**, 466–492.

Sears, R. R., Maccoby, E. E., & Levin, H. *Patterns of child rearing*. Evanston, Ill.: Row Peterson, 1957.

Sears, R. R., Whiting, J. W. M., Nowlis, V., & Sears, P. S. Some child-rearing antecedents of aggression and dependency in young children. *Genetic Psychology Monographs*, 1953, **47**, 135–234.

Segal, E. M., & Lachman, R. Complex behavior or higher mental processes: is there a paradigm shift? *American Psychologist*, 1972, **27**, 46–55.

Seligman, M. E. P., & Maier, S. F. Failure to escape traumatic shock. *Journal of Experimental Psychology*, 1967, **74**, 1–9.

Selye, H. *The physiology and pathology of exposure to stress*. Montreal: Acta, 1950.

Selye, H. The general-adaptation syndrome in its relationships to neurology, psychology, and psychopathology. In A. Weider (Ed.), *Contributions toward medical psychology*, Vol. I. New York: Ronald Press, 1953.

Selye, H. *The stress of life*. New York: McGraw-Hill, 1956.

Shaffer, L. F. Fear and courage in aerial combat. *Journal of Consulting Psychology*, 1947, **11**, 137–143.

Shaffer, L. F., & Shoben, T. R. (Eds.) *The psychology of adjustment*. Boston: Houghton Mifflin, 1956.

Sheldon, W. H. *The varieties of temperament*. New York: Harper, 1942.

Sheldon, W. H., Stevens, S. S., & Tucker, W. R. *The varieties of human physique*. New York: Harper, 1940.

Sherif, M. An experimental approach to the study of attitudes. *Sociometry*, 1936, **1**, 90–98.

Sherif, M., & Sherif, C. W. *An outline of social psychology* (rev. ed.). New York: Harper & Row, 1956.

Sherrington, C. S. *The integrative action of the nervous system* (2nd ed.). New Haven: Yale University Press, 1947 (first publ., 1906).

Shiffrin, R. M. Forgetting: trace erosion or retrieval failure? *Science*, 1970, **168**, 1601–1603.

Singh, J. A. L., & Zingg, R. M. *Wolf children and feral men*. New York: Harper, 1942.

Singh, S. D. Effect of urban environment on visual curiosity behavior in rhesus monkeys. *Psychonomic Science*, 1968, **11**, 83–84.

Skeels, H. H. Adult stature of children with contrasting early life experience: a follow-up study. *Monographs of the Society for Research in Child Development*, 1966, **31**, 3.

Skeels, H. M., & Dye, H. B. A study of the effects of differential stimulation on mentally retarded children. *Procedures of the American Association for Mental Deficiencies*, 1939, **44**, 114–136.

Skinner, B. F. On the rate of formation of a conditioned reflex. *Journal of General Psychology*, 1932, **7**, 274–285.

Skinner B. F. *The behavior of organisms*. New York: Appleton-Century-Crofts, 1938.

Skinner, B. F. *Science and human behavior*, New York: Macmillan, 1953.

Skinner, B. F. Teaching science in high school—what is wrong? *Science*, 1967a, **159**, 704–710.

Skinner, B F. What is psychotic behavior? In T. Milon (Ed.), *Theories of psychopathology*, p. 332. Philadelphia: Saunders, 1967b.

Skinner, B. F. *Beyond freedom and dignity*. New York: Knopf, 1971.

Skinner, B. F. On "having" a poem. In B. F. Skinner, *Cumulative record: a selection of papers* (3rd ed.). New York: Appleton-Century-Crofts, 1972.

Slater, E. A. review of earlier evidence on genetic factors in schizophrenia. In D. Rosenthal & S. S. Kety (Eds.), *The transmission of schizophrenia*, pp. 15–26. New York: Pergamon Press, 1968.

Snyder, F. W., & Pronko, H. H. *Vision with spatial inversion*. Wichita, Kan.: McCormick-Armstrong, 1952.

Sontag, L. W., Baker, C. T., & Nelson, V. L. Mental growth and personality development: a longitudinal study. *Monographs of the Society for Research in Child Development*, 1958, **23**(2), 1–85.

Spearman, C. E. General intelligence, objectively determined and measured. *American Journal of Psychology*, 1904, **15**, 201–292.

Staats, A. W. *Learning, language and cognition*. New York: Holt, Rinehart and Winston, 1968.

Stampfl, T. G., & Lewis, D. J. Essentials of implosive therapy: a learning-theory based psychodynamic behavior therapy. *Journal of Abnormal Psychology*, 1967, **72**, 496–503.

Starch, D. A demonstration of the trial and error method of learning. *Psychological Bulletin*, 1910, **7**, 20–23.

Stead, W. H., & Shartle, C. L. *Occupational counseling techniques*. New York: American Book, 1940.

Sternbach, R. A., & Tursky, B. Ethnic differences among housewives in psychophysical and skin potential response to electric shock. *Psychophysiology*, 1965, **1**, 241–246.

Sullivan, H. S. *The interpersonal theory of psychiatry*. New York: Norton, 1953.

Taylor, J., & Spence, K. W. The relationship of anxiety level to performance in serial learning. *Journal of Experimental Psychology*, 1952, **44**, 61–64.

Teitelbaum, P. Appetite. *Proceedings of the American Philosophical Society*, 1964, **108**, 464–471.

Terman, L. M. *The measurement of intelligence*. Boston: Houghton Mifflin, 1916.

Terman, L. M., & Merrill, M. A. *Measuring intelligence*. Boston: Houghton Mifflin, 1959.

Terman, L. M., & Merrill, M. A. *Revised Stanford-Binet intelligence scale* (3rd ed.). Boston: Houghton Mifflin, 1960.

Terman, L. M., & Oden, M. *The gifted child grows up*. Stanford: Stanford University Press, 1947.

Terwilliger, R. F. *Meaning and mind: a study in the psychology of language*. New York: Oxford University Press, 1967.

Thorndike, E. L. *Animal intelligence*. New York: Macmillan, 1911.

Thorndike, E. L. *The fundamentals of learning*. New York: Teachers College Press, 1932.

Thorpe, L., Katz, B., & Lewis, R. T. *The psychology of abnormal behavior* (2nd ed.). New York: Ronald Press, 1961.

Thouless, R. H. Phenomenal regression to the real object. *British Journal of Psychology*, 1931, **21**, 339–359.

Thurstone, L. L., & Chave, E. J. *The Measurement of attitudes*. Chicago: University of Chicago Press, 1929.

Tolman, E. C. *Purposive behavior in animals and men*. New York: Appleton-Century-Crofts, 1932.

Tolman, E. C. Cognitive maps in rats and men. *Psychological Review*, 1948, **55**, 189–208.

Tolman, E. C., & Honzik, C. H. Insight in rats. *University of California Publications in Psychology*, 1930, **4**, 215–232.

Tones, E. E., & Kohler, R. The effects of plausibility on the learning of controversial statements. *Journal of Abnormal and Social Psychology*, 1958, **57**, 315–326.

Triandis, H. C. Cultural influences upon cognitive processes. In L. Berkowitz (Ed.), *Advances in experimental social psychology*, Vol. I. New York: Academic Press, 1964.

Triandis, H. C., & Triandis, L. M. Some studies of social distance. In I. D. Steiner & M. Fishbein (Eds.), *Current studies in social psychology*, pp. 207–217. New York: Holt, Rinehart and Winston, 1966.

Tryon, R. C. Experimental behavior genetics of maze learning and a sufficient polygenic theory. *American Psychologist*, 1963, **18**, 442.

Tulving, E., McNulty, J. A., & Ozier, M. Vividness of words and learning to learn in free-recall learning. *Canadian Journal of Psychology*, 1965, **19**, 242–252.

Turnbull, C. M. Observations. *American Journal of Psychology*, 1961, **7**, 304–308.

Tyler, L. E. *The psychology of human differences* (3rd ed.). New York: Appleton-Century-Crofts, 1965.

Underwood, B. J. *Experimental psychology: An introduction*. New York: Appleton-Century-Crofts, 1949.

Underwood, B. J., & Richardson, J. The influence of meaningfulness, intralist similarity, and serial position on retention. *Journal of Experimental Psychology*, 1956, **52**(2), 119–126.

Underwood, B. J., & Shulz, R. W. *Meaningfulness and verbal behavior*. Philadelphia: Lippincott, 1960.

Vacchiano, R. B., Strauss, P. S., & Hachman, L. The open and closed mind: a review of dogmatism. *Psychological Bulletin*, 1968, **71**, 261–273.

Vaillant, G. E. Drug dependence and alcohol problems. *American Journal of Psychiatry*, 1966, **122**, 727–737.

Vidmar, N. Group composition and the risky shift. *Journal of Experimental Social Psychology*, 1970, **6**, 153–166.

Von Békésy, G. The ear. *Scientific American*, 1957, **197**(2), 66–78.

Von Senden, M. *Raum- und Gestaltauffassung bei opierten Blindgerbornen vor und nach der Operation*. Leipzig: Barth, 1932. (Trans. by P. Heath as *Space and sight*. Glencoe, Ill.: Free Press, 1960.)

Wagner, M. K. Survey of clinical psychologists' opinions regarding learning and deviant behavior. *The Clinical Psychologist*, 1970, **23**(3), 13.

Walker, C. E., Wolpin, M., & Fellows, L. The use of high school students as therapists and researchers in a state mental hospital. *Psychotherapy: Theory, Research and Practice*, 1967, **4**, 186–188.

Wallace, R. K., & Benson, H. The physiology of meditation. *Scientific American*, 1972, **226**(2), 84–90.

Wallach, H. the perception of motion. *Scientific American*, 1959, **201**(1), 56–72.

Wallach, H. The perception of achromatic colors. *Scientific American*, 1963, **208**(1), 107–116.

Wallach, M. A., & Kogan, N. *Modes of thinking in young children: a study of the creativity-intelligence distinction*. New York: Holt, Rinehart and Winston, 1967.

Wallach, M. A., Kogan N., & Bem, D. Group influence on individual risk taking. *Journal of Abnormal and Social Psychology*, 1962, **65**, 75–86.

Wallach, M. A., Kogan, N., & Bem, D. Diffusion of responsibility and level of risk taking in groups. *Journal of Abnormal and Social Psychology*, 1964, **68**, 263–274.

Wallas, G. *The art of thinking*. New York: Harcourt Brace Jovanovich, 1926.

Washburn, S., & Hamburg, D. Aggressive behavior in Old World monkeys and apes. In M. Wertheimer (Ed.), *Confrontation*. Glenview, Ill.: Scott Foresman, 1970.

Watson, J. B. *Behavior*. New York: Norton, 1924.

Watson, J. B. *Behaviorism*. New York: Norton, 1930.

Watson, J. B., & Rayner, R. Conditioned emotional reactions. *Journal of Experimental Psychology*, 1920, **3**, 1–14.

Watson, J. D. *The double helix*. New York: Atheneum, 1968.

Webb, W. B. *Sleep: an experimental approach*. New York: Macmillan, 1968.

Weber, E. H. De pulsu, resorptione, auditu et tactu: annotationes anatomicae et physiologicae (1834). In R. J. Hernstein & E. G. Boring (Eds.), *A source book in the history of psychology*, pp. 64–66. Cambridge, Mass.: Harvard University Press, 1965.

Wechsler, D. *The measurement of adult intelligence*. Baltimore: Williams & Wilkins, 1939.

Wechsler, D. *Wechsler Intelligence Scale for Children*. New York: Psychological Corporation, 1949.

Wechsler, D. *Manual for the Wechsler Adult Intelligence Scale*. New York: Psychological Corporation, 1955.

Weiner, B., & Kukla, A. An attributional analysis of achievement motivation. *Journal of Personality and Social Psychology*, 1970, **15**, 1–20.

Wenger, M. A., & Bagchi, B. K. Studies of autonomic functions in practitioners of yoga in India. *Behavioral Science*, 1961, **6**, 312–323.

Wenger, M. A., Jones, F. N., & Jones, M. H. *Physiological psychology*. New York: Holt, 1956.

Wenger, M. A., & Wellington, M. The measurement of autonomic balance in children: method and normative data. *Psychosomatic Medicine*, 1943, **5**, 241–259.

Wertheimer, M. *Productive thinking*, pp. 4–8. New York: Harper, 1945.

Westby, D. L., & Braungart, R. C. Class and politics in the family backgrounds of student political activists. *American Sociological Review*, 1966, **31**(5), 690–692.

Wheatley, M. D. The hypothalamus and

affective behavior in cats. *Archives of Neurological Psychiatry*, 1944, **52**, 298.

White, R. W. Motivation reconsidered: the concept of competence. *Psychological Review*, 1959, **66**, 297–333.

Whorf, B. L. *Language, thought, and reality* (J. B. Carroll, Ed.). New York: Wiley, 1956.

Wilkens, R. R., & Judson, R. E. The use of *Rauwolfia serpentina* in hypertensive patients. *New England Journal of Medicine*, 1953, **248**, 48–53.

Williams, R. J. *Biochemical individuality*. Austin: University of Texas Press, 1969.

Williams, R. B., & Eichelman, B. Social setting: influence on the physiological response to electric shock in the rat. *Science*, 1971, **174**, 613–614.

Winder, C. L., & Rau, L. Parental attitudes associated with social deviance in preadolescent boys. *Journal of Abnormal and Social Psychology*, 1962, **64**, 418–424.

Wittreich, W. J. The Honi phenomena. *Journal of Abnormal and Social Psychology*, 1952, **47**, 705–712.

Wohlwill, J. F. Developmental studies of perception. *Psychological Bulletin*, 1960, **57**, 249–288.

Wolf, M., Risley, T., & Mees, H. Application of operant conditioning procedures to the behavior problems of an autistic child. *Behavior Research and Therapy*, 1964, **1**, 305–312.

Wolfe, J. B. Effectiveness of token rewards for chimpanzees. *Comparative Psychological Monographs*, 1936, **12**, 50.

Wolfgang, M. Violence and human behavior. In M. Wertheimer (Ed.), *Confrontation*. Glenview, Ill.: Scott Foresman, 1970.

Wolpe, J. *Psychotherapy by reciprocal inhibition*. Stanford: Stanford University Press, 1958.

Wyatt, R. J., Murphy, D. L., Belmaker, R, Cohen, S., Donnelly, C. H., & Pollin, W. Reduced monoamine oxidase activity in platelets: A possible genetic marker for vulnerability to schizophrenia. *Science*, 1973, **179**, 916–918.

Zeigler, H. P., & Liebowitz, H. W. Apparent visual size as a function of distance for children and adults. *American Journal of Psychology*, 1957, **70**, 196–209.

Zimbardo, P. The human choice: individuation, reason and order versus deindividuation, impulse and chaos. In W. J. Arnold & D. Levine (Eds.), *Nebraska symposium on motivation*. Lincoln: University of Nebraska Press, 1969.

Glossary

All terms in **boldface** are defined in this Glossary.

ability test Measure of performance under standardized conditions. The two types of ability tests are achievement test and aptitude test.

ablation Surgical removal of a portion of an organ or system of organs; performed in studies of the nervous system.

abscissa The horizontal axis (x axis) of a graph; also the distance of any point on the graph from the horizontal axis. See also **ordinate**.

absolute refractory period Time immediately after a **nerve fiber** fires (responds to a stimulus), during which the nerve fiber is completely unresponsive to stimulation (from 0.001 to 0.01 second).

absolute threshold Least amount of stimulus necessary to be effective.

accommodation In vision, the change in shape of the **lens** to focus an image on the **retina**.

acetylcholine Substance in the **synapse** of nerve tissues that facilitates transmission of nerve impulses from one neuron to the next.

achievement drive Need to succeed, to perform well or better than others, based on standards set by the individual himself or by society.

achromatism Complete **color blindness** caused by the absence of **cones** in the **retina** of the eye.

acquired drives Drives that are acquired by the individual (as opposed to inborn drives); they include the numerous social, economic, personal, and intellectual drives that motivate people.

acquired fear Conditioned or learned fear.

acrophobia Fear of high places. See **phobia.**

acuity Ability to discriminate fine details in the field of vision; the keenness of vision we experience in daylight.

adaptation Adjustment to conditions of the environment. The sense organ becomes more or less sensitive depending on the conditions.

adaptation level Standard or reference level of stimulation to which an individual has become accustomed and which he then uses in judging other stimuli.

addiction Physical and psychological dependence on some substance, especially drugs.

adjustment Ability to cope with the environment and to satisfy one's own needs.

adolescence Period from puberty to maturity.

adrenal glands Endocrine glands located on top of the kidneys that produce **adrenalin** and **noradrenalin** in the adrenal medulla to control the body's flight-fight reactions (emotional arousal), and that also produce aldosterone and cortisone in the adrenal cortex to control the body's carbohydrate and salt metabolism.

adrenalin Hormone produced in the adrenal medulla. Adrenalin controls the body's flight-fight reactions (emotional arousal).

afferent neuron A neuron that carries **nerve impulses** to the central nervous system from a receptor cell. It receives external stimuli through its **dendrite** fibers, and its cell body is located on the nerve root. Also called the **sensory neuron.** See also **efferent neuron.**

afterimage The appearance of a hue after stimulation by that hue has ceased (positive afterimage); or the appearance of a hue's complementary color after stimulation by that hue has ceased (negative afterimage).

aggression Behavior related to feelings of anger and hostility that is usually a reaction to **frustration** and sometimes a response to threat.

agnosia Inability to recognize words and their meaning; caused by brain damage.

alcoholism Disorder in which the individual constantly needs alcohol to escape the hardships, frustrations, and emotional disturbances of his everyday existence.

alexia See **aphasia.**

all-or-none law Principle that **nerve fibers** respond completely or not at all.

alpha waves Brain waves having a frequency of about 10 hertzes and characteristically occurring when the person is awake and relatively relaxed.

ambivalence Feeling of conflict experienced by a person caught in an **approach-avoidance** conflict situation. The individual who wants to obtain and to reject the same goal is ambivalent toward that goal.

ambivert Alternating **introvert** and **extravert;** describes most individuals in a normal population.

amnesia Loss of memory that may be partial or total; many forms of amnesia are temporary. See **fugue; hysterical amnesia; repression.**

ampulla Bulging structure at the base of each **semicircular canal** in the ear. Conduction of sound waves to **nerve impulses** begins at the ampulla when it is stimulated by the fluid pressure in the canals.

anal fixation According to Freud's **psychoanalytic theory of personality development,** condition of an adult whose anal gratification was unfulfilled early in life; traits include stinginess, possessiveness, punctuality, excessive precision in organization, and sometimes **sadism.**

anal stage According to Freud's **psychoanalytic theory of personality development,** a stage of psychosexual development in which the infant's most intense pleasure comes from activities associated with elimination.

androgens Male sex hormones (for example, testosterone) that control the **secondary sex characteristics** and reproductive functioning; some are secreted by the **testes** and others by the adrenal cortex.

antagonistic muscles Muscles that are responsible for the movement of limbs. These muscles function in pairs; one member contracts while the other member expands.

anthropology Science of the origins of man and the manner in which he has developed his civilization.

antisocial reaction Severe and persistent personality disturbance in which the individual lacks a moral conscience, is not law-abiding, and seeks only to satisfy his own desires. Also called psychopathic reaction.

anxiety Experience of fear in the absence of any objectively noticeable fear stimuli. See **conditioned fear.**

anxiety hierarchy List of situations, ranked from least anxiety-producing to most anxiety-producing, for a particular person, compiled on the basis of an interview. The list is used in the process of **systematic desensitization.**

anxiety neurosis Disorder in which the individual cannot solve his conflicts, and his anxieties affect his overt behavior. The individual experiences continuing feelings of dread, and his behavior is technically defined as an anxiety reaction.

aphasia Disorder in which the individual is unable to use language, usually caused by damage to the left frontal lobe of the brain in righthanded persons.

apparent distance Perceived distance; the distance of an object as judged by the eye.

apparent motion Motion perceived because the observer sees an object in successively different positions rather than because the object is actually moving.

approach-approach conflict Conflict between two pleasurable or desirable goals.

approach-avoidance conflict Conflict caused by a situation that has both positive and negative aspects. The individual, who is both repulsed and attracted by the same goal, exhibits feelings of **ambivalence.**

approval motivation Seeking of praise in its many forms.

apraxia Disorder in which the individual is unable to perform purposeful movements, even though the motor pathways are undamaged; a result of damage to the **association cortex.**

aptitude test Type of **ability test** designed to predict potential for achievement.

archetype Jung's term for the universal models of prototypes in the individual's **collective unconscious.**

arousal level general level of neural activity, from very low during sleep to very high during extreme excitement.

assimilation The combining of verbal and visual stimuli in perception.

association cortex Area of the **cerebral cortex** thought to be responsible for the organizing, processing, and storing of information entering (sensory) and leaving (motor) the brain; it occupies more than three-quarters of the cerebral cortex.

association neurons Neurons that connect the impulses from the **axon** fibers of the **afferent** (sensory) **neurons** to the **dendrite** fibers of the **efferent** (motor) **neurons,** located within the brain and spinal cord. Also called **interneurons.**

associationism School of psychology that attempted to define learning and thinking solely in terms of the pairing of ideas.

astigmatism Visual defect in which either the vertical (up, down) or horizontal (left, right) degree of the **cornea** curvature is inconsistent with the **lens** curvature, resulting in a blurred image in whichever direction the distortion occurs.

attention Focusing of perception on certain aspects of the environment; attention has a focus in which events are clearly perceived, and a margin in which they are less clearly perceived.

attitude Tendency or predisposition to respond in a specific manner to particular **stimuli** (including people, objects, and situations); attitudes are learned, are reasonably long lasting, have specific referents, and are related to drives.

auditory aphasia Auditory disorder in which an individual can hear but not understand words. See also **word deafness.**

auditory area Area of the **cortex** stimulated by the auditory sensory neurons, located along the upper portion of the **temporal lobe** in the wall of the **fissure of Sylvius;** connects fibers from both areas.

auditory canal Canal leading from the external ear into the **middle ear** mechanism **(the eardrum).**

auditory nerve Nerve that carries impulses from the **cochlea** to the **brain.**

autism Psychological disorder in which the child withdraws into fantasy and is almost totally unable to

form relationships with other people; a form of **schizophrenia.**

autokinetic motion Motion created within the individual's own frame of reference caused by misinterpretation of stimuli.

autonomic nervous system The part of the peripheral nervous system that is primarily a motor system serving the **smooth muscles** and regulating the internal bodily organs; includes the **sympathetic division** and **parasympathetic division.**

aversion therapy A variation of **counterconditioning** in which negative reinforcement and punishment are used; for example alcoholics learn to associate alcohol with an exceedingly unpleasant experience and hence are conditioned to avoid alcohol.

avoidance-avoidance conflict Conflict between two equally undesirable or fear-evoking goals; the solution is often escape.

avoidance conditioning Learning to avoid an aversive stimulus by making the correct response to a warning signal.

axon Extended **nerve fiber** leading away from the body of a **neuron** cell. The axon's function is to send **nerve impulses** to the **dendrite** of the next neuron.

backward conditioning Classical **conditioning** procedure in which the **unconditioned stimulus** (US) precedes the **conditioned stimulus** (CS). Little or no conditioning actually occurs.

basic anxiety Karen Horney's term for the conflict between the individual and his environment. See also **neurotic need.**

basilar membrane A tissue in the ear that is vibrated by the cochlear fluid, activating the auditory receptors (hair cells on the **organ of Corti)** in the **cochlea;** it runs along the walls of the cochlea and transmits varying frequencies of sounds by means of its vibrations.

basket nerve ending Nerve endings enmeshed in the base of each hair on the skin, receptive to pressure and touch.

behavior Any detectable activity of the organism.

behaviorism School of psychology developed by J. B. Watson advocating the objective study of behavior.

behavior modification Technique used to change or adjust the behavior of individuals; based largely on principles derived from the psychology of learning. See **systematic desensitization; counterconditioning; modeling.**

behavior pathology A failure in some degree to adapt or adjust to life's demands.

behavior sample Technique to identify personality traits by observing an individual unknowingly placed in a situation where he will be behaving as he would in response to some similar future event.

(la) belle indifference Lack of concern that a person suffering from **conversion hysteria** feels toward his illness; results from the reduction of anxiety that occurs when the illness seems to solve the individual's problems.

binaural cues Direction perception cues involving both ears.

binocular cues Depth perception cues that simultaneously stimulate

both eyes; **retinal disparity** and **convergence** are binocular cues.

blastula A hollow sphere which develops from a division of the **gastrula.** See also **zygote.**

blind spot The part of the retinal surface with no **rods** or **cones;** a break in the retinal lining that allows the nerve ends to meet and tie together.

blur point Point 39 inches away from an old-sighted person, in front of which objects cannot be seen clearly. See also **presbyopia.**

brain Part of the **central nervous system** encased in the skull; involved in learning, perception, motivation, thinking, sensory experience and so on.

brightness How dark or light a color is; the degree of whiteness, grayness, or blackness of the color. See **hue; saturation.**

brightness constancy Perception of objects as maintaining the same brightness even though that brightness is not constant on the retina.

Broca's area Part of the left frontal lobe of the brain which controls aspects of speech that are essentially motor functions, such as moving the jaw and tongue.

camouflage Concealment of the real nature of an object through the use of misleading stimuli.

catch trial In **threshold** identification, a trial in which no signal occurs. See also **signal detection theory.**

catharsis In psychoanalytic theory, the release of emotional tension through expression of the emotion.

cell body Part of the **neuron** that contains the **nucleus, dendrites,** and **axons.**

central fissure See **fissure of Rolando.**

central nervous system The **brain** and **spinal cord.** See also **peripheral nervous system.**

cerebellum Area of the **hindbrain** controlling balance, posture, and body coordination.

cerebral arteriosclerosis Disorder of the aged in which the brain no longer receives enough oxygen or nourishment to maintain its function.

cerebral cortex Surface layer of cells (the gray matter) covering the **cerebrum.**

cerebral hemisphere The two halves of the **cerebrum** which are mirror images of each other and are separated by a groove from front to back; each half controls sensory and motor activity in the opposite side of the body and is composed of four lobes: the **frontal, occipital, parietal,** and **temporal.**

cerebrum Largest area of the forebrain, responsible for emotion, learning, thinking, remembering personality, and sense perception; composed of white matter (fiber tracts) and covered by the cerebral cortex. The cerebrum consists of a right and left hemisphere, each of which is divided into the **frontal, occipital, parietal,** and **temporal lobes** of the brain.

character disorder Relatively permanent pattern of socially unacceptable behavior. Character disorders include **alcoholism, antisocial reactions,** and drug addiction.

chemical senses Senses of taste and smell.

chemotherapy Treatment of be-

havior pathology involving the use of drugs. See **tranquilizers.**

chlorpromazine A strong **tranquilizer,** particularly effective in treating **schizophrenia.**

choroid Middle layer of the wall of the eye that provides protection against outside light; dark and opaque in color.

chromosomes Long, threadlike bodies located in pairs in the nucleus of the cell; the **genes**—the determiners of hereditary characteristics—are found on the chromosomes.

chronic anxiety reaction Neurotic disorder characterized by vague fears of impending disaster, constant emotional and physical tension, fatigue, the inability to concentrate, and so on.

chronological age Age in years, or calendar age.

classical conditioning Learning procedure in which an organism is repeatedly presented with a neutral stimulus **(conditioned stimulus)** paired with an **unconditioned stimulus** in a fixed order; the conditioned stimulus eventually elicits a **conditioned response** that is very similar to the **unconditioned response.** See **operant conditioning.**

claustrophobia Fear of closed places or of being shut in. See also **phobia.**

client-centered therapy Psychotherapeutic method in which the patient, or client, is free to direct the course that each session will take; the therapist accepts what the patient has to say and only rephrases or clarifies thoughts and feelings; also called nondirective psychotherapy. See **directive therapy.**

clinical observation A correlational method; the systematic observation of patients in clinical settings such as hospitals or in other situations involving diagnosis and therapy.

clinical psychology Branch of psychology emphasizing the study and treatment of behavior pathology: a clinical psychologist may specialize in diagnosis, in psychotherapy, or in a combination of both. As a psychotherapist, he may favor any one or a combination of the various schools and techniques of therapy ranging from **psychoanalysis** to **behavior modification.**

closure Tendency of individuals to see a whole object even when the stimulus is only partially complete.

coaction effects Effects on an individual's behavior caused by the presence of others performing the same activity; a branch of **social facilitation studies.**

cochlea In the inner ear, a snailshaped mechanism that is filled with fluid and that transmits vibrations from the oval window to the auditory receptors through displacement of the basilar membrane.

cochlear duct Canal in the cochlea of the ear.

cognitive development J. Piaget's stage theory in which the child masters certain mental operations at each stage. The five stages are **sensorimotor operations, preconceptual thought, concrete operations,** and **formal operations.**

cognitive dissonance A theory of attitude change holding that an individual's ideas tend to be consistent with each other and with his behavior; dissonance causes discomfort, and the individual will strive to restore balance and consistency by changing his attitude.

cognitive learning Acquisition of knowledge in terms of knowing what to do and of perceiving relationships among stimuli.

cognitive map Concept developed by Tolman to describe the individual's ability to store spatial associations and to retrieve those applicable to a particular problem. See also **perceptual learning.**

cognitive psychology School of psychology influenced by Tolman's reintroduction of the concept of purpose into the analysis of behavior. Cognitive psychologists are interested in thinking, language, problem-solving, perception, and learning.

collaterals **Axons** from **neurons** to other types of cells that also can transmit **nerve impulses,** so that the dendrite of one neuron may receive impulses from many other neurons.

collective unconscious Carl Jung's concept of the **unconscious** as extending beyond the structure of any individual's experiences to the experiences of mankind. Also called **racial unconscious.**

color blindness Inability to see certain, or sometimes all, colors; a sex-linked characteristic. See **achromatism.**

color solid A three-dimensional colored graphic design, such as a color wheel, on which all combinations of **hue, saturation** and **brightness** are related to each other.

community psychology Branch of applied psychology that deals with the individual in his reactions, relations, and adaptations to the social setting in which he lives.

compensation Defense mechanism in which a frustrated person, who may or may not be aware of his limitations, seeks a new goal that he can reach.

competence R. H. White's concept that each person desires to function as effectively as possible in the environment; closely related to the concept of **self-actualization.**

complementary colors Two hues that appear as gray when their wavelengths are combined.

compromise techniques Defense mechanisms that enable man to cope in some way with an anxiety-arousing situation, usually by changing or diluting the situation. See **compensation, projection, rationalization, reaction formation,** and **sublimation.**

compulsive reaction An irrational act that usually results from obsessive thoughts and may pervade the individual's behavior. See also **obsessive reaction.**

conception The fertilization of the female's **ovum** by the male **sperm** cell.

concordance Development of a specific characteristic by both twins of a twin pair.

concrete operations Fourth stage in Piaget's theory of **cognitive development** in which the child is able to understand and apply concrete rules to objects, events, or people. He understands the **conservation** of matter.

conditioned fear Fear of a previously neutral object that results from its association with an object that evokes a fear response. See **fear; anxiety.**

conditioned reinforcer A **stimulus** that becomes a **reinforcer** only after it has been associated with previous reinforcers.

conditioned response (CR) A response resembling the **unconditioned response** (UR) evoked by the **conditioned stimulus** (CS) as a result of repeated pairings of the CS with the unconditioned stimulus (US).

conditioned stimulus A neutral stimulus that for experimental purposes is presented to an organism together with a nonneutral stimulus (**unconditioned stimulus**) for the purpose of developing a **conditioned response** similar to the **unconditioned response** previously evoked by the US.

conditioning See **classical conditioning; operant conditioning.**

conduction deafness Disorder characterized by the inability to hear as a result of impairment in the conducting mechanism of the ear, for example, in the **eardrum** or the **ossicles.**

cones Receptor cells that dominate the **fovea** of the eye; they are receptive to daylight vision and are responsible for color vision and **acuity.**

confabulation Process of filling memory gaps by inventing or improvising, typical of **Korsakoff's psychosis,** as well as other forms of brain damage.

conflict frustration Condition arising from conflicting attitudes toward goal-directed activity.

connotative meaning The evaluative or emotional responses that a word elicits. See also **denotative meaning.**

consciousness Awareness of one's own internal processes.

conservation According to Piaget, a child's ability to perceive that an object, however it is transformed, is the same weight, and so on. See **concrete operations.**

consolidation theory Theory of memory that learned material is organized and stored in the brain for a period of time and, if the process is disrupted or interfered with, the material will not be recalled completely or correctly.

context Setting and surroundings in which a stimulus is perceived, which may significantly alter perception of the basic stimulus.

contiguity Principle that two events must occur together in space or time to be associated in learning.

continuation Tendency to group stimuli so as to make the fewest interruptions in contours.

continuous reinforcement A schedule of reinforcement in which every correct response is reinforced.

contour Boundary between a figure and its ground, used in organizing a pattern of stimuli.

contrast Noticeable variation in stimulation that enhances object perception.

control group Participants or conditions in a scientific experiment that, for the purposes of comparison with the **experimental group,** are not subjected to the **independent variable.**

convergence The process by which many neurons distribute several incoming impulses to a single **efferent neuron;** also, in vision, the process by which the eyes focus on close objects.

conversion hysteria Term originated by Freud to describe patients who had all the symptoms of physical illness but whose illness was psychological in origin. This illness occurs as the patient converts his unconscious conflict into an anxiety-reducing symptom; also called conversion reaction.

cornea Transparent outer coating in front of the **iris** of the eye.

corpus callosum Large, whitish area of the brain connecting the cerebral hemispheres, composed of myelin-sheathed axons. Cutting the corpus callosum splits the brain in two, so that each half no longer supports the activities of the other.

correlational method Method of investigation, using statistical evaluation of relationships between **variables.** Correlational methods are **clinical observation, naturalistic observation,** and **psychometric technique.**

cortex Outer covering. See **cerebral cortex.**

counterconditioning Extinguishing of an individual's originally conditioned responses before conditioning him to make new responses; a principle of learning applied in **behavior modification.**

CR See **conditioned response.**

cranial nerves Motor and sensory nerves originating in the brain stem.

crista Gelatinous, bud-shaped mass embedded with hair cells and located in the **ampulla** of a **semicircular canal** in the ear. Movement of the **endolymph** (canal fluid) affects the crista's hair cells, which by bending or otherwise moving stimulate the nerve fibers at the base of the ampulla. Necessary for bodily equilibrium.

criterion Standard of performance used as the basis for comparing actual performance to expected performance.

cross-cultural method Technique for determining similarities and differences in the cultural patterns of societies by selecting a certain universal problem or set of problems, sampling several cultures, and analyzing each culture's solution to the problem.

CS See **conditioned stimulus.**

cue Stimulus that sets the occasion for a **response;** an informal synonym for discriminative stimuli.

culture Set of customs, traditions, attitudes, and beliefs characteristic of a particular social group, usually the largest social group to which each person belongs. See **socialization.**

curare A drug that blocks transmission of impulses at the **motor end plate.**

dark adaptation Increased sensitivity of the eye to dark places; usually takes 30 to 45 minutes.

decibel Unit of sound intensity, or loudness.

decision tree Duncker's method of presenting the approach to a solution; begins with (1) a general understanding of what has to be done, which leads to an interpretation of (2) the general solution, and finally to (3) a specific solution.

decorticate To remove the **cerebral cortex.**

deduction In logical thinking, the process of deriving general principles from specific facts.

defense mechanism Reaction to **anxiety** or **frustration** that enables man to adjust to himself and society. See **compensation; fantasy; projection; rationalization; reaction formation; regression; repression; sublimation.**

deindividuation The tendency of membership in a large group to submerge the individuality of the single member.

delayed conditioning Classical conditioning in which the **conditioned stimulus** (CS) begins before the **unconditioned stimulus** (US) and continues at least until the US has started.

delirium tremens (DTs) Disorder commonly associated with long-term alcoholism and characterized by trembling, muscular weakness, and frightening hallucinations.

delusion A false, irrational belief characteristic of **paranoid reactions;** there are delusions of grandeur, influence, persecution, and reference.

dendrite Nerve fiber nearest the cell body of a **neuron,** which receives **nerve impulses** either from the **axon** of adjacent **neurons** or directly from some physical source.

denotative meaning The objective and identifiable stimuli elicited by a word. For instance, words denote objects, events, or relationships.

deoxyribonucleic acid (DNA) Chemical substance in the cell nucleus that determines hereditary characteristics as well as growth and development of the organism. See **genetic code.**

dependent variable In an experiment, the factor that the experimenter observes to see the effects of manipulation of the **independent variable.**

depolarization Neutralization of opposite charges. When a nerve cell is stimulated, its membrane becomes semipermeable and positive ions pass through the membrane to neutralize the negative ions.

depressant Any drug that tends to level off an individual's emotional experiences by raising the stimulus threshold so that less is perceived. Pain killers and sleeping pills are depressants.

depressive reaction A form of psychosis characterized by overwhelming feelings of sadness and futility. See **manic-depressive reaction.**

depth perception Perception of distance of an object from oneself; made possible by monocular and binocular cues. Despite the **retina's** two-dimensional images, such cues enable the individual to perceive three-dimensional objects and their distance from that individual.

descriptive behaviorism A system of thought founded by B. F. Skinner which is application oriented and uses **operant conditioning** as a kind of behavioral engineering. **Reinforcement** is a key concept in this system.

desensitization See **systematic desensitization.**

differential reinforcement The selective reinforcement of some responses but not others. See **discrimination.**

differential threshold Smallest difference in a stimulus that can be perceived; also called **just noticeable difference.**

diplopia (double vision) Visual defect caused by inability of the eye muscles to control incoming light so that only one retinal image is reflected; the brain receives two different impulses for unmatched sensory experiences.

directive therapy Psychotherapeutic method in which the therapist plays an active, directing role in his treatment of the patient. See **client-centered therapy.**

discrimination Differential response learned in the presence of a particular stimulus; occurs as a result of differential reinforcement.

discriminative stimulus The S^D (ess dee); the stimulus that sets the occasion for the reinforced response. By contrast, the SΔ (ess delta), the negative stimulus, is not accompanied by a reinforced response.

dissociative reaction Form of **hysteria** involving extreme **repression**; the person escapes anxiety by dissociating himself from the source of his anxiety.

double approach-avoidance conflict Conflict situation that involves two goals, each with its own positive and negative aspects.

double-blind technique Technique used in drug experiments to avoid bias. Neither the experimenter nor the subject is informed of which subjects receive the drug and which the **placebo.**

double vision See **diplopia.**

drive Stimulus that arises from a **need** and directs the organism toward a **goal**; the second stage of the motivation process; also called **motive.**

drive state Condition of the individual in relation to the fulfillment of his drives; often takes the form of an increase in the vigor or rate of responding.

drive-stimulus reduction theory Theory of reinforcement that states that reinforcement consists of the reduction of drive stimuli.

dyad Smallest **group**, consisting of two people interacting with one another.

eardrum Thin stretchable membrane in the middle ear which vibrates when sound waves exert pressure against it.

eclectic orientation Orientation in which one selects the best from various doctrines, theories, and so forth.

ectoderm The outer layer of cells of the embryo which forms the sense organs, skin, and nervous system. See also **mesoderm** and **endoderm.**

EEG See **electroencephalogram.**

efferent neuron A neuron that carries the impulse from the brain or spinal cord to the muscles. Also called motor neuron.

ego According to Freud's **psychoanalytic theory of personality development**, the rational self that satisfies the needs of the **id** and directs and controls the **libido** into effective behavior.

ego identity Erik Erikson's term for the adolescent's integration of his previous experiences to form a self-identity; the ego identity emerges from the psychosocial crisis of identity versus role confusion. See also **psychosocial crisis.**

eidetic imagery The ability to remember the minutest detail of a scene, the pages of a book, and so on; also called photographic memory.

electroconvulsive therapy Therapy that involves the induction of a convulsion and then a brief period of unconsciousness; the convulsion is produced by passing an electric current across the frontal portion of the cerebral cortex for a fraction of a second. Also called electroshock therapy.

electroencephalogram (EEG) Record of the electrical activity of the **cortex**; electrodes are attached to the scalp to detect changes in the electrical activity of the cortex and to record them graphically. The instrument for recording the electrical activity is called the electroencephalograph.

embryo An early stage in the development of an organism; in humans, from the second to the eighth weeks after conception. See **fetus; ovum.**

emotion Behavior that is influenced primarily by conditioned visceral responses.

empirical Based on observation, experimentation, and facts as opposed to reasoning or opinion.

endocrine glands Ductless glands that secrete hormones directly into the bloodstream; they include the adrenal glands, the gonads, the pancreas, and the parathyroid, pituitary, and thyroid glands.

endocrinology Study of the endocrine glands, their hormonal activities, and the results of their malfunctions.

endoderm The inner layer of cells of the embryo, which forms the digestive system. See also **ectoderm** and **mesoderm.**

endolymph Fluid in the **semicircular canals** of the ear, which helps to determine the **equilibratory sense.**

environmental frustration Condition arising when reinforcement is prevented by any of the numerous external objects or events.

environmental therapy Therapeutic approach that provides disturbed patients with continued social contacts in order to increase their chances of recovery; also called tertiary prevention.

equilibratory sense Sense of body balance, position, and movement. Also called labyrinthine sense; **vestibular sense.**

escape conditioning Learning to escape from a noxious stimulus by making the appropriate response.

escape techniques Defense mechanisms, such as **repression, fantasy,** and **regression,** that enable man to avoid or escape from situations that generate anxiety.

ESP See **extrasensory perception.**

estrogen Female sex hormone (produced by the ovaries) that controls the **secondary sex characteristics** as well as the reproductive function.

estrus Sexually receptive period in female animals triggered by the female hormone **estrogen**; commonly called **heat.**

ethnocentrism Attitudinal pattern in which the person glorifies groups to which he belongs and displays hostility toward groups to which he does not belong; tends to result from certain personality characteristics.

ethologists Biologists who study animal behavior by means of naturalistic observation.

Eustachian tube Tube that runs from the inside of the back of the mouth to the middle ear and equal-izes the pressure on both sides of the sensitive eardrum.

existential psychology An approach to psychology which centers on the way man deals with the reality of his own existence in the face of anxiety and death.

existential therapy Psychotherapy based on the view that a person's "sense of being" is the fundamental problem with which he and his therapist must deal; the therapist assists rather than guides or directs the patient.

expectancy Readiness of a subject to respond to a stimulus. See **set.**

experimental chamber An apparatus used in the study of **operant conditioning**; in the chamber, the organism has the opportunity to make responses (say, a lever press) in order to obtain **reinforcement.** Also known as a Skinner box.

experimental group Participants in a scientific experiment whose situation is altered for the purposes of comparison with another group of subjects, the **control group,** whose situation is not altered.

experimental method Scientific method in which the observer manipulates one set of variables to see if and how it affects another set of variables. The events being studied must be controlled, and extraneous and interfering factors minimized. See also **dependent variable; independent variable.**

experimental psychology Branch of psychology that is based on the experimental method. Although usually found in laboratory settings, it need not be confined to the laboratory. See **experimental method.**

exploratory drive The need to investigate a novel environment.

extinction Elimination of a **conditioned response** by repeatedly presenting the **conditioned stimulus** without the **unconditioned stimulus** (in **classical conditioning**) or without **reinforcement** (in **operant conditioning**).

extrasensory perception (ESP) Perception outside the usual sense organs, for example, clairvoyance, telepathy, and precognition.

extravert Jung's term to describe a personality that is realistic, conventional, sociable, and generally aggressive. See **ambivert; introvert.**

fantasy Defense mechanism in which the person is able to satisfy his needs by withdrawing into an unreal world.

farsightedness Visual disorder in which the eyeball is shorter than average and light rays are deflected to a point just beyond the surface of the **retina.**

feedback Information regarding performance on a learning task; also called knowledge of results; important to work and educational settings.

fetus The human organism in the womb during the fetal period (from the third month until birth).

field theory Theory of psychology proposed by Kurt Lewin, stressing the importance of interactions between events in the person's environment.

figural aftereffect Distorted perception due to overlong stimulation from a figure.

figure and ground relationship Perception typified by one feature standing out against a larger background.

fissure of Rolando Groove in the brain running from left to right between the frontal and parietal lobes; also called the central fissure.

fissure of Sylvius Deep groove on the lateral surface of the cerebral cortex, separating the temporal lobe from the frontal and parietal lobes; also called lateral fissure.

fixation A set inflexible pattern of perceiving objects, events, or situations because of previous reinforcement or frustration.

fixed-interval schedule In **operant conditioning**, a partial reinforcement schedule in which the organism is reinforced for the first correct response made after certain predetermined, fixed periods of time, regardless of the number of correct responses made during that period.

fixed-ratio schedule In **operant conditioning,** a partial reinforcement schedule whereby the organism is reinforced after a certain predetermined number of correct responses have been made.

forebrain Largest portion of the brain, composed of the most complex structures (the **cerebrum, thalamus,** and **hypothalamus**) and controlling all "higher level" behavior.

formal operations The last stage in Piaget's theory of **cognitive development** during which the child begins to think abstractly.

fovea Recessed area on the surface of the **retina** positioned almost centrally behind the **lens**; the **cones** are strongly concentrated in the fovea and are used in day and color vision, and the **rods** found around the fovea are used primarily for night vision.

fraternal twins Two children of the same parent, born at the same time, but with different hereditary characteristics and possibly of different sexes; they develop from different ova.

free association Psychoanalytic technique in which the patient is encouraged to allow his ideas to arise spontaneously and to express them without conscious restraint.

free nerve endings Structures below the surface of the skin that branch and tangle to cover the undersurface area; they are responsible for detection of pain, warmth, cold, and perhaps touch, to a degree.

fequency Dimension of vibrational stimuli; most often used for sound in terms of **hertzes.**

frequency theory Theory of audition emphasizing the **basilar membrane** as a vibrating unit that corresponds in number of vibrations per second to the original frequency of the sound wave stimulus.

frontal association area Portion of the **frontal lobe** of the brain that takes part in such complex behaviors as learning, thinking, and remembering.

frontal lobe Lobe in each hemisphere of the **cerebral cortex** located in front of the **fissure of Rolando** across the front of the brain.

frustration State that occurs when an individual is prevented by some obstacle from reaching a goal; may result in aggressive behavior. See **conflict frustration; environmental frustration; personal frustration.**

fugue Flight of an individual suffering from amnesia; a form of **hysteria.**

functional autonomy of motives G.

W. Allport's observation that acquired drives may cease to depend on their original associations with other drives and come to function independently.

functional fixedness Type of **set** that prevents individuals from using objects in novel ways; it may hinder problem-solving.

functional psychotic reactions Psychotic reactions that are not caused by an organic malfunction.

functionalism School of psychology that emphasizes the study of man's methods of adapting to his environment, as well as the ways in which man satisfies his needs and increases his abilities.

galvanic skin reflex (GSR) Change in the electrical resistance of the skin (usually, the palm) elicited by stimulus; it is most often associated with emotional arousal.

galvanometer Instrument that measures the electrical resistance of the skin or **GSR**.

ganglia Groups of neuron cell bodies outside the brain and spinal cord.

gastrula A cluster of cells resulting from the early cell division of the **zygote;** formed during the first 2 weeks of life.

general-adaptation syndrome Selye's term for the sequence of responses to emotional stress. There are three stages: the alarm reaction, resistance to stress, and exhaustion.

general paresis Psychosis produced by inflammation of the brain that develops as a result of a long-term syphilitic infection; characterized by loss of control of the fine muscles of the tongue and lips, confusion of speech and thinking, and delusions and hallucinations.

generative theory of language acquisition Noam Chomsky's theory that learning is a matter of understanding sentences or sequences of words and that the individual develops an ability to understand and produce groups of words (sentences) without continuous feedback from the environment.

genes Transmitter of hereditary characteristics; located on the **chromosomes,** occur in pairs, one from each parent.

genetic code The various combinations of the chemical elements of the DNA molecule; different combinations govern the transmission of different hereditary characteristics.

genital stage According to Freud's **psychoanalytic theory of personality development,** a psychosexual stage in which the **id** directs itself toward adult sexuality. This is the ultimate stage of psychosexual development.

germ cell Sperm or egg. Unlike other cells, the germ cell has only 23 single **chromosomes.**

Gestalt psychology School of psychology that emphasizes the whole as more than the sum of its parts; in learning, Gestaltists emphasize **insight;** in perception, organizations such as **figure and ground relationships.**

Gestalt therapy Based in part on Gestalt psychology, which emphasizes the study and analysis of a person's perceptions of his environment and his current problems; therapy is often carried out in a group setting.

goal Object or state toward which an organism directs itself. See **incentive.**

gonads Sex glands; **ovaries** in females and **testes** in males.

gradient of generalization Progressive loss in response strength to stimuli that are increasingly different from the original conditioned stimulus of S^D.

group Collection of people involved in a relatively long-term relationship. Members share in group activities and standards; remain within group attitude and behavior boundaries; and reject the same positions and people. A group has a structure or organization.

group therapy Psychotherapeutic method in which several patients meet regularly to work out problems through group interactions. See **environmental therapy.**

grouping Tendency of stimuli to be perceived in meaningful patterns, determined by such factors as closure, continuation, nearness, similarity, and symmetry.

GSR See **galvanic skin reflex.**

habit Conditioned or learned response to a particular stimulus, repeated each time that stimulus is presented.

habituation State of being accustomed to a particular situation.

hair cell Receptor cell located on the **organ of Corti** in the **cochlea** of the ear; transforms sound waves into electrical impulses for transmission to the brain.

halfway house A transitional situation in which patients released from a hospital can learn to adjust to community life before actually entering the community; usually run by ex-patients.

hallucination Imaginary or unreal perceptions, often experienced by psychotic individuals, such as schizophrenics.

hallucinogen Drug that induces distorted or exaggerated perceptions—for example, LSD and mescaline.

halo effect Influence that an interviewer's personal taste has on his objective observation of the interview.

heat See **estrus.**

hertzes (Hz) Frequency of wave vibrations; in audition, the number of hertzes (wave cycles per second) determines pitch.

heterogeneous group Group in which the members have different scores on ability or personality tests. See **homogeneous group.**

hierarchy of needs Abraham Maslow's listing of man's wants, beginning with the needs for physiological comfort, followed by safety needs, and primarily leading to needs for love, esteem, **self-actualization,** knowledge, and aesthetic pleasure.

higher-level reflexes Reflexes involving regions of the nervous system above the spinal cord.

higher-order conditioning Classical conditioning in which a conditioned stimulus (CS) is used as the unconditioned stimulus (US) for a third conditioning series, and so on.

hindbrain Portion of the brain concerned with the organism's survival; it controls breathing and blood circulation and includes the **cerebellum, medulla,** and **pons.**

homeostasis Process of maintaining the proper balance and rate of internal activities in the body.

homogeneous group Group in which the members have similar scores on ability or personality tests. See **heterogeneous group.**

homosexuality Sexual attraction between two members of the same sex.

hormones Substances secreted by the **endocrine glands** into the bloodstream.

hue Wavelength of a color; typified by a name, for example, green.

human relations training Methods used to improve interpersonal interaction by providing people with the resources for getting along with others. Three such methods are the **case method, sensitivity training,** and **role playing.**

humors See **temperament.**

hunger drive Unlearned drive for food which results from activity in the **hypothalamus,** caused by an imbalance in the chemical composition of the blood.

hypnosis Inducement of a trance-like state, sometimes used in psychotherapy as a quick method of uncovering unconscious material.

hypnotic regression Use of hypnosis to recall past experiences.

hypnotic suggestion After hypnosis, the patient's adoption of attitudes, conditions, or activities suggested by the therapist; it was once used to eliminate maladaptive symptoms or to substitute other less maladaptive symptoms. Often called posthypnotic suggestion.

hypothalamus Area of the forebrain concerned with maintaining the proper balance and rate of internal activities (homeostasis), mostly through the use of the endocrine system; it regulates the excitation or inhibition of hunger, sleep, temperature, thirst, and sex.

hysteria A neurotic disorder that may take the form of a **dissociative reaction,** such as multiple personality or amnesia, or a conversion reaction, which is characterized by physical symptoms.

hysterical amnesia Loss of memory such that the individual forgets personal memories such as his name, home, and occupation, but does not forget such things as how to read, how to drive, or the way he parts his hair; it is regarded by some as an extreme form of **repression.**

ICS See **intracranial stimulation.**

id According to Freud's **psychoanalytic theory of personality development,** the reservoir of man's basic instinctual urges; it contains the **libido,** which seeks immediate gratification. See **ego; superego.**

identical twins Two children that develop from the same **ovum** and have the same hereditary characteristics.

identification Process through which a child incorporates many of the parent's attitudes, particularly moral attitudes.

identity formation Erikson's theory of personality, which emphasizes that the unifying concept of individuality is a matter of knowing who one is at any particular time in one's life. See **integration of identity.**

illusion Perception that does not correspond with actual stimuli.

image Implicit (internal) representation of past experience; in vision, the representation of an object focused on the **retina.** See **percept.**

imageless thought theory Theory that some thinking occurs without images (as in rote association) and that some thinking is controlled automatically by an individual's state of readiness.

imitation See **modeling.**

implosive therapy Therapeutic technique which attempts to extinguish anxiety responses through the evocation of strong anxiety feelings.

imprinting Process of rapidly acquiring a response to a stimulus at an early **optimal period** of development; responses acquired in this way are apparently persistent and irreversible.

incentive A **reinforcer** that develops motivating features in its own right. See **goal.**

incus Hinged bony structure of the middle ear (familiarly called the anvil because of its shape) which receives pressure waves from the malleus and, in vibrating, causes the stapes to vibrate; with the **malleus** and **stapes,** called the ossicles.

independent variable In an experiment, the factor that is manipulated by the experimenter.

induced motion Motion perceived but not real, caused by misinterpretation of **figure and ground relationships.**

induction Process of deriving principles or rules from a collection of facts.

inferiority complex Deeply rooted feeling of inadequacy; according to Alfred Adler, such a complex may lead to strivings to dominate. See **power drive.**

informational social influence Pressure to accept other people's views of reality. See **normative group influence.**

inhibition Tendency of a response to occur less frequently with repetition of the response.

inner ear Innermost part of the ear containing the **cochlea, eustachian tube,** and **vestibular organs.**

insight Sudden understanding, as when one "sees through" a situation or "gets the idea"; often inferred from sudden improvement in learning; also, in psychoanalytic therapy, it is necessary for the patient to gain insight into his unconscious conflicts.

instinct Descriptive term for a complex, unlearned, adaptive response that is characteristic of a species.

instrumental conditioning See **operant conditioning.**

insulin coma treatment A form of therapy in which the patient is given a large dose of insulin to reduce his blood sugar level and to induce a coma in which brain metabolism is slowed; little used today.

integration of identity Erikson's concept that each individual's personality is an integration of various identities.

intelligence Term used to describe a person's general abilities in a number of different areas, including both verbal and motor skills.

intelligence quotient (IQ) Numerical value of the ratio of **mental age** to **chronological age,** multiplied by 100; the score 100 is the average IQ.

intensity In sensation, the strength of a stimulus impinging on a sense organ; in hearing, the loudness of a sound.

interference In learning theory, the

activities of the learner, either before, after, or during the learning process, that cause forgetting. See **proactive inhibition; retroactive inhibition.**

intergroup relations Term referring to the state of affairs that exists between two or more groups.

interneurons See **association neurons.**

interposition Obstruction of part of one object by another object, which enables us to judge the first object's apparent distance.

interstimulus interval In classical conditioning, the period of time between the onset of the **conditioned stimulus (CS)** and the onset of the **unconditioned stimulus (US).**

intracranial stimulation Electrical stimulation of the foreward portion of the **hypothalamus** and the limbic region of the brain, sometimes called ICS; it may be used as a reinforcer.

intragroup relations Relations between members of the same group, including the effects of the group on individual members and the effects of individuals on the actions of the group as a whole.

introspection The observing and reporting of one's covert behavior; self-observation.

introvert Jung's term to describe a personality that is shy, withdrawn, and interested in subjective cognitions and idealism. See **ambivert; extravert.**

intuitive thought The third stage of Piaget's theory of cognitive development, in which the child groups objects according to their outstanding perceptual qualities.

involuntary muscles Smooth muscles and cardiac muscles.

iodopsin Photosensitive material in the cones of the retina; important in daylight vision.

IQ See **intelligence quotient.**

iris Colored portion of the eye; the muscles that pad the inner circular boundary of the iris control the size of the pupil.

just noticeable difference (j.n.d.) See **differential threshold.**

kinesthesis Sense of position and movement in space, mediated by the receptors in the muscles, tendons, and joints.

Korsakoff's psychosis A disorder caused by brain damage and marked by progressive loss of memory; often accompanies alcoholism. The patient tends to fill memory gaps by inventing or improvising **(confabulation).**

kymograph Apparatus designed to record variations in activity intensity during a period of time; in its original form it was a rotating drum containing a strip of smoked paper on which marks were made by a recording pen.

labyrinthine sense See **vestibular sense.**

latency The elapsed time between the presentation of a stimulus and the appearance of a response.

latency period Fourth stage in Freud's **psychoanalytic theory of personality development** during which the libido is calm and there are no unconscious urges that might conflict with the individual's **superego.** The latency stage occurs between the age of 5 and the beginning of adolescence.

latent content Unpleasant or painful memories that the patient is hiding and that appear in symbolic form in the individual's dreams. The latent content of the dream finds expression in the disguised form of the **manifest content.**

latent learning Learning that appears to take place in the absence of reinforcement; however, it is manifested in performance when reinforcers are introduced.

lateral fissure See **fissure of Sylvius.**

lateral geniculate nucleus Portion of the **thalamus** involved in vision.

latitude of acceptance Degree of deviant behavior that a group will accept as compared to their social norm.

latitude of rejection Degree of behavior that deviates from the group norm, above which the individual will no longer be a member of that group.

law of effect E. L. Thorndike's principle that responses that lead to satisfying consequences will be learned. This idea set the stage for the principle of reinforcement.

learned drives See **acquired drives.**

learning Relatively permanent change in an individual's repertory of responses that results from past experience or practice.

lens Transparent focusing mechanism through which light stimuli must pass for vision to occur; it is in the black center of the visible eye. See **accommodation.**

lesion Damage to an organ or part of an organ caused by injury or disease.

libido According to Freud's **psychoanalytic theory of personality development,** the energy that serves the basic instincts and motivates every aspect of a person's behavior; it is basically sexual energy.

lie detector An instrument whose use is based on the idea that lying is often accompanied by the visceral components of fear or excitement; the detector indicates when a person's answers are accompanied by emotional arousal. See **polygraph.**

limbic system A large diffuse system of nerve cells often referred to as the "old cortex" because it is a more primitive region from the standpoint of evolutionary development; located in the cerebral cortex as well as parts of the thalamus and hypothalamus, it is involved in emotional reactions and, perhaps, in motivation and reinforcement.

linear perspective Perception of faraway objects as close together and nearby objects as far apart; it is important for depth perception as it enables the individual to estimate distances.

linear program An educational learning program that usually consists of constructed responses sequenced so that the student will respond correctly.

linguistic relativity hypothesis Theory that a language shapes the way in which speakers of that language view the world.

localized functions Specific bodily functions that are regulated by specific parts of the cerebral cortex.

logic A formal discipline that applies simple rules to **reasoning.**

long conducting neurons Afferent neurons and efferent neurons.

long-term memory Storage of information for relatively long periods of time. See **LTM-STM theory.**

LTM-STM theory Theory of remembering (also called the long-term memory—short-term memory theory) that certain material is retained for only a few moments, while other information is retained on a long-term basis.

Mach bands The light and dark bands that appear on either side of a border between a half-light, half-dark visual stimulus.

maladjustment General term describing mild as well as severe disorders in which the individual is unable to cope with his environment.

malleus Hinged, bony structure of the middle ear (familiarly called the hammer because of its shape), which receives pressure waves in the middle ear and transmits them to the incus; with the **incus** and **stapes,** called the ossicles.

manic-depressive reaction Psychotic reaction characterized by swings in emotion from the extreme of depression to the extreme of excitement.

manic reaction Psychotic reaction in which the individual exhibits exaggerated excitement; usually begins with a buildup of anxiety, sometimes emerging from a deep depressive episode.

manifest content Remembered portion of a dream, the actual sequence of events in the dream, as recalled by a person after he wakes up; a disguised form of the **latent content.**

marijuana A drug derived from the hemp plant which produces changes in perception and perceptual sensitivity.

masochism Behavior characterized by enjoyment of pain inflicted on oneself by another, often thought to have sexual overtones. See **sadism.**

maternal drive Tendency of female animals to care for and protect their young offspring; in human beings, it varies from one individual to the next and from one culture to another.

maturation Development of the bodily systems and processes; based on hereditary potential and somewhat influenced by learning and environment.

maze An arrangement of corridors consisting of correct pathways and blind alleys; it is used in the study of learning.

mean Average of a set of scores in a frequency distribution, computed by adding the scores and dividing by the number of scores.

median The score midway between the highest and lowest scores in a frequency distribution.

medulla Portion of the hindbrain that controls respiration, digestion, and circulation.

Meissner corpuscles Pressure-sensitive receptors found on the hairless parts of the body, the lips, eyelids, and tip of the tongue.

memory drum Device that rotates to show single words or pairs of words through a window; used in **serial memorization** or **paired-associate learning** experiments with **nonsense syllables.**

memory trace Hypothetical information pathway used to store **short-term memories** in the brain.

mental age (MA) Measuring unit of intelligence based on a norm; an MA of 8 means the individual has performed as well as the average 8-year-old.

mentally retarded Individual with an IQ below 70; approximately 3 percent of the population.

meprobamate A relatively mild tranquilizer used to induce relaxation.

mesoderm The middle layer of cells of the **embryo** which forms the blood, bone, and muscle. See also **ectoderm** and **endoderm.**

method of adjustment A psychophysical method in which the subject manipulates the stimulus until he thinks that it bears some required relationship to a standard.

method of constant stimuli A psychophysical method in which the subject, when presented with the stimulus, must report whether it is greater or less than some standard stimulus.

method of limits A psychophysical method in which the experimenter controls the stimulus and varies the amount of change above or below the intensity of the original stimulus, and the subject must report the relationship between the stimulus he perceives and the original stimulus.

microelectrodes Tiny electrodes surgically implanted in the brain to detect neural activity.

microspectrophotometer An instrument used to examine **cones** by directing different wavelengths of light through individual cones.

midbrain Area of the brain that controls visual and auditory responses; it involves the tracts between the cerebrum and the spinal cord and thus is part of the impulse conduction system.

middle ear Section of the ear containing the **eardrum** and the **ossicles.**

mode The most frequently scored value in a frequency distribution.

modeling Procedure of learning by imitating another person's responses; used in **behavior modification.**

mnemonic device A form of memory coding in which memorable phrases or associations are used to facilitate **recall.**

monaural cues Cues involving the use of one ear only.

monocular depth cues Depth perception cues that stimulate one eye independently; monocular cues are **linear perspective, clearness, interposition,** shadows, gradients of texture, movement, and **accommodation.** See **binocular cues.**

mood Emotional state that lasts longer than the emotion itself, but is generally not so intense as the emotion.

morpheme Smallest unit of meaning in a language; a morpheme may be a prefix, suffix, or root.

motivated forgetting Forgetting that is negatively reinforced; referred to as **repression** in psychoanalytic theory.

motivated remembering See **Zeigarnik effect.**

motivation General term that refers to driven behavior that seeks to fulfill a **need.** See also **drive.**

motivational traits Guilford's classification of traits that involve **needs, attitudes,** and interests. See also **temperament traits.**

motive See **drive.**

motor aphasia Disorder characterized by the inability to use spoken language.

motor area Primary area of the cortex responsible for motor functions, located in the **frontal lobe** to the front of the **central fissure**.

motor end plate Place at which the **axon** of the motor neuron connects with the muscle cell.

motor neuron See **efferent neuron**.

motor skill Skill involving coordination of the skeletal muscle system.

motor theory of thinking Theory that all thinking involves muscle movement, much of it covert.

multiple personality Dissociative reaction in which the individual's conflicts are so severe that he develops two or more distinctive personalities.

muscle Tissue that is the mechanism for responses; the three types are **smooth**, **striated**, and cardiac.

muscle tone Semiactive state of muscle cells which depends on the elastic strength and vigor of the muscle fibers.

myelin sheath Structure covering the membrane of the axon of some neurons, composed of a fatty substance and facilitating the conduction of impulses through the axon portion of the neuron; it is essential for the timing and patterning of these impulses.

narcosis Sleep or sleepiness that results from injection of such drugs as sodium amytal.

narcotherapy Type of medical therapy (also called narcoanalysis), in which the patient is injected with a sleep-inducing drug; half-awake and half-asleep he is able to recall or relive experiences that he could not otherwise remember. He may also be more responsive to suggestion.

nativism A position propounded by Gestalt psychologists that individuals are born with certain fundamental perceptual abilities.

naturalistic observation A correlational method that involves the observation of animals or people in their natural settings; the observer interferes as little as possible.

nearsightedness Visual disorder in which the eyeball is longer than average, and the light rays are deflected to a point just short of the surface of the **retina**.

need Physiological (internal) or environmental (external) imbalance that gives rise to a **drive**.

need reduction The satisfaction of one's internal or external needs.

negative reaction formation A **reaction formation** in which an individual who is unconsciously afraid of his drives defends his self-esteem by pursuing an overt behavior that he knows is socially acceptable and guilt free. See also **positive reaction formation**.

negative reinforcer In operant conditioning, a stimulus whose withdrawal strengthens responses leading to the withdrawal; see **positive reinforcer**.

negative transfer The learning of one task that disrupts or interferes with the learning of a later task.

neocortex See **cerebral cortex**.

neonate Infant less than 2 weeks old.

nerve Bundle of **nerve fibers**.

nerve cell See **neuron**.

nerve deafness Auditory disorder characterized by hearing loss of high-frequency sounds and caused by a malfunction of or damage to the inner ear or the auditory nerve.

nerve fibers Axons or dendrites from many **neurons** in the same loca-

tion of the body with the same path; they conduct **nerve impulses**.

nerve impulse Electrical impulse transmitted by **nerve fibers**, conducted through electrical changes in the membrane of the nerve fiber; it conforms to the **all-or-none law**.

nerve root Structure that connects the nerve cell with the spinal cord.

nerve trunk Bundle of **axons** that connect neurons running from within the spinal cord to the outer body areas.

nervous system The **brain, spinal cord,** and interconnecting **neurons** through which sensory and motor impulses are transmitted in varying degrees.

neurilemma Thick, porous membrane that covers the **neuron** and through which the electrochemical impulses are allowed to pass.

neurologist Physician whose major field of study is the nervous system; he is trained to recognize psychological disorders that may be caused in some degree by diseased tissue in the body.

neuron Specialized cell that conducts impulses; nerve cell.

neurosis See **neurotic reaction**.

neurotic need Karen Horney's term for the need of a person to adjust his behavior to deal with basic anxieties. See **basic anxiety**.

neurotic reaction Maladjustment that results from inability to cope with conflicts; no marked deviance is evident but it is often accompanied by symptoms of anxiety. Also called neurosis.

night blindness Loss of visual acuity under low illumination, caused by a deficiency of vitamin A.

nodes of Ranvier Interruptions in the myelin sheath covering the **axon** of a **neuron**.

nondirective psychotherapy See **client-centered therapy**.

nonsense syllables Random combinations of letters (usually two consonants and a vowel or three consonants) used in rote learning experiments; they were first employed by Ebbinghaus.

noradrenalin Hormone produced in the adrenal medulla which controls the body's "fight or flight" reaction.

norm Standard, or average, in terms of a given group of values; it allows for comparison of one individual to a larger group of individuals.

normative group influence Pressure to conform to the expectations of others; it serves the individual's need for social approval.

nuclei Large clusters of neuron cell bodies in the central nervous system; also refers to the chromosome-containing structure within cells.

nyctophobia Fear of the dark. See **phobia**.

obsessive-compulsive reaction See **compulsive reaction; obsessive reaction**.

obsessive reaction A neurotic reaction typified by a persistent, involuntary thought; the individual can think of nothing else and is characteristically lured away from productive and adjustive behavior. See **compulsive reaction**.

obstruction box Device for administering punishment to test the strength of a drive.

occipital lobe Lobe located at the lower back of each cerebral hemi-

sphere; visual impulses are organized in this lobe.

ochlophobia Fear of crowds. See **phobia**.

Oedipal stage See **phallic stage**.

Oedipus complex According to Freud's **psychoanalytic theory of personality development**, the tendency of a child in the phallic or Oedipal stage to have sexual desires for the parent of the opposite sex. See **phallic stage**.

old-sightedness See **presbyopia**.

olfactory sense organ Organ that is responsible for the sense of smell; situated high up on the walls of each side of the nasal cavity.

operant behavior Responses that produce **reinforcement**.

operant conditioning Conditioning based on the principle of **reinforcement**; the consequences of a **response** determine whether or not that response will persist; also called instrumental conditioning.

opinion A rather vague concept, falling somewhere between an attitude and a belief.

opponent-process theory Hering's theory of color vision that assumes three sets of **cones**, each set consisting of complementary (opposite) colors: blue-yellow, green-red, and black-white; each pair can react in two ways, and each way is incompatible with the other since each member of a pair opposes the other.

opsin Substance formed from breakdown of **rhodopsin** by light. It is useful in **dark adaptation**.

optic chiasma The junction at the base of the brain through which **nerve impulses** from the eye pass to the **occipital lobes**.

optic nerve Bundle of nerve fibers that originates in the retinal lining of the eye and connects to the brain.

optimal period Stage in development in which the organism is best ready to acquire certain forms of learned responses.

oral fixation According to Freud's **psychoanalytic theory of personality development**, condition of an adult whose oral gratification was unfulfilled early in life; traits include greed, dependence, overabundant speech or chatter, chewing, smoking, and a general desire to seek oral activities.

oral stage In Freud's **psychoanalytic theory of personality development**, the stage in which the most intense pleasures are derived from activities that involve the mouth— chewing, sucking, biting, and so on.

ordinate Vertical axis (y axis) of a graph; also the distance of any point on the graph from the vertical axis. See **abscissa**.

organ of Corti Structure attached to the **basilar membrane** of the ear; the hair cells in this structure are auditory receptors.

orienting reflex Changes in the bodily orientation elicited by the conditioned stimulus; the subject adjusts his sensory receptors for receiving the unconditioned stimulus, enabling him to be more attentive to stimuli.

ossicles Bony structures of the middle ear—the **stapes, malleus,** and **incus**—that transmit vibrations to the **cochlea**.

otoliths Stonelike structures in chambers near the **cochlea** which balance the fluid of the **utricle** and **saccule** to signal the position of the body

in space, exerting pressure when the body or head is not upright.

oval window Membrane separating the middle and inner ear through which sound pressures are transmitted to the auditory receptors. The oval window receives vibrations from the **ossicles**, whereupon it causes movement of the fluid in the **cochlea**.

ovaries Female sex glands; produce relaxin, estrogen, and progesterone, hormones that control **secondary sex characteristics** and the reproductive functions.

overcompensation Term used by Alfred Adler to describe an extreme form of the defense mechanism called **compensation**, in which the individual compensates for inferiority by developing a superiority in another area.

overlearning Practice that continues beyond the time learning has been achieved; it often improves retention.

ovum Female reproductive cell; also, the fertilized organism until the time at which it attaches itself to the human uterus, which occurs during the second week following conception.

paired-associate learning Learning of pairs of words or **nonsense syllables** in such a way that appearance of the first (stimulus) evokes the recall of a second (response).

papillae Bumps on the tongue that are actually clusters of taste buds. See **taste bud**.

paradoxical cold Perception of intense cold by receptor cells for cold when stimulated by a hot object a great deal above the indifference point in temperature.

paradoxical warmth Perception of intense heat by receptor cells for warmth when stimulated by a cold object a great deal below the indifference point in temperature.

paranoid reaction A general category of psychotic behavior marked by delusions; affected individuals often show logical-seeming thinking throughout their normal states and into their paranoid reactions. They may seem well adjusted, except when involved in a situation that stimulates their delusional behavior. See **delusion**.

parasympathetic division Part of the **autonomic nervous system** which arises from the cranial and sacral portions of the spinal cord; it is active during periods of bodily relaxation.

parietal lobe Lobe of each cerebral hemisphere located along the upper back of the brain.

partial reinforcement Reinforcing the correct response intermittently. See **schedules of reinforcement**.

pathophobia Fear of disease. See **phobia**.

peer group Group of equals in a particular social situation.

percept The stimulus that is perceived.

perception Process of becoming aware of and interpreting objects or events that stimulate the sense organs.

perceptual constancy Unchanging qualities of objects despite variations in sensory input; factors of constancy include size, shape, brightness, and color.

perceptual learning Process of problem-solving conceived as a sequence of changing perceptions. Each step toward a solution is characterized by a change in the individual's perceptions.

peripheral nervous system Part of the nervous system outside the brain and the spinal cord.

peripheral vision Vision in which stimuli are not observed directly through the center of the **lens** of the eye; light is focused on the area of the **retina** with fewer **rods** and **cones** than are in and around the **fovea.**

periphery Area of the **retina** with relatively few **rods** and **cones,** connected by multipurpose nerve cells.

personality The organized system of behavior patterns, attitudes, and values that characterize a given individual and account for his particular manner of functioning.

phallic fixation According to Freud's **psychoanalytic theory of personality development,** condition of an adult who was unable to resolve his **Oedipus complex** early in life; traits include an inability to distinguish or accept an adult sexual role and sometimes a tendency toward **homosexuality.**

phallic stage According to Freud's **psychoanalytic theory of personality development,** the period during which children are dominated by unconscious impulses of genital curiosity.

phenomenal field Carl Roger's term for a person's total realm of experience, which exists in the framework of his environment and his perception of himself.

phi phenomenon Tendency of individuals to see movement where none exists.

phobia Intense feelings of anxiety, associated with particular objects or situations.

phoneme Basic, linguistically significant unit of sound in a language.

phosphene A colored arc or circle seen in the eye on the opposite side of the area on which pressure has been applied. See also **afterimage.**

physiological psychology Branch of psychology closely associated with the biological sciences, particularly physiology, neurology, and biochemistry.

physiological zero point Normal temperature of the skin.

pitch Frequency of the vibrations of a sound wave; defined in terms of the number of wave cycles per second (**hertzes**); the more hertzes, the higher the pitch.

placebo A neutral substance that has no actual effect on the organism; often used as a control in drug experiments.

play therapy Special **psychotherapeutic method** developed to deal with emotionally disturbed children; by nonverbal activity, the child may reveal emotional conflicts and insecurities.

polarization Electrically, a situation in which part of an object has an excess of positive charge and part has an excess of negative charge. The neuron's membrane is negatively charged, the area surrounding it is positively charged; passage of positive ions through the membrane allows for passage of a nerve impulse.

polygraph Device consisting of several units, each of which is designed to record specific visceral changes, such as **galvanic skin reflex,** heartbeat, blood pressure, breathing; used

to detect emotional arousal, as in "lie-detection" test.

pons Area of the **hindbrain** that houses nerve fibers from both sides of the **cerebellum** as well as tracts and nuclei for impulses traveling between the upper brain and spinal cord.

population The entire group toward which a study is directed. A representative small group, called a **random sample,** is selected and is used to test a hypothesis. Then, with statistical inference, the conclusions are generalized to the population at large.

positive reaction formation A **reaction formation** in which socially acceptable behavior is exaggerated because of a person's guilt feelings for repressed hostility. See also **negative reaction formation.**

positive reinforcer In operant conditioning, a stimulus whose presentation strengthens the responses leading to its presentation. See **negative reinforcer.**

positive transfer Process in which the learning of one task facilitates the learning of a second task.

postingestional sensitivity Process in which signals in the bloodstream are translated into feelings of fullness in the stomach, thus leading to satiation of the hunger drive.

postsynaptic membrane Area in the synaptic region of a neuron to which the impulse is being transmitted.

power drive Alfred Adler's concept that man continually seeks compensation for his own feelings of inferiority.

preconceptual thought Jean Piaget's second stage of **cognitive development** during which representational thoughts begin to appear.

predisposition Tendency or leaning toward a previously learned or experienced perception. See also **set.**

prehension Grasping of objects with the hands and fingers; the first stage in motor development.

prejudice General term referring to a fixed, irrational **attitude** toward a person or group of people; usually used to mean a negative prejudgment.

prenatal period Time between **conception** and birth.

presbyopia Visual disorder involving the gradual development of farsightedness in an older person due to hardening of the **lens;** the individual cannot focus the lens by contracting it; also known as old-sightedness. See **blur point.**

presynaptic membrane Area in the synaptic region of a neuron from which the impulse is being transmitted.

proactive inhibition Interference of earlier learning with retention of current learning. See **negative transfer.**

probability sampling Polling technique in which people are chosen at random from the population under study and in which each person has the same numerical chance of being selected. See also **quota sampling.**

problem-finding An inventive ability stemming from the recognition that new approaches are needed, typically more demanding of originality than **problem-solving.**

problem-solving Behavior that is at an advanced stage of thinking; problem-solving can be divided into four stages: incubation, illumination, preparation, and verification.

process schizophrenia Categorization of schizophrenics who have undergone a progressive process of increasingly severe maladaptive behavior; the prognosis (prediction for recovery) is very poor. See also **reactive schizophrenia; schizophrenia.**

progesterone Female sex hormone produced by the ovaries; with relaxin, controls secondary sex characteristics and the reproductive functions.

programmed instruction Instructional technique based on the principles of **operant conditioning.** The material requires the student to make frequent responses, and the student receives immediate knowledge of the correctness or incorrectness of his responses.

progressive part learning Learning technique in which exceptionally long material is broken down into more meaningful smaller parts and each part is learned separately, and then the whole is combined.

projection Defense mechanism in which the individual remains oblivious to his own undesirable qualities by attributing them to others. In this way he reduces his own feelings of anxiety.

projection areas Specialized areas of the **cerebral cortex** that control particular sensory and motor activities.

projective techniques Tests using ambiguous stimuli to determine underlying personality factors and uncover unconscious conflicts. See **Rorschach inkblot test; Thematic Apperception Test (TAT).**

prolactin Pituitary secretion whose release into the female mammal's blood begins the production of milk to nurse the young when they are born.

proprioceptive sense Responsiveness to the kinesthetic and vestibular receptors within the body.

proximity A principle of perceptual organization; nearness or closeness of objects that leads the individual to perceive them in patterns.

pseudo-isochromatic plates specifically designed color arrangements used to test for color blindness.

pseudophone Device used for reversing the natural perception of sound waves; sounds coming from the right pass through the pseudophone and are heard by the left ear, and vice versa.

psychedelic drugs Drugs, such as lysergic acid diethylamide (LSD), with dramatic and complex effects, often producing psychotic-like behavior.

psychiatry Branch of medicine that deals with the treatment of individuals suffering from behavior pathology; it makes use of drugs as well as **psychotherapeutic methods.**

psychoanalysis Psychotherapeutic method devised by Sigmund Freud, involving intensive sessions between a **psychoanalyst** and his patient; the psychoanalyst attempts to make the individual aware of his unconscious motives, that is, to uncover the source of his conflicts and motives for repressing them. May involve analysis of **resistance;** dream analysis; **free association; transference.**

psychoanalyst Recognized **psychotherapist** who may be a psychiatrist or a clinical psychologist; he differs from other psychiatrists and psychologists in that he adheres to the **psychoanalytic theory of personality,** and he practices the psychoanalytic ap-

proach to therapy, as originated by Freud.

psychoanalytic theory of personality development Freud's theory that personality development is characterized by different psychosexual stages throughout an individual's growth years. Each stage represents a need for a different type of bodily gratification. See **anal stage; genital stage; latency period; oral stage; phallic stage.**

psychodrama Special form of **group therapy** that serves as a medium for releasing the "actor's" psychological conflicts; the patient acts out a particular scene that is thought to be crucial to his conflict; also used in **environmental therapy.**

psychodynamics Clinical approach to personality that sees personality as the end result of the conflicts existing within the individual; Freud's theories of personality are one of several psychodynamic theories.

psycholinguistics Study of language and how it is acquired and used, often through the observation of the development of language in children.

psychology Systematic study of the behavior of animals and human beings.

psychometric method Correlational method that samples behavior by means of tests. Tests may distinguish among the characteristics of several individuals or distinguish changes within one individual.

psychomotor abilities Abilities such as dexterity, strength, and coordination, measurable through testing.

psychoneurosis See **neurotic reaction.**

psychopathic reaction See **antisocial reaction.**

psychopharmacology The study of the effect of drugs on behavior. See also **chemotherapy.**

psychophysical methods Techniques used to determine the relationship between physical stimuli and the sensations they produce. See **method of adjustment; method of constant stimuli; method of limits.**

psychophysics Investigation of sensation to find the relationship between physical stimuli and the sensations they produce (developed by Gustav Fechner).

psychosexual stages According to Freud's **psychoanalytic theory of personality development,** the sequence of stages through which the child progresses; each stage—**oral stage, anal stage, phallic stage, latency period,** and **genital stage**—has its "zone of gratification."

psychosis See **psychotic reaction.**

psychosocial crisis A dilemma involuntarily faced by a person at each of the eight stages of Erik Erikson's human life cycle, based on real-life adjustments made necessary by the individual's social environment; the stages are trust versus mistrust; autonomy versus doubt; initiative versus guilt; industry versus inferiority; identity versus role confusion; intimacy versus isolation; generativity versus self-absorption; and integrity versus despair.

pychosomatic disorder Organic disorder caused by prolonged anxiety.

psychotherapeutic method Systematic attempt to have the individual understand his problems and adjust his behavior accordingly; the methods most commonly used are **behavior modification, client-centered therapy, group therapy, play therapy,** and **psychoanalysis.**

psychotic reaction Behavior pathology that becomes so extreme that it disrupts thinking and contact with reality. The individual may be disoriented to the extent that he loses his own identity or fails to distinguish between what is real and what is imagined.

psychotomimetic drugs Drugs that produce reactions that mimic psychoses, for example, LSD.

pupil Small opening in the **iris** of the eye through which light rays enter the eye.

pupillometrics Study of pupil size in relation to emotions; the pupil of the eye dilates (enlarges) when the eye is focused on an object pleasurable to the observer and contracts when focused on an unpleasant object.

purposive behaviorism E. C. Tolman's theory of learning, which emphasizes goal-directed behavior, stimulus-stimulus relationships, and also **cognitive maps.**

quota sampling Polling method in which a **representative sample** is selected that includes important sociological groups in the same proportions as they appear in the general population. See also **probability sampling.**

random sample Representative group chosen in such a way that each individual has an equal chance of being chosen; used as a basis for statistical inference.

rapid eye movement (REM) Quick movements of the eye in stage 1 of sleep, usually accompanied by dreaming.

RAS See **reticular activating system.**

rational psychotherapy Albert Ellis's psychotherapeutic technique which emphasizes the substitution of logical thought for irrational ideas.

rationalization Defense mechanism in which the individual attempts to apply the rules of reason to an unreasonable or irrational conclusion in order to hide the true motive for a particular behavior.

reaction formation Defense mechanism in which the individual disguises his repressed feelings by adopting an active belief in some opposite cause; used to protect the individual against his socially unacceptable desires.

reaction time Time lag between the onset of the stimulus and the organism's response.

reactive schizophrenia Category of **schizophrenia** in which the disorder has been triggered by a traumatic experience or a sudden personality collapse. See **process schizophrenia.**

reasoning Orderly thinking that enables us to adjust to the environment; the comprehension of symbolic relationships. See **logic.**

recall Measure of **retention** which involves the reproduction of previously learned material; the process of remembering without the benefit of extra cues.

recall stimuli Assumed stimuli, external or internal, conscious or not, that are responsible for recall.

receptor cell Structure in the nervous system that is tuned to particular

stimuli and transduces their energy into signals in the nervous system.

recidivism Tendency of offenders who are convicted of a crime to commit further crimes after release from prison.

reciprocal inhibition Technique of **behavior modification** that involves the inhibition of maladaptive responses while appropriate responses are strengthened.

reciprocal innervation Balance of impulses leading to the relaxation of one of a pair of antagonistic muscles as the other contracts.

recognition Measure of **retention** in which the individual perceives something as familiar; the ability to look at several things and select one that has been seen or learned before.

redintegration Process of recalling from fragmentary clues.

reflex Unlearned response that occurs rapidly and automatically to a particular stimulus.

reflex arc The circuit through which nerve impulses travel.

refractory period See **absolute refractory period; relative refractory period.**

regression Escape from frustrating or anxiety-provoking situations by retreat to earlier forms of behavior. Regression is a **defense mechanism.**

reinforcement Process of applying **reinforcers.**

reinforcer In **classical conditioning,** the unconditioned stimulus; in **operant conditioning,** the stimulus (positive or negative) that plays a role in increasing the probability of the response being conditioned. See also **negative reinforcer; positive reinforcer.**

relative refractory period Period of time after **absolute refractory period** when only very strong stimuli, well above **threshold,** will excite the nerve fiber, because complete repolarization of the membrane has not yet occurred.

relaxin A female sex hormone produced by the ovaries; with progesterone, controls secondary sex characteristics and reproductive functions.

relearning Process by which something previously learned is learned again more quickly; it is often the most sensitive measure of **retention.** See **savings method.**

reliability The quality of a test as a measuring instrument, determined by whether or not it produces the same or similar scores time after time for the same subject. See also **validity.**

REM See **rapid eye movements.**

representative sample In poll taking, the group of people that will reflect the attitudes of the population as a whole. There are two recognized ways to construct a representative sample: **probability sampling** and **quota sampling.**

repression Defense mechanism in which anxiety-provoking material is blocked from entering consciousness although it exists at an unconscious level. See **motivated forgetting.**

reserpine Drug used in **chemotherapy,** which may produce improved emotional control, better personality integration, decrease of inhibition, and increase in responsiveness.

resistance Refusal of individuals undergoing psychoanalysis to reveal certain thoughts; it may give the analyst a clue to his patient's **repressions.**

respondent conditioning See **classical conditioning.**

resting potential Difference in electrical charge between the negatively charged inside and the positively charged outside of an inactive nerve fiber.

retention Quantifiable aspect of remembering; the difference between what is remembered and what was originally learned. Retention is measured by **recall, recognition,** and **relearning.**

reticular activating system (RAS) System located in the brainstem extending upward to the thalamus and hypothalamus; it is involved in arousing the individual and is thought to play an important part in emotional excitement.

retina Innermost layer of the eye that receives light that has passed through the lens. The retina contains the receptor cells and nerve endings that are needed for transduction of the light stimulus into nerve impulses. See also **cones; fovea; rods.**

retinal disparity The difference in retinal images received by the two eyes; important in **depth perception.**

retinene Substances formed from the breakdown of **rhodopsin** by light. Useful in **dark adaptation.**

retroactive inhibition Interference of a later activity with the individual's recall of previous learning.

reverberating circuit Self-exciting neural circuit by which the impulse travels from afferent neuron to interneuron to efferent neuron and back around several times.

reward In conditioning, a **positive reinforcer;** all rewards are reinforcers, but all reinforcers are not rewards.

rhinencephalon Part of the brain located in the frontal lobe of the cerebral cortex; olfactory impulses are received in the front portion of the rhinencephalon. It is also believed to contain centers involved in emotional behavior.

rhodopsin Photosensitive substance in the **rods.** See **dark adaptation.**

ribonucleic acid (RNA) A molecule that sometimes acts as a messenger carrying the **genetic code** contained in DNA **(deoxyribonucleic acid).**

rods Receptor cells located near the **fovea** on the **retina** that are sensitive to tones of white, black, and some grays. See **cones.**

role Pattern of behavior typical of a given social status or occupational position; one's conception of a role is based on past experience and learning. See also **status.**

role diffusion Erik Erikson's term for an individual's failure to integrate his identity at a stage in human development. See also **psychosocial crisis.**

role playing In **psychodrama,** the patient's acting out of a role that will enable him to face some experience that is particularly disturbing to him; also, a human relations training technique.

Rorschach inkblot test Projective test consisting of 10 symmetrical inkblots in shades of gray or black or in color.

rote memorization Learning of material by repetitive practice without regard for meaning. **Paired-associate learning** and **serial memorization** are types of rote memorization.

round window An opening just below the oval window of the inner ear that equalizes pressures so that the **cochlea** does not burst.

saccule One of the double sacs (the other is the **utricle**) below the **ampulla** between the base of the **semicircular** canals and the beginning of the **cochlea;** it receives stimuli related to the upright position of the individual.

sacral nerves Motor and sensory nerves originating below the lower back.

sadism Behavior characterized by enjoyment of pain inflicted on others; often thought to have sexual overtones. See also **masochism.**

saturation Degree of pure color, or the amount of hue in a color; for example, a yellow green is less saturated than a pure green.

savings method A measure of **retention** arrived at by determining the difference between the number of trials originally needed to learn the material and the number of trials needed for **relearning.**

scapegoating Process of displacing aggression onto innocent persons, for example, aggression displaced onto a minority group.

schedule of reinforcement Pattern of reinforcement and nonreinforcement; the frequency with which a response is reinforced. See also **fixed-interval schedule; fixed-ratio schedule; variable-interval schedule; variable-ratio schedule.**

schemata Jean Piaget's term for the organizing frameworks of thinking, planning, and problem-solving; these schemata change successively in the course of cognitive development.

schizophrenia Diagnostic term used to refer to the psychotic reaction in which the basic symptoms are withdrawal from reality, distorted or disturbed contact with reality, regressive behavior, erratic thought, inconsistent emotional relationships, hallucinations, and delusions. See also **process schizophrenia; reactive schizophrenia.**

sclera Outermost covering, the "white of the eye," which is relatively hard and protects the shape of the eye.

scotoma A recurring blind spot somewhere in one's field of vision.

secondary motor areas Areas located in front of the primary motor area near the midline of the brain, representing the face, arms, and legs in proper (right side up) occurrence.

secondary prevention In community mental health, the method of providing early diagnosis and treatment of the individual with minor psychological disturbances to prevent the disturbances from becoming serious problems.

secondary sex characteristics Aspects of the body that differentiate the sexes but that have no direct sexual functions, such as body build, pitch of voice, and distribution of hair.

segregation Separation or isolation of an individual or a group from the rest of society.

selective perception In terms of preservation of attitudes, the tendency of people to perceive that which is consistent with their attitudes.

self-actualization Uniquely human drive to discover one's self and fulfill one's real potential, emphasizing the whole of human life.

self-concept Carl Roger's term for the individual's view of the world as a result of his interaction with the environment. The individual's perceptions tend to maintain his self-concept.

self-image The individual's view of himself, as influenced by his social group.

semicircular canals Structures near the **cochlea** in the inner ear that participate in the **vestibular sense** to maintain balance and position.

senile psychosis The most common organic psychosis, due to aging; damage to the brain is usually permanent and may lead to incomplete or defective memory, disorientation, disorganization, and delusions.

sensorimotor arc Path traveled by the nerve impulse from one or more **afferent neurons** to one or more **efferent neurons,** often including **interneurons;** the simplest is the **spinal reflex arc.**

sensorimotor operations The first stage in Jean Piaget's theory of **cognitive development,** during which the child is able to deal with material objects only.

sensory adaptation Adaptation of the sensory organs to a new environmental range of stimuli, so that once-powerful stimuli are ignored or very weak stimuli are noticed.

sensory associations Relationships among stimuli in which one **stimulus** evokes another stimulus.

sensory deprivation In perception studies, the temporary removal of the organism's sensory contact with the external world.

sensory gating The process in which strong inputs in one sensory channel interfere with inputs from another, resulting in selective perception of stimuli.

sensory neuron See **afferent neuron.**

sensory phase The time it takes a stimulus to travel from a sense organ receptor through the nervous system to the brain.

serial memorization Ebbinghaus's method of studying rote memory; the subject memorizes sequences of nonsense syllables, with each nonsense syllable serving as a stimulus for a response of the next syllable.

set Predisposition to respond in a certain way when confronted with certain stimuli.

sex hormones Substances secreted by the **gonads** for reproductive functions and determination of **secondary sex characteristics;** for example, estrogen in the female and testosterone in the male.

sex typing Learning of sex roles by young children.

sexual drive Drive induced by sex hormones and sexual stimuli. In humans, most sexual stimuli are conditioned.

shape constancy Perception of an object's shape as always the same, despite the actual shape of the image on the **retina** and the apparent tilt of the object.

shaping In **operant conditioning,** molding an organism's responses by reinforcing each successive approximation to a desired response until only the desired response is reinforced.

shock therapy See **electroconvul-**

sive therapy; insulin coma treatment.

short-term memory Storage of information during very short periods of time; thought to involve the hypothetical memory trace.

siblings Persons having a common parent.

sight screener Test for eye-muscle coordination, perception of depth, and the coordination of left-right (binocular) vision.

signal detection theory Method of **threshold** identification in which the subject's decisions are thought to depend on his sense organs, his expectations regarding the stimulus, the nature of the stimulus, and his motivation to be accurate in his decisions. Involves **signal trials** and **catch trials.**

signal trial In **threshold** identification, a trial in which a **stimulus** is presented. See **signal detection theory.**

silent area Largest section of the association areas, in the frontal lobes of the cerebral cortex, so-called because damage produces no sensory or motor loss; it is thought to be concerned with abstract reasoning and problem-solving.

simultaneous conditioning Classical conditioning procedure in which the **unconditioned stimulus** (US) and the **conditioned stimulus** (CS) are presented at the same time.

simultaneous contrast A phenomenon in which simultaneously presented, adjacent complementary colors affect each other in such a way as to appear much more vivid.

size constancy Tendency to adjust a frame of reference so that an object maintains a constant size from any vantage point.

skeletal muscles See **striated muscles.**

smooth muscles Muscles that control the internal organs, including the blood vessels.

Snellen eye chart A standard measuring device used to measure visual acuity.

social drives Acquired or learned drives that arise as a result of needs.

social facilitation studies Studies of the influence that a group has on individual behavior; studies concerned with audience effects, **coaction effects,** and group effects on motivation.

socialization Process of social learning through which a child acquires the attitudes, beliefs, and behaviors that are acceptable in his **culture;** the principal agents of socialization are the family, school, and peer group.

social needs General classification of learned needs activated by the presence of others.

social psychology Study of the individual's participation in the group and the group's influence on the individual.

sociology Study of people in groups; the group rather than the individual is the unit of study.

sociopathic disorder Character disorder that is expressed by lawlessness and disregard of the social code in which the individual must function. The sociopath is not usually troubled by anxiety or stress.

sodium amytal Drug sometimes used in narcotherapy to uncover unconscious conflicts ("truth serum").

somatic nervous system Sensory nerve fibers that connect receptors to

the spinal cord and the motor nerve fibers that connect the cord to the striated muscles.

somatosensory area Cortical center for body sense located from the top to the sides of the parietal lobe along the central fissure of the brain.

somatotyping Sheldon's system of body typing in which individuals are classified according to the degree to which their body build reflects certain physical characteristics (somatotypes). The three somatotypes are endomorph, mesomorph, and ectomorph.

sound waves Pressure changes that travel through the air and that emanate from vibrating objects, varying in intensity, wavelength, and duration; detected by the ear and ultimately interpreted as sounds.

source traits According to Cattell, the underlying traits that are expressed through **surface traits;** for example, responsiveness to people is a source trait.

sperm Male germ cell.

sphygmomanometer Instrument that measures blood pressure.

spinal cord Portion of the nervous system that runs up the spine and serves as the pathway through which nerve impulses from sensory organs pass to reach the brain and impulses from the brain are returned to reach the muscles and glands. Some impulses travel directly through the spinal cord to the muscles without passing through the brain (**spinal reflex**).

spinal reflex Reflex response in which the brain does not participate.

spinal reflex arc Path traveled by impulses in a **spinal reflex.**

split-half method of reliability Check of a test's reliability by comparing one half of the test scores with the other half.

spontaneous recovery In **classical conditioning,** the tendency of the conditioned response to regain some strength a short time after **extinction.**

S-R association Relationship between a **stimulus** and a **response.**

S-R psychology See **stimulus-response theories.**

S-S association Relationship between two or more **stimuli.**

Stanford-Binet Test Intelligence test originally devised by Binet and Simon, and later revised by Terman. This test heavily weights verbal skills.

stapes Hinged bony structure of the middle ear (familiarly called the stirrup because of its shape); the stapes, with the **malleus** and **incus,** receives the pressure waves vibrating through the middle ear. The three structures are known as the ossicles.

stereotyping Effect of evaluation caused by preexisting attitudes.

stimulant Drug or other substance that lowers the threshold for stimuli and increases the responsiveness of the individual.

stimulus (pl. **stimuli**) In general, any previous condition or "cause" of behavior that impinges on a sense organ; more specifically, environmental energy.

stimulus generalization Tendency for a stimulus similar to the conditioned stimulus (or the discriminative stimulus) to evoke or set the occasion for a response.

stimulus-response association See **S-R association.**

stimulus-response theories Theories that analyze behavior in terms of the responses of which behavior consists and the **stimuli** that evoke or set the occasion for these responses.

striated muscles Muscles that appear striped under the microscope and that are usually connected to the body skeleton; they control posture and movement of the skeleton and the movements of the tongue and eyes.

stroboscopic motion Apparent motion caused by the successive presentation of separate visual stimuli (as in motion pictures).

structuralism School of psychology that believes in the systematic study of the mind in terms of the elements of which the mind is composed; it made extensive use of introspection and was established by Wundt and brought to the United States by Titchener.

sublimation The **defense mechanism** in which the individual seeks to reach a secondary goal in order to satisfy his desires for some primary goal that is socially unacceptable or physically impossible.

successive contrast A phenomenon in which white light appears to take on the hue of a color.

summation Accumulation of weak impulses until they are strong enough to cross the **synapse.** Also, the tendency of two or three quick stimulations to the same area to produce only one efferent response.

superego According to Freud's **psychoanalytic theory of personality development,** the part of the personality that imposes on the individual the restraints and moral precepts of the external world.

surface traits Cattell's concept of traits that are close to the surface of the personality; they are more easily changed than **source traits.** Aggressiveness is an example of a surface trait.

syllogism A particular sequence in **logic** that derives its truth from a relationship between a major and a minor premise.

sympathetic division Part of the **autonomic nervous system** which prepares the organism for emergency reactions and, in general, acts in opposition to the **parasympathetic division.**

synapse Gap between neurons over which nerve impulses pass, specifically between the axon tip of a neuron and the dendrite of another neuron.

synaptic vesicles At the end of an **axon,** tiny sacs that release a transmitting substance which crosses the synaptic gap and causes the membrane of the receptor dendrite to react and produce an impulse in the dendritic fiber.

syndrome General term referring to a pattern of symptoms.

systematic desensitization Behavior modification technique in which the individual's fear of an object or person is gradually eliminated by replacing it with a more adaptive behavior, such as relaxation.

tachistoscope Device capable of presenting visual stimuli for very short periods of time.

taste buds Organs that receive the chemical stimuli for taste sensation; a cluster of taste buds forms a **papilla.**

taste cells Elongated cells that

compose the taste bud and that form an opening at the top of that taste bud.

taste neurons Neurons that carry nerve impulses from the taste bud sensory nerve fibers to the brain; they are characteristically grouped into several small bundles instead of a "gustatory nerve."

taste pore Opening formed by the taste cells at the top of a taste bud, through which chemical stimuli penetrate the gustatory sense organ.

TAT See **Thematic Apperception Test.**

temperament General description referring to an individual's overall emotional behavior. Also, Hippocrates' chemical typology for classifying personalities according to bodily conditions; he proposed that four basic bodily fluids, called humors, controlled personality types.

temperament traits Guilford's classification of traits that involve general, emotional, and social behavior. See also **motivational traits.**

temporal lobe Lobe of the cerebral hemisphere located at the lower sides of the brain, just inside that portion of the forebrain called the temples.

tertiary prevention See **environmental therapy.**

testes Male sex glands that produce androgens, hormones that control **secondary sex characteristics** and reproductive functions.

testosterone Male sex hormone that controls **secondary sex characteristics** and reproductive functions; one of the androgens.

test-retest reliability A reliability check in which a test is given on two separate occasions and the two sets of scores are then compared. It is used to check the reliability of a measuring instrument or test.

thalamus Part of the forebrain which sorts afferent and efferent impulses traveling into and out of the cerebrum.

Thematic Apperception Test (TAT) Projective personality test in which the individual is shown and a set of pictures, each deliberately drawn to serve as a stimulus for the telling of a story. Often a subject's narrative will reveal his own problems.

theory A way of organizing observations into a set of summary principles in order to predict relationships that have not yet been observed.

thirst drive Basic physiological drive caused by a need for water or other fluids.

threshold Point at which a stimulus is strong enough to produce a response.

timbre Quality of tones that enables the individual to tell one sound from another, even though both are of the same frequency; it depends on the pattern of the frequencies.

token economy Behavior-modification system based on the use of tokens as reinforcers.

trace conditioning Classical conditioning in which the **conditioned stimulus** terminates before the onset of the **unconditioned stimulus** (US).

trace theory Physiological theory of forgetting, stating that memory fades with time because some hypothetical trace disappears with time.

trait Particular and persistent feature of an individual's personality, a characteristic that can be measured and observed. See **source traits; surface traits.**

trait profiles Graphical depiction of the kind and degree of traits displayed by an individual.

tranquilizer Drug or other substance that raises the threshold for stimuli and decreases responsiveness.

transcendental meditation Technique for increasing individual awareness and relaxation. The individual achieves total concentration by attending in a particular way to a specific stimulus, sound, or thought.

transduction Process by which receptor cells transform physical energy into an impulse that the nervous system can carry.

transference In **psychoanalysis, the** patient's unconscious transfer of feelings from earlier interpersonal relationships to the analyst; the analyst uses this transference to further the therapy.

traveling-wave theory Von Békésy's theory (audition) that the sound wave displaces the **basilar membrane** a distance corresponding to the frequency of the sound wave.

trial and error Problem-solving technique in which all the seemingly appropriate solutions are tried one by one until the correct solution appears; this process may be covert.

tympanic canal Channel of the inner ear separated from the cochlear duct by the basilar membrane.

typologies Earliest classifications of personality based on the fact that certain human characteristics tend to occur together each time they occur.

unconditioned reinforcer A stimulus that is an effective **reinforcer** without benefit of previous association
with other reinforcers. See also **conditioned reinforcer.**

unconditioned response (UR) Response that automatically occurs when an **unconditioned stimulus (US)** is presented.

unconditioned stimulus (US) Stimulus that automatically produces a consistent response **(unconditioned response).**

unconscious Stimuli, responses, ideas, conflicts, and so on of which the individual is unaware; an important concept in psychoanalytic theory.

unlearned drives Innate, physiological drives of the individual, including hunger, thirst, and so on. Also called biological drives. See **drive; acquired drives.**

utricle One of the double sacs (the other is the **saccule**) below the **ampulla** between the base of the **semicircular canals** and the beginning of the **cochlea** of the ear; it receives stimuli related to the upright and nonmoving position of the individual.

validity Measure of the relationship of a test to some criterion; a test is valid if it measures what it is intended to measure.

variable Any factor that somehow affects an experiment; see **dependent variable** and **independent variable.**

variable-interval schedule Partial reinforcement schedule in which the first correct response after a variable time interval is reinforced; an average interval for reinforcement is established. There is a constant rate of responding under this schedule.

variable-ratio schedule Partial reinforcement schedule in which the first correct response after a variable number of correct responses is reinforced. The experimenter establishes the average number of correct responses needed for reinforcement.

verbal learning Learning involving the use of language, including nonsense syllables and numbers.

vestibular nuclei Vestibular nerve ends at the base of the brain where the nerve impulses break up and are sent to the eyes, internal organs, and brain; gray masses of matter.

vestibular organs Part of the **inner ear** necessary to the vestibular (balance) sense: the **semicircular canals** and the **otolith** organs.

vestibular sense Sense of body balance, position, and movement; it is also called the equilibratory or labyrinthine sense because of its function and location, respectively.

viscera Internal organs of the
body which are involved in maintaining and regulating everyday bodily functions and also emotional reactions.

visible spectrum Light energy frequencies that the human eye can perceive.

visual acuity See **acuity.**

visual area of the cortex Area that includes visual sensory neurons located primarily in the **occipital lobe**, with some centers in the **central fissure** and the **parietal lobe.**

visual cliff Device that tests depth perception by presenting an illusion of depth so that an individual's reaction to it may be observed.

visual field Part of the environment acting on the eyes at a given moment or during a period of time.

volley theory of audition Theory that holds that the frequency of nerve fiber discharge to the brain depends on groups of nerve cells that "fire" impulses at different times; these groups of fibers allow for the transmission of higher frequencies of sound. This theory applies for sounds up to 5,000 hertzes; after that, the place theory is needed.

voluntary muscles General name for the striated muscles that control the organism.

Weber's law Principle that for every stimulus there is some constant percentage of the stimulus that must be added to or subtracted from that stimulus for a difference to be detected.

word deafness Auditory disorder in which subject hears but does not understand words because of damage to the association cortex; it is also called auditory aphasia.

Yerkes-Dodson law Principle that optimum motivation for learning depends on the difficulty of the task. Efficiency is generally greatest when arousal is at some middle or intermediate level.

Young-Helmholtz theory of color vision Theory that the receptors for the three primary colors (red, green, and blue) are the basis for three corresponding types of absorption in cones; sensitivity to other colors is achieved by varying combinations and proportions of these three types of cones.

Zeigarnik effect Concept that uncompleted tasks are remembered better than completed ones.

zoophobia Fear of animals. See also **phobia.**

zygote Cell formed by union of **sperm** and **ovum.**

Subject index

Boldface page numbers refer to research abstracts; *italic* page numbers, to figures.

Name index